Entrepreneurship

ENTREPRENEURSHIP

FIFTH EDITION

Andrew Zacharakis
Babson College

Andrew C. Corbett
Babson College

William D. Bygrave
Babson College

VP AND EDITORIAL DIRECTOR	Mike McDonald
EXECUTIVE EDITOR	Lise Johnson
EDITORIAL MANAGER	Judy Howarth
CONTENT MANAGEMENT DIRECTOR	Lisa Wojcik
CONTENT MANAGER	Nichole Urban
SENIOR CONTENT SPECIALIST	Nicole Repasky
PRODUCTION EDITOR	Indirakumari, S.
COVER PHOTO CREDIT	© PitukTV/Shutterstock

This book was set in 10/12pt Times by SPi Global, Pondicherry, India and printed and bound by Quad Graphics.

Founded in 1807, John Wiley & Sons, Inc. has been a valued source of knowledge and understanding for more than 200 years, helping people around the world meet their needs and fulfill their aspirations. Our company is built on a foundation of principles that include responsibility to the communities we serve and where we live and work. In 2008, we launched a Corporate Citizenship Initiative, a global effort to address the environmental, social, economic, and ethical challenges we face in our business. Among the issues we are addressing are carbon impact, paper specifications and procurement, ethical conduct within our business and among our vendors, and community and charitable support. For more information, please visit our website: www.wiley.com/go/citizenship.

ISBN: 978-1-119-56322-8 (PBK)
ISBN: 978-1-119-60113-5 (EVALC)

Library of Congress Cataloging in Publication Data:
Names: Zacharakis, Andrew, author. | Corbett, Andrew C., author. | Bygrave, William D., 1937– author.
Title: Entrepreneurship / Andrew Zacharakis, Babson College, Andrew C. Corbett, Babson College, William D. Bygrave, Babson College.
Description: Fifth edition. | Hoboken, NJ : Wiley, [2020] | Includes index.
Identifiers: LCCN 2019038467 (print) | LCCN 2019038468 (ebook) | ISBN 9781119563228 (paperback) | ISBN 9781119601203 (adobe pdf) | ISBN 9781119563099 (epub)
Subjects: LCSH: New business enterprises. | Entrepreneurship. | Small business–Management.
Classification: LCC HD62.5 .B938 2020 (print) | LCC HD62.5 (ebook) | DDC 658.4/21–dc23
LC record available at https://lccn.loc.gov/2019038467
LC ebook record available at https://lccn.loc.gov/2019038468

SKY10059081_110123

To Frederic C. Hamilton and John H. Muller, Jr., pioneers, entrepreneurs, and benefactors of Babson College.

PREFACE

The green shoots of entrepreneurship give an economy its vitality. They give rise to new products and services, fresh applications for existing products and services, and new ways of doing business. Entrepreneurship stirs up the existing economic order and prunes out the dead wood. Established companies that fail to adapt to the changes cease to be competitive in the marketplace and go out of business.

Within the broadest definition, entrepreneurs are found throughout the world of business because any firm, big or small, must have its share of entrepreneurial drive if it is to survive and prosper. This textbook focuses on starting and growing independent new ventures. It is based on entrepreneurship courses taught at Babson College and at universities around the world.

One of the most common questions that entrepreneurship educators are asked is, Can entrepreneurship be taught? Our response is that anyone with a desire to become an entrepreneur will be more successful if he or she has taken a course on how to start and grow a new venture. About 30% of the students who have taken the new-venture course at Babson College since 1985 have gone on to start full-time businesses at some time in their careers. Many have started more than one.

Although this textbook empowers would-be entrepreneurs to start and grow their new ventures, it's not only for them. Any student who reads this book will learn about the entrepreneurial process and the role of entrepreneurship in the economy. We believe that all business students, regardless of whether they start a new business, will benefit from learning about entrepreneurship. After all, entrepreneurship and small business create most of the jobs in the U.S. economy and account for almost half the GDP. They are ubiquitous, and so integral to the economy that almost every student will work in one way or another with entrepreneurs and small businesses after graduation. This textbook will stand students in good stead—not only for starting their own firms, but also for dealing with startups as investors, bankers, accountants, lawyers, customers, vendors, employees, landlords, and in any other capacity.

An entrepreneurial revolution has transformed the economy since the mid-1970s. Central to that revolution is information technology, especially personal computers and the Internet. Information technology has profoundly changed the way companies do business, none more so than startup companies. Today's students were born after the personal computer and Internet came into common use. We believe they need an entrepreneurship text in which information technology is completely integrated all the way through.

This book combines concepts and cases to present the latest theory about entrepreneurship and relate actual experiences. The concepts cover what would-be entrepreneurs need to know to start and grow their businesses, and the cases illustrate how real entrepreneurs have gone out and done it. They cover all stages of the entrepreneurial process, from searching for an opportunity to shaping it into a commercially attractive product or service, launching the new venture, building it into a viable business, and eventually harvesting it.

Chapter 1 discusses the role of entrepreneurship in the U.S. economy and looks at the entrepreneurial competitiveness of nations throughout the world. Chapter 2 is an overview of the factors critical for starting a new enterprise and building it into a successful business.

Chapters 3 through 9 look in detail at what budding entrepreneurs need to do before they open their doors for business. The section starts with searching for opportunities and evaluating them, including through rapid prototyping. It explains how to build a workable business model and covers marketing, strategy, team building, financial projections, and business planning. At the end of this section students know how to write a business plan and how much startup capital they need to start their ventures.

The next section, Chapters 10 through 11, deals with financing businesses. Chapter 10 reviews the sources of financing for starting and growing businesses, including the nuts and bolts of raising money, particularly equity, to start and grow a business. Chapter 11 examines debt and other sources of financing.

Entrepreneurs need to understand the legal and tax issues associated with organizing a new business. They also need to know how to protect their intellectual capital. Chapter 12 explores these topics.

Anyone can start a new venture, but very few new businesses grow into substantial enterprises. Chapter 13 discusses what it takes to grow a business into a healthy company that provides financial rewards for the entrepreneur and good jobs for employees.

Finally, Chapter 14 looks at social entrepreneurship. Today, many students are looking at business ideas that may not only earn a profit, but also address a social concern.

Each chapter is accompanied by a case study of entrepreneurs in action. We chose the cases carefully, using these criteria:

- The entrepreneurs and their companies represent a spectrum of situations and industries that is as broad as we could make it.
- The judgment point in most cases occurs in the last decade— some as recently as 2019.
- All stages of the entrepreneurial process are covered, from pre-startup through harvest.
- Almost all the entrepreneurs in the cases are in their 20s and 30s; some are recent graduates.

There's no substitute for the experience gained from actually starting a business, but we believe that by completing the case studies in this book students will gain wisdom that would take years to pick up by trial and error as entrepreneurs starting and building businesses from scratch.

Each chapter ends with a unique Opportunity Journal. Here students can reflect on the lessons learned and think about how to apply them to their own entrepreneurial ventures or to managing their careers. Finally, a Web exercise builds on key concepts covered in each chapter.

New to this Edition

The fifth edition has been thoroughly updated and enhanced throughout. We have developed a completely new chapter on business models, incorporating the Business Model Wheel. Angelo Santinelli, a former venture capitalist, entrepreneur and currently a startup advisor brings his 30 years of new venture experience and wrote the chapter on a new way to consider business models.

We replaced half of the older cases. We have added cases on MightyWell, a medical apparel company looking to bring fashion to patients (Chapter 1), Vedavoo (Chapter 2) and ISlide (Chapter 3) that tracks product development in the sporting goods space, Gravyty, (Chapters 8 and 9) which shows a business planning process through the lens of artificial intelligence-based firm, Wefunder (Chapter 12) that looks at legal issues confronting crowdfunding, Esporte Interativo (Chapter 13) that illustrates a company striving to continue growth in a competitive industry and InnerCity Weightlifting (Chapter 14) that highlights a social venture changing the lives of young men prone to gang activity.

With these changes, we are confident that the fifth edition of Entrepreneurship, not only continues our mission of empowering and enabling young entrepreneurs, but enhances it.

Teaching Supplements

Case Teaching Notes Detailed teaching notes go into depth on the material covered in each chapter's accompanying case. They include discussion questions, classroom activities, and additional information on the businesses and entrepreneurs from the cases.

Test Bank With 60 questions per chapter, the test bank consists of multiple choice, true/false, and short answer questions of varying difficulty. A computerized version of this test bank is also available on the Instructor Companion Site so that you can customize your quizzes and exams. Access these resources on the Instructor Companion Site.

Additional Cases In addition to the 14 cases included in the book, additional cases, available on the book's companion site, give instructors more choices and give students more real-life examples. Cases available online include the following:

- *Adam Air*
- *Andres Galindo*
- *Ajay Bam*
- *Alexander Norman and Toni Randolph-Norman*
- *BladeLogic*
- *ClearVue*
- *College Coach*
- *Matt Grant*
- *Enox*
- *CardSmith*
- *Makers Mark*
- *Vayusa* (the *Ajay Bam* second case)
- *Beautiful Legs by Post*
- *Living Patio Rooms*
- *Malincho*
- *Neverfail*
- *Matt Coffin*
- *Jon Hirschtick*
- *SolidWorks* (the *Jon Hirschtick* second case)
- *David Pearlman*
- *StudentCity.Com*
- *Nancy's Coffee*
- *Earth Watch*

- *Zeo, Inc.*
- *Eu Yang Sang*
- Jim Poss
- Alison Barnard
- Vera Bradley
- P'kolino
- Crowdfunding: A tale of two campaigns
- Tessera
- LazyBones
- Earthwatch

Acknowledgements

A comprehensive textbook on entrepreneurship covers a very wide range of disciplines that require specialized knowledge, so we invited leading experts to write some of the chapters.

- Erik Noyes wrote Chapter 4 on Prototyping.
- As noted above, Angelo Santinelli wrote a new chapter on business models (Chapter 5)
- Entrepreneurial marketing was written by two leading experts: Abdul Ali at Babson College and Kathleen Seiders at Boston College, who wrote Chapter 6, "Entrepreneurial Marketing."
- Joel Shulman, Babson College, who specializes in entrepreneurial finance, contributed Chapter 11, "Debt and Other Forms of Financing."
- Legal, tax issues and intellectual property go hand in hand when setting up a new business; Richard Mandel, who is a Babson professor and a partner with the law firm Bowditch and Dewey that specializes in small business, wrote Chapter 12 along with Joseph Iandorio and Kirk Teska, who are patent attorneys in the firm that bears their names.
- Babson professors Donna Kelley and Edward Marram wrote Chapter 13, "Entrepreneurial Growth." Kelley is an expert on innovation, and Marram specializes in growing businesses.
- Professors Brad George and Candida Brush of Babson College wrote Chapter 14.

We thank all the contributing authors for their commitment and dedication to making this book as valuable as it can be for students.

We are forever indebted to everyone involved in the entrepreneurial process who has shared experience and wisdom with us. They include entrepreneurs from novices to old hands, informal investors, business angels, venture capitalists, bankers, lawyers, and landlords—indeed, anyone involved with entrepreneurs. We have learned so much from them. We're especially thankful for all the students and alumni we have worked with over the years. Their feedback has helped us shape what we teach and how we teach it.

We believe that entrepreneurs who successfully build businesses are inherently good coaches and teachers; they have to be if they are to develop and encourage employees. This generosity is borne out by their willingness to share their know-how with budding entrepreneurs. One important way in which entrepreneurs have done that is by allowing us to write cases about them and their companies, and then by coming to class when the cases are discussed. We thank all the case writers who researched and wrote the cases in this book and on its companion website. We'd also like to thank our student research assistants, who helped track down relevant examples in the popular press, acted as our first-draft readers, and worked hard on the instructional support materials. They are current and former Babson MBA students Alexey Amerikov, Eric Berglind, Mia Di Stefano, Rich Enos, Don Gourley, Sara Gragnolati, Andres Hinojosa, Mark Itkovitz, Kushal Manek, Mahmoud Mattan, Henry McGovern, Rich Palmer, Gabriel Quintana, Richard Raeke, Tommy Ripke, Ge Song, Steve Shafran, and Brian Zinn.

It is a pleasure to be members of the Arthur M. Blank Center for Entrepreneurship at Babson College. Our Babson colleagues are an inspiration. They are pioneers of entrepreneurship education who are continually coming up with new ways of teaching. The Babson faculty comprises a marvelous mix of academics and what we call "pracademics"— practicing academics— who are entrepreneurs, venture capitalists, angel investors, lawyers, and others associated day-to-day with starting and running businesses. Candida Brush, Provost of Entrepreneurship, has been highly supportive. We have benefited from discussions with Brian Abraham, Rob Adler, Matt Allen, Fred Alper, Lakshmi Balachandra, Craig Benson, Jean-Luc Boulnois, Dennis Ceru, Les Charm, Alan Cohen, Lily Crosina, Caroline Daniels, Mary Gale, Brad George, Len Green, Patricia Greene, Mike Gordon, Howard Gross, Tim Habbershon, John Halal, Neal Harris, Alisa Jno-Charles, Bill Johnston, Donna Kelley, Phil Kim, Julian Lange, Nan Langowitz, Bill LaPoint, Ray Marcinowski, Tim Marken, Ed Marram, Maria Minniti, Christopher Mirabile, Diane Mulcahy, Kevin Mulcahy, Kevin Mulvaney, Heidi Neck, Eric Noyes, Ernie Parizeau, Elizabeth Angela Randolph, Elizabeth Riley, Angelo Santinelli, Joel Shulman, Sid Vedula, and Yasu Yamakawa, all of whom teach at Babson College. We'd also like to acknowledge four of our biggest supporters and mentors who passed away since the earlier editions were published, Abdul Ali, Glenn Kaplus, Jeffry Timmons, and Natalie Taylor. Their long-time influence and contributions to Babson College was invaluable. We miss them.

The Babson administration and staff have supported our efforts: President Stephen Spinelli motivated us with his enthusiasm for entrepreneurship education. Michael Fetters, formerly provost, encouraged us to write this book and gave us permission to include the cases in the book.

We are thankful for the financial support we received from the benefactors of the Frederic C. Hamilton Chair for Free Enterprise, the John H. Muller, Jr. Chair for Entrepreneurship, and the Paul T. Babson Chair for Entrepreneurial Studies. We greatly appreciate all the help that we received from the staff at Wiley and its affiliates.

Finally, we are indebted to our families, our patient and supportive wives, and our beautiful and talented children. Thank you for being so understanding when we were pushing hard to meet our deadlines.

CONTENTS

8 The Business Planning Process 218

9 Building Your Pro Forma 275

10 Raising Money for Starting and Growing a Business 302

11 Debt and Other Forms of Financing 338

14 Social Entrepreneurship 442

Glossary G-1

Index I-1

The Power of Entrepreneurship

1

Photo Credit: © Jamel Toppin/The Forbes Collection/Contour RA/Getty Images

The founders of AirBnB; Nathan Blecharczyk, Brian Chesky, and Joe Gebbia

This is the entrepreneurial age. Each day across the globe, thousands of people embrace the power and liberation of entrepreneurship by pursuing their new business. The 2018/19 Global Entrepreneurship Monitor (GEM) reports that across the 49 countries investigated 12.6% of adults were in the process of working to start a new business or were running one they recently

This chapter was originally written by William D. Bygrave.

started. Hundreds of new businesses are born every hour of every working day in the United States.[1] Entrepreneurs are driving a revolution that is transforming and renewing economies worldwide. Entrepreneurship is the essence of free enterprise because the birth of new businesses gives a market economy its vitality. New and emerging businesses create a very large proportion of the innovative products and services that transform the way we work and live as they take advantage of tech opportunities within social media, virtual reality, and the Internet of Things or by creating new business models to transform "traditional industries" (e.g., Airbnb or Uber). Similarly, these same businesses created half of the new private-sector jobs in the United States in 2018.[2] As a backbone of the economy, entrepreneurs and small businesses played a leading role in helping the economy rebound from the recession of 2008. A 2015 report from the Small Business Association shows that entrepreneurs created 7 of 11 million new jobs since the 2008 recession.[3] Data suggest the same phenomenon is happening worldwide.[4]

There has never been a better time to practice the art and science of entrepreneurship. But what is entrepreneurship? Early in the 20th century, Joseph Schumpeter, the Moravian-born economist writing in Vienna, gave us the modern definition of an entrepreneur: "a person who destroys the existing economic order by introducing new products and services, by introducing new methods of production, by creating new forms of organization, or by exploiting new raw materials." According to Schumpeter, that person is most likely to accomplish this destruction by founding a new business but may also do it within an existing one.

Schumpeter explained how entrepreneurs had suddenly increased the standard of living of a few industrialized nations.[5] When the Industrial Revolution began in England around 1760, no nation had enjoyed a standard of living equal to that of Imperial Rome 2,000 years earlier. But from 1870 to 1979, for example, the standard of living of 16 nations jumped by sevenfold on average.[6]

Very few new businesses have the potential to initiate a Schumpeterian "gale" of creative destruction, as Airbnb is doing in hospitality and Uber is doing in the taxi industry. The vast majority enter existing markets. So, in this textbook, we adopt a broader definition of entrepreneurship than Schumpeter's. Ours encompasses everyone who starts a new business. Our

The Changing Economy

General Electric (GE), a once shining beacon of the power of a global conglomerate, exemplifies today what can happen to firms caught up in the destructive forces and aftermath of "Schumpeter's entrepreneurs." GE, founded in Schenectady, New York, in 1892, thrived in a number of industries and sectors including aircraft engines, locomotives, oil and gas, electrical distribution, health care, finance, and more. As late as 2018, GE was the 18th largest firm by gross revenue in the United States according to *Fortune* and was the 14th most profitable company and the 4th largest just a few short years ago. From the late 1990s through mid-2017, GE stock traded somewhere between $20 and $30. By the end of 2017, it was at $17 and at the start of 2019, GE stock was trading below $9 a share. What happened? Market shifts, bad investments, and direct competition to be sure, but also entrepreneurs and entrepreneurial firms creating Schumpeter's "gales of destruction" that upset the industries and markets where GE competes.

Companies have to react to the moves of a new market entrant and the combined changes over time by many different forces. Walmart and Amazon are currently in a fevered battle for the grocery store dollars of every American. Founded in 1962 by Sam Walton, Walmart was once a small startup retailer who became the world's largest retailer. Today as the company's sales move near $500 billion, they compete fiercely as a relative newbie in the world of e-commerce. Their primary competition? An online bookseller who just a few short years ago was not in the grocery business. However, with their 2017 acquisition of Whole Foods Market, Amazon is now the market leader in the online grocery business according to Forbes.

Sources: http://fortune.com/2018/05/22/fortune-500-companies-list-berkshire-hathaway; https://money.cnn.com/galleries/2011/fortune/1104/gallery.fortune500_most_profitable.fortune/14.html

entrepreneur is the person who perceives an opportunity and creates an organization to pursue it. And the entrepreneurial process includes all the functions, activities, and actions associated with perceiving opportunities and creating organizations to pursue them. Our entrepreneur's new business may, in a few rare instances, be the revolutionary sort that rearranges the global economic order, as Walmart, FedEx, Apple, Microsoft, Google, eBay, and Amazon have done and social networking companies such as Facebook and Twitter are now doing. But it is much more likely to be of the incremental kind that enters an existing market.

In this chapter, we next look at the importance of entrepreneurship and small business to the United States and the global economies. We then provide a foundation for today's entrepreneurial world by looking at some of the major historical markers that brought us to this point: we describe the entrepreneurial revolution, present a conceptual model for the entrepreneurial sector of the economy, and use it to explain major factors in the revolution. Finally, using data from the GEM, we will compare and contrast entrepreneurial activity among regions and different economies across the globe within the context of the conceptual model.

Entrepreneurship and Small Business in the United States

According to the U.S. Small Business Administration (SBA), there are 30.2 million small businesses in the United States today, which represents 99.9% of all businesses in the country.[7] In general, businesses with 500 or fewer employees are classified as small.[8] They account for half the private-sector workers and 47.5% of the private payroll, and they generate approximately half the nonfarm private GDP. The latest report from the U.S. Small Business Administration shows that these small businesses make a large impact not just in the United States but also across the globe as they generate a third of the United States $1.3 trillion in total exports.

Startups and small businesses are also an important driver of job growth. Since the turn of the century through 2017, small businesses created nearly twice as many jobs in the United States as large businesses: 8.4 million to 4.4 million, respectively. This growth comes in industries that are important to the future. In the latest three-year reporting window (2015–2017), small businesses outpaced large businesses in job growth and percentage increase in high-tech firms, software, pharmaceutical, scientific research & development, and computer systems design industries.[9] Not only are small businesses the engine for job creation, but they are also a powerful force for innovation. They hire 43% of all high-tech workers and produce approximately 16 times more patents per employee than large firms; those patents are twice as likely as large firm patents to be among the 1% most cited.[10]

Demonstrating a trend that can be seen in developed economies all over the world, more than a third of the 30 million small businesses in the United States come from the professional, technical, and other related services industries. The majority of businesses are non-employer firms run entirely by a single proprietor and approximately 17% of all firms have between 1 and 20 employees. Over a half million firms employ between 20 and 499 people. Health care, hospitality and food services, along with the retail sector, are leading small business employers.

At any one time, approximately 14% of all adults of working age in the United States can be classified as *nascent entrepreneurs,* that is they are trying to create a new business; they have conceived an idea for a new venture and have taken at least one step toward implementing their idea.[11] Many of them abandon their ventures during the gestation period and never actually open their businesses; nonetheless, each year at least 3 million new ventures are born, of which about 75% start from scratch. Most of the others are purchases of existing businesses.[12] Two in every three businesses are started in the owner's home. Most remain tiny because they are part-time businesses, but around 600,000 have at least one full-time employee.

Survival rates for new businesses have been the focus of several different studies.[13] One of the most thorough was done at the U.S. Census Bureau by Alfred Nucci, who calculated the 10-year survival rates of business establishments.[14] He found that 81% survive for at least one year, 65% for two years, 40% for five years, and 25% for ten years. The survival rate for independent start-ups was slightly lower. For example, the one-year rate was 79% instead of 81%. The chance of survival increased with age and size. Survival rates also varied somewhat with industry but not as strongly as with age and size.

Of course, survival does not necessarily spell success. In general, the median income of small business owners is almost the same as that of wage and salary earners. However, the income distribution is much broader for small business owners, which means that they are more likely to have significantly less income or significantly more income than wage and salaried workers.[15] But small business owners are also building equity in their companies as well as taking income from them, so it is possible that small business owners are better off overall than their wage-earning cohorts. However, a study of business owners disposing of their businesses through sale, closure, passing it on, and other methods found that comparatively few saw their standard of living changed by their business. Only 17% reported that their business had raised their standard of living, whereas 6% reported the opposite.[16] All these numbers aside, it is interesting to note that entrepreneurs and small business owners tend to be happier than others. On the whole, those who chose a path of entrepreneurship end up more satisfied with their life and see their life as being "excellent" and "close to ideal" compared to those who do not become entrepreneurs.[17]

Looking back at the new business formation index, we can see that it was stable through the 1950s and most of the 1960s; there was virtually no growth. By 1970, net new business formation was growing, and the growth continued through the 1970s and 1980s and into the 1990s.[18] No one noticed the change at the time. One of the first documented references to what was taking place was a December 1976 article in *The Economist* called "The Coming Entrepreneurial Revolution."[19] In this article, Norman Macrae argued that the era of big business was drawing to an end and that future increases in employment would come mainly from either smaller firms or small units of big firms. In 1978, David Birch published his book, *Job Creation in America: How Our Smallest Companies Put the Most People to Work*.[20] The title says it all. It captures the important finding from Birch's comprehensive study of business establishments.

No issue gets the attention of politicians more than job creation. Birch's findings and the stream of research that ensued forever changed the attitude of policy makers toward small business.[21] Until then, most of their focus had been on big business. After all, in 1953 Charles Erwin Wilson, then GM president, is reported to have said during the hearings before the Senate Armed Services Committee, "What's good for General Motors is good for the country." At the time, GM was one of the largest employers in the world—only Soviet state industries employed more people.[22] Today, in another example of Schumpeter's effect of entrepreneurship and its accompanying gales of creative destruction, GM employs less than 200,000 people down from its high of over 600,000 in the 1970s.

A recent study reported in MarketWatch showed that many Americans sit in their offices and dream of becoming their own boss. According to the survey

- 39% of employees hope to own their own business someday.
- More than 50% of respondents in their 20s who don't currently own their business aspire to do so.
- 50% of those in their 30s want to leave their job and start a business; the number is 35% for those in their 40s.

Source: http://www.marketwatch.com/story/40-of-employees-want-to-start-their-own-business-2014-08-05

Entrepreneurial Revolution

On November 1, 1999, Chevron, Goodyear Tire & Rubber Company, Sears Roebuck, and Union Carbide were removed from the Dow Jones Industrial Average (DJIA) and replaced by Intel, Microsoft, Home Depot, and SBC Communications. Intel and Microsoft became the first two companies traded on the NASDAQ exchange to be listed in the DJIA.

This event symbolized what is now called the *entrepreneurship revolution* that transformed the U.S. economy in the last quarter of the 20th century. Intel and Microsoft are the two major entrepreneurial driving forces in the information technology revolution that has fundamentally changed the way in which we live, work, and play. SBC (formerly Southwestern Bell Corporation) was one of the original "Baby Bells" formed after the U.S. Department of Justice antitrust action resulted in the breakup of AT&T. It is an excellent example of how breaking up a monopoly leads to entrepreneurial opportunities. And Home Depot exemplifies the big-box stores that have transformed much of the retail industry. In the continuing example of ongoing creative destruction, SBC has long since left the DJIA but today Intel, Microsoft, and Home Depot still remain and Chevron has retuned!

Companies like Intel, Microsoft, and Home Depot best exemplify the foundation of the entrepreneurial revolution. Intel was founded in Silicon Valley by Gordon Moore and Robert Noyce and funded by Arthur Rock, the legendary venture capitalist. Gordon Moore, the inventor of Moore's Law,[23] and Robert Noyce, one of the two inventors of the integrated circuit,[24] had been at the birth of Silicon Valley with William Shockley, the co-inventor of the transistor, when Shockley Semiconductor Laboratory was founded in Mountain View in 1956. They left Shockley in 1957 to found Fairchild Semiconductor, which in 1961 introduced the first commercial integrated circuit. In 1968, they left Fairchild to start Intel.

Ted Hoff, employee number 12 at Intel, invented the microprocessor in 1968. In 1971, Intel launched the first commercial microprocessor, heralding a new era in integrated electronics. Then, in 1974, it launched the first general-purpose microprocessor, the Intel 8080, which was the brain of the first personal computer,[25] the Altair 8800—a $439 hobbyist's kit—announced by MITS (Micro Instrumentation and Telemetry Systems of Albuquerque) on the front cover of the January 1, 1975, edition of *Popular Electronics*.

"When I was 19, I caught sight of the future and based my career on what I saw. I turned out to have been right."

—*Bill Gates*

According to personal computer folklore, Paul Allen, then working at the minicomputer division of Honeywell in Massachusetts, hurried to his childhood friend and fellow computer enthusiast, Bill Gates, who was a Harvard sophomore, and waving *Popular Electronics* with a mock-up of the Altair 8800 on its front cover, exclaimed, "This is it! It's about to begin!" Within a month or so, Gates had a version of BASIC to run on the Altair. He and Allen joined together in an informal partnership called Microsoft and moved to Albuquerque.

Microsoft grew steadily by developing software for personal computers. By 1979, it had moved to Bellevue, Washington, near Seattle, where Gates and Allen had grown up. It then had revenue of more than $2 million and 28 employees. It got its big break in 1980–1981 when, building on the core of a product acquired from Seattle Computer Products, Microsoft introduced MS-DOS for IBM's first PC. Fourteen years later, when Microsoft released Windows 95 in 1995, it sold 4 million copies in four days. Its success helped to move the personal computer into 250 million homes, businesses, and schools worldwide. In the early 1990s, Microsoft committed itself to adding Internet capabilities to its

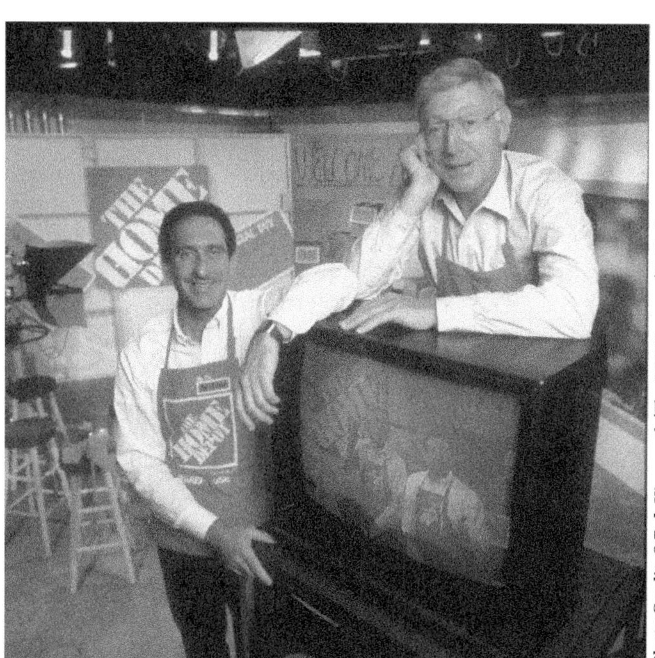

Photo Credit: © Rob Kinmonth/The LIFE Images/Getty Images

Bernard Marcus and Arthur Blank, founders of Home Depot

products. When Microsoft joined the DJIA in 1999, there were more than 200 million Internet users, up from 3 million just five years earlier.

Home Depot was founded in 1979 by Bernie Marcus and Arthur Blank. The chain of hardware and do-it-yourself (DIY) stores holds the record for the fastest time for a retailer to pass the $30 billion, $40 billion, $50 billion, $60 billion, and $70 billion annual revenue milestones. It is the fifth-largest retailer in the United States. And it almost set the record for the fastest time from starting up to joining the DJIA when it was only 20 years old. By comparison, Walmart was 35 years old when it displaced F. W. Woolworth in the DJIA. Along with Walmart, Home Depot has set the pace for the retail industry in the last three decades. Together, the two account for 2.7 million jobs.

At the turn of the 20th century, about 50% of U.S. workers were employed in agriculture and domestic service. Less than 100 years later, the number was about 4%. Much of this transformation came about because innovations, many of them introduced by entrepreneurs, made agriculture a shining example of increasing productivity, and labor-saving products such as the vacuum cleaner, gas and electric ranges, washing machines and clothes dryers, dishwashers, automobiles, lawnmowers, floor polishers, processed foods, microwave ovens, and services increased the productivity of household labor. The proportion of the workforce in manufacturing grew from 19% in 1900 to 27% in 1950, thereby providing alternative employment opportunities for farm laborers and domestic workers.

Today, only about 12% of U.S. jobs are in the goods-producing sector, and 80% are in the service-providing sector; the proportion of knowledge-based jobs is estimated to be more than 50%. The DJIA reflects the changing face of the U.S. economy: In 1896, the 12 companies that made up the DJIA reflected the dominance of agriculture and basic commodities; in 1928—the first time the DJIA comprised 30 companies—the members reflected the importance of manufacturing, retailing, and the emerging radio industry; and in 2019, the shift is toward knowledge-based industries, communications industries, and financial services.

Of course, only a few of the entrepreneurial giants ever get into the DJIA, which is composed of only 30 of the most widely held stocks. The following are some of the other legendary entrepreneurs and their companies that played important roles in the entrepreneurship revolution of the last 40 years.

Perhaps one of the most revolutionary entrepreneurial ideas outside of high-tech industries was Fred Smith's notion to deliver packages overnight anywhere in the United States.

Smith identified a need for shippers to have a system designed specifically for airfreight that could accommodate time-sensitive shipments such as medicines, computer parts, and electronics in a term paper that he wrote as a Yale undergraduate. Smith's professor did not think much of the idea and gave it a C. After tours of duty in Vietnam, Smith founded his company, Federal Express (FedEx) in 1971, and it began operating in 1973 out of Memphis International Airport. In the mid-1970s, Federal Express had taken a leading role in lobbying for air cargo deregulation, which finally came in 1977. These changes allowed Federal Express to use larger aircraft and spurred the company's rapid growth. Today FedEx ships 15 million packages a day on average and connects over 99% of the world's GDP by covering more than 220 countries and territories across the globe.[26]

In 1971, when Southwest Airlines began operations, *interstate* airline travel was highly regulated by the federal government, which had set up the Civil Aeronautics Board (CAB) in 1938 to regulate all domestic air transport as a public utility, setting fares, routes, and schedules. The CAB was required to ensure that the airlines had a reasonable rate of return. Most of the major airlines, whose profits were virtually guaranteed, favored the system. Not surprisingly, competition was

Dow Jones Industrial Average (DJIA) Companies

1896	1928	2019
American Cotton Oil	Allied Can	3M
American Sugar	Allied Chemical	American Express
American Tobacco	American Smelting & Refining	Apple
Chicago Gas	American Sugar	Boeing
Distilling & Cattle Feeding	American Tobacco	Caterpillar
General Electric	Atlantic Refining	Chevron
Laclede Gas Light	Bethlehem Steel	Cisco Systems
National Lead	Chrysler	Coca-Cola
North American	General Electric	Disney
Tennessee Coal, Iron & Railroad	General Motors	DuPont
U.S. Leather	General Railway	Exxon Mobil
U.S. Rubber	Goodrich	Goldman Sachs
	International Harvester	Home Depot
	International Nickel	Intel
	Mack Trucks	IBM
	Nash Motors	Johnson & Johnson
	North American	JPMorgan Chase
	Paramount Publix	McDonald's
	Postum	Merck
	Radio Corporation	Microsoft
	Sears, Roebuck	Nike
	Standard Oil (NJ)	Pfizer
	Texas Corporation	Procter & Gamble
	Texas Gulf Sulphur	Travelers
	Union Carbide	United Technologies
	U.S. Steel	United Health
	Victor Talking Machines	Verizon
	Westinghouse	Visa
	Woolworth	Walmart Walgreens

stifled, and almost no new airlines attempted to enter the market. However, *intrastate* passenger travel was not regulated by the CAB, so Southwest, following the pioneering path of Pacific Southwest Airline's (PSA) service within California, initiated passenger service within Texas. The success of PSA and Southwest in providing cheap airline travel within California and Texas provided powerful ammunition for the deregulation of *interstate* travel, which came about in 1981 as a consequence of the Airline Deregulation Act of 1978.[27] Since deregulation, more than 100 startup airlines have inaugurated interstate scheduled passenger service with jet aircraft.[28] Herb Kelleher, the charismatic cofounder of Southwest Airlines, is often credited with triggering airline deregulation by persevering with his legal battle to get Southwest airborne in the face of fierce legal opposition from Braniff, Trans-Texas, and Continental Airlines. Two of those airlines took their legal battle all the way to the U.S. Supreme Court, which ruled in Southwest's favor at the end of 1970.[29]

Robert Swanson was 27 when he hit on the idea that a company could be formed to commercialize biotechnology. At that time, he knew almost nothing about the field. By reading the scientific literature, Swanson identified the leading biotechnology scientists and contacted them. "Everybody said I was too early—it would take 10 years to turn out the first microorganism from a human hormone or maybe 20 years to have a commercial product—everybody except Herb Boyer."[30] Swanson was referring to Professor Herbert Boyer at the University of California at San Francisco, co-inventor of the patents that, according to some observers, now form the basis of the biotechnology industry. When Swanson and Boyer met in early 1976, they almost immediately agreed to become partners in an endeavor to explore the commercial possibilities of recombinant DNA. Boyer named their venture Genentech, an acronym for genetic engineering technology. Just seven months later, Genentech announced its first success, a genetically engineered human brain hormone, somatostatin. According to Swanson, they accomplished 10 years of development in seven months. Most observers say it was Swanson's entrepreneurial vision that brought about the founding of the biotech industry. Today there are over 20,000 biotech companies in the world with revenues of nearly $140 billion from the 700 hundred publicly traded U.S.-based firms alone.[31] At almost the same time that Swanson was starting Genentech in southern San Francisco, not many miles away Steve Jobs and Stephen Wozniak were starting Apple Computer in Silicon Valley. Their computer, the Apple I in kit form, was an instant hit with hobbyists. The Byte Shop—the first full-time computer store anywhere in the world, which opened in Silicon Valley in December 1975—ordered 25 of them in June 1976. The owner of The Byte Shop asked Jobs to put the Apple I computer board in a case because his customers were asking for complete units, not just kits. When they did so, both Apple and The Byte Shop had a hot product on their hands. The Byte Shop grew to a chain of 75 stores. "Without intending to do so, Wozniak and Jobs had launched the microcomputer by responding to consumer demand."[32]

Genentech's initial public offering (IPO) in October 1980, followed by Apple's IPO only two months later, signaled that something magical was stirring in the biotech and personal computer industries. It triggered a wave of venture capital investment and IPOs in both industries.

A tipping point in the infant personal computer industry was the introduction of the VisiCalc spreadsheet. Dan Bricklin conceived it when he was sitting in an MBA class at Harvard in 1978, daydreaming about how he could make it easier to do repetitive calculations. Bricklin designed the prototype software to run on an Apple II. Together with Bob Frankston, he formed a company, Software Arts, to develop the VisiCalc spreadsheet. When they introduced their first version in May 1979, it turbocharged the sale of Apple computers. Subsequently, sales of IBM PCs were rocketed into the stratosphere by Mitch Kapor's Lotus 1-2-3 worksheet.

The late 1970s and the early 1980s were miraculous years for entrepreneurial ventures in the computer industry. Miniaturization of hard-disk drives, a vital component in the information technology revolution, was pioneered by Al Shugart, first at Shugart Associates, then at Seagate Technology. Dick Eagan and Roger Marino started EMC Corporation in 1979, initially selling computer furniture, and with the seed money from that, they launched into selling Intel-compatible memory. From that beginning, Eagan and Marino built EMC into a company that during the 1990s achieved the highest single-decade performance of any listed stock in the history of the New York Stock Exchange. Today, after a merger that created Dell-EMC, it continues to redefine itself as the data storage industry evolves to a cloud-based industry.

Of course, Dell began in the 1980s as well. Michael Dell, while still a student at the University of Texas, Austin, in 1984, began selling IBM-compatible computers built from stock components that he marketed directly to customers. By concentrating on direct sales of customized products, Dell became the largest manufacturer of personal computers in the world, and Michael Dell was CEO longer than any other executive in the PC hardware industry.

Entrepreneurs were at the conception and birth of new products and services that have transformed the global economy in the last 50 years. However, what is turning out to be the biggest of them all began in 1989 when Tim (now Sir Timothy) Berners-Lee conceived the World Wide Web. The big four of today—Amazon, Apple, Facebook, and Goggle—would not have existed if not for Berners-Lee. Today, we are still in the midst of a revolution that is changing our lives more profoundly and faster than anyone could have imagined before the Web became operational in 1992. No major new product has been adopted as quickly by such a large percentage of the U.S. population as the Web.

Time for New Technologies to Penetrate 25% of U.S. Population	
Household electricity (1873)	46 years
Telephone (1875)	35 years
Automobile (1885)	55 years
Airplane travel (1903)	54 years
Radio (1906)	22 years
Television (1925)	26 years
VCR (1952)	34 years
PC (1975)	15 years
Mobile Phone (1983)	13 years
World Wide Web (1992)	5 years

Source: The Wall Street Journal, June 1997; http://en.wikipedia.org/wiki/Advanced_Mobile_Phone_Service; www.netbanker.com/2000/04/internet_usage_web_users_world.html.

Web: Three Revolutions Converge

In 1989, when Tim Berners-Lee wrote a proposal to develop software that resulted in the World Wide Web, he was not the first to conceive the idea. As far back as 1945, Vannevar Bush proposed a "memex" machine with which users could create information "trails" linking related text and illustrations and store the trails for future reference.[33]

As it turned out, he was 50 years ahead of the technologies that were needed to implement his idea. After all, the first digital computer was then only a couple of years old. Fifteen years later Ted Nelson, inspired by Bush's "memex," was the first person to develop the modern version of hypertext. He wrote—prophetically, as it turned out—in 1960 that "the future of humanity is at the interactive computer screen … the new writing and movies will be interactive and interlinked … we need a world-wide network to deliver it.[34]

But Nelson, too, was far ahead of the technology. In 1962, there were fewer than 10,000 computers in the world. They cost hundreds of thousands of dollars, they were primitive machines with only a few thousand bytes of magnetic core memory, and programming them was complicated and tedious. AT&T had a monopoly over the phone lines that were used for data communication. And the ARPANET, which was the forerunner of the Internet, had not yet been conceived.[35]

Berners-Lee was a 25-year-old physics graduate of Oxford University working as a consultant at CERN, the European Particle Physics Laboratory in Geneva, Switzerland, in 1980 when he wrote his own private program for storing information using the random associations the brain makes. His Enquire program, which was never published, formed the conceptual basis for his future development of the Web.[36] In 1980, the technology existed for implementing Berners-Lee's concept, but the power of the technology was low, and the installed base of computers was tiny compared to what it would be 10 years later. By 1989, when he revived his idea, three revolutions were ready for it. They were in *digital technology, information technology (IT)*, and *entrepreneurship*. The semiconductor revolution enabled the digital revolution, which in turn enabled the IT revolution. By 1992, when the Web was released by CERN, the Internet had 1 million hosts, computers were 1,000 million times faster, and network bandwidth was 20 million times greater than 20 years earlier. The entrepreneurship revolution meant that there was an army of entrepreneurs and would-be entrepreneurs, especially in the United States, with the vision and capacity to seize the commercial opportunities presented by the Web. In February 1993, the National Center for Supercomputing Applications (NCSA) released the first alpha version of Marc Andreessen's Mosaic. By December 1994, the Web was growing at approximately 1% a day—with a doubling period of less than 10 weeks.[37] In the next 10 years, Internet usage exploded.* By 2018, users numbered 4 billion, which was about half of the entire population of the world.[38]

Entrepreneurship Revolution Strikes Gold

Marc Andreessen moved to Silicon Valley in 1994, teamed up with veteran IT entrepreneur Jim Clark, and incorporated Mosaic Communications (later renamed Netscape Communications). Clark put $6 million of his own money into Mosaic, and venture capitalists added another $6 million.[39] Their intent was to create a browser that would surpass the original Mosaic. It was a classic Silicon Valley startup with programmers working 18-hour days, 7 days a week, sometimes even working 48 hours at one stretch just coding. In October 1994, the Netscape browser was posted as a download on the Internet. In no time at all, it was the browser of choice for the majority of Web users; in December 1994, Netscape Communications began shipping Netscape Navigator, which started to produce income.

Netscape Navigator was an instant success, gaining 75% of the browser market within four months of its introduction. Netscape Communications was only 16 months old when it went public in August 1995. Its IPO was one of the most spectacular in history and made Jim Clark the first Internet billionaire. According to an article in *Fortune*, "It was the spark that touched off the Internet boom."[40]

A gold rush was under way. "Netscape mesmerized investors and captured America's imagination. More than any other company, it set the technological, social, and financial tone of the Internet age."[41]A generation of would-be entrepreneurs was inspired by Netscape's success. What's more, corporate executives from established businesses wanted to emulate Jim Barksdale, the former president of McCaw Communications, who joined Netscape's board in October 1994, became CEO in January 1995, and made a huge fortune in just eight months. Investors—both angels and venture capitalists—hustled to invest in Internet-related startups. It seemed as if everyone was panning for Internet gold, not only in Silicon Valley but also throughout the United States—and a couple of years later throughout the rest of the world.

Netscape is a superb example of American venture capital at its best, accelerating the commercialization of innovations especially at the start of revolutionary new industries driven by technology. Venture capital was in at the start of the semiconductor and the minicomputer industries in the late 1950s and early 1960s and the biotech and personal computer industries in the late 1970s, and now it was eager to invest in what promised to be the biggest revolution of them all, the Internet and the Web.

Venture capital is not invested exclusively in technology companies. It was in at the beginning of the overnight package delivery industry with its investment in Federal Express, at the start

*The Internet and the World Wide Web (now usually called the Web) are two separate but related entities. However, most people use the terms interchangeably. The Internet is a vast network of networks, a networking infrastructure. The Web is a way of accessing information over the Internet. It is an information-sharing model that is built on top of the Internet.

of major big-box retailers such as Home Depot and Staples, and at the creation of new airlines including JetBlue. No wonder Jiro Tokuyama, then dean of the Nomura School of Advanced Management in Japan and a highly influential economist, stated that entrepreneurial firms and venture capital are the great advantages that Americans have.[42] Since the early 1970s, 42% of all public companies can trace their roots back to venture capital, and these same companies drive innovation as they account for 85% of all R&D spending of public firms.[43] The Web presented numerous opportunities that were soon being exploited by entrepreneurs. It created a huge demand for more and more capacity on the Internet, which in turn presented opportunities for hardware and software entrepreneurs. They were fortunate to find venture capitalists eager to invest in their startups. The period from 1996 through 2000 was a golden era for classic[44] venture capitalists and the entrepreneurial companies they invested in. It was golden both metaphorically and literally, as more and more venture capitalists and entrepreneurs seemed to have acquired the Midas touch. Some of the financial gains from venture-capital-backed companies were indeed of mythological proportions. For instance, Benchmark Capital's investment of $5 million in eBay multiplied 1,500-fold in just two years.[46] True, Benchmark's investment in eBay set the all-time record for Silicon Valley, but there were plenty of instances when investments increased at least a hundredfold and in some cases 1,000-fold. With investments such as those, overall returns on U.S. classic venture capital soared, with the one-year return peaking at 143% at the end of the third quarter in 2000, compared with average annual returns in the mid-teens prior to the golden era.

During a 1999 news conference at the World Economic Forum in Davos, Switzerland, reporters pestered Bill Gates again and again with variations of the same question: "These Internet stocks, they're a bubble?" An irritated Bill Gates finally confronted the reporters: "Look, you bozos, of course they're a bubble, but you're all missing the point. This bubble is attracting so much new capital to the Internet industry; it is going to drive innovation faster and faster."[45]

But the gold rush came to an end in 2000. The Internet bubble burst. Many companies failed, others were forced into fire-sale mergers, investors were hammered, many jobs were lost, and doom and gloom were pervasive. There was much hand-wringing about the incredible wastefulness of the U.S. method of financing new industries. However, by August 9, 2005—the 10th anniversary of Netscape's IPO—some companies founded during the gold rush were thriving. The market capitalization of just four of them—Google, eBay, Yahoo, and Amazon—was about $200 billion, which handily exceeded all the venture capital invested in all the Internet-related companies through 2000; what's more, it even topped the combined amount raised from venture capital and IPOs. Granted, there were many more losers than winners, but five years after the burst, it was clear that U.S. society as a whole had already benefited mightily and the best was yet to come—but not for everyone. As Schumpeter observed, revolutionary entrepreneurship creates new products, services, and business methods that undermine and sometimes destroy old ones.

Creative Destruction

The Web is blowing gales of creative destruction through many old industries, none more so than that of print newspapers, whose publishers were slow to recognize their business models were endangered—perhaps fatally—by the Web. Some long-established U.S. newspapers, such as the *Rocky Mountain News* and the *Tucson Citizen*, have shut down completely; others have drastically reduced their operations; and a few, including the *Christian Science Monitor* and the *Seattle-Post Intelligencer*, now publish only on the Web and no longer produce print editions. *Newsweek's* final print edition was published on December 31, 2012, ending almost 80 years in print. Several prominent newspaper chains, including the Tribune Company, the *Minneapolis Star Tribune*, Philadelphia Newspapers, and the Sun-Times Media Group, have filed for bankruptcy. The 2009 demise of *Editor and Publisher*, the 125-year-old trade magazine for the newspaper industry, seemed to symbolize the plight of the industry.

Newspapers had not only withstood potential competition from the introduction of other forms of news broadcasting, such as radio in the 1920s and 1930s, television in the 1950s, and 24-hour cable news channels in the 1980s and 1990s, but also actually prospered more and more, so why should they have foreseen in the early 1990s the havoc that the fledgling Web was about to wreak on their industry? What most print publishers did not foresee was that the Web would undermine the two basic sources of newspaper revenues, advertising and paid circulation; annual ad revenue, for example, plunged from its peak of more than $60 billion in 2000 to just over $16 billion in 2014.[47] The underlying cause is the changes in society brought about by the Internet, which was used by about 90% of the U.S. population in 2015 compared with less than 3% in 1993.[48] Twitter, Facebook, Instagram, bloggers, and all forms of social media give readers instant access to breaking news stories and often break news ahead of the old media; Google and other search engines make it easy to find stories from anywhere in the world at lightning speed; and perhaps best of all, it is free. For advertisers, the allure of the Web over print newspapers and magazines is that it allows them to target ads to individuals—every Web user is now a market segment of just one individual—and it provides much better metrics for tracking the effectiveness of ads.

Causes of the Entrepreneurial Revolution

The United States has always been a nation of entrepreneurs. But why has it become more and more entrepreneurial since the end of the 1960s—creating what is now called the entrepreneurial revolution?

First, we need to step back and look at the U.S. economy in the decades before the 1970s. The Great Depression, which followed the stock market collapse of October 1929, had an enormous effect on society. By 1932, when Franklin Roosevelt was elected president, over 13 million Americans had lost their jobs, and the gross national product had fallen 31%. The Roosevelt administration implemented many policies to try to bring the nation out of the Depression, but it was not until World War II that the nation once again started to become prosperous. The end of the war in 1945 heralded an era of economic growth and opportunity. But the memories left by the Depression meant that workers preferred secure jobs with good wages and benefits that medium-sized and big companies offered. And big business was booming.

The late 1940s and the 1950s and 1960s were the era of the corporate employee. They were immortalized by William Whyte in *The Organization Man*,[49] in which he "argued in 1956 that American business life had abandoned the old virtues of self-reliance and entrepreneurship in favor of a bureaucratic 'social ethic' of loyalty, security and 'belongingness.' With the rise of the postwar corporation, American individualism had disappeared from the mainstream of middle-class life."[50] The key to a successful career was this: "Be loyal to the company and the company will be loyal to you." Whyte's writing assumed the change was permanent, and it favored the large corporation.

Big American businesses were seen as the way of the future, not just in the United States but worldwide. John Kenneth Galbraith's seminal book *The New Industrial State*[51] and Jean-Jacques Servan-Schreiber's *Le D´efi Am´ericain* (The American Challenge)[52] both "became the bible to advocates of industrial policies"[53] supporting big business. Both books were instant best sellers. *Le D´efi Am´ericain* sold 600,000 copies in France alone and was translated into 15 languages. Galbraith wrote in 1967, "By all but the pathologically romantic, it is now recognized that this is not the age of the small man." He believed that the best economic size for corporations was "very, very large."

The works of Whyte, Galbraith, and Servan-Schreiber were required reading in universities through the 1970s. Schumpeter's work was hardly ever mentioned,[54] and when it was, it was his book, *Capitalism, Socialism, and Democracy*, published in 1942,[55] in which he was very pessimistic that capitalism would survive. Unlike Karl Marx, who believed the proletariat would bring about the downfall of capitalism, Schumpeter reasoned that the very success of free enterprise would create a class of elites, who would favor central control of the economy and thereby curb free enterprise. His first book, *The Theory of Economic Development*,[56] originally published in German in 1911, in which he endorsed entrepreneurship, was hardly ever mentioned. What's more, in the 1970s there was an abundance of university courses dealing with Karl Marx and almost none dealing with entrepreneurship. It's not surprising that the world was first alerted to the entrepreneurial revolution by a journalist, Norman Macrae, rather than by an academic scholar. About a decade later, researchers confirmed retrospectively that entrepreneurial activity had indeed been on the increase in the United States in the 1970s.[57]

Entrepreneurship did not disappear in the 1930s, 1940s, 1950s, and 1960s; it simply did not grow very much. What brought about the change in the economy that stirred up entrepreneurship around 1970? To try to understand what changes were taking place, we need to look at the social, cultural, and political context of an economy. A framework for this perspective is presented in Figure 1.1, the GEM model for the economy.[58]

The central argument[59] of the GEM model is that national economic growth is a function of two sets of interrelated activities: those associated with established firms and those related directly to the entrepreneurial process. Activity among established firms explains only part of the story behind variations in economic growth. The entrepreneurial process may also account for a significant proportion of the differences in economic prosperity among countries and among regions within countries.

When looking at the nature of the relationship between entrepreneurship and economic growth, it is important to distinguish between entrepreneurial opportunities and entrepreneurial capacity. What drives entrepreneurial activity is that people perceive opportunities and have the skills and motivation to exploit them. The outcome is the creation of new firms and, inevitably, the destruction of inefficient or outmoded existing firms. Schumpeter's process of creative destruction is

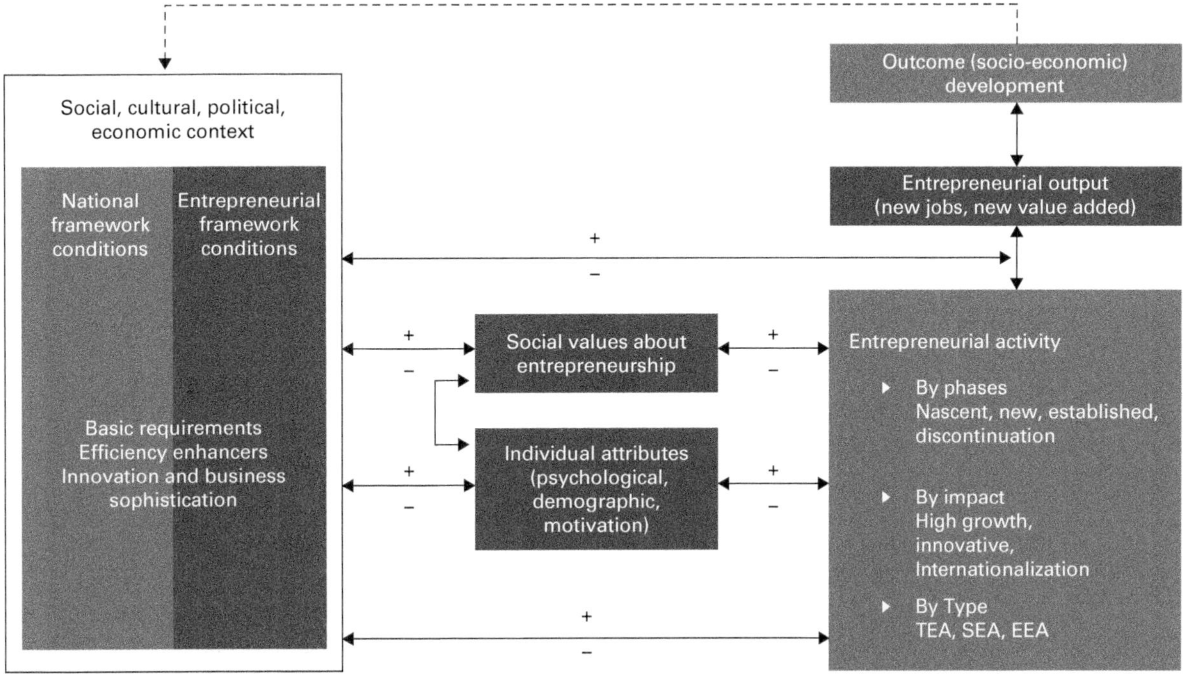

FIGURE 1.1 GEM Conceptual Framework.

captured in the model by business churning. Despite its negative connotation, creative destruction actually has a positive impact on economic growth—declining businesses are phased out as startups maneuver their way into the market. These dynamic transactions occur within a particular context, which the GEM model calls *entrepreneurial framework conditions* and which includes factors such as availability of finance, government policies and programs designed to support startups, R&D transfer, physical and human infrastructure, education in general, education and training for entrepreneurship, cultural and social norms, and internal market openness.

Changes in the Entrepreneurial Framework Conditions

Now let's look at some of the major changes in the framework conditions that have fueled the entrepreneurial revolution.

Cultural and Social Norms

First, let's consider the most important components, the entrepreneurs themselves. In the 1960s, a generation of Americans born in the late 1930s and the 1940s—including the first baby boomers—came of age. They had no firsthand memory of the Great Depression. When they were growing up, the economy was doing well most of the time, so they really had not experienced hard times like their parents had endured.

Hence, they were not as concerned about job security. Many were even rebelling against large corporations, some of which were seen as members of the military-industrial complex that was supporting the very unpopular war in Vietnam; some companies were trading with South Africa, where apartheid still prevailed; and others were under attack by consumer activists such as Ralph Nader.[60] It was a generation of Americans who were better educated than their parents, and for them, starting a new business was a credible career.

The *Fortune* 500 employed 20% of the workforce in the 1960s. That percentage began to decline in 1980 and has continued to do so every year since then, down to about 10% by 2005. Hence, jobs in big companies became scarcer. Many companies downsized, and according to George Gendron, who was the publisher of *Inc.* magazine during the 1980s and 1990s, 20% of downsized executives started businesses. Gendron also suggested that some of the executives who were retained—often the "best and the brightest"—became disillusioned by their career prospects in stagnant companies, and that led to a "second exodus" that produced more entrepreneurial activity.[61]

Other important social changes boosted entrepreneurship in the 1990s. More women became business owners, and the proportion of Asian-owned firms increased, as did Hispanic-owned and African American–owned firms. According to Gendron, for people with limited options in employment, entrepreneurship represents the "last meritocracy."

Today, many of the societal changes of the 1990s continue. Increasingly, digitization, shifts in business models, resources distribution, and a cultural evolution of workers and customers who expect outcomes beyond just pure economic drive our societal norms.[62]

Government

The 1970s were the decade when Washington bailed out Penn Central Railroad, Lockheed, and Chrysler. Washington seemed more concerned with big business than with small. But it did recognize the need to pay attention to startups with high potential, especially the ones funded by venture capitalists. There had been a burst of venture-capital-backed startups in the last half of the 1960s. But in the early 1970s, venture capital dried up to a trickle. Looking back from the perspective of 2012, when $26.7 billion of new money flowing into the venture capital industry seems routine, it is scarcely believable that only $10 million of new money was committed in 1975. Congress took urgent steps in 1978 to stimulate the venture capital industry, including reducing the capital gains tax and easing the ERISA prudent man rule, which had inhibited pension funds from investing in venture capital funds. The pension floodgates opened, and the inflow of venture capital increased to $4.9 billion by 1987. Likewise, venture capital invested in portfolio companies increased from a low of $250 million in 1975 to $3.9 billion in 1987—a 16-fold increase.[63]

The government asserted its role of ensuring *market openness* by minimizing anticompetitive behavior. We've already mentioned that legislation toward the end of the 1970s deregulated the airfreight and airline passenger industries. That was followed in the early 1980s by the U.S. Justice Department's move to break up AT&T's monopoly.

The government deserves immense credit for its funding of R&D in government, universities, and corporations, both directly and indirectly, through purchases of products. Its support was vital in the development of the computer, communications, biotech, and many other industries.

Washington activated the Small Business Innovation Research (SBIR) program in 1983 to ensure that small businesses shared some of the federal R&D dollars for new technology-based developments. Each year the SBIR has $2.2 billion set aside to support the financing of cutting-edge technologies developed by small businesses.[64] In general, funds awarded under the SBIR program go to develop new technologies that are high risk and high reward. Some might say it is pre-venture capital money. From that viewpoint, $2 billion is a significant amount when compared with $740 million that venture capitalists invested in 194 seed-stage companies in 2014.[65] Through 2015, SBIR support has resulted in "70,000 issued patents, close to 700 public companies, and approximately $41 billion in venture capital investments."[66] Symantec, Qualcomm, DaVinci, and iRobot received R&D funding from this program.

R&D Transfer

Commercial development of intellectual property resulting from federally funded research is a major benefit to the U.S. economy. It was given a major boost by the passage of the Bayh–Dole Act, implemented in 1980. The primary intent of that law was to foster the growth of technology-based small businesses by allowing them to own the patents that arose from federally sponsored research. Under Bayh–Dole, universities were allowed to grant exclusive licenses—a feature that was regarded as crucial if small businesses were to commercialize high technologies that were inherently risky propositions.[67]

Fruits of Federally Funded R&D

The success of Bayh–Dole goes far beyond the efforts of Bob Dole and Birch Bayh. This legislation combined the ingenuity and innovation from our university laboratories with the entrepreneurial skills of America's small businesses. Most importantly, this combination created the incentive necessary for private investment to invest in bringing new ideas to the marketplace. The delicate balance of ingenuity, entrepreneurship, and incentive on which the success of Bayh–Dole has depended must not be disrupted.

The year 2016 marked the 35th year since the implementation of the Bayh–Dole Act, and the Association of University Technology Managers estimates that universities have spun off 4,000 companies. They have patented nearly 20 new drugs in that time. It is estimated that 30% of the NASDAQ's total value comes from university-based and federally funded research that never would have happened if not for the Bayh–Dole Act. A few of the notable products to come from the act include the following:

- Taxol, the most important cancer drug in 15 years, according to the National Cancer Institution
- DNA sequencer, the basis of the entire Human Genome Project
- StormVision, which airport traffic and safety managers use to predict the motion of storms
- Prostate-specific antigen test, now a routine component of cancer screening
- V-Chip, which allows families to control access to television programming

Before 1980, U.S. universities were granted about 300 patents a year. In 2003, they applied for about 10,000. In 1980, 25 to 30 universities had offices for technology transfer. Today, more than 1,200 do.[68] *The Economist* hailed Bayh–Dole as "the most inspired piece of legislation to be enacted in America over the past half-century." *The Economist* estimated that Bayh–Dole had created 2,000 new companies and 260,000 new jobs and had contributed $40 billion annually to the U.S. economy.[69] That assessment was made almost 10 years ago, and more progress has been made since then.[70]

The government itself has technology transfer offices at most of its research laboratories,[71] and many large companies have licensing offices. IBM, for example, which annually spends about $6 billion on R&D, was granted 9,100 patents in 2018. It generates about $1 billion annually from licensing intellectual property, which comprises both patents and copyrights.

Photo Credit: Thomas Samson/Gammo-Rapho/Getty Images

Jack Dorsey, founder and chairman of Twitter at a conference in Paris in December 2009.

Physical Infrastructure

The biggest change in entrepreneurship in the last 20 years is due to the Web, the great equalizer. Small businesses now have at their fingertips a tool so powerful that it is leveling the playing field. Big businesses no longer enjoy as many scale economies as they did before the Internet. Information that could have been gathered only by a multitude of market researchers can now be found with a search engine and a couple of clicks of a mouse. Entrepreneurs don't have to spend a fortune to reach customers with print, radio, and television advertising; they can target their potential customers anywhere in the world via the Web. When they want to find a vendor, the Web is there to help them—as it is when they are seeking employees, bankers, and investors. Furthermore, the cost of communications of all kinds has plummeted since AT&T was broken up. A long-distance telephone call that cost 40 cents a minute in 1980 now can be made for as little as 1 cent. And if these entrepreneurs need to travel by air, they can shop the Web to find the cheapest ticket, automobile rental, and hotel room.

The worldwide distribution of goods and services is now open to everyone. The revolution of selling online that began in earnest with eBay now is driven by many online companies, most notably Amazon. Looking back, a 2005 study by ACNielsen International Research, reports that 724,000 Americans sell on eBay and that it is their primary or secondary source of income.[72] An American entrepreneur can sell merchandise to a customer anywhere in the world; PayPal (founded in 1998 and now part of eBay) can ensure that the entrepreneur receives payment speedily and securely online; the merchandise can be delivered to the buyer within a day or so; and buyer and seller can track the shipment online at each step of its journey. Amazon has allowed individual entrepreneurs to sell on their site since 2000, and today more than half of Amazon's sales come these third-party sellers.

Outsourcing services and goods makes companies more efficient and effective. Entrepreneurs can now focus on their company's core competency and let vendors take care of noncore items such as payroll, Web hosting, manufacturing, and distribution. There are even companies that will help entrepreneurs find outsource partners. Outsourcing enables small businesses to act like big ones, and some small companies are even called *virtual companies* because they outsource so much of their work.

For some entrepreneurs, business incubators combine many of the advantages of outsourcing. Incubators provide not only physical space but also shared services. Many incubators also provide ready access to human infrastructure. In 1980, there were only 12 business incubators in the United States; over the period between 1985 and 1995, the number of U.S. incubators grew 15-fold, from 40 to nearly 600[73]—and by 2006, there were some 1,115 incubators.[74] Today the International Business Innovation Association (INBIA) estimates that there are over 7,000 incubators worldwide. The Global Accelerator Report shows that nearly $200 million is invested annually across the globe by accelerators.[75]

Human Infrastructure

Access to human infrastructure is as important as access to physical infrastructure—maybe more so. The human infrastructure for entrepreneurs grew rapidly in the last 20 years or so, and gaining access to it has never been easier. Thirty years ago, starting a new venture was a lonely pursuit, fraught with pitfalls that would have been avoided by someone with prior entrepreneurial experience. Today numerous entrepreneurship experts gladly help people who are starting or growing companies. There are incubators, accelerators, support networks, both informal and formal, of professionals who know a lot about the entrepreneurial process.

Education, Training, and Professionalization

Entrepreneurship education and training is now readily available, part of the professionalization of entrepreneurship that has taken place over the few decades.[76] Entrepreneurs can get schooled in the art of business planning on campuses, at boot camps, in incubators and accelerators, and all sorts of programs. Today's training drives entrepreneurs to understand their opportunity and market, to understand how to create real value for their customers and themselves, and to develop the deliverables to communicate their vision. Successful entrepreneurs who grow will someday need a formal business plan but at the start it is more important that they understand business planning and the necessary tools they need to craft at the start (summaries, pitch decks, financial projections, etc.). The field has come a long way since the pioneers of entrepreneurship training put writing a business plan at the core of their programs in the 1970s.[77]

When Babson College and the University of Texas started their internal business plan competitions in 1985, only a few schools had entrepreneurship courses. Now more than 60% of four-year colleges and universities have at least one entrepreneurship course, and many have entrepreneurship centers.

The Accidental Entrepreneur

Like many other scientists and engineers who have ended up founding companies, I didn't leave Caltech as an entrepreneur. I had no training in business; after my sophomore year of college I didn't take any courses outside of chemistry, math, and physics. My career as an entrepreneur happened quite by accident.

There is such a thing as a natural-born entrepreneur.... But the accidental entrepreneur like me has to fall into the opportunity or be pushed into it. Most of what I learned as an entrepreneur was by trial and error, but I think a lot of this really could have been learned more efficiently.

—Gordon Moore (cofounder of Fairchild Semiconductor in 1957 and Intel in 1968)[78]

Financial

Raising money for a new business is seldom easy, but the process of raising startup and expansion capital has become more efficient in the last 30 years or so. In 1982, for instance, an economist at the National Science Foundation stated that venture capital was shrouded in empirical secrecy and an aura of beliefs.[79] The same held true for angel investing. In contrast, today there is an abundance of help. The National Venture Capital Association reports that in 2018 U.S. venture capital investment reached $131 billion surpassing the all-time high dot-com bubble year of 2000. And then there is crowdfunding, the global phenomenon where in just a few short years Kickstarter has facilitated individuals investing on over 150,000 projects to the tune of over $4 billion.[80] We do not have reliable numbers for business angel investors, but we do know that informal investors—everyone from parents to external business angels—now invest more than $100 billion annually in startup and baby businesses. Furthermore, informal investors are ubiquitous. Five percent of American adults report that they "invested" in someone else's venture in the last three years.[81] It is impossible to claim that the availability of financing has driven the entrepreneurial revolution, but it does appear that sufficient financing has been available to fuel it.

Churning and Economic Growth

Technological change, deregulation, competition, and globalization presented countless opportunities, which American entrepreneurs seized and commercialized. It caused a lot of *churning*, or Schumpeter's creative destruction. But 11 new businesses with employees were started for every 10 that died over the decade 1990–2000.[82] It is this churning that gives the economy its vitality. Only a society that willingly adapts to change can have a dynamic economy.

We can find examples of churning in every industry that is not a monopoly or a regulated oligopoly. Who can recall VisiCalc or for that matter Lotus 1-2-3? At the height of their fame, they were two of the most widely used software packages for PCs. Today Excel is the spreadsheet of choice. In one week alone in May 1982, when Digital Equipment Corporation (DEC) introduced its ill-fated Rainbow PC, four other companies introduced PCs.[83] At the peak of the PC industry frenzy in the early 1980s, more than 200 companies either had introduced PCs or were planning to do so. Only a handful of PC manufacturers exist today. DEC, which in 1982 was the second-largest computer manufacturer in the world, was eventually bought by Compaq, which in turn merged with Hewlett-Packard. In 2004, IBM sold its PC division to Lenovo, a company founded in 1984 by a group of academics at the government-backed Chinese Academy of Sciences in Beijing.

Entrepreneurial competition, according to Schumpeter, "strikes not at the margins of the profits … of the existing firms but at their foundations and very lives." Established companies that stick with their old ways of doing business self-destruct as their customers turn to new competitors with better business models.

"The power of Walmart is such, it's reversed a 100-year history in which the manufacturer was powerful and the retailer was sort of the vassal. It turned that around entirely."

— *Nelson Lichtenstein, University of California, Santa Barbara*

Not only did the advent of the PC churn up the entire computer industry, but also it virtually wiped out the typewriter industry. And it changed the way office work is organized. Secretaries had to learn computer skills or they were out of work.

And who knows what the future holds for the PC itself? Schumpeterian disruptions abound throughout the information technology space: The PC industry is being upset by mobile, and servers and data storage are being challenged by the cloud. More examples of churning: Southwest Airlines is now the most successful U.S. airline; two of its giant rivals in 1971 no longer exist, and the third, Continental, was bankrupt twice, in 1983 and 1990, and later merged with United Airlines. United Airlines, US Airways, Hawaiian Airlines, ATA Airlines (also known as American Trans Air), Delta, Northwest, Aloha Airlines, and American Airlines have all been in Chapter 11 bankruptcy, and only a handful of the 100 or so passenger airlines started up since deregulation are still around. Who goes to a travel agent to get a regular airline ticket or book a hotel room today? Where is the fax machine? Likewise, video stores and CD retailers are gone except in a few circumstances. Why are newspapers laying off workers? Who is buying a film camera?

Granted, churning causes a lot of disruption—and nowhere more than in the lives of those who lose their jobs as a result. But overall, society is the beneficiary. Entrepreneurship produces new products and services, it increases productivity, it generates employment, and in some cases, it keeps inflation in check. Economists estimate that Walmart alone knocked 20%—perhaps as much as 25%—off the rate of inflation in the 1990s.[84] According to Alfred Kahn, the father of airline deregulation, airline passengers are now saving $20 billion a year.[85] And with Skype and the Internet, you can "talk to anyone, anywhere in the world for free. Forever."[86]

Next we will look at how other nations as well as the United States are faring with entrepreneurship.

Global Entrepreneurship Monitor

The Global Entrepreneurship Monitor (GEM) was created in 1997* to study the economic impact and the determinants of national-level entrepreneurial activity. GEM is the largest coordinated research effort ever undertaken to study population-level entrepreneurial activity. Since its inception, a total of 99 economies accounting for approximately 95% of the world's GDP and 85% of its population have participated in GEM's annual study. This final section of Chapter 1 is based on the findings from the 20th anniversary of Global Entrepreneurship Monitor: the GEM 2018/2019 Global Report,[87] which explores the entrepreneurial activity from over four dozen economies around the globe. Because of this worldwide reach and rigorous scientific method, GEM has become the world's most influential and authoritative source of empirical data and expertise on the entrepreneurial potential of nations.[88]

The main objectives of GEM are to gather data that measure the entrepreneurial activity of nations and other data related to entrepreneurial activity, to examine what national characteristics are related to levels of entrepreneurial activity, and to explain how differences in entrepreneurial activity are related to different levels of economic growth among nations. GEM distinguishes between two types of entrepreneurial activity within the Total Early-Stage Entrepreneurial Activity (TEA)[89]:

- *Nascent entrepreneurs* are individuals who are actively trying to start a new business but who have not yet done so.
- *Owner–managers* are owner–managers of a new business that is no more than 3½ years old.

There are three main measures of entrepreneurial activity:

- TEA (total entrepreneurial activity) is the percentage of the adult population that is either nascent entrepreneurs or owner–managers or both. It measures the overall entrepreneurial activity of a nation.
- TEA (opportunity) is the percentage of the adult population that is trying to start or has started a business to exploit a perceived opportunity. They are classified as improvement-driven opportunity motivated if they additionally seek to improve their income or independence through entrepreneurship.
- TEA (necessity) is the percentage of the adult population that is trying to start or has started a business because all other options for work are either absent or unsatisfactory.

*GEM in itself is an example of not-for-profit (social) entrepreneurship. It was conceived in 1997 by Babson College and London Business School professors. It was prototyped with bootstrap funding and volunteers and was officially launched in 1998 with research teams from 10 nations and supported with funding raised by each team from national sponsors. It produces annual global reports on the overall state of entrepreneurship in those nations, country-specific reports, and reports on special topics such as female entrepreneurship, financing, and job creation. More than 100 global and regional reports can be read and downloaded at www.gemconsortium.org.

Principal Findings from GEM

For the 2018/19 Global Report, GEM researchers from dozens of countries across the world compiled data from individuals in 49 different economies, collectively representing all regions of the world and a broad range of economic development levels.* New features of this 20th anniversary report of GEM include the National Entrepreneurship Context Index (NECI), a composite measure of the health of the entrepreneurial context in each economy. Based upon a dozen framework conditions, NECI can be used to assess the environment for entrepreneurship in an economy. It allows policy makers and practitioners to benchmark results between peer economies and identify areas to address, as they seek to enhance an economy's entrepreneurial potential and impact. Peer economies are identified as low-income, middle-income, or high-income and as such provide cleaner comparisons and understanding. GEM 2018/19 also provides a first-time global look at entrepreneurship in the gig and sharing economy as well as entrepreneurial activity in family-based entrepreneurship, entrepreneurial employee activity, and solo entrepreneurship.

Activity

Total Entrepreneurial Activity (TEA) is a key indicator of GEM and is captured in the GEM Framework in Figure 1.2. It measures the percentage of adults (age 18–64) in an economy who are nascent and new entrepreneurs. In economies with low GDP per capita, TEA rates tend to be high, with a correspondingly higher proportion of necessity-motivated entrepreneurship. Conversely, high GDP economies show lower levels of entrepreneurship, but a higher proportion of those with opportunity-motivations. To at least some extent then, development levels are associated with particular patterns in the level and type of entrepreneurial activity. This relationship can be seen in Figure 1.3.

Some of the highest average TEA ranks and scores (see Table 1.1) are found in Middle East/Africa and Latin America/Caribbean. Angola and Guatemala came in with the highest TEA ranks and scores in these regions. The East and South Asia region shows a mix of TEA levels with Thailand ranking high but China and India coming in lower on the scale.

This table displaying the different rankings of entrepreneurial activity by regions also gives us a peek into the activity going on inside existing businesses. The Entrepreneurial Employee Activity (EEA) shows that high-income countries such as Canada, Ireland, and the United States report the highest EEA rates of more than 8% of their adult population. Overall, entrepreneurial activity among employees in existing companies is seen to be highest in Europe. In fact, in some European countries (Sweden and Germany, for instance), entrepreneurship is at least as likely to occur in organizations as it is in the "traditional" startup context. In other countries, entrepreneurship rates are strong regardless of context: see the Netherlands and Canada where levels of employee entrepreneurship complement similarly high TEA rates.

Necessity, Opportunity, and Gender

GEM defines necessity-driven entrepreneurs as those who are pushed into starting businesses because they have no other work options and need a source of income. Opportunity-motivated entrepreneurs, on the other hand, are those entering this activity primarily to pursue an opportunity.

*Some of the text in the following sections was excerpted and adapted from the *GEM 2018–19 Global Report*, http://www.gemconsortium.org/report.

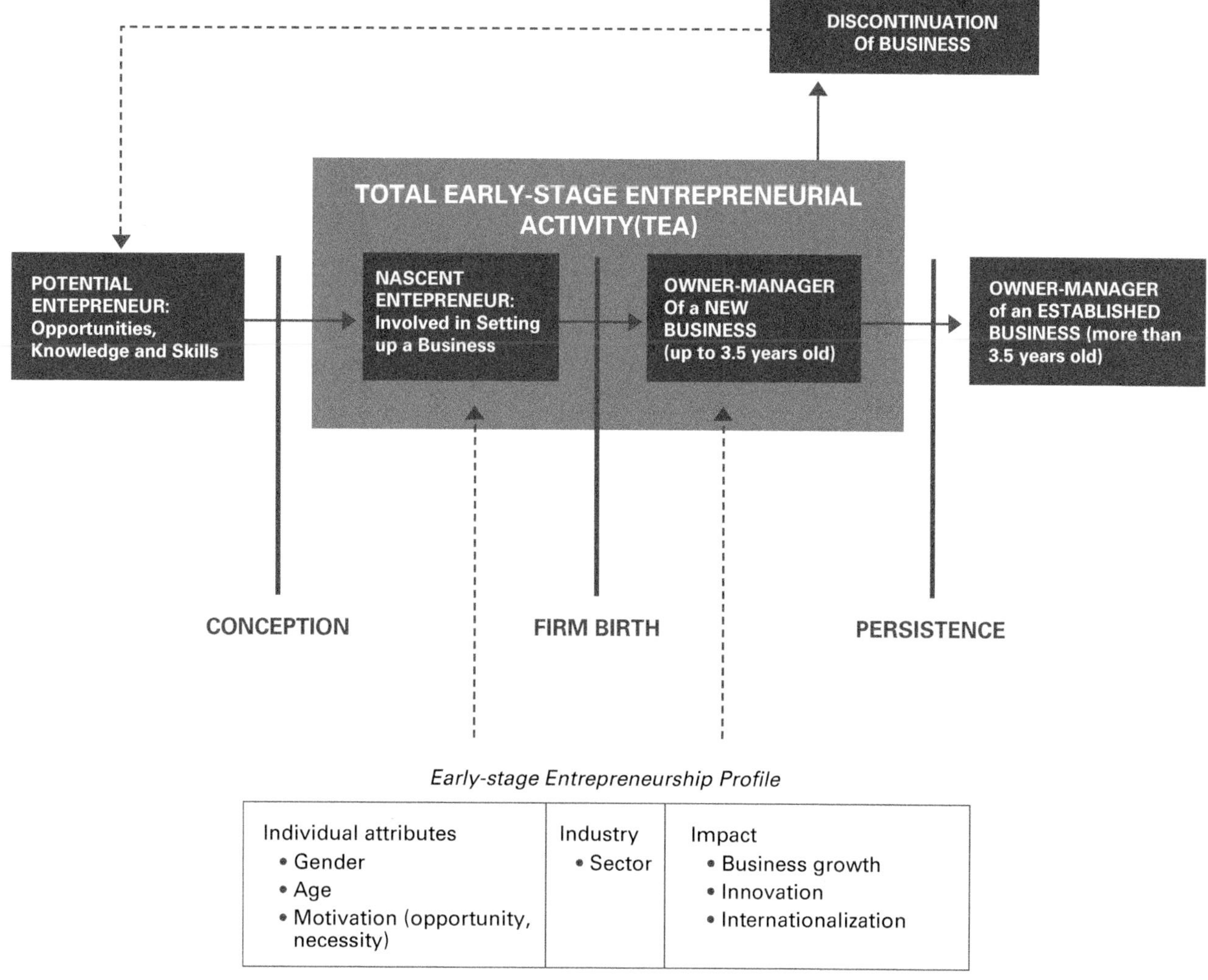

FIGURE 1.2 **Phases of the Entrepreneurship Process and GEM Indicators.**

The latter are further distinguished as improvement-driven opportunity motivated if they additionally seek to improve their income or independence through entrepreneurship.

Necessity-driven motives tend to be highest in low and sometimes middle-income economies. With greater economic development levels, the proportion of entrepreneurs with necessity motives generally declines, whereas improvement-driven opportunity increasingly accounts for a great proportion of motives. Geographic differences exist, however, even within the same region and sometimes at the same economic development level.

The GEM data also provides some insight into the issue of gender with respect to the rates of men and women who pursue necessity or opportunity-based entrepreneurial activities. Of all of the economies analyzed by GEM researchers, six show similar TEA rates between women and men (Table 1.2). With the exception of North America, they are split across the globe: two are in the East and South Asia region (Indonesia and Thailand), one is in Latin America (Panama), and three come from the Middle East and Africa region (Qatar, Madagascar, and Angola). It is also interesting to note that these countries cross all three income levels.

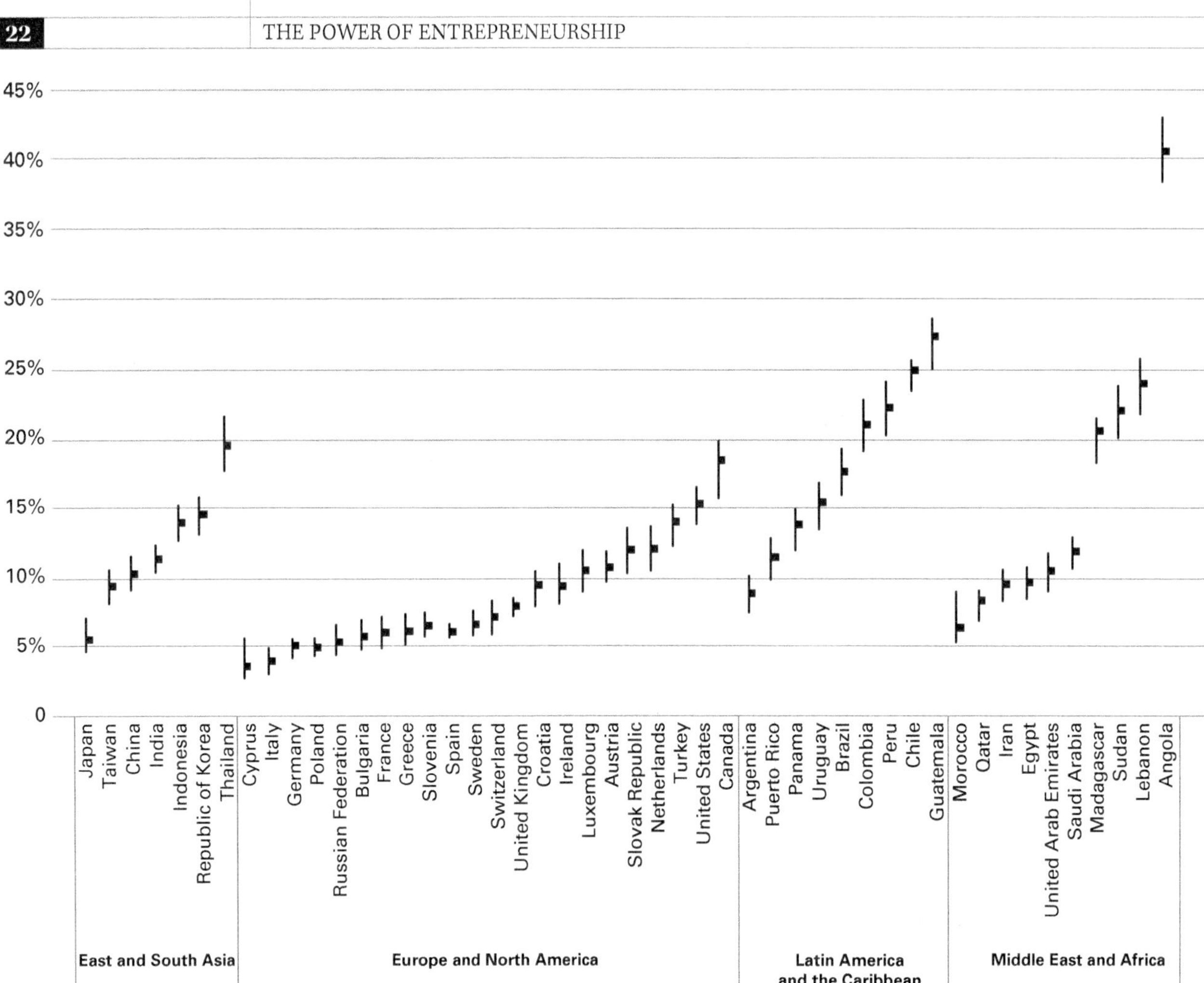

FIGURE 1.3 **Overall TEA Rates in Four Geographic Regions.**

Age Distribution of Early-Stage Entrepreneurial Activity

Although entrepreneurship is often seen through the lens of the popular press as a young person's domain, the data tells a story that again supports the entrepreneurial age we live in: People of all ages across all types of economies are engaging in entrepreneurial activity. Data consistently shows support for the idea that entrepreneurial activity is most prevalent for those in their early (age 25–34) and mid-career (age 35–44) affirming the thought that those with ambition and at least some experience, networks, and other resources view entrepreneurship as a productive path to follow. Those in their early careers may not have accumulated the resources, credibility, and connections of older entrepreneurs. Overall, however, it is interesting to note that rates in other age categories are not all that far behind.

Figure 1.4 shows an interesting comparison of entrepreneurs in countries whose activity is driven primarily by either younger or older entrepreneurs. On the left is a graph of TEA rates showing a high prevalence of entrepreneurial activity among the youngest adults for five countries. These graphs show high rates of entrepreneurship among those aged 18–24, with a steep decline in subsequent age groups, particularly in Canada, Brazil, and the Slovak Republic. The other side highlights countries where entrepreneurs thrive later in life. Here, the highest

Table 1.1 Phases and Types of Entrepreneurial Activity, GEM 2018

			Nascent entrepreneurship rate		New business ownership rate		Early-stage entrepreneurial activity (TEA)		EEA		Established business ownership rate		Discontinuation of businesses	
INCOME LEVEL	**REGION**	**ECONOMY**	**Score**	**Rank/48**	**Score**	**Rank/48**	**Score**	**Rank/48**	**Score**	**Rank/49**	**Score**	**Rank/48**	**Score**	**Rank/49**
low income	Middle East and Africa	**Angola**	22.8	1	19.5	1	40.8	1	3.2	25T	15.2	5	25.5	1
high income	Latin America and the Caribbean	**Argentina**	4.9	27	4.3	25	9.1	32	1.5	39T	9.1	16	3.9	24
high income	Europe and North America	**Austria**	6.8	20T	4.4	24	10.9	23	6.4	9	6.5	27T	5.0	17T
middle income	Latin America and the Caribbean	**Brazil**	1.7	47	16.4	3	17.9	11	0.7	45T	20.3	3	4.3	22T
middle income	Europe and North America	**Bulgaria**	2.4	46	3.7	30T	6.0	42	0.4	48	8.4	19T	1.8	43T
high income	Europe and North America	**Canada**	11.2	6	8.9	10	18.7	10	8.6	1T	7.5	22T	8.6	4
high income	Latin America and the Caribbean	**Chile**	16.0	3	10.1	9	25.1	3	4.2	21T	8.5	18	7.1	11
middle income	East and South Asia	**China**	4.7	28	5.9	17T	10.4	26	1.0	42	3.2	44	2.5	36T
middle income	Latin America and the Caribbean	**Colombia**	15.7	4	5.8	19T	21.2	7	2.0	32T	6.5	27T	4.7	20T
high income	Europe and North America	**Croatia**	5.8	24	3.9	27T	9.6	29T	5.3	15	4.2	40T	3.4	29T
high income	Europe and North America	**Cyprus**	1.2	48	2.7	39T	3.9	48	5.4	14	6.1	33T	2.3	41
low income	Middle East and Africa	**Egypt**	4.0	35T	5.9	17T	9.8	27	2.1	31	4.5	39	7.6	8T
high income	Europe and North America	**France**	4.0	35T	2.3	44T	6.1	41	4.3	19T	2.5	47	2.9	34
high income	Europe and North America	**Germany**	2.7	42T	2.4	43	5.0	46	5.2	16	7.5	22T	1.6	46T
high income	Europe and North America	**Greece**	4.2	30T	2.3	44T	6.4	38T	1.8	36	10.8	14	3.4	29T
middle income	Latin America and the Caribbean	**Guatemala**	13.7	5	15.0	4	27.5	2	2.0	32T	11.2	13	7.4	10
low income	East and South Asia	**India**	8.8	13	2.7	39T	11.4	22	0.8	44	7.0	24	4.9	19
low income	East and South Asia	**Indonesia**	3.1	40	11.1	7	14.1	16	1.3	41	11.8	11	1.4	49
middle income	Middle East and Africa	**Iran**	4.1	32T	5.7	21	9.7	28	0.9	43	12.3	9	6.1	13
high income	Europe and North America	**Ireland**	6.5	22	3.2	36	9.6	29T	8.6	1T	6.8	25T	3.8	25
high income	Middle East and Africa	**Israel**	–	N/A	–	N/A	–	N/A	7.2	6	–	N/A	5.0	17T
high income	Europe and North America	**Italy**	2.7	42T	1.6	47	4.2	47	3.2	25T	6.4	29T	1.6	46T
high income	East and South Asia	**Japan**	3.3	37T	2.2	46	5.3	44	2.2	30	6.2	32	1.8	43T
middle income	Middle East and Africa	**Lebanon**	6.9	19	17.6	2	24.1	4	1.7	37T	21.6	2	8.0	7
high income	Europe and North America	**Luxembourg**	7.1	17T	3.7	30T	10.7	24T	7.1	7	3.4	43	3.7	26T
low income	Middle East and Africa	**Madagascar**	10.3	9T	10.9	8	20.7	8	0.6	47	22.4	1	4.3	22T
low income	Middle East and Africa	**Morocco**	3.3	37T	3.5	34	6.7	37	4.8	17	4.2	40T	10.4	3
high income	Europe and North America	**Netherlands**	6.0	23	6.5	15T	12.3	18	7.9	4	12.0	10	2.5	36T
high income	Latin America and the Caribbean	**Panama**	7.4	14T	6.6	14	13.8	17	0.0	49	6.4	29T	3.4	29T
middle income	Latin America and the Caribbean	**Peru**	17.5	2	5.8	19T	22.4	5	1.5	39T	8.4	19T	7.6	8T
high income	Europe and North America	**Poland**	4.1	32T	1.1	48	5.2	45	1.9	34T	13.0	7	2.4	39T
high income	Latin America and the Caribbean	**Puerto Rico**	9.1	12	2.6	41	11.6	21	1.9	34T	1.9	48	3.1	32
high income	Middle East and Africa	**Qatar**	5.0	26	3.6	32T	8.5	33	6.3	10T	4.2	40T	3.0	33
high income	East and South Asia	**Republic of Korea**	6.8	20T	7.9	11	14.7	14	3.6	23	12.5	8	2.5	36T
middle income	Europe and North America	**Russian federation**	2.7	42T	2.9	38	5.6	43	0.7	45T	4.9	37	1.6	46T
high income	Middle East and Africa	**Saudi Arabia**	5.3	25	6.9	13	12.1	19T	2.8	28	3.1	45	8.5	5
high income	Europe and North America	**Slovak Republic**	9.2	11	3.1	37	12.1	19T	4.4	18	4.6	38	3.6	28
high income	Europe and North America	**Slovenia**	2.8	41	3.6	32T	6.4	38T	5.9	13	6.8	25T	2.4	39T
high income	Europe and North America	**Spain**	2.7	42T	3.8	29	6.4	38T	1.7	37T	6.1	33T	1.7	45
low income	Middle East and Africa	**Sudan**	10.3	9T	12.6	6	22.2	6	4.3	19T	10.2	15	17.3	2
high income	Europe and North America	**Sweden**	4.6	29	2.5	42	6.8	36	6.8	8	5.3	36	3.7	26T
high income	Europe and North America	**Switzerland**	4.1	32T	3.4	35	7.4	35	6.3	10T	11.5	12	2.0	42
high income	East and South Asia	**Taiwan**	3.2	39	6.5	15T	9.5	31	4.2	21T	13.9	6	5.4	14
middle income	East and South Asia	**Thailand**	7.3	16	13.2	5	19.7	9	2.4	29	19.6	4	8.1	6
middle income	Europe and North America	**Turkey**	7.4	14T	7.1	12	14.2	15	3.2	25T	8.7	17	5.2	15
high income	Middle East and Africa	**United Arab Emirates**	7.1	17T	3.9	27T	10.7	24T	6.3	10T	2.6	46	5.1	16
high income	Europe and North America	**United Kingdom**	4.2	30T	4.2	26	8.2	34	7.3	5	6.4	29T	2.7	35
high income	Europe and North America	**United States**	10.5	8	5.3	22	15.6	13	8.0	3	7.9	21	4.7	20T
high income	Latin America and the Caribbean	**Uruguay**	11.1	7	4.9	23	15.7	12	3.5	24	5.6	35	6.6	12

Source: 2018/19 GEM Global Report.

Table 1.2 **Gender Distribution of TEA, Opportunity TEA, and Necessity TEA**

			MALE TEA (% of adult male population)		FEMALE TEA (% of adult male population)		MALE TEA Opportunity (% of TEA males)		FEMALE TEA Opportunity (% of TEA females)		MALE TEA Necessity (% of TEA males)		FEMALE TEA Necessity (% of TEA females)	
INCOME LEVEL	REGION	ECONOMY	Score	Rank/48	Score	Rank/48	Score	Rank/48	Score	Rank/48	Score	Rank/48	Score	Rank/48
low income	Middle East and Africa	**Angola**	41.0	1	40.7	1	67.3	40	47.2	45	27.5	12	49.5	3
high income	Latin America and the Caribbean	**Argentina**	10.1	33	8.1	28	76.4	16	59.8	39	21.4	21	35.7	9T
high income	Europe and North America	**Austria**	13.9	23	7.9	29	74.3	24	77.0	16	16.5	37	14.9	36
middle income	Latin America and the Caribbean	**Brazil**	18.5	13	17.3	9	67.7	38	55.6	44	31.4	9	44.0	5
middle income	Europe and North America	**Bulgaria**	6.4	45	5.6	34	72.2	32	63.4	34	23.2	17	34.8	11
high income	Europe and North America	**Canada**	20.4	8T	17.0	11	75.9	17	83.3	5	16.8	35	10.0	42
high income	Latin America and the Caribbean	**Chile**	29.0	4	21.2	3	79.9	11	66.5	28	18.4	29	30.6	16
middle income	East and South Asia	**China**	11.4	29	9.3	18	68.9	37	72.4	22	29.4	10	25.9	24
middle income	Latin America and the Caribbean	**Colombia**	24.9	6	17.8	7	87.5	2	83.0	6	10.7	44	14.1	37
high income	Europe and North America	**Croatia**	12.1	27	7.1	31	63.3	42T	59.6	40T	32.4	7	32.2	15
high income	Europe and North America	**Cyprus**	4.8	48	2.9	47	83.4	7	86.6	2	12.4	40	9.8	43
low income	Middle East and Africa	**Egypt**	14.1	20	5.4	35T	48.4	47	45.0	46	47.3	1	48.5	4
high income	Europe and North America	**France**	7.0	41	5.3	37	77.5	15	66.9	27	21.1	23	23.9	26
high income	Europe and North America	**Germany**	6.6	44	3.3	46	69.9	36	69.7	24	17.1	32T	15.9	34
high income	Europe and North America	**Greece**	8.8	37T	3.9	43T	87.3	4	67.7	26	10.4	45	27.1	21
middle income	Latin America and the Caribbean	**Guatemala**	30.8	3	24.5	2	67.4	39	56.1	42	32.3	8	43.9	6
low income	East and South Asia	**India**	14.0	21T	8.7	21T	45.0	48	40.2	47	44.2	2	49.9	2
low income	East and South Asia	**Indonesia**	14.0	21T	14.1	12	75.2	19T	70.8	23	22.4	19	28.0	18
middle income	Middle East and Africa	**Iran**	12.9	25	6.5	32	59.0	46	64.9	30T	39.6	3	29.8	17
high income	Europe and North America	**Ireland**	11.9	28	7.5	30	75.2	19T	77.8	14T	19.6	27	19.3	31
high income	Europe and North America	**Italy**	5.5	47	2.8	48	82.2	8	78.6	12T	11.5	41	11.3	41
high income	East and South Asia	**Japan**	6.7	43	4.0	41T	73.3	28T	62.8	35	18.1	31	23.8	27
middle income	Middle East and Africa	**Lebanon**	31.3	2	17.4	8	63.3	42T	64.3	33	36.4	4	35.7	9T
high income	Europe and North America	**Luxembourg**	12.7	26	8.7	21T	78.8	13	82.4	8	17.1	32T	4.2	47
low income	Middle East and Africa	**Madagascar**	20.4	8T	21.1	4	70.3	34	64.4	32	28.5	11	33.9	13
low income	Middle East and Africa	**Morocco**	9.2	36	4.3	40	62.6	44T	68.3	25	32.8	6	27.7	19
high income	Europe and North America	**Netherlands**	16.2	16	8.3	27	79.3	12	82.8	7	8.6	46	9.7	44
high income	Latin America and the Caribbean	**Panama**	13.8	24	13.9	13	85.6	6	84.8	4	13.7	38	12.3	38
middle income	Latin America and the Caribbean	**Peru**	23.9	7	20.9	5	73.3	28T	73.1	21	23.1	18	23.1	28
high income	Europe and North America	**Poland**	6.0	46	4.5	39	87.9	1	95.0	1	10.8	43	5.0	46
high income	Latin America and the Caribbean	**Puerto Rico**	15.2	8T	8.4	24T	75.0	22T	64.9	30T	20.9	24	26.2	23
high income	Middle East and Africa	**Qatar**	8.6	39	8.4	24T	73.1	30	78.6	12T	16.7	36	15.8	35
high income	East and South Asia	**Republic of Korea**	17.0	15	12.2	16	77.6	14	77.8	14T	21.9	20	19.6	30
middle income	Europe and North America	**Russian federation**	7.3	40	3.9	43T	62.6	44T	39.8	48	33.1	5	51.1	1
high income	Middle East and Africa	**Saudi Arabia**	14.7	19	8.5	23	73.6	26T	59.6	40T	26.1	14	39.0	7
high income	Europe and North America	**Slovak Republic**	15.2	17T	9.0	19	64.4	41	61.7	37	26.6	13	27.6	20
high income	Europe and North America	**Slovenia**	8.8	37T	3.8	45	72.6	31	62.4	36	20.7	25	32.7	14
high income	Europe and North America	**Spain**	6.8	42	6.0	33	75.2	19T	65.7	29	18.9	28	26.7	22
low income	Middle East and Africa	**Sudan**	27.5	5	17.1	10	75.0	22T	55.9	43	21.2	22	38.3	8
high income	Europe and North America	**Sweden**	9.5	35	4.0	41T	70.7	33	80.0	10	12.5	39	1.3	48
high income	Europe and North America	**Switzerland**	10.0	34	4.7	38	87.4	3	86.4	3	5.5	48	11.5	39
high income	East and South Asia	**Taiwan**	10.2	32	8.8	20	75.6	18	75.3	18	24.4	16	24.7	25
middle income	East and South Asia	**Thailand**	20.1	10	19.3	6	80.3	10	79.6	11	17.1	32T	18.7	32
middle income	Europe and North America	**Turkey**	20.0	11	8.4	24T	73.6	26T	76.7	17	18.3	30	11.4	40
high income	Middle East and Africa	**United Arab Emirates**	11.0	31	10.1	17	73.9	25	73.8	20	20.3	26	21.4	29
high income	Europe and North America	**United Kingdom**	11.1	30	5.4	35T	85.7	5	81.0	9	11.1	42	16.6	33
high income	Europe and North America	**United States**	17.7	14	13.6	14	81.1	9	74.7	19	8.5	47	7.7	45
high income	Latin America and the Caribbean	**Uruguay**	19.4	12	12.3	15	70.2	35	60.5	38	25.7	15	34.7	12

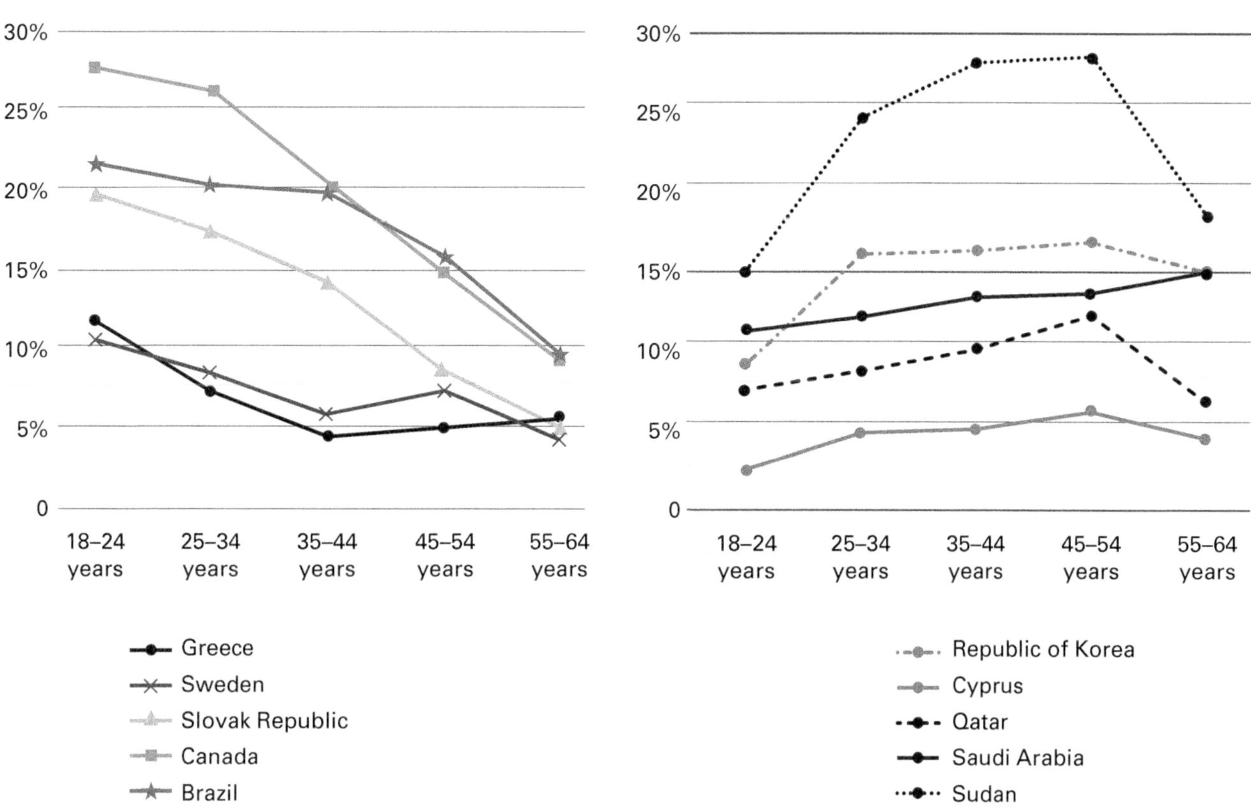

FIGURE 1.4 TEA by Age by Phase of Economic Development.

entrepreneurship rates occur among those in late careers, likely due to these individuals having particular strengths to leverage, as noted above.

Survey data alone does not allow one to definitively know why rates differ by age, but it is likely due to different sociocultural factors. The GEM report speculates that it could be that young people in the countries with high rates have the energy and motivation for entrepreneurship or there may be peers and an environment that celebrates young entrepreneurs. Or it could be that they simply have little to lose because they are at the beginning of their careers. As for the countries with high older entrepreneur rates, it may be that they are dissatisfied with their work situations and decide to venture out on their own or that they have only now accumulated the insight, wisdom, and networks to drive an entrepreneurial opportunity to fruition.

Growth Expectations and Job Creation

The power of entrepreneurship is derived from the positive impact it makes on the lives and well-being of people—not just the entrepreneurs themselves, but individuals throughout their communities. Most directly, as entrepreneurs build their businesses, they often create jobs for others, providing a broader economic impact for their region. Simply stated, entrepreneurship is a social good. When entrepreneurs create jobs, they contribute to employment and the overall well-being in their cities, towns, and regions. While TEA rates indicate how many entrepreneurs there are in each economy, growth expectations—measured in the GEM report as job creation projections—represent a quality measure of this activity. Entrepreneurs differ in their growth ambitions, and this can have significant potential impact on the employment growth and competitive advantage of each economy.

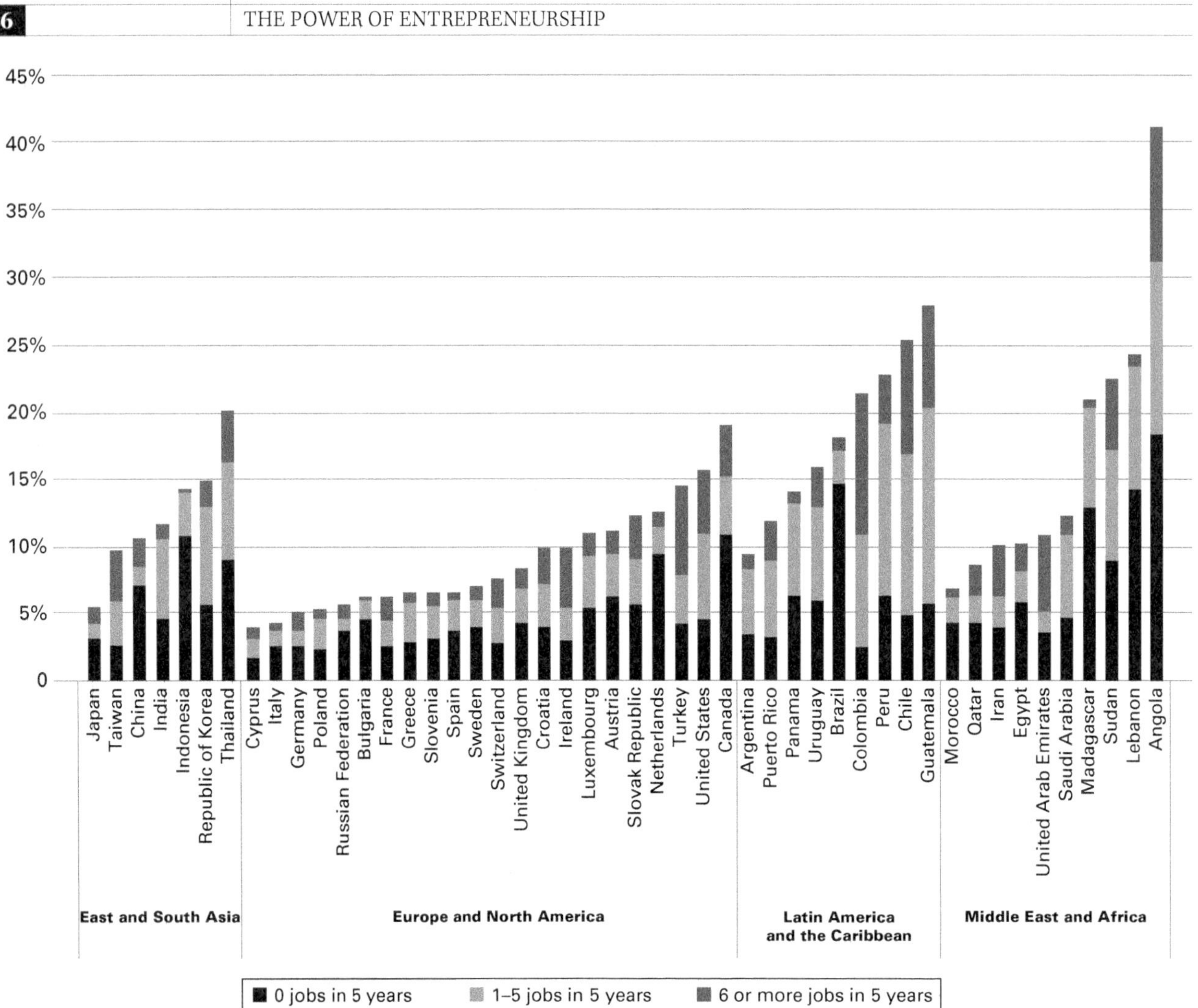

FIGURE 1.5 **Total Early-stage Entrepreneurial Activity with Three Level of Self-Reported Job Growth Expectations.**

The 2018/19 GEM Global Report allows us to see the ambitions and job creation intentions of entrepreneurs across the globe. The report classifies entrepreneurs into three groups: those who expect to create no new jobs in the next five years, those who expect to create at least one to five jobs in this time frame, and those who expect to create six new jobs or more. Figure 1.5 shows the job growth expectations of entrepreneurs by country across the four geographic regions of the study. Like other data we have examined, there is also great variation in the job creation expectations of entrepreneurs across regions and income levels.

Looking at regions and countries—and in line with the thoughts just noted—Brazil appears to be dominated by solo entrepreneurs (those not predicting any job creation), while the entrepreneurs in other countries in Latin America have more aggressive growth expectations.

Drilling down a bit more, in the Middle East and Africa, few entrepreneurs in Madagascar and Lebanon expect to add more than six jobs in the next five years. Alternatively, nearly a quarter of entrepreneurs in Sudan and Angola have these aspirations. Combined with high TEA rates, this accounts for much job creation potential in these economies. In the UAE, despite relatively low rates of entrepreneurship, over half of entrepreneurs project this highest level of job creation. This demonstrates that, even when entrepreneurship is less common in an economy, it can still have substantial impact.

As you examine Table 1.1 for your country and attempt to make sense of it relative to other parts of the world, it is always prudent to also remember that things may not turn out as the entrepreneurs expected. Some individuals are more optimistic than others. However, intention does matter, and to achieve growth, entrepreneurs need to have the ambition to grow!

Entrepreneurship Ecosystems and the Importance of Support

The cautionary notes regarding different factors outside the control of the individual entrepreneur that may affect their intentions to grow their business brings forward another important concept that all entrepreneurs must be aware of: the entrepreneurial ecosystem in which they reside. Similar to the biological ecosystem of the earth, atmosphere, animals, plants, and other organisms that work best in concert with each, entrepreneurial ecosystems include different elements that support each other. Public policy, financing, laws, education, development programs, and a host of other factors come together to create an environment of support for entrepreneurial activities. An entrepreneurial ecosystem can be defined as a multidimensional enterprise that supports entrepreneurial development through a variety of interrelated activities (education, financing, training, public policy and research, etc.)[90] between individuals, organizations, and institutions.

Although there may be different factors in each individual ecosystem, the GEM study assesses what are seen as some of the most relevant factors. In the 2018/19 GEM Global Report, researchers examined the following dozen factors across 54 different economies:

- Entrepreneurial financing
- Government policy support
- Taxes and bureaucracy
- Government entrepreneurship programs
- School-level entrepreneurship education and training
- Post-school entrepreneurship education and training
- R&D transfer
- Access to commercial and professional infrastructure
- Internal market dynamics
- Internal market burdens
- Access to physical and services infrastructure
- Social and cultural norms

Together these factors make a composite index, the National Entrepreneurship Context Index, which is designed to help policy makers—and all of us—better understand the strengths and weaknesses of their environment for entrepreneurship. Table 1.3 provides the NECI rankings and scores for all countries in the 2018/19 GEM Global Report. Most clear and striking to researchers was the importance of having healthy conditions across all aspects of the entrepreneurial environment. Researchers found that countries that had poor conditions in just a few of the overall factors can have a negative effect on the willingness and ability of people to start businesses, even with significant strengths in other areas. This reiterates the importance of an ecosystem that truly works in unison.

Table 1.3 GEM's National Entrepreneurship Context Index (NECI) Rankings

INCOME LEVEL	REGION	ECONOMY	NECI Rank	NECI Score (out of 10)
high income	Middle East and Africa	**Qatar**	1	6.7
low income	East and South Asia	**Indonesia**	2	6.6
high income	Europe and North America	**Netherlands**	3	6.5
high income	East and South Asia	**Taiwan**	4	6.3
low income	East and South Asia	**India**	5	6.2
high income	Europe and North America	**United States**	6	6.0
high income	Middle East and Africa	**United Arab Emirates**	7	5.9
high income	Europe and North America	**Luxembourg**	8	5.7
high income	Europe and North America	**Switzerland**	9	5.7
high income	Europe and North America	**France**	10	5.6
middle income	East and South Asia	**China**	11	5.6
high income	Europe and North America	**Canada**	12	5.5
high income	Europe and North America	**Austria**	13	5.5
high income	East and South Asia	**Republic of Korea**	14	5.5
middle income	East and South Asia	**Thailand**	15	5.5
high income	Europe and North America	**Spain**	16	5.4
high income	Europe and North America	**Ireland**	17	5.4
high income	Europe and North America	**Sweden**	18	5.4
high income	Europe and North America	**Germany**	19	5.4
high income	East and South Asia	**Japan**	20	5.3
high income	Latin America and the Caribbean	**Argentina**	21	5.2
high income	Europe and North America	**Latvia**	22	5.2
middle income	Latin America and the Caribbean	**Mexico**	23	5.2
high income	Europe and North America	**Poland**	24	5.2
high income	Europe and North America	**Slovenia**	25	5.2
high income	Latin America and the Caribbean	**Chile**	26	5.1
high income	Europe and North America	**Cyprus**	27	5.1
high income	Middle East and Africa	**Israel**	28	5.1
middle income	Europe and North America	**Turkey**	29	5.1
high income	Europe and North America	**United Kingdom**	30	4.9
middle income	Europe and North America	**Kazakhstan**	31	4.9
middle income	Latin America and the Caribbean	**Colombia**	32	4.8
high income	Latin America and the Caribbean	**Uruguay**	33	4.7
low income	Middle East and Africa	**Egypt**	34	4.7
middle income	Middle East and Africa	**Lebanon**	35	4.7

Table 1.3 (Continued)

INCOME LEVEL	REGION	ECONOMY	NECI Rank	NECI Score (out of 10)
middle income	Europe and North America	**Bulgaria**	36	4.7
middle income	Europe and North America	**Russian federation**	37	4.6
middle income	Latin America and the Caribbean	**Dominican Republic**	38	4.6
middle income	Latin America and the Caribbean	**Peru**	39	4.5
high income	Europe and North America	**Italy**	40	4.5
high income	Middle East and Africa	**Saudi Arabia**	41	4.4
high income	Europe and North America	**Greece**	42	4.3
high income	Europe and North America	**Slovak Republic**	43	4.3
middle income	Latin America and the Caribbean	**Guatemala**	44	4.3
low income	Middle East and Africa	**Sudan**	45	4.3
middle income	Middle East and Africa	**Iran**	46	4.3
low income	Middle East and Africa	**Morocco**	47	4.3
middle income	Latin America and the Caribbean	**Brazil**	48	4.2
low income	Middle East and Africa	**Madagascar**	49	4.1
low income	Middle East and Africa	**Angola**	50	4.1
high income	Latin America and the Caribbean	**Puerto Rico**	51	4.1
high income	Latin America and the Caribbean	**Panama**	52	4.0
high income	Europe and North America	**Croatia**	53	3.8
low income	Middle East and Africa	**Mozambique**	54	3.2

CONCLUSION

Entrepreneurial activity in the United States now accounts for much of the nation's prosperity and its competitiveness in the global economy. The disappearance of "old" jobs, particularly in mature manufacturing industries, and their replacement by "new" jobs, especially in service and knowledge-based industries, is disconcerting to workers whose jobs are threatened. But society has to accept *churning*—the creation of new enterprises and the destruction of obsolete ones—because it gives the U.S. economy its vitality. As seen in the GEM data, the same can be said for many other economies around the world. Across the globe, entrepreneurial framework factors combine to create entrepreneurship ecosystems and determine the degree of entrepreneurial activity in a nation, or for that matter in a region within a nation.

In this chapter, we have looked at the importance of entrepreneurship to national economies. In the following chapters, we will look at the specifics of how entrepreneurs start and grow their new ventures.

YOUR OPPORTUNITY JOURNAL

We are excited that you are exploring an entrepreneurial journey, one that may lead you to launch a business while in college, after graduation, or at some future point in your life. We know that all great entrepreneurs are avid readers and thinkers, and as such, we encourage you to capture some of your thoughts as you read this book. These thoughts may focus on a new venture that you are interested in creating, or they may focus more on your entrepreneurial career plan. In either event, we will close each chapter with space for you to reflect on what it means to you and your potential venture.

Reflection Point	Your Thoughts...
1. What world-changing industries or opportunities do you see developing over the next 5–10 years?	
2. What innovations or new technologies will drive these world-changing opportunities?	
3. Which regions of the world have the greatest potential for developing these opportunities? Which are you most interested in?	
4. What skills do you need to develop to take advantage of these opportunities?	

WEB EXERCISE

What do you think will be the next major innovation (that changes the way we live, work, and play)? Search the Web to identify trends, statistics, and other evidence to support your insight. (*Hint*: Venture capitalists in the United States have a knack for spotting emergent industries.)

NOTES

1. Estimate based on the 2015/16 Global Report and GEM Adult Population Surveys. http://www.gemconsortium.org/report.
2. https://www.sba.gov/advocacy/small-businesses-drive-job-growth-us.
3. https://www.sba.gov/blogs/small-businesses-create-2-million-jobs. Retrieved in August, 2016.
4. 2015/16 Global Entrepreneurship Monitor by Donna Kelley, Slavica Singer, and Mike Herrington.
5. Schumpeter, J. A. *The Theory of Economic Development*. Cambridge, MA: Harvard University Press. 1934. (This book was originally published in German in 1911.)
6. Maddison, A. *Phases of Capitalist Development*. New York: Oxford University Press. 1989. Baumol, W. J. Entrepreneurship and a Century of Growth. *Journal of Business Venturing*, 1(2): 141–145. 1986.
7. https://www.sba.gov/sites/default/files/advocacy/2018-Small-Business-Profiles-US.pdf.
8. For the Small Business Administration definitions of *small business* refer to www.sba.gov/gopher/Financial-Assistance/Defin/defi4.txt.
9. https://www.sba.gov/sites/default/files/advocacy/Frequently-Asked-Questions-Small-Business-2018.pdf.
10. Small Business Administration. *Frequently Asked Questions*. https://www.sba.gov/sites/default/files/advocacy/Frequently-Asked-Questions-Small-Business-2018.pdf
11. Global Entrepreneurship Monitor: 2017 United States Report.
12. It is impossible to establish a precise upper limit because many new ventures are abandoned very soon after they are started and never get entered into any data set that tracks startups.
13. Kirchhoff, Bruce A. *Entrepreneurship and Dynamic Capitalism*. Westport, CT: Praeger. 1994.
14. Nucci, A. The Demography of Business Closings. *Small Business Economics*, 12: 25–39. 1999.
15. *The Shape of Small Business*. www.nfib.com/object/PolicyGuide2.html. Retrieved in August 2005.
16. Dennis, W. J., Jr., and Fernald, L. W., Jr. The Chances of Financial Success (and Loss) from Small Business Ownership. *Entrepreneurship Theory and Practice*, 1: 75–83. 2002.
17. Global Entrepreneurship Monitor: 2013 United States Report.
18. *The Shape of Small Business*. www.nfib.com/object/PolicyGuide2.html. Retrieved in August 2005. The net business formation index was discontinued in 1995 when one of its two components was no longer available.
19. Macrae, N. The Coming Entrepreneurial Revolution. *The Economist*. December 15, 1976.
20. Birch, David L. *Job Creation in America: How Our Smallest Companies Put the Most People to Work*. New York: Free Press. 1978.
21. For example: Acs, Z. *The New American Evolution*. Washington, DC: U.S. Small Business Administration, Office of Economic Research. June 1998. Kirchhoff, Bruce A. *Entrepreneurship and Dynamic Capitalism*. Westport, CT: Praeger. 1994.
22. At one point, General Motors was the largest corporation ever to exist in the United States in terms of its revenues as a percentage of GDP. In 1953, Charles Erwin Wilson, then GM's president, was named by President Eisenhower as secretary of defense. When he was asked, during the hearings before the Senate Armed Services Committee, if as secretary of defense he could make a decision adverse to the interests of General Motors, Wilson answered affirmatively but added that he could not conceive of such a situation "because for years I thought what was good for the country was good for General Motors and vice versa." Later this statement was often garbled when quoted, suggesting that Wilson had said simply, "What's good for General Motors is good for the country." At the time, GM was one of the largest employers in the world—only Soviet state industries employed more people. *Source:* http://en.wikipedia.org/wiki/Charles_Erwin_Wilson.

23. "The observation made in 1965 by Gordon Moore, co-founder of Intel, that the number of transistors per square inch on integrated circuits had doubled every year since the integrated circuit was invented. Moore predicted that this trend would continue for the foreseeable future. In subsequent years, the pace slowed down a bit, but density has doubled approximately every 18 months, and this is the current definition of Moore's Law. Most experts, including Moore himself, expect Moore's Law to hold for at least another two decades." *Source:* www.webopedia.com/TERM/M/Moores_Law.html. Retrieved in August 2005.

24. Working independently and unaware of each other's activity, Jack Kilby at Texas Instruments and Robert Noyce at Fairchild Semiconductor Corporation invented almost identical integrated circuits at the same time. "In 1959 both parties applied for patents. Jack Kilby and Texas Instruments received U.S. patent #3,138,743 for miniaturized electronic circuits. Robert Noyce and the Fairchild Semiconductor Corporation received U.S. patent #2,981,877 for a silicon-based integrated circuit. The two companies wisely decided to cross-license their technologies after several years of legal battles, creating a global market now worth about $1 trillion a year." *Source:* http://inventors.about.com/library/weekly/aa080498.htm. Retrieved in August 2005.

25. The first personal computers were actually called microcomputers. The phrase "personal computer" was common currency before 1981 and was used as early as 1972 to characterize Xerox PARC's Alto. However, due to the success of the IBM PC, what had been a generic term came to mean specifically a microcomputer compatible with IBM's specification. *Source:* http://en.wikipedia.org/wiki/Ibm 5150.

26. https://about.van.fedex.com/wp-content/uploads/2019/01/FX_Corp_Brochure2018.pdf.

27. http://en.wikipedia.org/wiki/Airline Deregulation Act.

28. Jordan, W. A. *Airline Entry Following U.S. Deregulation: The Definitive List of Startup Passenger Airlines, 1979–2003*. www.trforum.org/forum/getpaper.php?id = 22&PHPSESSID = 119446d6d13ce93d6c6aea3df05010ce. Retrieved in August 2005.

29. www.tsha.utexas.edu/handbook/online/articles/SS/eps1_print.html.

30. Bygrave, W. D., and Timmons, J. A. *Venture Capital at the Crossroads*. Boston: Harvard Business School Press. 1992.

31. http://www.thinkbiotech.com/globalbiotech; https://www.ey.com/Publication/vwLUAssets/ey-beyond-borders-biotech-report-2017/$FILE/ey-beyond-borders-biotech-report-2017.pdf.

32. Rogers, E. M., and Larsen, J. K. *Silicon Valley Fever: Growth of High-Technology Culture*. New York: Basic Books. 1984.

33. Bush, Vannevar. As We May Think. *The Atlantic Monthly*. July 1945.

34. Nelson, Ted. The Story So Far. *Ted Nelson Newsletter, No.* 3. October 1994.

35. www.computerhistory.org/exhibits/internet_history/Internet_history_80s.html. Retrieved in August 2005.

36. Tim Berners-Lee, *Inventor of the World Wide Web, Knighted by Her Majesty Queen Elizabeth II*. www.w3.org/2004/07/timbl_knighted. Retrieved in August 2005.

37. *New Scientist Magazine*. December 17, 1994.

38. https://*www.internetworldstats*.com/stats.htm.

39. www.smartcomputing.com/editorial/dictionary/detail.asp?DicID = 17855.

40. Lashinsky, Adam. Remembering Netscape: The Birth of the Web. www.fortune.com/fortune/print/0,15935,108 1456,00.html. Retrieved in August 2016.

41. Ibid.

42. Gevirtz, D. *The Entrepreneurs: Innovation in American Business*. New York: Penguin Books. 1985. p. 30.

43. https://nvca.org/columns/the-true-impact-of-venture-capital. Retrieved in February 2019.

44. Classic venture capital is money invested privately in seed, startup, expansion, and late-stage companies. The term *classic* is used to distinguish it from money invested privately in acquisitions, buy-outs, mergers, and reorganizations.

45. www.forbes.com/2001/02/06/0207VC.html. Retrieved in August 2005.

46. Friedman, T. L. *The World Is Flat*. New York: Farrar, Straus and Giroux. 2005.

47. Pew Research Center for Journalism and Media. http://www.journalism.org/2015/04/29/newspapers-fact-sheet/. Retrieved in February 2019.

48. World Bank, *World Development Indicators*. www.google.com/search?hl = en& source = hp&q = Internet + users + united + states&aq = 2&oq = Internet + users + &aqi = g10.

49. Whyte, W. *The Organization Man*. New York: Simon & Schuster. 1956.

50. Postrel, V. How Has "The Organization Man" Changed? *The New York Times*. January 17, 1999.

51. Galbraith, J. K. *The New Industrial State*. Boston: Houghton Mifflin. 1967.

52. Servan-Schreiber, J. J. *The American Challenge*. New York: Scribner. 1968.

53. Macrae, Norman. *We're All Entrepreneurial Now-17 April 1982*. www.normanmacrae.com/intrapre-neur.html. Retrieved in August 2016.

54. For example, a mid-1980s study by Calvin Kent of the content of popular principles of economics "revealed that entrepreneurship was either neglected, improperly presented, or only partially covered." Kent, C. A., and Rushing, F. W. Coverage of Entrepreneurship in Principles of Economics Textbooks: An Update. *Journal of Economics Education*, 20, 184–189. Spring 1999.

55. Schumpeter, J. A. *Capitalism, Socialism, and Democracy*. Third edition. New York: Harper Torchbooks. 1950. (Originally published in 1942.)

56. Schumpeter, J. A. *The Theory of Economic Development*. Cambridge, MA: Harvard University Press. 1934. Reprinted edition, Cambridge, MA: Harvard University Press. 1949.

57. Blau, D. M. A Time-Series Analysis of Self-Employment in the United States. *Journal of Political Economy*, 95: 445–467. 1987. Evans, D., and Leighton, L. S. The Determinants of Changes in U.S. Self-Employment. *Small Business Economics*, 1(2): 111–120. 1987.

58. Acs, Z. J., Arenius, P., Hay, M., and Minniti, M. *The Global Entrepreneurship Monitor: 2004 Executive Report*. www.gemconsortium.org.

59. This is excerpted from Reynolds, P. D., Hay, M., Bygrave, W. D., Camp, S. M., and Autio, E. *Global Entrepreneurship Monitor: 2000 Executive Report*. www.gemconsortium.org.
60. Ralph Nader's best-selling book *Unsafe at Any Speed: The Designed-In Dangers of the American Automobile*, published in 1965, claimed that automobile manufacturers were ignoring safety features, like seat belts, and were reluctant to spend money on improving safety.
61. *George Gendron on the State of Entrepreneurship*. December 2002. www.pioneerentrepreneurs.net/bigidea_gendron.php. Retrieved in August 2005.
62. https://www.forbes.com/sites/sesilpir/2018/10/15/business-is-no-longer-an-island-four-trends-effecting-the-future-workforce/#2d536d7d5b54
63. Bygrave, W. D., and Timmons, J. A. *Venture Capital at the Crossroads*. Boston: Harvard Business School Press. 1992.
64. https://www.sbir.gov/birth-and-history-of-the-sbir-program. Retrieved in August 2016,
65. *National Venture Capital Association 2015 Yearbook*.
66. https://www.sbir.gov/birth-and-history-of-the-sbir-program.
67. Nelson, L. The Rise of Intellectual Property Protection in the American University. *Science*, 279 (5356): 1460–1461. 1998. www.sciencemag.org/cgi/content/full/279/5356/1460. Retrieved in August 2005.
68. Morris, D. Who Gets the Fruits of Public R&D? *Minneapolis Star Tribune*. November 28, 2004. www.ilsr.org/columns/2004/112804.html. Retrieved in August 2005.
69. Innovation's Golden Goose. *The Economist*. December 12, 2002.
70. Statement of Senator Birch Bayh to the National Institutes of Health. May 25, 2004. http://ott.od.nih.gov/Meeting/Senator-Birch-Bayh.pdf. Retrieved in May 2010.
71. www.nal.usda.gov/ttic/guide.htm. Retrieved in August 2005.
72. Singletary, M. How to Get the Most Bang from eBay. *Maine Sunday Telegram*. August 7, 2005.
73. Wiggins, J., and Gibson, D. V. Overview of US Incubators and the Case of the Austin Technology Incubator. *International Journal of Entrepreneurship and Innovation Management*, 3(1/2): 56–66. 2003. www.ic2.org/publications/Incubator%20Paper%20with%20Joel.pdf. Retrieved in September 2013.
74. National Business Incubation Association, *Business Incubation Frequently Asked Questions*. www.nbia.org/resourcelibrary/faq/index.php#3. Retrieved in May 2010.
75. https://www.forbes.com/sites/groupthink/2016/06/29/the-state-of-the-startup-accelerator-industry/#3fad1a0b7b44. Retrieved in February 2019.
76. *George Gendron on the State of Entrepreneurship*. December 2002. www.pioneerentrepreneurs.net/bigidea_gendron.php. Retrieved in August 2005.
77. Lange, J., Mollov, A., Pearlmuttter, M., Singh, S., and Bygrave, W. *Pre-Startup Formal Business Plans and Post-Startup Performance: A Study of 116 New Ventures*. Presented at the Babson Kauffman Entrepreneurship Research Conference, Babson College. June 2005.
78. Moore, G. E. The Accidental Entrepreneur. Originally published in *Engineering & Science* (California Institute of Technology), 57(4): 23–30. Summer 1994. http://nobelprize.org/physics/articles/moore. Retrieved in August 2005.
79. Boylan, M. *What We Know and Don't Know About Venture Capital*. American Economic Association Meeting, December 28, 1981, and National Economist Club, January 19, 1982.
80. https://www.kickstarter.com/help/stats.
81. Bygrave, W. D. *Global Entrepreneurship Monitor: 2004 Financing Report* (with Steve Hunt). www.gemconsortium.org.
82. www.sba.gov/advo/research/dyn_b_d8_902.pdf.
83. Rifkin, G., and Harrar, G. *The Ultimate Entrepreneur: The Story of Ken Olsen and Digital Equipment Corporation*. Chicago, IL: Contemporary Books. 1998.
84. Lichtenstein, N. Is Walmart Good for America? *PBS Frontline*. June 9, 2004. www.pbs.org/wgbh/pages/frontline/shows/walmart/interviews/lichtenstein.html. Retrieved in August 2005.
85. www.news.cornell.edu/stories/April05/HEC.05.cover.html. Retrieved in August 2005.
86. www.skype.com.
87. Global Entrepreneurship Monitor: 2018/2019 Global Report by Niels Bosma and Donna Kelley.
88. Autio, E. *Global Entrepreneurship Monitor: GEM-Mazars Special Report on High-Expectation Entrepreneurship*. 2005. www.gemconsortium.org.
89. Global Entrepreneurship Monitor: 2015/2016 Global Report.
90. https://hbr.org/2014/05/what-an-entrepreneurial-ecosystem-actually-is. Fetters, M., Greene, P., Rice, M., and Butler, J. *The Development of University-Based Entrepreneurship Ecosystems: Global Practices*. Northampton, MA: Edward Elgar Publishing. 2010.

Case MightyWell[1]

Introduction

As Emily Levy began to settle into her seat on a crowded train from Penn Station to Boston, a four-plus-hour commute that was now becoming a frequent event, she began to think of how far the company she had founded two years earlier had come. Graduating from college just months earlier in May 2016, Emily now found herself with a substantial investment offer that would allow her to grow her company, but she knew the next 12 months would be challenging. Emily had successfully developed and brought to market a product focused on improving the health-care experience for patients. She now wondered whether her company could rely on one product or whether she could disrupt a broader market within wellness wear.[2] Emily knew the decision she was about to make would have significant implications for the future success and sustainability of her company.

Early Years

To say that Emily Levy was born into a family of fashion industry entrepreneurs would be an understatement. While Emily was growing up, Emily's mother established a successful career in fashion, having helped open and run a Giorgio Armani store in the heart of Boston, Massachusetts, before transitioning into advertising roles at Hill Holiday, a leading advertising firm. While her mother focused on high-end fashion, Emily's father targeted more casual customers with his retail clothing store selling apparel to surfing, skateboarding, and snowboarding enthusiasts. Emily's brother, 12 years her senior, followed in the family's footsteps. After graduating from college, he launched his own sales representative company, "GL Sales," selling on behalf of O'Neill and other apparel companies. All three ventures provided Emily with direct insight and exposure to product design, manufacturing, wholesale and retail sales. Starting in the eighth grade, Emily balanced time at her father's store with her schoolwork, while also working with her brother to organize product samples for him on the weekends. Unfortunately, the recession of 2000 significantly affected her father's store, leading to bankruptcy. Emily recalled "seeing first-hand what being an entrepreneur was and how unforeseen macro risks can impact a company."[3]

In high school, Emily participated in three sports, including serving as captain for both field hockey and lacrosse, and completed a number of AP classes, including psychology. Emily had always been interested in humanities and the human element of history. While school never came easy to her, she took pride in her work ethic and never backed down from challenges. After graduating from high school, Emily considered a number of undergraduate business programs before accepting a four-year scholarship to Babson College as a Center for Women's Entrepreneurial Leadership (CWEL) scholar. The mission of CWEL is to "create a gender-enlightened business ecosystem where a diverse range of entrepreneurial leaders is encouraged to create economic and social value for themselves, their organizations, and society."[4] The Center provides female students with an opportunity to further develop and build confidence in their leadership skill. Knowing that she wanted to start her own business eventually, Emily believed Babson's focus on women entrepreneurs would help her accomplish her dream. It was at Babson that Emily began to surround herself with a number of mentors who worked at the Center, often reaching out to them for feedback and advice.

Following her freshman year of college, Emily's focus on social entrepreneurship continued to grow as she took part in a three-week program that sent female students to Rwanda to teach entrepreneurship. In 2010, Babson had partnered with the Rwanda Private Sector Federation to establish the Babson Rwanda Entrepreneurship Center (BREC) with the mission of strengthening Rwanda's entrepreneurial environment:

> BREC will partner with Babson's Center for Women's Leadership Program to send a team of 5–8 of Babson's Women's Leaders from across campus to Save, Rwanda for three weeks in the Summer of 2013 for the second year in a row to teach entrepreneurship, leadership and academic skills to 9th and 10th grade Rwandan students, conduct a women's leadership seminar at the National University of Rwanda, work alongside aspiring and successful female entrepreneurs of Rwanda, and engage with women empowerment organizations all while getting the opportunity to explore the nation's capital of Kigali and other unique Rwandan experiences.[5]

Reflecting on her time in Rwanda, Emily recalled her participation in this program and the unique timing of this trip, "I loved to see how resilient the people in Rwanda were. They taught me that just because you have a bad situation, it doesn't

[1] This case was written by Andrew Zacharakis and Alan Simonian of Babson College with financial support from the John H. Muller, Jr. Chair in Entrepreneurship, Babson College. Copyright Babson College, 2017.

[2] Wellness wear—clothing that complements or facilitates medical well-being.

[3] Emily Levy, interview by author, Wellesley, MA, November 10, 2016.

[4] Babson College, "Center for Women's Entrepreneurial Leadership," Babson College website, http://www.babson.edu/Academics/centers/cwel/Pages/home.aspx, accessed January 29, 2017.

[5] Babson College, "Babson Rwanda Entrepreneurship Center," Babson College website, http://www.babson.edu/about-babson/global/Pages/Babson-Rwanda-Entrepreneurship-Center.aspx, accessed January 13, 2017.

mean you can't have a positive life. I definitely have taken that into my own business and personal philosophy."[6]

Between her sophomore and junior years in college, Emily traveled to Israel for a three-month internship. When she arrived in Israel, it was a time of peace, but that soon changed as Hamas began firing rockets toward Israel, eventually leading to the 2014 Israel–Gaza conflict. Emily recalled:

> It was a life changing experience. I was there when there was conflict and remember how I just kept working, even though I had friends who kept going into Gaza after being called into the military. One weekend we were surfing with some friends and the next weekend one of them was injured in the conflict and lost his hearing. Just seeing how they kept on working in the face of adversity made me realize that I could embody this attitude too. It's something I'll never forget.[7]

Diagnosing an Opportunity

In seventh grade, Emily had been bitten by a tick, but there was no physical evidence of the bite; doctors had failed to notice symptoms of common diseases associated with tick bites. Throughout high school, Emily had constantly found herself tired and clumsy, often complaining of body pains. In an effort to diagnose and treat her ailments, Emily had met with physical therapists, psychological therapists, holistic doctors, and even had attempted acupuncture, to no avail. For seven years, Emily had struggled physically and mentally to cope each day with fatigue and pain. Prior to leaving for Rwanda in 2013, Emily had completed additional tests; once she returned home, she learned that she had tested positive for Lyme disease.

Lyme disease is prevalent in the United States. "The Centers for Disease Control and Prevention estimate that 300,000 people are diagnosed with Lyme disease in the US every year. That's 1.5 times the number of women diagnosed with breast cancer, and six times the number of people diagnosed with HIV/AIDS each year in the United States. However, because diagnosing Lyme can be difficult, many people who actually have Lyme may be misdiagnosed with other conditions. Many experts believe the true number of cases is much higher."[8]

Treatment for Lyme disease can vary but in severe cases can require intravenous medication delivered directly to a patient's heart via a peripherally inserted central catheter (PICC line). Doctor insert a PICC line, a sterile, flexible catheter, into a vein in the patient's arm and thread it up to the heart, where it can remain in place for days, months, or years depending on the treatment. While PICC lines prevent patients from undergoing IV injections for each treatment, they leave the patient with an exposed end of the catheter outside of the body. Doctors commonly use PICC lines to deliver nutrients and medication for chemotherapy; PICC lines also allow easy access for drawing blood.

In December of her sophomore year, Emily received her first PICC line, which was scheduled to last for six months. Following the placement of the line, nurses and doctors told Emily to wear a cut-off sock over her arm if she wanted to cover the entry port, which she tried when returning to campus. During her freshman year, Emily had been involved in numerous clubs on campus and had actively participated in social scenes. With a cut-off sock added to her fashion wardrobe, everything began to change. Fellow students and friends began inquiring about the sock-covered PICC line and would often stare at her when she had to administer her treatment in public areas. Emily rapidly saw her extroverted personality become much more introverted. As Emily worked to complete her sophomore year, she began to question whether a cut-off sock was the best option to cover her PICC line.

Creating a Solution

In the spring of 2014, Emily and fellow Babson student, Yousef Al-Humaidhi, started to explore options to cover her PICC line. They purchased a number of products that were intended to cover PICC lines, but quickly concluded that they failed to meet Emily's needs. In many cases, Emily even preferred the cut-off sock to some of the products they evaluated. This initial product research pushed Emily and Yousef to design their own solution. In the fall of 2014, they created their first prototype, which Emily personally used and tested, prior to Babson's annual Rocket Pitch event.[9] Following the three-minute pitch of their business concept, Emily received strong positive feedback from a number of attendees who told her that the market needed her prototype and business idea and urged her to continue to move forward. Emily left that day with renewed motivation to bring her PICC line cover to market.

In the spring of 2015, Emily took the prototype with her to attend classes at Babson's San Francisco campus. Throughout the semester, she continued developing the company by using

[6] Emily Levy, interview by author, Wellesley MA, November 10, 2016.

[7] Ibid.

[8] LymeDisease.org, "About Lyme Disease," LymeDisease.org website, https://www.lymedisease.org/lyme-basics/lyme-disease/about-lyme, accessed March 24, 2017.

[9] The Rocket Pitch event is a college-wide half-day event where over 100 students and alumni have three minutes to pitch an opportunity to an audience of over 400 people, including other students, faculty, investors, and entrepreneurs. The event is immediately followed by a networking hour where the presenters have a table to demonstrate their product/service and answer follow-up questions.

her product for class projects. Through this experience, fellow Babson student Maria del Mar Gomez Viyella joined Emily and Yousef to further build the venture. Emily was fortunate to have Professor Jim Poss, founder and CEO of Big Belly Solar and WeModifi, as her mentor while on the West Coast, absorbing valuable guidance, insights, and encouragement to "just go" and take action.

While in San Francisco, and subsequently when she returned to Boston after the semester, Emily began to focus on raising seed capital to fund her first manufacturing purchase order of $10,000, which ultimately rose to $16,000. Until now, Emily and Yousef had funded the company with an initial investment of $11,000. The majority of this capital had already been invested in designs and prototype development, so Emily needed to look elsewhere.

- Kickstarter—Emily established a 30-day online Kickstarter campaign with the goal of raising $10,000. The campaign was completed under the company's former name PICCPerfect. She chose Kickstarter over other crowdfunding platforms for three primary reasons: Kickstarter was a known and recognizable global platform, their campaign fees were comparable to other global fundraising sites, and the site had proven successful for entrepreneurs developing physical consumer products. Prior to launching, she received advice from previous entrepreneurs who attempted to raise their own funding; they recommended that she spend time and resources to create a comprehensive marketing plan for the campaign. This advice was reinforced in conversations with many individuals she spoke with who had failed to complete a Kickstarter campaign successfully and subsequently had faced roadblocks from future investors who quickly took notice of their failed funding attempts. In light of this, Emily invested $2,000 to develop professional marketing materials and videos, with the intent of leveraging these for future marketing purposes. Following Kickstarter's 30-day period, Emily's campaign was oversubscribed and raised $13,200, with both domestic and international donors pledging funds. The final campaign generated net proceeds of $12,188 for her company, with 70% of funds generated from friends and family and the remaining 30% from individuals who wanted to purchase the product for themselves or someone else. After creating and shipping all pledge rewards for donors and deducting the cost of marketing materials, Emily's profits from the campaign were $9,249 (see Exhibit 1.1 for details).
- Business competitions—In addition to funding the company through Kickstarter, Emily entered several business competitions in the Greater Boston area. Between 2015 and 2016, Emily participated in 17 business competitions and won first prize in 15. These competitions provided the company with $225,000 in funding and in-kind professional services and did not dilute Emily's ownership or that of her co-founders (see Exhibit 1.2 for details). While Emily invested significant resources and time away from her business to attend these competitions, she gained increased publicity and guidance from industry peers, successful entrepreneurs, and investors.

Soon thereafter, Emily's market research uncovered that 2.5–3 million patients in the United States receive PICC lines each year.[10] This information, along with feedback she had received from patients, nurses, mentors, and the Kickstarter campaign, led her to realize, "This isn't just Emily who has this problem, it's an addressable market of 3 million potential customers."[11]

Emily returned to Boston for the summer before her senior year at Babson to participate in Babson's Summer Venture Program (SVP). Graduate and undergraduate students accepted into this program receive housing, work spaces, and access to advisors over the course of an intensive 10-week period designed to foster meaningful advances for their ventures. Since launching in 2009, this program has assisted over 150 students in the development of 109 ventures, including companies such as Virool and ThinkLite in 2010 and HigherMe in 2014.[12] Subsequent to SVP, HigherMe was accepted into Y Combinator, which invests small amounts into new ventures and runs the

Exhibit 1.1a Kickstarter Campaign

Gross Funds Pledged	$13,200
Kickstarter Fee[a]	($660)
Payment Processing Fee[b]	($442)
Net Proceeds Generated	$12,098
Pledge Rewards	($869)
Marketing Materials	($2,000)
Net Profits from Campaign	$9,229

Source: Alan Simonian and Andrew Zacharakis, based on data from MightyWell™.

[a] Standard Kickstarter fee for successful campaigns that reach their goal: 5% of pledged funds.

[b] Payment processing fees: 3% of pledge amount plus $0.30 per pledge (5% of pledged funds and $0.05 for pledges under $10.00).

[10] Emily Levy, interview by author, Wellesley MA, November 10, 2016.

[11] Ibid.

[12] Babson College, "Summer Venture Program," Babson College website, http://www.babson.edu/Academics/ centers/blank-center/venture-accelerator/summer-venture-program/Pages/summer-venture-program.aspx, accessed January 26, 2017.

Pledge $5 or more

-Thank you snapchat!

ESTIMATED DELIVERY
May 2015

5 backers

Pledge $10 or more

-Name on our sponsor wall of fame on our website (can opt for a thank you email)

ESTIMATED DELIVERY
May 2015

24 backers

Pledge $20 or more

-Name on our sponsor wall of fame on our website (can opt for a thank you email)
-Personalized handwritten thank you card with the story and picture of a life that you are impacting
-Personalized social media video shout out!

ESTIMATED DELIVERY May 2015
SHIPS TO Anywhere in the world

14 backers

Pledge $30 or more

-Name on our sponsor wall of fame on our website (can opt for a thank you email)
-PICCPerfect cover sent to you or donated to a PICC line patient in your name

ESTIMATED DELIVERY May 2015
SHIPS TO Anywhere in the world

12 backers

Pledge $50 or more

-Name on our sponsor wall of fame on our website (can opt for a thank you email)
-PICCPerfect T-Shirt and PICCPerfect cover donated to a PICC line patient in your name

ESTIMATED DELIVERY May 2015
SHIPS TO Anywhere in the world

13 backers

Pledge $100 or more

-Name on our sponsor wall of fame on our website (can opt for a thank you email)
-PICCPerfect T-Shirt or PICCPerfect cover sent to you or donated to a PICC line patient in your name
-Blog Post Dedicated to your story or on a person of your choosing

ESTIMATED DELIVERY May 2015
SHIPS TO Anywhere in the world

11 backers

Pledge $200 or more

-Designed Named After You!

ESTIMATED DELIVERY
May 2015

8 backers

Pledge $1,000 or more

-Designed Named After You!
-PICCPerfect cover donated to a PICC line patient in your name
-PICCPerfect T-Shirt
-Blog Post Dedicated to your story or on a person of your choosing
-Personalized handwritten thank you card with the story and picture of a life that you are impacting
-Name on our sponsor wall of fame on our website (can opt for a thank you email)

ESTIMATED DELIVERY May 2015
SHIPS TO Anywhere in the world

1 backer

EXHIBIT 1.1b Rewards from Kickstarter Campaign.
Source: PICCPerfect Kickstarter campaign, https://www.kickstarter.com/projects/piccperfect/piccperfect-fashion-meets-function-for-picc-line-

companies through an accelerator program, and Virool successfully raised over $27M in two rounds of funding led by venture capital firm, 500 Startups.

SVP provided an environment for the participants to not only learn from the mentors (successful entrepreneurs, investors, and professors) but also from other teams in SVP. Like Professor Poss in San Francisco, mentors in SVP pushed Emily to attend industry conferences to market her company and product. One of the first industry meetings she attended was targeted to vascular access nurses. This conference opened Emily's eyes even further as she began to question whether a broader market existed outside of PICC line covers. She continued to hear from existing customers of PICC lines who urged Emily to consider developing products and solutions for other medical conditions and treatments. The question Emily now faced was whether she could pivot and transform her young company from a single-product venture into a larger company focused on wellness wear for patients.

PICC Line Cover Product Overview

PICCPerfect™ was designed to provide a functional and fashionable solution to PICC line covers. The product was manufactured using four-way stretch, antimicrobial, nontoxic, moisture wicking fabric to keep the site dry and sanitary. Each machine-washable cover was designed to stay in place at all times using medical-grade elastics. The product's double-way fold feature made treatment easier by fully concealing the PICC

Exhibit 1.2 Selected Business Case Competitions

Month/Year	Competition Name	Location	Prize Received	In Kind Services Received
Apr/2015	Purdue University Big Sell	West Lafayette, IN	$3,000	$24,100 in professional services
Oct/2015	Beantown Throwdown	Boston, MA	$0	$12,500 in legal services, 4 months shared office space, and digital marketing consulting services
Dec/2015	InnovateHER Massachusetts	Boston, MA		Chance to compete in Washington DC if selected by the SBA
Feb/2016	Shark Tank from Combined Jewish Philanthropies	Boston, MA	$1,000	
Mar/2016	Rhode Island Business Plan Competition	Providence, RI	$15,000	$31,650 in professional and consulting services
Apr/2016	Smith College's Tim and Melissa Draper Business Competition	Northampton, MA	$10,000	
Apr/2016	Babson B.E.T.A Challenge	Boston, MA	$20,000	Additional professional services provided by Microsoft, BizLand, Cummings Properties, and MassChallenge
Apr/2016	Girls Geek Boston	Boston, MA	$0	
June/2016	MassChallenge	Boston, MA		$1,000 UPS Domestic Shipping, office space and mentoring
Aug/2016	SheKnows Media Video Pitch	National	$5,000	Funding in the form of video and media feature
Sept/2016	UPS XPort Challenge (Northeast Region)		$10,000	Funding in the form of free international shipping
Oct/2016	Babson Breakaway Challenge	Boston, MA	$250,000	>$20,000 in TV, digital and print campaigns, brand consulting services, and work space
Jan/2017	Draper U: Silicon Valley Intensive Pitch Competition	San Mateo, CA	$10,000	Funding in the form of scholarships for Emily & cofounders

Source: Alan Simonian and Andrew Zacharakis, based on data from MightyWell™.

line and creating a barrier between the tubing and a patient's skin (see Exhibit 1.3 for examples of the PICCPerfect™ product).

Target market of MightyWell™ was women in the United States between the ages of 18 and 36, a market segment Emily identified based on a combination of industry data and historic purchasing demographics from the company's initial sales. To date, the company had relied on word-of-mouth advertisement, business competitions, and free press from their Kickstarter campaign as means to sell their first 1,000 units during Emily's senior year. The majority of these initial sales were direct to consumer through the company's website and e-commerce platforms such as Amazon, priced at $29.95.

Following her first production order, Emily evaluated the effectiveness of their current manufacturer, based in California. She uncovered numerous units in their first order that had been incorrectly manufactured and failed to meet quality standards. In 2016, Emily decided to change manufacturers and selected a firm based in Providence, Rhode Island, for their next order of 2,500 units. This change reduced production costs by 40%, which increased gross margins from 47% to 68%. While further cost reductions may have been possible by moving manufacturing overseas, Emily had committed to keep manufacturing in the United States for all products that touch patient wound sites. The challenge that MightyWell™ faced with their new manufacturer was their company's size and purchasing power relative to the size of other companies their new manufacturer worked with. The small order size of MightyWell™ limited the company's negotiating power with its supplier. However, Emily knew the increase in product quality and expansion of gross margin that MightyWell™ gained significantly outweighed longer manufacturing times and delays.

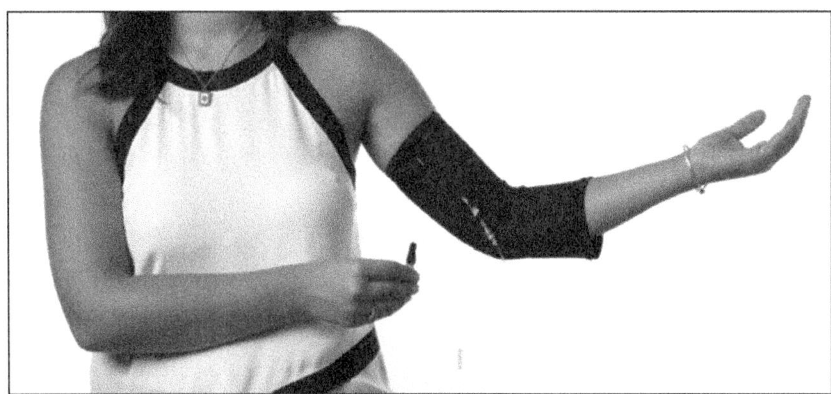

concealed
treatment

antimicrobial,
moisture wicking
material

reinforced
elastic

machine
washable
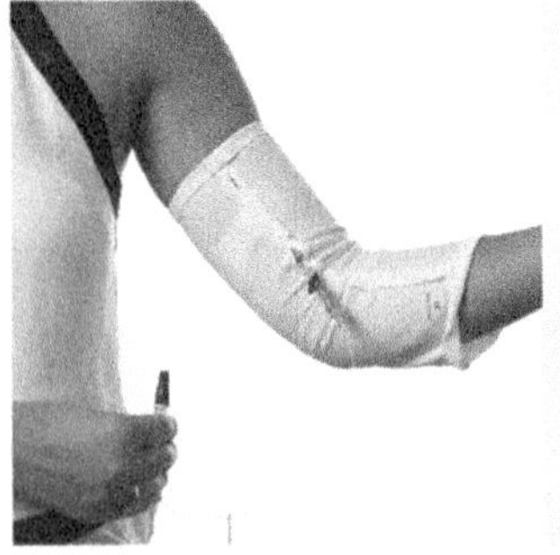
line is pulled through the access hole & wrapped around arm for concealed treatment

two-way fold provides seamless coverage that's easy to pull down for line access
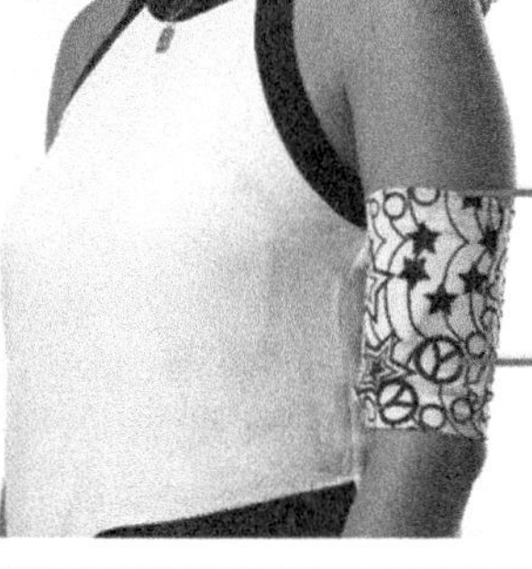
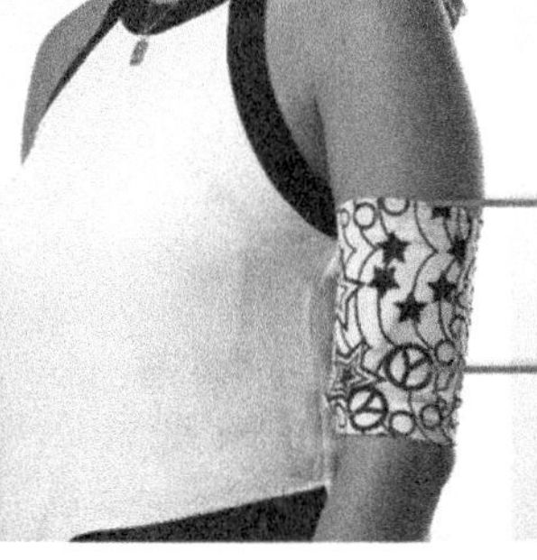
medical grade elastic keeps the cover securely in place

four way stretch fabric keep site dry & sanitary

EXHIBIT 1.3 Examples of MightyWell Products.
Source: Reproduced with permission of Mighty Well

Industry Overview

The majority of new ventures in the fashion and wellness industries can be segmented into two categories, those that clearly fall within one of the above industries and those that span multiple industries. MightyWell™ was in the second category, with influences from multiple industries and sectors including health care, wholesale manufacturers, and retail, as the company sold directly to consumers.

Health Care and PICC Lines

Since the 1970s, doctors and nurses had commonly used PICC lines to deliver antibiotics directly to the heart. With an estimated U.S. annual volume of 2.5 million and 5 million on an international scale, PICC line usage is growing rapidly.[13]

While the rate of bloodstream infections associated with PICC line patients was less than those experienced via similar procedures, doctors and nurses recommended that patients keep the wound site clean. Numerous studies had shown patients who receive PICC lines in an outpatient setting and subsequently returned home had a lower rate of infection compared to those who remained in hospital settings.[14] Given these statistics, a segment of PICC line patients admitted to hospitals for extended periods of time may have presented MightyWell™ with an opportunity to target this customer base.

Wholesale Manufacturers

The North American Industry Classification System (NAISC) identified "Women's, Children's, and Infants' Clothing and Accessories Merchant Wholesalers" as a sector within the Wholesale Trade industry classification. In Q2 of 2016, this sector created 249 startups within the United States with average annual sales exceeding \$3.9M. Most new ventures within the "small business" category employed four employees, with average annual sales per employee exceeding \$996,000. In aggregate, these 249 startups generated annual revenues of approximately \$988M, representing 4.6% of the sector's \$21B total revenue.[15]

[13] U.S. Department of Health and Human Services, "Preventing PICC Complications: Whose Line Is It?" U.S. Department of Health and Human Services website, https://psnet.ahrq.gov/webmm/case/289/ preventing-picc-complications-whose-line-is-it, accessed January 26, 2017.

[14] The Traux Group Healthcare Consulting, "January 21, 2014 The PICC Myth," The Traux Group Healthcare Consulting website, http://www.patientsafetysolutions.com/docs/January_21_2014_The_PICC_Myth.htm, accessed February 12, 2017.

[15] "Industry Market Research - [424330] Women's, Children's, and Infants Clothing and Accessories Merchant Wholesalers." *Bizminer*. November 2016. http://reports.bizminer.com/temp/pdf/6533411560.pdf, accessed June 2, 2017.

Between 2013 and 2015, the number of wholesale companies in this sector, both small and large businesses, remained flat, with less than a 1% overall change. However, the industry's average two-year cessation rate, that is, firms who failed to stay in businesses, was 12.3%. This rate had remained constant over recent years, with the most recent data from 2015 showing 164 startups still in operation compared to the same 186 that had been started in 2013.[16]

The U.S. textile, apparel, and luxury good market had maintained average gross margins between 46% and 49% over the last five years, but had increased margins 650 basis points since 2006. Industry experts expected future margin improvement based on advances in technology and falling commodity prices. Many believed that "companies with strong brands, differentiated products, and attractive price-value propositions are likely to outperform their peers."[17] Furthermore, the industry's historical average earnings before interest and taxes (EBIT) margin over the last 10 years was 12.75%. The industry EBIT margin was highly impacted by the 2009 U.S. recession, as industry averages fell below 11% before rebounding to a peak of 14.25% in 2014.[18]

Retail

According to a 2016 Mintel Market report, the U.S. clothing industry generated revenue of \$239.9 billion in 2015, representing a 4.1% year over year growth rate. This sector was forecasted to experience a 2.9% compound annual growth rate (CAGR) through 2020, reaching \$284.3 billion, with increases in spending per capita of the U.S. population and increases in the consumer price index driving many of the advances.[19] The U.S. clothing market has three main segments: women, men, and children. The following values reflected sales and growth between 2008 and 2015:

- Women comprised 53.3% of industry sales, growing at 1.71% CAGR.
- Men comprised 27.4% of industry sales, growing at 2.49% CAGR.
- Children comprised 19.3% of industry sales, growing at 1.51% CAGR.[20]

[16] Ibid.

[17] Tuna N. Amobi, "Industry Surveys – Textiles, Apparel & Luxury Goods," *CFRA*, January 2017. https://gskkr.files.wordpress.com/2015/01/apparel-footwear-retailers-brands.pdf, accessed January 23, 2017.

[18] Ibid.

[19] Diana Smith, "Women's Clothing: US, May 2015," Mintel Group Ltd., http://www.mintel.com, accessed January 2017.

[20] Ibid.

A high volume of suppliers, brands, and retailers fragmented the women's clothing market. The Mintel report identified an opportunity for companies to focus on women between the ages of 18 and 34, as this market segment was the most engaged and involved in shopping for fashion. Furthermore, the report suggested, "the notion of self-gifting is a ripe opportunity for marketers that can tap into both rational and emotional mindsets. Nearly one in three bought clothing as a treat or reward, and this can be amplified through direct marketing communication." The highest concentration of women purchasing clothing as a self-gift was within the age range of 35–44, as 42% of respondents stated they purchase clothing as a treat or reward.[21]

The U.S. women's retail sector continued to see a shift in purchasing trends, moving from in-store purchases at traditional brick-and-mortar locations to online e-commerce purchases. In 2015, 24% of women purchased clothing directly through Amazon, with 66% of women having purchased at least one article of clothing online. This trend had risen 300 basis points, up from 63% in 2013.[22]

Successes to Date

During the summer of 2016, MassChallenge accepted Emily's venture as one of 128 ventures, out of over 1,700 applicants; MassChallenge was a global startup accelerator for early stage entrepreneurs that did not receive an equity position from companies in exchange for their participation in the program. While in this program, Emily began to rebrand her company and implement a marketing strategy to transform the company from a single-product identity with the PICCPerfect cover to a comprehensive consumer brand for patients, caregivers, and health professionals. The transformation not only included branding, changing her company name from PICCPerfect to MightyWell™, but also a number of new products scheduled to launch in 2017–2018 that included PortPerfect™, for patients undergoing chemotherapy, and PillPerfect™, a new version of a pill box.

Months later, in September, MightyWell™ entered the Babson Breakaway Challenge, a business competition sponsored by CWEL at Babson College and Breakaway, a Boston-based brand capital firm. This competition promoted gender parity and awards $250,000 in convertible debt to women entrepreneurs and ventures with consumer-facing businesses. MightyWell™ was one of 23 semifinalists, then one of five finalists, and subsequently became the 2016 winner of the Babson Breakaway Challenge. In addition to the funding, Emily received in-kind business services that included TV and digital advertising campaigns, print media campaigns, legal services, and use of shared workspaces. Upon receiving the $250,000 in convertible debt funding, she also gained access to a team of experienced branding experts who continued to mentor and help her navigate MightyWell™'s transformation and growth.

Moving Forward

Emily was proud of her achievements and the journey she had started years earlier. While she saw the benefits of expanding and diversifying via new product lines, she questioned what types of products made sense. Emily worried that expanding too quickly might lead her to neglect her current emerging product and existing customer base. Could she manage all these elements at once? Could she successfully grow MightyWell™ in the next 12 months while ensuring the long-term sustainability for her company?

Discussion Questions

1. What are the advantages and disadvantages of adding new product lines?
2. If she goes forward, how would you advise Emily to identify these lines?
3. What criteria should she use in deciding what products to add?
4. How can Emily balance expanding her existing base of PICCPerfect customers while educating new markets of customers with other medical needs?
5. Does a hybrid market opportunity exist for MightyWell™'s wellness wear?
6. What are the positives and negatives for the way in which Emily has bootstrapped her company up to this point?

---

[21] Ibid.

[22] Ibid.

The Entrepreneurial Process

2

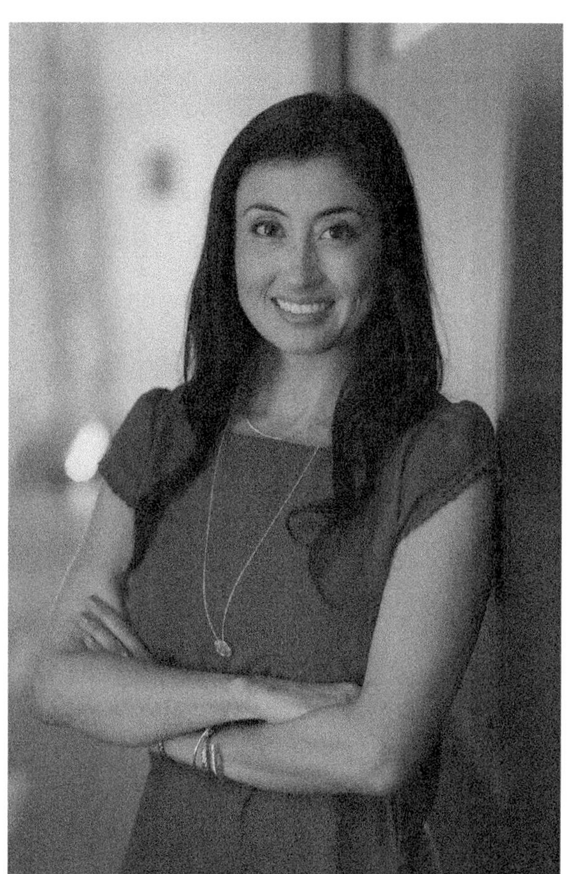

Photo Credit: © David Paul Morris/Bloomberg/Getty Images

CEO Katrina Lake of Stich Fix

An **entrepreneur** is someone who perceives an opportunity and creates an organization to pursue it. The **entrepreneurial process** includes all the functions, activities, and actions that are part of perceiving opportunities and creating organizations to pursue them. But is the birth of a new enterprise just happenstance and its subsequent success or failure a chance process? Or can the

This chapter was written by William D. Bygrave.

art and science of entrepreneurship be taught? Clearly, professors and their students believe that it can be taught and learned because entrepreneurship is one of the fastest-growing new fields of study in American higher education. A study by the Kauffman Foundation found that 61% of U.S. colleges and universities have at least one course in entrepreneurship.[1] It is possible to study entrepreneurship in certificate, associate's, bachelor's, master's, and PhD programs. Moreover, there are 9,000 faculty members teaching over 5,000 entrepreneurship courses to over 400,000 students.[2]

That transformation in higher education—itself a wonderful example of entrepreneurial change—has come about because a whole body of knowledge about entrepreneurship has developed during the past four decades or so. The process of creating a new business is well understood. Yes, entrepreneurship can be taught. No one is guaranteed to become the Collison brothers (founders of the payment processor Stripe) or a Katrina Lake (founder of Stitch Fix, which started as a business school project and reached $1B in revenue and IPO'ed in 2017) any more than a physics professor can guarantee to produce an Albert Einstein or a tennis coach can guarantee a Serena Williams. But students with the aptitude to start a business can become better entrepreneurs.

Critical Factors for Starting a New Enterprise

We will begin by examining the entrepreneurial process (see Figure 2.1). These are the factors—personal, sociological, organizational, and environmental—that give birth to a new enterprise and influence how it develops from an idea to a viable enterprise. A person gets an idea for a new business through either a deliberate search or a chance encounter. Whether he or she decides to pursue that idea depends on factors such as alternative career prospects, family, friends, role models, the state of the economy, and the availability of resources.

Origins of Whatsapp

In 2009 Brian Acton was turned down for a job at Facebook. He took to Twitter to express his perspective at the time, calling the experience, "...a great opportunity to connect with some fantastic people. Looking forward to life's next adventure." Acton had previously worked at Yahoo! with Jan Koum, a Ukrainian-born engineer who had also been turned down by Facebook. The two of them quickly developed a mutual respect for each other, and in 2007, they each left Yahoo! in search of another challenge. It was in 2009 that Koum and Acton, by this time great friends, ultimate-frisbee buddies, and, of course, members of the "Facebook Reject Club," reconnected around an idea that Koum had been slowly bringing to life. It was a mobile application that allowed users worldwide to share their mobile status with their contacts. They had also hit on something bigger—that users could connect with messages over data networks rather than via SMS, all without sharing any more personal information than a name and phone number. This has been attributed to Koum's desire to stay connected to his family back home in Ukraine, without personal information being snatched by authorities. By 2014, they had 450 million monthly average users. Their app, which began as a modest rebuttal to similar ad-based or fee-based services was soon worth nearly $19 billion and acquired by Facebook, the same company that had declined to offer jobs to Koum and Acton just five years prior.[4,5,6]

There is almost always a *triggering event* that gives birth to a new organization. Perhaps the entrepreneur has no better career prospects. For example, Mary Ellen Sheets was a working, single mother who had just seen her sons head off to college. What they had left behind was a pickup truck and a small moving business they had started to earn extra money. Though her boys had moved on,

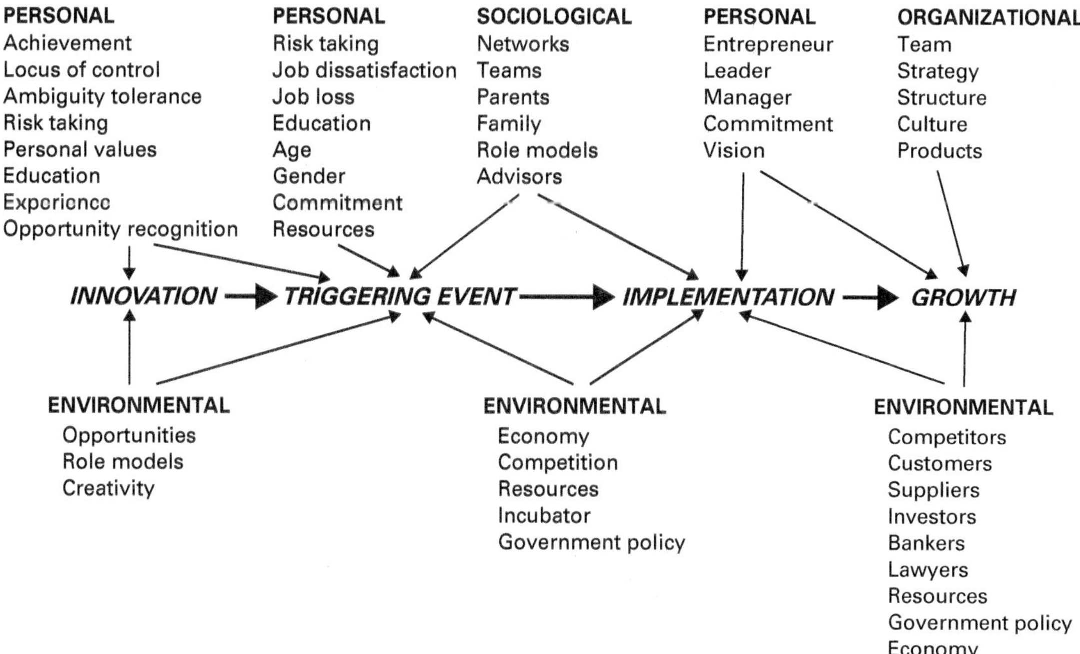

FIGURE 2.1 A Model of the Entrepreneurial Process.
Source: Adapted and elaborated on Carol Moore's Model.[3]

the requests for their services kept coming in. Mary Ellen recognized the opportunity and quickly hired two movers to take the place of her college-bound sons.[7] Her business, Two Men and a Truck, grew to nearly 380 franchises and over 2,800 trucks. Her sons, along with her daughter, all joined the executive leadership team and have been an integral part of the company's success.

Sometimes the person has been passed over for a promotion or even laid off or fired. Brent Schuldecker was one of many people left without a job when Pfizer closed its facility in Terre Haute, Indiana, in 2008. With colleagues of his, who had also been laid off, Schuldecker leveraged his specialized skills to start a contract laboratory services company—even buying and using some of the equipment from Pfizer to get started.[8] When Paul Tasner was let go from his senior level position at a San Francisco-based manufacturing firm he had over 30 years of supply chain experience under his belt. Tasner was not ready to retire, so instead he focused his attention on solving a serious problem in manufacturing: the toxic side effects of plastic packaging. At 66, he founded PulpWorks, Inc., a company that designs and manufactures biodegradable packaging for consumer goods. "Five years later, I'm thrilled and proud to share with you that our revenues have doubled every year, we have no debt, we have several marquee clients, our patent was issued, I have a wonderful partner who's been with me right from the beginning, and we've won more than 20 awards for the work that we've done. But best of all, we've made a small dent—a very small dent—in the worldwide plastic pollution crisis," said Tasner.[9]

For some people, entrepreneurship is a deliberate career choice. Babiators, which manufactures aviator-style sunglasses for children, was formed by college friends Carolyn Guard and Molly Fienning. Guard had been pondering her next endeavor when Fienning and her husband, Ted, a Marine fighter pilot at the time, came up with the idea for stylish, protective sunglasses. Along with Carolyn's husband, Matthew, they launched in 2010, and their sunglasses have become even more fashionable thanks to the attention from celebrity children who have been spotted wearing Babiators.[10]

Where do would-be entrepreneurs get their ideas? More often than not it is through their present line of employment or experience. A study of the *Inc.* 500—"America's [500] fastest growing companies"—found that 57% of the founders got the idea for their new venture in the industry they worked in, and an additional 23% got it in a related industry. Hence, 80% of all new high-potential businesses are founded in industries that are the same as, or closely related to, the one in which the entrepreneur has previous experience. That is not surprising because it is in their present employment that entrepreneurs will get most of their viable business ideas. Some habitual entrepreneurs do it over and over again in the same industry. David Neeleman founded Morris Air in 1984 and, along with it, a revolutionary concept at the time—electronic ticketing. Following the sale of Morris Air to Southwest, he cofounded Canadian low-fare airline WestJet. His most successful and well-known airline venture, of course, was JetBlue, which was consistently lauded by the likes of J.D. Power and Conde Nast Traveler as a top American airline throughout his tenure as CEO. And even though bad weather and an underperforming stock spelled the end for him at the helm of the company he founded, Neeleman did not allow that to subdue his passion for the airline industry. Shortly after leaving JetBlue, he founded Brazilian airline Azul Linhas. His efforts—successes and failures—gave rise to his inclusion on *Inc.'s* list of Entrepreneurs of the Decade, a list that includes Steve Jobs, Mark Zuckerberg, and Jeff Bezos, among others.

What factors influence someone to embark on an entrepreneurial career? Like most human behavior, entrepreneurial traits are shaped by *personal attributes* and *environment.*

Personal Attributes

There is no neat set of behavioral attributes that allows us to separate entrepreneurs from nonentrepreneurs. A person who rises to the top of any occupation, whether an entrepreneur or an administrator, is an achiever. Granted, any would-be entrepreneur must have a need to achieve, but so must anyone else with ambitions to be successful.

It does appear that entrepreneurs have a *higher internal locus of control* than nonentrepreneurs, which means that they have a stronger desire to be in control of their own fate.[11] This has been confirmed by many surveys in which entrepreneurs said independence was a very important reason for starting their businesses. The main reasons they gave were entrepreneurship suited my skill set (33%), they had an idea they just had to try (18%), wanted to be their own boss/independence (11%), wanted financial success (10%), admired other successful entrepreneurs (9%), and a variety of other factors (19%).[12] For many entrepreneurs, starting one's own business is a calling that they have always felt, whether it originates from within or is inspired by a role model. Hiscox's Global DNA of an Entrepreneur report reveals that 52% of respondents always thought they would start their own business, while 30% started their business because they "couldn't find a suitable job," and 26% were influenced by a parent who ran a business. Interestingly, 35% reported they were influenced by a role model other than a parent and that statistic jumps to 50% when looking only at American respondents.[13] The most important characteristics of successful entrepreneurs are shown in Figure 2.2.

Environmental Factors

Perhaps as important as personal attributes are the external influences on a would-be entrepreneur. It's no accident that some parts of the world are more entrepreneurial than others. The most famous region of high-tech entrepreneurship is Silicon Valley. Because everyone in Silicon Valley knows someone who has made it big as an entrepreneur, role models abound. This situation produces what Stanford University sociologist Everett Rogers called "Silicon Valley fever."[14] It seems as if everyone in the valley catches that bug sooner or later and wants to start a business. To facilitate the process, there are venture capitalists who understand how to select and nurture high-tech entrepreneurs, bankers who specialize in lending to them, lawyers who understand

Dream	Entrepreneurs have a vision of what the future could be like for them and their businesses. And, more important, they have the ability to implement their dreams.
Decisiveness	They don't procrastinate. They make decisions swiftly. Their swiftness is a key factor in their success.
Doers	Once they decide on a course of action, they implement it as quickly as possible.
Determination	They implement their ventures with total commitment. They seldom give up, even when confronted by obstacles that seem insurmountable.
Dedication	They are totally dedicated to their businesses, sometimes at considerable cost to their relationships with friends and families. They work tirelessly. Twelve-hour days and seven-day workweeks are not uncommon when an entrepreneur is striving to get a business off the ground.
Devotion	Entrepreneurs love what they do. It is that love that sustains them when the going gets tough. And it is love of their product or service that makes them so effective at selling it.
Details	It is said that the devil resides in the details. That is never more true than in starting and growing a business. The entrepreneur must be on top of the critical details.
Destiny	They want to be in charge of their own destiny rather than dependent on an employer.
Dollars	Getting rich is not the prime motivator of entrepreneurs. Money is more a measure of success. Entrepreneurs assume that if they are successful they will be rewarded.
Distribute	Entrepreneurs distribute the ownership of their businesses with key employees who are critical to the success of the business.

FIGURE 2.2 **The 10 Ds—The Most Important Characteristics of a Successful Entrepreneur.**

the importance of intellectual property and how to protect it, landlords who are experienced in renting real estate to fledgling companies, suppliers who are willing to sell goods on credit to companies with no credit history, and even politicians who are supportive.

Knowing successful entrepreneurs at work or in your personal life makes becoming one yourself seem much more achievable. Indeed, if a close relative is an entrepreneur, you are more likely to want to become an entrepreneur yourself, especially if that relative is your mother or father. At Babson College, more than half of the undergraduates studying entrepreneurship come from families that own businesses, and according to Hiscox' DNA of an Entrepreneur Report, 33% of American entrepreneurs are influenced by business-owning parent.[15] But you don't have to be from a business-owning family to become an entrepreneur. Bill Gates, for example, was following the family tradition of becoming a lawyer when he dropped out of Harvard and founded Microsoft. He was in the fledgling microcomputer industry, which was being built by entrepreneurs, so he had plenty of role models among his friends and acquaintances. The United States has an abundance of high-tech entrepreneurs who are household names. One of them, Meg Whitman (eBay and Hewlett-Packard), is so well known that she was the gubernatorial candidate preferred by 41% of California voters in 2012. Some universities are hotbeds of entrepreneurship. For example, Massachusetts Institute of Technology (MIT) has produced numerous entrepreneurs among its faculty and alums. Companies with an MIT connection transformed the Massachusetts economy from one based on decaying shoe and textile industries into one based on high technology. In fact, if MIT entrepreneurs were an independent country, they would be the 10th largest economy in the world.[16] Moreover:

> *As of 2014, MIT alumni have founded over 30,000 currently active companies, employing 4.6 million individuals and generating $1.9 trillion in revenue. Approximately 31% of MIT alumni companies are located in Massachusetts and 21% in California.*
>
> *Approximately 25% of all MIT alumni are entrepreneurs, of which 40% identify as serial entrepreneurs, with an average of 3.25 startups each.*

It is not only in high tech that we see role models. Consider these examples:

- At least 400 Dunkin Donuts stores are said to have been opened as result of the efforts of just one family. The Andrade family, from the Portuguese village of Villa Franca, encouraged family, friends, and Villa Franca natives to move to the United States and buy Dunkin Donuts franchises.[17]
- The vacation town of Myrtle Beach, South Carolina, stakes its claim as the Miniature Golf Capital of the World, with over 50 miniature golf courses along a 20-mile stretch of U.S. Highway 17.[18]
- Drinking that Colorado whiskey? Denver, CO's metro area contains 15 liquor distilleries, meeting the demand for locally sourced alcohol that Millennials gravitate towards.[19]
- Hay-on-Wye—a tiny town in Wales with 1,900 inhabitants—has 21 secondhand bookstores. It claims to be the "largest used and antiquarian bookshop in the world." It all began in 1961 when Richard Booth, an Oxford graduate, opened his first bookstore.[20]

African Americans make up 13.6% of the U.S. population but owned only 9.4% of the nation's businesses in 2012.[21] One of the major reasons for that low number is the lack of entrepreneurial role models. A similar problem exists among Native Americans. Fortunately, this situation is rapidly improving. Between the 2007 census and 2012 Survey of Business Owners, the number of minority-owned businesses grew from 5.8 million to about 8 million firms, with a 46.3% increase in Hispanic-owned firms and a 34.5% increase in black or African American owned firms during that time.[22] According to the 2012 Survey of Business Owners, Hispanics/Latinos owned 12% of the nation's businesses, African Americans owned 9.4%, Asian Americans owned 6.8%, and American Indians and Alaskan Natives owned 1%.[23]

Other Sociological Factors

Besides role models, entrepreneurs are influenced by other sociological factors. *Family responsibilities* play an important role in the decision to start a company.[24] It is a relatively easy career decision to start a business when you are 25 years old, single, and without many personal assets and dependents. It is a much harder decision when you are 45 and married, with teenage children preparing to go to college, a hefty mortgage, car payments, and a secure, well-paying job. And at 45+, if you fail as an entrepreneur, it will not be easy to rebuild a career working for another company. But despite the risks, plenty of 45-year-olds are taking the plunge; in fact, the median age for entrepreneurs founding a company is 41.9 and that of the founders of the high-growth companies is 45 according to a 2018 study of over 2.7 million entrepreneurs by MIT.[25]

Another factor that determines the age at which entrepreneurs start businesses is the trade-off between the *experience* that comes with age and the *optimism* and *energy* of youth. As you grow older you gain experience, but sometimes when you have been in an industry a long time, you know so many pitfalls that you are pessimistic about the chance of succeeding if you decide to go out on your own. Someone who has just enough experience to feel confident as a manager is more likely to feel optimistic about an entrepreneurial career. The best-performing businesses owned by Babson alumni, for example, were started when the entrepreneurs had 10 years management experience after graduation. Perhaps the ideal combination is a beginner's mind with the experience of an industry veteran. A beginner's mind looks at situations from a new perspective, with a can-do spirit.

Twenty-seven-year-old Sara Blakely, an aspiring stand-up comic with no previous experience in retail or fashion, wanted to reinvent the way women's hosiery was designed, manufactured, and marketed. With the simple step of cutting the feet out of a pair of pantyhose, she created Spanx. Just as she had realized that producers at the time were not meeting the specifications of their customers, she enthusiastically set out to disrupt the competitive landscape by appearing in retailers with her product and its flashy, red packaging backing her up. Blakely took the competition by surprise by representing the voice of the customer—in this case, women—where before their collective voice was not heard. In 2012, *Forbes* recognized Blakely as the youngest, self-made, female billionaire; in the same year, *Time* magazine honored her as one of the 100 Most Influential People in the World.[26] As of 2018, Blakely is #21 on the list of America's Richest Self-Made Women, as ranked by Forbes.

Reid Hoffman had a beginner's mind in 2003 when, after stints with Apple, PayPal, and his own failed entrepreneurial venture, Socialnet, he cofounded LinkedIn. He produced a vision for online professional networking that until then had proven difficult for other entrepreneurs to create. Eventually, Hoffman's vision, technical expertise, and creativity were joined with Jeff Weiner's leadership and entrepreneurial wisdom. The pair turned out to be an awesome combination. LinkedIn boasted 500 million members as of April 2017 and was acquired by Microsoft in December 2016 for $26 billion. The company had become not only a networking phenomenon but also a social media powerhouse.

We cannot specify how much managerial expertise it takes to become a skilled entrepreneur. But we do know that venture capitalists recognize that neophyte high-tech entrepreneurs, especially very young ones, do not have enough experience, so they often recruit seasoned entrepreneurial managers to guide them. An example is Google, where Eric Schmidt was hired as CEO to guide Page and Brin.[27] Then after 10 years at the helm, Schmidt announced he would step aside to allow Page to take over the reins as CEO in 2011.

Before leaving secure, well-paying, satisfying jobs, would-be entrepreneurs should make a *careful estimate of how much sales revenue* their new businesses must generate before they will be able to match the income they presently earn. It usually comes as quite a shock when they realize that, if they are opening a retail establishment, they will need annual sales revenue of at least $750,000 to pay themselves a salary of $70,000 plus fringe benefits such as health care coverage, retirement pension benefits, and long-term disability insurance. Seven hundred and fifty thousand dollars a year is about $15,000 per week, or about $2,500 per day, or about $250 per hour, or about $4 per minute if they are open 6 days a week, 10 hours a day. Also, they will be working much longer hours and bearing much more responsibility if they become self-employed. Forty-two percent of the CEOs of the *Inc*. 500 said they worked 80 hours a week or more in their company's first year. Only 25%, however, began paying themselves a salary immediately on launching their business.[28]

When they actually start a business, entrepreneurs need a host of *contacts*, including customers, suppliers, investors, bankers, accountants, and lawyers. So it is important to understand where to find help before embarking on a new venture. A network of friends and business associates can be of immeasurable help in building the contacts an entrepreneur will need. They can also provide human contact, which is important because opening a business can be a lonely experience for anyone who has worked in an organization with many fellow employees.

Fortunately, today there are more organizations than ever before to help fledgling entrepreneurs. Often that help is free or costs very little. The Small Business Administration (SBA) has Small Business Development Centers in every state, it funds Small Business Institutes, and its Service Core of Retired Executives provides free assistance to entrepreneurs. Many colleges and universities also provide help. There are hundreds of incubators and accelerators in the United States where fledgling businesses can rent space, usually at a very reasonable price, and spread some of their overhead by sharing facilities such as copying machines, secretarial help, answering services, and so on. Incubators are often associated with universities, which provide free or inexpensive counseling. There are numerous associations where entrepreneurs can meet and exchange ideas.

Evaluating Opportunities for New Businesses

Let's assume you believe that you have found a great opportunity for starting a new business. How should you evaluate its prospects? Or, perhaps more important, how will an independent person such as a potential investor or a banker rate your chances of success? The odds of succeeding appear to be stacked against you because, according to small business folklore, only 1 business in 10 will ever reach its 10th birthday. This doesn't mean that 90% of the estimated 3 million

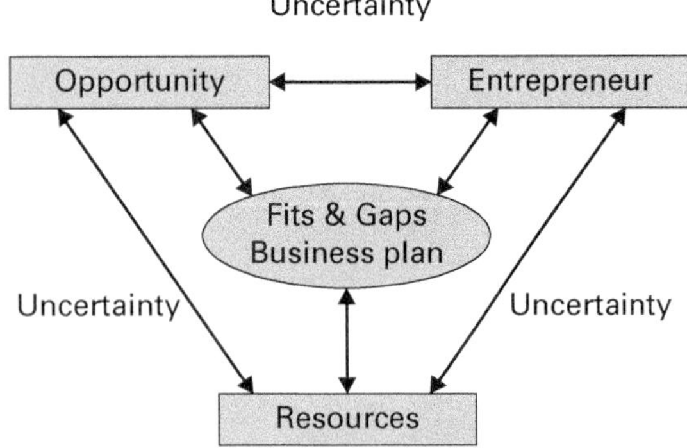

FIGURE 2.3 Three Driving Forces (Based on Jeffry Timmons's Framework).[32]

businesses that are started every year go bankrupt.[29] We know that even in a severe recession, the number of businesses filing for bankruptcy in the United States has never surpassed 100,000 in any year. In an average year, the number is about 35,000. Even in 2008, when small businesses were hit hard by a severe recession, the number of bankruptcies was fewer than 45,000.[30] So what happens to the vast majority of the ones that do not survive 10 years? Most just fade away: They are started as part-time pursuits and are never intended to become full-time businesses. Some are sold. Others are liquidated. Only 700,000 of the 3 million are legally registered as corporations or partnerships—a sure sign that many of the remaining 2.3 million never intended to grow because, in general, an entrepreneur will go to the bother and expense of registering a new venture as a separate legal entity only if it is expected to become a full-time business with employees. Hence, the odds that your new business will survive may not be as long as they first appeared to be. If you intend to start a full-time, incorporated business, the odds that the business will survive at least eight years are 41%.[31]

But survival may not spell success. Too many entrepreneurs find that they can neither earn a satisfactory living in their businesses nor get out of them easily because they have too much of their personal assets tied up in them. The happiest day in an entrepreneur's life is the day doors are opened for business. For unsuccessful entrepreneurs, an even happier day may be the day the business is sold—especially if most personal assets remain intact. What George Bernard Shaw said about a love affair is also apt for a business: Any fool can start one, but it takes a genius to end one successfully.

How can you stack the odds in your favor so that your new business is a success? Professional investors, such as venture capitalists, have a talent for picking winners. True, they also pick losers, but a start-up company funded by venture capital has, on average, a four-in-five chance of surviving five years—better odds than for the population of start-up companies as a whole. Very few businesses—perhaps no more than one in a thousand—will ever be suitable candidates for investments from professional venture capitalists. But would-be entrepreneurs can learn a lot by following the evaluation process used by professional investors. There are three crucial components for a successful new business: the opportunity, the entrepreneur (and the management team, if it's a high-potential venture), and the resources needed to start the company and make it grow. These are shown schematically in Figure 2.3 the basic Timmons framework. At the center of the framework is business planning, the method of integrating the three basic ingredients into an iterative process to launch and grow the new business. The parts must fit together well. It's no good having a first-rate idea for a new business if you have a second-rate management team. Nor are ideas and management any good without the appropriate resources.

The crucial driving force of any new venture is the lead entrepreneur and the founding management team. Georges Doriot, the founder of modern venture capital, used to say something like this: "Always consider investing in a grade-A man with a grade-B idea. Never invest in a grade-B man with a grade-A idea." He knew what he was talking about. Over the years he invested in about 150 companies, including Digital Equipment Corporation (DEC), and watched over them as they struggled to grow. But Doriot made his statement about business in the 1950s and 1960s. During that period, there were far fewer start-ups; U.S. firms dominated the marketplace, markets were growing quickly, there was almost no competition from overseas, and most entrepreneurs were male. Today, in the global marketplace, with ever-shortening product life cycles and low growth or even no growth for some of the world's leading industrial nations, *the crucial ingredients for entrepreneurial success are a superb entrepreneur with a first-rate management team and an excellent market opportunity.*

It's often said that entrepreneurship is largely a matter of luck. That's not so. We do not say that becoming a great quarterback, a great scientist, or a great musician is a matter of luck. There is no more luck in becoming successful at entrepreneurship than in becoming successful at anything else. In entrepreneurship, it is a question of recognizing a good opportunity when you see one and having the skills to convert that opportunity into a thriving business. To do that, you must be prepared. So in entrepreneurship, as in any other profession, *luck is where preparation and opportunity meet.*

When co-CEOs Dave Gilboa and Neil Blumenthal founded Warby Parker with two other Wharton MBA classmates in 2008, the idea of buying a pair of glasses online was unheard of. As an MBA student and former finance guy, Gilboa was shocked when his new pair of glasses cost more than an iPhone. Meanwhile his classmate Blumenthal had worked for VisionSpring, a nonprofit that produced affordable glasses for low-income people. Armed with Blumenthal's experience in designing glasses and connections to manufacturers, and access to entrepreneurial resources at Wharton, the Warby Parker team decided to challenge Luxxotica, the multi-billion-dollar glasses company that had dominated the eyewear market from Ray-Bans to Sunglass Hut for decades. Blumenthal's enabled Warby Parker to tap into the supply chain and order their first inventory of frames, economically priced at $95 a pair.[33] To ease the pain of buying online, Warby Parker started with a "try before you buy" online ordering model.

One bit of luck came in 2010 when GQ approached Warby Parker about an article just before the eyeglasses company was set to launch its website, and months before its co-founders' graduation from business school. The team quickly put a website together but forgot to add a "sold out" button. GQ dubbed Warby Parker "the Netflix of eyewear" on February 10, 2010, causing so much traffic to the website that the company met its year-long sales goal in three weeks with a waitlist of 20,0000 orders.[34, 35]

By 2014, Warby Parker had sold over 1 million pairs of eyeglasses and donated 1 million more pairs under its Buy A Pair, Give A Pair model. As of 2018, Warby Parker has sold over 4 million pairs of glasses and another donated 4 million more.[36]

The Opportunity

Perhaps the biggest misconception about an idea for a new business is that it must be unique. Too many would-be entrepreneurs are almost obsessed with finding a unique idea. Then, when they believe they have it, they are haunted by the thought that someone is just waiting to steal it from them. So they become super-secretive, reluctant to discuss it with anyone who doesn't sign a nondisclosure agreement. That makes it almost impossible to evaluate the idea, and many counselors who provide free advice to entrepreneurs refuse to sign nondisclosure agreements. Generally speaking, these super-secret, unique ideas are big letdowns when the entrepreneurs reveal them. Some notable recent examples were "drive-through pizza by the slice," "a combination toothbrush and toothpaste gadget," and "a Mexican restaurant in Boston." One computer programmer said he had a fantastic new piece of software for managing hairdressing salons. He was completely floored when he found that less than a month previously another entrepreneur had demonstrated a software package for exactly the same purpose. Another entrepreneur had an idea for fluoride-impregnated dental floss. Not three months later, the identical product turned out to be available in Boots—Britain's largest chain of drugstores and a major pharmaceutical manufacturer.

Almost any idea a would-be entrepreneur might have will also have occurred to others. In fact, some of the most revolutionary thoughts in the history of humankind occurred to more than one person almost simultaneously. Newton and Leibnitz independently invented calculus within a few years of each other; Darwin was almost preempted by Wallace in publishing his theory of evolution; Poincare´ formulated a valid theory of special relativity about the

- The crucial ingredients for entrepreneurial success are a superb entrepreneur with a first rate management team and an excellent market opportunity.
- In entrepreneurship, as in any other profession, luck is where preparation and opportunity meet.
- The idea in itself is not what is important. In entrepreneurship, ideas really are a dime a dozen. Developing the idea, implementing it, and building a successful business are the important things.
- Would-be entrepreneurs who are unable to name a customer are not ready to start a business. They have found an idea but have not yet identified a market need.

same time Einstein did; and the integrated circuit was invented in 1959, first by Jack Kilby at Texas Instruments and then independently by Robert Noyce at Fairchild a few months later. And as we read in Chapter 1, Berners-Lee was not the first person to introduce the concept of hypertext.

Alexander Fleming discovered penicillin by chance but never developed it as a useful drug. About 10 years later Ernst Chain and Howard Florey unearthed Fleming's mold and immediately saw its potential. They soon were treating patients in England with it, and before the end of World War II, penicillin was saving countless lives. It was a most dramatic pharmaceutical advance and heralded a revolution in that industry.

According to the late Stanford Professor Rajeev Motwani, who mentored Sergey Brin and Larry Page, "At some point these guys said, we want to do a company. Everybody said you must be out of your minds. There are like 37 search engines out there and what are you guys going to do? And how are you going to raise money, how will you build a company, and these two guys said, we'll just do it and they went off and did it. And then they took over the world."[37]

The Customer

Many would-be entrepreneurs fail to think carefully enough about who makes up the market for their product or service. They should have a very specific answer to this question: "Can you give me the names of prospective customers?" If they have a consumer product—let's say it's a new shampoo—they should be able to name the buyers at different chains of drugstores in their area. If they are unable to name several customers immediately, they simply have an idea, not a market. There is no market unless customers have a real need for the product—a proven need rather than a hypothetical need in the mind of a would-be entrepreneur. A few rare cases may be revolutionary new products with markets waiting to be formed, but most entrepreneurial ideas are for existing products with improved performance, price, distribution, quality, or service. Simply put, customers must perceive that the new business will be giving them better value for their money than existing businesses.

The Timing

Time plays a crucial role in many potential opportunities. In some emerging industries, there is a definite window of opportunity that opens only once. For instance, about 40 years ago, when videocassette recorders (VCRs) were first coming into household use in the United States, there was a need for video stores in convenient locations where viewers could pick up movies on the way home from work. Lots of video retail stores opened up on main streets and in shopping centers. They were usually run by independent store owners. Then the distribution of videos changed. National chains of video stores emerged. Supermarket and drugstore chains entered the market. Then the technology changed, and VCR cassettes were replaced by digital video discs (DVDs), which are much less bulky. You could get DVDs via postal mail, download them via the Internet, or pick them up at vending machines and conventional video stores. Just as quickly as DVDs came, they are dying and being replaced by video on demand. Today the window of opportunity for starting a video store is closed.

In other markets—high-quality restaurants, for example—there is a steady demand that does not change much from year to year, so the window of opportunity is always open. Nevertheless, timing can still be important because, when the economy turns down, those kinds of restaurants are usually hit harder than lower-quality ones; thus, the time to open one is during a recovering or booming economy.

If the window of opportunity appears to be very brief, it may be that the idea is a consumer fad that will quickly pass away. It takes a very skilled entrepreneur indeed to make money out of a fad. When Lucy's Have a Heart Canvas of Faneuil Hall Marketplace in Boston introduced shoelaces with hearts on them, they flew off the shelves. Children and teenagers could not get enough of them for their sneakers. The store ordered more and more of them. Then demand suddenly dropped precipitously. The store and the manufacturer were left holding huge inventories that could not be sold. As a result, the store almost went under.

The Snuggie Fad...

Entrepreneur Scott Boilen credits social media with much of the success of his signature invention—the Snuggie.[38] Boilen's company, Allstar Products (where he is its CEO), has brought over 100 products to market since he founded the company in 1999. Many of them have been sold via television networks QVC and HSN, but Allstar Products also boasts deep relationships with retailers, including Walmart, Home Depot, Target, and Bed Bath & Beyond, just to name a few. The Snuggie was brought to market in 2008 and quickly sold millions of units. In fact, nearly 4 million units were sold during the holiday season in 2008.[39] The good sales numbers, however, could not ward off the jokes from media and celebrities. Longtime host of *The Tonight Show*, Jay Leno, mocked the product's apparent lack of ingenuity on his show, "Why don't you just put your robe on backwards!"[40] However, the company used the silliness and simplicity of the Snuggie to its advantage as it became known as much for its quirky commercials as it did for its intended use. Says Boilen, "They're going to buy it because it's a blanket with sleeves, they're going to watch the commercial 'cause it's funny."[41] It has not been all laughs and good times. The company ran into trouble with the Federal Trade Commission (FTC) over claims about pricing for the wearable blanket. It cost Allstar Products $8 million to settle the claims, just a fraction of total Snuggie sales, but it once again underscored the nature of marketing fad products vis-à -vis their utility and popularity.

Most entrepreneurs should avoid fads or any window of opportunity they believe will be open for a very brief time because it inevitably means they will rush to open their business, sometimes before they have time to gather the resources they will need. That can lead to costly mistakes.

The Entrepreneur and the Management Team

Regardless of how right the opportunity may seem to be, it will not become a successful business unless it is developed by a person with strong entrepreneurial and management skills. What are the important skills? First and foremost, entrepreneurs should have experience in the same industry or a similar one. Starting a business is a very demanding undertaking indeed. It is no time for on-the-job training. If would-be entrepreneurs do not have the right experience, they should either get it before starting their new venture or find partners who have it.

Some investors say the ideal entrepreneur is one who has a track record as a successful entrepreneur in the same industry and who can attract a seasoned team. Of the CEOs included in the 2015 *Inc.* 500, 60% have started at least one additional business other than their present firms.[42] Named by *Inc.* 5000 as the ninth fastest-growing company of 2018, Scientist.com is an online platform that connects buyers and sellers of scientific research services like gene editing. Scientist .com is founder Kevin Lustig's third biotech start-up. Lustig launched his first enterprise, a drug discovery company called Kalypsys, in 2001, when the biotech industry was just beginning. In 2013, to help other life scientists launch ventures, Lustig co-founded Bio, Tech, and Beyond, a nonprofit incubator equipped with a research facility.[43]

Without relevant experience, the odds are stacked against the neophyte in any industry. An electronics engineer thought he had a great idea for a chain of fast-food stores. When asked if he had ever worked in a fast-food restaurant, he replied, "Work in one? I wouldn't even eat in one. I can't stand fast food!" Clearly, he would have been miscast as a fast-food entrepreneur. True, there are entrepreneurs who have succeeded spectacularly with no prior industry experience. Jeff Bezos of Amazon, Anita Roddick of The Body Shop, Ely Callaway of Callaway Golf, and Richard Branson of Virgin Airlines are four notable examples. But they are the exceptions.

Second to industry know-how is *management experience*, preferably with responsibility for budgets or, better yet, accountability for profit and loss. It is even better if a would-be entrepreneur has a record of increasing sales and profits. Of course, we are talking about the *ideal* entrepreneur. Very few people measure up to the ideal. That does not mean they should not start a new venture. But it does mean they should be realistic about the size of the business they should start. In 2010, a team of Harvard Business School students won second place in the HBS Annual Business plan competition for their idea to create an obstacle course adventure race. There was no prize money involved, just the pride of completing the course. The business plan estimated that 500 souls would sign up for the grueling course, a number that professors thought was too high. One of the HBS team members, a Brit who had previously worked as a counterterrorism expert named Will Dean, decided to take the idea and put it into action. He believed it would work because an even more grueling event called the Tough Guy race had existed in England for over 20 years. Dean partnered with his friend from boarding school turned corporate lawyer, Guy Livingstone, to plan the first event. They rented out a ski resort and invested $8,300 in Facebook ads targeting specific demographics like firefighters, extreme athletes, and military professionals, hoping for at least 300 attendees. Over 4,500 competitors signed up for the first event, which paid for itself before the first Tough Mudder even took place. Tough Mudder now holds more than 50 events per year with thousands of attendees and a loyal following.[44]

Photo Credit: © Handout/Getty Images

Participants competing in a Tough Mudder.

Entrepreneurial frugality requires
- Low overhead
- High productivity
- Minimal ownership of capital assets

Resources

It's hard to believe that Whatsapp, a company that was purchased by Facebook for $19 billion, started with only $250,000 of start-up capital. Founders Jan Koum and Brian Acton built a company that, as of 2015, had 900 million monthly active users.[45]

The modest beginnings of the company also included a period of time in which the Whatsapp team worked from a cafe´ in Mountain View, California, writing the code and developing the nascent messaging service. They eventually moved into subleased space at the nearby headquarters of software company Evernote, from which they were booted when Evernote's own success necessitated more space.[46]

Successful entrepreneurs are frugal with their scarce resources. They keep overheads low, productivity high, and ownership of capital assets to a minimum. By so doing, they minimize the amount of capital they need to start their business and make it grow.

Determining Resource Needs and Acquiring Resources

To determine the amount of capital that a company needs to get started, an entrepreneur should first assess what resources are crucial for the company's success in the marketplace. Some resources are more critical than others. What does the company expect to do better than any of its competitors? That is where it should put a disproportionate share of its very scarce resources. If the company is making a new high-tech product, technological know-how will be vital, and the most important resource will be engineers and the designs they produce. Therefore, the company must concentrate on recruiting and keeping excellent engineers and on safeguarding the intellectual property they produce, such as engineering designs and patents. If the company is doing retail selling, the critical factor will most likely be location. Choosing the wrong initial location for a retail store just because the rent is cheap can be a fatal mistake because it's unlikely there will be enough resources to relocate.

When Southwest Airlines started up in 1971, its strategy was to provide frequent, on-time service at a competitive price between Dallas, Houston, Austin, and San Antonio. To meet its objectives, Southwest needed planes that it could operate reliably at a low cost. It was able to purchase four brand-new Boeing 737s—very efficient planes for shorter routes—for only $4 million each because the recession had hit the airlines particularly hard, and Boeing had an inventory of unsold 737s. From the outset, Southwest provided good, reliable service and had one of the lowest costs per mile in the industry.

Items that are not critical should be obtained as thriftily as possible. The founder of Burlington Coat Factory, Monroe Milstein, likes to tell the story of how he obtained estimates for gutting the building he had just leased for his second store. His lowest bid was several thousand dollars. One day he was at the building when a sudden thunderstorm sent a crew of laborers working at a nearby site to his building for shelter from the rain. Milstein asked the crew's foreman what they would charge for knocking down the internal structures that needed to be removed. The foreman said, "Five." Milstein asked, "Five what?" The foreman replied, "Cases of beer."

A complete set of resources includes everything the business will need, but a business does not have to do all of its work in-house with its own employees. It is often more effective to subcontract the work. That way it doesn't need to own or lease its own manufacturing plant and equipment or to worry about recruiting and training production workers. Often, it can keep overhead lower by using outside firms to do work such as payroll, accounting, advertising, mailing promotions, janitorial services, and so on.

Even start-up companies can get amazingly good terms from outside suppliers. An entrepreneur should try to understand the potential suppliers' marginal costs. *Marginal cost* is the cost of producing one extra unit beyond what is presently produced. The marginal cost of the laborers who gutted Milstein's building while sheltering from the rain was virtually zero. They were being paid by another firm, and they didn't have to buy materials or tools.

Google founders Larry Page and Sergey Brin bought a terabyte of disks at bargain prices and built their own computer housings in Larry's dorm room, which became Google's first data center. Unable to interest the major portal players of the day, Larry and Sergey decided to make a go of it on their own. All they needed was a little cash to move out of the dorm—and to pay off the credit cards they had maxed out buying a terabyte of memory. So they wrote up a business plan, put their PhD plans on hold, and went looking for an angel investor. Their first visit was with a friend of a faculty member.

Andy Bechtolsheim, one of the founders of Sun Microsystems, was used to taking the long view. One look at their demo and he knew Google had potential—a lot of potential. But although his interest had been piqued, he was pressed for time. As Sergey tells it, "We met him very early one morning on the porch of a Stanford faculty member's home in Palo Alto. We gave him a quick demo. He had to run off somewhere, so he said, 'Instead of us discussing all the details, why don't I just write you a check?' It was made out to Google Inc. and was for $100,000."

The investment created a small dilemma. Because there was no legal entity known as "Google Inc.," there was no way to deposit the check. It sat in Larry's desk drawer for a couple of weeks while he and Sergey scrambled to set up a corporation and locate other funders among family, friends, and acquaintances. Ultimately, they brought in a total initial investment of almost $1 million.

On September 7, 1998, more than two years after they began work on their search engine, Google Inc., opened its door in Menlo Park, California. The door came with a remote control, as it was attached to the garage of a friend who sublet space to the new corporation's staff of three. The office offered several big advantages, including a washer and dryer and a hot tub. It also provided a parking space for the first employee hired by the new company: Craig Silverstein, who, after 12 years, left Google to join another start-up, Khan Academy in 2012.

Excerpted from *Google History*.[47]

Photo Credit: © David Paul Morris/Bloomberg/Getty Images

Photo Credit: © Brooks Kraft/Getty Images, Inc.

Google founders Sergey Brin and Larry Page

A small electronics company was acquired by a much larger competitor. The large company took over the manufacturing of the small company's products. Production costs shot up. An analysis revealed that much of the increase was due to a rise in the cost of purchased components. In one instance, the large company was paying 50% more than the small company had been paying for the same item. It turned out that the supplier had priced the item for the small company on the basis of marginal costs and for the large company on the basis of total costs.

Smart entrepreneurs find ways of controlling critical resources without owning them. A start-up business never has enough money, so it must be resourceful. It should not buy what it can lease. Except when the economy is red hot, there is almost always an excess of capacity of office and industrial space. Sometimes a landlord will be willing to offer a special deal to attract even a small start-up company into a building. Such deals may include reduced rent, deferral of rent payments for a period of time, and building improvements made at low or even no cost. In some high-tech regions, landlords will exchange rent for equity in a high-potential start-up.

Start-up Capital

You've developed your idea, you've carefully assessed what resources you will need to open your business and make it grow, you've pulled all your strategies together into a business plan, and now you know how much start-up capital you need to get you to the point where your business will generate a positive cash flow. How are you going to raise that start-up capital?

There are two types of start-up capital: **debt** and **equity**. Simply put, with debt, you don't have to give up any ownership of the business, but you have to pay current interest and eventually repay the principal you borrow; with equity, you have to give up some of the ownership to get it, but you may never have to repay it or even pay a dividend. So you must choose between paying interest and giving up some of the ownership.

In practice, your choice usually depends on how much of each type of capital you can raise. Most start-up entrepreneurs do not have much flexibility in their choice of financing. If it is a very risky business without any assets, it will be impossible to get any bank debt without putting up some collateral other than the business's assets—and most likely that collateral will be personal assets. Even if entrepreneurs are willing to guarantee the whole loan with their personal assets, the bank will expect entrepreneurs to put some equity into the business, probably equal to 25% of the amount of the loan. If your personal assets are less than the amount of the loan, the bank might recommend an SBA-guaranteed loan, in which case you would have to put in more equity.

The vast majority of entrepreneurs start their businesses by leveraging their own savings and labor. Consider how Apple, one of the most spectacular start-ups of all time, was funded. Steve Jobs and Stephen Wozniak had been friends since their school days in Silicon Valley. Wozniak was an authentic computer nerd. He had tinkered with computers from childhood, and he built a computer that won first prize in a science fair. His SAT math score was a perfect 800, but after stints at the University of Colorado, De Anza College, and Berkeley, he dropped out of school and went to work for Hewlett-Packard. His partner, Jobs, had an even briefer encounter with higher education: After one semester at Reed College, he left to look for a swami in India. When he and Wozniak began working on their microcomputer, Jobs was employed at Atari, the leading video game company.

Apple soon outgrew its manufacturing facility in the garage of Jobs's parents' house. Their company, financed initially with $1,300 raised by selling Jobs's Volkswagen and Wozniak's calculator, needed capital for expansion. They looked to their employers for help. Wozniak proposed to his supervisor that Hewlett-Packard produce what later became the Apple II. Perhaps not surprisingly, Hewlett-Packard declined. After all, Wozniak had no formal qualifications in computer design; indeed, he did not even have a college degree. At Atari, Jobs tried to convince founder Nolan Bushnell to manufacture Apples. He too was rejected.

However, on the suggestion of Bushnell and Regis McKenna, a Silicon Valley marketing ace, the two partners contacted Don Valentine, a venture capitalist, in the fall of 1976. In those days, Jobs's appearance was a holdover from his swami days; he definitely did not project the image of Doriot's grade-A man, even by Silicon Valley's casual standards. Valentine did not invest. But he did put them in touch with Armas Markkula, Jr., who had recently retired from Intel a wealthy man. Markkula saw the potential in Apple, and he knew how to raise money. He personally invested $91,000, secured a line of credit from Bank of America, put together a business plan, and raised $600,000 of venture capital.

> *[Mike Markkula] emphasized that you should never start a company with the goal of getting rich. Your goal should be making something you believe in and making a company that will last.*
> *Steve Jobs.*[48]

The Apple II was formally introduced in April 1977. Sales took off almost at once. Apple's sales grew rapidly to $2.5 million in 1977 and $15 million in 1978. In 1978, Dan Bricklin, a Harvard business student and former programmer at DEC, introduced the first electronic spreadsheet, VisiCalc, designed for the Apple II. In minutes, it could do tasks that had previously taken days. The microcomputer now had the power to liberate managers from the data guardians in the computer departments. According to one source, "Armed with VisiCalc, the Apple II's sales took off, and the personal computer industry was created." Apple's sales jumped to $70 million in 1979 and $117 million in 1980.

In 1980, Apple sold some of its stock to the public with an initial public offering (IPO) and raised more than $80 million. The paper value of their Apple stock made instant millionaires of Jobs ($165 million), Markkula ($154 million), Wozniak ($88 million), and Mike Scott ($62 million), who together owned 40% of Apple. Arthur Rock's venture capital investment of $57,000 in 1978 was suddenly worth $14 million, an astronomical compound return of more than 500% per year, or 17% per month.

By 1982, Apple IIs were selling at the rate of more than 33,000 units a month. With 1982 sales of $583 million, Apple hit the *Fortune* 500 list. It was a record. At five years of age, it was at that time the youngest company ever to join that exclusive list.

Success as spectacular as Apple's has never been equaled. Nonetheless, its financing is a typical example of how successful high-tech companies are funded. First, the entrepreneurs develop a prototype with personal savings and **sweat equity**, or ownership earned in lieu of wages. Then a wealthy investor—sometimes called an *informal investor* or *business angel*, who knows something about the entrepreneurs, or the industry, or both—invests some personal money in return for equity. When the company is selling a product, it may be able to get a bank line of credit secured by its inventory and accounts receivable. If the company is growing quickly in a large market, it may be able to raise capital from a formal venture capital firm in return for equity. Further expansion capital may come from venture capital firms or from a public stock offering.

The vast majority of new firms will never be candidates for formal venture capital or a public stock offering. Nevertheless, they will have to find some equity capital. In most cases, after they have exhausted their personal savings, entrepreneurs will turn to family, friends, and acquaintances (see Figure 2.4). It can be a scary business. Entrepreneurs often

	All Nations	U.S.
Close family member	40%	44%
Other relative	11%	6%
Work colleague	10%	9%
Friend/Neighbor	28%	28%
Stranger	9%	7%
Other	2%	6%
	100%	100%

FIGURE 2.4 Relationship of Investor to Entrepreneur.
Source: Global Entrepreneurship Monitor.[50]

find themselves with all their personal net worth tied up in the same business that provides all their income.

That is double jeopardy because if their businesses fail, they lose both their savings and their means of support. Risk of that sort can be justified only if the profit potential is high enough to yield a commensurate rate of return.

Would-be entrepreneurs sometimes tell us that they did not start their ventures because they could not raise sufficient money to get started. More often than not, they were unrealistic about the amount of money that they could reasonably have expected to raise for their start-up businesses. We tell them that many of the best companies started with very little capital. For example, 61% of companies on the 2013 list of companies founded by CEOs included in the *Inc*. 500 were started with less than $10,000; 86% of those companies were funded with money from the entrepreneurs, 21% with money from family and friends, 13% with bank loans, 9% with angel funding, and only 6% with venture capital,[49] which is by far the rarest source of seed-stage investment. It is estimated that at most only 1 in 10,000 of all new ventures in the United States has venture capital in hand at the outset, and only 1 in 1,000 gets venture capital at any stage of its life.

Profit Potential

The level of profit that is reasonable depends on the type of business. On average, U.S. companies make about 5% net income. Hence, on one dollar of revenue, the average company makes a five-cent profit after paying all expenses and taxes. A company that consistently makes 10% is doing very well, and one that makes 15% is truly exceptional. Approximately 50% of the *Inc*. 500 companies make 5% or less; 13% of them make 16% or more. Profit margins in a wide variety of industries for companies both large and small are published by BizMiner, so entrepreneurs can compare their forecasts with the actual performance of similar-sized companies in the same industry.

Any business must make enough profit to recompense its investors (in most cases that is the entrepreneur) for their investment. This must be the profit after all normal business expenses have been accounted for, including a fair salary for the entrepreneur and any family members who are working in the business. A common error in assessing the profitability of a new venture is to ignore the owner's salary. Suppose someone leaves a secure job paying $70,000 per year plus fringe benefits and invests $100,000 of personal savings to start a new venture. That person should expect to take a $70,000 salary plus fringe benefits out of the new business. Perhaps in the first year or two, when the business is being built, it may not be possible to pay $70,000 in actual cash; in that case, the pay that is not actually received should be treated as deferred compensation to be paid in the future. In addition to an adequate salary, the entrepreneur must earn a reasonable return on the $100,000 investment. A professional investor putting money into a new, risky business would expect to earn an annual rate of return of at least 40%, which would be $40,000 annually on a $100,000 investment. That return may come as a capital gain when the business is sold, or as a dividend, or as a combination of the two. But remember that $100,000 compounding annually at 40% grows to almost $2.9 million in 10 years. When such large capital gains are needed to produce acceptable returns, big capital investments held for a long time do not make any sense unless very substantial value can be created, as occasionally happens in the case of high-flying companies, especially high-tech ones. In most cases, instead of a capital gain, the investor's return will be a dividend, which must be paid out of the cash flow from the business.

The cash flow that a business generates is not to be confused with profit. It is possible, indeed very likely, that a rapidly growing business will have a negative cash flow from operations in its early years, even though it may be profitable. That may happen because the business may not be able to generate enough cash flow internally to sustain its ever-growing needs for working capital and the purchase of long-term assets such as plant and equipment. Hence, it will have to borrow or raise new equity capital. So it is very important that a high-potential business intending to grow rapidly make careful cash-flow projections to predict its needs for future outside investments. Future equity investments will dilute the percentage of ownership of the founders, and if the dilution becomes excessive, there may be little reward remaining for the entrepreneurs.

Biotechnology companies are examples of this problem: They have a seemingly insatiable need for cash infusions to sustain their research and development (R&D) costs in their early years. Their negative cash flow, or *burn rate*, sometimes runs at $1 million or more per month. A biotechnology company can easily burn up $50 million before it generates a meaningful profit, let alone a positive cash flow. The expected future capital gain from a public stock offering or sale to a large pharmaceutical company has to run into hundreds of millions of dollars, maybe into the billion-dollar range, for investors to realize an annual return of 50% or higher, which is what they expect to earn on money invested in a seed-stage biotechnology company. Not surprisingly, to finance their ventures, biotechnology entrepreneurs as a group have to give up most of the ownership. A 2017 study of venture-capital-backed biotechnology companies found that after they had filed to go public, the entrepreneurs and employees were left with less than 22% of the equity, compared with 44% for a comparable group of computer software companies.[51]

We've said that most businesses will never have the potential to go public. Nor will the owners ever intend to sell their businesses and thereby realize a capital gain. In that case, how can those owners get a satisfactory return on the money they have invested in their businesses? The two ingredients that determine return on investment are (1) the amount invested and (2) the annual amount earned on that investment. Entrepreneurs should invest as little as possible to start their businesses and make sure that their firms will be able to pay them a "dividend" big enough to yield an appropriate annual rate of return. For income tax purposes, that "dividend" may be in the form of a salary, bonus, or fringe benefits rather than an actual dividend paid out of retained earnings. Of course, the company must be generating cash from its own operations before that dividend can be paid. For entrepreneurs, happiness is a positive cash flow. And the day a company begins to generate **free cash**—that is, more cash than needed to sustain operations and purchase assets to keep the company on its growth trajectory—is a very happy day in the life of a successful entrepreneur.

- For entrepreneurs, happiness is a positive cash flow.

Awash with Cash

Apple is an awesome money machine. Apple's stash of cash kept piling up so that by 2017 its cash and marketable securities stood at $ $252.3 billion. It was enough money to give each household in the United States $2002, or put another way, it was enough to purchase a MacBook Pro, two iPads, a cup of coffee, and a sandwich for every man, woman, and child in North America.

In 2017, Apple generated $5.3 billion of cash flow from operations per month on average—almost $36,805 per second on the basis of a five-day working week, eight hours per day. No wonder Apple, with a market capitalization of more than $920 billion, was the most valuable company in history.[52]

Ingredients for a Successful New Business

The great day has arrived. You found an idea, wrote a business plan, and gathered your resources. Now you are opening the doors of your new business for the first time, and the really hard work is about to begin. What are the factors that distinguish winning entrepreneurial businesses from the also-rans? Rosabeth Kanter prescribed Four Fs for a successful business,[53] a list that has been expanded into the Nine Fs for entrepreneurial success (see Figure 2.5).

First and foremost, the founding entrepreneur is the most important factor. Next comes the market. This is the "era of the other," in which, as Regis McKenna observed, the fastest-growing companies in an industry will be in a segment labeled "others" in a market-share pie chart. By and large, they will be newer entrepreneurial firms rather than large firms with household names; hence, specialization is the key. A successful business should focus on niche markets.

The rate of change in business gets ever faster. The advanced industrial economies are knowledge based. Product life cycles are getting shorter. Technological innovation progresses at a relentless pace. Government rules and regulations keep changing. Communications and travel around the globe keep getting easier and cheaper. And consumers are better informed about their choices. To survive, let alone succeed, a company has to be quick and nimble. It must be fast and flexible. It cannot allow inertia to build up. Look at retailing: The historical giants such as Kmart are on the ropes, while nimble competitors dance around them. Four of the biggest retailing successes are the late Sam Walton's Walmart, Ingvar Kamprad's IKEA, Howard Schultz's Starbucks, and Tadashi Yanai's Fast Retailing, the parent company of Uniqlo. Entrepreneurs such as these know that they can keep inertia low by keeping the layers of management as few as possible.

Small entrepreneurial firms are great innovators. Big firms are relying increasingly on strategic partnerships with entrepreneurial firms to get access to desirable R&D. Microsoft, for example, has been aggressive in its acquisitions of businesses that will allow the company to expand its mobile product offerings, virtual reality (VR) and video gaming, artificial intelligence, and cloud-based products.[54] Its $7.5 billion purchase of code-hosting service company GitHub in 2018[55] enabled Microsoft to leverage GitHub technology to support and enhance the capabilities of its enterprise and cloud-based products by bringing Microsoft code developers to new audiences. In June 2018, Microsoft announced its acquisition of four gaming companies, Ninja Theory, Playground Games, Undead Labs, and Compulsion Games to strengthen their game development for their Xbox platform.[56] In the first nine months of 2018, Microsoft had acquired 11 companies altogether.[57]

When it comes to productivity, the best entrepreneurial companies leave the giant corporations behind in the dust. According to Capital IQ, as of 2018, Apple's revenue per

Founders	Every start-up company must have a first-class entrepreneur.
Focused	Entrepreneurial companies focus on niche markets. They specialize.
Fast	They make decisions quickly and implement them swiftly.
Flexible	They keep an open mind. They respond to change.
Forever-innovating	They are tireless innovators.
Flat	Entrepreneurial organizations have as few layers of management as possible.
Frugal	By keeping overhead low and productivity high, entrepreneurial companies keep costs down.
Friendly	Entrepreneurial companies are friendly to their customers, suppliers, and employees.
Fun	It's fun to be associated with an entrepreneurial company.

FIGURE 2.5 The Nine Fs for Entrepreneurial Success.

employee was an astonishing $2,075,398 and Alphabet's was $1,391,206, while Hewlett-Packard generated just over $463,121 and Western Digital's was $288,365. Whether you hope to build a big company or a small one, the message is the same: Strive tirelessly to keep productivity high.

But no matter what you do, you probably won't be able to attain much success unless you have happy customers, happy workers, and happy suppliers. That means you must have a friendly company. It means that everyone must be friendly, especially anyone who deals with customers. In the world of technology, many companies have long promoted a fun working environment that includes perks to keep employees happy and productive, while also promoting collaboration and loyalty. Two notable examples are Google and LinkedIn, who also happen to be neighbors in Mountain View, California. Among the perks at LinkedIn are free food and workout facilities. Furthermore, the company demonstrates its commitment to the career development of its employees. "We want all LinkedIn employees to be able to transform their career trajectory through learning and development. We offer a transformation plan through an online learning platform, which we call LearnIn, so our employees can create a plan for their career journey, track their progress and share with their managers."[58] Google, meanwhile, topped the list of *Fortune*'s 100 Best Companies to Work For in 2017 for the sixth time.[59] Larry Page, cofounder and CEO, has emphasized the importance of creating a family-like atmosphere for employees, whereby they have not only perks like free food but also generous benefits for things like sick leave and parental leave. "You treat people with respect, they tend to return the favor to the company. And that goes for families."[60]

Most new companies have the Nine Fs at the outset. Those that become successful and grow pay attention to keeping them and nurturing them. The key to sustaining success is to remain an entrepreneurial gazelle and never turn into a lumbering elephant and finally a dinosaur, doomed to extinction.

CONCLUSION

It is easy to start a business in the United States; anyone can do it. What distinguishes successful entrepreneurs from less-successful ones is the ability to spot an opportunity for a high-potential venture and then to develop it into a thriving business. As the business grows, the successful entrepreneur is able to attract key management team members, to motivate employees, to find more and more customers and keep them coming back, and to build increasingly sophisticated relationships with financiers.

YOUR OPPORTUNITY JOURNAL

Reflection Point	Your Thoughts...
1. What life events might trigger your entrepreneurial career?	
2. What ideas do you have for a new business?	
a. What ideas can you draw from your past work experience?	
b. What ideas can you draw from your family's work experience?	
3. Which of your personal attributes will most help you succeed as an entrepreneur?	
4. Which attributes do you think you need to further develop?	
5. Who are your entrepreneurial role models? Can you foster any of them into mentors?	
6. Is your idea an opportunity? Explain.	
7. Is the timing right to launch your venture?	
8. What are some cost-effective ways for you to get started?	

WEB EXERCISE

There are many self-assessment exercises on the web that indicate whether you have the skills necessary to be a successful entrepreneur. The reality is that these exercises often tell more about whether you'll be successful in any endeavor, whether that is entrepreneurship or a career with a large multinational, the military, or any other type of organization. Take a look at this assessment (http://www.psychometrictest.org.uk/entrepreneur-test/). Think about why these four parameters might make you a successful entrepreneur. Would they also lead to success in other career endeavors?

NOTES

1. According to the 2002 Kauffman study, 1,992 two- and four-year colleges and universities offered at least one course in entrepreneurship, up from about 300 in the 1984–1985 academic year. http://money.cnn.com/magazines/fsb/fsbarchive/2006/03/01/8370301/index.htm.
2. https://www.kauffman.org/what-we-do/research/2013/08/entrepreneurship-education-comes-of-age-on-campus.
3. Moore, Carol. "Understanding Entrepreneurial Behavior." In J. A. Pearce II, and R. B. Robinson, Jr., eds., *Academy of Management Best Paper Proceedings*. Forty-sixth Annual Meeting of the Academy of Management, Chicago, 1986.
4. http://nymag.com/daily/intelligencer/2014/02/jan-koum-brian-acton-whatsapp-billionaires.html.
5. http://www.forbes.com/sites/parmyolson/2014/02/19/exclusive-inside-story-how-jan-koum-built-whatsapp-into-facebooks-new-19-billion-baby/.
6. http://www.pcmag.com/article2/0,2817,2453710,00.asp.
7. http://www.womenyoushouldknow.net/moving-on-up-with-mary-ellen-sheets/.
8. http://www.bloomberg.com/ss/09/03/0313 rebounders/14.htm.
9. https://www.ted.com/talks/paul_tasner_how_i_became_an_entrepreneur_at_66.
10. http://www.huffingtonpost.com/2012/06/11/babiators-aviators-sunglasses-babiesn1581728.html.
11. Brockhuas, R. Risk-Taking Propensity of Entrepreneurs. *Academy of Management Journal*, 23: 509–520. 1980.
12. http://www.inc.com/magazine/201409/inc.500-2014-inc-500-ceo-survey-results.html.
13. https://www.hiscox.com/documents/DNA-of-an-Entrepreneur-Report-2017.pdf.
14. Rogers, E. M., and Larsen, J. K. *Silicon Valley Fever: Growth of High-Technology Culture*. New York: Basic Books. 1984.
15. https://www.hiscox.com/documents/DNA-of-an-Entrepreneur-Report-2017.pdf.
16. http://web.mit.edu/innovate/entrepreneurship2015.pdf.
17. http://search.proquest.com.ezproxy.babson.edu/docview/1563808804?pq-orig site=summon (Swidey, Neil. **Boston Globe** [Boston, Mass] 21 Sep 2014: R.20).
18. https://www.roadsideamerica.com/story/28020.
19. https://theknow.denverpost.com/2018/03/07/colorado-spirits-trail-map-52-distilleries-prize-2018/178528/.
20. http://www.hay-on-wye.co.uk/bookshops/ for population: https://www.citypopulation.de/php/uk-wales.php?cityid=K05000002.
21. https://factfinder.census.gov/faces/tableservices/jsf/pages/productview.xhtml?pid=SBO_2007_00CSA01&prodType=table.
22. https://www.census.gov/newsroom/press-releases/2015/cb15-209.html.
23. https://www.census.gov/newsroom/press-releases/2018/annual-business-survey.html.
24. http://www.adweek.com/socialtimes/infographic-the-social-profiles-of-inc-500-ceos-vs-fortune-500-ceos/114501.
25. http://mitsloan.mit.edu/uploadedFilesV9/180325%20Age%20and%20Successful%20Entrepreneurship.pdf, also https://www.businessinsider.com/young-startup-founder-myth-average-age-of-entrepreneurs-42-mit-study-2018-4.
26. https://www.businessinsider.com/linkedin-reaches-a-half-billion-users-2017-4.
27. It is also an excellent example of what venture capitalists call value-added.
28. http://www.inc.com/magazine/201409/inc.500-2014-inc-500-ceo-survey-results.html.
29. In fact, 33% of all businesses survive intact for 10 years. According to the U.S. Bureau of labor Statistics, a little bit more than 33% of businesses survive past 10 years: https://www.bls.gov/bdm/entrepreneurship/bdm_chart3.htm.
30. www.sba.gov/advo/research/rs204tot.pdf.
31. Detailed information on survival rates can be found at: https://www.bls.gov/bdm/entrepreneurship/bdm_chart3.htm.
32. Timmons, Jeffry A. *New Venture Creation: Entrepreneurship for the 21st Century*, 5th ed. Boston: McGraw-Hill. 1999.
33. https://www.prosperity.net/articles/magic-surveys-warby-parker-disrupted-eyeglass-monopoly.
34. https://www.inc.com/magazine/201505/graham-winfrey/neil-blumenthal-icons-of-entrepreneurship.html.
35. https://www.prosperity.net/articles/magic-surveys-warby-parker-disrupted-eyeglass-monopoly—source for 1 mSource for 4m: https://www.warbyparker.com/buy-a-pair-give-a-pair.
36. http://finance.yahoo.com/q/ks?s=tsla+key+statistics.
37. Obituary: Professor Rajeev Motwani. June 9, 2009. www.telegraph.co.uk/news/obituaries/technology-obituaries/5487846/Professor-Rajeev-Motwani.html.

38. http://www.marketwatch.com/story/allstar-products-group-scott-boilen-named-one-of-drtvs-industry-leaders-to-watch-2015-08-31.
39. http://abcnews.go.com/GMA/Weekend/story?id=6716994&page=1.
40. http://www.nytimes.com/2009/02/27/business/media/27adco.html? r=0.
41. http://finance.yahoo.com/blogs/daily-ticker/secret-snuggie-success-revealed-124324161.html.
42. http://www.inc.com/uploadedfiles/inlineimage/0915LAUInfogfinal31031.pdf.
43. https://www.inc.com/profile/scientistcom, https://www.crunchbase.com/person/kevin-lustig#section-overview.
44. https://www.nytimes.com/2010/04/29/sports/29mudder.html?_r=2& and https://mudder-guide.com/guide/tough-mudder-facts-and-trivia/.
45. http://www.statista.com/statistics/260819/number-of-monthly-active-whatsapp-users/.
46. http://www.forbes.com/sites/parmyolson/2014/02/19/exclusive-inside-story-how-jan-koum-built-whatsapp-intofacebooks-new-19-billion-baby/.
47. www.google.com/corporate/history.html.
48. Isaacson, Walter. *Steve Jobs*. New York: Simon and Schuster, 2011. p. 78.
49. http://www.inc.com/magazine/201309/numbers-from-inc.500-companies-first-year.html.
50. The information in Figure 2.4 was extracted from the Global Entrepreneurship Monitor data set. www.gemconsor tium.org.
51. https://arxiv.org/pdf/1711.00661.pdf.
52. https://www.moneyshow.com/articles/guru-47817/, and https://www.marketwatch.com/investing/stock/aapl/financials/cash-flow.
53. Kanter, Rosabeth Moss. *Change Masters: Innovation and Entrepreneurship in the American Corporation*. New York: Simon & Schuster. 1985.
54. http://www.informationweek.com/software/operating-systems/6-microsoft-acquisitions-what-do-they-mean/d/d-id/1318999?image number=1.
55. Capital IQ.
56. Capital IQ.
57. Capital IQ.
58. http://www.bizjournals.com/sanfrancisco/best-places-to-work/news/2015/04/14/best-places-to-work-largest-linkedin-social-networ.html.
59. http://fortune.com/best-companies/2017/google/.
60. http://fortune.com/2012/01/19/larry-page-google-should-be-like-a-family/.

Case Vedavoo[1]

Introduction

Five years after buying his first sewing machine, Scott Hunter was telling friends about the conversation with Yvon Chouinard, the legendary rock climber and environmental advocate who founded the global apparel and equipment brand Patagonia. Years before—while a student in the MBA program at Babson College—he had sought to interview Chouinard for a paper he had to write, but was unable to connect. After graduation, Hunter began work on designs for backpacks to be sold under his newly launched brand, Vedavoo. He worked with outside designers, and struggled to identify an offshore factory to manufacture his bags. One of these in China looked promising, but ultimately rejected his project after Nike bought all unused capacity. In another case, he shipped a prototype bag that had cost him thousands to another potential partner in Vietnam, only to have the design stolen and the intermediaries he was expecting to do business with disappear. After months of effort, Hunter found himself down to his last $700 with little to show for the time and capital invested to that point.

By fate or divine guidance, Hunter received a very unexpected call.

> Mr. Chouinard's assistant called me and said, "Yvon's got 20 minutes this afternoon. If you've got time, he would be happy to speak with you." So I jumped on it, and the conversation lasted about an hour. We swapped stories about hiking and climbing in Wyoming before he asked, "Okay, tell me about your business." I told him what I was working on, and the challenges I'd faced. He said, "If you can't build something with your own hands, you have no business being in business. You've got to learn what's involved in making it, how it goes together and why things are the way they are so that you can figure out ways to build it better, easier, and more cost effective. How can you expect others to make something for you if you don't even know what your designs will force them to do? Go buy a sewing machine and learn to sew!"

Inspired by Chouinard's advice, Hunter went straight to Craigslist and used $300 of his remaining funds to purchase a used sail-making machine. He drove from his home west of Boston down to Providence, Rhode Island, to pick it up. He returned home, and following the time-honored, classic American entrepreneur tradition, set up the machine in his garage. Filled with determination, he used another $300 to purchase enough materials to make a few backpacks, paid his website up for the year to come, and began teaching himself to sew with a $12 safety net. He explained his plans for the company, which he named VEDAVOO, after an area in the Medicine Bow Routt National Forest in Wyoming.[2] "I decided it's going to be made in America, and we're going to use American-sourced goods. We're going to build on-demand. We're going to follow this path whether it's custom goods or our core products" (see **Exhibit 2.1**).

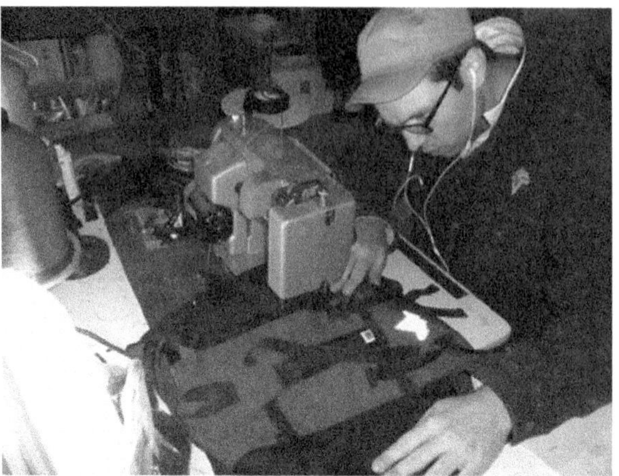

Photo Credit: Courtesy of Scott Hunter

EXHIBIT 2.1 Scott Hunter Sewing in Basement Workshop.

Company Background

Scott Hunter grew up in Wyoming, spent much time outdoors hunting and fishing, and graduated from the University of Wyoming in 2005. During his senior year, he was a finalist in a business plan competition with his concept for Changing Leaf Designs,[3] a start-up that would make large modular backpacks for backpacking. Though he did not win the competition, the effort established an entrepreneurial passion in his heart to be pursued in time.

Upon graduation, Hunter took a job in Wyoming as an Internet salesman, ultimately moving up within the company to a Project and Account Management position developing wireless telecommunications systems for the oil business. Finding little personal value in this work, Hunter left the business and returned to his initial plan to make backpacks. He applied to Babson College, hoping to enroll and learn skills he would need as an entrepreneur launching a start-up. To his surprise, he gained acceptance to the one-year program and promptly moved to Massachusetts.

[1] This case was written by Martha Lanning, Caroline Daniels, and Scott Hunter. *Copyright © Babson College.*

[2] Vedauwoo was an area of distinctive rock outcrops in southeastern Wyoming, popular for rock climbing. Hunter changed this word slightly for the name of his company.

[3] Pingora Peak was a prominent granite tower in the Cirque of the Towers in the Wind River Range in Wyoming. Hunter chose the name of this peak for his company.

In 2009, Hunter launched his backpack company while finishing his program at Babson. His plan was still to make large, modular trekking packs. After facing many challenges, including bad advice from respected experts and losing money in deals with unscrupulous offshore agents, Hunter reframed his business plan to focus on building smaller, simpler designs that would be designed internally for domestic production. By 2014, Hunter had established and begun to grow a successful enterprise fabricating fly fishing packs from his home base in Lancaster, Massachusetts. He noted, "We just try to keep evolving and let the market dictate."

Sales revenue had not yet reached one million, but product orders were growing and the company had high expectations. Hunter summed it up. "Coming back to my passions and to the things I love has been incredible. Knowing we're creating new jobs and new opportunities in the state is unbelievably fulfilling for me."

The Entrepreneurial Process

Generating the Idea: Outdoor Life Shapes the Entrepreneurial Vision

During his early years in Wyoming, Scott Hunter hiked, fished, and camped in the mountains and rivers of his home state. He was active in Boy Scouts of America and in their service branch, the Order of the Arrow,[4] building trails and portages and other conservation projects. He was elected state president, then five-state regional president, then the National Vice-Chief in 2001. He taught leadership skill development and advocated conservation minded outdoor programs from this platform.

Heading off to the University of Wyoming, Hunter planned to study aeronautical engineering. He commented, "Frankly, after one semester, I realized it was completely wrong for me. I'm a people person. I couldn't sit behind a desk with a calculator all day and just crunch numbers. I needed to get out and talk to folks and be me." He enrolled in the College of Business and studied Business Administration.

In his senior year, Hunter pursued and was granted special clearance to substitute the traditional capstone thesis with a business plan to be entered in the Wyoming $10K entrepreneurship competition during the academic year 2004–2005. Previously during a summer internship in Washington, D.C., he had worked for Senator Mike Enzi from Wyoming. While in Washington, Hunter frequently heard people talk about the decline of American manufacturing and outsourcing. His concern grew, and he resolved not to outsource.

> I knew I needed to write a business plan, so I tried to pick something I had a lot of passion for, something I loved. I decided that starting a bag and pack business with everything made in the USA could be the way to go. At the time, a lot of things were going overseas. I saw manufacturing jobs leaving, and you couldn't buy a *Made in the USA* backpack anymore. That really bothered me! I was selected a finalist with the first iteration of what would become Vedavoo. I got to pitch to local angel investors, but was graciously told I was far from ready. So I went back to finish my undergraduate study and to look for a real job to gain some experience before I took it forward again.

Transition from Desk Job to Entrepreneur

Hunter turned down a marketing job in D.C. and took a job near Lander, Wyoming, as an Internet salesman. "It wasn't the most glamorous opportunity, but I wanted to be close to the outdoors, to stay close to what I loved." He moved up the ranks quickly and was transferred to a sister company in wireless telecommunications system consulting and design for oil fields. As director of business development, he met with clients and worked on big-ticket contracts, but knew he was not fulfilled. "It was a big jump in a short time, and it was very good work. But at the end of the day, I was killing myself for very little personal value."

He decided to chase his dreams as an entrepreneur. His plan was to reframe his early plan to build large trekking packs that could be converted to other uses such as a tent or a sleeping bag. "My concern as a backpacker was that I would hike in with this huge pack that weighed a lot, but once I got to camp it had no useful purpose." Hunter arrived at Babson College, bringing with him his concept for the backpack company, now named Pingora Pack Company.

Outsourcing vs. Personal Values

Hunter used his time to prepare his company for launch while at Babson. Soon, he was forced to change the name of the venture again after learning that another pack company had rights to the name "Pingora." He drew inspiration for a new name from another of his favorite areas in his home state of Wyoming, the area known as Vedauwoo in the Medicine Bow Routt National Forest. Hunter opted for an easier to pronounce and spell variation of the park's name, choosing "VEDAVOO" for the brand under which he would focus on building modular backpacking equipment. Prospective financiers for his venture and advisers alike strongly encouraged him to go overseas for manufacturing. Through a contact at Babson, Hunter identified a design studio in California with the capability to convert his ideas into prototypes, and to further coordinate material selection, sourcing, and fabrication in China. Hunter explained, "They were a one-stop-shop. They could help me select materials for my bag. They could do all the coordination and sourcing themselves, and then take it to a factory in China. I wasn't thrilled to give up on keeping production

[4] The Order of the Arrow (OA) was the honor society of Boy Scouts of America. Among other goals, OA promoted responsible use of the outdoors, environmental stewardship, and service.

domestic, but at that point it seemed more important to win the battle first, then come back to the US with production later when we had the brand and the resources to support the move."

Although it meant sacrificing his personal values at least temporarily, Hunter decided to proceed with the California design firm. "So I went to the designer with a patent pending technology for a modular backpack, and spent hours trying to make it real. Everything was looking up for the brand, and people were getting excited about our first products, but the pack proved too complicated for him to build a sample or to attract interest from capable factories overseas. There were too many things that had to work together just right. There was a huge fear the pieces wouldn't operate the right way and that we would have a high waste ratio because of the number of pieces that had to fit together perfectly. So factories pushed us away, the designer was pushing us away, and we went back to the drawing board. Looking back—this was a blessing in disguise. Even if it had been produced, it would have retailed around $700 in a niche that really only accounted for about 5% of the global pack market at that point."

Reframing the Strategy

Looking for simple alternatives to bring to market after the abandonment of the modular trekking pack, Hunter worked with the designer on three other options. The first was a *bear bag* he had developed with a team of fellow students in Babson's Product Design & Development class. This bag was designed to be suspended from a tree, thus holding food and other "smellable" cooking and camping items at a height above the reach of bears. The second was a shoulder sling with removable storage pouch based on a concept he had envisioned while fly fishing. The third was a new hiking backpack design with modular padding that gave users the ability to customize their pack to better fit their bodies and comfort preferences. He pursued a provisional patent on this, and worked again with the California designer to generate final designs and prototypes for each of the products.

The California designer also worked in parallel for other notable brands such as Marmot, CamelBak, REI, and Eastern Mountain Sports and was therefore unable to complete work quickly for Hunter. Turnaround for prototypes of the designs took several months to receive and cost thousands of dollars. The single backpack prototype (see Exhibit 2.2) alone cost Hunter $5800. Though each of the new options was much simpler in design, the California designer still struggled to locate suitable manufacturing overseas. Potential factories viewed the projects as too complex and the company too small to offer adequate return. After several months without progress, Hunter and the design firm found the challenges too great and ended their relationship.

> If I wanted to be a success, I had to reduce my dependence on outside sources, and be able to do more myself. I needed to have the ability to work directly with potential factories so that I could work through potential hang-ups. I needed to be able to do my own sourcing. I went back to the Outdoor Retailer show on a mission to find myself a factory.

Photo Credit: Courtesy of Scott Hunter

EXHIBIT 2.2 Vedavoo Exhibit at the IFTD Show in 2014. Scott Hunter Wearing Red Sling Pack.

Another New Beginning

In January of 2010, now approaching a year into the business without serious revenue, without sellable packs, without a factory, and without a designer, Hunter attended the Outdoor Retailer Winter Market Show in Salt Lake City. Carrying the prototypes of the modular padding backpack and bear bag, he spoke with several potential partners before coming to an agreement with a group from South Korea that managed a pack factory in Vietnam. This factory was known for work they did for Mont-Bell, another notable, premium brand. Through a translator, they agreed Hunter would send the only existing sample of his modular padding backpack, and using this, they would develop a line of three sizes of backpacks built to use the same customizable padding technology that was in the prototype. Hunter shipped the pack and never heard from the company again. He related the saga.

> I tried to fight it for a little while, but it became clear that the South Korean company was just an intermediary. They had sold themselves as the owner of the factory when in reality they were just a contractor using the factory's resources. At some level, the design got stolen. So picture this: I had put in a year, spent an exorbitant amount of money, and had nothing to show for it! I didn't even have the backpack anymore to be able to try and figure out how to rebuild it!"

In March of 2010, having spent so much of his capital in the efforts to that point, Hunter reached a point when he had only $700 left in the company account. After the struggles to that point, he was faced with giving up on his dream, or finding a way to keep it alive. He remembered his early conversations with others who had followed similar paths like Wayne Gregory (the founder of Gregory Packs), and drew heavily on his conversation with Yvon Chouinard. Each in their own way had encouraged him to follow a similar path. "Learn to sew!" He also returned to his early goal of producing all of his products in the United States. Taking the advice and his values to heart, he bought a used industrial sewing machine off Craigslist for $300, bought $300 worth of materials, and paid his website up for another year. With a $12 safety net and limited revenue from the sale of Vedavoo t-shirts, Hunter went to his garage and taught himself how to sew.

Using old daypacks and duffel bags from Goodwill and garage sales, Hunter studied how packs and bags were made. He cut them apart, made patterns out of brown paper grocery bags, and tried to recreate them using his own fabrics. He learned to understand how curves worked to create depth. He learned how square cutouts could be used to make corners. He learned the importance of sewing consistently straight lines, and just how difficult it was to make them.

Though Hunter struggled with reproducing existing products, he had to be able to do much more than copy other products for Vedavoo to succeed. He wanted to learn how to design products himself so that he could use the machine to turn his ideas into realities without outside help. Joining several pieces of two dimensional fabric into a single three-dimensional shape was a significant challenge that outweighed the sewing itself. When weeks of practice gave him a reasonable grasp on this, he then taught himself how to refine those shapes so that they would each fit together perfectly. He reflects.

> Those days were so hard. I had no money. I had no experience building gear. All I had was my dream, my passion, and a commitment to keep the company alive. Having never sewn before, my early products were as could be expected—but they laid a foundation that I use still today.

His greatest challenge at this stage, however, was finding a niche with genuine opportunity for an American Made bag company to succeed and developing products that would deliver real value for customers there. He reflects.

> After we struggled to find traction in backpacking, I wasn't sure where to turn next. I knew I still wanted to keep the venture in the outdoor industry, but it was tough to narrow down to a niche I could work in. Vedauwoo—the inspiration for the company's name—is known for many types of outdoor adventure, but more than anything, it's known for rock climbing. So I was getting all kinds of interest from rock climbers through social media. I decided to follow the energy there and to focus my efforts on building rope bags, duffels, chalk bags, and simple backpacks for climbers to carry their gear in. I knew little about the sport, but they gave me great ideas and the energy they brought in support of our new brand convinced me.

Through this process, Hunter learned the ins and outs of how to build gear: how to pattern, how to build, how to prototype, how to put things together. "I learned how to do all that, and instead of paying $5,800 for a single pack, now I had my own patterns, the ability to make my own prototypes, and for the first time, I had products that were truly my own designs."

Serendipity Strikes

Armed with a line of packs and bags for rock climbers, Hunter raised new capital and went a second time to the Outdoor Retailer Trade Show in the summer of 2011. This time he had his own booth. However, a few problems became apparent.

> They put me on the back wall in a corner from hell because I was a first-timer. There was no light above the booth. I got my stuff set up, and the few people who actually made

it back that far started saying, "If I can buy a similar pack made in China for $40, why would I pay $80 for yours?" American Made wasn't enough to justify the difference for a sport where the bulk of the money is spent on things that keep climbers from falling. To put it mildly, I was feeling like a complete failure. As I neared the end of the show, I had no sales, no serious interest, and was ready to give up and move on. But late on the last day, a gentleman came by the booth with a wheelchair. He had his video camera mounted to it so it worked like a rolling tripod. Though he was definitely soliciting me to pay him for other videos later, he offered to do the first video for free, and I said, "Sure." At that point, I had nothing left to lose. Much to my surprise, he scanned the packs on display and kept walking. He pointed at the back of the booth, where a sling pack I had built for myself to use fly fishing after the show was hanging. He said, "I want to do the video on that!" I didn't even have it named until he asked me what it was called while filming.

Another Surprise Phone Call

A week after the show, Hunter received a phone call from a person who ran the International Fly Tackle Dealer (IFTD) Show.[5] He told Hunter, "We have the show next week in New Orleans, and I want you to be there. I saw this video online, and I'm really impressed. I think you'd be perfect for this market. We need new guys and new blood in the industry, and I think you'd be fantastic!" Hunter had spent nearly all his money on his Outdoor Retailer booth and said he could not afford to attend. The Fly Tackle Show manager offered Hunter a booth for free. ("Just don't tell anybody.")

Hunter grabbed one of his climbing designs, altered it slightly to work as a fly fishing daypack, developed a simple lanyard, grabbed his personal sling pack, and went to New Orleans. He thought, "We'll see what happens." To his immense surprise, the gear was a hit. "People loved what we were doing. They loved the ideas and the new brand. Our designs were different. Plus, we found that fly fishermen had a lot more money to spend than climbers did!"

Hunter learned this market, unlike rock climbing, was not composed of college kids with no money. Instead it was 35- to 40-year olds and up with discretionary income to spend. Hunter thought back to his conversation with Yvon Chouinard and how he had mentioned among other plans that he considered building packs for fly fishing. Chouinard had told him not to touch it, that fly fishing was a "dying market." The show clearly proved otherwise. In fact, Hunter saw that fly fishing was changing. It was no longer solely for 35+ year old men. A new market segment was emerging that was younger, passionate, and interested in having gear that was different and designed better and more durably than the gear their fathers and grandfathers used. Stores and media professionals quickly took note, and Hunter got his first legitimate orders.

Hunter identified a factory in Pennsylvania and placed preliminary orders with them to build the fly fishing products that had enjoyed success at the trade show: the sling pack, the chest pack, and the day pack. Two days before the order was scheduled to ship, Hunter telephoned the factory to confirm billing details and learned they had not yet begun production. Hunter exclaimed, "So here I am again, I've had my first real glimmer of success, then the factory I was counting on so desperately completely dropped the ball! I fired my factory, called all of my first customers, told them what was happening, and told them my plans to bring everything back in-house." Hunter reflects.

> It was so tough in 2012 because every pack shipped I had built myself. But it was truly a blessing in disguise. I was a one-man show, so I built only what actually sold because I didn't have time to build up an inventory. It took me probably five times what it should have, but I made sure that I built it right so that it would last. And at least I was building it myself! I didn't have that cost, and I wasn't depending on an outside source. I was able to build on demand and keep moving forward. This established the baseline for the business model we have now, giving us the opportunity to build on demand with only minimal inventory. We get paid up front for sales, build to order, and stay nimble and cash efficient with everything we do!

Strategy Decisions

In early 2016, as Hunter looks back on the five years since he bought his sewing machine, he reviewed how Vedavoo had progressed and recognized two things: he was building packs, which had been his initial dream; and he was sourcing everything he could in the United States, in line with his personal values. There had been many challenges along the way, well more than many would deem worth fighting through, but also a few lucky breaks that no one could have planned.

Key strategy decisions had sometimes evolved organically without deliberate planning. They had allowed the business to stay true to its original focus, and also to scrape through when the going got tough.

1. Product focus: Abandoned backpacking and rock climbing in favor of a central focus on fly fishing. Relaunched in 2012 with two products that sold immediately: a chest pack and

[5] The International Fly Tackle Dealer Show was the largest gathering in the world for fly fishing manufacturers, retailers, sales reps, media, and industry organizations. The yearly shows featured people, products, emerging trends, innovations, leading brands, seminars, and more for the fly fishing industry.

a sling pack. Followed with a Daypack, and several simple storage solutions that also saw quick success. Continues to keep line simple, but innovates regularly to keep the line fresh while developing new solutions for greater market share (see **Exhibit 2.3**).

2. Pricing: Looked at other packs on the market and set Vedavoo prices only slightly higher, typically around 10 dollars more, to suggest greater value but not so far removed from competitors that higher numbers seemed unreasonable. "The pricing worked, and we've been able to increase our price more on some things. People continued to buy, and sales actually went up when we increased the price. It's a shame that I underpriced a bit upfront, but without knowing clearly what my costs were, I just did my best. As we've grown, we've learned new tricks that help us be more efficient with our most expensive input—labor hours—and we've found ways to make new products easy to build and standing products easier to build so we can be more profitable."
3. Quality control: Built everything "to perfection" to assure no returns and to protect brand reputation.
4. Customization: Decided early on to offer customization. Customers asking for specific features gave Hunter new ideas for product improvement and development. "We were

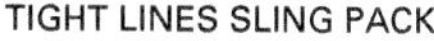

TIGHT LINES SLING PACK

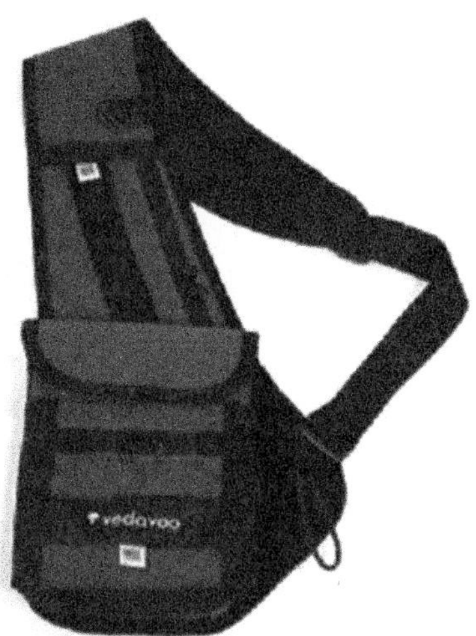

TIGHT LINES SLING PACK DELUXE

The Tightlines Sling Pack was designed to be the one pack that can cover your needs for 90% of the fishing you do. Worn over your non-dominant shoulder (left if you're right handed), the pack rides comfortably in the small of your back. When you need access to your gear, you pull the sling around to the front–where it lies comfortably and level across your chest. This gives you quick and easy access to your tools, flies, and tippet, but keeps your front clean and tangle free while you fish.

Frustrated by other "circular"slings that creep around or flop forward on you, our design was built to stay put on your back. Our offset design connects to the body of the pack at a point above the center of gravity–which means that the weight is already past the point of turn, and must be PULLED around to the front.

Minimalist, but not restrictive, designed to carry two full size flyboxes from Cliff Outdoors (ideal with a Super Days Worth and a Standard Cliff Flybox) in the gear pouch. The strap is built with two key pockets:
1) Behind the gear pouch is a velcro closure pocket ideal for thin items you need (but don't want in your way). Things like leader wallets, granola bars, pocket flasks, peanut butter sandwiches, etc fit nicely here.
2) A small zipper pocket to hold your loose gear and other accessories you need to have quick access to. Stash your indicators, weight, chapstick, floatant and more here.

ON THE DELUXE MODEL: The Deluxe Gear Pouch has the same internal dimensions as the standard gear pouch, but it comes with several additional features that make it a great addition. The Pouch has a front tuck pocket, a front zippered pocket, two stretch fabric side pockets (for easy access / storage of indicators, etc.), two additional tool loops (perfect for dry fly floatant and a Cliff Strait-N-Dry), and a large ARC Loop giving you the ability to add on any of our ARC Accessories like the ARC Fly Pack.

Every pack is hand-built order in our workshop using 1000D American woven Cordura fabrics and American made hardware, straps, and closures. Even the thread used to sew your pack is American Made. We're looking forward to building yours!

EXHIBIT 2.3 Vedavoo Top Sellers

Source: Courtesy of Scott Hunter

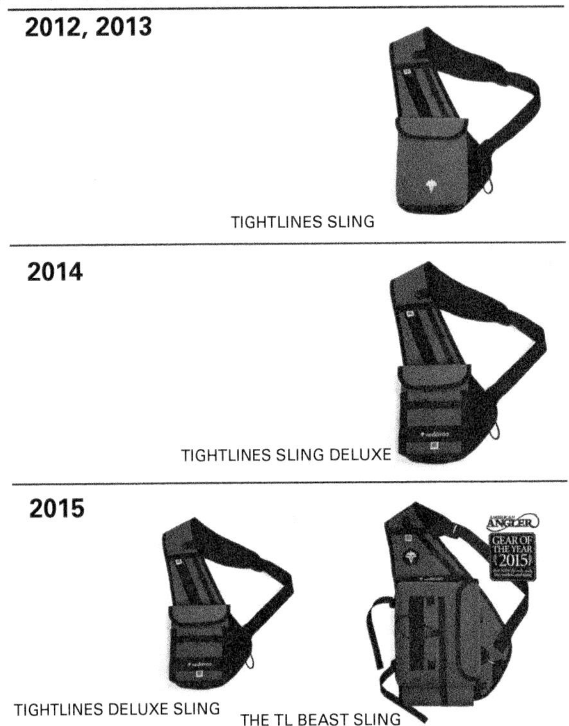

EXHIBIT 2.3 (Continued)

able to make continuous iterations, compared to a company with a lot of inventory made overseas that they are stuck with for a year."

5. American sourcing: "If I was going to hang the flag, it had to represent the entire picture." Initially all packs were built in Massachusetts. Later, Hunter added other work-from-home sewers from around New England and as far South as Maryland. Further, he used American-made inputs wherever possible. Heavy duty, 1,000 denier military grade Cordura nylon that was "more than double the thickness and density of the best pack cloth on the market" improved durability, and 500 denier cordura was used for linings. Buckles, zippers, Velcro, webbing, and even the sewing thread used to make the products came from U.S. manufacturers. Nonfabric products were also U.S.-made, for example, bottles from the Pacific Northwest, and apparel produced in Southern California.

Future Growth

Hunter discussed how Vedavoo was positioned to grow. "We have grown no less than 83% per year since 2012—at least doubling in every other year. More business comes with added costs and greater need for a strong team. Could we grow faster if we went out and got a big angel? Probably. Do we want to grow faster? Not really. Organic growth has been excellent, and is letting our team develop and grow in a positive way together as we take on more work."

> My expectation was to come to Babson for the one-year program, graduate, and move back. I expected to launch the business out west, use Wyoming-based manufacturing, and work with folks I already had contact with from the local business council. But, we made the decision to stay in Massachusetts and have built a community around ourselves. It was definitely not the ideal location for a new outdoor brand, but it's been perfect for American craft manufacturing, and I've found other people here that have helped make the dream a reality.
>
> New England has this strong manufacturing mindset, and people and facilities here were part of that culture. It has been a good place to develop our business. Things may have gone downhill when all the factories closed, but the people who sewed here remain. We've been fortunate enough to gain staff from factories long since outsourced, and they already know the craft when they sit down to sew their first sling. We have stay-at-home moms and grandmothers, single ladies, and college kids. It's been awesome. The best example is a stay at home mother of three that lives in the same town I do, and we met at a local festival. Her husband came through and said, "Hey, I want that pack!" and she followed with "I can sew that." So I asked her on the spot if she wanted an interview. She's

> become my right-hand in the business and works as our production team manager now.

Cash remained a challenge, and Vedavoo was covering bills with incoming revenue. Capacity to build for large orders had begun to loom as a growth concern.

> Every day we are challenged by new orders and less time to build them. As strong as our team is, it wasn't built overnight. Finding skilled and talented professionals is difficult and takes time. Our greatest risk is growing too fast, but we've been slowly planning for the storm since 2014.

Hunter began a program to develop and grow as the business grows. His "workshop team" handles day-to-day manufacturing on an at will basis. Historically, this team did it all. With significant growth and the increase in partner and retail orders, it became clear that a quick spike in ordering could quickly overwhelm this team. He linked with a manufacturing facility in western Massachusetts late in 2014, and has continued to work with the factory on large-scale projects since that time. The factory had run successfully for many years but was forced to close when the outsourcing movement began. Hunter appreciated New England's rich manufacturing history that extended from the 19th through the 20th century.

Vedavoo now focused on fly fishing products. Seasonality and geographic region were important to this market. Hunter noted that certain times of year were busier than others.

> Our biggest season starts at Thanksgiving and goes through Easter. That's by far our heart and soul. Christmas buying season is followed immediately by consumer show season. In 2014, we did ten of these events, and they were a huge success. That year we surpassed 2013 net before we got to the end of the first quarter. Our slow down happens thereafter through mid-summer. We have used this time to build for cobranded projects, new orders for retailers, and some inventory for the holiday to come. Every minute sewing is a minute making money—and we try to keep everyone running smooth and even all year, buffering the seasonality. By the time we hit fall, people start ramping up again leading into Thanksgiving.

Customer interest in Vedavoo had begun in New England and the Northern Rocky Mountains where freshwater fishing was practiced, then strong sales developed in the Southeast. Hunter said about 75% to 80% of customers were male, parallel to industry participation. "People going out for saltwater fishing have also picked up our stuff. They've been very happy with it, so a lot of new potential, and recently expansion into international markets as well." Discussing competition, Hunter named standby industry leaders like Orvis[6] and Fishpond[7] he tries to focus on his work so that he always competes with himself. Hunter often invited potential customers at trade shows to try on a competitor's pack, then come back and try on a Vedavoo pack. At the beginning, Hunter thought *Made in the USA* would be the primary driver of sales, but he learned gear functionality was the real key to winning a customer.

> In our case, the weight stays put on your back better because of the way our pack is shaped. You can lean over and the pack still stays put, whereas with the others, the pack flips to the front and gets in your way, or slides down your back. We also designed the pack to keep your front clean and free, with the pack riding flush on your back until you need it.

On the future of the industry, Hunter believed Vedavoo held a good place.

> Fly Fishing was probably considered "a dying industry" because the active angler was getting older, and products homogenized. When we entered the industry, you could look at two sling packs from different companies, they look very similar, all built by Asian factories. They were feature rich but over so. These companies lost sight of the critical piece, which was how it felt, carried, and functioned once the user was there. Conditions were ripe for new entrants—and this coupled with a huge emergence of fly fishing as a "cool" active sport in the 18–35 demographic. Seeking "different" than their fathers and grandfathers, and driving demand for *Made in America* product. We started as that wave started and we've been fortunate as a result. Getting more younger people and kids into the sport is the center pin of our longevity.

Discussion Questions

1. Does Scott have the right characteristics to be an entrepreneur? Discuss his entrepreneurial process. Is it effective?
2. Is Vedavoo an opportunity? Why or why not?
3. Evaluate Vedavoo using the Timmons Framework. How would you move forward if you were Scott?

---

[6] The Orvis Company, worldwide leader in fly fishing, was founded in Vermont in 1856. Orvis was America's oldest mail order outfitter and longest-operating fly fishing business. In 2014, Orvis was a multinational company with 1,700 employees and $350 million in sales (2012).

[7] Fishpond was a small enterprise based in Colorado and focused on the fishing industry.

3 Opportunity Recognition, Shaping, and Reshaping

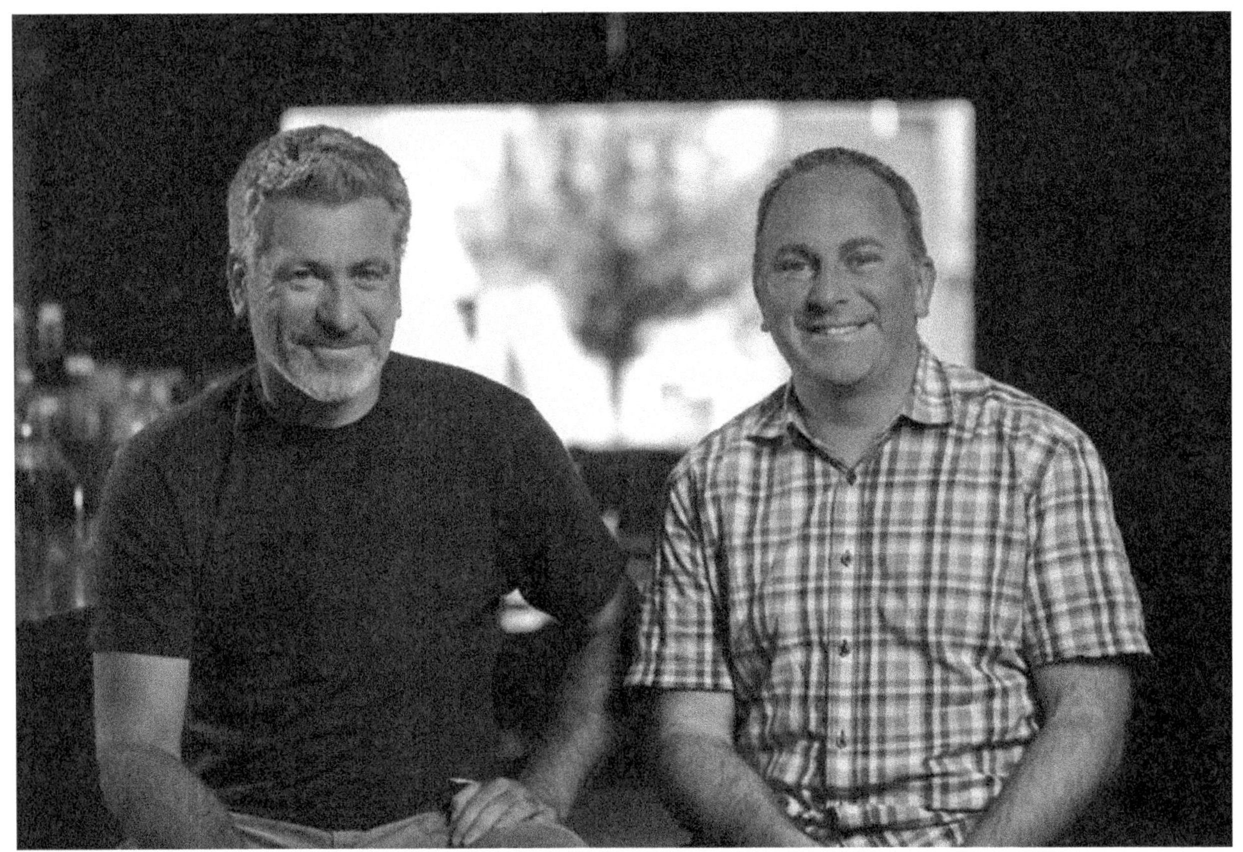

Photo Credit: © Reproduced with permission of Yaymaker

Paint Nite founders Daniel Hermann and Sean McGrail

This chapter was written by Andrew Zacharakis.

Entrepreneurship is all about opportunity. Would-be entrepreneurs often have one of two things on their minds: "How do I come up with a good business idea?" and "Is this idea big enough to make a successful business?" This chapter focuses on evaluating ideas and assessing whether they are indeed good opportunities. Although an idea is necessary to entrepreneurship, it is not sufficient. To have a successful entrepreneurial endeavor, your idea needs to be an opportunity.

Belief in your idea is a great thing; but first, step back and ask a more important question: "Is this idea an *attractive* opportunity?" Moving from an idea to a viable opportunity is an iterative process. Entrepreneurs need to conduct a series of tests—what we refer to as **market tests**—to identify interesting ideas and then see whether they are viable opportunities. Each test is an escalation of commitment, an important step to successfully launching the venture. So the process of recognizing, shaping, and reshaping an opportunity combines thought and action to take the idea from formulation to execution. Both are critical as you embark on your entrepreneurial adventure. In this chapter, we will lay out the process from the very beginning—the idea—and move through opportunity shaping and reshaping.

From Glimmer to Action: How Do I Come Up with a Good Idea?

We said in the preceding chapter that most successful ideas are driven by the entrepreneur's personal experience. Entrepreneurs gain exposure to their fields through their jobs and use this experience to identify possible opportunities for a new venture. Considering that many students have limited work experience, you may not have the knowledge base to generate a new idea. So how, then, does a student find a worthy idea?

Start by looking inside yourself and deciding what you really enjoy. What gives you energy? What can you be passionate about for the many years it will take to start and grow a successful company? For those who lack this professional experience or who find they haven't enjoyed their professional life to date, it takes effort to find the answers to these questions.

Finding Your Passion

Think long-term. What are your goals for your degree, and where would you like to be 5 and 10 years down the road? Most students have difficulty envisioning the future. They know they want an exciting job with lots of potential (and, of course, above-average pay), but they haven't really thought about their careers in detail. Students often have a general idea of which industries and types of jobs are interesting to them (say, "something in finance"), but they lack a clear sense of what type of company they want to work for after college (culture, customers, and so forth). After all, school is a time of self-discovery, and this self-discovery is critical for both undergraduates and MBAs. In fact, many people enroll in MBA programs with the express goal of switching careers or industries and use the graduate program as a stepping-stone toward a field they are more passionate about. It can thus pay dividends to spend time thinking beyond the next exam, semester, or year.

Launching an entrepreneurial venture takes a tremendous amount of time and energy, and you will have difficulty sustaining that level of energy if you aren't passionate about the business. How do you go about finding your passion? There are two primary ways. First, think deeply about all the things that give you joy. What do you do in your spare time? What are your hobbies? What types of articles or social media do you read? The reality of our capitalistic society is that all those things you enjoy likely have ancillary businesses around them. Some are obvious. Many students have a passion for investment finance. They have been tracking stocks for a number of years and trade them for their personal portfolio. There are many viable businesses associated with personal finance, ranging from directly trading stocks to providing an analysis of the industry through a blog, for instance.

Other passions may not have as many clear-cut examples of ancillary businesses. You may have a passion for the outdoors and enjoy hiking on the weekends. On the surface, hiking seems like a free endeavor, yet there are numerous ancillary businesses that support this activity. Take AllTrails, for example. Russell Cook started the online platform sometimes described as "Yelp for the Outdoors" to solve a problem he experienced personally: as an amateur hiker, it was difficult to find weekend hiking spots within his experience level.[1] In Fall 2011, Cook raised a $400,000 seed round from investors such as 500 Startups. However, AllTrails soon hit a snag when Google Maps, the provider it had been using for mapping data, announced a new payment monetization strategy outside of AllTrails' price range.[2] What seemed like an insurmountable barrier turned into a great opportunity as AllTrails entered into a strategic partnership with TOPO!, National Geographic's topographic map tool, and began providing detailed trail maps.

Co-branding with National Geographic enabled AllTrails to partner with retail outlets for sporting goods like REI and Sport Chalet, catapulting its install base from 200,000 to 1,000,000 within six months. By 2018, AllTrails boasted 9 million active users across 100 countries for a range of outdoor activities from hiking to mountain biking to trail running. In October 2018, a private equity firm called Spectrum Equity invested $75 million in AllTrails to take the company to even greater heights.[3]

The world is full of examples of enterprising individuals who turned their passions into a lifetime of fulfilling work. After your initial search of "self," you may still have a fuzzy sense of what you're passionate about. To help refine your self-analysis, talk to people in your sphere of influence.

Although it is often difficult for people to be introspective about what they love, your strengths may be clearer to those who know you well. The first place to start is your family. They have watched you grow and have seen what you excel at and enjoy. Ask your parents what they see as your greatest strengths. What weaknesses do they think you are blind to? What activities over the years have given you the greatest joy? Just keep in mind that although your parents and other family members clearly know you best, their perspective may be somewhat biased. Michael Dell of Dell Computers originally enrolled in premed courses while in college to please his father, who was an orthodontist.[4] He would hide his computers in his roommate's bathtub when his parents came to visit.[5] In your search, also go outside your family and ask your friends, teachers, and former work associates (even if the latter group is limited to your old manager at McDonald's). How do they perceive you? The insight others provide is usually surprising. We all have blind spots that prevent us from seeing ourselves in a clear light. Seeking the opinions of others can help us overcome those blind spots and better understand our true passions.

During your search of "self," you may realize that you are passionate about something but haven't yet developed the skill set to successfully translate that passion into a viable business. For example, you may fall in love with a new restaurant idea—say, fast-casual Thai—but never have worked in a restaurant. Opening a restaurant is a worthy goal, but many students don't want to put in the effort to learn about the business. Instead of going to work as a waiter in a restaurant on graduation, they will take a corporate job with a life insurance company. They rationalize that the pay is better and this will give them the nest egg needed to launch their restaurant. Although we don't want to downplay the importance of cash flow, if you or others on your team haven't earned some deep experience in the operations of a restaurant, you will burn through your nest egg quickly and likely fail. Instead of taking the bigger paycheck, go work at a restaurant. You'll learn what customers like and how to deliver it cost effectively, while also earning a bit of money. More important, you will have an "apprenticeship" at a successfully run restaurant and will learn many of the major areas that you need to watch out for when the time comes to launch your own restaurant. This apprenticeship won't make you rich in the short term, but it will provide a platform for greater personal wealth and fulfillment in the long run. If you truly want to be an entrepreneur, you will need to make countless sacrifices. One of the first may be bypassing a higher-paying job for the opportunity to roll up your sleeves and gain hands-on experience in your field of choice. Just remember that the knowledge you gain will be far more valuable than the salary you give up.

Paint Nite Startup Story

After going out to a casual painting and wine night with a group of friends in 2011, Daniel Hermann and his friend Sean McGrail were inspired. "We both fell in love with it—and realized that there were some hidden gems in it—where people were actually doing something instead of just sitting there," said Hermann, Paint Nite's CEO.[6]

The two hosted the first "Paint Nite" in March 2012 in Boston's Back Bay, and the idea immediately took off. Within the first month, they had hosted 20 Paint Nites, bringing together groups of friends in local bars on "off-nights" when the bars might not otherwise be full. Hermann and McGrail decided to license the event, providing the online ticketing platform, painting supplies, and brand marketing to their partners, "creative entrepreneurs" who work with networks of local artists to host Paint Nites across the country. Each event ranges from $45 to $65, and Paint Nite splits ticket revenue 30/70 with its partners.

Social painting took off in part due to the viral nature of social media: customers loved to share pictures of their art and wine-filled camaraderie that brought them together. Social media was the perfect vehicle to reach their target audience of 20–30-something women in need of a girls' night out. Within the first 18 months, Paint Nite had expanded to 20 cities across the United States and Canada, with 50 artists hosting 250 events per week.

By 2014, Paint Nite was approaching $25 million in annual revenue and Hermann sought an investment to scale their national licensing model. Paint Nite raised $13 million in a round led by Highland Consumer Fund in 2015 to expand their operations. As of 2016, the company's revenue had grown to $55 million, 36,555% increase from 2012. Paint Nite counts 110 employees at its Somerville, Massachusetts headquarters, who work with 250 creative entrepreneurs to manage a network of over 1,000 artists hosting Paint Nites in 1,600 cities across the world.[7]

Once you identify your passions, you have a strong base to start to identify ideas for business opportunities. Today's business environment is intensely competitive, and simple replication (another app company) is often a recipe for failure. You will need to work on developing ideas that are unique and have something in them that can be a source of sustainable competitive advantage. This process is the focus of the next section, and it will help you understand how to take a basic idea and turn it into a great opportunity.

Idea Multiplication

All great ideas start with a seed of an idea. The trick is moving from that seed to something that is robust, exciting, and powerful. Doing so requires input from others, such as your fellow cofounders, trusted mentors, friends, and family. Spend as much time as possible brainstorming your idea with this group. These informal conversations help you think through the idea and flesh it out. You will learn more about some of the shortcomings or challenges of the business idea, and you will also gain new insights on how it might grow beyond that first product or service.

We offer one caution, however: Avoid becoming a "cocktail-party entrepreneur." This is the individual who always talks of becoming an entrepreneur or brags of the ideas he or she thought of that others turned into exciting, profitable ventures. In other words, a cocktail-party entrepreneur is all talk and no action. Anybody can be a cocktail-party entrepreneur because it doesn't require any effort or commitment, just a few people who are willing to listen. To become a true entrepreneur requires effort beyond that first conversation. It requires continual escalation of commitment.

We have found a few useful processes that help move you beyond the simple initial idea. The first is called **idea multiplication** and is best exemplified by IDEO, the idea think tank responsible for many of the product innovations we take for granted. For instance, that thick, grippable toothbrush you use every morning was developed by IDEO, as was the design of your computer monitor and any number of other products you use every day. Figure 3.1 highlights the top IDEO

Product	Year	Description
Computer mouse	1981	A computer mouse for navigating a computer desktop.
Compass	1982	The precursor to the modern-day laptop.
Aerobie football	1992	Foam football with fins to stabilize the ball in air.
Yeoman XP-1	1997	GPS system for map plotting.
Leap	2000	Scientifically designed desk chair for enhanced comfort and back support.
Apollo booster	2001	Redesign of children's car seats for Evenflo.
MoneyMaker Deep Lift Pump	2003	Human-powered irrigation pump for use in impoverished regions.
Windows home computing concept	2005	Computer interface linking personal entertainment and home computing units.
Shimano coasting bicycle	2006	Comfortable and low-maintenance bicycle to attract casual cyclists.
"Keep the Change" Service for Bank of America	2006	The service rounds up purchases made with a Bank of America debit card to the nearest dollar and transfers the difference from individuals' checking accounts into their savings accounts.
Eli Lilly KwikpenTM	2007	Discreet, prefilled insulin device to help patients deliver their insulin.
Healthy Choice Fresh Mixers for Conagra	2008	Innovative packaging configuration is comprised of a strainer, bowl, and sauce container. The unique design delivers a fresher, more flavorful product.
Tendril Vision Home Energy-Management Solution	2009	A revolutionary digital display that promotes household energy savings.
Node Chair for Steel Case	2010	A reconfigurable seat/desk combo that complements the way students learn—and the tools they use.
Designing the Ideal Home for "Wounded Warriors" for Clark Reality Capital	2011	Making housing truly accessible for disabled U.S. military veterans and their families.
In-Home Sanitation Solutions for WSUP and Unilever	2011	A collaborative R&D effort for a portable toilet and collection service for low-income families in Kumasi, Ghana.
Smartphone-Charging Handbag Design for Vodafone and Richard Nicoll	2012	A purse that fuses technology with high-end fashion for London Fashion Week.
Smarter Hand Washing for Hospitals	2013	Refined SwipeSense digital hand-sanitizing system.
The Infinite Museum	2014	Throwing open the Royal Academy's doors and letting the world flow in.
A Powerful New Use for Nuclear Waste	2015	Helping Transatomic Reset the Course for Smart Communications.
Bill and Melinda Gates Foundation	2015	Helping entrepreneurs design tools that students like and teachers need.
Designing for Smarter Mobility for Ford Motor Company	2016	Pay-as-you-go insurance offer and a digital tracker that captures how bikes, cars, and public transport interact.
Video Games that Build Kids' Emotional Strength	2017	Harnessing the knowledge of psychologists, game designers, and engineers to gamify emotional development.
Genomic insights based on a person's unique DNA sequence	2017	Identified what users need most from personalized DNA testing.

FIGURE 3.1 **IDEO Innovations over the Years.**[8]

innovations over the years. IDEO, founded by Stanford engineering professor David Kelley, is hired by leading corporations worldwide to develop and design new products. We can learn a lot by observing its process. There are four basic steps: (1) gather stimuli, (2) multiply stimuli, (3) create customer concepts, and (4) optimize practicality. Let's talk about each.

Gather Stimuli. All good ideas start with the customer. Most often, entrepreneurs come across ideas by noting that there is some product or service they would like but can't find. This is your first interaction with a customer—yourself. To validate this idea, you need to go further by gathering stimuli.[9] IDEO does this through a process called *customer anthropology*, in which the IDEO team goes out and observes customers in action in their natural environment and identifies their pain points.[10] For example, in an ABC *Nightline* segment about IDEO, the team went to a grocery store to better understand how customers shop and, more specifically, how they use a shopping basket. The team's mission was to observe, ask questions, and record information. They did not ask leading questions in hopes that the customer would validate a preconceived notion of what that shopping cart should be. Instead, the questions were open ended.

Beware the leading question. As an entrepreneur who is excited about your concept, you may find it all too easy to ask, "Wouldn't your life be better if you had concept X?" or "Don't you think my product/service idea is better than what exists?" Although this might be a direct way to validate your idea, it requires that people answer honestly and understand exactly what they need. Most people like to be nice, and they want to be supportive of new ideas—until they actually have to pay money for them. Also, many times people can't envision your product/service until it actually exists, so their feedback may be biased.

During the "gathering stimuli" phase, act as if you were Charles Darwin observing finches on the Galapagos Islands—just *observe*. Ideally, you'll gather stimuli as a team so that you have multiple interpretations of what you have learned.

Multiply Stimuli. The next phase in the IDEO process is to multiply stimuli. Here, the team members report back on their findings and then start brainstorming on the concept and how to improve on the solution. One of our colleagues shared with us the trick of comedy improv for facilitating this process. A group of actors (usually three to four) poses a situation to the audience and then lets the audience shout out the next situation or reply that one actor is to give to another. From these audience suggestions, the actors build a hilarious skit. The key to success is to always say, "Yes, and…." Doing so allows the skit to build on itself and create a seamless and comical whole. Likewise, multiplying stimuli requires the team to take the input of others and build on it. Be a bit wild-eyed in this process. Let all ideas, no matter how far-fetched, be heard and built on because even if you don't incorporate them into the final concept, they might lead to new insights that are ultimately important to the product's competitive advantage.

Remember that "Yes, and…." means that you build on the input of your colleagues. All too often in a group setting it is easy to say, "That won't work because…." These kinds of devil's advocate debates, although important in the later phases of business development, can prematurely kill off creative extensions in this early phase. Also beware of "Yes, but…." statements, which are really just another way of saying, "Your idea won't work and here's why…." The key to this phase of development is to generate as many diverse ideas as possible.

As you go through this multiplication stage, *brain-writing* is a useful technique to avoid prematurely squashing interesting extensions. The process is like brainstorming, but the focus is on written rather than verbal communication. The biggest shortcoming of brainstorming is that it opens up the opportunity for the most vocal or opinionated members of the group to dominate the conversation and idea-generation process. In contrast, brain-writing ensures that everyone has a chance to contribute ideas. To start, the team identifies a number of core alternative variations to the central idea (if you have a disparate team, as you might for an entrepreneurship class, use each member's favored idea). Put the core ideas onto separate flip-chart sheets and attach them to the wall. Then the team and trusted friends, or classmates, go around and add "Yes, and…." enhancements to each idea. Keep circulating among the flip-chart sheets until everyone has had an opportunity to think about and add to each idea. At the end of that cycle, you'll have several interesting enhancements to consider. Instead of publicly discussing the ideas, have everybody vote on the three to five they like best by placing different-colored sticky notes on the sheets. In essence, this is another "market test" in which your team and other interested parties are gauging the viability of the idea.[11]

Create Customer Concepts. Once you've narrowed the field to the idea and features you think have the most potential, the next step is to create customer concepts. In other words, build a simple mock-up of what the product will look like. This helps the team visualize the final product and see which features/attributes are appealing, which are detrimental, and which are nice to have but not necessary. Keep in mind that this mock-up doesn't need to be functional; it is just a tool to solidify what everybody is visualizing and to help the team think through how the product should be modified.

When your team is developing a service, your mock-up won't necessarily be a physical representation but rather some kind of abstract modeling of what you hope to achieve. For example, the initial mock-up for a restaurant is often just a menu. Entrepreneurs who want to take the research process even further will often test the product or service in a low-cost way. This process allows for rapid-fire prototyping of ideas, and it also provides the luxury of failing early and often before making substantial investments in a bricks-and-mortar establishment. We discuss prototyping in more detail in Chapter 4.

Optimize Practicality. Quite often at this stage people "overdevelop" the product and incorporate every bell and whistle that the team has come up with during the brainstorming process. This is fine—the next and last step is to optimize practicality, when the team will identify those features that are unnecessary, impractical, or simply too expensive.

This is the phase in which it is important to play devil's advocate. As the IDEO developers state, it is a time for the "grown-ups" to decide which features are the most important to optimize. If the previous steps have gone well, the team has learned a tremendous amount about what the customer may want, and that means they have a deeper understanding of the features/attributes that create the greatest value for the customer.

The entire idea-generation process is iterative. At each of the four steps we've presented, you learn, adjust, and refine. You start to understand the critical criteria that customers use in their purchasing decision and the pain points in building your product or delivering your service. This process allows you to identify and refine your idea with relatively little cost, compared to the costs you'd incur if you immediately opened your doors for business with what you believed to be the most important attributes. Nonetheless, up to this point you still don't know whether your idea, which is now very robust and well thought out, is a viable opportunity.

Is Your Idea an Opportunity?

Whereas the idea-generation process helps you shape your idea so that it is clearer and more robust, it is only part of the process. The difference between venture success and failure is a function of whether your idea is truly an opportunity. Before quitting your job and investing your own resources (as well as those of your family and friends), spend some time studying the viability of your idea. There are five major areas you need to fully understand prior to your launch: (1) customers, (2) competitors, (3) suppliers and vendors, (4) the government, and (5) the broader global environment (see Figure 3.2). We'll discuss each of these areas in turn.

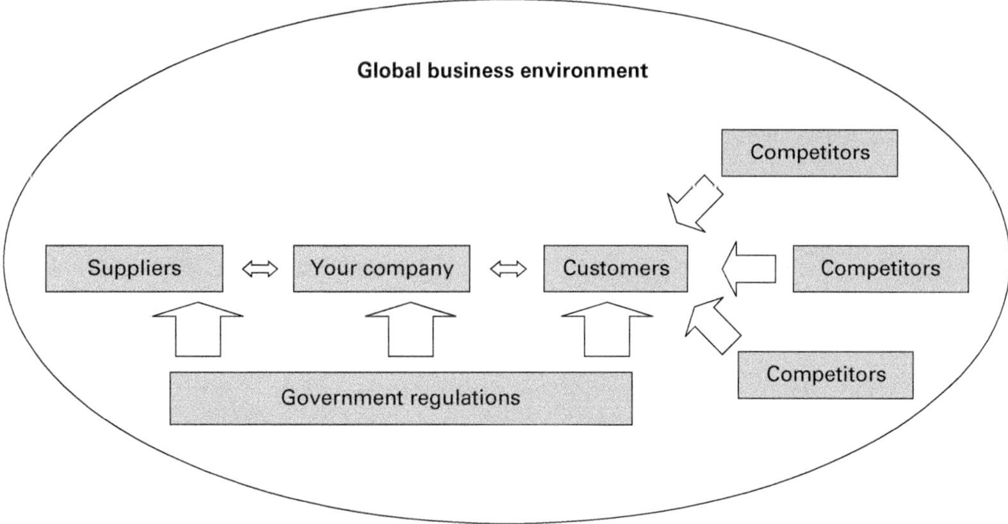

FIGURE 3.2 The Opportunity Space.

The Customer

Who is your customer? This broad question, the first you must answer, can be problematic. For instance, you might be tempted to think, if you're hoping to open a restaurant, that anyone who would want to eat in a restaurant is your customer: in other words, just about everyone in the world except for the few hundred hermits spread out across the country. But you need to narrow down your customer base so that you can optimize the features most important to your customer. So a better question is, "Who is your *core* customer?" Understanding who your primary customer is lets you better direct your efforts and resources to reach that customer. You can further refine your definition.

Starting with your initial definition, break your customers down into three categories: (1) core customer group or primary target audience (PTA), (2) secondary target audience (STA), and (3) tertiary target audience (TTA). Most of your attention should focus on the PTA. These are the customers you believe are most likely to buy at a price that preserves your margins and with a frequency that reaches your target revenues. Let's consider our fast-casual Thai restaurant example. The sector is growing as consumers seek less-expensive food that does not sacrifice quality. Fast-casual restaurants usually have larger footprints (more square feet) than fast-food restaurants and food-court outlets. Thus, you want a customer willing to pay a bit more than a fast-food customer for perceived higher quality. A wise location might be a destination mall with tenants like Trader Joe's, Pottery Barn, and other stores that attract middle-income and higher-income shoppers. Your core customer, in this situation, might be soccer moms (30–45 years old, with household incomes ranging from $50,000 to $150,000). These women tend to shop, watch what they eat, and enjoy ethnic food.

During the investigation stage, you would focus your attention on better understanding your core customer. How often do they shop? How often do they eat out? What meals are they more likely to eat outside the home? What other activities do they participate in besides shopping and dining out? What you are collecting is information about things like income and ethnicity (demographics), and about personality traits and values (psychographics).[12] Both categories help you design and market your product or service. During the launch phase, you would design the decor in a manner that most appeals to your core customer. You would create a menu that addresses their dietary concerns and appeals to their palette. During operations, you would market toward your core customer and train your employees to interact with them in an appropriate and effective manner. Note that the efforts across the three stages of your venture (investigation, launch, and operations) are different than they would be if you were launching a fast-food restaurant or a fancy sit-down French restaurant because your target audience is different.

Although you should focus most of your attention on your PTA, the STA group also deserves attention. The PTA may be your most frequent, loyal customers, but to increase your revenues, you'll want to bring in some of your STA as well. In the restaurant example, your STA may be men with similar demographics as your PTA, older couples who are active and near retirement age, and younger yuppie post-college working professionals (see the box entitled "Fast-Casual Demographics"). These groups are likely to find your restaurant appealing but may not attend with the same frequency (possibly more on weekends or during the dinner hour versus lunch). Your STA may also be part of your growth strategy. For instance, after you get past your first two to three restaurants, you may choose to expand your menu or your location profile (urban centers, for instance). Understanding which STA is the most lucrative helps you make better growth decisions.

Fast-Casual Demographics

The most-often-cited reason for the growth in the fast-casual segment is the generation of consumers who grew up on fast food and won't eat it anymore. Add the aging baby boomers who are looking for healthier alternatives and who can afford to pay a little more for better quality. The price of a meal in a moderately priced restaurant has dropped; it's now only 25% more than the price of a meal purchased in a grocery store and prepared at home... making dining out an economically viable alternative. Other fast-casual demos:

- Fast-casual price points are $9 –14 vs. $3 –9 for fast food.
- Millennials (18–35) are most likely to opt for fast casual and make up 42% of the traffic at such outlets compared to Baby Boomers at 26%.
- Fast-casual customers have more discretionary income to treat themselves to a meal: 44% of fast-casual customers report making $75,000 a year or more—compare that to 33% of all restaurant-goers.
- Fast casual offers digital convenience: 75% of fast-casual customers check the menu on their phone before visiting a new location and almost 40% say they will pay with their phone if they can.
- Casual dining is too slow for kids...parents don't want to eat fast food.
- Fast casual is diversifying customers' palates: 66% of customers reported frequently trying new ethnic cuisines.
- Casual dining companies are responding to the fast-casual trend by aggressively marketing takeout business.
- Casual dining has now become an event...not a spur-of-the-moment dining decision.
- Fast casual has grown 1243% since 1999 with 2016 sales of $47B, revenues more than doubled from 2014 to 2016.
- Fast casual is 18% of market in 2016, up from 4% in 2000.

Sources:
https://www.restaurantbusinessonline.com/consumer-trends/fast-casual-consumers-who-are-they.
https://www.restaurant.org/Downloads/PDFs/Events-Groups/17_SHOW_PPT_5-4-compressed.pdf.
https://www.franchisehelp.com/industry-reports/fast-casual-industry-analysis-2018-cost-trends/.

Finally, your TTA requires a little attention. During the investigation and launch stage, you shouldn't spend much time on the TTA. However, once you begin operating, a TTA may emerge that has more potential than you originally realized. Keeping your eyes and ears open during operations helps you adjust and refine your opportunity to better capture the most lucrative customers. In our Thai restaurant example, you might find that soccer moms aren't your PTA but that some unforeseen group emerges, such as university students. If you segment your customer groups throughout the three stages as we have outlined, you'll be better prepared to adapt your business model if some of your preconceptions turn out to be incorrect.

Demographics	Psychographics
Age	Social group (white collar, blue collar, etc.)
Gender	Lifestyle (mainstream, sexual orientation, materialistic, active, athletic, etc.)
Household income	Personality traits (worriers, Type As, shy, extroverted, etc.)
Family size/family life cycle	Values (liberal, conservative, open minded, traditional, etc.)
Occupation Education level Religion Ethnicity/heritage Nationality Social class Marital status	

FIGURE 3.3 Common Demographic/Psychographic Categories.

We've said that it's important to understand your audience's demographics and psychographics. Part of your investigation phase should include creating customer profiles. Figure 3.3 provides a sampling of the types of demographics and psychographics that might be used in describing your customer.

Trends. Customers aren't static groups that remain the same over time. They evolve; they change; they move from one profile to another. To best capture customers, you need to spot trends that are currently influencing their buying behavior and that might influence it in the future. When considering trends, look at broader macrotrends and then funnel down to a narrower focus on how those trends affect your customer groups. Trends might also occur within customer groups that don't affect the broader population.

One of the most influential trends in the macro environment within the United States over the last 70 years has been the life cycle of the baby boom generation. Born between 1946 and 1964, the country's 77.6 million baby boomers are usually married (69.4%), well educated (college graduation rates hit 19.1% at the end of the boomer generation, compared to just 6% for prior generations), and active (46% of boomers exercise regularly).[13] What links them as a generation is the experience of growing up in post–World War II America, a time of tremendous growth and change in this nation's history. Because they represent such a large percentage of the U.S. population, it is no wonder that they have created numerous new categories of products and services. For example, in the 1950s, the disposable diaper industry emerged and then exploded to the point where it is projected to globally reach $64 billion in sales by 2022.[14] In the late 1950s and through the 1960s, the rapidly growing population created a need for large numbers of new schools, which in turn led to a building frenzy (Now you know why so many schools were named after former President John F. Kennedy). In the late 1960s and the 1970s, the rock-and-roll industry exploded. Then in the 1980s, as these baby boomers became parents, a new car category was created (the minivan), which saved Chrysler from bankruptcy. In the 1990s, the boomers were in their prime working years, and new investment categories emerged to help them plan for their retirement and their children's college educations. Today, as the boomers age, we see growth in pharmaceuticals and other industries related to the more mature segment. According to one market research firm, "Boomers are expected to change America's concepts of aging, just as they have about every previous life stage they have passed through."[15] How does this macro trend influence your idea?

Numerous macro trends affect the potential demand for your product or service. Trends create new product/service categories, or emerging markets, that can be especially fruitful places to find strong entrepreneurial opportunities. The convergence of multiple trends enhances the power of an opportunity like the Internet boom. First, the personal computer (PC) was common in the workplace, and as a result, many Americans grew comfortable using it. That led to a proliferation of PCs in the home, especially for children and teenagers, who used it for school, work, and video games. Although the Internet had been available for decades, the development by Tim Berners-Lee of the World Wide Web (WWW or Web) system of hyperlinks connecting remote computers, followed by the development of the Mosaic Web browser (the precursor to Netscape and Explorer) and the proliferation of Internet service providers like Prodigy and AOL created huge opportunities for commerce online. Social media exploded in the early 2000s with the advent of Facebook, Instagram, and a proliferation of others. Now, with smartphones, people are on the Web nonstop. From the very first domain name—symbolics.com—assigned in 1985, the Web has evolved into an integral component of the modern economy. Even though many dot-coms failed, others, like eBay and Amazon, have established themselves as profitable household names. That many of these successful businesses have become multi-*billion*-dollar companies in less than a decade speaks to the incredible power of convergent trends.

The launch of smartphones has also created new business opportunities for entrepreneurs. When Apple launched the iPhone in 2007, there were only 800 apps available. Today, there are more than 2 million apps published in the Apple App Store and more than 2.1 million apps in Google Play. Although the Apple App Store lags behind Google Play in number of apps, the revenue generated by consumer spending in Apple App Store reached $38.5 billion in 2017, nearly double Google Play's $20.1 billion.[16]

Trends also occur in smaller market segments and may be just as powerful as macro trends; in fact, they may be precursors to larger macro trends. For example, there is a trend of U.S. Hispanic consumers to be early adopters of new technologies. Hispanics are 70% more likely to visit technology-related websites than the average online adult. Therefore, companies like Google, Apple, and Virgin Mobile offer online visitors the option to translate their websites to Spanish because these consumers prefer to search and read in their native language.[17] As the U.S. immigrant population continues to add new ethnicities with differing mother tongues there are going to be more and more opportunities to reach these customers in their native language.

Another important trend is the changing demographics of the U.S. population. According to the U.S. Census Bureau, the projected Hispanic population of the United States will reach 133 million by 2050. According to this projection, Hispanics will constitute 30% of the nation's population.

With the incredible growth in both size and purchasing power of this untapped market, it's no wonder that companies are scrambling to serve emerging opportunities. The past decade has seen a proliferation of media outlets targeting the Spanish-speaking U.S. population, and because some pundits believe the Hispanic population could emerge as the next middle class, it's likely more and more companies will find ways to capture this enormous demographic.

Trends often foretell emerging markets and suggest when the window of opportunity for an industry is about to open. Figure 3.4 lists some influential trends over the last 50 years. However, it is the underlying convergence of trends that helps us measure the power of our ideas and whether they are truly opportunities.

How Big Is the Market? Trends suggest increasing market demand. Thus, one of the questions that distinguishes ideas from opportunities asks whether there is sufficient market demand to generate the level of revenues necessary to make this an exciting career option. As we pointed out in Chapter 2, an entrepreneur typically needs the new venture to generate a minimum of $750,000 per year in revenue to meet market rates on his or her forgone salary of $70,000 plus benefits. Although this level might make a nice "mom-and-pop" store, many students are interested in creating something bigger. The larger your goals, the more important your market-demand forecasts. To accurately gauge your demand, start at the larger macro market and funnel demand down to your segment and your geographic location. Granted, as you expand, you'll likely move beyond your segment and your geographic origins, but the most critical years for any venture are its first two. You need to be certain that you can survive the startup, and that means you need to be confident of your base demand.

Trend	Impact
Baby boom generation	Pampers, rock 'n' roll, television, minivans, real estate, McMansions
Personal computing	Internet, electronic publishing, spreadsheets, electronic communication
Obesity	Drain on healthcare system, growth of diet industry, changes in food industry, health clubs, home gyms
Dual-income households	Child care, home services—landscaping, housecleaning, prepared foods
Smart phones	Apps, location-based couponing, NFC (near field communication) and mobile payments, E-commerce retailers moving to mobile, voice-activated commands
High-speed Internet	Cloud computing, streaming media, free online education—Khan Academy, edX.org (free online courses from Harvard, MIT, Cal Berkeley, and University of Texas)
Touch computing	Tablet computers and eReaders—iPad, Blackberry Playbook, Windows Surface, Amazon Kindle Fire, Samsung Galaxy, Motorola Xoom. Touch-based operating systems—Windows 8 and Mac OS X Lion
Social media	Widespread popularity of Facebook, Twitter, LinkedIn, Pinterest, Google+. "Frictionless sharing" through social media apps like Spotify, Social Reader, and Gilt
Sharing economy	Connecting people to excess capacity, like Uber, Lyft, Airbnb
Big Data	Predictive analytics, artificial intelligence, and machine learning from analyzing big data, changing social mores surrounding data privacy, and an increased awareness of cybersecurity risks for both companies and individuals
Internet of Things	"Smart" objects from personal assistants such as Amazon's Alexa and Google Home, to Internet-connected washing machines inside our homes
Blockchain	Cryptocurrency, decentralization of information, supply chain innovations

FIGURE 3.4 Important Trends Over the Last 50 Years.

Let's go back to our Thai fast-casual restaurant example to begin to understand how large our market demand might be. Figure 3.5 steps through the demand forecast. It is best to start with the overall market size—in this case, the size of the entire restaurant industry in the United States. Next, segment the industry into relevant categories. We are interested in both the relative size of the fast-casual segment and the size of the ethnic segment. It would be ideal to find the size of the fast-casual-ethnic (or better yet, Thai) segment, but as you narrow down to your opportunity, there is likely to be less information because you may be riding new trends that suggest future demand that has yet to materialize. Finally, during your initial launch, you'll likely have some geographic focus. Extrapolate your overall market data to capture your geographic market. In this case, we took the population of the towns within a five-mile drive along the major thoroughfare on which our restaurant would be located and multiplied that percentage of the state population by the total spent in the state (Massachusetts). Basically, for this last step, you should try to assess the number of soccer moms in your geographic reach. The U.S. Census makes this very easy, as it breaks out demographics by town. Thus, it appears that there are roughly 14,000 soccer moms in this target market.

Market Size Today and into the Future. Although it is important to size your market today, you'll also need to know how big it will be in the future. If you are taking advantage of trends, your market is likely growing. Attractive opportunities open up in growing markets because there is more demand than supply, and a new firm doesn't need to compete on price. In the early years, when the firm is going through a rapid learning curve, operational expenses will be proportionately higher than in later years, when the firm has established efficient procedures and systems. Furthermore, market growth means that your competitors are seeking all the new customers entering the market rather than trying to steal customers away from you.

Projecting growth is notoriously difficult, but you can make some educated guesses by looking at trends and determining overall market size as described earlier. Then make some estimates of

Restaurant industry sales projections in 2017	$799 Billion[18]
Size of market segments	
Eating places	$551.7 Billion
Table service restaurants	$263 Billion
Quick service restaurants including fast-casual	$233.7 Billion
Retail, vending, recreation, mobile	$70.2 Billion
Managed services	$53.6 Billion
Lodging place restaurants	$36.1 Billion
Bars and taverns	$19.8 Billion
Other	$62.4 Billion
Market share for ethnic restaurants	$249.41 Billion[19]
Market share by state Massachusetts	
Overall restaurant sales	$17 Billion[20]
Ethnic	$7.68 Billion
Natick (we are opening in Natick shopping district) Massachusetts population................. 6.86 M	
Natick population.......................... 33 K	
Framingham population.................. 68 K	
Wellesley population...................... 28 K	
Natick, Framingham, Wellesley population is 2% of total Massachusetts population	
Natick, Framingham, Wellesley ethnic restaurant sales	$153 Million
Soccer moms (women between 30 and 45)....... 14 K or	$16.83 Million
11% of Natick, Framingham, and Wellesley population	

FIGURE 3.5 Market Size for Thai Fast-Casual Restaurant.

what type of market penetration you might be able to achieve and how long it will take you to get there. If all else fails, the easiest thing to do is to verify past growth. As trend analysis tells us, past growth is usually correlated with future growth, which means you can make reasonable estimates based on historical numbers. The **S-curve** is a powerful concept that highlights the diffusion of product acceptance over time.[21] When a product or innovation is first introduced, few people are aware of it. Typically, the firm has to educate consumers about why they need this product and the value it offers. Hence, the firm concentrates its effort on early adopters. It is expensive to develop the right concept and educate the consumer, but the firm can offset this cost somewhat by charging a high price.

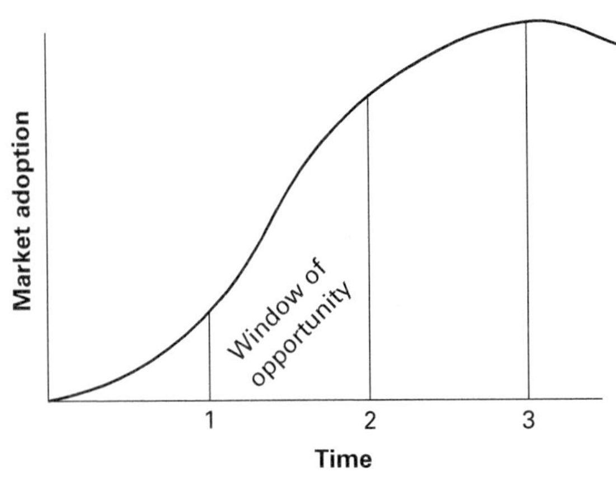

FIGURE 3.6 S-curve.

As customers react to the concept, the company and other new entrants learn and modify the original product to better meet customer needs. At a certain point (designated as point 1 in Figure 3.6), customer awareness and demand exceed supply, and the market enters a fast-growth phase. During this time (the time between points 2 and 3 in Figure 3.6), a dominant design emerges, and new competitors enter to capture the "emerging market." Typically, demand exceeds supply during this phase, meaning that competitors are primarily concerned with capturing new customers entering the market. After point 3, market demand and supply equalize, putting price pressure on the companies as they fight to capture market share from each other. Finally, innovations push the product toward obsolescence, and overall demand declines.

Frequency and Price. Market size and growth are important, but we also need to think about how often our average customer buys our product or service and how much he or she is willing to pay. Ideally, our product or service would have perfectly inelastic demand: The customer would pay any price to have it. For a product with elastic demand, the quantity demanded will go down if the price goes up, and vice versa. Inelasticity results in the opposite—whether prices increase or decrease, the demand for the product stays stable. Consider front row seats for your favorite baseball team or theater production. Nearly everyone would like to sit in the front row, but most of us can't or don't because the price is too high. However, if the price were lowered by a certain amount, we might be more than happy to buy the tickets. This is an example of elastic demand: As price decreases, demand for that product increases.

In contrast, consider gasoline. People who rely on a car to get to work have little choice but to pay the prices charged at the pump. If prices go down, they are unlikely to buy more gas, and if prices go up, they will still need to buy enough gas to get to work and run errands. Although not perfectly inelastic, the demand for gasoline is relatively inelastic. In reality, there will almost always be elasticity in customer demand, and our price will be a function of that elasticity. We need to determine the optimal price that encourages regular purchases, accounts for the value inherent in our product, and allows us to earn an attractive margin on the sale. These three variables are highly correlated, and an imbalance would hurt the profitability and even the viability of the firm.

In a classic mistake, some entrepreneurs use a penetration-pricing strategy. They reason that to pull customers from existing alternatives, the firm needs to price lower than the competition. Then, once the product is able to gain acceptance and market share, the company can raise prices to increase gross margins and better reflect underlying value. There are a number of flaws in this logic. First, as we've noted, attractive ventures are often launched in emerging markets where demand exceeds supply. This means that price is relatively inelastic. Consumers want the product and are willing to pay a premium for it. Second, many new products are designed to be better than existing alternatives. These products offer greater value than competitive products, and the price should reflect this greater value, especially because it usually costs more to add the features that led to it. Third, price sends a signal to the customer. If a product with greater value is priced lower than or the same as competing products, customers will interpret that signal to mean it isn't as good, despite claims that it has greater value.

Fourth, even if customers flock to the low-priced product, this rapid increase in demand can sometimes cause serious problems for a startup. Demand at that price may exceed your ability to supply, resulting in stock-outs. Consumers are notoriously fickle and are just as likely to go to a competitor as wait for your backlog to catch up.[22] Finally, these same customers may resist when you try to recapture value by raising prices in the future. They will have developed an internal sense of the value of your product, and they may take this opportunity to try other alternatives. The last thing you want is a business built around customers who are always searching for the lowest price. These will be the first people to leave you when a competitor finds a way to offer a lower price.

Many technology companies enter the market by adopting new business models. One of the most common is a freemium model. The idea is simple; give your base product away for free to attract new customers and then try to upsell them to premium services. Dropbox is a great example. Since its founding in 2007, Dropbox has attracted over 5.4 billion registered users worldwide and generated estimated revenues of $1.1 billion in 2017, or $2.2/year/user. It is estimated that only 2.2% of its users convert to paying for Dropbox. The market opportunity for cloud storage, collaborative applications, and content management is huge, expected to reach $50 billion by 2019. Dropbox's saving grace is its customer retention: Dropbox Business Teams represent approximately 100% in revenue retention, and other businesses boast revenue retention of

90%.[23] This "lock-in" effect is likely in part due to the switching costs of changing cloud storage, a huge advantage for Dropbox. Dropbox had raised $617M in equity capital and IPO'd at $21 per share in March of 2018.[24] While Dropbox has become cash flow positive in recent years by cutting capital expenditures and increasing revenue, it counts Microsoft, Apple, Amazon, and Alphabet (Google) among its top competitors for cloud storage and content collaboration. The success of the company will depend upon continuing growth of its paid user base and development of complementary content management tools that differentiate it from its competitors.

The argument many unsuccessful Internet entrepreneurs make is that the "number of eyeballs" using a service is more important than profitability, which firms figured will come later as they developed a critical mass of customers. These firms reason that they could charge lower prices (or free) to get people using the service and then convert them to paying customers. Although in theory this should work, it is often hard to get customers to pay for what was previously free. Moreover, the high user base attracts new competitors to the marketplace, further making it difficult to charge higher prices.

Finding the right price to charge is difficult. It requires understanding your cost structure. You cannot price under your cost of goods sold (COGS) for an extended period of time unless you have lots of financing (and are certain that access to financing will continue into the future). Thus, your minimum price should be above your COGS. Some firms look at their cost to produce a unit of the product and then add a set percentage on top of that cost to arrive at the price. This is called **cost-plus pricing**, and the problem is that it may set your price lower or higher than the underlying value of your product or service. For example, if you price at 40% above marginal cost, that may result in your product being a great value (software usually has gross margins of 70% or better) or drastically overpriced (groceries often have gross margins in the 20% range).

A better approach is to assess market prices for competing products. For instance, consider GMAT test-preparation courses that help students strengthen their business school applications. At the time of this writing, a quick scan of Kaplan and Princeton Review reveals that prices for their classroom GMAT programs range from $1,449 to $1,600. Given the similarities of the content, structure, and results of these programs, it is no surprise that their prices are comparable. Over the years, Kaplan and Princeton Review have gained deep insight into what parents will pay. For an entrepreneur entering this marketplace, Kaplan and Princeton Review provide a starting point in deciding what price can be charged. The entrepreneur would adjust his or her price based on the perceived difference in value of the offering.

Many entrepreneurs claim that they have no direct competition, so it is impossible to determine how much customers might pay. In such cases, which are very rare, it is essential to understand how customers are currently meeting the need that you propose to fill. Assess how much it costs them to fulfill this need and then determine a price that reflects the new process plus a premium for the added value your product delivers.

Margins. For new ventures, research suggests that gross margins of 40% are a good benchmark that distinguishes more-attractive from less-attractive opportunities. It is important to have higher gross margins early in the venture's life because operating costs during the early years are disproportionately high due to learning curve effects. For instance, no matter how experienced they are in the industry, your team will incur costs as you train yourselves and new hires. Over time, the team will become more efficient, and the associated costs of operations will reach a stability point. Another reason for keeping margins high is that the new venture will incur costs prior to generating sales associated with those costs. For instance, well before you are able to generate any leads or sales, you will need to hire salespeople and invest time and money training them. Even if you are a sole proprietorship, you will incur costs associated with selling your product or service before you receive any cash associated with the sale. For instance, you may have travel expenses like airline tickets or gasoline for your car and infrastructure expenses like a new computer and office furniture. This lag between spending and earning creates a strain on cash flows, whether you are a one-person shop or a growing enterprise, and if your margins are thin to begin with, it will be harder to attract the investment needed to launch.

It typically takes three to five years for a firm to reach stability and for operating costs to stabilize. At this point, strong firms hope to achieve net income as a percentage of sales of 10% or better. If the net income margin is lower, it will be hard to generate internal cash for growth or to attract outside investors, to say nothing about generating returns for the founding team. The exceptions to this rule are businesses that can generate high volumes. During the 1980s and 1990s, many new ventures sought to replicate the Walmart concept. Staples, Office Max, Home Depot, and Lowe's are good examples. Gross margins on these businesses range from 10% to 33% and net income margins from 1.8% to 6.5%. However, the stores do such enormous volumes that they are still able to generate huge profits. For example, in the 12-month period ending on January 31, 2018, Walmart projected operating income of $20.4 *billion*, which is more in profits than the vast majority of all U.S. companies had in sales, and it was able to do so because it generated $495.7 billion in sales during the same period. Walmart's gross profit margin of 24.68% is small by most measures, but its sales and profit numbers are clear indicators that its business strategy is working.

The performance of these big companies suggests another kind of industry structure that can be very attractive—fragmented industries. Prior to the launch of Home Depot, people filled their hardware needs through mom-and-pop companies. These small enterprises served small geographic regions and rarely expanded beyond them. The big-box stores entered these markets and offered similar goods at much lower prices against which mom-and-pop firms couldn't compete.

Although entering a fragmented industry and attempting to consolidate it, as big-box stores do, can create huge opportunities, the financial and time investments required are substantial. For instance, Arthur Blank and Bernard Marcus founded Home Depot in 1978 in the Atlanta area. Although its individual stores had enormous sales and profit potential, the company needed significant up-front capital for the initial building costs and inventory, and it raised venture capital, followed by $7.2 million from its 1981 public offering (which translates to $19.4 million in 2018 dollars). Almost 10 years later, Thomas Stemberg founded Staples and followed a nearly identical path in office supplies. Here, again, the startup costs were enormous, and the company relied heavily on its founders' experience in retailing. Staples raised $33.83 million in venture capital before it went public in April 1989, raising $51.3 million.[25] The bottom line is that such opportunities are rarer than in emerging markets, and they require a team with extensive industry experience and access to venture capital or other large institutional financing resources.

Reaching the Customer. Reaching the customer can be very difficult, even for the most experienced entrepreneur. Take the example of the founder of Gourmet Stew.[26] After completing her MBA, she spent many years with one of the top three food producers in the country, where she gained a deeper understanding about the industry. In the 1980s, she joined a small food startup company that developed a new drink concept that became widely successful and was ultimately acquired by Kraft Foods. Still a young woman, she cashed out and started her own venture, Gourmet Stew. Its first product was beef stew in a jar, like Ragú spaghetti sauce. The product tasted better than competitors like Hormel Stew (in a can). Despite her extensive entrepreneurial and industry experience and even though her product tasted better, the entrepreneur couldn't overcome one obstacle: how to reach the customer.

Stew in a jar is usually distributed in grocery stores, but this is a very difficult market to enter on a large scale. The industry is consolidated and mature, with only 19 chains throughout the entire country. Large product and food companies like Procter & Gamble and General Mills control much of the available shelf space, due to their power and ability to pay the required slotting fees.[27] Grocery stores also have an incentive to deal with fewer rather than more suppliers because it improves their internal efficiency.

Given that, companies that sell only a few products, such as Gourmet Stew, have a more difficult time accessing large chain stores. And even though smaller chains may find a unique product

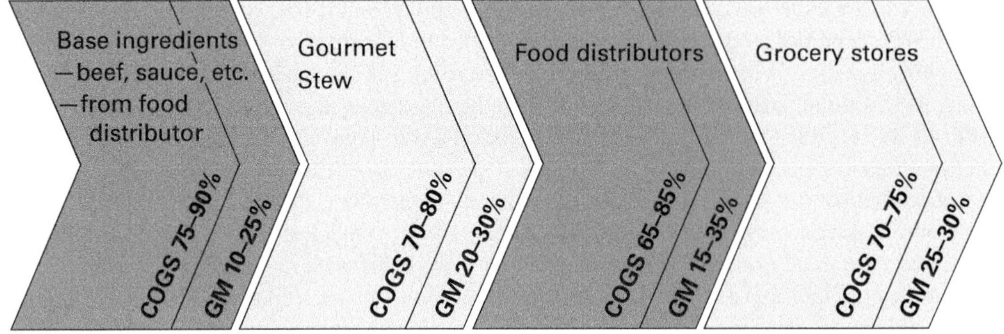

FIGURE 3.7 Value Chain of Gourmet Stew.

like Gourmet Stew appealing, it costs one-product companies more to distribute through these channels because they have to deal with multiple vendors instead of sealing a few large distribution agreements. Alternatively, Gourmet Stew could work with a large food brokerage company, but that would mean giving a portion of its margins to the brokerage. With all these options, the economics of distribution make it almost impossible to generate a decent margin on this type of company.

Stacy's Pita Chips Gaining Widespread Distribution

Stacy's Pita Chips didn't start out as a snack food maker. Instead, Stacy Madison, a social worker by training, and Mark Andrus, a psychologist, wanted to open a restaurant. Their first venture was a small food cart that sold pita bread wraps in downtown Boston. They were instantly successful and soon had long lines of hungry customers waiting for their freshly made wraps. Some of these potential customers tired of waiting in line and would give up before placing an order. To minimize the number of lost customers, Stacy and Mark started serving seasoned pita chips, baked from the bread they had left at the end of each day. The pita chips were a hit. In addition to great roll-up sandwiches, customers had a delicious incentive while they waited in line. Eventually, the couple was running two businesses and had to make a choice. They chose the pita chips, figuring they'd be able to gain national growth more rapidly. A new venture was born.

Even though Stacy and Mark had a great product, the question was, "How could they reach the end consumer en masse?" Most people buy chips in the grocery store, but getting space in the snack aisle is nearly impossible. Large distributors sell to grocery stores, and they are interested only in products that their buyers (the grocery stores) want. Recognizing this problem, Stacy decided that there was another way into this channel; Stacy's would place its chips in the natural food aisle and the in-store delis.

Stacy and Mark attended trade shows and made direct contact with grocery stores, sold them on their product, and secured trial placements in the stores. Stacy supplied display racks for her chips to each store and worked hard to increase consumer awareness by giving sample chips to shoppers. Without a distributor, Stacy's Pita Chips often shipped their product via UPS, but once they secured 10 or more stores in a particular geographic region, they went to the stores and asked who distributed snacks to them. The stores often contacted the distributors on Stacy's behalf, asking them to handle the product for them. Stacy noted, "Having customers that the distributor sold to gave us leverage. They wanted to carry our products because we created customer demand for them." Once Stacy's had a few large distributors in line, the company gained momentum, and other stores and distributors wanted to carry the product. In 2005, Stacy's hit $60 million* in sales, and Frito-Lay, the largest snack food maker in the world, finalized the acquisition of the company in January 2006.

Compiled from a personal interview with Stacy Madison, March 22, 2006.

*Frito-Lay Is Extending Its Healthy Snack Offerings with the Acquisition of Stacy's Pita Chips, Randolph, Mass., for an Undisclosed Sum. *Brandweek* 46.43: 5(1). Nov. 28, 2005.

One of the most overlooked keys to entrepreneurial success is distribution. How *do* you reach the customer? Although Gourmet Stew might have been able to reach the customer through alternative distribution channels like the Internet, these are likely to generate lower sales volume and higher marketing expenses because you have to educate the customer not only about what your product is but also about where to find it.

It is important to understand the entire value chain for the industry you are competing in. You need to lay out the distribution of your product from raw materials all the way to the end consumer. Figure 3.7 captures the value chain for Gourmet Stew.[28] From the figure, you can see the respective gross margins of the players—note that their net income margins would be much lower if based on their operating costs. The higher gross margins of the grocery stores indicate their relative power. Consider whether there is a variation on your business idea that would allow you to enter the portion of the value chain where greater margins are available. In sum, you must understand the entire value chain to determine where opportunities to make a profit might exist.

Although Gourmet Stew wasn't successful at gaining distribution, the box featuring Stacy's Pita Chips shows how a small food company can slowly gain distribution and build momentum to the point where it achieves a successful harvest for the entrepreneurs.

The Competition

Would-be entrepreneurs often say, "I have a great idea, and the best part is there's NO COMPETITION." If that were true, then as long as you have a customer, you have a license to print money. However, most nascent entrepreneurs turn out to be defining their competition too narrowly. For example, an overly optimistic entrepreneur might suggest that Gourmet Stew has no competition because there are no other companies producing stew in a jar. That doesn't account for Hormel canned stew (direct competition). It doesn't account for the multitude of frozen pizzas and other prepared foods that customers can bring home from the grocery store (more direct competition). It ignores the customers' options of preparing their own secret recipe for stew (indirect competition) or going out to eat (substitute). In other words, Gourmet Stew's competition isn't just stew in a jar; it is all the other businesses competing for a share of the consumer's stomach. Entrepreneurs ignore these competitors and substitutes at their peril.

To fully identify the competition, start with the customer. How is the customer currently fulfilling the need or want you intend to fill? You must identify direct competitors, indirect competitors, and substitutes. The number and strength of your competitors mirror the market structure. In a mature market, the industry is likely consolidated, and the power of existing competitors is likely strong. From the Gourmet Stew example, the industry is highly consolidated. Two top soup makers, Campbell Soup and General Mills, control more than 43% of the market. Entering this market is difficult, as we saw earlier, because the major competitors control the primary channel of distribution.

Even if you successfully enter the market, the strength of your competitors enables them to retaliate. Competitors, because of their economies of scale and scope, can lower prices to a point that makes it difficult for new ventures to compete. They can spend more on their advertising campaign and other marketing expenditures and increase their visibility due to greater resource reserves or easier access to capital. The good news is that many times strong competitors won't bother with new startups because they're so small that they aren't noticeable or because they don't feel threatened in either the short or the medium term. However, entrepreneurs should plan for contingencies just in case the larger competitors retaliate earlier than expected.

When markets are emerging, like the smart home market sparked by Nest and Ring, fewer products compete for customers primarily because the demand exceeds the supply. The main struggle within these markets is trying to find and own the dominant design that will become

Year	Android (Google)	Blackberry (RIM)	iOS (Apple)	Symbian (Nokia)	Windows Mobile (Microsoft)
2007	0%	10%	3%	64%	12%
2009	4%	20%	15%	47%	9%
2011	46%	11%	19%	20%	2%
2013	80%	3%	13%	N/A	3%
2015	83%	0.30%	14%	N/A	2%
2017	85%	N/A	15%	N/A	N/A

FIGURE 3.8 Smartphone Operating Systems Move Toward a Dominant Design.[31]

the customer favorite. A recent example of convergence toward a dominant design is the smartphone industry. In the early years, there were a multitude of potential operating systems that used different network providers and different phone manufacturers. In 1993, IBM and Bell South partnered to create the world's first smartphone. Dubbed Simon, the smartphone featured a touchscreen, predictive text, and apps like maps, stock prices, and a camera that could be used by plugging software cards into the phone. From 1996 to 2000, Nokia and Ericsson entered the smartphone market with a number of unique phones running on the Symbian Operating System. From 2001 to 2003, Palm and Microsoft both introduced a line of phones running on their own operating systems, Palm OS and Microsoft Windows Mobile. From 2003 to 2006, Blackberry dominated the smartphone market with the introduction of the first smartphone optimized for wireless e-mail use. In 2007, Apple changed the smartphone game with its release of the first generation iPhone. In 2008, Taiwanese smartphone manufacturer HTC unveiled the first smartphone powered by Google's Android OS.[29]

According to the research firm IDC, Google's Android is the world's most popular smartphone OS. In 2018, Android accounted for over 1,240.6 million units shipped and 84.8% of the smartphone OS market share. Apple's iOS took 15.1% market share while Research in Motion, Linux and Microsoft accounted for a collective 0.1% market share.[30]

Figure 3.8 shows some of the competing mobile operating systems and their market shares for eight years. Note that in 2007 the Symbian OS controlled 64% of the marketplace, Windows Mobile had 12%, Blackberry 10%, and Linux 10%. Symbian became the dominant operating system primarily because it was included in the most popular smartphones at the time, the Nokia smartphones. With the instant popularity of the open source Android OS in 2008, smartphone manufacturers converged toward the Android OS, existing smartphone manufacturers and new manufacturers alike adopted the Android platform. This example highlights the evolution of most marketplaces. Once a dominant design is in place, the market moves rapidly to maturity.

Emerging markets are characterized by "stealth" competitors. Entrepreneurs often believe their idea is so unique that they will have a significant lead over would-be competitors. But just as your venture will operate "under the radar" as it designs its products, builds its infrastructure, and tests the product with a few early beta customers, so will a number of other new ventures likely be at similar stages of development. Although it is relatively easy to conduct due diligence on identifiable competition, it is extremely difficult to learn about competition that isn't yet in the marketplace. Thus, it is imperative for new ventures to scan the environment to identify and learn about stealth competition.

There are several sources of intelligence you can tap. It is probable that your competition is using inputs, and thus suppliers, similar to what you are. As you interview your potential suppliers, make sure to query them about similar companies with whom they are working. Although the suppliers may not divulge this information, more often than not they don't see it as a conflict of interest to do so. Outside professional equity capital can also help you determine competitors.

Angels and venture capitalists see many deals and have knowledge about how an industry is developing, even if they haven't funded one of your stealth competitors. Again, you can talk to professional investors about who they see as strong emerging competitors. Furthermore, a number of widely available databases track and identify companies that receive equity financing. PricewaterhouseCoopers publishes MoneyTree,[32] which allows you to screen new investments by industry, region, and venture capitalists making the investment. *Fortune* Term Sheet and PEHub are two daily e-mail newsletters that track current deals—and the best part is that they are free.[33] The smart entrepreneur will diligently monitor his or her industry and use these resources, as well as many others, to avoid being surprised by unforeseen competition. An excellent source of industry gossip is trade shows.

Although your direct competition is most relevant to your success, you also should spend some time understanding why your target customer is interested in your indirect competitors and substitutes. As you increase your knowledge of the total marketplace, you will start to understand the key success factors (KSFs) that distinguish those firms that win and those that lose. KSFs are the attributes that influence where the customer spends money. If we think once again about Gourmet Stew, customers base their food purchasing decisions on a number of factors, including taste, price, convenience (time to prepare and serve), availability (the distribution channel issue discussed earlier), and healthy attributes of the food, among other factors. As you gather data on these factors, constructing a competitive profile matrix to identify the relative strength of each will help you decide how to position your venture in the marketplace (see Figure 3.9). Gauge how well your competitors are doing by tracking their revenues, gross margins, net income margins, and net profits. Note that we don't yet know what the figures are for Gourmet Stew because it has yet to hit the marketplace. Likewise, "homemade stew" in the figure is the creation of the consumer, who buys all the ingredients separately at the grocery store.

As you examine the competitive profile matrix, you understand the competitors' strategy and which customers they are targeting. Hormel, for example, is targeting price-sensitive, convenience-minded consumers. Typical customers might include males living on their own, college students, or others who don't have the time or desire to cook but are living on a budget. Homemade stew, on the other hand, falls in the domain of persons who enjoy cooking and have more time. Stay-at-home parents may have the time to shop for all the ingredients and to cook the stew from scratch, or weekend gourmets might like to have something special for guests or family. Gourmet Stew might appeal to families where both parents work outside the home. They want quality food but don't have the time to cook it from scratch and are not as sensitive to prices. Last, DiGiorno pizza (a higher-quality pizza) is targeting families who want something in the freezer for those nights that they just don't have time to cook. Although there are many more

	Gourmet Stew	Hormel	Homemade	DiGiorno Pizza
Taste	Good	Fair	Excellent	Fair
Price	High $3.50	Medium $1.89	Low	Very high $6.50
Convenience	High	High	Low	High
Availability	Low	High	High	High
Healthy	Medium	Low	High	Medium
Revenues		$2.2 billion*		CHF91.6 million*
Gross Margins		17%*		48%*
Net Income Margins		6.5%*		15.3%
Net Profit		$602 million*		CHF14 million*

*Financial figures for Hormel and DiGiorno are for the whole company, not just the product.

FIGURE 3.9 Competitive Profile Matrix.

competitors than we have highlighted in the matrix, it is often best to pick representative competitors rather than to highlight every potential company. The matrix is a tool to help you understand the competitive landscape by drilling down deep on a few key competitors. Although you'll want to be aware of every potential competitor and substitute, focusing on a few in depth will help you devise a successful strategy.

From this information, you can start to get the broad guidelines of the competitors' strategies—Hormel is pursuing a low-cost strategy—and of what might be an appropriate strategy for Gourmet Stew. It might pursue a differentiation strategy of better quality at a higher price. Moreover, considering the difficulties of entering the distribution channels, it might focus on a niche strategy. Maybe Gourmet Stew could access health-oriented grocery stores like Whole Foods. Understanding the marketplace helps you formulate a strategy that can help you succeed.

Suppliers and Vendors

Understanding the customers and competition is critical to determining whether your idea is indeed an opportunity, but other factors also need consideration. Referring back to the value chain we created for Gourmet Stew (see Figure 3.7), you'll notice that suppliers are providing commodity goods such as beef, vegetables, and other food products. These types of vendors usually have limited power, which means that more of the ultimate gross margin in the chain goes to Gourmet Stew. A sudden rise in the market price of beef, however, could have a negative impact on your margins even though your power over suppliers is strong. A diversified offering that includes vegetarian stew, for example, can guard against such problems.

In other instances, your suppliers can have tremendous power, and that will directly affect your margins. For example, Microsoft, as the dominant operating system and core software provider, and Intel, as the dominant microprocessor supplier, have considerable power over PC manufacturers. Microsoft has gross margins of 65.94%, and Intel has gross margins of 64.50%[34,35] whereas average gross margins for computer hardware manufacturers average a 35% margin.[36] Putting aside the strong competition in the mature PC market for a moment, the fact that suppliers have so much power lessens the opportunity potential for entrepreneurs entering the PC market—unless they find an innovation to supplant the Microsoft operating system or the Intel chip.

The Government

For the most part, the U.S. government is supportive of entrepreneurship. Taxes are lower than in most nations in the world, the time required to register a new business is shorter, and the level of regulations is generally lower. However, in certain industries, government regulation and involvement are significantly higher, such as in pharmaceuticals and medical devices. For example, consider a startup company that produces a stent that more quickly and effectively removes kidney stones. To bring this product to market, you would have to guide your product through Food and Drug Administration (FDA) approval. The approval process is often lengthy, taking on average 12 years and over $350 million to get a new drug from the laboratory onto the pharmacy shelf.[37] During this time, the startup company is incurring costs with no revenue to offset the negative cash flow, increasing the time to break even, and also increasing the amount of money at risk if the venture fails. Although the up-front time and expense are entry barriers that reduce potential future competition, your company benefits only if the product proves successful in gaining both FDA approval and adoption by doctors. Thus, as an entrepreneur, you need to be aware of government requirements and their impact on your business. If the requirements are stringent, such as getting FDA approval, and the potential margins you can earn are relatively low, it is probably not a good opportunity. In the preceding case, the stents command a very high margin, so the company can more than recoup its investment if it successfully navigates FDA approval and secures wide doctor adoption.

The Global Environment

As the world marketplace becomes global, your opportunity is increasingly strengthened by looking overseas. What international customers fit within your PTA, STA, and TTA? How easy is it to reach them? When might you go international? On the flip side, you also need to be aware of your international competitors. Have they entered your market yet? When might they? It is increasingly common for entrepreneurial firms to use an outsourcing strategy, which means that you may need to evaluate international vendors and their relative power.

The Opportunity Checklist

Figure 3.10 summarizes the concepts we have covered in this chapter. Use it to evaluate your idea to see whether it is a strong opportunity or to evaluate several ideas simultaneously to see which one has the greatest promise. Although your opportunity would ideally fit entirely in the middle column under "Better Opportunities," there will be some aspects where it is weak. Examine the weak aspects, and see how you can modify your business model to strengthen them. In the end, of course, the goal is to be strong in more areas than you are weak.

"I Don't Have an Opportunity"

After doing a thorough analysis, some entrepreneurs conclude that the marketplace isn't as large or accessible or that the competition is much greater than they expected, and they quickly reach the conclusion that they should abandon their dreams. But in fact, if you analyze every aspect of the business and if you do your assessment completely, you'll always find a reason for the business to fail. There is no perfect business. There will be areas of weakness in any business model, and it is human nature to amplify those weaknesses until they seem insurmountable. Step back, take a second look, and ask yourself two questions: First, how can you modify your business model so that it isn't as weak in those aspects? Second, what can go right as you launch your business? The entrepreneurial process is one of continuous adjustment.

Many times entrepreneurs stick stubbornly to an idea as it was originally conceived. After a thorough customer and competitive analysis, you need to find ways to modify the business concept so that it better matches the needs of your customer and so that it has advantages over your competitors. The more you learn about the opportunities that exist for your product, the more you must refine your business plan. For instance, as you open your doors and customers come in and provide feedback, you'll find more ways to improve your business model. If you ignore feedback and remain tied to your initial concept as you originally visualized it (and possibly as you wrote it in your plan), you are more likely to fail. The business planning process is ongoing, and you'll learn more about your opportunity at every step along the way. Therefore, to prematurely abandon your concept after some negative feedback from your analysis is a mistake unless the negatives far outweigh the positives in Figure 3.10.

Your prelaunch analysis is just a starting point. You need to understand the variables in your business model, how they might be greater or less than you initially imagine, and what that might mean for your business. In Chapter 5, we will define and examine business models—how you make money and what it costs to generate revenues.

Analysis and criticism are of no interest to me unless they are a path to constructive, action-bent thinking. Critical type intelligence is boring and destructive and only satisfactory to those who indulge in it. Most new projects—I can even say every one of them—can be analyzed to destruction.

—Georges Doriot, Founder of the modern venture capital industry

Customer	Better Opportunities	Weaker Opportunities
Identifiable	Clear "core" customer	Several possible customer groups
Demographics	Clearly defined and focused	Fuzzy definition and unfocused
Psychographics	Clearly defined and focused	Fuzzy definition and unfocused
Trends		
Macromarket	Multiple and converging	Few and disparate
Target market	Multiple and converging	Few and disparate
Window of opportunity	Opening	Closing
Market structure	Emerging/fragmented	Mature/decline
Market size		
How many	Core customer group is large	Small core customer group and few secondary target groups
Demand	Greater than supply	Less than supply
Market growth		
Rate	20% or greater	Less than 20%
Price/Frequency/Value		
Price	Gross margin >40%	Gross margin <40%
Frequency	Often and repeated	One time
Value	Fully reflected in price	Penetration pricing
Operating expenses	Low and variable	Large and fixed
Net Income Margin	>10%	<10%
Volume	Very high	Moderate
Distribution		
Where are you in the value chain?	High margin, high power	Low margin, low power
Competition		
Market structure	Emerging	Mature
Number of direct competitors	Few	Many
Number of indirect competitors	Few	Many
Number of substitutes	Few	Many
Stealth competitors	Unlikely	Likely
Strength of competitors	Weak	Strong
Key success factors		
Relative position	Strong	Weak
Vendors		
Relative power	Weak	Strong
Gross margins they control in the value chain	Low	High
Government		
Regulation	Low	High
Taxes	Low	High
Global environment		
Customers	Interested and accessible	Not interested or accessible
Competition	Nonexistent or weak	Existing and strong
Vendors	Eager	Unavailable

FIGURE 3.10 Opportunity Checklist.

CONCLUSION

All opportunities start with an idea. We find the ideas that most often lead to successful businesses have two key characteristics. First, they are something that the entrepreneur is truly passionate about. Second, the idea is a strong opportunity as measured on the opportunity checklist. To be sure of having a strong opportunity, entrepreneurs need a deep understanding of their customers, preferably knowing the customers by name. Better opportunities will have lots of customers currently (market size) with the potential for even more customers in the future (market is growing). Furthermore, these customers will buy the product frequently and pay a premium price for it (strong margins). Thus, entrepreneurs need to be students of the marketplace. What trends are converging, and how do these shape customer demand today and into the future?

Savvy entrepreneurs also recognize that competitors, both direct and indirect, are vying for the customers' attention. Understanding competitive dynamics helps entrepreneurs shape their opportunities to reach the customer better than the competition can. As this chapter points out, the entrepreneurial environment is holistic and fluid. In addition to their customers and competitors, entrepreneurs need to understand how they source their raw materials (suppliers) and what government regulation means to their business. If all these elements—customers, competitors, suppliers, and government—are favorable, the entrepreneur has identified a strong opportunity. The next step is successfully launching and implementing your vision.

YOUR OPPORTUNITY JOURNAL

Reflection Point	Your Thoughts...
1. What do you really enjoy doing? What is your passion? Can your passion be a platform for a viable opportunity?	
2. What do your friends and family envision you doing? What strengths and weaknesses do they observe? How do their insights help lead you to an opportunity that is right for you?	
3. What ideas do you have for a new business? How can you multiply the stimuli around these ideas to enhance them and identify attractive opportunities?	
4. Put several of your ideas through the opportunity checklist in Figure 3.10. Which ideas seem to have the highest potential?	
5. How can you shape, reshape, and refine your opportunities so that they have a greater chance to succeed and thrive?	
6. Identify some early, low-cost market tests that you can use to refine your opportunity. Create a schedule of escalating market tests to iterate to the strongest opportunity.	

WEB EXERCISE

Subscribe to the free listserve like *Fortune* Term Sheet (http://fortune.com/tag/term-sheet/). Track the stories on a daily basis. Which companies are receiving venture capital? What trends does this flow of money suggest? How might these trends converge to create new opportunities?

NOTES

1. https://tech.co/athletepreneur-passion-hiking-business-2017-04; https://www.businessinsider.com/alltrails-national-geographic-2012-1.
2. https://readwrite.com/2012/01/17/alltrails_partners_with_natgeo_maps_after_googles-3/.
3. https://outdoorindustry.org/press-release/alltrails-com-announces-1-million-mobile-installs-and-retail-launch-of-the-ultimate-outdoor-mapkit/.
4. www.fastcompany.com/magazine/44/dell.html.
5. Boyett, Joseph, and Jimmie Boyett. *The Guru Guide to Entrepreneurship: A Concise Guide to the Best Ideas from the World's Top Entrepreneurs*. New York: Wiley. 2001. p. 258.
6. https://www.inc.com/christine-lagorio/2016-inc5000-paint-nite.html.
7. https://www.inc.com/christine-lagorio/2016-inc5000-paint-nite.html; https://www.marketwatch.com/press-release/paint-nite-expands-to-18-new-markets-as-the-industry-leader-in-social-painting-event-phenomenon-2013-06-18.

8. Compiled from IDEO Web site at http://ideo.com/portfolio and from Edmondson, Amy C. "Phase Zero: Introducing NewServices at IDEO." Boston: Harvard Business School Publishing. December 14, 2005, p. 13.
9. The four-step process outlined in this chapter—gather stimuli, multiply stimuli, create customer concepts, and optimize practicality—comes from a process outlined by Doug Hall. See Hall, D. *Jump Start Your Brain, 2.0*. Cincinnati, OH: Clerisy Press. 2008.
10. *Pain points* are those aspects of a current product or service that are suboptimal or ineffective from the customer's point of view. Improving on these factors or coming up with an entirely new product or service that eliminates these points of pain can be a source of competitive advantage.
11. For those of you who are interested in learning more about brainwriting, visit www.mycoted.com/Brainwriting.
12. Psychographic information categorizes customers based on their personality and psychological traits, lifestyles, values, and social group membership. It helps you understand what motivates customers to act in the ways they do and is important because members of a specific demographic category can have dramatically different psychographic profiles. Marketing strictly based on demographic information will be ineffective because it ignores these differences. Our use of soccer moms captures both the demographic and the psychographic attributes of a broad customer profile.
13. *The U.S. Baby Boomer Market: From the Beatles to Botox*. Third edition. Rockville, MD: Packaged Facts. November 2002, pp. 8–10.
14. https://www.grandviewresearch.com/press-release/global-baby-diapers-market.
15. Ibid.
16. https://www.statista.com/statistics/276623/number-of-apps-available-in-leading-app-stores/https://techcrunch.com/2018/07/16/apples-app-store-revenue-nearly-double-that-of-google-play-in-first-half-of-2018/.
17. http://www.experian.com/assets/simmons-research/white-papers/marketig-services-hispanic-demographic-report-11-2012.pdf.
18. https://www.restaurant.org/Downloads/PDFs/News-Research/2017_Restaurant_outlook_summary-FINAL.pdf.
19. https://www-statista-com.ezproxy.babson.edu/statistics/808240/fsr-unit-share-by-cuisine-type-us/.
20. https://www.restaurant.org/Downloads/PDFs/State-Statistics/Massachusetts.pdf.
21. Brown, R. Managing the "S" Curves of Innovation. *Journal of Consumer Marketing*, 9(1): 61–72. 1992.
22. *Backlog* is the sales that have been made but not fulfilled due to lack of inventory to finalize the sale.
23. https://medium.com/@alexfclayton/dropbox-ipo-s-1-breakdown-3c74742b10ac.
24. https://www.marketwatch.com/story/dropbox-ipo-five-things-to-know-about-the-cloud-storage-company-2018-02-26.
25. VentureXpert.
26. The names of the company and the entrepreneur are disguised.
27. Slotting fees are fees that supermarket chains charge suppliers for providing shelf space in their stores.
28. Information for this value chain was gathered from financial data on sample industry companies found at http://biz.yahoo.com/ic/340.html and linked pages.
29. www.businessweek.com/articles/2012-06-29/before-iphone-and-android-came-simon-the-first-smartphone#p1.
30. https://www.idc.com/getdoc.jsp?containerId=prUS43856818.
31. Ibid.
32. https://www.pwcmoneytree.com/MTPublic/ns/index.jsp.
33. https://pages.email.fortune.com/newsletters/?source=FO_CMS_Cha_Footer and https://www.pehub.com/.
34. https://ycharts.com/companies/MSFT/gross_profit_margin.
35. https://ycharts.com/companies/INTC/gross_profit_margin.
36. https://csimarket.com/Industry/industry_Profitability_Ratios.php?ind=100241 www.drugs.com/fda-approval-process.html.
37. www.drugs.com/fda-approval-process.html.

Case ISlide, Inc.[1]

"Stand in what you stand for."—ISlide, Inc. Company Motto

In August 2014, Justin Kittredge, whose e-mail signature read, "President, CEO, and Janitor—ISlide, Inc.," reflected on the whirlwind of the past 20 months. Justin started ISlide, a manufacturer/distributor of customized athletic sandals known as "slides," in January 2013. By the summer of 2013, he had lined up a slide supplier in China who could manufacture the slides with the level of quality he wanted, and he had found a local printer who could customize the slides. In December 2013, he purchased a printer so that he could customize the slides in-house. He expected 2014 to be the first profitable year for ISlide, Inc. As he looked toward 2015, Justin wondered how to increase the momentum of his nascent company and create a new brand.

The Founder's Background

Justin Kittredge grew up in Barnstable, Massachusetts. Like many of his peers, he played a number of sports growing up, including basketball, baseball, tennis, and soccer. Justin was always tall for his age; by high school with a height of 6'4", he was towering over most of his classmates. Justin attended Barnstable High School for his freshman and sophomore years and then transferred to Northfield Mount Herman School (NMH). According to the NMH website,

> "NMH is considered the best combination of academics and basketball in the United States."[2] In 2013, NMH won the national championship and in 2012, they were the New England (NEPSAC AAA) champions. Further, in 2013–2014, NMH had more than two dozen former graduates playing basketball at Division 1 schools.

When asked why he transferred to NMH, Justin noted, "Northfield Mount Herman was a better match for me from an academic and athletic standpoint. It had a strong academic profile and one of the top rated basketball programs. I wanted to play basketball at a Division 1 college or university and NMH helped me realize that dream."

After graduating from NMH in 1996, where he was voted MVP of the prep school's very successful basketball team in his junior year, Justin attended James Madison University. At James Madison, he played on the JV basketball team, where he was captain during his senior year. In college, Justin majored in hotel and hospitality management and spent his summers doing landscaping. He realized in his senior year of college that he needed to get a "real" job and decided that he wanted to do something related to basketball. Justin recalled, "I applied for a position at Reebok. The interviewer told me there seemed to be no reason to hire me but he invited me to participate in a Reebok League basketball game. The next day, I played my heart out and he offered me an internship."

After the summer internship, Justin received a job offer in the fall and took it. He then spent four years in various sales and marketing positions at Reebok International, one of the largest athletic shoe companies in the world. Justin focused on sales and marketing at Reebok, and following his big corporate experience at Reebok, he decided to move to a small local footwear company, Atsco Footwear Company, where he spent approximately two years as a sales manager and product manager. In 2006, Reebok offered him a position that would give him a big step up in terms of responsibilities and would give him a way to focus on his passion of basketball. So he returned to Reebok to serve as Director of Product Development for Performance Basketball Shoes. In that role, he managed the overall process of design, development, and marketing of high-end basketball shoes, primarily worn by pros and other basketball aficionado athletes. In that role, Justin worked closely with footwear designers at Reebok, supervised the field testing of proposed shoes, travelled to China to meet with the managers in the factories that produced the shoes, and interacted with NBA basketball players. In fact, he was often responsible for developing custom shoes for specific players. According to Keith Regan, a journalist who wrote an article about Justin and ISlide for the *Boston Business Journal*, "As jobs go, the one Justin Kittredge held at Reebok wasn't so bad. The former college athlete plied his trade in the sports world, always scored tickets to the biggest games, and spent time interacting with celebrities from the sports and entertainment worlds."[3] When asked by a reporter for Nice Kicks[4] what his favorite project at Reebok was, Justin replied:

> Number one was probably EuroCamp. To spend a week in Italy with NBA GMs, presidents, and players in a laid back atmosphere is something I could definitely do 365 days a year. Aside from that, I think the process of sitting down with professional athletes and talking about what the inspiration could be from their shoe to seeing it come to fruition

[1] This case was written by Donna Stoddard and Lakshmi Balachandra of Babson College. *Copyright by Babson College* 2016.

[2] http://www.nmhschool.org/athletics/winter/basketball-boys.

[3] http://www.bizjournals.com/boston/print-edition/2014/02/14/emerging-leader-justin-kittredge-of.html?page=all.

[4] http://www.nicekicks.com/2013/10/18/industry-interview-justin-kittredge-taks-reebok-starting-islide/.

Exhibit 3.1 Christopher Clunie, Davidson College

More Than Just a Game: Basketball as a Force for Change in the World

South Africa, Argentina, Japan, Italy

I will examine basketball as a tool for change within global politics. People are using basketball to confront social, ethnic, economic, and political boundaries, educate youth on the significance of issues such as AIDS and racism, and foster international solidarity. By working with basketball outreach programs, looking at the implications of professionalism and social mobility, and experiencing the international competitive aspect of basketball, I will better understand how and why basketball is so powerful in creating change in the world today.

Source: http://www.watsonfellowship.org/site/fellows/06_07.html.

> over the course of 18 months when it actually hits retail with marketing behind it. Just to see a guy like John Wall tweet about it and talk about it on his own and to see how proud he was to have his own shoe—to have a team make that dream a reality for him. Not even just John, even guys like Jason Terry or Jameer Nelson who still have things that are very close to them. To add those elements to the shoe and see how proud they were to wear the shoe was great. That took so much hard work from the design and development team, the marketing team, and even the team overseas in China.

Euro Camp in Italy featured the best players from Europe and attracted NBA coaches and general managers. While at the Euro Camp in 2009, Justin met Chris Clunie, a former NCAA basketball player for Davidson College who was working with the National Basketball Association as a coordinator for their International Operations. Clunie had won a Thomas Watson Fellowship upon graduating from Davidson College, a fellowship that allowed him to travel the world and see how basketball impacts international cultures (see **Exhibit 3.1**). Meeting Chris and learning about his experience with the Watson Fellowship inspired Justin with the goal of using basketball to change the world.

After college, Justin coached AAU[5] basketball teams and found that he really liked mentoring and coaching young players. As he typically had one or two kids who needed financial assistance to play on the team, he built funding these players into his team's financial model. Since he had access to the Reebok facility, he would offer kids on financial aid free basketball clinics, where they attended weekly skill and drills sessions and a week-long summer basketball camp with legendary coach, Bob Hurley Sr. "I realized that I could change lives by coaching," noted Justin. He started to envision establishing a nonprofit organization that would enable him to do this. He realized:

> I was really influencing their lives, not just helping the kids with basketball. I had high expectations of my kids and they lived up to those expectations. Kids who had been in trouble, stayed out of trouble, they started to do better in school, they started helping others; in essence, I could see they were becoming better people.
>
> After meeting Chris, my wife Lindsey and I formalized the structure of Shooting Touch. We envisioned Shooting Touch as a basketball Peace Corps, of sorts. We formed a board that, in August 2014, included a number of high-profile current and former basketball players, coaches, and franchise owners, including Hall of Famer, Coach Bob Hurley, Sr.; Head Coach of University of Buffalo, Bobby Hurley, Jr.; former NBA player and Franchise Owner, Wayne Embry; Celtics player, Kelley Olynk, and others [see **Exhibit 3.2**]. Annually, we accept applications from recent college graduates and give them $25,000 to go to a third-world country and use basketball to make a difference.
>
> We had our first Gala in 2010. We raised enough money to send our first grantee, Tome Barros, to Senegal, Brazil, and Cape Verde where he built and refurbished basketball courts and used the game of basketball to teach life skills to over 2,400 youth. In 2011, Leah Westerbrook went to South America and Zimbabwe. By 2012, we changed our approach and decided to commit to one country, Rwanda, for five years. We were able to raise enough to send two grantees to Rwanda, Casey Stockton and Isaura Guzman. Pricilla Dodoo and Kevin Ketti, the 2013 grantees, are on the ground now making a difference building courts and holding camps and clinics for kids in Rwanda."[6]

Starting ISlide, Inc.

By the time Justin decided to start ISlide, in 2013, he had 13 years of experience in the footwear industry. Justin described how he decided to start the venture.

[5] According to Wikipedia, "The Amateur Athletic Union (AAU) is one of the largest non-profit volunteer sports organizations in the United States. The AAU offers participants sports teams in their local community that they can join and compete with other athletes their own age. There are teams in most sports ranging from 9U to 18U, allowing children to play for championships in sports against other children similar in age and athletic development."

[6] http://www.shootingtouch.com/what-we-have-done-grantees/.

Exhibit 3.2 Shooting Touch Mission and Board of Directors[7]

Mission

Shooting Touch, Inc. harnesses the power of basketball to improve the lives of youth in the areas of health, education, and character around the world. In Boston, Shooting Touch has established a year-round presence through programs that provide youth with opportunities for development, both on and off the court.

Internationally, The Shooting Touch Sabbatical Program, known as the "Basketball Peace Corps," provides the opportunity for gifted college graduates to work in Rwanda for one year. There, they provide places to play by constructing courts, and train local coaches and youths in both basketball and our off-court curriculum of gender equality, health and fitness, disease prevention (HIV/AIDS, malaria, hand washing), the importance of education, and leadership skills.

Board of Directors

- KENNY ATKINSON, Assistant Coach for the NBA's Atlanta Hawks
- AMADOU FALL, Head of NBA Africa
- WAYNE EMBRY, NBA Hall of Fame Inductee and Former General Manager of the Cleveland Cavaliers and the Toronto Raptors
- FRAN FRASCHILLA, ESPN Basketball Analyst and Commentator
- COACH BOB HURLEY, National Championship Coach for the St. Anthony Friars and Naismith 2010 Hall of Fame Inductee
- BOBBY HURLEY, JR., Head Men's Basketball Coach for University of Buffalo
- JACKIE MACMULLAN, ESPN Author and Commentator
- KELLY OLYNYK, Forward for the Boston Celtics
- PETE PHILO, Director of International Scouting for the NBA's Indiana Pacers
- SAM PRESTI, Executive Vice President and General Manager of the Oklahoma City Thunder
- BARBARA STEVENS, Head Women's Basketball Coach for Bentley University
- JAY TRIANO, Assistant NBA Coach Portland Trailblazers and Head Coach for Canadian National Team

In December 2012, Reebok announced that it was slowly moving away from its Basketball Division. At some level, that was not surprising since Adidas, which purchased Reebok in 2005, also had a basketball line. Over the years, I had toyed with starting my own footwear company, but I had signed a noncompete with Reebok. When I was laid off in 2012, I realized this was my opportunity. I had spent my entire career in footwear; I understood the product development cycle and had relationships with manufacturers in China. Footwear was a category that I knew, so it made sense to create a company in that space.

I decided that slides would be my first product because athletic sandals were a small category that I felt was poised for growth. Further, my product would be different because it is customizable.

Even with my background, and the relationships that I had with footwear manufacturers in China, it took me six months to get up and running. I had to design the slides, find a supplier that could make them, conduct a field test, and determine the best technology to customize the slides. Initially, we outsourced the printing on the slides, but earlier this year we acquired a printer so we now customize the slides in house.

The Product

ISlide sells customizable athletic sandals that are known as "slides." While other companies such as Nike, Reebok, and Under Armour, among others, made and sold slides, in 2014, ISlide, Inc. was the only company that sold *customizable* athletic sandals (see **Exhibit 3.3** for pictures of the ISlide product). As noted in the ISlide catalog, "The outsole (bottom) of the shoe is sneaker inspired with forefoot and heel, herring bone accents."[8] Such sandals are popular among both amateur and professional athletes. Performance basketball shoes, which in August 2014 cost $40–$275 on www.finishline.com, were designed to be worn on indoor basketball court surfaces to give the players traction and agility. Hence, serious players wore sandals, flip-flops, or other shoes to and from a game in order to protect the integrity of their basketball sneakers; many basketball players would not even think of wearing their performance sneakers outdoors. Soccer, football, and baseball players also wear specially designed athletic shoes—like high-technology shoes called cleats—that are designed to

[7] http://www.shootingtouch.com/board-of-directors/.

[8] October 2013 ISlide Product Catalog.

Photo Credit: © Reproduced with permission of Islide

EXHIBIT 3.3 **Photos of Islides.**

be worn only on the field and are similarly priced at expensive price points. These athletes also typically wear sandals or other shoes when not on the field or turf.

In 2014, what distinguished the ISlide product from the other slide sandals on the market was its high-end comfort design and its ability to be completely customizable. Customers could have any design they liked printed on the top flap of the sandals as well as a different image on the side of the flaps. Teams could have their logos on the shoes, or even the team logo on one sandal and the athlete's name on the other. The website www.ISlideUSA.com offered a library of graphics to choose from as well as fonts for writing whatever customers wanted.

Customers could also upload their own image or designed logo that they wanted printed on the slides. Justin noted, "We know that if this [customizable athletic sandal line] takes off, we will have competition from others. This is why we are hoping to get a head start and to establish ISlide as the 'go to' brand for customizable athletic sandals."

In August 2014, ISlides retailed for $49.99 for one pair and the company offered a discount on bulk sales. Justin based his pricing on a similar product on the market, the Nike Air

Experience Slides, which were adorned with the Nike swoosh, and were sold for a retail price of $50.00.

Building the Company

By December 2013, just 11 months after Justin started the company, he had five employees: Justin was CEO; Hope and Jackie, who were responsible for graphic designs; Steve, who ran operations; and Demitri, who was responsible for marketing and ISlide's significant social media efforts. In starting the company, Justin used a strategy of hiring smart, motivated, college students to work during the summer as interns. ISlide had employed over 16 college students or recent college graduates from a number of schools, including Babson, Bentley, Boston College, Drexel, Emerson, George Mason, Harvard, and Villanova. Justin described his interest and experience in working with interns:

> I love working with interns. First, it is great for my financials since they are unpaid. Second, it gives me the opportunity to learn from others. I appreciate their input; life is too short to make all the bad decisions alone. However, I have to hire a certain type of person. I need people who will do whatever we need from packing or unpacking slides, identifying sales leads, selling, helping with a social media campaign, or cleaning the bathroom. The interns know this is not a 9–5 job, rather a 7am–11pm position, if necessary.
>
> I ask a lot of the interns, but in return, I try to give them as much exposure to the business as I can. For example, as I'm currently fundraising, I had an opportunity to present my funding pitch to professors with venture capital investing experience who are faculty of the Blank Center at Babson College. I brought every member of the ISlide team, including the interns, to that session as I wanted them to hear the feedback and understand the fundamentals of my business. I had asked Babson if it was OK if I brought my team…but I think the Babson folks were shocked when 18 of us showed up!

Justin launched the business in an office space in Wellesley, Massachusetts. He noted, "When I left Reebok, a part of my package was an office for six months at an outplacement firm in Wellesley." He explained further, "The office space, internet, and telephone were all free. However, once my interns joined me in the space—well, the space was not designed for multiple people and we were asked to leave after five months."

In September 2013, Justin moved ISlide to the Winsmith Mill Market in the Norwood Commerce Center. According to the *Norwood Town News*,

> In years gone by, the area was the home of the Winslow and Smith Brothers tannery. Today, it is a revitalized set of mill buildings, a section of which is appropriately devoted to warehouses filled with antique, vintage and repurposed furniture, accessories, tools, "doohickeys," etc. Another section houses artist lofts. The remaining portions house manufacturing and commercial businesses.[9]

As described in the article, the Winsmith Mill Market houses an eclectic group of businesses and shops. There are numerous antique shops and galleries in the complex, which open for business on the weekends, Friday to Sunday. ISlide's location was on the third floor of one of the buildings in the back; it was essentially a walk up since only someone familiar with the manually operated elevator would even consider getting on it. Justin described his rationale for moving to the Norwood antique warehouse location:

> In this location I am paying $4.50 per square foot and that includes utilities. As you can see, we have plenty of space for our inventory. Our printing approach is proprietary; we have a secure room where we house our printer. We have an office here for Shooting Touch, the basketball-based not for profit that I started in 2006. And, given the expansive space, we can host events. For example, in a few weeks we will have a pizza-eating contest. People will pay $25 to enter; the winner will receive a pair of ISlides and all proceeds will go to support a charity.

Social media and celebrity endorsements had provided a very cost-effective way for Justin to get the word out about ISlide and market the new business. *Slam* and *Dime* magazines ran print ads for ISlide and ISlide advertised on their websites, which were popular among basketball enthusiasts. Similarly, ISlide placed ads on other basketball aficionado websites such as HoopRootz (www.hooprootz.com). Further, Justin and his staff frequently updated the ISlide Instagram page, and many custom sandals were produced for Boston Celtics players, NCAA draft players, and other athlete celebrities such as Tom and Gisele Brady. Justin noted:

> A unique aspect of our business is that we can customize one pair of ISlides or 500 pairs of ISlides. To that end, we have a website that allows customers to go online and customize one or many pairs of ISlides. Our slogan is "Stand in What You Stand For." As such, if we are making shoes for a basketball team, we can put the team name on our shoes. A player might want to put his jersey number on his shoes, or his name on one shoe and his jersey number on the other shoe. As we state in our catalog, we offer "Endless Custom Options, your logo, your brand, your team, even your wildest dream.

In 2013, ISlide sold approximately $50K of slides. Most of those sales were to individual customers. The company hoped to achieve revenue between $250 and $350K in 2014,

[9] http://www.norwoodtownnews.com/content/winsmith-mill-market-revitalization-historic-winslow-brothers-tannery.

and while they still sold to individuals, they were increasingly targeting teams and other bulk-sale opportunities. Justin's sales approach was to be constantly on the road attending basketball tournaments and trade shows and calling on large companies that supply uniforms and equipment to teams. For example, Dick's Sporting Goods, a large sporting goods chain retailer, has a division that focuses on team sales and volume purchases. Justin noted, "A deal with the team sales and volume purchases division of Dick's Sporting Goods would be huge for us." Justin also used an independent sales representative for team athletic wear, a father and son, who carried the ISlide line in their shoe offerings. As independent sales representatives, they were paid a percentage of the ISlide shoes they sold. Justin felt that was a great way to get the line in front of customers, for a minimal cost. In late 2013, ISlides with the logo "Boston Strong" were available at The Tannery and at Puritan Cape Cod, two local shoe retail chains. A portion of the proceeds, from the Boston Strong line of ISlide, would be donated to the Boston Strong foundation.

Justin shared his view on how he envisioned growing the company. He noted,

> I love the "Life is Good" model. They started selling t-shirts out of the back of their car. They had a cool logo that caught on. Now they sell a wide variety of products. I hope we have a similar trajectory. Currently, we have one product but I hope to expand. Like "Life is Good," my plan is to build a company. Of course, if we get an outrageous offer, I would consider selling ISlide. **Exhibit 3.4** summarizes Justin's professional journey and shows the parallel journey that Justin and Lindsey experienced with Shooting Touch.

The Future

Justin used his own funds to start ISlide. He noted, "I made some good investments early in my career that I used to start ISlide. Thus far, I have not taken a salary from the business. I am currently seeking investors, both friends and family and venture capitalists; an influx of capital will provide the funds I need to grow the business."

Exhibit 3.4 Justin's Journey

	Professional	Shooting Touch
2000	Graduated from James Madison University. Accepted entry-level sales position at Reebok International.	Volunteered to coach a high school boys AAU team.
2004	Left Reebok as he accepted a sales management position with Atsco, a footwear company.	
2006	Hired back by Reebok International to return as "Director of Product Development" for the Performance Basketball Division.	
2009	Attended Euro Camp for his work as Director of Product Development for the Performance Basketball Division at Reebok. Met George Clunie and learned about his Watson Fellowship, enabling Clunie to travel the world and observe how basketball impacts international cultures.	Justin and wife, Lindsey, decide to a start a basketball nonprofit, Shooting Touch. Lindsey will be the executive director of Shooting Touch. July 2009, Shooting Touch hosted the first annual "Coach Bob Hurley Basketball Camp" for boys and girls of grades 3–8. Sixty kids attended; all camp proceeds to Shooting Touch.
2010		Hosted the first annual Shooting Touch Gala. The first Shooting Touch "fellow" selected and sent to sites in Senegal, Brazil, and Cape Verde.
2011		The second Shooting Touch "fellow" selected and sent to sites in South America and Zimbabwe.
2012	December 2012, Reebok announces it will be eliminating Justin's division, the performance basketball division.	Hosted third annual Gala; decided to commit to work in one country, Rwanda, for five years. Raised enough money to send two grantees to Rwanda.
2013	January 15, 2013, Justin launches ISlide in Wellesley, Massachusetts. June 2013, Justin moved ISlide and Shooting Touch to larger office space in Norwood, Massachusetts.	

Justin continued,

I am proud of what we have accomplished so far, but I wonder what we should do to grow and scale this business. Should we add other products and if so what kinds of products? Should we develop strategic partnerships, and if so, with whom? Should we focus on selling to retailers and if so, how can we reach them and manage the relationship with those companies while maintaining appropriate margins? Or should we stay the course and focus on selling to the end user?

Discussion Questions

1. Is Justin an entrepreneur? Why or why not?
2. Who is Justin? What does he enjoy? Where is his passion?
3. What aspects of his background can you identify that led him to start ISlide?
4. What resources does Justin use to start ISlide? How does he research what he needs to do?
5. Whom does Justin know? Whom has he engaged so far to help him with his ISlide journey?
6. What should Justin do next?

4 Prototyping Your Ideas

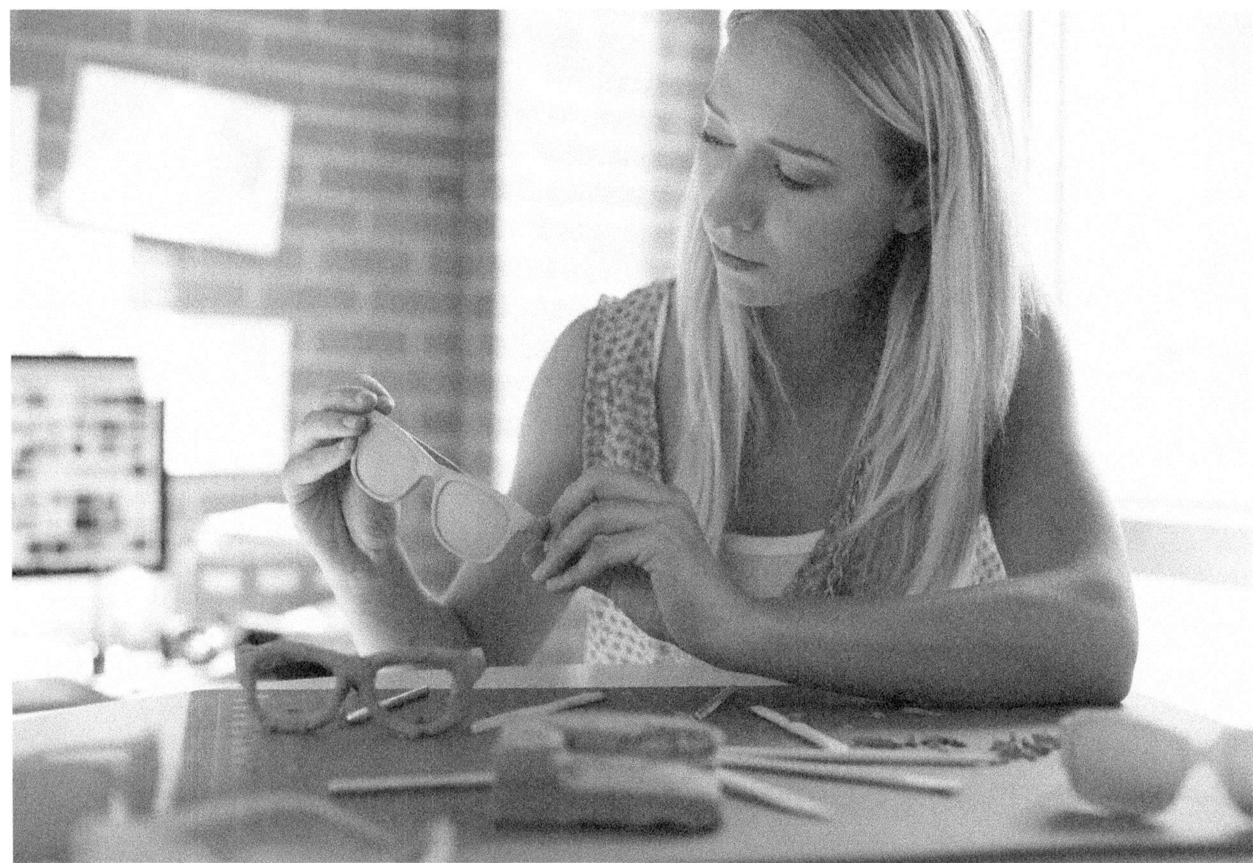

Photo Credit: © Hero Images/SuperStock

A Looks-like Prototype of Sunglasses.

Innovation—the creation of new and useful products and services—is often at the heart of entrepreneurship. To create economic and social value, entrepreneurs develop new products, processes, and business models to satisfy unmet needs in the marketplace.

This chapter was written by Erik A. Noyes.

Introducing a new product or service involves substantial risk, and upwards of 50–90% of innovations fail, depending on industry.[1] Also, there is often a large gap between what the entrepreneur believes is valuable and what the target customer—the ultimate judge—perceives.

Prototyping, both products and services alike, is one strategy to test key assumptions about what a customer will value and be willing to buy. Although you may think of a prototype as an elaborate model that requires special technical skills to create, with a little creativity, any entrepreneur can make a basic prototype to answer a range of vital questions, including the following:

- Does my target customer want the new product I propose creating?
- How might I alter the product or service to make it more attractive to my target market?
- And how does my proposed innovation compare against existing solutions in the marketplace?

This chapter discusses the importance of the *prototyping process* in exploring and shaping entrepreneurial opportunities, with a special emphasis on steps entrepreneurs can take to reduce their risk. Prototyping can lead to new insights about an entrepreneurial opportunity, signal venture readiness to potential investors, and shorten time-to-market.

What Is Prototyping?

Prototyping is the process of quickly putting together working models (i.e., prototypes) *to represent ideas, test various aspects of a design, and gather early customer feedback.* Prototyping can help entrepreneurs develop, test, and refine their entrepreneurial idea, ideally resulting in the confirmation of an entrepreneurial opportunity. In many cases, a prototype can be as simple as a sketch of a product concept, the basic design for a web landing page, or a simulation of new service concept.

The core purpose of the prototyping process and developing a prototype is to get a *response* from a target customer or user—in other words, feedback that can be acted on. Taken together, responses from many potential customers can help an entrepreneur decide what directions to pursue (or not pursue) with a new innovation or venture. Too often entrepreneurs are narrowly focused on their pet product and venture idea; the prototyping process forces the entrepreneur to get out in the field and engage potential customers, all with the intent of learning and iterating rapidly.

The prototyping process focuses on the representation and testing of *assumptions*, ultimately to drive deeper learning about an entrepreneurial opportunity (see Figure 4.1). If you think about it, any new product (the iPhone, cloud storage, a consumer good) is just a set of assumptions about what a target customer values and is willing to pay for. If the core assumptions are correct, then that product is much more likely to succeed in the marketplace. Conversely, products and services that fail in the marketplace are generally based on incorrect assumptions about what a target market values.

For example, an automobile manufacturer such as Ford, long before finalizing its design for a new minivan, will show its target customers (e.g., fathers and mothers who have children) prototypes to seek detailed feedback. The parents might be shown a table-sized model of the minivan to see if they appreciate its exterior styling. Similarly, they might be asked to try out a new design for a flip-down/flip-up seating system to make moving large items easier. They might be shown detailed images of a novel dashboard design and be asked to offer critiques.

Critically, the whole minivan need not be built—which would be very costly—to know if the target customer would want one. Collectively, *many* prototypes conveying core aspects of the new design can help confirm the desirability of the new minivan concept.

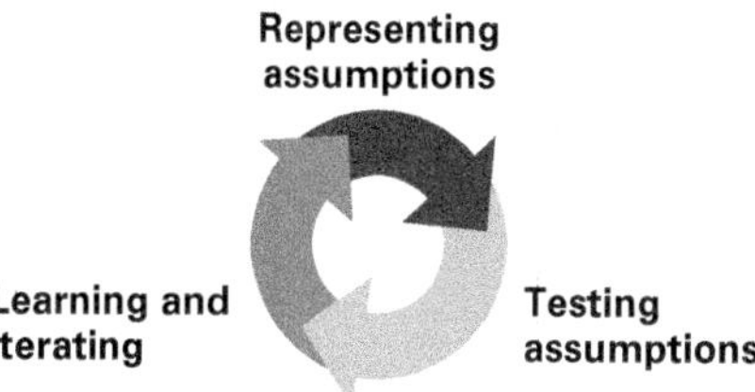

FIGURE 4.1 The Prototyping Process: Representing and Testing Assumptions.

Similarly, 3-D and 2-D prototypes, such as models and sketches, respectively, can help an entrepreneur represent—and therefore explore and test—key assumptions about their innovation. Variables to test can range from pricing assumptions to assumptions about product benefits and product use, as well as how a new product concept stacks up against existing competition.

In sum, despite the myth of the entrepreneur who thinks of a perfect new product or service in a flash of brilliance, almost all new products and services require significant trial and error to develop before they are ready for the target market. For this reason, the third and most vital stage in the prototyping process is *learning and iterating*. Many responses from target customers will show some aspects of a concept to be desirable and others not to be. As such, the challenge becomes one of quickly learning and developing additional prototypes—likely many times in succession—and gathering more feedback.

Low- Versus High-Fidelity Prototypes

The prototyping process often involves the creation of not one but several prototypes to explore a potential entrepreneurial opportunity. Some models are referred to as *low-fidelity prototypes* because the prototype expresses the rough product concept, either in two- or three-dimensional form, often in material as basic as paper (see paper prototyping in Figure 4.2). The purpose of low-fidelity prototyping is for the entrepreneur to get ideas out rapidly and to see how potential customers and different stakeholders react. With a new product concept, even low-fidelity, or rough, prototypes can help confirm desirable, as well as undesirable, product characteristics (e.g., forms, colors, benefits, and features).

In contrast, *high-fidelity prototypes* are designed to look like a final completed product concept. Here, the aim is to represent final, detailed assumptions about the product (e.g., the final materials and production process) and even potentially use the prototype in promotion to customers, partners, or investors.

For example, a low- or medium-fidelity prototype of a new teleconferencing device might be crafted of foam simply to examine its size and form, where a later high-fidelity prototype may have color, finishes, and a sample screen image added.

Generally, when testing and developing a new product, an entrepreneur moves from several low-fidelity prototypes to increasingly detailed high-fidelity prototypes to clarify the existence of a customer need and market opportunity. As you can see the video (see Figure 4.3) on the prototyping challenge focused on 10- to 12-year-old children, you can gather enormously useful intelligence from rough, low-fidelity prototypes, particularly in the *early* stages of idea generation. The process of representing and then testing assumptions is meant to be repeated many times (with the target market) to drive deeper learning and uncover unexpected insights.

Photo Credit: Peter Hermes Furian/ Alamy Stock Photo

Photo Credit: Maciej Frolow/Getty Images

FIGURE 4.2 The Goals of Low- and High-Fidelity Prototyping.

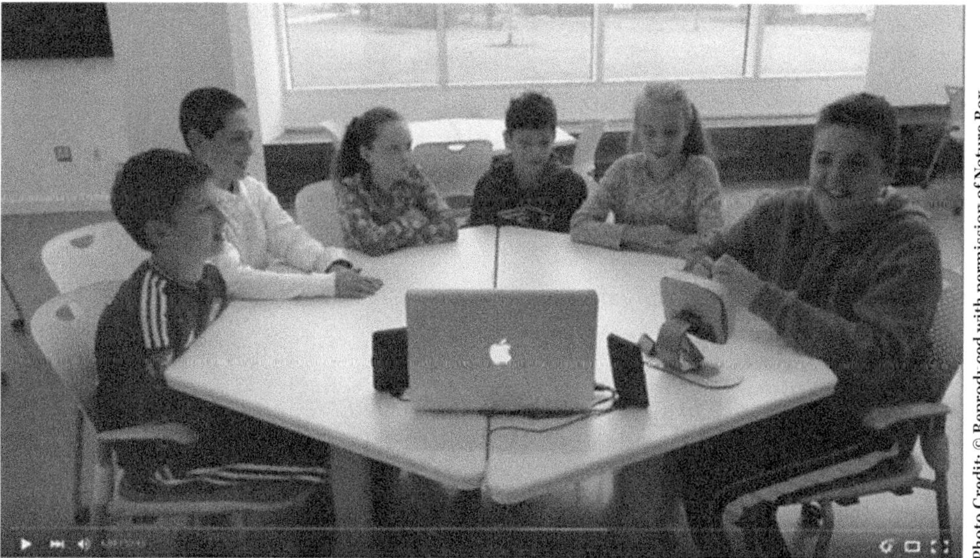

Photo Credit: © Reproduced with permission of Nature Box

FIGURE 4.3 An undergraduate prototyping challenge at Babson College. Going from idea generation to low-fidelity prototypes in only 45 minutes, teams developed paper prototypes to be shared with children aged 10–12 years old. Want to see prototyping in action? Watch this 14-minute video: youtube.com/watch?v=gomjd3GEEP8.

Photo Credit: © Epa European Pressphoto Agency B.V./Alamy Stock Photo

FIGURE 4.4 Looks-Like Prototypes of Google Glass.

Looks- and Works-Like Prototypes

As discussed, prototypes are simplified versions of product concepts, and often many prototypes emphasizing different product elements are needed to confirm a final product design. Product developers distinguish between *looks-* and *works-like* prototypes. A looks-like prototype (Figure 4.4), as suggested by its name, appears similar or identical to a final product but does

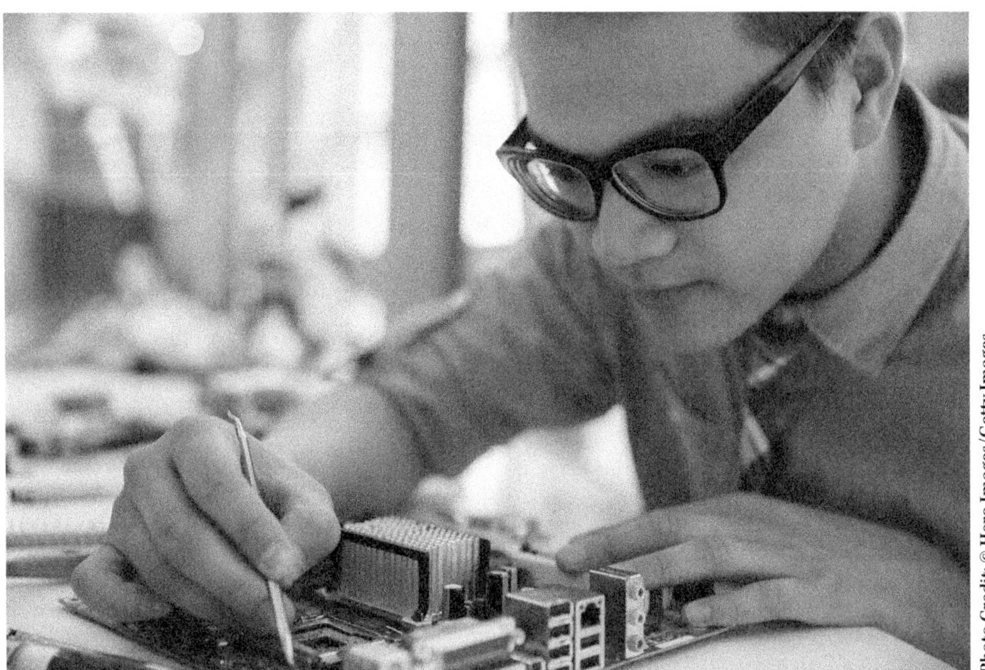

Photo Credit: © Hero Images/Getty Images

FIGURE 4.5 Works-Like Prototype.

not function as the final product is expected to. It may be made of paper, foam, or potentially 3-D printed. For instance, a looks-like prototype of a new consumer electronic product would have the outer appearance of the device but would not include the electronics and power source of the final, produced product. Looks-like prototypes are valuable to test market acceptance of a design before costly, detailed product development is started.

In contrast, a works-like prototype operates like the final intended product design—demonstrating product functionality or usability—but often does not appear at all like the end product.

In developing and testing new product concepts, it is wise to seek feedback on both works- and looks-like prototypes, which collectively suggest the desirability of the end product design. There are challenges and limitations in seeking target customer feedback with each type of prototype. Presenting a looks-like prototype alone requires the customer to imagine the functioning, usability, and in-use benefits of the product. Similarly, a works-like prototype (Figure 4.5) without a final design requires the target customer to imagine the final, designed product, for example, how it looks and feels or is merchandized or packaged in a store.

Consistent with our discussion of opportunity shaping and market testing in the previous two chapters, an entrepreneur should first proceed by creating and testing basic prototypes (e.g., paper prototypes), only thereafter escalating commitments, and investments to develop more refined prototypes. One key point of this chapter is that it is foolish to jump straight from idea or concept to final product design, incurring all the costs and risks of a full product development effort. Although it is true that there are an array of creative services available to entrepreneurs (e.g., product and industrial design services, web design services), simple and low-cost is almost always the best way to start. Time and money invested should be increased only *after* confirming that a product is desirable to the target market.

Types of Prototyping

Paper Prototyping

As demonstrated in the video in Figure 4.3, many product concepts can be richly explored through *paper prototyping*. Paper prototyping, as the name suggests, is the representation of a concept using simple materials such a paper or cardboard, markers, and tape. Quick and directionally correct is the objective, not perfection. The goal is to get the basic idea out into the world to get a response from a target customer and to explore what is valuable to the target customer—and to see if there is a real willingness to pay.

A paper prototype can help an entrepreneur consider different design configurations and trade-offs with the product, particularly before higher-cost prototyping methods are used (see 3-D printing). Critically, a paper prototype can help an entrepreneur consider what market tests to run and where to put time and energy. In reading this, you may think that paper prototyping requires certain technical training to get started. It does not—anyone can create and test paper prototypes to explore an entrepreneurial idea!

Mobile Apps

One area where paper prototyping is common and particularly useful is mobile application development for smart phones and tablets (see Figure 4.6). Too often, entrepreneurs think they must fully code and develop their application to see if it is valued by the market when in fact a simple paper prototype can answer basic questions such as: Does my target customer want or value this app? How can the app be dramatically improved to take into account the unique expectations and wishes of my target market? And what are the most likely use-cases, and therefore needed areas of development for the app? Simply put, you do not need to spend thousands of dollars to actually *build* an app to get insights from your customer. Basic smart phone and tablet templates, known as wireframes, can help you map out and test user interactions and user experiences.

3-D Printing

In recent years, the costs and complexity of 3-D printing have fallen dramatically. In 3-D printing, a 3-D object is printed, for example, in plastic, from a digital file (see Figure 4.7). Working independently or with support from a 3-D designer, an entrepreneur can mock up looks-like and even works-like prototypes to share with target customers.

3-D printing is a type of "additive manufacturing," where a medium, such as plastic, ceramic, or even metal, is extruded through a computer-controlled tool head, which lays down the medium in layers, thus building up a 3-D object.

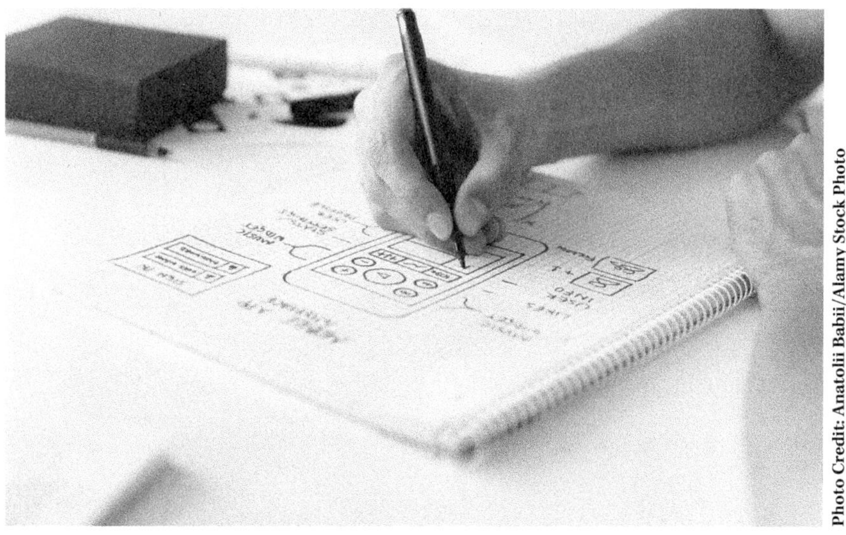

Photo Credit: Anatolii Babii/Alamy Stock Photo

FIGURE 4.6 Smart Phone and Tablet Templates Can Help You Create a Paper Prototype of Your App Concept.

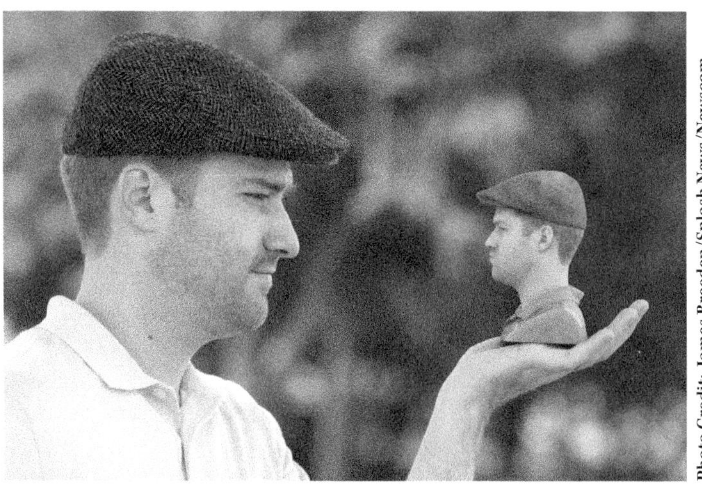

Photo Credit: James Breeden/Splash News/Newscom

FIGURE 4.7 A Color 3-D Printed Model. This Model was Created by Taking a 3-D Digital Scan of the Man Shown in the Picture.

Currently, Makerbot Industries offers an array of 3-D printers costing between $1,000 and $5,000 that print in an array of plastic types and colors (see Figure 4.8). Also, FormLabs offers a resin printer, a different technology than that used by Makerbot, for $3,500 to create higher-resolution prints.

Although historically 3-D printing has been for prototyping and model-making, increasingly 3-D printing is becoming an end manufacturing platform, where entrepreneurs can produce (i.e., print) their own final products for sale. Year by year, the print envelope (volume of the printed object) is becoming larger, the print resolution is becoming finer, and the stability and ease-of-use of consumer-oriented 3-D printers are improving. These developments have created new opportunities for craft as well as high-tech entrepreneurs to develop and sell their wares. Kacie Hultgren, uses 3-D printing to design and sell custom doll house furniture, which she markets, online (www.shapeways.com/shops/prettysmallthings). Another venture, Athletics 3D (https://www.athletics3d.com/) offers customized athletic gear for biathletes and para-biathletes.

It is important to note, an entrepreneur need not purchase a 3-D printer to create a 3-D printed prototype or model. Due to growing market interest, new 3-D printing services have emerged that can address either one-time printing needs or the desire for small batch production without the cost of printer ownership and maintenance. Online services company Shapeways

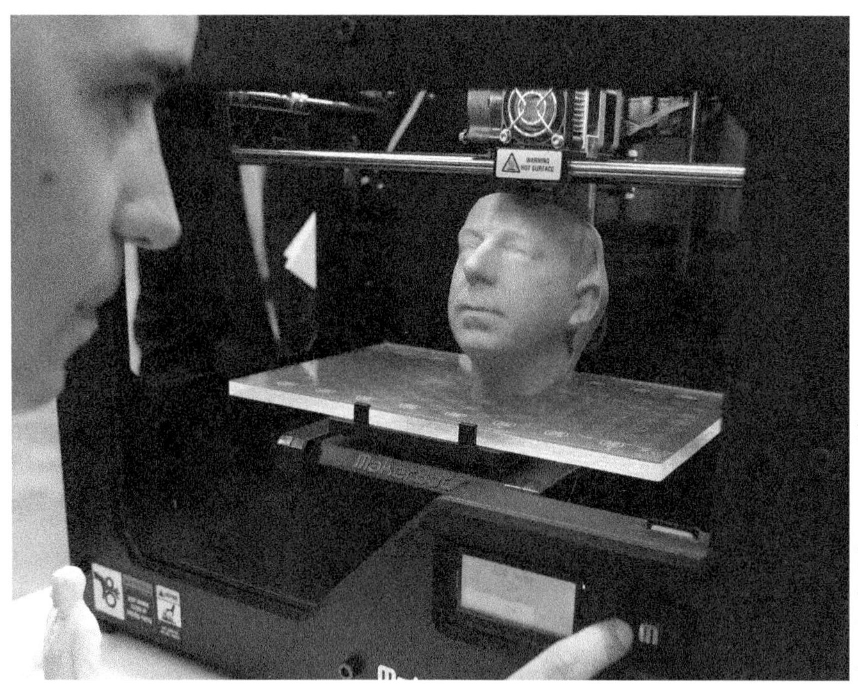

Photo Credit: Fabrizion Bensch/Newscom

FIGURE 4.8 3-D Printers Offered by Makerbot Industries.

(www.shapeways.com) will print in a wide range of media, including ceramics and even metals (gold, silver, and titanium). Also, 3DHubs (www.3dhubs.com), a global network of independent 3-D printing entrepreneurs, list individuals by geography, often just two to three miles from where you live, who will quote and complete 3-D printing work.

Finally, free software programs that allow nearly anyone to design and print 3-D objects include TinkerCad and SketchUp. Most software are cloud based, and the design files can be accessed or modified from anywhere.

Although much has been made about 3-D printing and the technology offers new opportunities for entrepreneurs and designers alike, a 3-D printer is just another tool. Chances are it first makes sense to develop and test a paper prototype, which can address many questions quickly and efficiently before investing time and money into a more elaborate 3-D model.

Electronics Prototyping

In recent years two new open-source projects, Arduino (launched in 2005) and Raspberry Pi (launched in 2012), have created new possibilities for prototyping electronic devices. Arduino promotes itself as an electronics prototyping platform, and its microcontrollers allow DIYers and "hackers" to connect a wide range of sensors (components that detect something) and actuators (components that do something in the real world) to explore and test new product and service concepts.

In basic terms, an Arduino is a simple computer (see Figure 4.9) that, if set up to do so, can, for example, alert you by text if your basement is flooding or remotely measure the soil humidity in your greenhouse to tell you if your tomatoes need watering. A basic Arduino controller costs as little as $15, and some are miniaturized to be as small as a quarter. Some of the added communication capabilities require the connection of "shields" to the microcontroller (i.e., special-purpose components), but the point is that powerful electronic prototyping has come to the masses. You only need time, not a degree in electrical engineering, to explore concepts for novel electronic products and services. Arduino is a particularly useful technology for creating works-like prototypes—a basic system that functions similar to the final product.

Low-cost electronic prototyping technologies like Arduino and Raspberry Pi are spurring new waves of product and service development and contributing to the emerging Internet of Things (IoT) industry. Raspberry Pi, a "computer on a chip," costs as little as $5–$30 and is a technology similar to Arduino but where the emphasis is placed on computing. For only the cost of a keyboard and display, an owner of a Raspberry Pi can have a fully functional computer, running the Linux operating system, which is perfectly capable of running productivity software such as MS Office. DIYers, tinkerers, and entrepreneurs are constantly exploring the possibilities and promise of these low-cost prototyping platforms (see Figure 4.10).

Photo Credit: Khim Hoe Ng/Alamy Stock Photo

Photo Credit: Premier/ Alamy Stock Photo

FIGURE 4.9 Raspberry Pi and Arduino.

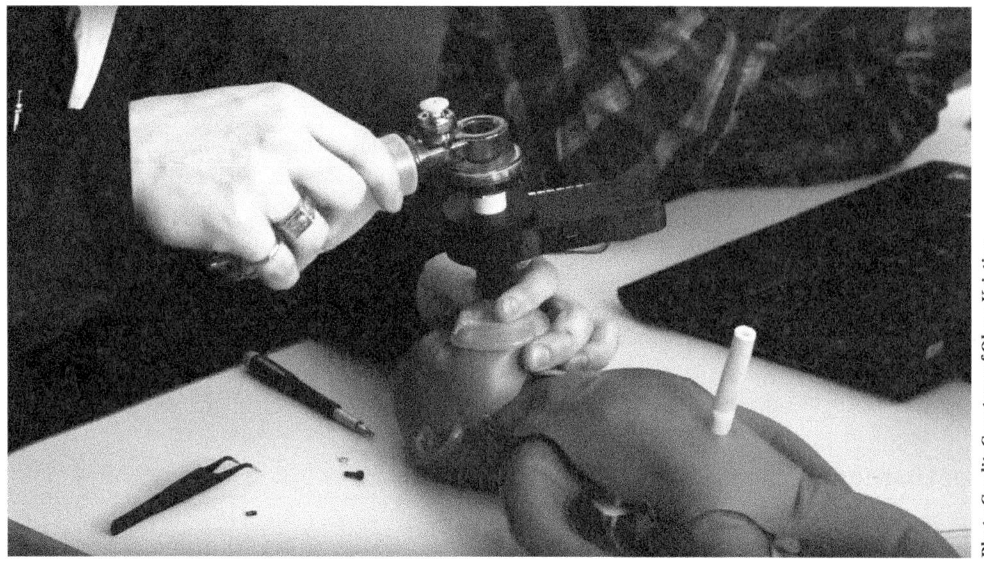

Photo Credit: Courtesy of Olson Kristian

FIGURE 4.10 An Arduino microcontroller was used to prototype the Augmented Infant Resuscitator or "AIR" in Uganda, which aims to combat infant asphyxia. An air-flow meter connected to an Arduino and LED-indicator strip helped convert what historically had been a "dumb" medical device, the air mask, into an intelligent, interactive device that provided real-time feedback to the medical professional, thus dramatically increasing the rate of correct device use.

Looks-Like Prototyping in Crowdfunding

The growth of online crowdfunding (e.g., Kickstarter and Indiegogo) and pitch videos, which are central to crowdfunding campaigns, have highlighted the value of prototypes in securing funding for a project or venture. In rewards-based crowdfunding, backers financially support a new product campaign often before the final product has been produced or sometimes even before a final product design has been chosen.

To demonstrate a new product and its benefits, creators of crowdfunding campaigns often must develop and feature looks-like prototypes to not only convey their creative vision but also signal their professionalism and dedication to their project. A well-designed prototype, particularly one that has received positive feedback from potential customers, is a strong signal of an entrepreneur's commitment to bring an innovation to market. In addition, it conveys that an entrepreneur has thought through the production plan, going from idea to final manufacture.

For example, Ryan Grepper, creator of The Coolest Cooler, which became the most funded project on Kickstarter in 2015 by raising over $13 million dollars, designed a high-end outdoor cooler with a built-in blender for making mixed drinks and Bluetooth speakers, available for a contribution of $249. The final product did not exist when the campaign launched—it had yet to be produced. An experienced industrial designer, Grepper leveraged multiple prototypes in his Kickstarter pitch video to communicate his innovative design, his passion for the project, and—through extensive prototyping—that he was ready and able to move quickly into production with known production partners.

Up until 2015, Kickstarter prohibited the use of photorealistic, digitally rendered prototypes to guard against campaign fraud. Kickstarter insists on physical prototypes, which, they believe, provide a stronger signal of the preparedness of the project creators. Although most prototypes are developed to test the attractiveness of product ideas with target customers, prototyping is also tremendously important in the move to commit to a final product design and consider the costs and methods of manufacturing. Production prototypes (i.e., comparatively late-stage prototypes) assist in the final planning of production and consider if the product has been designed, for example, to minimize the number of parts, chances of product failure and breakage, and the costs to produce.

Co-Creation

Up to this point, it might sound as if entrepreneurs should independently develop their prototypes and only later present them for feedback to target customers. This is consistent with the notion of designing *for* a target audience. In fact, often it is most useful to design *with,* meaning alongside, your target audience to not only validate their needs but also to discover unexpected entrepreneurial opportunities. This idea of customer engagement is at the center of the product design process sometimes referred to as *co-creation*, where product concepts are "co-created" with target customers.

In co-creation, target customers are engaged early and continuously in the process of idea generation and product development. They are asked to share their unique problems, wishes, and aspirations to get deep insights about their wants and needs *often before any product design is developed.* Unlike traditional market research methods, which rely on surveys and systematic data collection, co-creation relies on building trust and intimacy with your target customers such that they can guide and shape the innovation process. Best practices in co-creation are to involve target customers in problem/need clarification, idea generation, early prototyping, late prototyping, and even market strategy/market planning. As shown in the box, "Prototyping, Co-Creation, and Social Entrepreneurship," co-creation is particularly critical when you are looking to develop an innovation or entrepreneurial offering for an unfamiliar need or market.

Prototyping, Co-Creation, and Social Entrepreneurship

Social entrepreneurs focus on creating social value in areas such as health care, education, and the environment. The prototyping process is equally helpful in social entrepreneurship where the aim is to develop new products or services that have positive social impact.

In a course offered jointly by Babson College and Olin College of Engineering, known as Affordable Design and Entrepreneurship, one social venture aimed to generate income and reduce physical burden for gari-producing women in Ghana. Gari, which comes from grating and frying a starchy root vegetable known as cassava, must be pressed after grating to squeeze extra water from the pulp and aid in the removal of a naturally occurring toxin from some varieties. For well over a hundred years, female gari entrepreneurs—those who do the back-breaking work of preparing gari—have relied on a traditional system of pressing, whereby cassava mash is placed in porous sacks and squeezed with large rocks (refer figure. 4.11 shown in the next page), typically weighing a minimum of 80 lb. each. Often these women are dependent on help from family members or friends to prepare gari for market.

Asking, "How can gari pressing be done more rapidly, independently, and safely?" a team of undergraduate students partnered with gari-producing women in Ghana to consider new, improved approaches (see Figure 4.11). Engaging in a co-creation process with these women and through several rounds of prototyping, the team came up with an affordable, food-safe design with two lead screws and cranks that easily lets women independently press large amounts of cassava mash.

It is important to note that the women were engaged in every step of the process, including as experts on their needs during user research, during idea generation to consider novel designs and solutions to address their challenges, in evaluation to assess a number of works-like prototypes, and to recommend final product direction and pricing.

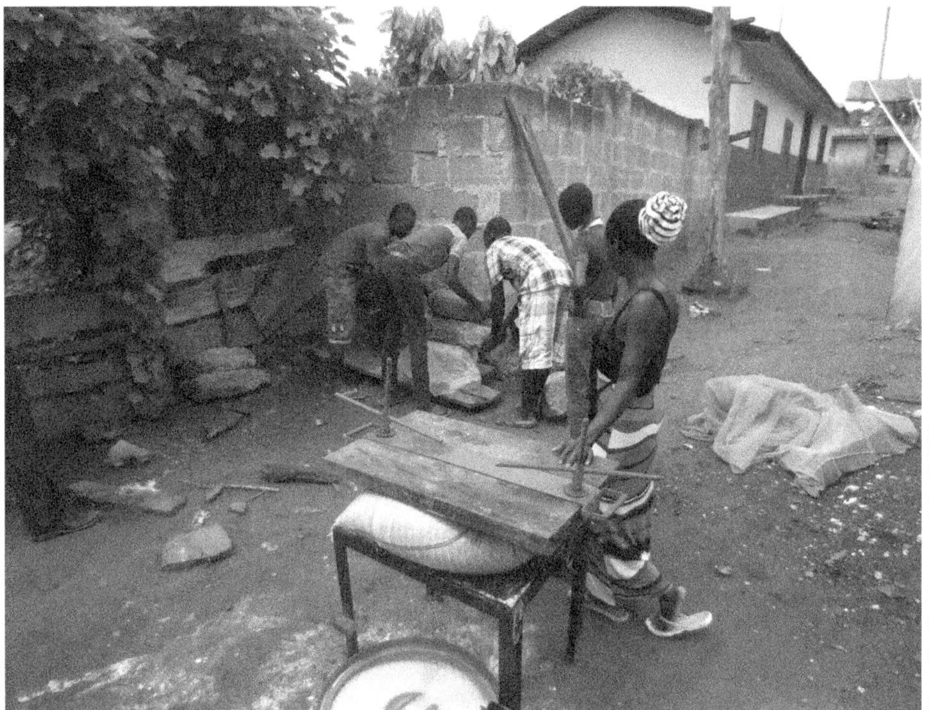

FIGURE 4.11 Working Prototype of a Gari Press.

Photo Credit: Courtesy of Dr. Erik Noyes

Prototyping Services

Up this point, we have focused almost exclusively on prototyping products. However, major elements of *services* can be prototyped as well. For example:

- A plumbing company wishing to experiment with a new 30-minute "arrival guarantee" for plumbing emergencies can set aside a plumber for rapid response to test the desirability of this new service.
- An entrepreneur with a new pickup-and-delivery concept for a dry cleaner can first experiment with just the pickup-and-delivery aspect of the service without building and operating an entire cleaning operation. For example, an existing dry cleaner/cleaning operation can be used to do the cleaning itself.
- A design company wishing to charge a fixed price for 30 design treatments of a company logo (e.g., 99Designs) can line up many designers to provide rapid turnaround on logo design ideas before building out a complete and costly coordination platform.

In the preceding service business examples, a works-like prototype might be offering a *simulation* of how a service is performed (and even actually delivering the service!) all to better understand the needs, wants, and wishes of the target customer. In fact, many ventures provide a mix of products and services, so there is much that can be prototyped to explore and shape an entrepreneurial opportunity. Given that services are one of the fastest-growing sectors of the global economy, we can easily extend our thinking about the prototyping process to services as well.

Minimum Viable Product

As we have discussed in this chapter, entrepreneurs should resist the temptation to develop a full product when exploring a venture idea. Not only is it generally time-consuming and costly to develop fully created products for potential customers, but it is also extremely risky to proceed down such a path without deep validation of value from the target market. We have also laid out the many tools and resources available to entrepreneurs for their prototyping process.

As an output of the prototyping process, many entrepreneurs aim to develop a **minimum viable product**, or "MVP," one that drives early engagement and rapid learning with customers. Eric Reis defines a minimum viable product as *that version of a new product concept that allows a team to collect the maximum amount of validated learning about customers with the least effort.*[2] As such, the minimum viable product can be one that is developed "just enough" (i.e., a product sketch, a hand-drawn representation of a mobile application) to seek customers' feedback.

Others view a minimum viable product as a more evolved prototype that *can be used by the customer and actually deliver value to a customer*, even in a rough form. For example, Zappos's founder Nick Swinmurn's minimum viable product was a basic website he built where he simply posted pictures of shoes available in a store near his home. If a customer placed an order—which they did—he just ran down to the shoe store, bought the shoes, and shipped them to the customer. Core to his concept for Zappos, Nick wanted to see if customers *were willing to order shoes online*, which they were! Many potential investors and partners told him customers would never order shoes online—but they did. This vital and relatively straightforward market experiment with a minimum viable product helped him confirm his entrepreneurial opportunity and ultimately guided the development of the final Zappos shoe-shopping platform (Figure 4.12).

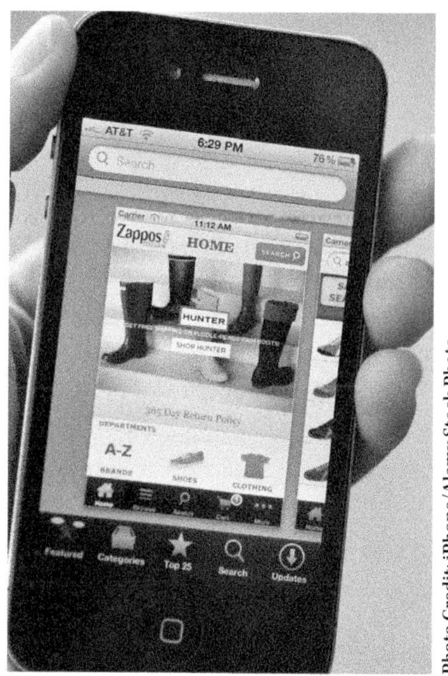

Photo Credit: iPhone/Alamy Stock Photo

FIGURE 4.12 Zappos's Website was First Tested as a Minimum Viable Product.

Nick Swinmurn did not need to go through the time, cost, and trouble of building a complete site and carrying an expensive inventory of shoes to test his core concept.

Instead, validation of the entrepreneurial opportunity came from a simple experiment—doing the bare minimum that was central to his concept. Launched in 1999, Zappos now has over 1,500 employees and carries over 150,000 styles of shoes. In 2009, Zappos was acquired by Amazon for $1.2 billion.[3]

The purpose of developing an MVP is for an entrepreneur to rapidly screen out—or reconfigure—a product or service concept. It is a market testing strategy that is used to evaluate product ideas very soon after their generation. Developing and testing an MVP focuses on *customer engagement first*—establishing your customer's true needs and willingness to pay—and product development second.[4]

This perspective of developing an MVP is radically different from more traditional notions of first developing a product, engaging customers about its desirability, and thereafter then positioning the product in the market to maximize its chances of success. The assumption is that early learning and multiple rounds of iteration—versus costly product development—is the priority early in the exploration of an entrepreneurial opportunity. A clear understanding of the customer's wants and needs is the absolute priority over any additional product development. For this reason, an MVP can be viewed as the *product with the highest return on investment risk* as it seeks to maximize the information learned about the customer per dollar spent.[5] Developing an MVP *first,* and testing it early and repeatedly, lines up with the earlier discussion on the importance of low-fidelity prototyping to explore and validate innovative product or services. Similarly, the development of an MVP and focus on customer engagement aligns with the approach of co-creation.

In short, an entrepreneur creates an MVP to avoid building a product that nobody wants. At the core, your MVP is a vehicle to drive *accelerated learning* about your entrepreneurial opportunity. The idea of developing an MVP is the humble acknowledgment that few entrepreneurs get things perfect out of the gate, so the fastest route to establishing a viable venture is to learn and iterate rapidly. General George Patton once said, "A good solution applied with vigor now is better than a perfect solution applied ten minutes later." Hopefully this chapter has caused you to think about options and approaches to prototype your entrepreneurial ideas.

CONCLUSION

In sum, prototyping is a *process,* and prototypes can be thought of in many ways:

- As market research and exploration tools
- As physical embodiments of a set of assumptions
- As fundraising tools for Crowdfunding efforts
- As a coordination device within an entrepreneurial team to identify research and development priorities

Entrepreneurs face the challenge of how to embody their ideas to seek vital feedback from customers. Although first-time entrepreneurs often doubt their abilities to create prototypes, with a little effort and creativity, most individuals can develop prototypes to clarify an entrepreneurial opportunity.

YOUR OPPORTUNITY JOURNAL

Reflection Points	Your Thoughts...
1. How might you leverage prototyping to explore your idea for an entrepreneurial venture?	
2. What simple prototype could you develop *today*, or this week, to test some core aspect of your concept?	
3. How might you develop multiple prototypes to seek a wide range of feedback from your target customer?	
4. How do you think 3-D printing might change how entrepreneurs develop prototypes as well as final products?	
5. How might you co-create opportunities with your target customer, that is, involve them early in your idea generation?	
6. How might you develop and test a minimum viable product (MVP) for your product or service concept?	

WEB EXERCISE

Watch this two-minute video example of how to demonstrate on how to get started with simple paper prototyping: https://www.youtube.com/watch?v=-RmY6F_2zhU. Remember, simple, low-fidelity prototyping is always the place to start.

Look at Fiverr.com to discover a wide range of affordable design services, including graphic design, industrial/product design, 3-D design, and Web development. If you did not already, look at 3Dhubs.com and Shapeways.com to learn more about 3-D printing services, some of which are likely available in your city. How might you leverage these resources to advance your innovation?

NOTES

1. Markham, S. K. & Hyunjung, L. *Product Development and Management Association's 2012 Comparative Performance Assessment Study*, 30: 412. 2013. Castellion, G. & Markham, S. K. New Product Failure Rates: Influence of Argumentum ad Populum and Self-Interest. *Journal of Product Innovation Management*, 30(5): 978. September 2013.
2. Ries, Eric. *Minimum Viable Product: A Guide*, http://www.startuplessonslearned.com/2009/08/minimum-viable-product-guide.html, August 3, 2009.
3. www.zappos.com, http://www.zappos insights.com/files/accounts/zappos/assets/ files/approved/MediaKit.pdf.
4. Blank, Steve. *The Four Steps to the Epiphany: Successful Strategies for Products that Win*, K&S Ranch Publishing. 2013.
5. Robinson, Frank. SyncDev, http://www. syncdev.com/minimum-viable-product/.

Case Balanced Snacking[1]

In a small apartment in Santa Monica, California, Gautam Gupta and Ken Chen found themselves at a crossroads. "Do we pursue this business idea or call it quits?" They had just finished running a simple experiment to test the willingness of the market to adopt their new business idea—healthy snacking direct to the consumer. Using Facebook to launch an advertisement, the pair sat back and waited to see what the public had to say. Much to their surprise, they were now faced with the task of fulfilling over 100 orders. Excitement gripped the two, but reality quickly set in.

The Beginning

Gautam Gupta started his entrepreneurial journey as a child in Orange County, California. Growing up, Gautam was largely uninterested in sports and struggled with his weight. In lieu of time spent playing outdoors, he took up an interest in trying to hustle different products on the playground. What started with selling pencils in second grade grew to selling candy and other items that might interest his classmates. In high school, he continued his journey by creating mix tapes of current popular music and selling them to fellow peers. Throughout school, he was an average student; he found far more validation in his entrepreneurial rather than academic endeavors.

Gautam's entrepreneurial aspirations were largely influenced by his family. His grandfathers both started companies in the steel industry of India. His mother worked for Silicon Valley Bank, which actively supports early-stage entrepreneurial companies. His father worked in the technology industry. Family conversations were always around business and opportunities.

College Years

Based on his entrepreneurial aspirations, Gautam chose to attend Babson College. Babson immersed Gautam in all things entrepreneurship. While coursework deepened his knowledge, extracurricular opportunities such as the entrepreneurship affinity dormitory, E-tower, which grouped like-minded students together, were a huge influence.

Life at Babson reinforced my entrepreneurial aspirations. All the businesses I started as a kid were fun, but at Babson I realized I could do something much bigger. Not only were the classes focused on entrepreneurship, but everyone at the school was talking about starting a business.

E-Tower and other Babson student organizations strive to provide resources for entrepreneurs including networking, conferences, speaker series, and mentorship. One of the key events that helped shape Gautam's collegiate experience was the annual rocket pitch event where students and alumni give a three-minute business pitch in front of interested investors and collaborators.

We called it pitching to the bullpen. It allowed you to pitch ideas and get feedback from fellow students, professors, experienced entrepreneurs, and investors.

At his first rocket pitch, Gautum formed a connection that fundamentally altered his path. It just so happened that a partner from the venture capital (VC) firm General Catalyst was judging pitches that day. Although Gautam was not actually pitching at this event, he was helping with the logistics and happened to strike up a conversation. The partner was so impressed by his conversation with Gautam that he invited him to intern at General Catalyst. From his junior to senior year, Gautam interned part-time during the school year and full-time during the summer. Upon graduation, Gautam was offered and accepted a full-time position with General Catalyst, where he was exposed to numerous startup enterprises.

General Catalyst

It was 2007 when Gautam stepped into this first full-time position with General Catalyst. Things were going really well for him and the company right up until the economic crash of 2008. General Catalyst became very conservative in their approach, as many businesses were struggling at the time.

There was a sense of fear that had come over the firm and the venture capital industry as a whole. Every investment decision was met with questions building on more questions.

During 2008, VC firms were reluctant to deploy capital into new investments and starting "pruning the bush," meaning they cut follow-on investments to all but the most promising of their portfolio companies. However, General Catalyst persevered and in 2010 decided to expand their operations beyond Boston. Gautam was given the opportunity to move to Silicon Valley and open the new office for General Catalyst.

He embraced this experience as he was the sole employee at this newly founded location for about six months. During this time Gautam was tasked with developing the West Coast brand of General Catalyst. He spent his time finding potential investments that focused on e-commerce and software as a service (SaaS) business models. One company left an impression on Gautam, The Honest Company, which is a direct-to-consumer (D2C) company focused on baby products (founded by, among

[1] This case was written by Eric Berglind and Andrew Zacharakis with support from the John H. Muller, Jr. Endowed Chair in Entrepreneurship at Babson College.

others, Jessica Alba). The D2C business model intrigued Gautam. In D2C, a company forms a strong relationship with the customer. The Honest Company wasn't reliant on distribution channels, like Walmart, that often had too much power in the relationship. D2C companies didn't have to fight for shelf space with other competitors. Instead, companies like The Honest Company had direct connections to the customer allowing them to collect customer desires and modify their offerings accordingly. Gautam wanted to explore this business model more deeply.

A Partnership in the Making

Ken Chen had known Gautam since college. Ken grew up in an entrepreneurial family, although the family was entrepreneurial by necessity as opposed to choice. Ken's family immigrated to America when Ken was young. They came looking for a better life and journeyed to where other relatives had gone. Upon arrival, with little English proficiency, Ken's parents relied on their family ties in the United States to gain employment. All of Ken's relatives were in the restaurant business at the time, so by association Ken's family was in the restaurant business. Soon, Ken's family started its own restaurant that Ken worked in while he was growing up.

Ken, like Gautam, found extracurricular activities more fulfilling than his studies. He was elected student council president and enjoyed playing basketball in high school. He found identity and philosophy in sports over all of his other exploits. He mentioned,

Sports teaches about hard work and merit, there is not much luck involved. If your coach yells at you, you learn not to take it personally. He is trying to help you improve so that the team will win. If you're benched, it means you're not as good as the player in front of you. I like that merit-based system. It motivates me to be my best enabling me to contribute to the team effort.

Ken viewed business similarly to sports; it should be merit based. If you're the best you can be and you have a strong team, you can win. That attitude drew him to Babson College, where he met Gautam. Both students lived in the E-tower and ultimately become roommates. Even before entering Babson, Ken pursued entrepreneurial ventures. He acquired a Realtor license, and during college, he continued to pursue real estate in addition to involvement at school. He had a particular interest in residential real estate and was easily able to raise funds via credit cards to acquire, renovate, and flip homes.

Ken graduated from Babson in 2006 and immediately went to work for JP Morgan in real estate finance. While he pursued his passion for real estate, Ken explored other entrepreneurial interests after work hours. Around 2008, he noticed that with the emergence of Facebook and social media, advertising was moving online versus offline. It just so happened that other Babson-based companies were doing well in this space, so Ken thought that he would pursue it further. Over the next few months, Ken moonlighted by working with advertising agency companies on improving their online advertising for clients. He learned how to execute online advertising more effectively than the agency companies for which he moonlighted. The inflection point came when Ken's revenue from his side activities grew greater than his income from his day job. He thought to himself,

I have to create my own agency. This is a new industry and because I'm young and unbiased by how things have always been done, I have the ability to learn it better than a seasoned marketing veteran. Experienced ad people are stuck in their offline world. My youth and understanding of the online world will allow me to leap ahead of existing players. I had an unfair advantage.

With the help of some friends from Babson, Ken launched his online advertising agency in 2009, W Media, which developed a performance advertising platform that empowered its clients to cost effectively access consumers across digital media channels. W Media became one of the first advertisers for Facebook. When W Media hit revenues in the tens of millions, Ken sold the firm and started looking for his next venture. Throughout his entrepreneurial journey, Ken and Gautam kept in touch. Ken recalls,

I saw Gautam as an exceptionally strong team member. He was articulate, was reliable, and carried himself in such a way that he earned respect from all he worked with.

Gautam, likewise, felt deep professional respect for his old college friend and roommate, Ken. They knew that they wanted to start a company together, but the question was, what kind of company?

The Seeds of an Idea

Armed with years of investor experience and industry knowledge, Gautam was ready to pursue his own venture. However, he wasn't sure what kind of business to start. Simultaneously, Ken was selling W Media and thinking of his next move. Gautam and Ken connected and started brainstorming new business ideas that they could pursue together. The timing was perfect as Gautam was still working at General Catalyst but trying to nail down the right business idea, and Ken was available to pursue something new. Gautam recalls,

We met up and started laying out the criteria for our new business idea. We wanted to work on something we were passionate about, but most of all we wanted to love what we were working on.

With that mind-set at the core of their brainstorming, they started exploring shared interests. It just so happened that they both were passionate about food, but this love of food stemmed from very different origins. Ken grew up working in a family restaurant, where he developed a love for working with food. Gautam actually struggled with food earlier in life, given that he was not very active and had poor dietary habits. He developed a weight problem that plagued him until his senior year of high school. Six months before Gautam started attending Babson College, he drastically changed his eating habits and worked hard to bring his weight down. Gautam successfully lost 70 pounds by the time he started college through food management versus crash dieting and extreme exercising. Gautam's habits transitioned from unhealthy snacking to a more balanced diet. With Ken's experience in the restaurant industry and Gautam's analytical approach to a balanced diet, food was where they wanted to work, but where in this large opportunity space should they launch a new business?

With a mutual mission, they proceeded to do as much market research as possible. They formed a new question, "What is not being done in the food industry?"

Their secondary research showed some interesting statistics about the industry as a whole. The U.S. snack food industry brought in $37.6B worth of revenue in 2015 and was projected to continue growing by 3.6% annually.[2] A study conducted by the University of North Carolina analyzing snacking trends between 1977 and 2006 showed that children were snacking as many as three times a day, whereas adults were snacking only two times; however, for both groups, this was one more snack per day than in 1977.[3] With the steady growth in leisurely snacking, obesity rates in the United States had grown as well. In 2012 the obesity rates were at 34.7% of the entire U.S. population.[4] Snacking seemed to be a lucrative industry, but was also the main cause of obesity and associated diseases. Class-action lawsuits against the snack and fast-food industries started to rise. The first one, *Pelman v. McDonald's Corporation*, was targeted at the fast-food giant McDonald's. However, this case was defended by McDonald's as the court ruled that eating McDonald's food and snack/fast food in general is the choice of the individual not the responsibility of the company.[5] This precedent has held for the myriad other cases brought against large fast-food and snack food companies to date. Based on lawsuits and obesity rates, yet a desire to still snack, there seemed to be an eager population searching for alternatives to traditional snacking. Would people want healthy options?

Gautam and Ken were intrigued. They continued to investigate the industry, now focusing on competitors and what they were doing in the market. Walking around a grocery store, they saw a clear division in foods that were for sale. There was fresh produce and packaged goods. They quickly decided against entering into the fresh produce area due to the lack of differentiation. Ken mentioned,

People pay a premium for branded packaged goods. It doesn't make sense to enter non-branded fresh food portion of the market. Margins are low, and it is expensive to brand produce.

With that in mind they decided to analyze packaged foods competitors. This market was much more attractive as all the products were highly differentiated from brand to brand, and there was lots of choice. They found that the margins for packaged foods were much higher than those of produce.

Gautam and Ken recognized that there were plenty of exciting businesses within the snacking industry. They could create a new brand, like a fellow Babson alum Pete Lescoe, who founded Food Should Taste Good. They could get into the huge market of dieting, which brought in $6.7B worth of revenue in 2015.[6] The two needed some time to brainstorm. They both flew to Santa Monica, California, where another former classmate offered his offices for them to use. During their long weekend, they started hashing out how they could answer the question of how to make snacking healthier. Taking a break from their brainstorming, the duo walked through the Santa Monica farmers' market. While strolling by the various vendor stands, Gautam noticed some almonds that had been uniquely flavored and was intrigued. This experience sparked two different ideas where Gautam was thinking of how new and unique flavors could be incorporated into snacks like the almonds he had seen. Ken was wondering, "How can farmers' market quality food be brought to the masses?"

With a more focused direction, they went to local grocery stores and observed what consumers were doing when purchasing snack foods. They noticed that customers were consistently checking the labels to determine allergy/dietary constraints. This key finding formed a theory that if they could create a way for people to tell them their allergy and dietary

---

[2] Ibisworld.com. Snack Food Production in the US. 2016.

[3] Crowley, C. The Snack Food Nation: A Culture of Near-Constant Eating Contributes to the Obesity Epidemic. Mar 26, 2012. Retrieved from: http://www.timesunion.com/living/article/The-snack-food-nation-3430561.php.

[4] Obesity Rates & Trends Overview: Obesity Rates Still High. 2016. Retrieved from: http://stateofobesity.org/obesity-rates-trends-overview/.

[5] WIlensky, S. and O'Dell, K. Where's the Beef?—The Challenges of Obesity Lawsuits. *Bloomberg*. Jul 18. 2013. Retrieved from: http://www.bna.com/wheres-the-beef-the-challenges-of-obesity-lawsuits/.

[6] Ibisworld.com. Weight Loss Services. 2016.

restrictions, then they could offer products tailored to match each individual customer. Another variable that additionally stoked their fire was that they noticed a lot of businesses were moving online (books, electronics, etc.); however, online food was still underdeveloped.

Testing Ideas

The biggest thing the duo had to do now was prove that they could garner interest in their new ideas. They quickly ruled out trying to develop a product that would go on a grocery store shelf. Grocery stores charged for shelf space, called slotting fees. Slotting fees gave power to the distribution channel. Moreover, it would be difficult to get deep intelligence on a customer if you had to go through the distribution channel to acquire that information. The time it would take to research and develop a variety of healthy snacks and develop partners that would display those snacks on their shelves would take months if not years. They determined there was no way to develop an unfair advantage over the competition with this model. Gautam recalled The Honest Company. Maybe it made sense to go D2C. Why not build a company that provided healthy snacks through the mail to customers on a monthly basis. The next logical step was to test the hypothesis that online snacks would sell.

Utilizing Ken's deep experience in online media and with Facebook, they set up a landing page with some snack options (see **Exhibit 4.1**). The first test was successful, and over 100 people signed up and asked to join, agreeing to pay a $22 monthly subscription fee. Gautam and Ken could either respond with an email explaining that the company didn't yet exist, which had the potential to frustrate these would-be customers and possibly lead to an online backlash, or they could try to fulfill these orders; in essence, testing the hypothesis that they could produce a product that customers wanted.

They ran to the local Costco and other bulk food stores to pull together enough product to start creating four to five different types of snack bags to offer potential customers. They packed each type of snack into one box so that each box provided a variety of healthy snacks. With labels bought at the local Staples, they started naming their new products and quickly displayed them on a single-page website (**Exhibit 4.2**). The whole endeavor cost them very little—just the cost of buying and repacking the snacks and the personal time to put up the webpage and Facebook sites. This small test seemed to confirm that people would be willing to buy snacks online and, better yet, would be willing to do so on a regular, monthly basis, but online food had a troubled history.

Photo Credit: Brian Macdonald/ Getty Images

EXHIBIT 4.1 Snack Options

Photo Credit: © Reproduced with permission of Nature Box

EXHIBIT 4.2 Packaged Snacks

One of the pioneers in the online food service market was Webvan. This company offered premium food products at reasonable prices to be shipped directly to your home or office. The idea was to try to save customers time and effort for their regular grocery shopping by taking advantage of the proliferation of Internet-based startups during the late 1990s. Contrary to what Gautam and Ken were proposing, Webvan gave its customers the ability to go online and order groceries and have them delivered to your home in 30 minutes or less. It seemed that Webvan was set to flourish with one of the largest predicted IPOs in the Silicon Valley history but unfortunately the company went bankrupt in 2001 due to high capital costs and over-expansion, spending over $800 million in the process. Amazon has since acquired the company and is still operating it today, however with some constructive changes.[7] Gautam and Ken thought that the problem with Webvan was that it was just a distribution channel. It sold goods that you could buy in a grocery store, meaning that there was little margin and very high operating costs. With recorded business failures in the market, Gautam and Ken had to answer, "Why can we do this better?"

Exhibit 4.3 Pro Forma Income Sheet

		2016		2017		2018		2019		2020
Subscribers (yr avg)		10,000		20,000		40,000		100,000		250,000
Revenue										
Subscription	$	2,394,000	$	4,788,000	$	9,576,000	$	23,940,000	$	59,850,000
Less discount	$	(299,250)	$	(598,500)	$	(1,197,000)	$	(2,992,500)	$	(7,481,250)
E-commerce	$	300,000	$	500,000	$	750,000	$	1,500,000	$	2,500,000
Total Revenue	**$**	**2,394,750**	**$**	**4,689,500**	**$**	**9,129,000**	**$**	**22,447,500**	**$**	**54,868,750**
Cost of Goods Sold	**$**	**1,677,600**	**$**	**2,995,800**	**$**	**5,272,800**	**$**	**13,182,000**	**$**	**32,955,000**
Gross Profit	**$**	**717,150**	**$**	**1,693,700**	**$**	**3,856,200**	**$**	**9,265,500**	**$**	**21,913,750**
Margin		*30.0%*		*35.4%*		*40.3%*		*38.7%*		*36.6%*
OpEx	**$**	**750,000**	**$**	**1,250,000**	**$**	**2,000,000**	**$**	**3,000,000**	**$**	**6,000,000**
Marketing Spend	$	1,000,000	$	2,000,000	$	3,000,000	$	3,000,000	$	4,000,000
EBITDA	**$**	**(1,032,850)**	**$**	**(1,556,300)**	**$**	**(1,143,800)**	**$**	**3,265,500**	**$**	**11,913,750**
EBITDA %		−43%		−33%		−13%		15%		22%
Assumptions										
Subscription Rate	$	19.95	$	19.95	$	19.95	$	19.95	$	19.95
Intro. Discount (3 mos)		50%		50%		50%		50%		50%

What's Next

Lots of other questions still had to be answered. Would, as they expected, a D2C model like The Honest Company work for snacks? How would you scale such a business, especially sourcing raw ingredients? How many different varieties of snacks would you need? Would they need to be changed every month? Could you build your own branded snacks, which would allow higher margins, or would people prefer brands they already knew? Gautam put together a simple pro forma income sheet of what the business might look like (**Exhibit 4.3**), and it seemed promising, but there were lots of assumptions that needed validation. Gautam and Ken wanted to proceed, but how could they start validating these assumptions at a low cost?

Discussion Questions

1. How should Gautam and Ken address the questions they've raised? What kind of hypotheses, prototypes, and market tests can they run at a low cost to further prove the business model?
2. What other questions should Gautam and Ken be thinking about?
3. When and how should they scale the business? Will they need to raise outside capital? Where would it come from?

5 The Importance of Business Models

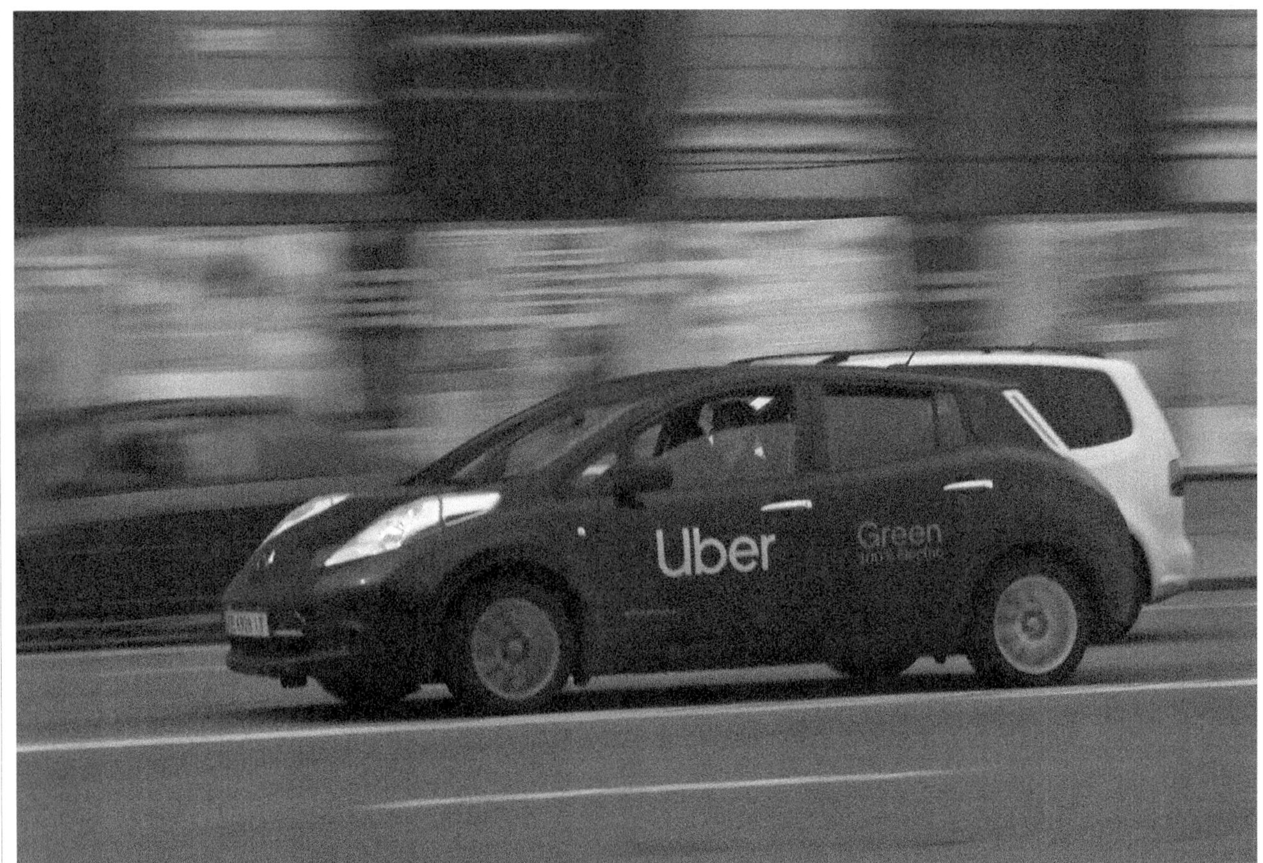

Photo Credit: Kharchenko/NurPhoto via Getty Images

Uber disrupts the taxi industry with an innovative business model.

Introduction

Once you've identified your opportunity, the next step is to devise a strategy to pursue that opportunity. Although you're probably familiar with the basic strategy categories from previous coursework—differentiation, low cost, niche—many would-be entrepreneurs fail to grasp the

This chapter was written by Angelo Santinelli

intricacies of devising and implementing their strategy. All strategies are driven by the company's business model. At the heart of any successful startup is a business model that generates enough cash to sustainably grow and gain market share.

Many entrepreneurs focus too much on writing a pitch or business plan for the sole purpose of raising money, rather than to prove out for themselves that there is a large and growing market with an important need or problem to be addressed. When using this approach neither the pitch, nor the business plan hold up to the scrutiny of investor inquiry because the most important questions and analysis are being put off to some future time after ample cash has been raised. While this approach might work well when money is in abundant supply, it ignores the most important depleting asset of any entrepreneur, time. The desire to execute on an idea sometimes outweighs the importance of discovering precisely what you should be building and for whom. By putting the cart before the horse, you run the risk of building the wrong product for the wrong market and having to "pivot," which is a term that has become synonymous with "we screwed up and will have to spend more time and money to do the right thing."

The Problem with Pivots

Though there have been many successful high-profile pivots namely Twitter, Paypal, Instagram, and Pinterest, the truth is that most fail. The pivots that do work usually occur during the customer discovery phase of a startup's life. This should be a period when the company is rapidly and inexpensively testing several ideas to determine which will resonate. During this phase when the company is in search of a repeatable, scalable business model, cash burn should be at a minimum. This ensures that if your first idea fails, you'll have time and money to try something else.

It's when a company tries to pivot during the execution phase that the chance of success become less, because a lot of real and political capital has been spent—the organization and operations have already scaled and the initial product is fully developed. At this point in the life of the company it has already raised two or perhaps three rounds of funding, scaled sales and marketing, and the company profile is higher than it would be in the discovery phase.

Pivoting at this point presents several challenges: (1) Investor fatigue and loss of confidence. Pivot once during the discovery phase and it can be interpreted as learning and adapting to the findings. Pivot two or three times and investors begin to wonder if it is worth continuing, especially if the pivot comes too late and after most of the capital has been used. (2) The best employees head for the door. There are two critical jobs in a startup—the people who make things and the people who sell things. The first do not enjoy scrapping everything that they have worked on previously in favor of a new thing. Simply put, developers hate to be whipsawed. You can usually sell one new vision, but too many times and they lose faith and move on. Salespeople, especially the good ones, will not hang around if the prospect of making money has once again been pushed off into the future. They will also protect their reputations with their best customers and not want to sell them and resell them a new story. Take too long to get the product right and once again the best people head for the door first.

The lesson here is do more experimenting, hypothesis testing early and you might preserve enough trust and money to try successfully pivoting once.

Building a company from scratch is always a challenging task and one that deserves a thoughtful and thorough approach to understand that various elements that comprise your business model. Figures 5.1 and 5.2 represent the critical elements of any business model, how they relate to the competitive and industry context, and help to support a comprehensive financial strategy. There are a series of questions that accompany each element that need to be answered. Think of the Business Model Wheel as an experiment, or multiple experiments, each with a hypothesis that you plan to either prove or disprove. The purpose is to work through answering the most critical questions related to each element, assess their fit, and to try and find a model that is scalable and repeatable. It is an iterative process. This approach allows you to address several potential opportunities simultaneously, constantly iterating to discover what the customer wants and is willing to pay to solve an important problem. Once a working business model is found, it can

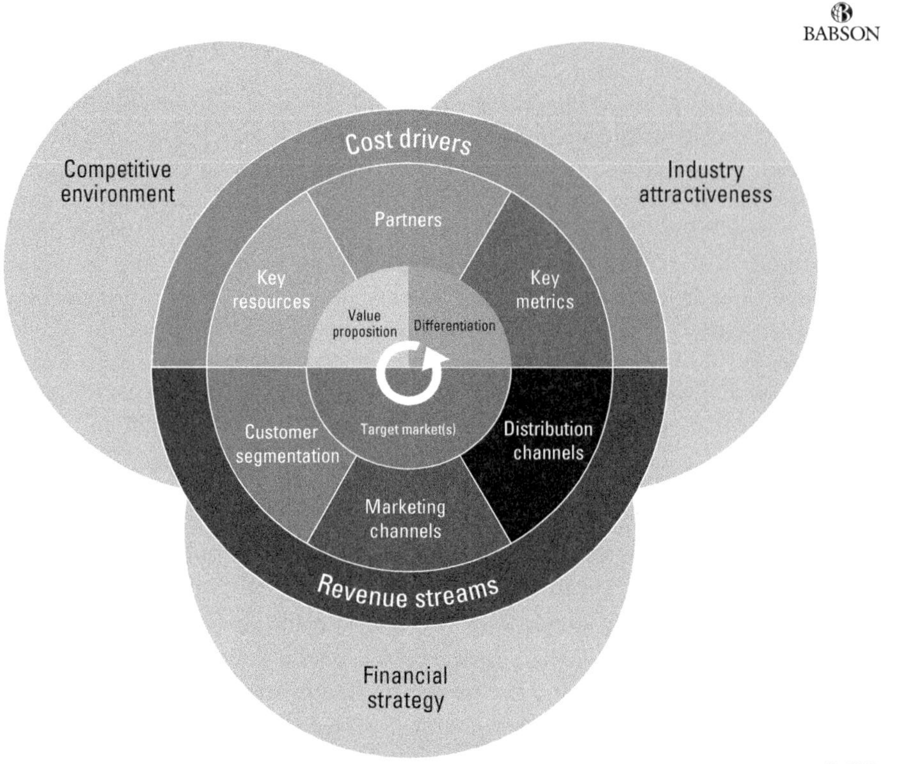

FIGURE 5.1 Babson Business Model Wheel.

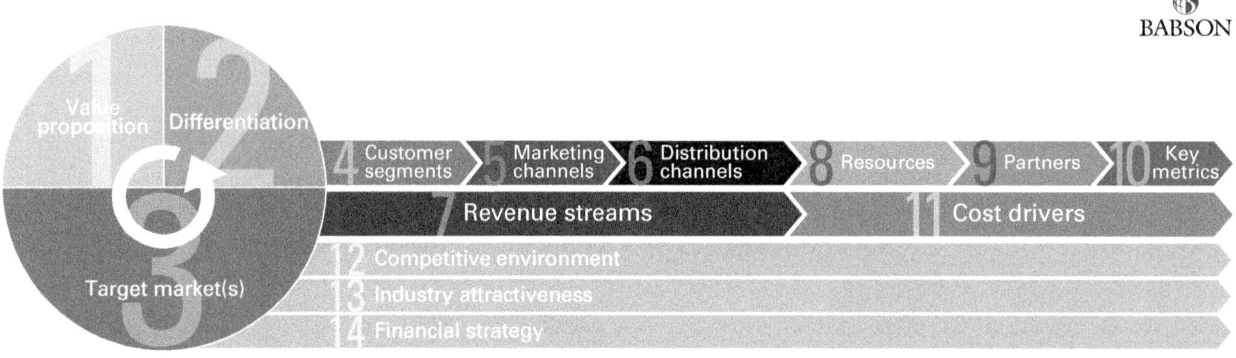

FIGURE 5.2 Steps to Develop your Business Model Wheel.

be translated into an operating plan that the company can execute, while business plans have a tendency to go into a file cabinet.

So, what is the difference between a business plan, a business model and an operating plan? It's all in the approach, timing and use. Business model exploration is an iterative process that should yield incredible knowledge and confidence in your idea. It can then be put into a tactical operating plan that can be shared with the company, executed, and monitored.

The Core *(Steps 1, 2, and 3)*

At the core of the business model wheel is the foundation upon which every great business is built—*The Value Proposition, Differentiation, and Target Market*. These are not necessarily created in the sequence in which they appear. It is best to work on them simultaneously and in concert with customer interactions.

The Value Proposition addresses the reasons why customers will purchase whatever it is that you are selling. It answers several key questions:

- *What is it?*
- *Who is it for?*
- *Why do they need it?*
- *How does it work?*
- *What is unique or different?*

The first four questions allow you to consider the product offering, the target audience, the compelling reason for them to take action, and the experience that you hope for them to have while using your product. Customers require a reason to purchase—an unmet need, a problem to be solved, an experience they desire to have. Your value proposition can be thought of as a collection of reasons as to why customers will part with their hard earned money. The benefits of what you are providing must clearly outweigh the costs. In a world with endless possibilities and businesses competing for a share of wallet, your solution must address the customer's problem in a manner that focuses on the most important needs in new and different ways that yield the best results.

Value Proposition Example: Uber's Unique Customer Value Proposition

Although Uber is widely criticized for its work culture, corporate governance, and treatment of its drivers, its Customer Value Proposition is simple and easy-to-understand. The message, "Move the way you want," which is taken from the company's homepage conveys to drivers and passengers alike what the service is and for whom.

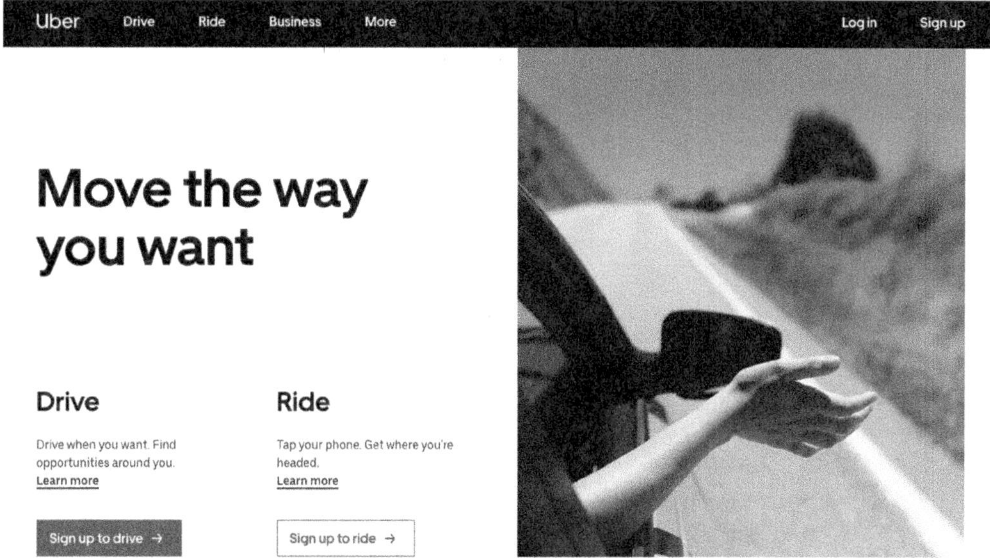

Below the tag line it clearly outlines why they need this service. For drivers they can set their own hours of operation and work where they like. For passengers it conveys simplicity, "Tap your phone. Get where you're headed. If you want to know more, just click and find out how it works and, without explicitly stating, how it is unique and better than a typical cab."

Why ride with Uber

Rides on demand

Get a reliable ride in minutes, at any time and on any day of the year.

Budget-friendly options

Compare prices on every kind of ride, from daily commutes to special evenings out.

An easy way to get around

Tap and let your driver take you where you want to go, worry-free.

Differentiation is broken out as its own rather than being lumped in with the value proposition even though differentiation is an important part of the overall value proposition. This is done specifically to bring attention to one of the most overlooked and misunderstood elements of the value proposition.

Your differentiation must be something that is truly not easily copied in short order, or easily procured. It must be something that satisfies an important customer want or need in a significantly unique and beneficial way. To start, think of your differentiation as addressing one or more of three needs—*Air, Aspirin*, or *Addiction*. Air is a necessity. You need it to survive. Aspirin addresses a pain. Addiction is neither a necessity, nor a pain reliever, but something that you feel a strong desire to use. If you are addressing a necessity, you should ask yourself how the customer is solving the problem today and does your solution create enough of a benefit to convince them to switch? If you are addressing a pain, a good question to ask is, if you are addressing an issue that has, or will have, dire consequences if not addressed? In other words, are you solving a "top 3 problem" with adverse personal or economic ramifications for the customer? Addiction is more difficult to predict, but if achieved can have enormous market potential. For instance, who could have ever imagined that billions of people around the world would have Facebook accounts, or post photos regularly to Instagram?

Your differentiation must also *resonate* with the customer. It is not enough to say that your product has 25 features, while your competitor's product only has 15. What is important is to have those few key features that the customer can't live without, or perhaps have high switching costs. For example, media measurement firm Nielsen Holdings Plc, moved 56,000 employees from Microsoft Corp.'s business software to the paid versions of Google's G Suite. Nielsen executives realized that 60% of their employees were under the age of 35 and had years of experience using the free versions of Gmail and Google Docs. Despite having fewer features, the Google's products focus on "new ways of working" and more fashionable office trends, like remote work and consumer-style applications that millennials are more accustomed to using.[1]

Last, in order to close the deal, you should be able to *substantiate* any claims that you make about your product or service. Most customers do not like taking risk and will require more proof of the claims that you are making. Substantiation can be accomplished in any number of ways. Customer case studies and testimonials are just two that are often used along with product awards or more complex substantiation research. However, do not be tempted to push the limits when it comes to substantiation and it is probably good to even avoid simple *puffery*.[2] Remember that competitors, regulators, and consumers will place a high level of scrutiny on any claims that you make. So be certain to establish and comply with a clear approval and due diligence policy for claims that you make about your product or service.

Lack of Substantiation

It is never good to deceive the public by pushing the truth or making unsubstantiated claims. When companies cross the line it can cost them millions of dollars and lost trust from the negative publicity that usually accompanies scandals.

Take for instance Volkswagen who falsely advertised environmentally friendly diesel cars. In March of 2016, the Federal Trade Commission (FTC) filed a lawsuit against the company claiming that VW had deceived customers with false claims of "Clean Diesel" vehicles. Prior to the lawsuit, it was exposed that the company had been cheating on emissions test for at least seven years.

The company was fined $4.3 billion in the United States to resolve criminal and civil penalties and an additional $1.18 billion by German authorities.[3]

If your value proposition includes clear differentiation that resonates with the customer and can be substantiated in a believable manner, the probability of making a sale are greatly enhanced.

The Market *(Steps 4, 5, 6, and 7)*

A common flaw of business plans and presentations, in particular in the high-tech industry, is the hyper-focus on the product or idea. Any seasoned investor will tell you that they invest first in teams and second in potentially large and growing market opportunities. While the idea is important, it does not paint a complete picture of the opportunity. As a first step, you should identify the target market, or markets for whom you are creating value. Even though this is a first step, the analysis should go much deeper than to simply identify what is commonly referred to as the *Total Available Market (TAM)*. The TAM is best defined as the total market demand for a product or service. However, the biggest way to lose credibility with investors is to recite someone else's market research and then proclaim that you will get 1% or 2% of the TAM. This type of over simplified thinking will only serve to increase perceived risk in the minds of investors. Instead, do your own analysis of the market. At a minimum, drill down to the next level of market segmentation, the *Serviceable Available Market (SAM)*. The SAM is the segment, or segments, of the TAM that you plan to target your product or service for sale. Initially, the targets identified are within realistic reach given your company's budget and location. This level of segmentation helps you identify those customer segments for whom the value proposition resonates and are likely prospects. Then, as will be explained in step #4, you can drill down even deeper to determine the portion of the SAM you can likely capture as customers. This segment is referred to as the *Serviceable Obtainable Market* (SOM).

For example, let's assume that you are going to open a specialized fitness studio for women in your town that you hope to expand in the future. Your TAM would be the worldwide fitness market. If you were the only game in town and had the ability to expand into every country, then the TAM would be your market, but this is not realistic.

If you are starting off in your town then demand for your studio will be based upon certain segments of the female population and their exercise habits. You might also make some comparisons to similar types of studios in towns with similar demographics to yours. Therefore, your SAM would be the estimated demand for your type of studio within your geographic area.

Since you are likely not the only exercise offering in your area, you would have to further segment the market by taking into consideration how far women are willing to travel to your studio and what other opportunities exist for them to get exercise. This narrower target would be your SOM.

The next three steps focus on outward customer facing elements of the business model. The purpose here is to build atop the foundation that you created in steps 1–3 by further identifying your customer segments and considering how you plan to communicate with them to build awareness, trial and purchase. Another element to consider is sales and distribution of your product or service and the ongoing relationship that your customer wishes to have with you. Finally, how to do you make money? What are the drivers of revenue and how will you price your product or service?

Customer Segments *(Step 4)*

In the early stages of a startup, both the customer and the offering are continuously being explored. As you begin to narrow down both, individual customer segments, especially those most likely to be early innovators and adopters of your product become better understood. We call this the *Serviceable Obtainable Market (SOM)*. By understanding individual segment personas, size, and growth potential you can begin to answer critical questions related to how, why and where they will purchase? What and how they will pay? What is the extent of the relationship required and other services they wish for you to provide? And, how profitable each segment might be now and in the future?

Questions to consider:

- *What is the Serviceable Obtainable Market?*
- *Where do they purchase?*
- *How do they purchase?*
- *Why do they purchase?*
- *What and how do they pay?*
- *What relationship is required for each?*
- *What other products or services do they want you to provide?*
- *How profitable is each segment?*

Marketing Channels *(Step 5)*

In the 1989 movie, *Field of Dreams*, an Iowa farmer, hearing voices, interprets them as a command to build a baseball diamond in his fields; he does and the 1919 Chicago White Sox show up along with hundreds of fans to watch them play without spending a dime to reach them! How you plan to communicate with the target customer(s) to build awareness, trial and purchase, and at what cost, is another consideration that is often overlooked especially by new entrepreneurs. A *Field of Dreams* marketing strategy rarely works. Even in some situations where lightning strikes and an inexpensive video goes viral, which happened with Dollar Shave Club's first video, this initial success must be followed up with a more comprehensive marketing strategy to build brand awareness.

Depending upon the type of business, the cost of customer acquisition can be a significant operating expense. Careful consideration and planning must be given to the target audience, the message, the appropriate channels, content types, and frequency necessary to build awareness of your brand.

Questions to consider:

- *What are the best ways to reach our target segments?*
- *What are their sources of information?*
- *Whom do they trust?*
- *What is the cost of customer acquisition (CAC)?*
- *What is the customer lifetime value (CLTV)?*

CAC and CLTV

The Cost of Customer Acquisition (CAC) and Customer Lifetime Value (CLTV) are two important measures of sales and marketing efficiency. These measures answer the simple question: Is the lifetime value of a customer (CLTV) more than the cost to acquire that customer (CAC)? You might also see this expressed as a ratio CLTV:CAC. In any case, you want your CLTV to be significantly higher than your CAC. If you are using the ratio, a good rule of thumb is that CLTV should be at least three times more than the CAC, or a ratio of 3:1.

For founders this simple calculation provides answers to other important questions that are part of the business model like:

- Do I have the right go-to-market strategy?
- How much can/should I invest in sales and marketing?
- Which customers should I target and with which products/services?

These and other questions will cause you to think more about where you spend both your time and money to capture each additional customer.

There are a couple of ways to calculate CLTV. The first is with the formula:

CLTV = Average Revenue per Customer/Customer Churn

or you can calculate CLTV using the following formula:

CLTV = Average Revenue per Customer x Average Customer Lifetime

For example, assume that you are selling a subscription to a mobile app for $6.00 per month and the average customer lifetime is 24 months. The CLTV is:

$6 x 24 = $144

CAC can be calculated using the formula:

CAC = Total Sales and Marketing expense/Number of New Customers

Let's assume that you spent $5,000 on online marketing to attract 135 new customers. Therefore, your CAC would be:

$5,000/135 = $37

The CLTV:CAC ratio would then be $144/$37 = 3.89

Distribution Channels *(Step 6)*

How do you plan to sell to your customer(s)? Will you build a sales force and sell direct, or sell through indirect channel partners? Is your business well suited to an Omni-channel[4] approach? Determining the most appropriate and cost-effective channel is another consideration that will affect both cost and revenue potential. Today's customers want speed and convenience of purchase. It is important to understand the relationship and services that customers desire and factor it into your business model.

Questions to consider:

- *How will you reach the customer? Each segment?*
- *How are they reached today? Direct? Indirect? Owned? Partnered?*
- *What services/relationship is offered with each?*

- *Which channels work best?*
- *Are the channels integrated?*
- *Which channels are most cost efficient?*

Revenue Streams *(Step 7)*

Revenue is often represented in the business plan as a series of annual numbers that grow exponentially year-over-year. When displayed graphically the revenue line resembles a "hockey stick." Ask how the numbers were determined and, at best, there might be some estimates of unit growth. Probe more deeply into the support for the numbers and the business case typically falls apart.

Revenue drivers, streams, pricing and margins need to be well understood and estimates based on primary, as well as secondary, research and comparable data. What drives revenue is customer demand. Customer demand is driven by market size and growth, and your ability to best meet market needs at a price and place that is amenable to the customer. Other things to consider are sales cycle time, frequency of purchase, volume of purchase, and breakeven points.

Streams of revenue relate to the variety of ways in which you make money by selling your product or service. Having multiple streams is often preferred to a single stream of revenue. Following are several examples of revenue streams:

- Unit Sales—Sell a product or service to customers on a per unit basis
- Advertising Fees—Sell opportunities to distribute messages
- Franchise Fees—Sell and support a replicable business for others to invest in, grow, and manage locally
- Utility Fees—Sell goods and services on a per-use or as-consumed basis
- Subscription Fees—Charge a fixed price for access to your services for a period of time or series of uses
- Transaction Fees—Charge a fee for referring, enabling, or executing a transaction between parties
- Professional Fees—Provide professional services on a time-and-materials contract
- License Fees—Sell the rights to use intellectual property

Pricing must also be given careful thought and be market tested, as it will affect margins. Here too there are a number of ways to determine the appropriate fixed or dynamic pricing methods. Perhaps the best example of dynamic pricing is Uber's "Surge Pricing." Employing an algorithm to set price proportionate to demand, prices increase during peak periods to encourage more drivers to go online.

As you can see there is a lot more to understanding revenue than the typical "hockey stick" graph might imply.

Questions to consider:

- *What are the drivers of revenue*[5]*?*
- *What are customers willing to pay? What are the pricing mechanisms?*
- *How do they pay? Are there alternative methods of payment?*
- *What is the average time to a sale? Frequency of purchase? Volume of purchase?*
- *What is the contribution margin?*

- *What are the breakeven points? (unit volume, sales volume)*
- *Where is there leverage in the revenue model?*

Product and Operations *(Steps 8, 9, 10, and 11)*

Now that you have an understanding of the various customer segments and their needs, the question that remains is can you build a product or service cost effectively? Understanding resource needs and potential partnerships are necessary steps in answering this question. Understanding the resources necessary, their availability, and their associated costs are an important series of steps in understanding your business model.

Resources *(Step 8)*

Understanding resource intensity is another important element of your business model. Resources tend to cluster around four categories: (1) human resources; (2) physical resources; (3) intellectual resources; and, (4) financial resources.

In some businesses people costs can add up to 70–80% of total operating expenses. Understanding how and when to recruit and onboard people is an extremely important exercise that can have a large impact on cash burn. As part of your overall operating plan, take time to understand what human resource are required at the various phases of company launch and growth. The hiring process takes time and finding the right fit is paramount for young companies.

Capital expenses can also weigh heavily on cash burn. Think about what assets truly need to be owned, versus rented or borrowed especially in the early years. For instance, do you really need to sign a two or three-year lease for space when you are just starting out? Or, would it make more sense to sublet space from another company that over-estimated their space needs? Low capital intensity can be a real advantage.

Know what intellectual resources need to be protected. Patents can be expensive to file and expensive to defend. In some industries (i.e., software) there is an ongoing debate over patent reform. Be sure to stay up-to-date on changes to the laws and get legal advice.

Understanding the financial resources required to launch and grow your business is a necessary exercise. Undertaking the task of building an integrated pro forma financial statement is well worth the time and effort. It is imperative that you accurately estimate the total capital required to get to breakeven and how you plan to source that capital over time. Too many startups underestimate the capital requirements to achieve significant milestones that will allow them to raise additional capital at a higher valuation. This can lead to significant dilution for the founders at best, and bankruptcy at worst.

Questions to consider:

- *What key assets are required to deliver on the value proposition? (Human, financial, physical, intellectual)*
- *Are these resources available to you at a reasonable cost?*
- *What can be rented, leased or borrowed rather than purchased?*

Partners *(Step 9)*

Knowing what alliances, joint ventures and agreements with outside entities are required to deliver on the value proposition are important as they can affect time to market and cost to build and deliver your product or service. Understand the activities that are worth outsourcing versus those activities and capabilities that should be developed in house. Can you reduce risks and uncertainties through partnering? Especially in the early stages of company development it is helpful to understand what capabilities need to be owned and controlled and which are better off done by a trusted partner.

Questions to consider:

- *Who are your key partners?*
- *What value is delivered by each?*
- *How critical are partners to delivering the value proposition?*
- *What key resources or activities are delivered by each?*
- *What risks or uncertainties are reduced?*

Key Metrics *(Step 10)*

There is a wise adage that you can't manage what you can't measure. Recall that the business model is initially a hypothesis that you are trying to prove or disprove. Even after a working business model is found you must monitor your progress to plan. Most businesses are fairly good at monitoring financial results, but financials are a backward look at progress. Understand the most critical elements of your business model that inform your financials and build a dashboard to monitor those elements in near real-time. This will help you understand patterns in your business that may help you address issues before they show up in your financial statements. Figure 5.3 shows a dashboard that captures key metrics for a business.

Questions to consider:

- *What are the key measures of business model success?*
- *How will value delivery to the customer be measured?*
- *How are performance standards developed?*
- *How do these metrics inform your revenue and costs?*

Cost Drivers *(Step 11)*

Few startups cease to exist because the product doesn't work. When most startups fail it is because they ran out of money before achieving significant milestones that gave investors the confidence they needed to continue their support. Similar to revenue, you must understand what activities and resources drive costs. Unit costs to produce and deliver your product or service should be well understood. Every entrepreneur should understand how to calculate breakeven, cost to acquire a customer, and customer lifetime value, as well as other key metrics that drive costs and affect overall financial viability.

Questions to consider:

- *What are the cost drivers? (Activities, resources, standards)*
- *What is the resource intensity of producing your product or service?*
- *What is the unit cost structure?*
- *Are there economies of scale or scope?*
- *What costs are fixed? Which costs are variable?*
- *Is the value proposition cost driven or value driven?*
- *Where is there leverage in the cost model?*

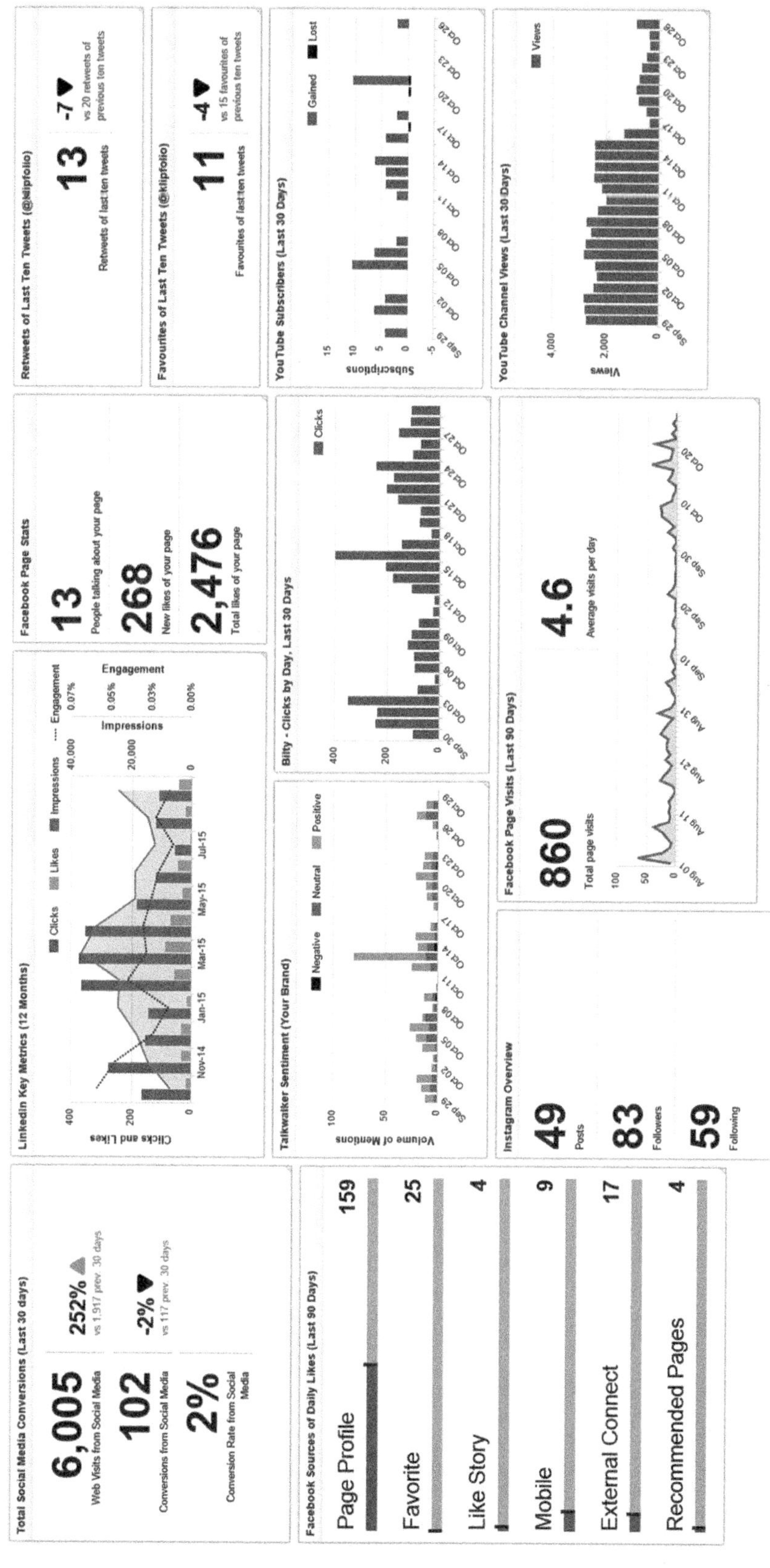

FIGURE 5.3 Dashboard Example
Source: Mikhail_Grachikov/Depositphotos

- *What is the cost to acquire a customer (CAC)?*
- *What are the working capital requirements?*

The External Enviroment and Financial Strategy *(Steps 12, 13, and 14)*

Competitive Environment *(Step 12)*

No business model should be developed in a vacuum. Context is everything, especially as it relates to the competitive environment and industry attractiveness. To say that you have no competitor is naïve and another signal that will raise perceived risk to investors. While you may believe that you have no direct competitors there are likely substitutes, potential new entrants and those existing players with the means to react to new market opportunities as they arise. At a minimum, having the customer remain with the status quo solution can be considered competition. A thorough and honest competitive review will leave you with an understanding all potential competitive threats now and in the future.

Questions to consider:

- *Who are the known competitors?*
- *Who might enter the market?*
- *Are there possible substitutes to your product or service?*
- *What are their strengths, weaknesses?*
- *What resources do they have?*
- *What will the intensity of the rivalry be like?*
- *How might they react to competitive pressures?*

Industry Attractiveness *(Step 13)*

A bad business can usually be fixed. A bad team can be replaced. A bad industry should be avoided. Some industries have structural and regulatory challenges that simply make it extremely difficult for new entrants to compete effectively. Again, it is important to investigate the contextual factors that exist in your industry. Note the trends that may be helpful and those that may be harmful. Understand barriers to entry and exit and the industry structure. While there may be opportunities for disruption, be certain that size of the prize is worth the cost to play the game.

Questions to consider:

- *What if any contextual factors exist that are favorable/unfavorable for the business?*
- *Possible regulatory changes?*
- *Global economic changes?*
- *Consumer and business trends?*

Financial Strategy *(Step 14)*

The financial strategy is the last step in the process and it should support the execution of the business model. The plan should clearly document all of the critical assumptions made in the business model, as well as the effect that changes to these assumptions will have on capital requirements. Is the amount of capital required under different scenarios available at a reasonable cost? What can go right? What can go wrong? What can you do to mitigate risks?

Questions to consider:

- *How much capital is needed to execute the business model?*
- *Is this capital accessible and at a reasonable cost?*
- *What are the critical assumptions in our financial model?*
- *What is the financial impact of positive/negative changes to these assumptions?*

CONCLUSION

Once you have an idea for a business and you've deemed it an opportunity, the next step is to assess how you will execute and develop that business. The Business Model Wheel (BMW) helps you understand the various elements of the business and how they all fit together. Figure 5.1 shows the various steps in the BMW and the questions associated with those steps. Just as with the Opportunity Checklist (Chapter 3) and Rapid Prototyping (Chapter 4), building your BMW is an iterative process. As you initially answer the questions associated with the various steps, you'll likely be making a number of assumptions. Your task to successfully execute on your business is to validate those assumptions with rigorous research and interactions with your targeted core customer. If you need to raise outside capital, you can rest assured that your investors will ask many of the questions raised in the BMW. Your ability to answer with authority will go a long way to giving the investors (and you) the confidence to support your venture.

YOUR OPPORTUNITY JOURNAL

Reflection Point	Your Thoughts...
1. Describe your business model. What are your primary sources of revenue? What are your revenue drivers? Your expenses?	
2. What is your customer value proposition? How does this lead to differentiation?	
3. What is your overall strategy? Why does this strategy help you sell to customers? What is your cost to acquire customers (CAC)? Does this exceed the customer lifetime value (CLTV)?	
4. What kind of partners and resources will you need? When will you need these?	
5. How will you measure success? What are the most important key metrics for your business?	

WEB EXERCISE

Pull the income sheets from three companies in the industry that you are interested in entering. Try to find companies that are pursuing different strategies. Examine their business models, and see if you can identify the drivers that they are influencing to achieve their strategy. What lessons can you learn for your own venture? What new elements can you incorporate into your business model? How do you tie these elements to your strategy?

NOTES

1. https://www.itprotoday.com/collaboration/google-grabs-nielsen-business-apps-user-microsoft.
2. Puffery: General, favorable statements of exaggeration that cannot be proven and are not likely to be relied upon by consumers. Includes general claims of superiority that are understood by consumers as merely an expression of opinion.
3. https://www.reuters.com/article/us-volkswagen-emissions-dieselgate/vw-fined-one-billion-euros-by-german-prosecutors-over-emissions-cheating-idUSKBN1J92AI.
4. Omnichannel refers to a type of retail that integrates the different methods of shopping available to consumers (e.g., online, physical location, mobile).
5. Revenue drivers refers to the financial metrics used to identify the sources of revenue generation in a business. For instance, revenue drivers for a restaurant might include the number of diners, the menu items they choose, and the amount paid for each item.

Case Zumba Fitness[1]

Alberto Perlman walked out of the old warehouse that served as the offices of Zumba Fitness and into the hot Miami sun. He had just finished meeting with his two partners, and the company that they had started with such a bang four years earlier seemed on the ropes. The agreement they had with the marketing company that produced and promoted their exercise videos had broken down, and despite selling millions of dollars' worth of videotapes featuring their unique Latin-based exercise routine called Zumba, the company had not been able to provide enough profitability for it to do more than scrape by. One of his partners, Alberto Aghion, was even looking at starting a medical billing company. With only about $14,000 left in the bank, they needed to figure out how to either make this business profitable or start looking for other opportunities.

Childhood Friends

The Salesman: Alberto Perlman

Alberto Perlman was born and raised in Bogota, Colombia, where his family was very involved in business and entrepreneurship. His great-grandfather had immigrated to Bogota from Jerusalem in the pursuit of business opportunities. Starting out by selling textiles door-to-door, his grandfather gradually built the second largest retail store in the country. It was clear that growing up in this environment had a great influence on Alberto. From the beginning, Perlman seemed destined for business. When he was 6 years old, his father bought him a digital watch with a game on it. The enterprising young Perlman proceeded to loan it to a classmate on weekends in exchange for 750 pesos (approximately $10). When his parents found out, they apologized to the boy's mother and made Alberto return all the money, but a budding entrepreneur was born. In high school, Perlman noticed a vacant lot near the school that was being occupied by a number of homeless people. At his school, like many others, it was cool to have a car and drive to school. However, Perlman realized that many of the students couldn't drive their cars because they could not find a place to park. He approached the people living in the lot and offered a deal. He would pay them if they would let students park there and keep an eye on the cars. He then charged his classmates 90,000 pesos (about $45 at that time) each month to park. This venture, too, was short-lived.

> *Unfortunately, the people found out what I was charging, and they started going direct. So, I figured out that being a middle man is not a good deal.*

Despite these early setbacks, it was apparent to everyone that he was destined to be an entrepreneur.

> *I always knew I was going to do business, but I was a bit rebellious as a teenager and I told my mom I was going to study philosophy. My mom said, "I would never tell any of my kids this, but YOU ... I'm telling you. You were born to do business. I would never force any of my kids to do anything, but I'm forcing you to do business. So go find a business school."*

After graduating from high school, Perlman went backpacking through Europe with his childhood friend, Alberto Aghion, who would figure prominently in a number of his subsequent business ventures. Following the trip, Perlman enrolled in Babson College, a business school located outside of Boston, MA, known for its Entrepreneurship program.

Although his official studies were in finance and MIS, Perlman continued his entrepreneurial ways in the United States. He was fascinated with the Internet, and in 1995–1996, while studying at Babson, he got together with two other students and started a Web design company called Cyber Spider Designs.

> *We went up and down Newbury Street trying to sell Web sites at a time when nobody had Web sites. We did the Web site for Boston Proper Real Estate. We did a flower site. It was all right. It paid the bills, but nobody was paying good money for that at the time.*

It was also at Babson that Perlman made an impression on Professor Prichett, who ended up indirectly playing a key role in the founding of Zumba Fitness. Professor Prichett was impressed with his calculus student and introduced Perlman to his son, who worked at a New York consulting firm called the Mitchell Madison Group and who subsequently offered Perlman a job with the firm.

One of the first projects Perlman was given was working on direct response television advertising[2] for the First USA

[1] *This case was written by Professor Bradley George as a basis for class discussion rather than to illustrate either effective or ineffective handling of an administrative situation. Funding was provided by the Teaching Innovation Fund at Babson College.*

[2] Direct response television (DRTV) is television advertising that asks consumers to respond directly to the company, typically by either visiting a website or calling a toll-free number. DRTV can be either short form (a commercial that is two minutes in length or less) or long form (any commercial that is longer than two minutes with a common form being the 30-minute infomercial).

division of Bank One. While on this project, he spent considerable time analyzing the business model and operation of successful infomercial companies. Reflecting on his grandfather's retail business and his own experience as a middleman in his short-lived parking venture, he fell in love with the idea of direct marketing to consumers via television.

> *I always saw how difficult it was for suppliers to get their products into the stores. The infomercial industry was fascinating because you didn't have to go through a store. You didn't have to go to a big supplier like Walmart. You did it on your own merit. You bought media, created the commercial and it's your product.*

By this time Alberto's father was working at a nearby private equity firm, and he was meeting with a Chilean newspaper company that was interested in developing an Internet strategy. Knowing his son's knowledge of the latest technologies, he asked if Alberto would be willing to talk with them. After meeting with them and helping them with their strategy, he realized that his expertise in emerging Internet technologies coupled with his background and connections in Latin American markets provided a unique opportunity for him to once again set out on his own. So, after 10 months, he left his job with the Mitchell Madison Group to pursue Internet opportunities in Latin America.

Initially, Perlman, together with his brother and another friend, focused on building an Internet events company in which they would put on conferences for companies, entrepreneurs, and investors who were interested in Internet businesses in Latin America. This provided a way for him to both make money and make connections for future business opportunities.

> *We started calling companies like IBM and said, "Hey! Do you want to sponsor an event? It's called Latin Venture. We'll have all the entrepreneurs from Latin America there." And they said, of course ... how much? Twenty-five thousand dollars. Done. So we sold, and that's when things were going like crazy and we made a couple hundred thousand dollars at our first event.*

After the success of the Latin Venture event, Perlman used the money he had made to start an Internet incubator in which he raised money to invest in launching technology companies in Latin America. He was able to raise about $8 million, which they used to eventually fund nine different companies. It was also at this time that he convinced his long-time friend Alberto Aghion to turn down a job offer with Merrill Lynch and join him in one of the incubator's companies.

The Problem Solver: Alberto Aghion

Alberto Aghion grew up with Perlman in Bogota. They attended the same schools, had the same group of friends, and started becoming close friends in their early teens. When Perlman left for Babson following their European adventure together, Aghion decided to continue travelling and eventually ended up at the Hebrew University in Jerusalem, where he took courses in history, studying the Arab–Israeli conflict, and working odd jobs to make ends meet.

> *I had some crazy experiences. I went hiking in Africa. I hiked Kilimanjaro. I mean, I had a really interesting year. When you're 18 years old, you have no real responsibilities and it was an adventure in life. I'm really glad I took that year to do that because if I hadn't done that at that age, at that stage in my life, I couldn't have done that.*

After spending a little more than a year abroad, Aghion returned to Colombia ready for a new challenge. He was always interested in looking at ways to solve problems of all kinds. He excelled in math and physics in high school, so as soon as he returned, he applied to study Industrial Engineering at the Universidad Javeriana in Bogota with the belief that an engineering education would give him a good foundation in problem-solving techniques that he could apply to a number of different situations. However, he soon found out that he did not enjoy the teaching philosophy at the school. As with many engineering programs, there seemed to be a focus on filtering out students early in the program. In addition, it was difficult adjusting to life back at home after more than a year on his own. He felt out of place and restless in Bogota, so he talked to his friend Perlman, who was in his second year at Babson. Perlman seemed to be happy in Boston, so Aghion decided to visit him and look into opportunities in the United States.

> *I went to a few colleges. I mean I checked out Northwestern. Boston College. A few interesting schools. And on the way back, I stopped in Miami and I saw the palm trees, the ocean. So, I also went to UM and FIU and I checked out those schools and actually I decided, you know what, I think I like Miami better. I'm not a cold weather fan.*

He was accepted at both the University of Miami and Florida International University (FIU), but FIU was less expensive and they agreed to transfer his credits both from Bogota and from Israel, allowing him to graduate a year sooner, so he chose FIU where he majored in finance and international business.

I wanted to be an entrepreneur. I wanted to do different things. But I had no idea what I wanted to study. Also, I guess I got a little burned out at the university in Colombia. I mean, I like problem solving. I guess maybe if I would have gone to a different school and had a different experience with engineering, I might have stayed with that career. But, because I didn't enjoy that methodology in Colombia, I said, you know what, this is not for me. And at the end of the day, I just wanted to do business. I had picked engineering because I was good at physics and calculus and problem solving, not necessarily because I wanted to be an engineer.

Aghion excelled in the new environment, getting straight As for the first two years and graduating with a job offer from Merrill Lynch. He was considering this offer when he got a phone call from Perlman.

I spoke with Perlman, he was launching this whole incubator. Really exciting. Internet boom. All this interesting stuff. And he tells me, "Why the hell are you going to go work for a boring bank? Come work with me." So I said OK.

One of the first ventures Perlman and his partners invested in was FonBox, which was a service for providing a virtual office anywhere in Latin America. Aghion was asked to help develop FonBox, and he did a significant amount of work helping them develop the infrastructure for the business. They eventually sold it to J2 Communications for a loss.

By March 2001, they were working on nine different businesses when the Internet bubble burst. Most of their companies were early-stage companies in their first or second round of funding, and the capital for additional investments in Internet firms quickly dried up. With no funding available, a lack of new businesses to invest in, and $4M of the original investor's money remaining, they decided to continue to work with the firms they had invested in on the chance that one of them would be successful. They could then return what was left of the money to their investors rather than risk the remaining funds and the relationships with the investors they had worked so hard to establish.

The Third Alberto

Alberto "Beto" Perez grew up in Cali, Colombia, as the son of a young, single, working mother. Always an energetic child, he loved to perform. He would take his mother's hairbrush and use it like a microphone as he would sing and dance. In the same way that Perlman seemed destined for a career as an entrepreneur, Beto seemed born to dance. As his mother recalls,

When he was seven, I took Beto to see the movie Grease. *The next day, he was out on the street teaching John Travolta's dance moves to kids who were much bigger than he was.*

Growing up in Cali in the 1980s was difficult. Drugs and violence were common on the streets. Beto saw this firsthand when his mother got into an abusive relationship with a drug addict. When he was 14, his mother was hit by a stray bullet, and he had to work multiple jobs to help support the two of them. Despite these hardships, dance was a constant presence in his life.

As a teenager in the 1980s, I was always sneaking out to nightclubs to dance, and my mom was trying to keep me at home, safe.

When Beto was 16, his mother took a job in Miami, but he wanted to stay in Cali to pursue a career in dance. They would keep in touch via telephone and letters, but it would be a long, hard 10 years before they would see each other again. During this time, Beto continued to try to make it as a dancer. When he was 17, he couldn't afford rent so he slept in the ice cream shop where he worked. He thought he finally had his big breakthrough when he was chosen to represent Colombia at a Latin dance competition in Miami. However, after spending his entire savings on costumes, his U.S. visa request was denied and he was unable to compete.

Because he couldn't afford to attend a dance academy, he worked as a courier in the morning and taught private dance lessons in the evening. The owner of the gym where Beto prepared his dance routines offered him an opportunity to teach a children's class in the summer. Because he was so popular, he was invited to teach more classes. A modeling agent gave him his first job as a choreographer and he gained national attention after winning a lambada competition at the age of 19. Eventually, he saved enough money to attend and graduate from the Maria Sanford Brazilian Dance Academy with a degree in choreography.

Although dance was his passion, it was a series of fortuitous events that led to the creation of what is now known as Zumba. One evening a local gym owner telephoned Beto and asked if he could substitute for one of her aerobics instructors who had been injured. Although Beto had never taught aerobics, he needed the money so he accepted the job. He immediately went to a book store and bought a copy of Jane Fonda's *Workout Book* and tried to copy the moves in the book coupled with some of his own dance steps. The class went well, and soon Beto was regularly teaching aerobics classes as well as dance. Then fortune struck again. As Beto recalls,

At one of those sessions, I forgot to bring the music, and all I had were salsa and merengue tapes in my backpack. So I improvised, and that was the beginning of Zumba.

Beto called his new style of aerobics "Rumbacize" as a tribute to the Latin influences behind many of the moves. As Beto's popularity increased, he found himself traveling to Bogota to do television commercials. Eventually, he moved there and began teaching at one of the top gyms in the city where one of his early students was Alberto Perlman's mother.

In 1994 Mrs. Perlman was taking my class in Bogota and announced, "This is the best class in the world!" I'll never forget that.

In addition to his Rumbacize classes, he was gaining attention for his dancing and choreography. He was hired by Sony Music to work with some of their singers, and he helped with the choreography for singer-songwriter Shakira's breakthrough album, "Pies Descalzos." During this time, he began traveling more outside of Colombia and fell in love with the idea of moving to Miami, so he decided to sell everything and move to the United States. However, his lack of English skills made the transition difficult, and he had a hard time finding work.

I love Miami, and I knew this is where I wanted to live. At first it was not easy. No one knew who I was, I did not speak English and I ran out money. I even slept on the street one time.

His big break came one afternoon when one of the gym managers decided to see what Beto could do, so she gave him an impromptu audition. It was the middle of the afternoon and she told Beto to teach a class to one student. Herself.

It was 3 p.m., and the gym was empty. Soon a passerby wandered in to watch, then two, three, four. After 20 minutes I had about 15 people. They thought it was a new class and wanted to sign up.

The manager was impressed and offered Beto a job teaching Saturday mornings. Beto's passion, energy, charisma, and lively exercise programs became increasingly popular, and he soon found himself teaching classes of up to 160 students at gyms throughout the Miami area. Investors were approaching him about opening up his own gym.

The Birth of Zumba Fitness

Following the end of Perlman's incubator venture, Perlman and Aghion found themselves trying to decide what to do with their lives. Reflecting back on his brief time with the Mitchell Madison Group, Perlman was drawn back to the idea of an infomercial-based company. Perlman approached Aghion, who was considering going back into the finance world. Aghion was interested so they began brainstorming potential ideas. As Aghion recalls,

I still don't have a family. I still don't have anything. I want to take a risk. Things are happening and I was really interested in the infomercial industry. I thought that it was a good opportunity. And I remember talking to Perlman and saying, why don't we do an infomercial or something? If we make it, we could make a lot of money. And then we can figure something else out.

During this time, Perlman's family had moved to Miami, and his mother was once again taking Beto's classes. One day his mother suggested that he meet Beto. "Beto has something special," she told him. So Perlman arranged to meet Beto at a Starbucks to learn more. Beto's energy and passion were contagious and Perlman could envision his aerobics routines and personality as a great combination for his infomercial concept. Following their meeting, he immediately called his friend Aghion to see what he thought about the idea.

I remember my stomach saying, I LOVE IT. Ricky Martin was singing "Living La Vida Loca" at the Grammy's. Latin music is crossing over in the U.S. Tae Bo. Fitness. Beto. It clicked in my head immediately.

As Perlman recalls:

It was a gut decision. We were two out-of-work businessmen with no contacts in the fitness industry and a dancer who couldn't speak a word of English, and here we were deciding to launch a fitness business together. But we knew if we could capture the excitement of his class on video, people would go crazy for the music and the moves.

With little money between them, they decided to create their own video, which they would then use to as a marketing vehicle for launching the business. They spent the night laying down boards on the beach and the next morning made a video of Beto teaching a class. They then renamed the program "Zumba," which rhymed with "rumba," meaning "party" and Zumba Fitness was born.

Table C5.1 **Forms of Exercise**

Fitness Activity	1998	2000	2004	2005	1yr change (%)	Change from 1998 (%)
Aerobics (High Impact)	7460	5581	5521	5004	−9.4	−32.9
Aerobics (Low Impact)	12774	9752	8493	9071	6.8	−29.0
Aerobics (Step)	10784	8963	8257	7062	−14.5	−34.5
Aerobics (Net)	21017	17326	15767	15811	0.3	−24.8
Other Exercise to Music	13846	12337	16365	14428	−11.8	4.2
Aquatic Exercise	6685	6367	5812	6237	7.3	−6.7
Calisthenics	30982	27790	25562	24854	−2.8	−19.8
Cardio Kick Boxing	n.a.	7163	4773	4163	−12.8	n.a.
Fitness Bicycling	13556	11435	10210	10211	0.01	−24.7
Fitness Walking	36395	36207	40299	36348	−9.8	−0.1
Running/Jogging	34962	33680	37310	37810	1.3	8.1
Fitness Swimming	15258	14060	15636	14553	−6.9	−4.6
Pilates Training	n.a.	1739	10541	10355	−1.8	n.a.
Stretching	35114	36408	40799	42266	3.6	20.4
Yoga/Tai Chi	5708	7400	12414	14656	18.1	156.8

Fitness Industry Business Models[3]

The fitness industry consists of a wide range of activities that people engage in for exercise. In general, most forms of exercise have experienced a decline in participation in recent years in the United States (Table C5.1). Notable exceptions are Pilates and yoga, which have seen dramatic increases in participation. Aerobics, although popular in the 1980s and 1990s, has seen a decline in participation since 1998, whereas other forms of exercising to music have remained relatively steady.

Companies in this industry have used a variety of approaches to enter and compete in this industry. Due to the fact that many of these forms of exercise can be done individually or in groups, companies can target instructors or participants as their primary customers. Revenue models can range from unit sales models to franchising models, each with their own implications. Following are some of the approaches firms in this industry have used.

Franchise Model

Developed in 1969 by Judi Sheppard Missett, Jazzercise, Inc. is the world's leading franchiser of dance and fitness classes with over 5,000 franchises worldwide.[4] After creating the program, demand for her classes eventually exceeded her ability to single-handedly teach all her students, and she began training some of her early students to become teachers. These instructors agreed to pay a start-up fee and 30% of their gross revenues to Missett in exchange for the permission to use the Jazzercise brand.

In 1979, Jazzercise formally incorporated and in 1983 it formalized its franchise relationship with its certified instructors. Jazzercise instructors would pay a $500 franchise fee and, as with the early instructors, a royalty fee of 30% of gross revenues. In 1988, the company reduced the royalty fee to 20% paid monthly. In exchange for this, the company would provide corporate support to the franchisees in the form of marketing materials, national advertising on radio and TV, choreography, choreography notes, and business advice. The company maintains strict control over the brand and the routines, with instructors agreeing to only use corporate-developed choreography.

Instructor Training Model

First developed by circus performer and boxer Joseph Pilates while in an English internment camp in World War I, Pilates has become an increasingly popular form of exercise. Joseph was said to be inspired by the ancient Greek ideal of man perfected in development of body, mind, and spirit and incorporated elements

[3] It should be noted that gyms and fitness clubs account for a major portion of the revenue in the fitness industry. However, these businesses do not specialize in a single form of exercise but rather differentiate themselves on the variety of offerings available. They require a physical location, equipment, and instructors, and members typically have access to most classes and equipment in exchange for a monthly membership fee.

[4] Gale Group.

of Eastern philosophies into his exercise routines, which he called "contrology."[5] He expresses this holistic approach in his book, *Return to Life Through Contrology*, when he writes, *Contrology develops the body uniformly, corrects wrong postures, restores physical vitality, invigorates the mind, and elevates the spirit.*

After moving to New York City in 1925, Pilates established a studio where he continued to teach his form of exercise until his death in 1967. During and after this time, a number of his students opened their own studios (with Joseph's permission), teaching classical Pilates. Eventually, some of his original students developed their own unique methods, such as the Fletcher Method (Richard Fletcher) and the Gentry Method (Eve Gentry). Today there are a number of different businesses focused on Pilates in various forms, but each uses essentially the same business model.

Unlike Jazzercise, companies such as Balanced Body Pilates and Pilates Institute of America do not offer franchises, but rather generate revenue from individual instructor training and certification. This is similar to a unit sales revenue model, with the "unit" being the instructor. Certification costs generally run between $3,000 and $7,000, with specialty certifications adding additional costs for the instructor. Once an instructor is certified, he or she is not required to pay any additional amounts to the company. Instructors can then teach individual or group classes once certified. Some of these firms generate additional revenue through the sales of equipment that is used in special forms of Pilates.

Due to the various forms of Pilates certification available, a major cost for these firms is brand management and differentiation. The company provides the instructors with training materials and runs training classes that result in certification, so other costs typically include facilities for training, instructors, and training materials.

Exercise Video Model

Another popular business model in this industry is a unit sales model through the production and sales of exercise videos and DVDs. Although the revenue model is fairly straightforward, the cost structure can be more complicated. In this type of model, consumer awareness and distribution are critical. Distribution can be accomplished through direct sales via the Internet, sales through retail channels, and/or direct sales through infomercials. In each of these cases, creating brand awareness through marketing is a critical success factor. If infomercials are used, then the costs of producing and airing the infomercial need to be considered. In the case of retail sales, potential slotting fees and gaining access to retail outlets can constitute a significant cost. For exercise programs that utilize music, companies also need to consider music licensing costs.[6]

Zumba Fitness—The Early Years

Following their initial idea to establish an infomercial-based business, Perlman and Aghion built a website, and Perlman began going to the gyms in Miami marketing the video. Beto was teaching classes at Crunch South Beach at the time, and his boss, Donna Cyrus, introduced them to the founder of Crunch gyms. The founder was interested in their new fitness program and subsequently introduced them to a representative from a large firm that produced infomercials for various fitness products.

Perlman flew out to meet with them and show them the video. The company was impressed, and they entered into an agreement where the company would produce and air the infomercials and pay Zumba Fitness a royalty for each of the videos they sold. Within six months, they had sold hundreds of thousands of copies of the videos. Despite its popularity, the videos were barely making enough to cover the production costs for the infomercials, so Zumba Fitness was asked to forgo its royalty so that they could spend the money on marketing the videos via retail outlets. They agreed, but as a result of some miscommunication, the firm failed to get all of the necessary licenses for one of the songs. As a result, the company had to discontinue selling the videos. Following lengthy legal discussions, Zumba Fitness eventually bought back the rights to its fitness program in 2003 and started over on its own, this time using its own music.

After remaking the videos, Perlman, Aghion, and Beto continued selling a handful of videos online each day, packaging them themselves and driving them to the post office. Eventually, they partnered with a Colombian firm to produce an infomercial for the Latin American market. This went well for a while, but piracy became a big issue and sales dropped off. From there they tried to expand into the U.S. Hispanic market and met with some success. It was also during this time that they got another important break.

[5] Ogle, Marguerite. "Joseph Pilates: Founder of the Pilates Method of Exercise," Ask.com.

[6] There are two different types of music licenses that need to be considered for each song when producing a video or DVD. A mechanical license allows you to make multiple copies of the recording. This fee is used to pay royalties to the owner of the song's copyright. If you are pairing music with video or other media, this requires a synchronization license. In this case, the synchronization license replaces the mechanical license. If you are using an artist's actual recording, then a master license is required, which is paid to the owner of the master recording, typically the record label. If you hire someone to record a cover version of a song, the master license is no longer needed.

So we were in Aghion's garage, which was our office, and we get a call from this lady saying she was from Kellogg's. We thought it was a scam, of course. She says that she wants to meet with us. She is from the ad agency for Kellogg's in Miami. She tells us that the CEO's wife bought the tapes off our infomercial and she loves them. And he had an idea that he could use Zumba as part of a health and fitness campaign. So we started talking and it ended up being a great deal over four years. That was totally the amount of money that we needed to survive from 2003 to 2006.

The company had also begun receiving calls from fitness instructors who had purchased the Zumba tapes and wanted to teach classes. So in 2003, Zumba Fitness held its first instructor training session. To their surprise, more than 150 people flew to Miami to learn firsthand from Beto. They continued to hold the training sessions every few months and this, coupled with the money from Kellogg's and the video sales, kept them afloat. Despite this, they still felt like they were not tapping the full potential of the business and money was getting tight.

At the Crossroads

Perlman thought about their predicament. On the one hand, there was no doubt about the passion of the Zumba enthusiasts. Once people tried it, they fell in love with it. When they began offering the instructor training, they were amazed to see the same instructors come back again and again, even though they had already been trained. They even began setting up their own cameras and recorders at Beto's classes to capture the new moves and the music. On the other hand, they weren't making much money with their current model and their cash flow was unpredictable. Perlman's thoughts strayed back to the medical billing company Aghion had mentioned. This is ridiculous, he thought. We're not going to let this go. We have to do something. All these instructors keep coming back to Miami, and they are just in love with Zumba. We *have* to be able to come up with something to make this work.

Discussion Questions

1. What business models could Zumba use?
2. Develop a revenue and cost model diagram for each of the options.
3. Which of these models would you recommend that they implement and why?
4. What are the key revenue and cost drivers for your recommended model?
5. What do you feel are the key aspects to implementing this model?

Entrepreneurial Marketing

6

Photo Credit: © Alexander Klein/AFP/Getty Images

Entrepreneurial at its core, Red Bull has always emphasized creativity over spending large amounts of cash in its marketing efforts.

Marketing is at the heart of an organization because its task is to identify and serve customers' needs. In essence, marketing spans the boundaries between a company and its customers. It is marketing that delivers a company's products and services to customers and marketing that takes information about those products and services, as well as about the company itself, to the market.

This chapter was written by Abdul Ali and Kathleen Seiders.

In addition, it is marketing's role to bring information about the customers back to the company. Although many people relate the term *marketing* to advertising and promotion, the scope of marketing is much broader. The American Marketing Association defines marketing as:

> *An organizational function and a set of processes for creating, communicating, and delivering value to customers and for managing customer relationships in ways that benefit the organization and its stakeholders.*[1]

Successful entrepreneurs select and optimize the marketing tools that best fit their unique challenges. Marketing practices vary depending on the type of company and the products and services it sells. Marketers of consumer products, such as carbonated soft drinks, use different tools than marketers of business-to-business products, such as network software. Companies in the services sector, such as banks, market differently from companies that sell durable goods, such as automobile manufacturers.

Why Marketing Is Critical for Entrepreneurs

Marketing is a vital process for entrepreneurs because no venture can become established and grow without a customer market. The process of acquiring and retaining customers is at the core of marketing. Entrepreneurs must create the offer (design the product and set the price), take the offer to the market (through distribution), and, at the same time, tell the market about the offer (communications). These activities define the famous **Four Ps** of marketing: product, price, place (distribution), and promotion (communication).

Entrepreneurs often are faced with designing the entire "marketing system"—from product and price to distribution and communication. Because it is difficult and expensive to bring new products and services to market—especially difficult for new companies—they need to be more resourceful in their marketing. Many entrepreneurs rely on creativity rather than cash to achieve a compelling image in a noisy marketplace.

An important part of gaining the market's acceptance is building brand awareness, which, depending on the stage of the venture, may be weak or even nonexistent. Entrepreneurs must differentiate their company's product or service so its distinctiveness and value are clear to the customer. This is the job of marketing.

Marketing also plays a central role in a venture's early growth stages when changes to the original business model may be necessary. Companies focused on growth must be able to switch marketing gears quickly and attract new and different customer segments.

Entrepreneurs Face Unique Marketing Challenges

Entrepreneurial marketing is different from marketing done by established companies for a number of reasons. First, entrepreneurial companies typically have limited resources—financial as well as managerial. Just as they rarely have enough money to support marketing activities, they also rarely have proven marketing expertise within the company. Most entrepreneurs do not have the option of hiring experienced marketing managers. Time—as well as money and marketing talent—is also often in short supply. Whereas larger corporations can spend hundreds of thousands or even millions on conducting extensive marketing research, testing their strategies, and carefully designing marketing campaigns, new ventures find creative and less costly means to validate their ideas and reach customers.

Most entrepreneurs face daunting challenges. Their companies have little or no market share and a confined geographic market presence. As a result, they enjoy few economies of scale; for example, it is difficult for small companies to save money on "media buys" because their range of advertising is so limited. Entrepreneurs usually are restricted in their access to distributors—both wholesalers and retailers. On the customer side, entrepreneurs struggle with low brand awareness and customer loyalty, both of which must be carefully cultivated.

Not only is market information limited, but also decision making can be muddled by strong personal biases and beliefs. Early-stage companies often stumble in their marketing because of a product focus that is excessively narrow. Companies frequently assume that their products will be embraced by enthusiastic consumers when, in reality, consumer inertia prevents most new products from being accepted at all. Research has shown that common marketing-related dangers for entrepreneurs include overestimating demand, underestimating competitor response, and making uninformed distribution decisions.

Entrepreneurs market to multiple audiences: investors, customers, employees, and business partners. Because none of these bonds is well established for early-stage companies, entrepreneurs must be both customer oriented and relationship oriented. A customer orientation requires understanding the market and where it is going. A relationship orientation is needed to create structural and emotional ties with all stakeholders. *Thus, marketing helps entrepreneurs acquire resources by selling their ideas to potential investors and partners. It also allows entrepreneurs to leverage scarce resources through innovative business approaches.*

In this chapter, we consider entrepreneurial marketing in depth. Building on the opportunity-defining and -refining discussion in Chapter 3, we provide direction on market research—that is, collecting information useful in making marketing and strategy decisions. We do so because regardless of where you decide to promote and/or advertise your offerings, every entrepreneur must first understand her customers, the value they expect, and other critical issues before developing and executing marketing plans. What customer segments are most likely to buy? How should we price our products? Answers to these and other fundamental questions need to be answered first. After examining marketing research, we focus on implementing marketing strategies that make the most of these opportunities. We also examine value propositions, social media, and guerilla marketing techniques. Finally we explore how certain marketing skills serve to support a new company's growth.

Acquiring Market Information

An entrepreneur needs to do research to identify and assess an opportunity. Intuition, personal expertise, and passion can take you only so far. Some studies show that good pre-venture market analysis could reduce venture failure rates by as much as 60%.[2] But many entrepreneurs tend to ignore negative market information because of a strong commitment to their idea. Whereas Chapter 2 defined what an opportunity is and Chapter 3 presented a checklist for assessing how attractive your opportunity might be, this chapter provides a drill-down on how you collect data to validate your initial impressions of the opportunity.

We define **marketing research** as the collection and analysis of any reliable information that improves managerial decisions. Questions that marketing research can answer include the following: What product attributes are important to customers? How is customers' willingness to buy influenced by product design, pricing, and communications? Where do customers buy this kind of product? How is the market likely to change in the future?

There are two basic types of market data: **secondary data**, which marketers gather from already published sources like an industry association study or census reports, and **primary data**, which marketers collect specifically for a particular purpose through focus groups, surveys, or experiments. You can find a great deal of market information in secondary resources. Secondary research requires less time and money than primary research, and it should be your first avenue. Entrepreneurs sometimes use databases at college libraries to collect baseline information about product and geographic markets (Figure 8.5 in Chapter 8 lists some common databases).

Stage	Examples of Effective Questions
Introduction	• Think of the last time you purchased Product X. • What prompted or triggered this activity? • How often do you use X?
Rapport Building	• What are some of the reasons for so many products in this industry?
In-Depth Investigation	• Here is a new idea about this market. In what ways is this idea different from what you see in the marketplace? • What features are missing from this new product? • What would you need to know about this idea in order to accept it?
Closure	• Is this focus group discussion what you expected?

FIGURE 6.1 Focus Groups Stages & Questions.

Some types of primary data are easy to collect, for instance, with personal interviews or focus groups, but keep in mind the limitations of such data, such as observer bias and lack of statistical significance (because the samples are small). To ensure that they obtain high-quality data, some entrepreneurs hire marketing research firms to perform research studies. Lower-cost alternatives do exist: For example, online surveys can be made pretty cheaply these days (see tools like Qualtrics that many university libraries support or SurveyMonkey) or if you are on campus, a business school professor might assign the company's project to a student research team. In choosing a research approach, balance your quality and time constraints with the possible cost savings.

The appendix at the end of this chapter provides a list of possible questions to address in a customer research interview. You can structure such an interview as a one-on-one interaction or as a focus group. In focus groups, a discussion leader encourages 5 to 10 people to express their views about the company's products or services. The focus group has distinct stages, and you will need to ask specific questions to get good-quality information from the group participants. Figure 6.1 displays these stages and provides some example questions to use when conducting a focus group.

Market Research for Revolutionary New Products?

Henry Ford is reputed to have said that if he had asked potential customers for his yet-to-be-introduced automobile what they wanted, they would have replied, "a faster horse." Market research may be valuable for existing products and incremental improvements to them, but what is its value for revolutionary new products? By definition, a revolutionary new product has no SIC classification, so it is virtually impossible to gather meaningful data from secondary sources. And what use are the opinions of primary sources who are unfamiliar with the product because it is different from anything they have ever used? Steve Jobs (along with other Apple executives) had no faith in market research for the radically new products that he introduced. Here is what he had to say on that subject:

"Some people say 'give the customers what they want.' But that is not my approach. Our job is to figure out what they're going to want before they do."[3]

When asked, "Should [Apple] do some market research to see what customers wanted?" [Jobs] replied, "No, because customers don't know what they want until we've shown them."[4]

On the day he unveiled the Macintosh, a reporter from *Popular Science* asked Jobs what kind of market research he had done. Jobs responded by scoffing, "Did Alexander Graham Bell do any market research before he invented the telephone?"[5]

Jonathan Ive, Apple's senior vice president of industrial design, who gave Apple products their sleek, minimalist form, says that Apple has a good reason for not doing focus groups: "They just ensure that you don't offend anyone, and produce bland inoffensive products."[6]

FIGURE 6.2 Understanding the Customer Choice Process.

Customer acceptance of an entrepreneur's idea is proof that the opportunity is worth pursuing. Entrepreneurs must understand the customer decision-making process and how to influence the customer's choice. Such customer understanding enables entrepreneurs to develop the right products at the right prices (create and capture value) and then market these products to the right customers in the right place (communicate and deliver value). Further, such knowledge of customers' behavior at each stage of the decision-making process helps entrepreneurs to be effective and efficient with their communication strategy to reach the target customers. Figure 6.2 provides an illustration of the role that marketing tools play in the customer choice process.

Marketing Strategy for Entrepreneurs

A company's marketing strategy must closely align with its resources and capabilities. Entrepreneurial companies with limited resources have little room for strategic mistakes. Segmentation, targeting, and positioning are key marketing dimensions that set the strategic framework. We begin this section by discussing these three activities and their role in marketing strategy. Then we examine the widely studied marketing elements known as the marketing mix: product, price, distribution (place), and communications (promotion). Finally, we conclude this section by connecting these concepts and exploring the concept of value and the development of a value proposition for entrepreneurial firms.

Segmentation, Targeting, and Positioning

Segmentation and *targeting* are the processes marketers use to identify the "right" customers for their company's products and services. In Chapter 3, we talked about the segment your opportunity would initially target, what we call the primary target audience (PTA) or core customers. As we move beyond opportunity recognition into implementation of a marketing strategy, we need to revisit our initial conceptions and refine what that core customer segment really means. A **segment** is a group of customers defined by certain common bases or characteristics that may be demographic, psychographic (commonly called *lifestyle characteristics*), or behavioral. Demographic characteristics include age, education, gender, and income; lifestyle characteristics include descriptors like active, individualistic, risk taking, and time pressured. Behavioral characteristics include consumer traits such as brand loyalty and willingness to adopt new products.

Marketers identify the most relevant bases for segmentation and then develop segment profiles. It's common to define a segment using a combination of demographic and lifestyle characteristics: for example, high-income, sophisticated baby boomers or environmentally conscious millennials. Marketers also segment customers based on where they live (geography), how often they use a product (usage rates), and what they value in a product (product attribute preferences).

Targeting compares the defined segments and then selects the most attractive one, which becomes the core customer. Target market definition is essential because it guides your company's *customer selection* strategy. The attractiveness of a segment is related to its size, growth rate, and profit potential. Your targeting decisions should also reflect your company's specific capabilities and longer-term goals. Accurate targeting is important for entrepreneurs; however, it is not always clear which customer segment(s) represents the best target market, and finding out may require some research and some trial and error. As we noted in Chapter 3, it is wise to identify secondary target audiences (STAs) in case the core customer segment doesn't meet expectations. Nevertheless, identifying the appropriate target market early on is critical because pursuing multiple targets or waiting for one to emerge is an expensive strategy.

To display segmentation and targeting, let's look at the example of Red Bull, the energy drink company cofounded by Dietrich Mateschitzan, an Austrian entrepreneur, and Chaleo Yoovidhya, a Thai entrepreneur and originator of Red Bull. For Red Bull, the most relevant segment characteristics are age, health, and behavior (in this case, extreme sports). Red Bull, originally a Thai energy drink was mainly consumed by truck drivers and then later modified for a larger population who preferred to boost their energy while enjoying the taste as well. Red Bull positioned itself as a drink suitable for stretching the human limits for doing things and associated the drink with the activities that require a tremendous amount of energy and strength. As Red Bull gained popularity among younger consumers, it connected itself to extreme sports, which is highly popular with youngsters. Also, the relation with high-adrenaline adventure sports strengthened its position as a high-priced premium energy drink. Red Bull hosts several extreme sports events all around the world as part of its international marketing campaign. They have also entered into the video game industry to promote the drink in a younger population that forms the future market segment for the drink.[7]

Whereas segmentation and targeting profile a company's customers, **positioning** relates to competitors and to customers' *perceptions* of your product. Positioning usually describes a company's offering relative to certain product attributes—the ones customers care about most. Such attributes often include price, quality, and convenience, all of which can be scaled from high to low. For example, if brands of single-serve beverages were shown on a positioning map (see Figure 6.3) with the two dimensions of *price* and *quality*, Red Bull would be positioned in the high-price, high-quality (upper-right) quadrant, whereas a store-brand offering other price-focused brands would likely be positioned in a low-price, low-quality (lower-left) quadrant.

The Marketing Mix

The marketing mix—the Four Ps of product, price, place, and promotion—is a set of tools your company can use to achieve its marketing goals. In fact, the marketing mix is so basic to a company's business model that *marketing* strategy often defines company or corporate strategy. In this section, we discuss the individual elements of the marketing mix, shown in Figure 6.4. Our focus is on the particular challenges entrepreneurial marketers face.

Product Strategy

We can divide product strategy into the **core product** and the **augmented product**. The core product is the essential good or service, whereas the augmented product is the set of attributes

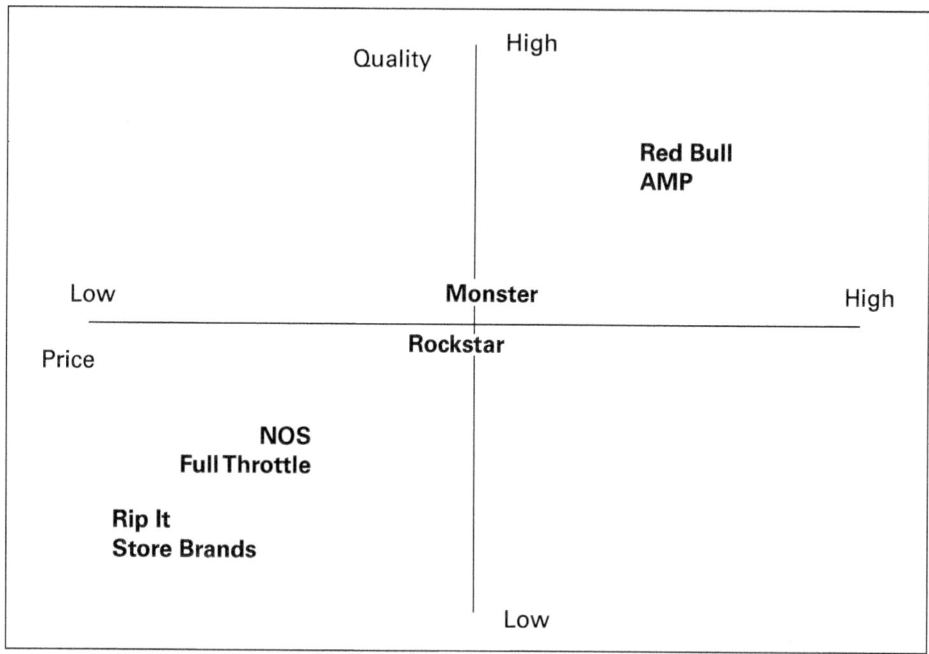

FIGURE 6.3 Red Bull's Position Map.

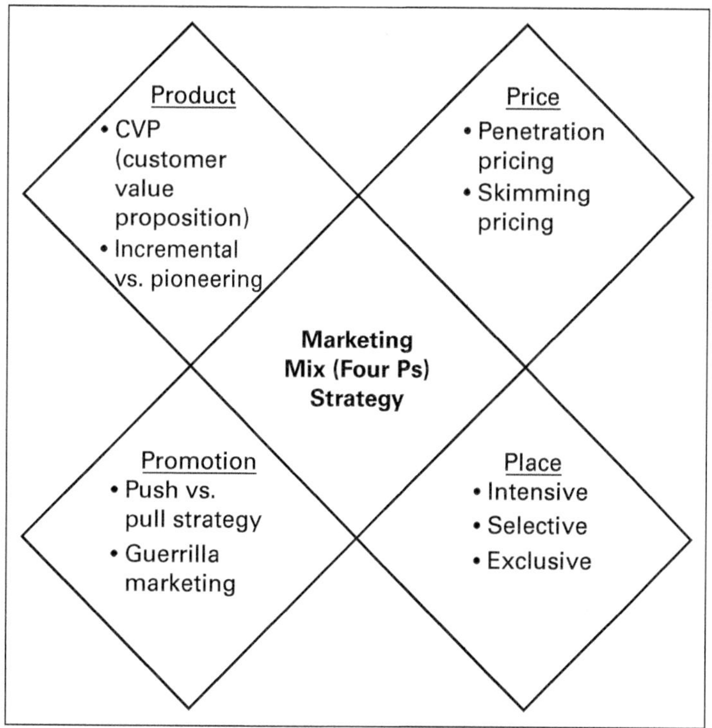

FIGURE 6.4 Marketing Mix Strategy for an Entrepreneur.

peripherally related to it. For example, Apple manufactures and markets its iPhone, the core product, but it also provides App Store for downloading applications for the phone and an iPhone upgrade program as augmented services. The strategies can apply in the business-to-business space as well. For instance, Caterpillar manufactures and markets heavy earthmoving machinery to construction companies as its core product and provides training to the company operators as an augmented product/service.

Another way to look at the product variable part of the marketing mix is in terms of goods and services (the word *product* here can refer to either a service or a good). Whereas beverages and computers are obviously tangible goods, supermarkets, travel booking companies, and banks are services *and* offer service products, such as food, shopping, flight/hotel bookings, and debit accounts. The line between products and services has been eroding for some time. Furthermore, we live in a service economy, and a large part of the gross national product and new job creation are tied to services.

In your product strategy, you'll pay attention to the strength of the *value proposition* you are offering customers and make sure your products are clearly *differentiated*. You'll also be guided by the *product life cycle* in crafting your strategy and by *product diffusion theory* in assessing how fast consumers will adopt your products. Finally, from the beginning, you should be obsessively focused on *quality*.[8]

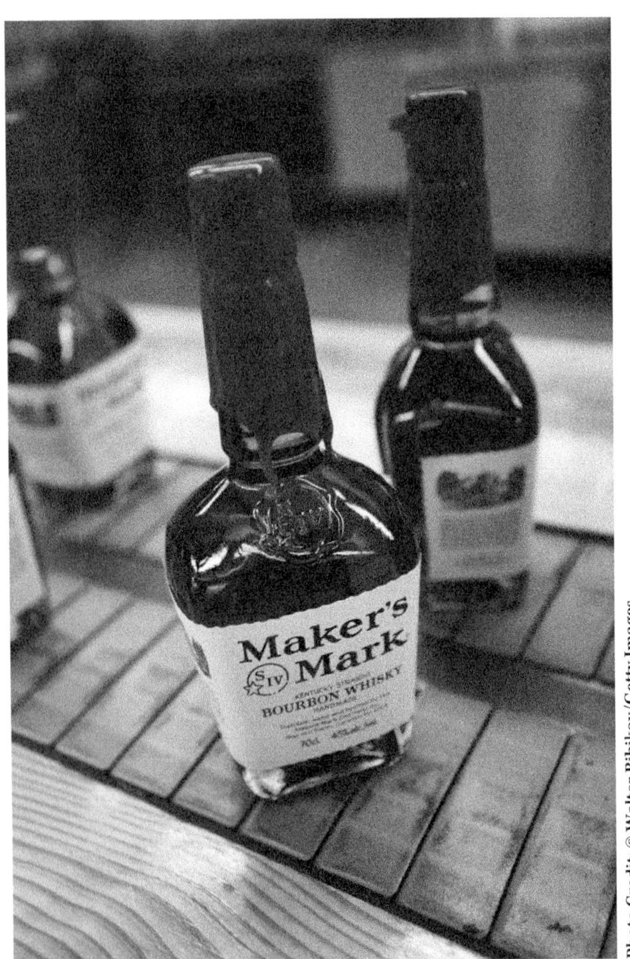

Photo Credit: © Walter Bibikov/Getty Images

Maker's Mark whiskey.

Many entrepreneurs establish companies based on a new product or product line. When developing any new product, your company must ensure that it is truly addressing an "unmet consumer need"—that there is a real **customer value proposition (CVP)**. **Customer value** is the difference between total customer benefits and total customer costs, which are both monetary and nonmonetary. A product attribute is not a benefit until consumers buy into the advantage.

Identifying a CVP, also known as a *positioning statement*, is an essential step in the marketing of a product or service regardless of your industry. Any positioning statement has four elements: (1) target group and need, (2) brand, (3) concept, and (4) point of difference. The formula is straightforward. Entrepreneurs need to know which attributes customers consider important and how customers rate the company's products—and competing products—on each attribute.

Product differentiation is important for initial product success as well as for longer-term brand building. In its early days, Maker's Mark, a sixth-generation, family-run Kentucky bourbon producer, leveraged the product-related attributes that make its bourbon unique (for e.g., wheat instead of rye, six-year fermentation, and small-batch production) to build a distinctive image for the brand. For decades, the company has been able to rely on these product differences to reinforce its quality position.

A venerable framework for understanding product strategy is the **product life cycle**. The stages of the

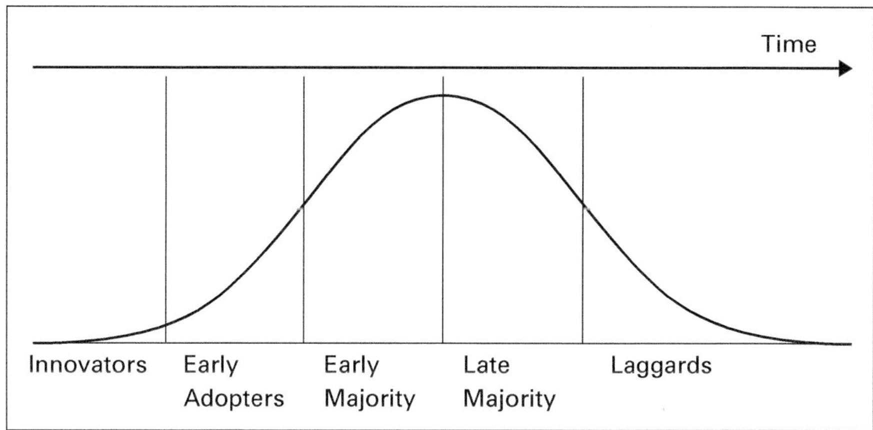

FIGURE 6.5 Product Diffusion Curve.

product life cycle are **introduction**, **growth**, **maturity**, and **decline**. Product life-cycle analysis can help you recognize how marketing requirements differ at each stage of a company's growth. During the introduction stage, marketers must educate the customer and secure distribution. During the growth stage, they must cultivate customer loyalty and build the brand. Differentiation is important during the maturity stage, and marketing efficiency is critical during the decline stage.

In a business environment with intense global competition and fast-paced technology, entrepreneurs must continue to develop new products to maintain a profitable market position, even after creating a winning new venture. New product development is critical for market longevity. Entrepreneurship combined with innovation equals success. Naturally, entrepreneurs need to understand new product opportunities and the new product development process if they are to ensure their venture's survival.

Because new products have varying levels of *newness* to both the company and the marketplace, entrepreneurs must make different kinds of *risk-return* trade-offs. At one extreme, pioneering or radical innovation represents a technological breakthrough or "new-to-the-world" product. Although pioneering products may be risky investments, they can produce handsome returns. At the other extreme, entrepreneurs may develop *incremental* products, which are modifications of existing products, or *product line extensions.* Incremental products are less risky to develop but typically produce a more modest return. Regardless of the type of new products you develop, bringing products to market quickly—by mastering the new product development process—is critical for gaining a competitive advantage.

If you introduce highly innovative products, be particularly attentive to consumer adoption behavior. Consumer willingness to adopt a new product is a major factor in the realm of technology products. The **product diffusion curve** (see Figure 6.5) captures adoption behavior graphically, showing customer segments called innovators, early adopters, early majority, late majority, and laggards. A number of factors affect the *rate of diffusion*, or how fast customers adopt a new product. If a product represents risk or is complex or is not completely compatible with existing products, then the market usually will adopt it at a fairly slow rate.

Incremental Improvement versus Radical Innovation

In September 2010, 58.7 million Americans had smart phones, and 37% of them were BlackBerrys. From that peak, U.S. sales of BlackBerrys slowed down, whereas sales of Apple iPhones accelerated. By April 2011, more Americans were using iPhones than BlackBerrys; and by May 2015, less than 1% of the smart phone market share in the United States were BlackBerrys.[9]

Apple's initial radical innovation and continued incremental improvements allowed it to evolve along the life cycle, and it forced Blackberry to a different market. After the Blackberry OS 10 fizzled out, it was made clear that the company was going to concentrate on selling software and services to corporations and governments. After years of marketing to position itself as the ideal business smart phone, Blackberry finally gave up in 2015 by launching PRIV, a smartphone powered by ANDROID.[10] Blackberry most recently announced they will no longer provide tech support for the PRIV and can only guarantee support on their BB10 model through 2020.[11] Nearly 40% market share to out of business in 10 years!

Entrepreneurs sometimes err in being overly product focused, concentrating on the product as they conceive it rather than as customers may want it. One way to offset the danger of this mindset is to involve the customer in the design process. Custom Research, a Baldrige National Quality Award—winning marketing research firm, performs a comprehensive survey of each of its clients prior to beginning a project. This allows the company to learn exactly what the client expects and hopes to gain from its investment. The practice of studying the customer up front not only results in better service quality but also enables you to deliver a highly customized product.

Finally, perhaps the most important product attribute for entrepreneurs is quality, which serves as a powerful differentiator and is needed to gain the recommendation of customers. Positive word-of-mouth recommendations are essential because most customers are not yet familiar with the company. Entrepreneurial companies with a quality orientation also find it easier to engage in internal marketing: Employees are more enthusiastic about and proud to be selling high-quality products than products of mediocre quality.

Pricing Strategy

Developing an optimal pricing strategy is a daunting challenge for even the most sophisticated entrepreneurial company. Figure 6.6 shows various price-setting options.

Entrepreneurs incur many costs in starting a venture. Some are *fixed costs*, which do not change with the volume of production (such as facilities, equipment, and salaries), and some are *variable costs*, which do change with the volume of production (such as raw materials, hourly labor, and sales commissions). The price of a product/service must be higher than its variable cost (point A in Figure 6.6), or you will sustain losses with the sale of each additional unit. To operate successfully, an entrepreneurial venture must not only recover both fixed costs (point B) and variable costs (point A) but also make a reasonable profit (point C). The crash of many early dot-com

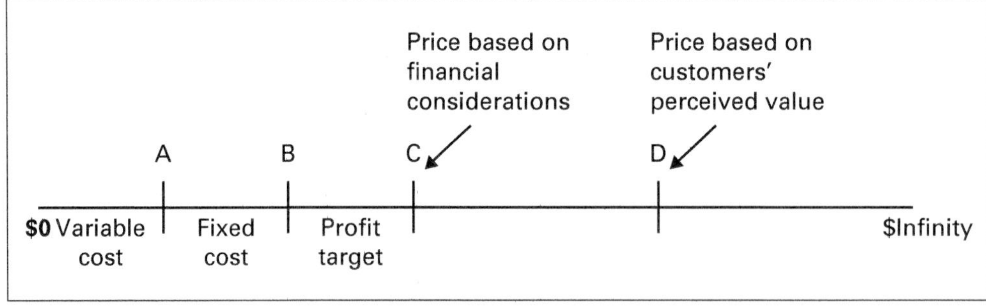

FIGURE 6.6 Pricing Decision for an Entrepreneur.

businesses illustrates this simple financial logic, as a number of these companies followed a "get-big-fast" strategy by aggressively selling their products below cost. Online grocery businesses such as Webvan fell into this trap: The expense of filling and delivering each order exceeded the profitability of the sale. They could never fit the price and operations to the value the customer expected, and now this market is being filled by companies like Instacart, whose smarter infrastructure allows them to price right and make a profit.[12]

Many entrepreneurs, in setting prices, use a *cost based method*, marking up a product based on its cost plus a desired profit margin (point C in Figure 6.6). Another method, often used in conjunction with a markup, is matching competitors' prices. A common problem with these methods is that they allow entrepreneurs to price too low, thereby "leaving money on the table." Pricing too low can hurt the long-term profitability of the venture. Of course, pricing too high also has a serious downside, as it can create a purchase barrier and limit sales.

So what choices does an entrepreneur have in identifying the most appropriate price? An alternative to cost-based and competitive pricing is *perceived value pricing* (point D), which is especially viable for pricing a new or innovative product or service. Entrepreneurs also can pursue strategies that trade off high profit margins for high sales, or vice versa. Determining the full value of a product/service and then using effective communications to convince target customers to pay for that value are challenging tasks even for an established company.

If possible, approach perceived value pricing with premarket price testing, estimating the number of units customers will purchase at different price points. Two well-known pricing strategies, which represent opposite ends of the pricing spectrum, are price skimming and penetration pricing. **Price skimming** sets high margins; you can expect to gain limited market share because your prices will be relatively high. **Penetration pricing** aims to gain high market share with lower margins and relatively lower prices. For entrepreneurs with a product that brings something new to the marketplace, a skimming strategy is usually best. Unless your channels of distribution are very well established, a penetration strategy, generally reserved for mature products, is hard to implement.

We can represent price in a variety of ways. There are basic **price points** (also called *price levels*) for products, which are standardized or fixed, and there are **price promotions**—a tool by which marketers can achieve specific goals, such as introducing a product to a new customer market. Price promotions are short term and use regular price levels as a base to discount from; they provide a way to offer customers good deals. Price promotions let you increase sales, reward distributors, gain awareness for a new product, and clear excess inventory. Periodically, Nike lists products from the previous stock under "CLEARANCE" on its website at a discounted price to push the sales of the old stock and make way for the new stock of sporting goods and apparel. This type of promotion typically increases sales on the older products and increases the penetration of the new stock in the market, benefiting both the company and the consumers. Price promotions often are necessary to maintain good relationships with distributors: Both wholesalers and retailers must offer price promotions to stay competitive. In business-to-business markets, companies often reward their business customers with volume discounts applied to the ongoing purchase of particular goods and services. Promotions are an important tool for entrepreneurs, too, who often use them to gain an initial position in the marketplace. Amazon offers a six-month free trial period for its product Amazon Prime, a yearly subscription service for users to have access to entertainment, online shopping benefits, and so on. Amazon Prime provides this promotion to motivate the users to try the product in hopes of locking them in for the long term.

A common pricing strategy is **price discrimination**: charging different prices to different customer segments. Examples of this practice are highly varied and include the lower prices charged to shoppers using store loyalty cards and the differing price structures used to charge airline passengers. *Couponing* is a widely used form of price discrimination that rewards customers who care about receiving a discount but does not reward those who don't care enough to put forth the extra effort to redeem the coupon.

Pricing is important to entrepreneurs not just because it affects revenue and profit but also because it plays a role in how consumers perceive a product's position in the market. Price serves as a quality cue to consumers, especially when they have had limited experience with the product. The *economic perspective* views consumers as rational actors who buy when the perceived benefits of a product exceed its price. Those who study consumer behavior, however, understand that consumers' *willingness to pay* is not totally rational but is affected by a variety of psychological factors.

Entrepreneurs can use some marketplace wisdom relative to pricing. First, the selling effort for a product must match its price. Price skimming, for example, must be accompanied by a sophisticated, effective selling process. It is easier to lower than raise prices because customers are resistant to price increases. The more established the differentiation and/or quality of a product or service, the more price insensitive the consumer—if he or she values the perceived benefits. Customers also are less price sensitive when products and services are bundled into a single offer because this makes prices more difficult to compare. A good entrepreneur will be aware of both the pricing practices of competing companies and the pricing-related purchase behavior of consumers.

Distribution Strategy (Place)

Distribution presents special challenges for entrepreneurs because channels of distribution often are difficult to set up initially. Figure 6.7 shows the structure of traditional distribution channels for consumer and business-to-business marketing. Although established businesses may introduce new products, price points, and communications strategies, they usually rely on existing channels of distribution. For example, Crest, a Procter & Gamble brand, may introduce a new type of electric toothbrush with a distinctive price position and an innovative advertising campaign, but it will use its existing network of wholesalers and retailers to actually distribute the product. Entrepreneurs usually don't have this luxury.

Finding the right channel can be far less difficult than breaking into the right channel. Entrepreneurs who want to market food products, for instance, face enormous barriers when they try to get their products on supermarket shelves, as the Gourmet Stew case in Chapter 3 illustrated. Most supermarkets are national chains that charge large slotting fees. Even when brokers and distributors accept new products into their lines, they may be unwilling to dedicate much effort to selling them when the products are unknown.

Distribution can be problematic for entrepreneurial service companies as well as for those that manufacture goods. Distribution decisions for a service company often are location decisions because many services require that service providers interact directly with customers. Effective distribution is the availability and accessibility of a service to its target customers. As early-stage service companies grow, new locations often are the most important means of attracting new customers and increasing sales.

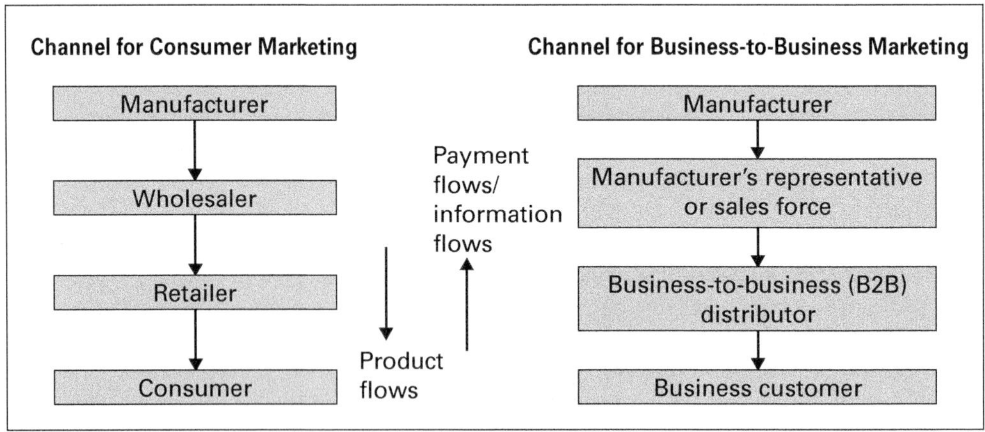

FIGURE 6.7 Traditional Distribution Channels.

Starbucks is an international services-sector company with thousands of stores; nevertheless, the service is sold locally, and one location may be more or less successful than another. If a Starbucks location is unsuccessful, the company can cancel its lease and open an alternative location in that neighborhood or focus on locations in other neighborhoods. But if an entrepreneur makes a bad location decision for his first or second or even third location, the financial loss can paralyze the company.

There is a great deal of *interdependency* in a distribution channel: Each channel member has a particular function to perform, and each relies on the others. Entrepreneurs especially are inclined to rely on other companies to fulfill certain distribution tasks. Many companies were able to enter the Internet retailing sector quickly because they could outsource *fulfillment*—warehousing, packing, and delivering the order—to another company, allowing them to maintain *virtual* companies with low fixed costs. In business-to-business channels, entrepreneurs often outsource their selling efforts to sales brokers who work for a marketing firm rather than investing the time and money to build their own sales force. There are disadvantages to this kind of outsourcing, though: Quality is hard to control, the information flow between you and your customer is interrupted, and longer-term cost economies are harder to achieve.

Sometimes channel partners turn out to be more expensive for your business than you expect. In the case of Amazon, the urgency to have a delivery network of their own was initiated due to delivery failures during the Christmas rush. Relying completely on third-party logistics companies for delivery was increasing the risk of not satisfying customers and also driving financial losses due to compensation for missed deliveries. Amazon now provides the "Last Mile" delivery of its goods themselves to have more control over consumers' shopping experiences. This small trial of having their own delivery network has the benefit of potentially transforming the company from an online retailer to a full-fledged logistics company.[13]

Distribution channel strategy includes three types of **channel coverage**: intensive, selective, and exclusive. The appropriate strategy depends on the type of product or service that you will sell. **Intensive** coverage works for consumer goods and other fast-moving products. The carbonated soft drink category is one of the most intensively distributed: Products are sold in supermarkets, drugstores, convenience stores, restaurants, vending machines, sporting event concessions, and fast-food outlets. **Selective** distribution brings the product to specific distributors, often limiting selection geographically by establishing a dealer network. Kate Spade sells her handbags and other fashion accessories to high-end, luxury department stores, as well as Kate Spade specialty stores, but not to mainstream retailers or mass merchandisers. Selective distribution can protect dealers and retailers from competition, while helping manufacturers maintain prices by thwarting price competition. The third coverage strategy, **exclusive** distribution, is often used for luxury products. For some time, Neiman Marcus had exclusive rights to distribute the Herme`s line of fashion accessories.

Channel partnerships (or *relationships*) have important implications for entrepreneurs. Often the channel member with the most power will prevail; for this reason, **channel power** is an important concept in distribution strategy. Although channel partnerships can speed a young company's growth, preserve resources, and transfer risk, entrepreneurs must be careful not to sacrifice their direct relationship with customers. Most important, entrepreneurs must carefully manage their relationships with channel partners and monitor them over time.

Another widely applied concept, **channel conflict**, refers to situations where differing objectives and turf overlap, leading to true disharmony in the channel. Channel conflict was a high-profile phenomenon in the early days of the Internet, when many startup companies were using the strategy of **disintermediation**—cutting intermediaries out of traditional distribution channels by selling directly to customers. Amazon, the online bookseller, created conflict between book publishers and distributors and traditional book retailers. Because Amazon could buy in volume and avoid the high occupancy costs retailers pay, it could offer an enormous assortment at deeply discounted prices. Amazon's volume allowed it to negotiate low prices from publishers and wholesalers, who in turn alienated their other customers, the traditional book retailers in the channel.

Entrepreneurs succeed with their distribution strategies when they have a strong understanding of channel economics. Giro, the bicycle helmet company that outfitted both Greg LeMonde and Lance Armstrong—famous American winners of the Tour de France and in Armstrong's case subsequently discredited for using performance-enhancing drugs—gained initial access to the retail channel by offering high margins and selective distribution to preferred bike shops. This allowed the company to maintain its premium prices and establish loyalty among experts and cycling enthusiasts.

Current practice reflects a focus on multichannel distribution, which gives a company the ability to reach multiple segments, gain marketing synergies, provide flexibility for customers, save on customer acquisition costs, and build a robust database of purchase information. J.Crew, for instance, has been successful diversifying its store-based business to include strong catalog and online channels. But a multichannel strategy adds operating complexity and demands more resources, so entrepreneurs are best to approach these opportunities cautiously and be careful that their timing is in line with their capabilities and resources. For example, Dell Computers built its business model on direct sales of computers—which was different than the industry norm and eliminated the middleman standing between the company and the customer. By the early 1990s, their growth trajectory solely through direct distribution faltered, and Dell entered the retail channel in pursuit of revenue growth. Although the growth strategy worked in the beginning and revenue grew 50% in the next four years, it started suffering losses because it lost margins through retail channels. Dell realized that the retail channel was not profitable for other computer corporations as well due to low margins and supply chain costs. Dell pulled out of the retail channel in 1994 and dramatically changed its approach to customers, gearing its business to serve only the most profitable segments, such as big companies.[14] Today, Dell is a private company again but reports suggest large companies are still its biggest channel.

Research shows that many of the most serious obstacles to entrepreneurial success are related to distribution. Specifically, entrepreneurs tend to be overly dependent on channel partners and short on understanding channel behavior in their industry. It is critical that entrepreneurs take the time to learn about distribution and make fact-based decisions about channel design and channel partnerships to overcome these threats to good distribution strategy.

Marketing Communications Strategy (Promotion)

Marketing communications convey messages to the market—messages about the company's products and services as well as about the company itself. The marketing communications element of the marketing mix is a mix within a mix: The **communications mix** is defined as *advertising, sales promotion, public relations, personal selling*, and *direct marketing* (sometimes included with advertising). The marketing communications mix and some of its key elements are shown in Figure 6.8.

The components of the communications mix, like those of the marketing mix, are often referred to as *tools*, and the use of these tools by marketers differs substantially across business and industry contexts. To illustrate, consumer product companies' communications are often aimed at mass markets and include advertising and sales promotions, whereas business-to-business companies use more customized, interactive tools, such as personal selling by a sales force. Of course, the communications a marketer uses are closely aligned with the specific type of product the company is attempting to sell as well as with the company's marketing objectives.

It is common marketing wisdom to use a variety of tools in marketing any product or service. Because of this focus on multiple methods and the need to integrate and coordinate these methods, we often call the process **integrated marketing communications**. A range of factors—including cost, timing, and target market—determines the selection of a company's key communications tools. The question you must answer is, "What is the most effective way to communicate with my customers and influence their actions?" And the sooner you can answer this, the better.

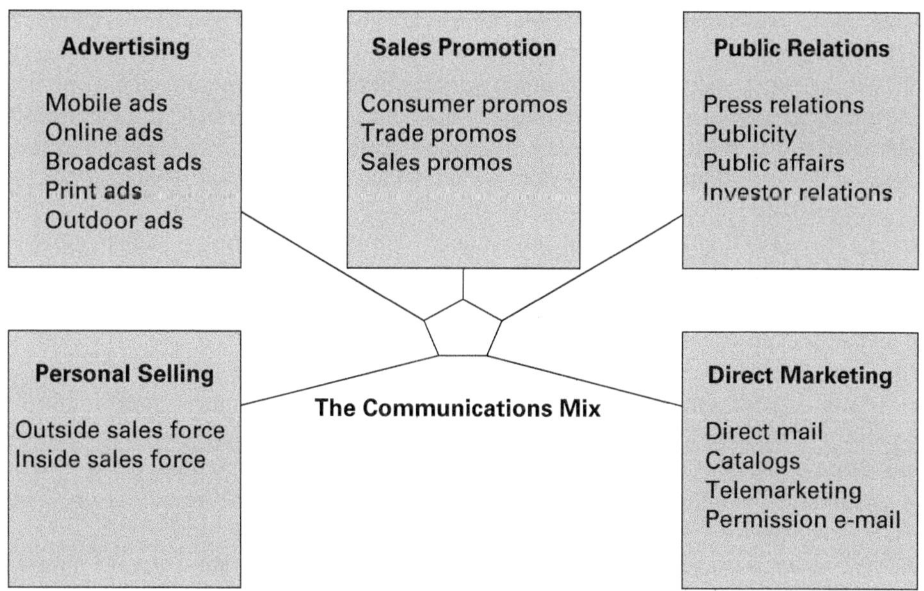

FIGURE 6.8 Marketing Communications.

Two fundamental communications strategies are *push* and *pull*. A **push** strategy aims to push a product through the channel using tools such as trade promotions, trade shows, and personal selling to distributors or other channel members. A **pull** strategy's goal, on the other hand, is to create end-user demand and rely on that demand to pull the product through the channel. Pull strategies, which are directly targeted to end users, include advertising and consumer sales promotions, such as in-store specials. These strategies also are relevant for service companies. Fidelity Investments, for example, can push its mutual funds through brokers or advertise them directly to investors, who, the company hopes, will then request them.

Marketing communications is a broad and sophisticated field. Many of the most visible tools are primarily accessible to large companies with deep marketing budgets and in-house marketing talent. This is usually the case for large, national television and print advertising online and mobile ads, and high-penetration direct mail campaigns. Probably the greatest breadth of tools exists within the domain of advertising, which includes everything from mobile advertising on your smart phone to billboards to Web sites to local newspapers to Super Bowl commercials. There also are various direct marketing tools, including catalogs, direct mail and e-mail, telemarketing, and infomercials (vehicles for direct selling).

Traditional advertising outlets have options geared toward recent changes with online newspapers and advertising opportunities on all sorts of mobile platforms. In addition, entrepreneurs have the option to advertise directly to consumers who are searching online by using Amazon Ads, Google AdWords and other services. These advertising offerings allow you to connect directly to people who are searching online using words connected to your product.

What *advertising* choices are available to an entrepreneur? Anything that is appropriate, affordable, and measurable, or at least possible to evaluate. Entrepreneurs can use traditional major media by focusing on scaled-back options, such as regional editions of national magazines, locally broadcast commercials on cable television stations, and local newspapers and radio stations. The disadvantage is that it's almost impossible to achieve advertising economies of scale. But you can efficiently conduct strongly targeted campaigns with a focus on cost control. AdWords and online options allow you to target very tightly but it can be costly, and scale will likely be expensive as well.

In addition to regionalized or localized major media of both the traditional and electronic type, you have a number of minor media options. These include "traditional" options such as classified ads, the Yellow Pages and online information services, brochures, flyers, online bulletin boards, local canvassing (for business-to-business), and educational seminars or demonstrations. As mentioned earlier, most marketing experts support using multiple methods in combination, in part because different methods have particular strengths and weaknesses. But even though the media are varied, the message and the brand image you want to communicate should be strictly consistent. Two terms that are frequently mentioned in relation to advertising objectives are *reach* and *frequency*. **Reach** is the percentage of a company's target market that is exposed to an ad campaign within a specific period of time. **Frequency** is the number of times a member of your target market is exposed during that time period.

When selecting media, entrepreneurs match their communications goals to media capabilities. Radio is more targeted and intimate than other traditional advertising media; it allows flexibility but requires repetition for the message to get through. Television has a large reach and is good for demonstrating product benefits but is usually expensive and entails substantial production costs. Many magazines with a long shelf life are well targeted (consider how many times a magazine may be read in a doctor's waiting room).

Newspapers are good for geographical targeting and promotional advertising but have a very short shelf life. Some mobile advertising opportunities have the reach of and frequency metrics of newspapers because they have similar traits (news stories within a 24-hour period). Infomercials, which we may also consider a direct marketing tool, have production costs and a short life span but are persuasive and good for telling the product story. Ad words and online advertising allows companies to reach a specific and often desirable customer market. Figure 6.9 presents brief guidelines for the strategic use of advertising media.

Even entrepreneurs often go to marketing experts for advice about how to execute campaigns and how to frame an effective message. Although some early-stage companies use established advertising agencies, others contract with freelance marketing professionals, many of whom have experience in the entrepreneurial domain. You'll want to learn the basics of advertising, public relations, and marketing research to be able to select and evaluate agencies or individuals you bring in to assist your company with its early-stage marketing.

The three primary types of **sales promotion** are *consumer promotions, trade promotions*, and *sales force promotions*. **Consumer promotions** are deals offered directly to consumers to support a pull strategy. **Trade promotions** are deals offered to a company's trade or channel partners—such as distributors or retailers—to support a traditional push strategy. **Sales force promotions** motivate and reward the company's own sales force or its distributors' sales forces.

There are two basic types of sales promotions: price and nonprice. We discussed price promotions earlier in the section on pricing strategy. *Consumer* price promotions include coupons, rebates, and loyalty rewards; *trade* price promotions include discounts, allowances, buyback guarantees, and slotting fees. Types of *consumer* nonprice promotions include product sampling, advertising specialties (such as T-shirts with a brand logo), contests, and sweepstakes. *Trade* nonprice promotions include trade shows and sales contests.

The effects of sales promotions differ from the effects of advertising. In general, sales promotions produce more immediate, sales-driven results, whereas advertising produces a more long-term, brand-building result. Sales promotions have become increasingly popular with companies in the last couple of decades.

Many entrepreneurs derive great value from using **public relations (PR)** as a strategic communications tool. PR has two major dimensions: *publicity* and *corporate communications*. When Google founder Larry Page introduced Google Pack at the 2006 Consumer Electronics Show, that was a corporate communication designed to move users away from competitor, Microsoft. When Google joined the O3b (other 3 billion) consortium—a group of companies that support web access for Africa—it did so to gain positive publicity. Bill Samuels, Jr.,

Advertising Medium	Key Factors for Entrepreneurs to Consider
Brochures and flyers	• Allow creative flexibility and focused message • Production quantity and distribution must be well planned
Direct mail and e-mail	• Permits precise targeting and encourages direct response • Results are measurable and can guide future campaigns
Infomercials	• Effective for telling a story and communicating or endorsing product benefits • Costly to produce but measurable and good for collecting data
Internet communications	• A variety of options, such as banner ads and permission e-mail marketing • Superior for collecting data and measuring responses
Magazines	• Can easily be targeted, are involving for readers, and have a long shelf life • Offer budget flexibility but involve a long lead time
Newsletters	• Good creative opportunities and maximum control • Cost factors (time and money) should be carefully considered
Newspapers (including mobile or online news)	• Best medium for advertising promotions and reaching a geographically based or local market • Shelf life is fairly short, and ads are usually not carefully read
Outdoor	• Can have strong visual impact and repeat exposure; this medium is believed to offer a high return on investment • Targeting is difficult because ads are location bound
Radio	• Good potential for creativity and connecting with the audience; message can be easily varied • Excellent for targeting, but ads must be repeated to be effective
Search (i.e., Google AdWords)	• People are searching for you, but clicks do not equate to sales • Can be done on a budget, but limited by character space, and cost of clicks can add up quickly
Telemarketing	• Interactive communication with one-on-one selling capabilities • A direct response method that has faced increased regulation because it is seen by many to be intrusive
Television	• High media and production costs but superior reach; most effective way to present and demonstrate a product • Commonly used for brand building
Yellow Pages	• An important local medium used as a basic reference by consumers; necessary for credibility • Low cost, but standardized format limits creativity

FIGURE 6.9 Strategic Use of Advertising Media.

the CEO of Maker's Mark Bourbon, used a personal connection and an elaborate plan to gain major-league publicity:

> *Dave Garino covered the Kentucky area for The Wall Street Journal. Bill Jr. discovered that he and Dave had a mutual friend, Sam Walker, with whom Dave had gone to journalism school. Bill Jr. knew Dave was going to be in town covering an unrelated story and decided to try a unique approach to persuade him to do a story on Maker's Mark. Bill Jr. staged an event at the distillery and awarded exclusive rights to cover the show to a local news station. He found out which hotel Dave Garino was staying in and had Sam Walker arrange to meet Dave for cocktails in the hotel's bar. Next, Bill Jr. convinced the bartender to turn all the televisions above the bar to the local station that was covering the distillery show. When Dave saw the news footage, he asked Sam what Maker's Mark was and why, if there was so much interest in this distillery, had he never heard of it. When Sam replied that it was the local favorite and offered to introduce him to Bill Jr., he accepted. Subsequently, Dave and Bill Jr. spent three days developing a story that was published on the front page of The* Wall Street Journal.

Bill Jr. recalled: "From that one story we received about 50,000 letters inquiring about our product. The phone lines didn't stop ringing for weeks. We had one salesman at the time and we were trying to figure how to best capitalize from all this publicity."

And the rest, as they say, is history.[15]

Maker's Mark Waters Down Image, but Boosts Brand Recognition

When Maker's Mark announced that it would be diluting the strength of its bourbon from 45% to 42% by volume and thereby increasing its output, they set off a public relations rollercoaster! The announcement outraged some loyal drinkers, who immediately vented their anger via social media; reports of their protests soon spread to conventional media. One week later Bill Samuels, Jr., Maker's Mark Founder and Chairman Emeritus, and Rob Samuels, COO, in a Tweet headed "You spoke, we listened" handsomely apologized to their customers for their misstep and reversed their decision by stating that they would make it "just like we've made it since the very beginning."

According to BrandIndex data, Maker's Mark attention score shot up from 8 before the dilution announcement to 24 in less than three weeks, indicating that 24% of the population age 21 and over had heard something good or bad about the brand in the last two weeks. The threefold increase caused a few skeptics to question whether Maker's Mark's initial announcement was a deliberate marketing move to boost its name recognition rather than a public relations blunder. That was unlikely as it damaged Maker's Mark's image. Also the last thing that Maker's Mark needed before it could increase production capacity was more demand that would result from increasing brand recognition. More likely it was following the lead of Tennessee whiskey icon, Jack Daniel's, which diluted its strength from 43% to 40% in 2004 with little adverse reaction from drinkers.

The Samuels's swift and effective response is a good illustration of how to handle a public relations disaster in the Internet age when bad news and rumors go viral at lightning speed on the Web.

It is often argued that publicity is an entrepreneur's best friend, more valuable than millions of dollars of advertising. The reason is that PR is perceived as more credible and more objective; a reporter's words are more believable than those of an advertising agency. Also, the argument goes, PR is free! This, of course, is not true—it takes a significant amount of time and effort, sometimes money, and always the ability to leverage connections to generate good PR. If this were not the case, there would not be so many public relations firms charging high fees and battling for the media's attention. Savvy entrepreneurs with fledgling companies are good at managing their own PR. For example, they send out press releases announcing new products, key executive hires, and other significant company events to newspapers, trade magazines, and online media outlets.

For companies operating in a business-to-business environment or those that need to sell into an established distribution channel, *personal selling* is a core component of the communications mix. Although some companies separate sales and marketing, a company's sales force is often its primary marketing tool. Establishing and managing a sales force requires decisions related to sales force size, training, organization, compensation, and selling approaches.

A sales force is often considered to be a company's most valuable asset. Maintaining a strong sales force is an expensive proposition, though, and startup companies often face a difficult decision: whether to absorb the expense and sell directly or hire manufacturers' representatives (*reps*, sometimes called *brokers*) to sell the company's products (along with those of other companies) on commission. Reps are advantageous in that they have existing relationships with customers, but a company has more control—and a closer relationship with its customers—if it invests in its own sales force. A sales force may be organized geographically, by product line, by customer size, or by customer segment or industry. Compensation is usually some mix of base salary and commission, and incentives may be linked to gaining new customers, exceeding sales quotas, or increasing profitability. Current marketing practice places a high value on selecting and retaining customers based on their profit potential to the company. The sales force typically should have access to effective selling materials, credible technical data, and sales automation software that will ensure an effective and efficient selling process.

Personal selling is an important activity for entrepreneurs on an informal, personal level—through professional networking. Leveraging personal and industry connections is a key success factor, especially in the startup or early growth stage of the venture. But this is a time-consuming and often laborious process, which is often neglected and rarely fully optimized. Giro's helmets founder, Jim Gentes, personally attended top triathlons and other high-profile races across the country, demonstrating his helmets and giving them to the best cyclists. He was ahead of his time in understanding the value of endorsements from world-class athletes.

Entrepreneurs can implement *direct marketing* campaigns to be broad based or to be local or limited in scope. Direct marketing methods include direct mail, catalogs, telemarketing, infomercials, and permission e-mail (where consumers "opt-in" to receive messages). The effectiveness of direct media is easy to measure, and these media are ideal for building a database that can be used for future marketing and analysis. Direct marketing is an important tool for communicating with new or existing customers, whom you can target for mailings that range from thank-you notes to announcements of future promotions.

With the increased use of technology and databases in marketing, and the growth of the Internet channel, the practice of "one-to-one" marketing has become pervasive. This type of marketing is interactive and has qualities similar to personal selling: Your company can address a customer on an individual level, factoring in that customer's previous purchasing behavior and other kinds of information, and then respond accordingly. It is the use of databases that allows marketers to personalize communications and design customer-specific messages.

Customer relationship management (CRM) systems are designed to help companies compile and manage data about their customers. Although CRM systems are usually large scale and expensive, an astute entrepreneur can set up a more fundamental system to capture and use customer data to facilitate relationship building. Part of this process is capturing the right metrics—for example, *cost of customer acquisition* or *average lifetime value of a customer*—and knowing how to act on them.

Value Proposition: Articulating the Entrepreneurial Strategy[16]

Understanding the nascent firm's strategy for segmenting, targeting, and position is critical; so too is having your 4Ps well defined. However, entrepreneurs need to go beyond thinking about these aspects as disparate parts and instead bring them together to clearly articulate the value they will bring to their customer segment(s). As noted at the start of this section, connecting these concepts can provide the foundation for thinking about how you will position the value you will bring to your primary target audience.

Early on during the process, entrepreneurs will often cycle through many different customer segments and different ways to position to these segments. During this process you are trying to find out what value the customer wants and expects from your product, but it is not only about the product. Distilling down to the best match between a customer segment and the value they expect brings along the other Ps as well. What price do they expect to pay (Price)? Where do they expect to get the product; what channel (Place)? How can I reach them (Promotion)?

Let's look again at Red Bull. Total sales figures released in 2019 show that Red Bull is still the world's leading energy drink, with 26.4 percent[17] in the United States alone. Across the globe, they sold 6.8 billion cans in 171 different countries in 2018.[18] You can find Red Bull in virtually any channel that distributes canned or bottled drinks. Can *you* hope to get that kind of distribution? Unlikely at the start, but that's okay. Accessing the right channel, connecting with the primary target audience, and doing so at the right price with the product they want, can be a constant game of trial-and-error at the start. As we addressed in earlier chapters, by talking to potential customers and other stakeholders in the process, you can perform low-cost probes to learn. What you learn allows you to develop a value proposition that incorporates the 4Ps while understanding how to target and position your value to the intended segment.

Uncovering and developing the right value proposition for your venture is an evolving process. When Red Bull was in the concept stage in the early 1980s, or even later in the decade as it began in earnest, do you think its leaders had such clarity of message? No. Today, it is positioned around the world as an energy drink for high-adventure, action sports athletes and others who want a boost from their drink. The company promotes dozens of events and sponsors many teams—from car rallies and cliff diving championships to extreme athletes and the New York Red Bull soccer club.

However, the start was different. Red Bull began when Austrian Dietrich Matechitz travelled through Thailand in the early 1980s and came across a local energy drink called "krating daeng" (red bull), which had become a popular pick-me-up for local blue-collar workers. After striking a deal with the Thai pharmaceutical company that owned this early version, he went to work shaping it, reformulating the product taste for Western palates, and figuring out the right value for the right segment. Red Bull began to spread across Europe in the mid-1990s; during this time its value proposition slowly began to resemble what we see today. Still, when it came to the United States, it was essentially locked out of traditional supermarket channels due to dominant competitors. Instead, Red Bull found initial distribution success in gas stations and local bodegas. It was pitched through dance clubs and purposefully through smaller independent outlets as opposed to large national chains.[19] Some clubs had Red Bull and others did not. This "exclusivity" play in distribution was eventually married with their sponsorship of athletes and other sports and music events that comprised their promotional efforts. This was the beginning of the evolution of Red Bull's value proposition into what we know it is today: a high-quality energy drink for extreme athletes and other like-minded enthusiasts.

Building Your Value Proposition. Potential customers look at more than your product and its price when consciously or subconsciously determining its value. We know that some folks will pay a premium, but others may not. Some want a basic standard of quality, whereas others want the absolute best. Value is a deeper concept than just the price–quality trade-off, however. People buy for all sorts of reasons: Sometimes they buy to have the newest: the newest phone, latest technology gadget, or even to be one of the first to go to the newest, hottest restaurant or club in town. Think about the lines of folks waiting for the latest Apple product to release. Or what about LVMH? LVMH Moe¨t Hennessey Louis Vuitton SE comprises some of the world's leading houses of design focused on fashion, accessories, spirits, and more. Whether it's Veuve Clicquot or Dom Pe´rignon champagne, Louis Vuitton bags, Donna Karan clothes, Christian Dior perfumes, De Beers diamonds, or TAG Heuer watches, LVMH builds their value proposition on a foundation of luxury.

For entrepreneurs beginning to build their company, discovering the venture's value proposition takes work, as a value proposition cannot always be captured in one simple word. Think about Apple again: For some people it may be that they buy because they want to have the latest or newest gadget. Others will tell you they buy because of Apple's beautifully minimalist design. Still others might say it's their functionality or ease of use. Few will likely admit that they buy Apple products for status, but we suspect that status plays a part. For many companies, their value proposition is a combination of different factors. Sometimes there might be clearly differentiated customer segments that buy the same product but extract different value (some might buy Nike running shoes for their performance, whereas others might buy them based purely on fashion and how they look). In many instances people will see more than one value point: Some people purchase Diet Coke both for the taste and as a low-calorie option.

Entrepreneurs need to know what their market looks like and how it might be segmented as a precursor to trying to figure out what value each group of customers truly values. How do you bring this all together? What is the value you are delivering for your venture? The list in Figure 6.10 gives some examples of traditional forms of value that firms deliver. How then do you go about figuring out what value your venture wants to bring to its customers? What is the value your venture is trying to deliver?

Entrepreneurs can begin to discover the unique value they can deliver to their customers by following a relatively simple three-step approach of (1) examining the total benefits their venture could offer, (2) differentiating it from the existing competitors, and (3) validating it with their customers.

As startups, we don't have the benefit of a track record with existing customers like most of our established competitors. These firms have data on what customers have bought in the past, and they have *some* sense of what customers expect and what they will pay for going forward. With this data in hand, these firms are in a good position to figure out exactly what value proposition resonates best with their customers.[20]

- Accessibility
- Brand/Status
- Convenience
- Cost reduction
- Customization
- Design
- Environmental/Green
- Exclusivity
- Newness
- Performance
- Price
- Risk reduction
- Safety
- Socially responsible
- Trust
- Usability

FIGURE 6.10 Classic Forms of Value.

For a new venture, a good first step is to begin to list all the potential benefits your offering could deliver to the market. Although a list of benefits on its own does not make a value proposition, for those of us trying to start a new venture, this is actually a good place to begin. We do not yet have the benefit of knowing any existing customer segments well. We may not even know the exact segment to approach yet. So crafting a list of a venture's potential benefits allows us to document what we believe we can deliver and why it provides value to our intended customers. The **venture's total benefits** list gives us a starting point of all of the value we *could* deliver into the marketplace. As you are initially shaping your venture, you should be able to begin to shape such a list from your initial customer interviews and interactions with others in the marketplace and industry. Being purposeful by developing a list like this allows entrepreneurs to work with their first customers or potential customers to begin to hone in on a number of different forms of value.

With this data in hand, entrepreneurs can then begin to winnow the list down by comparing what they can do in contrast to what others are offering. We do not want to enter the marketplace with a "me too" offering, so we need to understand what we do differently and potentially better than the alternatives. Here we are trying to analyze how we might create value that is different or better than competitors. A **differentiated value grid** can illustrate how we stack up against competition. Again, being purposeful in this manner allows us to see where our strengths are relative to others. It is likely that we have some strengths and some weaknesses relative to our competitors, and being able to easily compare and contrast them leads us to our final step.

Our goal is to try to develop a value proposition that truly resonates with our customers. When they think about your venture you want them to immediately think about the value they are getting. You want to be able to easily articulate this value to them through all of your marketing and outreach. From the prior work, your list of total benefits and the grid that outlines how you are differentiated from your competitors, you need to focus in on one or two points of **superior customer value**. The ideal is to determine through your work with customers and all stakeholders across the entire value which segment you can deliver value to above and beyond anyone else.

A clear value proposition can come from cycling though the different options your venture has in order to segment, target, and position your product offering and venture. Going through the three steps outlined earlier will allow you to align your 4Ps with your plan for positioning to create a clear value proposition as part of your overall marketing strategy.

Social Media

Almost every entrepreneur today will use some form of social media to market their firm and its products and services. And with good reason: social media can improve your communication with stakeholders, drive sales, increase brand awareness, increase your traffic, and bolster your search engine rankings. Here, we'll outline some basics and a few reminders, but as we said at the start of this chapter, good marketing research needs to come first and be at the foundation of your marketing plan. Social media is just a set of tools you use, and how well you make use of them is dependent upon how well you *really* know you customers, your offering, and the value you may bring.

There was a time when it looked like the Internet and then social media and mobile apps would replace the guerilla marketing techniques of the prior generation of entrepreneurs. That is simply not the case. These tools may make it easier to find folks who might be interested in your product or service, but they are not necessarily cheap. Social media marketing is mainstream and a desirable channel for companies of all types and sizes. As such, cost-per-click and auction-based pricing models do not always make social media your most effective marketing avenue.

Linda Orr, a researcher at the University of Akron, notes that the return on many big social media platforms may not be attainable for an entrepreneur that is cash-strapped and just starting out.[21] She explains that average cost per click on a Facebook ad is $1.72 and that there is a 0.77% conversion rate on these clicks. Therefore, a quick calculation shows that it costs $223.37 to gain just a single customer from Facebook, and that does not include the cost to create and manage the ad.

Given this, you need to think about your social media presence just like any other marketing tool at your disposal. Social media and the resulting data that comes from it should be part of an overall plan to reach, interact with, and learn from your customers, potential customers, and various other stakeholders. As an entrepreneur, you have to remember what you own and can control and other things that you can use and perhaps borrow. Your website, your e-mail list and contacts are assets you own. Social media are tools you can use to achieve your objectives so you start first with how it can help you achieve the objectives and goals you have for your firm.

Nascent and start-up entrepreneurs need to use social media strategically and efficiently. You need to rely upon the foundational marketing principles in this chapter to figure out exactly who your target customer is, what she wants, how she wants it delivered, and more. Some of the more common social media options for entrepreneurs are listed in the accompanying box.

Social Media Options for Entrepreneurs

- Amazon ads
- Blogging
- Facebook
- Instagram
- Google adwords
- LinkedIn
- Pinterest
- Reddit
- Twitter
- YouTube

Make sure you know your target market, research exactly what each of the tools can do for you, and make your choices accordingly. Obviously, an advantage of social media usage is the data that will be available to you when you use some of these outlets. With this data, you can use social media metrics to measure attitudes, preferences, and trends. Common metrics like hits, page views, bounce rates, click paths, conversion rates, and keyword analysis will allow you to make the choices that are right for you. The ubiquity of data can be dizzying, but a big benefit is that it can be analyzed pretty simply and it can be easily adapted to fit your needs if circumstances warrant a change.

As you venture grows, or if resources allow, you might also want to use some form of social media management tool to help you become more efficient with this part of your marketing mix. There are dozens of social media tools and social media management platforms to help you manage your promotion and advertising: Salesforce Social Studio, HubSpot Social Media Tools, BuzzSumo, Hootsuite, and more. While each is differentiated, most provide primary functions such as allowing you to schedule your social media posts and promotion, monitor comments, get relevant data on your brand, and provide you with detailed analytics of your social media usage.

The most critical aspect of social media marketing is start with a clear plan and objectives. Are you trying to build your authority as an industry expert via LinkedIn? Do you want to start a conversation on Facebook that might lead folks to your services? Do you want to show appreciation to your customers via Instagram? Or maybe you want to be an influencer via Pinterest or YouTube? Whatever it is you want to achieve, you need to be clear about that goal and then find the right outlet for you. Choosing the "right" outlet is also critical: for your message might get lost or your goals and objectives might be unfulfilled and diluted if you are spread across too many platforms. It's a good idea to try find out where your target customers spend their time online: is it Facebook, LinkedIn, Reddit, Twitter, or somewhere else? Go there, try to dominate, and make a real connection and presence before dispersing yourself across too many other outlets. Hootsuite, one of the purveyors of social media management tools, guides entrepreneurs to remember the acronym: SMART. They remind us that you want to be **S**pecific about your goals; make sure your goal is **M**easurable; that these goals are **A**ttainable from both a cost and time perspective; that they are **R**elevant in that they connect to larger objective and strategy of the venture; and that they are **T**imely because they help you achieve milestones that you need to achieve now.

In summary, you need to align your social media goals with your overall marketing goals and the broad strategy for your venture. This alignment should include an initial acknowledgment of who is going to handle your social media. Do you have the time? Ability or interest? If not, consider delegating it to a team member. Regardless, of who will oversee it, start with your top marketing objectives, then evaluate the different social media options and how each one may help you achieve your marketing goals.

Guerrilla Marketing

As social media marketing quickly became a mainstream activity, where and how can resource-limited entrepreneurs efficiently market their products and services? Guerrilla marketing is marketing activities that are nontraditional, grassroots, and captivating—that gain consumers' attention and build awareness of the company.

Guerrilla marketing is often linked to "creating a buzz" or generating a lot of word-of-mouth in the marketplace. The terms *buzz, viral,* and *word-of-mouth marketing* aren't interchangeable. According to the Word of Mouth Marketing Association (WOMMA), the three concepts are defined as in the accompanying box.[22]

Types of Guerrilla Marketing

- Word-of-mouth marketing: Giving people a reason to talk about your products and services and making it easier for that conversation to take place.
- Buzz marketing: Using high-profile entertainment or news to get people to talk about your brand.
- Viral marketing: Creating entertaining or informative messages that are designed to be passed along in an exponential fashion, often electronically or by e-mail.

Entrepreneurs may use all of these nontraditional promotion campaigns to get people's attention, especially younger generations who may not pay attention to TV campaigns and print media. Guerrilla marketing is also attractive to entrepreneurs because often they have to work with a limited or nonexistent promotion budget, and traditional media are very expensive. Unfortunately for entrepreneurs, such nontraditional promotional methods are getting the attention of big marketers, who want to break through the clutter of existing media. BzzAgent, a Boston-based word-of-mouth marketing agency, has more than 500,000 agents who will try clients' products and then talk about them with their friends, relatives, and acquaintances over the duration of the campaign. It has worked with companies like Anheuser-Busch, General Mills, and Volkswagen. Procter & Gamble's (P&G's) four-year-old Tremor division has a panel of 200,000 teenagers and 350,000 moms who are asked to talk with friends about new products or concepts that P&G sends them. Some experts suggest that traditional marketers underused public relations or used it only as an afterthought, thus opening the door for creative guerrilla marketers.

It is easier to define what guerrilla marketing *does* than what it *is*. Guerrilla marketing is heard above the noise in the marketplace and makes a unique impact: It makes people talk about the product and the company, effectively making them "missionaries" for the brand. It creates drama and interest and positive *affect*, or emotion—all pretty amazing results. But in fact, truly good guerrilla marketing is as difficult as—and maybe more so than—good traditional marketing. Because lots of companies are trying to do it, it's harder to break free of the pack.

Think of guerrilla marketing as guerrilla *tactics* that you can apply to various media or elements of the communications mix rather than as entirely different communications tools. You can use guerrilla tactics in advertising (riveting posters in subways) and in personal selling (creative canvassing at a trade show), but you'll most likely use them as a form of PR—as tactics that garner visibility and positive publicity. The president of Maker's Mark practiced guerrilla marketing when he inspired *The Wall Street Journal*'s reporter to learn about and write the story of his bourbon. Red Bull is a master of promotion, including many extreme sports–related events including the Stratos Project. With Stratos, Red Bull organized to create the world record for the highest skydive from a record height of 128,000 ft. The entire event was branded as a Red Bull Event while being viewed by over 12 million individuals on YouTube.

Much of what we now call *event marketing* is in the realm of guerrilla marketing because it is experiential, interactive, and lighthearted. But as we noted earlier, guerrilla tactics are becoming more and more difficult for entrepreneurs to execute because every corporate marketing executive is trying to succeed at guerrilla marketing too and has a much larger budget to employ. Sony Ericsson Mobile executed a guerrilla marketing campaign in New York City in which trained actors and actresses pretended to be tourists and asked passersby to snap a picture with the company's new mobile phone/digital camera product. Deceptive? Yes, but too commonplace a tactic to truly be controversial.

Not every guerrilla campaign escapes controversy. When Cartoon Network's Adult Swim launched a guerrilla marketing campaign to promote the show *Aqua Teen Hunger Force*, they ended paying more than a traditional marketing campaign may have cost. The campaign used battery-powered electronic light boards of a middle-finger-waving moon man hidden in various areas around 10 cities. People in Boston mistook the packages for bombs, and the police responded. Turner Broadcasting, the owner of Cartoon Network, was forced to pay $2 million to the city of Boston not only to cover the costs of police and bomb squad but also as a show of goodwill.[23] An elaborate guerrilla marketing campaign in Toronto, designed to promote an HBO comedy series, featured street teams with TV-equipped backpacks to show pedestrians 30-second promotional clips, chalk drawings promoting the series at major intersections, and ads in the bathrooms of major media agencies that showcased giant quotes from reviews of the show. The attempt by large corporations and advertising agencies to set the standard for guerrilla marketing makes these tactics less accessible to small companies. Still, as long as entrepreneurs are sparked by creativity, guerrilla successes can still be possible, even though they require a continuous stream of ideas and energy.

In conclusion, entrepreneurs who create successful marketing strategies must have a clear vision of their goal. They also must understand how one strategic element affects another because if the marketing mix elements of product, price, distribution, and communications are not perfectly compatible—if the mix is not internally logical—the strategy will not work. Even a good beginning strategy is not enough, however, because the marketplace is dynamic. Entrepreneurial companies, more so than mature businesses, must constantly reevaluate their strategy and how it is affecting growth.

Marketing Skills for Managing Growth

It is beyond the scope of this chapter to offer a comprehensive discussion of the next step: the marketing processes and capabilities a young company needs to pursue strong growth. However, two key areas for you to focus on are *understanding and listening to the customer* and *building a visible and enduring brand.*

Understanding and Listening to the Customer

Although intuition-based decision making can work well initially for some entrepreneurs, intuition has its limitations. Entrepreneurs must be in constant touch with their customers as they grow their companies. When a company decides to introduce its second product or open a new location, for example, it needs to be able to determine whether that product or location will be welcomed in the marketplace. Entrepreneurs with a successful first product or location often overestimate demand for the second, sometimes because their confidence encourages them to put too much confidence in their own intuition.

Entrepreneurs must obtain information that will allow them to understand consumer buying behavior and customer expectations related to product design, pricing, and distribution. They also need information about the best way to communicate with customers and influence their actions. Finally, they need information about the *effectiveness* of their own marketing activities so they can continue to refine them. Marketers build relationships in part by using information to customize the marketing mix. Good entrepreneurial marketers do whatever it takes to build relationships with customers.

Entrepreneurs following a high-growth strategy need to continuously find new customer segments to support that growth. Bill Samuels, Jr., recognized that for Maker's Mark to grow significantly, the company would have to reach a new segment—drinkers of other types of alcohol—because the bourbon connoisseur market was near saturation. Rather than relying on his own intuition, Samuels studied the consumer market to understand where he would find his new customers and how he would attract them.

There are a number of ways to listen to customers; some require formal research, and others use informal systems for soliciting information and scanning the market environment. Leonard Berry cites a portfolio of methods that entrepreneurs can use to build a *listening system.*[24] These include

- *Transactional surveys* to measure customer satisfaction with the company
- *New and lost customer surveys* to see why customers choose or leave the firm
- *Focus group interviews* to gain information on specific topics
- *Customer advisory panels* to get periodic feedback and advice from customers
- *Customer service reviews* to have periodic one-on-one assessments
- *Customer complaint/comment capture* to track and address customer complaints
- *Total market surveys* to assess the total market—customers and noncustomers

Building the Brand

All entrepreneurs face the need for **brand building**, which is the dual task of building brand awareness and building brand equity. **Brand awareness** is the customer's ability to recognize and recall the brand when provided a cue. Marketing practices that create brand awareness also help shape **brand image**, which is the way customers perceive the brand. **Brand equity** is the effect of brand awareness and brand image on customer response to the brand. It is brand equity, for example, that spurs consumers to pay a premium price for a brand—a price that exceeds the value of the product's tangible attributes.

Brand equity can be positive or negative. Positive brand equity is the degree of marketing advantage a brand would hold over an unnamed competitor. Negative brand equity is the disadvantage linked to a specific brand. Brand building is closely linked to a company's communications strategy. Whereas brand awareness is created through sheer exposure to a brand—through advertising or publicity—brand image is shaped by how a company projects its identity through its products, communications, and employees. The customer's actual experience with the brand also has a strong effect on brand image.

Maker's Mark used its communications strategy, implemented through humorous, distinctive print advertising in sophisticated national magazines like *Forbes* and *Business Week*, to create a brand image that would help establish a high-end market for bourbon where none had existed in the past. The company created a likable, genuine brand personality for its bourbon. Because many of the advertisements were in the form of an open letter from Bill Samuels, Jr., to his customers, Samuels was able to represent and personalize the brand.

CONCLUSION

Marketing is often described as a delicate balance of art and science. Certainly developing the expertise to be a master marketer is difficult, especially for entrepreneurs who are constantly pulled in a thousand directions. Nevertheless, the task remains: to have customer knowledge and PR mastery and to recognize effective advertising as well as effective experiential promotion. Entrepreneurial marketers must, first and foremost, be able to sell: sell their ideas, their products, their passion, their company's long-term potential. And they must learn the skill of knowing where the market is going, now and into the future.

Early-stage companies often find it necessary to scale up or change focus. In these scenarios, competition can be a potent driver of marketing decisions, whether you are staying under the radar screen of giant companies or buying time against a clone invasion. But successful entrepreneurs will have a strong, focused marketing strategy—a consistent strategy—and therefore will not easily be thrown off course.

YOUR OPPORTUNITY JOURNAL

Reflection Point	Your Thoughts...
1. How do you learn about your customer?	
2. What secondary sources can you use?	
3. What primary data will you collect?	
4. How do you segment your market? Who's your PTA, your core customer? Who are your STAs?	

Reflection Point	Your Thoughts...
5. How will you price your product?	
6. How will you distribute your product?	
7. What channels are available? Which channels are best? When will you add new channels?	
8. What is your marketing communications strategy? What mix of advertising, PR, personal selling, and direct marketing is most effective?	
9. Can you create a list of your venture's total benefits? A differentiated value grid? One or two points of superior customer value for your intended customer segment?	
10. What guerrilla tactics can you use to create a buzz? How will you get your product's buzz to be heard above the noise?	
11. Articulate what you would like your brand to be. How will you build it during launch? During growth?	

WEB EXERCISE

Scan the Web and identify the Internet marketing techniques of two to three companies. Start with the company's home page. What functionality does the page contain (just information, online selling interface, etc.)? Evaluate the home page's communications effectiveness. Next go to your favorite search engine. What key search terms bring this company up on the first two or three pages? Does the company use paid Internet advertising? Affiliate programs? Are there any other unique aspects about the company's Internet strategy? How does what you've learned inform your Web strategy?

APPENDIX: CUSTOMER INTERVIEW

To whom should we ask the questions?

What possible information would we ask about?

Should the questions be open ended or structured?

How should the questions be sequenced?

GENERAL OUTLINE: IT NEEDS TO BE TAILORED TO MEET YOUR RESEARCH NEEDS

1. Opening discussion (introduction and warm-up):
   Briefly describe research purpose, introduce self, ensure confidentiality of response, and state expected duration of the interview session.
   Opening statement: Think of the last time you purchased or used such a product. What prompted or triggered this activity? What specific activities did you perform to get the product or service? What was the outcome of your shopping experience?
2. Current practice:
   How do you currently purchase or use a product/service of interest? How did you go about deciding on what to buy? How frequently do you buy/use this product/service? How much do you buy/use each time? Where do you buy?
3. Familiarity/awareness about product/service:
   What other products/services/stores have you considered before deciding on the final product/service you bought?
4. Important attributes: If you were shopping for such a product, what would you look for? What is important? What characteristic(s) are important to you?
5. Perception of respondents:
   How would you compare different products/services? How well do you think of the product/service you bought compared with those of its competitors with respect to these attributes?
6. Overall satisfaction with or liking of the product/service:
   Ask satisfaction level and preference ranking among competitive products.
7. Product demo/introduction/description:
   Purpose: Get reactions to the product concept and elicit a response that may identify additional decision drivers.
   What do you like about this idea? What do you dislike? Does listening to this idea suggest some factors that you would consider important and that we have not discussed so far?

Does it change the importance you attach to different factors before choosing a product or service?

Purpose: Determine the purchase intent of new product or service.

What will be the level of interest or willingness of respondents to buy or use this new product/service? At what price?

We would like to know how likely it is that you would buy such a product or service.

- Would definitely buy
- Would probably buy
- Might or might not buy
- Would probably not buy
- Would definitely not buy

We would like to know now how much you would be willing to pay for such a product or service:

- Would definitely pay $.

Please note that comparable products are priced at $.Now how much would you be willing to pay for such a product or service?

- Would definitely pay $.

8. Media habit:
   How do you find out about a product or service? What media do you read, listen to, or watch?
9. Demographic information:
   Personal information should be asked at the end of the interview. Age, income, occupation, gender, education, etc.

   Size of the firm (revenue, total full-time staff, research and development staff), resources, experience, skills, etc.
10. Wrap-up:
    Any final comments or ideas?

NOTES

1. American Marketing Association. 2004. www.marketingpower.com/content21257.php.
2. Lodish, Leonard M., Morgan, Howard Lee, and Kallianpur, Amy. *Entrepreneurial Marketing*. Hoboken, NJ: Wiley, 2001, p. xi.
3. Isaacson, Walter. 2011. *Steve Jobs*. New York: Simon and Schuster, p. 567.
4. Ibid.
5. Ibid.
6. www.macworld.com/article/1141509/jonathan_ive_london.html.
7. www.Redbull.com, http://www.kratingdaeng.com/en/index.php?page=about, http://www.cnn.com/2012/03/17/world/asia/thailand-red-bull-founder-dead/.
8. Adapted from John A. Martilla and John C. James. Importance-Performance Analysis. *Journal of Marketing*, www.beverage-digest.com/editorial/020329.php: 77–79. January 1977.
9. http://bgr.com/2015/05/27/blackberry-vs-android-vs-ios-market-share/.
10. Source: Incremental Improvement versus Radical Innovation, p. 165: Smartphone Market Statistics: http://www.gartner.com/newsroom/id/3061917.
11. https://www.theinquirer.net/inquirer/news/3023217/blackberry-will-support-bb10-until-2020-but-the-priv-has-been-flushed
12. "Rebuilding History's Biggest Dot-Com Bust," *Wall Street Journal*, Jan. 12, 2015.
13. Traditional Distribution Channels: p. 168, e.g., Amazon—"Amazon, in Threat to UPS, Tries Its Own Deliveries" *Wall Street Journal*, April 24, 2014, www.wsj.com/articles/SB10001424052702304788404579521522792859890.
14. Gadiesh, Orit and Gilbert, James L., "Profit Pools a Fresh Look at Strategy." *Harvard Business Review*, May–June 1998.
15. Seiders, Kathleen (1999), "Maker's Mark Bourbon" (case study and teaching note), Arthur M. Blank Center for Entrepreneurial Studies, Babson College.
16. The Value Proposition section written by Andrew Corbett.
17. https://www.statista.com/statistics/306864/market-share-of-leading-energy-drink-brands-in-the-us-based-on-case-volume-sales/
18. https://energydrink-us.redbull.com/en
19. Red Bull case, by Richard, R. Johnson and Jordan Mitchell, 2002, Darden Case Collection.
20. Anderson, James C., Narus, James A., and van Rossum, Wouter. "Customer Value Propositions in Business Markets." *Harvard Business Review*, March 2006.
21. https://www.entrepreneur.com/article/330032
22. Taylor, Catherine P. Psst! How Do You Measure Buzz? *AdWeek*, October 24, 2005.
23. Turner, Contractor to Pay $2M in Boston Bomb Scare. February 5, 2007. www.cnn.com/2007/US/02/05/boston.turner/index.html.
24. Berry, Leonard L. *Discovering the Soul of Service*. New York, NY: Free Press. 1999. pp. 100–101.

Case Theo Chocolate[1]

Four years after moving from Boston to Seattle to join her ex-husband in running an organic, Fair Trade chocolate factory, Debra Music felt both a sense of accomplishment and one of foreboding. Theo Chocolate began producing its first Fair Trade–certified, single-origin and blended dark chocolate bars in March of 2006 and by the fall of 2009 had built a unique brand that was particularly strong in the Pacific Northwest region. Seattle, with its young, well-educated, and socially conscious population, had proved to be a perfect base for a company rooted in socially responsible, sustainable business practices. The company had increased sales each year since its inception (see Exhibit 6.1[2]), and in the wake of large customer orders that were coming in, production had been recently ramped up. As the Vice President of Sales and Marketing of Theo Chocolate, Debra had reason to be proud of what the company had achieved.

She also had reason to be concerned. Despite a unique value proposition, a skilled and fervent management team, growing brand strength, numerous awards, and an endorsement from a well-known celebrity, Theo Chocolate had yet to turn a profit by the fall of 2009. Joe Whinney, Debra's ex-husband and Theo's CEO, had strong feelings about how the chocolate industry operated. Theo was designed from the outset to completely change the way people thought of and purchased chocolate products; Joe's explicitly stated goal was to do for cacao (the fruit from which chocolate is made) and chocolate what Starbucks had done for coffee. He had built a company that implemented sustainable, Fair Trade practices at every stage of its value chain—a model totally unique in the highly competitive chocolate industry. In fact, Theo Chocolate's Web site boasted that it was "the only organic, Fair Trade, Bean-to-Bar chocolate factory in the United States."[3] Theo's entire marketing and branding strategy—indeed, its reason for existence—was based on these principles.

With some indication that the company might soon turn the corner and get "in the black" for the first time in its existence, Debra was faced with a key decision: Should the company stay true to its socially responsible roots, or would it have to compromise some of its core principles to become and stay financially profitable? As the person Joe had entrusted with building the Theo brand, much of the responsibility of this decision had fallen to Debra. The decision would determine the strategic direction the company would take and, ultimately, how the company would market itself and its products. Perhaps most important, it would determine whether Joe and the rest of the management team could make a profit while maintaining their values.

Joseph and the Chocolate Factory

Background

Like any startup, Theo Chocolate (named after the Greek name for the cacao tree, *Theobroma Cacao*, or "food of the Gods") spent the first few years of its existence struggling to make a name for itself. Its first few years had been unprofitable as the company made investments in plant, people, and marketing, pushed by Joe's vision to keep going. See Exhibit 6.1 for select financial measures of the company, 2006–2009.

For Joe Whinney, the journey to CEO of a chocolate company had truly been a unique one. An avid sailor, Joe decided to go work for a conservation foundation while sailing around Central

Exhibit 6.1 Select Company Financials 2006–2009

	Year 1 (July 06–June 07)	Year 2 (July 07–June 08)	Year 3 (July 08–June 09)
Net Sales	$ 1,125,808	$ 2,669,264	$ 3,096,194
Gross Margin	157,294	767,179	857,788
% of Net Sales	*13.6%*	*28.7%*	*27.7%*
Sales & Marketing Expenses	504,634	940,693	1,097,359
General & Admin Expenses	749,619	1,018,024	1,079,063
Total Operating Expenses	1,254,253	1,958,717	2,176,422
Opex as % of Net Sales	*111.4%*	*73.4%*	*70.3%*
Operating Income (Loss)	(1,096,959)	(1,191,358)	(1,318,634)
Net Income (Loss)	(1,241,901)	(1,368,125)	(1,499,450)

[1] Case was written by *Gary Ottley and Michael Cummings of Babson College.*

[2] All financial information has been disguised.

[3] https://www.theochocolate.com/

America in his early twenties. His very first job was volunteering to help indigenous cocoa farmers in Belize. Always environmentally conscious and a self-described "tree-hugger," Joe quickly found his passion in cacao working with farmers and saw firsthand the impact of a pure-profit motive on the members of an industry value chain. He saw the business opportunity in an alternative business model very early:

> *[Back in 1991] I saw the problem—the need for profit, combined with short-term thinking, is making everybody—from the subsistence farmer in Central America who has to buy books for his kids for school and has a small cash requirement, all the way up to CEOs of Fortune 100 companies—they all have exactly the same mindset. I thought it made sense—good business sense—for business to be done differently. I thought, if people are paid a fair price, they can invest [in their business] for the long term and not have these short-term, paycheck-to-paycheck behaviors, and there's this group of consumers who respect this—I thought, why not just make it happen? To me, it was just pure common sense. It wasn't this "I'm going to change the world" thing; I just thought that it was so silly that this hadn't happened yet.*

Theo Chocolate was not Joe's first attempt at running a company devoted to this ideal. He had tried being a "value added broker," sourcing organic cacao for 10 of the largest processors of cocoa beans in the United States. His company, Organic Commodity Products, purchased beans from farmers and provided partially or totally processed cocoa and chocolate products to those processors to be sold under their labels. The company ultimately succumbed to the economic forces in play in 2001 and 2002. The dot.com bust froze OCP's equity financing, customers started looking for less-expensive sources, and the company closed in 2002.

The experience did little to dampen Joe's passion for his vision: to convince consumers that where chocolate came from, and how it was made, made a difference—in taste, in quality, and in the impact it had on each stage of the supply chain. In fact, after dealing with large-scale cocoa processors, it had increased. Joe wanted nothing less than to cause a major shift in how consumers thought of and consumed chocolate and often cited Starbucks as an exemplar because of what it had done to shift perceptions of another so-called commodity product: coffee. He wanted to increase the perceived value of, as he put it, "this really special, incredibly delicious agricultural product called cocoa beans." He was convinced that "converted" consumers would be willing to pay more, for a higher quality product, which would have a direct impact all the way down the chain to the farmers. Despite the failure of OCP, Joe still felt that there was a way to do this profitably, and he felt that at the heart of it all, the consumer held the key to that profitability.

> *At the heart of this is a consumer issue. We can point fingers at industry, but at the heart of it, business is designed to give people what they want in the most efficient way possible at the highest level of profit. The big guns—they're just trying to give people what they think the people want. Now—companies have some influence, and can and should take an active role to change consumers' perceptions—but at the end of the day what it's going to take is consumers putting a value—a higher value—on where all of their things come from, and the decisions they make and how they impact the future. To me, that's a cultural movement—and a very, very tall order.*

Joe realized that he needed to build a brand that personified and exemplified these ideals to do all this—to not only control the message going out, but also the supply chain feeding it and the facility making it. If quality was to be the differentiator, the only way he could be sure of the quality was to control as much of the supply chain as he could. For the next three years after OCP folded, he consulted to companies in the organic food industry while he refined his ideas and made connections.

Then in 2005, a group of investors with interests in some of those companies decided to partner with Joe in an organic chocolate company run on the principles of quality, sustainability, and Fair Trade. Joe had little trouble finding smart people to come work in a real chocolate factory with strong ideals and socially responsible principles in Seattle. What was missing was additional executive skill—"adult supervision," as Debra had playfully described it. Joe was great at articulating a vision, infusing enthusiasm into his endeavors and in motivating others to go along with them—and of course, at the technical elements of chocolate making. When it came to running a company on a day-to-day basis, and especially to the marketing of the company's products, even he would admit that those weren't strong suits for him. Debra, however, had a graduate degree in psychology and a strong background in social marketing and consumer brand building, and she had held numerous marketing positions in Boston in the 18 years she lived there. When Joe decided to move to Seattle, he had no hesitation in offering a Sales and Marketing VP position to Debra—who gladly consented.

They spent the next 18 months building the factory in a historic building, the former home of the Red Hook Brewery, in the quaint, eclectic, and artsy Fremont[4] district of Seattle. Joe

[4] According to the website gonorthwest.com, Fremont is "home to several prominent Northwest businesses such as Adobe Systems and Getty Images and numerous local and international nonprofit organizations" and is "known best for its offbeat and irreverent parades, parties and sidewalk art…such as the Annual Solstice Parade, which is famous for its nude cyclists and quirky celebrations; and the Fremont Troll Monument."

envisioned controlling his chocolate "from bean to bar," and a factory was an integral and necessary part of Joe's plan to differentiate Theo from other, much larger, chocolate makers. In March 2006, the company began producing its first Fair Trade–certified, single-origin, and blended dark chocolate bars at that factory.

2006–2009

Debra's job was a challenging one from the get-go: find customers for the products made at this quirky factory—a new and unknown brand that was very different from what others in the industry represented. She was meticulous about the customers she targeted, matching Theo's value proposition and values with customers in the Pacific Northwest with whom she felt they would resonate. Beginning with organic supermarkets and cooperatives in the Seattle area, and the distributors that served them, Debra painstakingly built Theo sales each quarter. Given the seasonal nature of the chocolate market, Theo monitored its growth by quarter, year over year, comparing a given quarter to the same quarter in the previous year.[5] By that measure, Q3 FY09 (January–March 2009) was the only quarter in Theo's three-year history in which sales had not increased substantially since the corresponding quarter the previous year (see Table C6.1).

Sales came primarily from distributors (who got them into retail establishments such as supermarkets) and through Theo's retail store in Fremont. The store was in the same building as the factory and served as both a retail front and the gateway to factory tours run by employees known as "Theonistas."

By June 2009, between 75% and 80% of annual sales came from these two channels (see Table C6.2). Direct sales, which accounted for about 25% of annual sales (on average), came from small, mostly local stores and a few large chain stores. Copacking (i.e., the production of chocolate to be sold under another company's brand), although accounting for a negligible amount of total sales, nevertheless was proving to be very beneficial to the company as it learned how to manage its capacity and drive down production costs. Copacking arrangements allowed for longer runs, and thus for better management of contribution and of capacity.

Joe, Debra, and Theo's management team were eagerly anticipating the results for the second half of 2009. Despite the economic recession that had gripped the country that year, all indications were that Q4 FY'09—traditionally Theo's busiest quarter because of Halloween, Thanksgiving and the end-of-year holidays—would be Theo's first "in the black" and that FY2010 might be Theo's first profitable year.

The Chocolate Industry

Brief History

Cocoa was originally developed by the Mayans almost 2,000 years ago. Although the first U.S. chocolate production began in New England in 1765, the modern chocolate industry originated during the Industrial Revolution when new machinery allowed for the mass production of chocolate-based confections at a fraction of pre-Revolution costs.[6] By the mid-1860s, two firms, Cadbury and Nestle, produced what was to become the most consumed form of chocolate—milk chocolate. Product

Table C6.2 Sales by Channel, Q4 FY09

Channel	% of Total (Q4)	Δ from Previous Year
Theo Retail Store	39%	35%
Direct (to retailers)	18%	–29%
Distribution	39%	60%
Copacking	4%	–17%
Total	100%	20%

Table C6.1 Net Sales by Quarter

	Sep 06	Dec 06	Mar 07	Jun 07	Sep 07	Dec 07	Mar 08	Jun 08	Sep 08	Dec 08	Mar 09	Jun 09
Qtr Ending	Q3 CY06	Q4 CY06	Q1 CY07	Q2 CY07	Q3 CY07	Q4 CY07	Q1 CY08	Q2 CY08	Q1 CY09	Q2 CY09	Q3 CY09	Q4 CY09
Net Sales ($000, rounded)	150	310	330	340	450	700	350	670	620	970	690	801
Δ Over Same Quarter in Prev. Year	n/a	n/a	1142%	1142%	206%	123%	159%	99%	38%	40%	–19%	21%

[5] As of July 2008, Theo's financial year ran from July to June the following year.

[6] fieldmuseum.org.

knowledge, including scale production techniques, soon spread to America where, in 1894, Milton Hershey used chocolate to cover his caramels. Chocolate was widely available in all developed nations by the end of World War II. In addition, Cadbury continued to develop large-scale distribution in most of the former British Empire nations.

Value Chain Activities

Theo Chocolate's strong desire to control its value chain elements as much as possible was a key foundation block of its value proposition. The chocolate industry value chain was a well-defined set of closely integrated processes from cultivation to final consumer consumption by the 1920s. Cocoa cultivation was confined to areas approximately 20 degrees north and south of the equator, with the most robust areas of production present in Western Africa and South America.

Farming

Cocoa was generally grown on small farms in hot rainy environments near the equator. Many growers were subsistence farmers, surviving at the margins and extremely vulnerable to price fluctuations, crop failure, and downstream distribution power. Historically, farm labor conditions were characterized as primitive with numerous documented cases of extreme abuse of labor, especially child labor. Prior to the 1990s however, cocoa prices were protected by government price controls providing some measure of insulation from market-based forces. In the late 1990s international agreements led to market-based pricing. The resulting impact of these agreements was that farm gate prices were subject to greater fluctuations during the 10-year period from 1998 to 2008 due to currency valuations, local market structures, distance from port, and quality impacting price. Basic supply approximately matched demand, however. Although supply and demand remained in balance, price volatility placed additional burdens on subsistence farmers living and working close to the margins. In 2009 Ivory Coast, the world's largest cocoa producer, introduced proposals to re-establish price controls where farmers are paid a predetermined price at the start of the harvest.[7] Supply uncertainty combined with incumbent price volatility pressured downstream production quality and raw input costs.

Intermediate Processing

Intermediate processors source cocoa directly from growers using the cocoa to produce products such as cocoa butter, cocoa powder, and cocoa liquor. Depending on a firm's market position, these intermediate products are sold to downstream manufacturers for use in products as diverse as sun tanning products, food products, and alcoholic beverages or a portion retained for in-house use. Intermediate processing was highly concentrated with three large firms controlling 40% of the origin grindings. Archer Daniels Midland (ADM) operates cocoa processing plants globally and sells its products under the De Zaan brand. Swiss-based Barry Callebaut is a processing and chocolate confectionery firm. Approximately two-thirds of the firm's production is for in-house usage, whereas the balance is sold to downstream food producers. The firm has long-term contractual arrangements as a strategic supplier with both Nestle and Hershey. U.S.-based Cargill grinds 14% of world cocoa bean production. The firm purchased Nestle´'s primary cocoa processing plant in 2007. Cargill also recently developed processing capabilities in Ghana.[8]

Finished Chocolate Production

Finished chocolate products' broad classifications include candy/chocolate bars, block chocolate, box chocolates, other chocolate-based confections, and chocolate spreads. By market share, candy and chocolate bars captured the largest market share (44.2%) with differentiation among products typically created by the presence of additional inputs into the final product.[9] The largest producers such as Mars added value through the addition of inputs to the intermediate products purchased from upstream manufacturers.

Outside of the four largest industry players (see following), the market for chocolate was widely distributed with no one firm holding greater than a 1% market share. However, large chocolate-consuming nations experienced a change in consumption behavior from the late 1990s through 2009. In the United States, demand for high-end organic chocolate was increasing. Specifically, health research suggested that dark chocolate with higher cocoa content had substantial health benefits associated with moderate consumption including reduction in LDL (bad cholesterol) oxidation. In addition, antioxidants present in chocolate reduce the risk of cancer similar to health claims associated with red wine consumption. Growth estimates of high-cocoa-content chocolate products were 24% from 2001 to 2005, as opposed to the more modest growth rates of 3% for the more traditional milk chocolate products sold by the major competitors.[10]

[7] "Ivorian Cocoa Committee Wants Industry Run by State"; Bloomberg.com, December 10, 2009.

[8] Report to the Executive Committee, International Cocoa Organization, April 2008.

[9] IBIS World Industry Report July 2, 2009, Confectionery Production from Purchased Chocolate in U.S.

[10] AC Nielsen estimates.

Distribution

The majority of products were distributed through confectionery wholesalers (76.8%) with the largest U.S. distributor, McLane Company, responsible for 26% of Hershey's total sales distribution. Distributors supplied a wide variety of retail outlets including supermarkets, convenience stores, discount stores, pharmacies, and other specialty stores. Distributors forged links to all the various retail outlets developing long-term relationships with their customers. Increasingly, small producers sought to bypass complex distribution channels with the increased usage of online direct-to-end-user sales.

Retail

Grocery, supermarket, and convenience stores accounted for 14.6% of confectionery sales in 2009. Larger chain operators, aided by increased online purchasing efficiency, increased their share of industry revenue. Aided by increased volume, large retailers bought increasing amounts of product directly from manufacturers.[11]

Competition

Large Competitors

The United States was the largest chocolate market in 2008. Competition was fierce among the major industry competitors with Hershey, Mars, Nestle, and Russell Stover holding a combined market share of 51.7%. The major firms sought to increase market power through increased brand loyalty and widening their product offerings. Operating worldwide, the major competitors combine high-intensity marketing, strong product portfolios, and key contractual arrangements with large retailers to wield considerable market power.

Although industry growth was thought likely to continue, large players were increasingly concerned with the negative publicity associated with the health aspects of candy. Media coverage of childhood obesity issues led to concerns voiced by health advocates over the consumption of snack foods such as candy and chocolate by school-age children. Responsible marketing to children was an increasingly important industry issue.[12] Recognizing the threats associated with stakeholder concerns with candy combined with the emergent data on the health benefits of certain kinds of chocolates, large competitors began to focus on growing niche markets in the chocolate industry. Nestle's strategy emphasized wellness products shifting from low-end commodity-based consumer products to high-margin health-based products. Chocolate was designated as a key product category in this effort.[13]

For all major competitors, organic growth was challenging, with most growth coming from existing or acquired brands. As competitors tried to differentiate themselves, large established firms sought a foothold in the organic chocolate segment. In addition to Cadbury's acquisition of Green and Black's,[14] Hershey entered the market with the acquisitions of Dagoba Organic Chocolate and Scharffen Berger Chocolate Maker. As large candy producers continued to purchase smaller brands, other firms such as Campbell's exited the market, selling their Godiva brand to a private equity firm in 2007. Clearly there was opportunity in the organic/niche brand space.

Niche Competitors

Recognizing a market opportunity, smaller players emerged during the late 1990s to fill the market need for high-content cocoa products. Competitors' approaches to satisfy market demand varied widely among the new entrants. Early entrants into the organic chocolate market such as UK's Green and Black's had sales of £22 million by 2004 before selling to Cadbury's for £20 million in 2005.[15] (Appendix 6.4 provides a background of the terms as applied to the chocolate industry and its standard requirements and definitions.)

In the United States, new market entrants into the gourmet segment reached 25 by 2008. Seeking to capitalize on demand for high-quality chocolate, producers entered the market as retailers, midstream producer and fully integrated producers of high cocoa content chocolate products. Firms such as Fran's Chocolates, from Seattle, Washington, chose to compete primarily via retail outlets in the Pacific Northwest, whereas other firms such as Jacques Torres concentrated on one local retail market: New York. Most other finished product producers bought chocolate from intermediate producers adding additional inputs before final shipment to retail outlets. A few new entrants chose to fully integrate production from contracting directly with growers to in-house grinding and finished product manufacturing.

Theo Chocolate in 2009

By mid-2009, Joe, Debra, and the rest of the "Theonistas" (the name the employees of Theo adopted for themselves, and for all fans and followers of the company's products) had carved a

[11] IBIS World Industry Report July 2, 2009—Confectionery Production from Purchased Chocolate in U.S.

[12] candyusa.com (website for the National Confectioners Association Washington, DC).

[13] "The Unrepentant Chocolatier," *The Economist*, November 2009.

[14] Since the writing of the case, Kraft Foods has acquired Cadbury's.

[15] independent.co.uk.

niche within the huge and competitive chocolate industry. From its inception, Theo held to the tenets that had defined it in the first place[16]:

- *Using only pure ingredients that are grown sustainably. We source our ingredients locally whenever possible, Fair Trade whenever applicable.*
- *Partnering with our growers by ensuring they earn a living wage and have access to education for their families.*
- *Honoring and respecting our employees and suppliers. This is possible due to the unique fact that we control every step of our own manufacturing process.*
- *Using green energy sources to power our factory.*
- *Using sustainable packaging and printing methods.*
- *Educating about social and environmental accountability 7 days a week through public tours of our artisan factory.*

By 2009, Joe had surrounded himself with people who were both as passionate about the business as he and Debra were and skilled in necessary business areas. Apart from himself and Debra, the company's executive management team included Andy McShea, its Chief Operating Officer and Head Scientist, and Charles (Chuck) Horne, its CFO. Andy was a Harvard-trained molecular biologist with expertise in genetic and chemical analysis who had left a routine research career to assume the COO role at Theo. His credo "Better Science Through Chocolate," was sewn onto his lab coat. Chuck came to Theo first as an investor and then as CFO, after an illustrious 25-year career in senior financial leadership in companies such as Safeco, Dell, and Silicon Graphics. (See Exhibit 6.2 for a company organization chart.) A total of 40 people worked at Theo in the fall of 2009. Most worked in the factory or in the store; less than 10 worked in a managerial or administrative capacity.

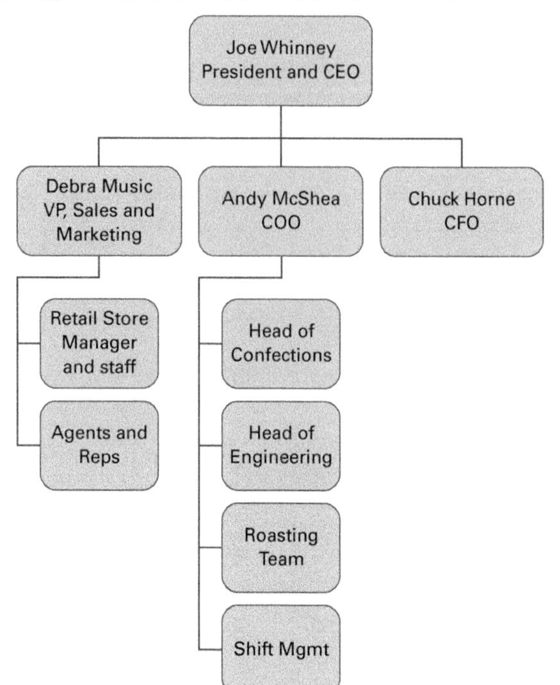

EXHIBIT 6.2 Theo Chocolate Organization Chart, Fall 2009.

Production and Operations

Theo considered its production processes a core competency and publicized them at every opportunity. The company prided itself on using only the best-quality beans from key growing regions of the world, made into chocolate in small batches in the company's Fremont factory. Theo's chocolate-making process truly started with the cocoa beans, sourced from farms in Africa, Central America, and South America. Much emphasis was placed on where beans originated, how they were cultivated, and ultimately, their quality. Terms like *Fair Trade* and *organic* weren't just platitudes to the Theonistas; they defined the company's chocolate products and were the bedrock of its operations and marketing. Exhibit 6.3 shows the meanings Theo

PLACE: *The meaning of Origin*
The heart of Theo resides in the cocoa-growing regions of the world, which we lovingly refer to as "origin." We buy our cacao direct from farmers and grower cooperatives. Building long–term business partnerships benefits farmers financially and technologically as we work together to perfect the art of growing quality cocoa beans. Economic stability keeps children in school, improves nutrition, and allows farmers to invest in equipment and land.

PEOPLE: *The meaning of Fair Trade*
Our founding principle is that the finest artisan chocolate in the world can (and should) be produced in an entirely ethical, sustainable fashion. We believe that every gold medal we win is a testament to both our commitment to excellence and to the people and families who grow and harvest our cacao. The social benefits of Fair Trade are far reaching. The child who gets adequate nutrition and access to healthcare and education today also gains access to a world of opportunities. Fair Trade enables farmers to take their livelihoods to the next level in sophistication, blending the benefits of modern techniques with artisanal practices, while participating in greater social change through the democratic Fair Trade cooperative organization.

PLANET: *The meaning of Organic*
Focus on sustainable growing practices benefits both our fragile environmental ecosystem and all of the people inhabiting our

EXHIBIT 6.3 Theo Foundation Principles.[17]

[16] theochocolate.com.

[17] www.theochocolate.com.

planet. Integrated pest management protects farmers and the environment from damaging pesticides. Shade grown cacao allows for biodiversity and much needed forest habitat for many species such as migratory birds. Reforestation helps offset worldwide air pollution and has a positive impact on global warming.

THEO: *The meaning of Bean to Bar*
Theo's small batch chocolate production is truly an art form. We take great time and care to steward our cocoa beans through the entire manufacturing process, add only the finest, sustainably produced ingredients, and are proud to offer chocolate we can guarantee is equal parts ethical and delicious!

EXHIBIT 6.3 (Continued)

ascribed to these and other words and how they impacted how the company made and sold chocolate.

The factory in Fremont was a 20,000-square-foot facility, which also housed Theo's offices and its retail store. The company could expand to 28,000 square feet if it needed to. Its capacity was between 700,000 and 800,000 pounds of chocolate per year, and in 2008, it was running at about 33%, producing 250,000 pounds (120 tons) of chocolate. It was turning over inventory about 10 times per year.

On the factory floor, cacao beans went through a number of production stages before being transformed into chocolate. Exhibit 6.4 diagrams Theo's chocolate production process.

Marketing Theo Chocolate

Product Categories

Theo made and sold chocolate products in six categories (see Exhibit 6.5). Table C6.3 illustrates the volume distribution of each product category in Q1 FY10.

Who Is the Theo Customer?

As might be expected, Theo's target customer fit a defined profile, despite the company's lofty goal of repositioning chocolate in everyone's eyes. They tended to be younger than 40, were

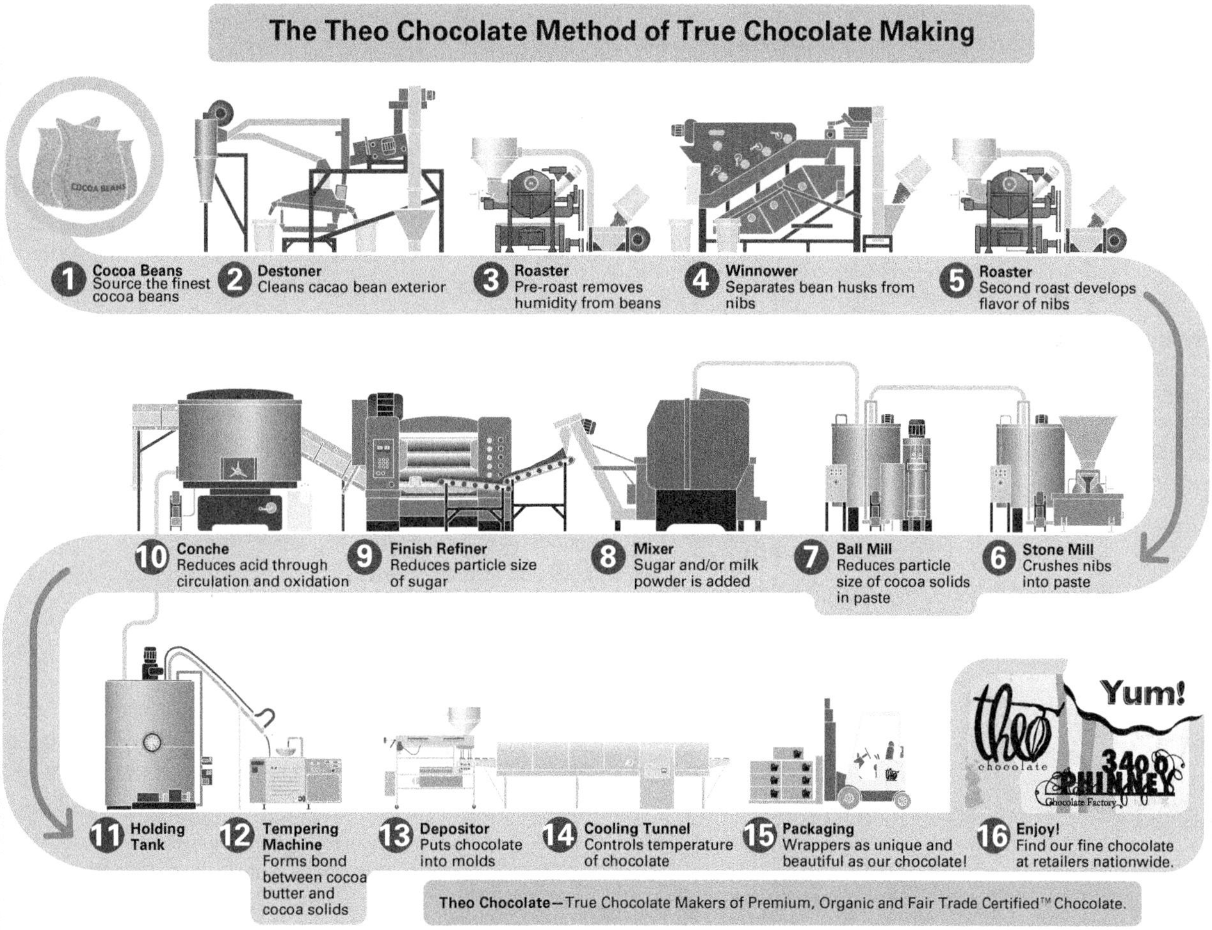

The Theo Chocolate Method of True Chocolate Making

1 Cocoa Beans
Source the finest cocoa beans
2 Destoner
Cleans cacao bean exterior
3 Roaster
Pre-roast removes humidity from beans
4 Winnower
Separates bean husks from nibs
5 Roaster
Second roast develops flavor of nibs
6 Stone Mill
Crushes nibs into paste
7 Ball Mill
Reduces particle size of cocoa solids in paste
8 Mixer
Sugar and/or milk powder is added
9 Finish Refiner
Reduces particle size of sugar
10 Conche
Reduces acid through circulation and oxidation
11 Holding Tank
12 Tempering Machine
Forms bond between cocoa butter and cocoa solids
13 Depositor
Puts chocolate into molds
14 Cooling Tunnel
Controls temperature of chocolate
15 Packaging
Wrappers as unique and beautiful as our chocolate!
16 Enjoy!
Find our fine chocolate at retailers nationwide.
Yum!

Theo Chocolate—True Chocolate Makers of Premium, Organic and Fair Trade Certified™ Chocolate.

EXHIBIT 6.4 Theo Chocolate Production Process (Shown at each factory tour).

"**Origin**"—Theo's signature line consisted of dark chocolate bars that feature the flavor notes of cacao from different parts of the world: Costa Rica (91% cacao); Ghana (84%); and Madagascar (74%). The 3-ounce bars offered "a truly uncompromised chocolate experience, rich in both satisfying flavor and antioxidants."

"**3400 Phinney**"—Named for the address of the Theo chocolate factory, these 2-ounce milk and dark chocolate bars came in bold and innovative flavors: Hazelnut Crunch; Vanilla; Chai; Bread and Chocolate; Coconut Curry; Nib Brittle, Coffee; and Fig, Fennel, and Almond. Dark chocolate bars had a minimum 65% cacao content; the milk chocolate bars had a minimum 40% cacao content.

"**Classic**"—Theo Classic Flavor Combinations were inspired by loyal customers who requested the taste of chocolate with other, well-known flavors. The 3-ounce dark chocolate bars came in Orange, Mint, Cherries and Almonds, and Spicy Chile flavors; the Classic line also included a 45% Milk Chocolate and a 70% Dark Chocolate bar.

"**Confections**"—These were small, bite-size squares of dark and milk chocolate and chocolate combinations that came in a variety of flavors, such as Scotch, Sage, Burnt Sugar, Lemon, Jalapeno Lavender, Saffron Caramel, Chinese Five Spice, Chipotle Spice, and Pear Balsamic. The Confections line included caramels, peanut butter/chocolate and marshmallow/chocolate combinations, sipping chocolate, and cocoa nibs (used in savory cooking). Most confections were sold only through the Theo retail store (in-person or online).

"**Specialty**"—Specialty products are typically products other than chocolate bars, that were sold only in Theo's retail store or direct, not through distribution. There are some handmade bars that also fall into this category, such as its Theo/Nicobella Vegan Confections. Seasonal flavors, sipping chocolate, and handmade bars would also fall into this category.

"**Miscellaneous/Other**"—This category was the catchall for all the other/nonchocolate items sold in the retail store, such as T-shirts and mugs with the Theo logo, cobranded beauty products, wine tasting kits, and so on.

EXHIBIT 6.5 Theo Chocolate Product Lines.

Table C6.3 Distribution of Product Orders and Shipments, Q1 FY10 (Jul–Sep '09) (totals may not equal 100% due to rounding)

Product Category	Shipments ($)
Classic	32%
3400 Phinney	25%
Origin	10%
Confections	13%
Specialty	6%
Misc./Other	11%
Copack	1%
Total	**100%**

educated (i.e., college or postgrad), and/or were "ecominded." The recent focus on the "green movement" in the United States meant that more people were seeking out products that were made using sustainable practices, which fit Theo's value proposition perfectly. Of course, one of the key questions facing Debra and Theo Chocolate[18] was that of who they should target going forward. Although the company's value proposition and branding messages connected with this group of customers, catering exclusively to this population had not been profitable up to this point. There was obviously some uncertainty on whether the firm could afford to continue to target just these customers, and if so, how to reach more of them to become profitable.

Reaching the Customer

As Table C6.2 illustrated, Theo marketed its products through four main channels: food distributors to retailers (39%); direct to retailers (18%); copacking arrangements (4%); and through its retail sore (39%). Debra had also built a network of brokers and representatives across much of the United States, whose job was to facilitate sales at the retail level.

Retailers

Between product distributed to them and product sold directly to them, third-party retail (i.e., retail sales outside of Theo's retail store) accounted for almost 60% of all of Theo's sales. Customers could buy Theo's products in higher-end food retail stores, such as Whole Foods, and some specialty retail stores, such as REI or Pier 1 Imports. It also had discovered a potentially lucrative retail channel in bookstores (more on this later).

At the retail level, price of a typical Theo bar was about $4; Single Origin bars were about 25% more expensive, whereas the smaller 3400 Phinney bars sold for between $3 and $3.50 each. There was no significant difference in COGS among the bars—they all were between $1.20 and $1.25 per bar. However, where and how a bar was sold had a large impact on Theo's bottom line. Distribution and direct-to-retail costs, including discounts and chargebacks, could run as much as 50% of the price of a bar (although they typically accounted for 40%–45%) and thus had significant impact on Theo's returns.

Brokers

Food brokers were independent sales agents who negotiated sales for producers and manufacturers of food and food products, usually in a specified geographic area. They provided a service to both food producers and buyers by facilitating sales to chain wholesalers, independent wholesalers, and retail stores.

[18] www.theochocolate.com.

Suppliers often found it less expensive to sell through food brokers rather than directly because it saved the cost of paying a sales staff to market their products. Brokers tended to represent between 15 and 30 brands, so wholesalers and retailers saved time, energy, and resources by dealing with one broker rather than with many manufacturers' representatives.

Theo employed a network of food brokers that served the natural food channel on the East Coast, in the Rocky Mountain region, and the West Coast (as of the fall of 2009, Theo did not have a presence in the Midwest, the Southwest, or the South). Brokers tended to pay a disproportionate amount of attention to the larger, more established brands. Brokers were classified as "A," "B," and "C" brokers, according to size and focus. Theo was too small and not so well known as to attract "A" class brokers and tended to be sought out by "B" brokers.

Independent Bookstore Representatives

In the summer of 2009, Debra decided to hire an independent bookstore sales representative to handle accounts on the East Coast (Maine to DC) and on the West Coast. The rep handled book sales to small, independent bookstores; because they were not involved in food sales, they didn't handle other chocolate brands. The idea to use reps for bookstores that might sell chocolate as a complementary item seemed to be getting some traction; Theo's West Coast book rep had access to 1,200 accounts, and the typical customer of an independent bookstore matched Theo's "ideal" customer profile to a large degree.

Direct-to-Retail

About 18% of Theo's revenues came from direct sales to retailers. Most direct sales were made to small, independent food retailers, many of whom liked to have relationships with their suppliers. Theo had established especially strong ties with cooperative supermarkets. These were owned and operated by groups of individuals with similar interests and tended to have a strong regional/neighborhood focus. Theo also had a few large "house" accounts, which it served directly.

Distributors

Distributors such as United Natural Foods[19] would take delivery of product on pallets for distribution to large food retailers, such as Whole Foods (which used UNFI exclusively). In the Pacific Northwest, where Theo was widely available, the company used a number of smaller, regional distributors; as the company looked to the national stage and was attempting to break out of the Northwest, distribution and transportation became the key issue.

Getting into large grocery stores and supermarket chains had proven to be a unique challenge because of how Theo's distribution was managed. Distributors "owned" a chain's entire product set; one distributor would provide a chain's entire candy inventory, for example, as it was the only way the chains could manage the logistics involved. Grocery store chains (with the exception of Whole Foods) never dealt with Theo directly. These chains purchased from distributors, not producers. A company like Theo would have to enter into a contract with a distributor, usually at prices well below what it charged retailers. As such, margins on sales to distributors were significantly less than to retailers. For example, for a bar with a suggested retail price of $4, a typical direct-to-retailer price might be between $2 and $2.50, depending on volume. The same bar would cost a distributor between $1.50 and $2.00.

Still, Theo was very optimistic about potential arrangements with the top 100 stores in the Safeway chain (the third-largest supermarket chain in the country, behind Walmart and Kroger[20]) and Costco. Theo was in talks to create a new private-label product for the Costco brand. In addition, the company had begun selling through Amazon in the fall of 2009 and was discussing options for cobranding with other major brands.

Trade Shows

Because over 60% of its sales were made "business-to-business," Debra had put in a lot of face time at food trade shows to build Theo's network of players in the industry. By late 2009, however, she was doing less of them because she thought their results were mixed, at best. Still, as the company looked toward the future and envisioned a "'national" brand, Debra would have to think about the best way to use trade shows to her advantage.

The Factory Store

Located in the same building as the chocolate factory, Theo's own retail store (see Exhibit 6.6) was by far the most important marketing vehicle for the company. The store was the face of Theo to the public, and its layout had been designed to showcase the Theo story and its products.

The store accounted for about 40% of Theo's total revenues. Everything that was available in other retail establishments was on sale at the factory store. Since starting operations in 2006, Debra had put a lot of effort into local outreach to drive foot traffic to and through the store and the factory. Although supported mainly by local patrons, the store and factory tour

[19] UNFI is Theo's largest distributor and has an investment stake in the company.

[20] International Dairy.Deli.Bakery Association, "What's In Store 2009."

Photo Credit: Courtesy of Gary Ottely

Photo Credit: Courtesy of Gary Ottely

EXHIBIT 6.6 Theo Factory Store.

attracted a booming tourist trade, especially in the summer. In fact, Theo's chocolate factory had become so well known and respected by 2009 that it was listed in the top 10% of Seattle tourist attractions at tripadvisor.com, a popular travel rating Web site.[21] Seattle convention organizers and cruise-ship lines[22] actively promoted Theo as an attraction.

The typical, "core" customer in the factory store tended to be someone who wanted to support a local business and who cared about "green," organic, and Fair Trade products. Seattle-based customers typically had found out about Theo through word-of-mouth (WOM, either from a friend who had visited or from social media outlets such as Twitter or Yelp.com) and sought out the store for gifts and keepsakes for holidays known for involving chocolate and sweets (the end-of-year holidays, Valentine's Day). Non-Seattle customers were directed to the store by their tour organizers or convention organizers and/or had found out about it via the Internet. In fact, Theo's advertising had been entirely WOM and relied on Twitter and Facebook posts and blog entries by satisfied customers.

Factory Tours

Theo offered factory tours, which were key to the store's revenues. The tours were conducted by Theo employees and covered not only the production facility, but also a description of where the chocolate was coming from, the farming practices that went into producing the raw cacao, and tastings of chocolate made with cacao from different regions of the world. They were immensely popular: in the summer and on weekends (Friday to Sunday), they ran every day, four times a day; during the week in the other seasons, they operated twice daily. Reservations were required, and although walk-ins were accommodated as space allowed, the tours were usually filled up a week or two in advance. On weekends, as many as 25% of the people who came to the store took the tour.

Theo charged $6 a head for its daily tours and $12 for private tours. Tours were limited to 20 people (25 for private tours). In the summer of 2009, Chuck Horne instructed the store employees to start asking customers buying chocolate if they had taken the tour. When he ran the numbers, he realized that for every dollar the tour itself brought in, tour guests spent another $1.50 to $2.00 on chocolate products. Table C6.4 shows a typical breakdown of the sales by product line from the retail store.

The factory tours made staffing the factory store a challenge. Audrey Lawrence, the retail manager, had a supporting staff of 10 in the store, and there were plans to hire more given the tours' popularity. The factory store employees tended to be female and were usually in their early to mid-twenties. These weren't high-paying jobs, but Audrey and Debra found that there was no shortage of applicants for customer service positions in an organic, Fair Trade chocolate factory. People who worked at Theo, and especially those who worked in the factory store, felt a deep and strong connection to the Theo brand. That connection manifested itself and was visible in the enthusiasm with which Theonistas conducted the factory tours and fielded tough questions from customers on the tours.

Table C6.4 Sample Percentage Quarterly Breakdown of Factory Store Sales (totals may not equal 100% due to rounding)

Product Category	% of Sales
Classic	15
Phinney	22
Theo Origins	5
Confections	21
Specialty	13
Misc. Other	23
TOTAL	**100**

Events

The 1,500 square foot retail store space was available for private functions after 6 p.m. The space could hold 100 people standing or 70 seated and was often rented out for gatherings and parties. Events were often catered. The room rental rate was $125 per hour.

Theo Chocolate University

As part of its mission to "demystify chocolate and help consumers understand where cacao comes from and the captivating process it undergoes in its transformation to becoming a most beloved indulgence,"[23] Debra and Andy had recently revamped a series of classes on chocolate, and Theo was now offering them under the banner of "Theo Chocolate University" at the factory store. The classes covered such topics as the health benefits of chocolate, the cocoa and chocolate industry, and the science behind tasting chocolate. The classes were split into series that increased in complexity as one progressed through the series (much like a series of college classes). Each class

[21] In late 2009, Theo was listed at #31 of 331 Seattle tourist attractions on tripadvisor.com.

[22] Seattle was a stop for cruises along the western coast of North America.

[23] theochocolate.com.

cost $40 (some required additional lab fees), were 2 hours long, and required reservations, because they too were very popular, and spaces filled up quickly. Exhibit 6.7 lists the classes offered by Theo Chocolate University in late 2009. Chocolate U was staffed solely by Theo personnel.

Series 1: Chocolate Science
Learn all about the science behind the flavor and health benefits of this complex fruit.

CHOC101 THE REAL THING
An in-depth description of what constitutes "real chocolate," Dr. McShea will truly separate craft chocolate making from industrial "mockolate." Using chemical analyses of cocoa beans and chocolate, this class explores the chemical intricacies of artisan chocolate versus industrial chocolate. Dr. McShea also answers questions about addictive properties of chocolate and our psychological responses to cacao.

CHOC102 CHOCOLATE FOR NERDS
This class gets into the nitty-gritty chemistry of fermentation and taste analysis of quality cacao. Dr. McShea will connect the dots of fermentation to finished chocolate flavor as it relates to the chocolate-making process. You will also explore the chemical make-up of cocoa beans from different regions of the world explaining why beans from different regions have such dramatic flavor differences. A tasting of poor versus well-fermented cacao will follow the lecture.

Series 2: Chocolate in the World
Learn about the cocoa and chocolate industries in the marketplace internationally

CHOC201 COCOA, UP CLOSE AND PERSONAL
Joe Whinney, founder of Theo Chocolate, will investigate how the complex web of politics, economics, and traditions of growing and selling cacao have brought us to where we are today. We will follow cacao from its first uses in Mayan and Aztec times through the European industrialization, up to present-day manufacturing. Mr. Whinney will explain from firsthand experience at origin the importance of sourcing Fair Trade and organic cocoa beans.

CHOC202 THEO TALES FROM THE TRENCHES
Debra Music, VP of Sales and Marketing for Theo Chocolate will share stories and insights on the trials, pitfalls, and victories encountered from the inception of the Theo brand through to the company's present stage of growth. Gain an inside look at the development of Theo's logo and brand concepts, the block and tackle of launching products into distribution, and the challenges in launching a consumer brand in today's economy. To experience the marketing of chocolate in an edible way, we'll sample some of our latest and freshest chocolate treats. You will even get to sample some new products we are developing and offer your expert opinion on their market viability.

EXHIBIT 6.7 **Theo "Chocolate University" Class Listing (Fall 2009).**

Series 3: The Art Of Making Chocolate
Behind the closed doors of manufacturing chocolate from bean to bar to confection.

CHOC301 FACTORY SECRETS
During this class our chief engineer, Erin Holzer, takes us inside the factory and explains the detailed inner workings of all of Theo's chocolate-making equipment. He will conduct demonstrations of many of the machines and let you have your own hands-on experience of making chocolate in our factory. This also provides the unique experience of tasting chocolate through all of the stages of processing bean to bar.

CHOC302 GANACHE MAKING
Learn from our top chocolatiers the techniques of making Theo's award-winning ganache recipes. Watch and learn as our talented kitchen staff go step-by-step through each stage of the ganache-making process and take home the secrets you'll need to wow your friends and family. Of course, we will be tasting chocolate throughout the night.

CHOC303 HOMEMADE CHOCOLATE
Homemade chocolate is a workshop that reproduces the industrial process of chocolate making in your home kitchen. Our product development wizard, Nathan Palmer-Royston, will give detailed demonstrations on how to roast, winnow, mill, conche, and temper your own homemade chocolate.

Series 4: Chocolate Connoisseur
An exceptional exploration into the heart of chocolate sensory evaluation.

CHOC401 TASTING LIKE A PROFESSIONAL
Bring your appetite as our CEO Joe Whinney and food scientist Abby Cumin walk you through an extensive tour de taste of Theo's finest chocolates and confections. Learn to taste chocolate like a true connoisseur as they describe the in-depth qualities of mouth feel, temper, balance, and finish. By the time you leave, you will have the knowledge to pick out the right chocolate for any tasting or pairing event.

CHOC402 BEYOND DESSERT; CHOCOLATE AS A SAVORY INGREDIENT
We explore chocolate beyond dessert as our very own chef and chocolatier Chad Fureck sets the table with a four-course savory chocolate exploration. He will walk you through his menu and recipes as well as give hints on to how to use chocolate in your own savory creations. But fear not, no meal would be complete without a spectacular dessert, and Chef Chad won't let you down.

CHOC403 EXOTIC & EROTIC
Our grand finale evening, we explore the exotic and erotic side of chocolate with special guests Lisa Francoise of Sweet Beauty and the babes from Babeland. The workshop begins with a discussion on the benefits of chocolate and cocoa butter for your skin and body. Then we move into a hands-on demonstration of Sweet Beauty's chocolate lotions, scrubs, and facial masks. Finally our sexy instructors will demonstrate more

EXHIBIT 6.7 **(Continued)**

creative uses of chocolate like body painting and sensual eating and talk about the real scientific relationship between chocolate and love.

All classes are held at:

Theo Chocolate

3400 Phinney Avenue North in the Fremont neighborhood of Seattle Wednesday evenings from 6:30–8:30 p.m.

All classes are $40 (+tax). If you register for 5 classes or more we offer a 10% discount.

***There is an additional $15 lab fee for choc302, choc401, and choc402 and an additional**

$30 lab fee for choc301.

EXHIBIT 6.7 (Continued)

Theo Chocolate's Branding Strategies

At the epicenter of Theo Chocolate's branding strategy was its organic, Fair Trade positioning. The company proudly boasted that it was the only organic, Fair Trade, bean-to-bar chocolate producer in the United States. Each of the key elements of Theo's carefully crafted and meticulously executed positioning had a particular meaning—see Exhibit 6.3.

By definition and by design, Theo's products were more expensive than those of their mass-producing competitors. Part of the company's mission was to increase the positive perception of chocolate and to convince consumers that there was intrinsic value in a product's origin and production processes. Joe was actively attempting to do with chocolate what Starbucks had successfully done with coffee: change the perception of the base product (cacao) from a "commodity" and of the finished product (chocolate) from "candy." By sticking to its sourcing and production principles, Theo's products had a significantly higher cost of production, necessitating higher prices—but as Joe put it, "We sell our chocolate at a price that reflects the true cost of making chocolate." As they saw it, Theo chocolates were priced to reward the company for the higher quality it provided. Table C6.5 lists the retail prices of a 3-oz. Theo bar and a sampling of those of its competitors.

Table C6.5 Sample of Competitors' Retail Prices

Firm	Brand	Weight	Retail Prices
Theo	Dark Chocolate (Orange)	3 oz	$4.00
Cadbury	Green and Black	3 oz	$3.69
Hershey	Hershey Bar	2.6 oz	$1.19
	Symphony	4.25 oz	$1.69
	Extra Dark	3.25 oz	$2.50
Nestle	Crunch	4.40 oz	$1.25
Mars	Twix	3.02 oz	$1.19
	Snickers	3.25 oz	$1.19

Source: Case Writer Field Observations.

Jane Goodall "Good For All" cobranding

Jane Goodall was a well-known leader of the environmental movement for over 40 years and a United Nations Messenger of Peace. She was best known for her study of chimpanzees and her efforts to protect them and to preserve their natural habitats, but she was also associated with numerous charitable causes that are supported by the Jane Goodall Institute, which she established in 1977.

Jane Goodall had created her own "Good For All" seal to reflect her personal commitment to supporting high-quality, ethically produced products from the developing world. Two of Theo's chocolate bars carried the "Good For All" seal—a major coup for a small company like Theo. The partnership between Theo and Jane Goodall was inspired by "Cocoa Practices," a Theo Chocolate initiative that brought together small-scale cocoa farmers, larger producers, and nongovernmental organizations from the world's cocoa-producing regions. Cocoa Practices was designed to give farmers the tools they needed to grow high-quality cocoa beans while conserving indigenous wildlife and other natural resources in the tropical rain forest ecosystems that provided both their livelihoods and their homes. As such, the "Good For All" seal was a natural fit with Theo.

Proceeds from the sale of these chocolate bars (would benefit cocoa farmers, promote conservation in the tropical rain forest, and directly contribute to the Jane Goodall Institute's efforts to save chimpanzees, develop community-centered conservation efforts, and direct youth education programs around the world.

Private Labels

Despite Debra's desire to grow the brand to such a degree that the factory could reach capacity making Theo-branded products, the company was not yet at that stage. It had recently entered into a private-label agreement with a large chocolate maker that would serve to increase throughput significantly and reduce the company's overhead burden. Debra and Joe were hopeful that Theo could use its excess capacity in the next few years for similar arrangements.

What's Next for Theo?

The three years leading to expected profitability had been rocky and fraught with uncertainty—but also exhilarating and fun. Theo was being recognized in food and other circles for its chocolate (see Exhibit 6.8); Joe had come a long way from the rain forests of Central America and his first, unsuccessful foray into the world of chocolate. He had built a company that was becoming more and more well known and respected; he was literally living his dream.

The dream was, however, rooted in a harsh reality: Joe had a company that had been unprofitable for its first 3 years, and he now was responsible for 40 people working for him. The bedrock on which Theo had built its foundation—socially responsible business practices throughout the value chain—had yet to prove that it was strong enough to support a profitable business. The next few years, and especially the next year, would be crucial. Chuck was still crunching the numbers for Q1 FY10 (July–September 2009), but they looked very promising, and given the orders coming in, the last 3 months of 2009 was expected to be Theo's best quarter ever.

Joe had always been focused on the internal operations of the company, trusting Debra with the marketing and sales of his products. It was Debra who needed to find and capitalize on Theo's growth opportunities. But first, she had to determine whether Theo could continue to operate with its current business model—or whether that growth necessitated compromise on some level. All signs pointed to *eventual* profitability, with steady and significant increases in sales—but Theo was still hemorrhaging. Did Theo have "something" worth persevering with its unique positioning? Its vision and strategy were certainly laudable—but were they viable? Could Theo withstand more unprofitable quarters to achieve its vision—or would it have to take measures to stop the bleeding, and thus compromise its principles?

With Theo's busiest period fast approaching, Joe and the rest of the management team were expecting to hear her opinion, and a plan for moving ahead, soon.

- Best Chocolate Creation of the Year 2009, *Seattle Magazine*
- Jane Goodall Institute Global Award for Corporate Social Responsibility 2009
- National Association for Specialty Foods, Silver Medal Outstanding Confection, Silver Medal Outstanding New Product
- Silver Medal Outstanding Organic Product 2009
- Pastry Scoop New York, Silver Medal 2009
- WEB MD, Outstanding Dark Chocolate 2009
- London Academy of Chocolate Awards, 5 medals 2008
- "O".e Oprah Magazine Best List 2008
- *Time* Magazine Style and Design Top 100 2008
- *Forbes* Traveler "Chocolate Paradises Around the World" 2008
- Time Out NY Critics Pick 2008
- Rachel Ray Snack of the Day 2008
- Northwest Source People's Picks 2008
- *Evening Magazine* Best of the Northwest 2008
- Best of Seattle 2008
- Grist List "Top Ten Green Business Leaders, Joseph Whinney" 2008
- National Association for Specialty Foods, Gold Medal "Outstanding Chocolate" 2007
- *Food and Wine Magazine* "Eco-Epicurean Award" for making the world "a better—and more delicious—place" 2007
- Food Network "Top 3 Hottest Chocolate Companies" 2007
- Gallo Family Gold Medal Awards Finalist 2007
- Pastry Scoop New York Silver Medalist 2007
- London Academy of Chocolate Awards, 3 medals 2007
- Best of Seattle 2007
- Best of Seattle 2006

EXHIBIT 6.8 List of Awards for Theo Chocolate.

Appendix 1 *Background and Explanations of* Organic *and* Fair Trade *in the Chocolate Industry*

Organic Chocolate

Market demand for certified organic cocoa developed rapidly from 2003 to 2009. General definitions of organic agriculture were not restricted to chemical free but encompassed a more complex set of requirements:

> *Organic agriculture is a holistic production management system which promotes and enhances agro-ecosystem health, including biodiversity, biological cycles, and soil biological activity. It emphasizes the use of management practices in preference to the use of off-farm inputs, taking into account that regional conditions require locally adapted systems. This is accomplished by using, where possible, agronomic, biological, and mechanical methods, as opposed to using synthetic materials, to fulfill any specify function within the system.*
>
> World Health Organization 1999

Tying into chocolate products' health attributes, firms sought organic cocoa from an increasing limited supply base. Although over 400 organizations provided certification services, legislative changes during the decade resulted in a smaller number of suppliers able to meet the increased requirements. Tougher import permits requirements squeezed out small growers. In 2006 U.S. per ton import costs of organic cocoa were $200 per ton more than nonorganic cocoa. The

$200 per ton premium was a fixed price over market prices of nonorganic, which generally fluctuated between $100 and $300 per ton.[24]

Production of organic cocoa was estimated at 0.5% of total cocoa production in 2006. Although small, industry estimated organic cocoa production exceeded Fair Trade cocoa production. Seventy percent of organic cocoa production originated in South America. A small portion of organic cocoa production was thought to be Fair Trade certified.

The Fair Trade Movement

Although Fair Trade has been generally considered a recent social movement with a market-based approach, the genesis of the Fair Trade movement has roots in the early 20th century. In 1910, William Cadbury, the founder of Cadbury Chocolate, initiated discussions among U.S. and UK chocolate manufacturers to boycott the purchase of cocoa from plantations with harsh working conditions. That same year, the U.S. Congress banned the import of chocolate from areas using slave labor.[25] However, subsistence farming combined with labor practices generally considered unfair in developed nations continued during the 20th century and early 21st century. Fair Trade, rooted in the justice movement, sought to increase awareness of substandard practices while introducing practices designed to ensure equitable treatment of workers with fair financial returns for farmers. The Fair Trade movement initially sought to target coffee growers. The movement has since expanded to include numerous agricultural products including chocolate. Fair Trade has been criticized by free-market economists who suggest it encourages growers to produce commodities where prices are artificially propped up, which leads to overproducing and long-term price decreases.[26]

Ignoring economic arguments against Fair Trade costs, consumer products firms including high-end chocolate producers recognized a potential market opportunity during the last 10 years to align their brands with the Fair Trade movement. Consumers who purchased Fair Trade products tended to have more education and wealth, which allowed firms to increase prices to compensate for the additional costs associated with Fair Trade practices.[27]

Fair Trade Practices

Fair Trade practices were distinct from organic trade practices, although there was alignment between the two movements. Fair Trade was principally concerned with economic viability. The goal was to use collective bargaining through a cooperative organization of farmers to generate a sustainable price per pound guarantee, irrespective on market forces, although the movement did incorporate some elements of environmental stewardship into their programs. Activists used high-intensity marketing, including public relation tactics to appeal to "conscious consumers" to buy Fair Trade products while working to convince high-profile firms such as Walmart and McDonald's to purchase and sell Fair Trade products. In 2007 50% of UK consumers were aware of the Fair Trade movement, whereas only 20% of U.S. consumers were.[28]

[24] Report to Executive Committee, International Cocoa Organization, September 2006.

[25] fieldmuseum.org.

[26] "Good Food? Ethical Food," *The Economist*, December 2006.

[27] Sarah Glazer. "Fair Trade Labeling." *CQ Researcher,* 17, no. 19 (May 18, 2007).

[28] Sarah Glazer, "Fair Trade Labeling." *CQ Researcher,* 17, no. 19 (May 18, 2007).

7 Building The Founding Team

Photo Credit: © Scott Mc Kiernan/ZUMA Wire/Alamy Stock Photo

U.S.A. Women's hockey celebrating its gold medal during the 2018 Olympics.

This chapter was written by Andrew Zacharakis.

Despite the glowing tributes to superstar entrepreneurs that we all read about in the popular press, entrepreneurship is a team sport. Even Mark Zuckerberg, one of the richest men in the world, did not start Facebook by himself. Mark Zuckerberg, started the social networking site Facebook in 2004 as a sophomore college student at Harvard University. He launched the company on his strengths: a passion for technology and computer programming, which was self-taught. He also started with some partners who added to and complemented his strengths. Co-founder and former Vice President of Engineering, Dustin Moskovitz, was his roommate at Harvard. Former Facebook Chief Technology Officer Adam D'Angelo was Zuckerberg's friend in high school, where they wrote software for the MP3 player Winamp that learned your personal music listening habits and then automatically created a custom playlist to meet your tastes. Other cofounders, Chris Hughes and Eduardo Saverin, helped in the early years to promote Facebook.[1] Although all were young, together they brought an understanding of technology and how young people like to connect and communicate with each other.

Arguably, one of the best tactical decisions Mark Zuckerberg made was to bring in Sheryl Sandberg, then VP of global sales and operations at Google as Facebook's Chief Operating Officer. Drawing upon a decade of experience in tech, Sandberg was instrumental in transforming Facebook from a start-up into a multibillion-dollar technology company. Her first task was to create a sustainable business model for the social network, and she held round-the-clock meetings to discuss how to monetize Facebook, from e-commerce to subscription services. Just one month after she was hired, Facebook settled on advertising.[2] Under her guidance, Facebook grew from $56 million in losses in 2008 into a multibillion-dollar technology company with profits of $15.93 billion in 2017.[3] As of the third quarter of 2018, Facebook had over 2.27 billion active users.[4]

Power of the Team

Teams provide multiple benefits. First and foremost, a team enables the entrepreneur to do more than he or she could accomplish alone. No matter how strong the entrepreneur, how many hours she puts into the business, or how many days a week she is willing to work, at some point a team becomes necessary to increase the capacity of the business. Y Combinator founder Paul Graham named solo founders as the No. 1 mistake that kills start-ups, because a team is critical to gathering new perspectives and to weathering the highs and lows of entrepreneurship.[5] Data from the Global Entrepreneurship Monitor (GEM) confirms a trend that we see year after year: On average, ventures founded by teams tend to generate more revenue, be more profitable, and create more jobs within growth and future oriented industries than those founded by single individuals.[6] Moreover, team-led start-ups are quicker to scale and also more successful at fundraising, in part due to the different skillsets that multiple co-founders can leverage.[7] The size of your organization is also directly correlated to the amount of revenue your business can derive. For example, if you are launching a retailing business, your average sales per person will range from $ 138,593 per employee for a restaurant in 2018 to $909,090 per employee for a new car dealer in 2017.[8] So if you hope to grow a million-dollar business, you'll need to build up an organization capable of generating that kind of revenue. For a restaurant, that means you'll need 10-plus employees. Keep in mind that these figures are revenue and not profits. Thus, if you want $100,000 or more in profits each year, you'll likely need a much larger business. For a full-service restaurant, that has generated an annual average net income margin of 6.1%[9] before taxes, you'd need sales of $1.64 million per year to pull out $100,000 in profits. Understanding these relationships going into your business will help you set goals and objectives for growing your company.

For growth, it's important to add employees who generate revenue. Too often, firms add support staff. Although such employees can improve the effectiveness of the people they work for, their impact on revenue is often not large enough to pay for their salary, especially for the early-stage entrepreneurial company. Instead, hire a salesperson who will directly lead to new revenue. In most new ventures one of the founders is almost certainly going to be the first and best early salesperson for the firm. This mind-set should permeate so that in the early years, it is critical to be focused on revenue-generating employees.

That said, the power of the team extends beyond adding sales. Solo entrepreneurs suffer from a number of shortcomings, including a limited perspective, little moral support, and a small network. Research finds that teams have a higher chance of success due to an increased skill set,[10] an improved capacity for innovation,[11] and a higher social level of support,[12] among other factors.

Entrepreneurs benefit by hearing and evaluating suggestions from others about how to better define and shape their business concept. No matter how brilliant your idea is, it can be better. Solo entrepreneurs often fail to get feedback on their idea that could help them better match customer needs and thereby increase product demand. Remember, initially your concept is based on your own perception of a customer need. Just because you are enthralled with the idea doesn't mean that it will generate widespread demand. Your team provides a good initial sounding board for ways to improve your idea. Granted, you can solicit this feedback from people outside your founding team (and you should), but you're likely to find that team members will provide more detailed suggestions because your success directly affects their own well-being. Moreover, your team members can help you evaluate the feedback you receive from outsiders. As we discussed in Chapter 3, your idea will continue to evolve during the entire entrepreneurial process, from pre-launch all the way through rapid growth. Getting different perspectives on the opportunity will help you come up with a more robust product or service.

Starting a business is hard work. You'll face a roller coaster of emotion as you achieve important milestones (your first sale) and hit unexpected pitfalls (your first unhappy customer). Unfortunately, most new ventures encounter far more pitfalls than milestones in the launch phase. It is all too easy to fold up and find regular employment when you hit a particularly tough problem. Having a team around you provides moral support. You're all in this together. You have a shared responsibility to work hard on each other's behalf because if the business fails, it is not only you who needs to find alternative employment or opportunities but the rest of the team as well. Furthermore, a team means there are people you can confide in and share your frustrations with because they are facing them as well. The sympathetic ear enables you to let off steam and then refocus your attention on the problem at hand. Finally, it is more fun and rewarding to share the successes with a group of people who have been working toward the same goals. The power of a team is its shared vision of success.

Business is all about relationships. You need to establish relationships with suppliers, distributors, customers, investors, bankers, lawyers, accountants, and countless others. Although well-networked individuals make better entrepreneurs, a team dramatically multiplies the size of even a good network. If you build your team wisely, you will gain access to a broader range of contacts that can help your business. This is often most evident in the fund-raising phase. Early on, you will likely need to raise equity capital, and the bigger your team, the more contacts you have as you embark on finding that investment. At the very least, your team is a great source for co-investment. In the *Inc.* magazine list of the 500 fastest-growing firms, 17% of the entrepreneurs reported that co-founders were a source of seed financing. Even if the co-founders don't invest directly, they can tap their own friends and family for start-up capital, as was the case at 10% of the companies on the *Inc.* listing.[13] Today, you and your team can more easily extend your network for capital through crowdfunding, where thousands of dollars are raised every hour.[14] Thus, the power of the team greatly enhances your network, which connects directly to the lifeblood of any business (capital).

A team also rounds out the skill set needed to launch a business. Most lead entrepreneurs have a vision of the initial product, and many even have the skills necessary to build a prototype—as when a software engineer identifies an opportunity for new video game or app. But it is almost impossible for one individual to possess all the skills necessary in the launch phase. For instance, a person with strong technical skills may lack the business know-how required to successfully introduce a new product to market, or a business guru may see a product need but lack the technical skill to build it. Even a business superstar is unlikely to possess all the business skills needed for long-term success. For example, a financial expert likely will need team members with marketing, sales, operations, and production experience, among others. The key is to understand your own strengths and weaknesses. Know what you know, and more important, know what you *don't* know. Once you have a strong sense of who you are, you can create a strategy to construct a powerful team. As you start to build up your team, identify the critical skills for success. Create job descriptions and a time line of when you need these people. Then work through your network to find the right candidates.

Where Do You Fit?

Just because the business is your idea doesn't mean you must be the CEO. Every entrepreneur needs to take a hard look at himself or herself and decide how to best contribute to the venture's success. Rob Kalin, founder and original CEO of Etsy.com, is a case in point. He took his concept of an online open craft fair that gave sellers personal storefronts to Union Square Ventures in November 2006. After raising $1M in Series A funding, Kalin began to scale Etsy by focusing on handmade and vintage items, as well as art and photography.[15] In November 2007, buyers spent $4.3 million by purchasing over 300,000 items for sale on the marketplace.[16] Etsy's rapid growth created the need for management with senior experience in large organizations. In 2008, Etsy hired Former NPR executive Maria Thomas as COO, and Kalin quickly promoted her to CEO. Thomas grew Etsy into a profitable company and increased revenues sevenfold within two years.[17] In 2009, Thomas stepped down as CEO and returned the seat to Ex-CEO Rob Kalin. Was Kalin the right person to lead Etsy all along? The future would prove otherwise. In July 2011 Etsy's Board of Directors asked Chad Dickerson the company's CTO to take over the role of CEO.[18] Before joining Etsy, Dickerson served as Senior Director of Yahoo's in-house start-up incubator, Brickhouse & Advanced products team. Although Kalin's innovative nature nurtured and led the company's first few years of growth, Etsy's Board of Directors and investors felt the company's potential could best be reached by an experienced executive like Dickerson who still leads the company today.

Granted, creating a new venture requires most people to develop new skills on the job, but you'll be encountering a plethora of new challenges in the launch process, and you need to understand your personal limits. Stubbornly keeping the CEO job could limit the potential of your venture and may even lead to its premature demise. So the question is, "How do you gauge what you already know and what you can comfortably grow into as your business evolves?"

The first thing to do is to update your resume. This document best captures your skill set to date. The key to revising and reviewing your resume is to do an *honest* and complete assessment of your demonstrated skills. This is not the time to exaggerate your accomplishments because the only person you're fooling is yourself. You need to understand how your skill set will help you achieve success.

A second thing to keep in mind as you update your resume is, "What do you really like to do and what do you dislike?" Too many product people fail as CEO because they don't like to sell. These entrepreneurs want to design a product—and then redesign it over and over until it is perfect. Although there is definitely a place for this type of founder within a new venture, it's not in the CEO role, which is about selling your company to customers, investors, and vendors. Even if you're still a student and have limited work experience, building your resume will help you examine what you have achieved. Do you see patterns in your resume that suggest some underlying strengths? Can you leverage these strengths as you try to launch a start-up? Even if you are relatively young, recognize that many young entrepreneurs built companies large and small starting from their strengths. Pete Lescoe, a Babson MBA student, created Food ShouldTaste Good, Inc., in 2006 with the goal of making a unique new snack with great taste, real ingredients, and sophisticated flavor. Lescoe started from humble beginnings by creating multigrain and jalapeño chips in his tiny apartment kitchen in Waltham, MA. After months of revising recipes, calling stores, and handing out samples, Lescoe finally made his first sale to a grocery store. Soon after, Food Should Taste Good won the Best New Product award at the Natural Products East Expo.[19] Sales began to grow, and Lescoe started to create new innovative chip flavors such as olive, chocolate, sweet potato, and cinnamon. Focusing on the growing health concerns in the United States, Lescoe ensured that all chip varieties were gluten free, cholesterol free, and had zero grams trans fats. Plus, many varieties are certified vegan. Food Should Taste Good started to become a household name after being featured in magazines like *Better Homes and Gardens*, *Good Housekeeping*, *Shape*, and *Women's Health*.[20] The brand's increased popularity did not go unnoticed; in February 2012 General Mills acquired Food Should Taste Good for an undisclosed amount.[21] Today Food Should Taste Good continues to thrive at General Mills with double-digit sales growth under the continued leadership of Lescoe.[22] Looking back, we can see that Lescoe's strengths lay in his ability to bootstrap the business, his persistent never-give-up sales attitude, and his ability to continually innovate new products that stay true to his vision.

Lescoe started modestly and grew his businesses incrementally (at least in the beginning), which allowed him to develop his own skills in line with the growth of the business. Yet Lescoe had a key strength he could leverage in the early days, a platform from which he could launch his business. As you examine your resume, what key strength pops out at you? Is that strength a strong platform from which you can develop the skills necessary to be the company's CEO, or might you be better off taking another role, such as Rob Kalin did, and bringing in a more seasoned leader? Can you sell, or are you better suited to another role? You can't build a successful team until you understand your strengths and the best place for you in the company today at its launch and in the future as it progresses through various stages of growth.

Although most people are pretty good at identifying their own strengths, they often have trouble understanding their weaknesses. Peter Drucker, the deceased management guru who published over 30 books and received the 2002 Presidential Medal of Freedom, suggested that we can all improve our own self-awareness by conducting feedback analysis.[23] His methodology is simple: Every time you make a major decision or take a significant action, record what you expect to happen. For instance, as you decide to take an entrepreneurship class, write down what you expect to learn and what grade you believe you will earn. Several months later, after an outcome has occurred, compare it to what you originally recorded. Are your expectations and your actual results similar? What's different, and why is it different? Drucker's exercise focuses you on performance and results so you can identify your strengths and work to improve them. Although this exercise and others can help you understand your own strengths, many times people who know you are better judges of you than you are.

Talk to those people in your sphere of influence, people who know you well and whom you respect. Talk to your parents, friends, bosses, employers, coaches, professors, and others who can gauge your capabilities. Ask them, "What do you see me doing? What are my strengths and how can these attributes translate into launching a successful venture? What areas do you think I need to work on, and how should I go about it?" It is also important to ask them about your weaknesses: "What characteristics might impede my success? How can I work to rectify them?" Understanding your weaknesses will help you devise a plan to overcome them, whether that be through self-improvement or by hiring the right people to compensate for your weaknesses.

When it comes to self-awareness, there are two types of people. First, there are those who are overly conscious of their own weaknesses; they are their own worst critics. This group may be reluctant to pursue a venture because they fear their own shortcomings will lead to failure. In contrast, the second group seems oblivious to their own weaknesses. Although this group may be more likely to launch a business, they are also more likely to fail once they do so because they won't seek help or even recognize that they need help. It is important to strike the right balance between these two extremes. The key to doing so is to develop deep self-awareness.

In addition to self-reflection and feedback from friends and family, there is a wide array of psychological and personality tests available. Some classic examples are the DiSC Profile test, Myers Briggs Personality Type Indicator, the California Personality Inventory, and the Personal Interests, Attitudes and Values (PIAV) profile. These tests, which vary widely in cost, are designed to help individuals understand things like their underlying interests, motivations, leadership, and communication styles. They can provide valuable insights, but there are several important caveats to keep in mind when using them. First, always remember that no test, no matter how carefully designed and applied, can accurately predict an individual's likelihood for success in an entrepreneurial endeavor. Few things in life are as dynamic and unpredictable as an entrepreneurial environment, and for this reason, expect these tests only to give you a deeper understanding of your own strengths and weaknesses. Second, should you decide to take advantage of these resources, industry newsletter *HRfocus* strongly recommends that you have a trained professional administer and interpret the test for you and that you insist on a test that has been statistically validated. This is a field with little regulation, and as a result, it is essential that you use assessments that have a proven track record.[24]

Finally, keep in mind that no single personality or demeanor is best suited for entrepreneurship. In fact, a study by *Inc.* magazine found that many of the most common assumptions about entrepreneurs were misleading or wholly inaccurate. For instance, a classic label applied to entrepreneurs is that of risk taker. In reality, the study found that CEOs of the *Inc.* 500 companies varied widely in their levels of risk tolerance. A *Wall Street Journal* article debunks another myth explaining how many entrepreneurs and CEOs are either self-admitted introverts or have so many introvert qualities that they are widely thought to be introverts.[25] All entrepreneurs are not risk takers or extroverts, and they are not necessarily overly optimistic, or big self-promoters; entrepreneurs do not come from a single mold. What many had in common, however, was an ability to work well under highly stressful conditions.[26] They tend to be resilient. The lesson here is that entrepreneurs come in all shapes and sizes, and you need to be careful about letting common myths about entrepreneurs dissuade you from starting a business. Tests can't tell you whether you will be successful, but they can provide you with insights that you can use to help ensure your success. The key thing to remember is that entrepreneurship is hard work. You will not become a millionaire overnight—or in five years. As Walter Kuemmerle notes, entrepreneurship requires patience.[27] It can be a mistake to grow too big too fast. It is cheaper to test the business model when a company is small and then shift strategies quickly to better adapt the model to the market reality.[28] Today's technology allows for quicker, cheaper, market tests, but building a venture still is more like a marathon than a sprint. It will take years, not months. So you need to ask yourself whether you have the patience and resilience to be an entrepreneur—this can be harder for the young and brash.

Once you understand who you are and what skill set you bring to the venture, the next step is to identify what other skills are necessary to successfully launch the business. Create a staffing plan that not only identifies key roles but also tells you when you need to fill those roles. Figure 7.1 provides an example, but staffing plans vary based on the type of company, stage of development, type of industry, and so on. Early on, you likely need only one or two other team members. At this stage, each team member needs to understand that early-stage companies are flat and nonhierarchical. It is more important to know what needs to be done than to worry about who should do it. Nonetheless, the roles for these members should be complementary, and each co-founder should also participate extensively in shaping the vision of the business. An ideal combination might have team members coming from different disciplines such as science and business. Or if they are in the same major field of study, they might have different functional specialties, such as finance and marketing or biology and microbiology. The co-founders will work together on the overall direction of the business, but it is also wise for them to identify and

Role	Primary Duties	Person Filling Role	When Needed
Product Development	Develop prototype	Lead entrepreneur	Now
Market Development	Customer research Channel development	Founder	Now
Finance	Raise outside capital	To be determined	Next month
Production	Identify manufacturing partners	To be determined	Three months from now

FIGURE 7.1 Staffing Plan.

divide primary responsibilities. Many co-founders make the mistake of working on every task and decision together, which often leads to frustration and inefficiency. Although everyone's input is valuable, consensus is often a deterrent to success. Someone needs to be in charge.

The sample staffing plan in Figure 7.1 is a working document that grows and evolves as the founding team achieves milestones and moves on to new tasks. The value in creating the staffing plan is that it helps you to anticipate where the company is going and to plan for those needs. Note that not all the positions are currently filled. It is wise in the launch stage to conserve resources, especially cash. Thus, the founders may take on some of the future roles as their skills permit. If, for example, the team needs a strong finance person with previous experience raising equity capital, it makes sense to start identifying that person early on but to delay bringing him or her onto the team until needed (which might be when the company raises a significant round of financing from angels or through a private placement).

How to Build a Powerful Team

Your staffing plan is the first step in building a powerful team. Your next challenge is to identify the individuals to fill the gaps. How do you identify the best candidates? The simple answer is to tap your personal network and the network of your advisors, but you'll want to go outside that network to broaden the pool of quality candidates. Work with your professors to make contacts with alumni. Search your college's alumni database to find people in the right industry and with the right kind of position. More often than not, alumni are willing to speak with current students. Even if the alumnus isn't willing or able to join your team, she may be able to recommend someone from her network. You should also check with your investors, accountant, lawyer, or other people affiliated with your efforts (if you have these people lined up already). Oftentimes, entrepreneurs will hire a lawyer or accountant earlier than they might need that individual just to tap into his or her network. Moreover, many law firms are willing to work for promising new ventures pro bono, at reduced rates, or for deferred compensation. Thus, it may make sense to hire your lawyer early in your launch process. The key to your success is continually building your network. This will help you meet challenges beyond filling out your team.

A natural place to find co-founders and other team members is your family and friends. A look at the *Inc.* 500 shows that 58% of entrepreneurs teamed up with a business associate, 22% with a personal friend, and 20% with their spouse or other family members.[29] Just remember that working with a close friend or family member can be a double-edged sword. On the plus side, you know these people well, so you have a strong sense of their work ethic and personal chemistry. This was definitely the case for Ben Cohen and Jerry Greenfield. The co-founders of the eponymous Ben and Jerry's ice cream brand met in seventh grade gym class and lived in Manhattan together before drifting apart. After Jerry failed to get into medical school, the friends reunited in Saratoga Springs, NY. Ben, then working as a potter in upstate New York, suggested they start a food business. Ben and Jerry took a $5 ice cream-making correspondence course with mail-in lessons and raised $12,000 from personal funds and a small business loan. In 1978, they moved to Burlington, Vermont, a college town with no ice cream parlor, to start without competition.[30]

"We learned a lot from these little brochures that the Small Business Administration put out back in those days. They were 20 cents a piece, you could get them at the Post Office, and one would be about how to calculate your break-even point, another would be about how to manage your books. That was pretty much our business education," said Ben.[31] By 1980, Ben & Jerry's was selling pints to local grocery stores and in 1981, the first Ben & Jerry's franchise opened. Ben & Jerry's differentiated itself with its socially conscious mission and signature flavors like Cherry Garcia and Chunky Monkey, which were invented by Jerry without test marketing. Ben & Jerry's became synonymous with premium ice cream. The company also relied on guerrilla marketing tactics like giving away samples of the flavor "Economic Crunch" for free on Wall Street after the stock market crash of 1987. By 1987, sales had reached $32 million and by the following year, Ben & Jerry's was operating in 18 U.S. states.[32]

By 1997, Ben & Jerry's had reached sales of $174 million. In 2000, the brand was sold to Unilever for $326 million,[33] but retained its own CEO and Board of Directors to continue its social mission. Ben and Jerry continue to be involved in an advisory capacity, and Ben & Jerry's has grown to 577 Scoop Shops in 38 countries as of 2017.[34]

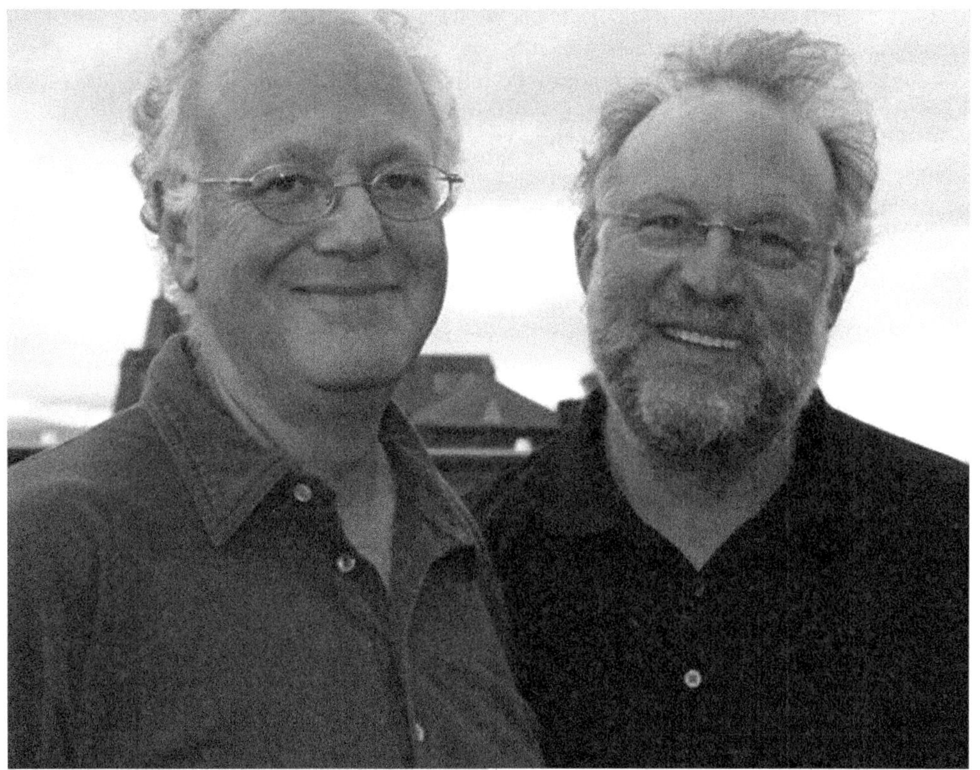

Photo Credit: © SIPA/Newscom

Ben Cohen and Jerry Greenfield, founders of Ben and Jerry's Ice Cream

Another good source is working with family members. It can be difficult because you are mixing a professional relationship with an already existing personal/familial relationship. Diane Lansinger was busy running her own second start-up when her father, a former automotive engineer for Chrysler, asked her for advice on how to move forward with his own business idea. After taking a look at his patents, she agreed to come on board, with one caveat: "I'm all in, but I want to be in charge," she informed Jere Lansinger. "I want you to work for me—I think you'll be happiest with that." He agreed.[35]

A former Microsoft employee, Diane felt their talents combined "Midwest automotive muscle and Silicon Valley hustle" would be a winning formula. Together, they run SEEVA Technologies, an automotive engineering company that focuses on autonomous vehicles. "we have that yin and yang in terms of business and engineering, said Diane. "I'm the front of the house—my flow state is figuring out how we get our product in the market, figuring out our sales pitch. He's in the back of the house, our innovation and engineering person."[36] SEEVA was accepted into Techstars Mobility program in 2017, and the father-daughter pair became roommates when they moved into an AirBnB in Detroit to complete the accelerator. In 2018, SEEVA raised $2 million to pursue the self-driving car market.[37] Similar dynamics occur when you hire friends. You need to relate to your friends in a different manner—a more professional manner—and this can stress the friendship. Recognizing the consequences of this new dynamic is the first step toward managing it, but there is more that you can do.

Before entering into a team relationship with family or friends (or anyone, for that matter), lay out as much as possible the previous accomplishments, industry profile, and years of experience that person has and the roles and responsibilities that person will fill in your organization going forward. Define decision and reporting responsibilities. We are not saying you need to have a highly formalized structure at an early stage of your venture's development, but you do need to clearly state expectations, tasks, and objectives. We have seen more teams self-destruct because of personal conflicts than because of lack of funding.

Although the circumstances surrounding the fallout between Facebook co-founders Mark Zuckerberg and Eduardo Saverin remain mysterious, Zuckerberg forced Saverin from the company. Saverin then sued Zuckerberg and Facebook.[38] The moral of the story is that founder conflict occurs and can escalate to the point of endangering the company. Setting expectations and responsibilities in advance of engaging in a relationship can help to mitigate damaging conflict.

It is not at all uncommon for friends to dive into starting a business before they have really considered how it could affect their relationship. An excellent example unfolds in the movie *Startup.com*. This outstanding documentary follows two close friends through the rise and fall of their company and provides a dramatic example of how working together can affect the relationship of two lifelong friends. Although Kaleil Tuzman had to make the difficult and painful decision to fire his friend and co-founder, Tom Herman, the two were ultimately able to piece their friendship back together. This is just one example of the difficulties you may face. Again, the key is to have clear expectations of each other and understand that pitfalls will test your friendship.

Once you have identified the right co-founders or team members, there is still the hurdle of opportunity costs. The best candidates often are already employed in good jobs, frequently in the industry where you will be competing. That means at some point they will need to leave a well-paying job to join your venture, and most new businesses can't afford to pay market rates during the cash-strapped start-up phase. In addition, there is much greater risk that a new business will fail, which compounds the personal opportunity costs that co-founders and early team members face. As the lead entrepreneur, you need to convince potential candidates that the job itself is intrinsically rewarding and growth oriented (team members get to do something they like and be part of creating something new and exciting) and that in the long run the financial payoff will be much greater. A young company offers potential team members opportunities to grow into higher management positions (and therefore higher deferred tax–advantaged pay) than might be possible at their current company and to have some ownership in the new venture (through either options or founder stock). These are both powerful tools for convincing talented candidates to take a risk with your company. The more successful the targeted candidate, the harder it will be for you to successfully make these arguments; yet many people are willing and eager to jump into the entrepreneurial fray for the right opportunity. Make sure to present your best case. Sell candidates on the vision, and back that up by showing them what you've accomplished to date, such as building and testing a prototype or securing outside financing.

Bootstrapping: Building the Team Based on Stage-of-Venture Life

Building your team requires resources, which are scarce in most nascent ventures. Co-founders must often live off their savings or their spouse's income during the early days, as it may be impossible to draw a salary. Recognizing that difficulty, you are likely to find that it is better to bootstrap your team build-out rather than putting everyone in place from day one. It's common for founders of smaller companies to stay at their current jobs and work on the business part-time at night and on weekends. Many companies are able to successfully develop prototypes or raise the first round of outside investment while the founders are still at their current job (although you should not continue working for a firm that you'll directly compete with).

Be careful, though, not to commingle activities. When you're at your current job, your attention should be focused on those duties that help your employer succeed. You should *not* use your employer's resources, like computers and copiers, without explicit permission. You should *not* expropriate intellectual property from your current employer to use in your new venture. And you most certainly should *not* solicit your employer's customers while you are still taking a paycheck from that employer. If you handle your start-up well, you will often find that your current employer is supportive, especially if the business isn't directly competing with your proposed venture. Thus, you should notify your employer of your intentions as soon as possible.

Another means of earning a salary during the early days is to take a part-time job. Although this may mean working as a waiter or for a temp agency, entrepreneurs will often consult in a related field until their main product or service is ready to go to market.

As a lead entrepreneur, you need to prepare for a diminished personal cash flow during the early years of your business, as you will often have to defer drawing a salary. Continuing to work for your current employer, building up a savings war chest, and delaying purchases of new cars or a house all contribute to sustaining you during the beginning. Although painful, this frugality is often a small trade-off to pursue your dream, and if you are successful, you will likely receive a future payoff that will be well worth the initial risk and sacrifice.

Perhaps the most common means to protect your personal cash flow is to continue working in a full-time job during the early phases. The weekend and nighttime entrepreneur is common, but at some point you have to quit and work on your dream full-time. For example, Ruthie Davis, founder of DAVIS by Ruthie Davis, an ultra-modern footwear company, continued to consult for Tommy Hilfiger where she had been Vice President of Marketing and Design for Women's Footwear. Ruthie's phenomenal success in launching "Tommy Girl Shoes" garnered the attention and support of the entrepreneur and founder Tommy Hilfiger. When Ruthie decided to launch her own firm, Tommy Hilfiger asked her to remain as a consultant for six months. This consulting agreement allowed Ruthie to maintain a salary, contacts, and focus on building her brand.[39]

The trade-offs of this approach are clear. Although you do maintain your personal income, every waking hour is devoted to either your regular job or your new venture. This dual-job strategy usually works only during the planning stages of your new venture—you can write a business plan, build a prototype, and start to make some key vendor and customer contacts, but you likely can't launch the business while working full-time elsewhere.

In addition to the time constraints, there are other issues to consider. If you are being paid, that means your time and effort should go toward your current job. Make sure to work on the start-up on your own time. There is also the potential for a lawsuit if your new business uses intellectual property developed on the company's time. Once you leave your full-time job, your previous company may feel like a jilted lover. Working to maintain a relationship with your former company is difficult—but not impossible. Follow the example of Ruthie Davis. She not only informed Tommy Hilfiger but also got his blessing to work on her business while continuing to consult for his. The risk of informing your current company, of course, is that you might be immediately terminated, but for the long term, it is better to be straight with those affected by your decision.

When you're bringing on team members, many of the same principles apply. Examine your staffing plan to assess when you need that individual on a part-time basis and when you need her on a full-time basis. If the person is critical to building your product, you'll need her sooner. If she will be your primary salesperson, you won't need her until you go to market. Accurately timing when different people join the team conserves company cash and helps the new hire manage her own personal finances. There are trade-offs, however. First, you need to plan ahead. It often takes four months or more to identify and hire key employees. Second, it is easy for a part-time worker to become disengaged from the start-up. If your team member is still at his current job, that one will likely take priority over your venture, especially if some special projects come up. Third, people who are already working on the start-up full-time may resent that the other person isn't as heavily involved in the sweat and tears that characterize the venture. They may feel this person is getting a free ride. As the lead entrepreneur, you need to manage these perceptions and work to keep the part-time and future team members fully apprised of what is happening. Finally, until a person signs up, she is at greater risk of either changing her mind about joining the venture or walking away for another new opportunity. Understanding these risks will help you manage them and still preserve your cash flow. One way to handle these situations is to develop a compensation plan that excites your current and future team members.

Compensation

As resource constrained as new ventures are, you are likely hard-pressed to think about compensation for you and your team. At some point, however, you'll need to pay yourself and others in your organization. The more powerful your team members, the more compensation they will expect, whether that is in salary or in equity (but usually a combination). So how does a start-up company determine what to pay its employees? How does it choose among wages, salary, bonuses, equity, or some combination of these options? The answers to these questions depend not only on the nature of your company but also on the nature of your team and employees.

Equity

There are several good reasons why most new ventures distribute equity to at least some of their employees. First, new companies often can't pay market rates for salary and wages. Equity can induce people to work for below-market rates with the expectation that at some point in the future they will be handsomely rewarded. As Lalitha Swart of Silicon Valley Bank put it, "People don't leave large corporations and take on risk without knowing there is an upside in stock."[40] Second, including some equity in the compensation package aligns the employee's interests with those of the company. Basically, the employees become owners, and their stock or options increase in value as the company prospers. Finally, the sense of ownership boosts morale, as employees perceive that everybody is in this together. This added camaraderie helps the team to stick together during the inevitable rough times in the early-launch phase. Of course, distributing equity throughout an organization isn't costless. It dilutes the founders' and investors' equity. You need to understand the trade-offs among motivating employees, conserving cash flow, and preserving your own equity. Understanding the trade-offs helps you develop a compensation plan.

There are two basic ways of distributing equity: founder shares and an option pool. As the name implies, **founder shares** are equity earned by founders of the company at the time it is officially established or when the first outside equity capital is invested (usually when it is first incorporated, although the shares may vest over time). Founder shares are most often given with no or minimal investment (maybe one cent per share) and are an acknowledgment of the "sweat equity" that the founders have invested in turning their idea into a company or of the track record and value of the founders. There are several considerations to keep in mind when granting founder shares. First, remember that granting shares to new parties dilutes your personal ownership, but this dilution is more than offset if you are granting shares to valuable co-founders who can help the company grow. For example, if you are opening a French restaurant and you have front-room experience as a maître d', it makes sense to co-found the restaurant with an accomplished French chef who can design and run the kitchen. It makes less sense to award founder shares to waiters, dishwashers, busboys, and other staff who are more transient and less central to the restaurant's competitive advantage. Founder shares should be reserved for those team members who are essential to turning the idea into reality.

How many people should get founder shares? It's a serious question. We advise entrepreneurs to keep this group small, usually no more than three people. Again, keep in mind the principle of preserving your equity by avoiding dilution. Once the founding team gets to be five or more, dilution can dramatically affect the capital appreciation that each founder receives, especially if the company needs to raise outside equity. Investors like to see founders with a significant stake in the company because "having skin in the game" focuses entrepreneurs on growing the company's future value rather than on maximizing current salaries. If, after a few rounds of outside investment, each of the founders has only 1% to 5% of the equity, they may start to recognize that no matter how big the company becomes, the long-term gain won't be sufficient to compensate them for all the hard work of getting the company to that point. Therefore, the founders might be more inclined to leave the new venture for greener pastures, and disruption in the leadership team is very difficult for emerging ventures to survive. The smaller the group of people who receive founder shares, the smaller this dilution problem. This is not to say that other team members should be precluded from equity participation, just that founder shares are not the best way to distribute equity to employees. Options are a better choice, and we'll touch on that topic shortly.

A third consideration regarding founder shares is how to divide them between the founders. Many first-time entrepreneurs fall into the trap of evenly dividing the shares among the founders. So if you have four founders, you might give each person 25% of the founder shares. A number of problems can arise from equal distribution. First and foremost, if each founder has an equal share, it can be hard to make important decisions because the group will want to have consensus. Even if one founder has been designated CEO, the others may perceive that their input needs to be given full consideration. At a minimum, this situation slows the decision-making process, but it can sometimes lead to disaster as the team stalls and becomes incapable of taking action. Another factor is that ambitious people tend to benchmark themselves against their peers. This means that a CEO will benchmark her compensation against that of other CEOs. If the founder shares are equally distributed, it is only a matter of time before the CEO recognizes that she is doing as much work as her peers but has less potential upside. This discrepancy acts as a disincentive to maintaining the level of commitment required by start-ups.

Although there are no hard-and-fast rules for splitting founder stock, keep in mind these guiding principles centering on past contribution and expected future contribution. First, acknowledge the time and value of past contributions.[41] The entrepreneur who initiated the idea, started doing the legwork and enticed co-founders to join deserves consideration for all these efforts and also for her expected contribution going forward—maybe as much as 50% if the founder also continues in a major role as CEO or some other high-level manager. Second, the founder who is CEO should have most of the equity, often as much as 50% of the founder shares. Next, the founder who brings in the intellectual capital—say, a patent or invention—should have 20% to 30% of the founder shares. As you can see, it is difficult to put hard-and-fast rules on founder shares because founders may assume multiple roles. Although these principles can guide the distribution, the final split comes down to a negotiation. Detail each founder's past and expected future contributions and the role he will assume in the organization, and then divide the founders' stock accordingly. It can be useful to engage a lawyer with experience in this area. The lawyer can help you benchmark against other companies and offer outside validation that each founder is getting her due share.

Because you will want to minimize the distribution of founder shares, another way to reward other employees and future hires is through an option pool. An **option pool** is equity set aside for future distribution. Options basically give the holder the right to buy a share in the company at a below-market rate. The option price is often determined by the market price of the stock on the day the employee is hired (or in the case of a private company, the price at the last round of financing).

The principles we discussed about founder shares apply to options as well. An option pool will dilute the founders' equity—but to a much lower degree than broadening the number of people who receive founder shares. Granting options also helps align the employees' interests.with those of the founders by making the employees partial owners of the company. In addition, to exercise their options, recipients must pay for the shares, which brings money into the company (although the amount is usually too small to be considered as a source of growth capital). Sometimes macroeconomic factors or poor company performance leads to lower share prices. In such instances, many employees may find their options "under water," meaning that the exercise price is greater than the current market price for the share. If options lose their value, they cease to be an incentive and retention tool. When this happens, employees are more likely to leave to seek new opportunities. However, if a company is growing, the value of the options should continue to grow, which increases the incentive and value for the employees.

Because granting options can mean giving up a significant piece of the organization, it is essential that owners know how to use these motivational tools effectively. The worst-case scenario is one in which the entrepreneur gives up equity in the company and receives little or none of the value that equity is supposed to create. Many rank-and-file employees have difficulty understanding exactly how they contribute to the value of the organization. Communicating with employees about the importance of their roles, and training everyone about how they can increase shareholder value, is essential.

According to the Beyster Institute, a nonprofit organization dedicated to improving the use of employee ownership, entrepreneurs can take several key steps to ensure that options improve organizational performance. First, employees need to fully understand the stock ownership program and how they will participate in it. Related to this point, employees should have a solid understanding of how the company is performing. Second, the staff must know how to measure company success and receive training on how to achieve it through their individual roles. Third, as we have mentioned, one of the great benefits of offering options is that it makes employees owners of the company and therefore encourages them to think like owners. However, the key here is that owners are typically more motivated to find solutions to problems or to develop innovations. An entrepreneur who offers options and doesn't harness or listen to this highly motivated workforce is failing to capitalize on the greatest benefit of offering ownership. Fourth, a stock ownership plan should offer employees a true opportunity to earn a financial reward. This potential for financial windfall is the key to stock-ownership plans.[42] Once the company decides it wants to use options to motivate and reward employees, the question becomes how many options to issue and to whom. Research suggests that issuing options generates increased overall company value through gains in employee productivity and that this increased value offsets the dilution effect.[43] It is common for many technology firms to put aside 15% to 20% of their equity for employee options after a major investment round. From that pool, the company can decide to distribute options to all or just key employees. Don't make the mistake of distributing all the options to existing employees, but anticipate how many new hires you'll make over the coming years. Then you can come up with a distribution plan based on employee level. Higher-level employees—say, vice presidents and other upper-management employees—will get more options than lower-level employees. Keep in mind that you'll vest shares over an employee's tenure.

Although options are the most commonly used form of equity compensation, Financial Accounting Standards Board (FASB) regulations make them more expensive for both private and public companies. Specifically, companies must list options at fair-value as an expense on their income sheet rather than just as a footnote to their financials.[44] Although it appears that the FASB rule hasn't dampened the use of options, there are other similar means to reward employees, including restricted stock, stock appreciation rights, and phantom stock.[45] **Restricted stock** is actual shares, rather than the option to buy shares, that are vested over time. The upside is that the expense is the current share price rather than the expected exercise price of an option. The downside is that the recipient gets the stock regardless of company performance, whereas employees exercise options only when the company's stock price increases. **Stock appreciation rights** accrue to employees only if the stock price increases (similar to options). Their advantage over options is that they tend to be lower cost to the company. Finally, **phantom stock** isn't really issued equity but a cash bonus paid to employees if the stock price appreciates over a set period of time. Phantom stocks are expensed over the vesting period, but they have the benefit of lowering dilution. The downside is that you'll need cash once the phantom stocks are exercised, and for a resource-constrained start-up, cash is at a premium.

One of the main reasons to award options, founder stock, or one of the hybrids just mentioned is to keep key employees with the firm. However, what happens if you decide that someone needs to be fired due to poor performance, nonperformance, or any variety of other reasons? If it is a co-founder, that person likely has a sizable chunk of equity and any voting rights associated with it. That may mean the person can interfere with the operations of the business. An important means to protect you from an employee or co-founder who doesn't pan out as expected is to create a vesting schedule. **Vesting** basically means that people earn their shares or options over time, usually over four or more years. For example, if a co-founder is entitled to 25% of the company's shares, you may vest those shares in equal chunks over four years. That way if the person leaves or is fired in the first year, he walks away with only a quarter of the shares he would have been entitled to if he stayed. This maintains the unvested shares for distribution to future hires.

You can also structure an employment contract to permit the company to repurchase the employee's shares at cost, or some other predetermined rate, when she leaves or is dismissed from the company. You may negotiate a right of first refusal that gives the company or other existing shareholders the right to buy the equity of an ex-employee at the prevailing market rate. It is important for your employment agreement to state that the employee is an at-will employee, regardless of her ownership position in the company, in case you would need to fire that employee in the future. Failure to take this step can open your company up to the possibility of a minority shareholder lawsuit. To avoid lawsuits, you should define *fired for cause*, touching on what the company considers to be fraud, negligence, nonperformance, and so forth. Lawsuits aside, having a right of first refusal or the option to repurchase shares when the employee leaves preserves all the shares for redistribution among the remaining founders and employees. To avoid the time and energy of litigation, companies usually buy out fired co-founders after they reach a settlement.

The Dilution Effect: An Example

This hypothetical example shows what happens to an entrepreneur as her firm achieves various milestones/ benchmarks of a successful launch and moves on to a harvest/ liquidity event. To demonstrate dilution, assume valuations at different rounds (valuation is covered in detail in Chapter 10). The following are some typical milestones that a successful venture might reach.

Milestone Events

1. Entrepreneur entices technology partner to join her firm, gives him **40%** of the equity.
2. Raises **$200,000** in equity from family and friends. The idea is valued post-money at **$1.0 million**.
3. Idea is technically feasible. Needs to hire **software engineers** to build a working prototype. Raises **$1 million** from

angels on a **$2.5 million** post-money valuation. Establishes a **15%** option pool to provide equity to current engineers as well as future hires.

4. Prototype looks promising, and company successfully raises **$3 million** of venture capital on a **$7 million** post-money valuation to start sales. The venture capitalist imposes the following terms: Company needs to hire an experienced CEO, CFO, and VP of Sales, giving the three options worth **10%, 3%**, and **7%**.
5. Sales growth is on plan, and the firm needs to ramp up to meet increasing demand. Raises **$10 million** of additional venture capital on a **$30 million** post-money valuation.
6. Firm receives acquisition offer from a large company (e.g., Google, Facebook) for **$100 million in the large company's stock**.

Note that although our entrepreneur is being diluted, the increasing value of her firm offsets this dilution.

This example highlights a successful venture. Founders who distribute equity wisely grow the value of their firm, which leads to a higher return for all involved, even as dilution occurs. However, student entrepreneurs often make the mistake of giving too much founder stock to too many different people. If, for example, the firm started with five student founders with equal ownership and still progressed through each step, the final harvest value for each founder would be $1 million. Although this sum is attractive, keep in mind that this growth projection likely takes five or more years, and in the early years, the founders will be paid below-market salaries (and probably no salaries until the angel round).

Also, if there is any kind of problem that leads to a lower valuation than projected here, the final payoff for the founders is greatly impacted. If, for example, the valuation that the firm receives when the first venture capital comes in is only $5 million versus $7 million, the entrepreneur (as sole initial founder) earns a harvest value of $2.8 million. If there were five initial cofounders who get equal shares, each would earn a bit less than $600,000 for many years of hard work and below-market pay. The lesson is to distribute equity wisely. Make sure that all cofounders will contribute throughout the entire time it takes to build and harvest the company and that each can increase the value of the company.

Event	Entr. Share	Co-founder	Family/ Friends	Angels	Option Pool	CEO	CFO	VP Sales	VC Rnd1	VC Rnd2	Total	Valuations (000)	Ent's Value
1	60%	40%									100%		
2	48%	32%	20%								100%	$1,000	$480
3	22%	14%	9%	40%	15%						100%	$2,500	$540
4	8%	5%	3%	15%	6%	10%	3%	7%	43%		100%	$7,000	$562
5	5%	4%	2%	10%	4%	7%	2%	5%	29%	32%	100%	$30,000	$1,605
6	5%	4%	2%	10%	4%	7%	2%	5%	29%	32%	100%	$100,000	$5,349
Harvest Value for All Stakeholders	$5,349	$3,566	$2,229	$9,905	$3,714	$6,667	$2,000	$4,667	$28,571	$33,332			

Salary

Although equity can compensate for a below-market salary, most of your team will need at least a subsistence salary during the launch phase. The difficulty is trying to set that initial salary. You can start by researching the current market rate for the position you are trying to fill at online resources such as www.salary.com. The website provides general parameters for the position and then allows you to personalize your search by company size, industry, and other factors. For instance, an information technology director might earn anywhere from $172,014 to $212,969 in the Boston metropolitan area.[46] The person's salary would be adjusted by her previous work experience, the industry focus of your company, and other mitigating factors specific to the individual or your company. You can also double-check your market figure by looking at some of the Internet job sites like www.linkedin.com, www.monster.com, and, again, www.salary.com.[47] A scan of these sites found that a chief information technology officer position pays anywhere from $252,989 and $371,268.[48] The market rate is a reference parameter, and you'll adjust it by considering the person's expertise and perceived contribution to the company. A younger, less-experienced co-founder will earn well below the market rate. A more senior, experienced co-founder with a long record of success might earn close to or above the market rate, but paying the market rate is probably impossible for a start-up.

Once you know the market rate, you can negotiate a current salary and expected increases based on your company's improving cash flow. For instance, you might tie an increase to closing the next round of funding. Other increases might be linked to increasing cash flow due to improved sales. Instead of making firm commitments to future salary increases, consider using performance-based bonuses in the early years. This further aligns the team's efforts with the venture's overall goals and preserves cash flow. If team members successfully execute, the venture should have increasing sales, which in turn can lead to rapid growth in bonuses and other profit sharing. The key is to be creative and motivate your team to work toward common goals. That means deferred current income (lower salaries), with the promise of larger returns in the future (bonuses, appreciation of equity, and options).

Although start-ups should negotiate below-market salaries, it can be helpful to understand the implications of a fully loaded business model. When constructing your pro forma financials, see what happens to your expected profitability if you paid everyone their market rates. All too often, entrepreneurs launch into a business expecting attractive profit margins only to realize that these margins are a mirage; once people are paid according to the market rate (say, in the fifth year), the profits disappear. Some entrepreneurs choose to promise market rates but defer payment until cash flow improves. In this case, they are creating a deferred liability that obligates the company to make up for the lower-than-market salary in the future. This means the market-rate salary is reflected in the income statement, the actual pay is shown on the cash flow, and the remainder appears on the balance sheet as a deferred liability. However you decide to compensate your team, be cognizant of the full range of possibilities, and keep in mind that you need to preserve cash flow in the early years to fund growth.

Other Compensation Considerations

In addition to equity and salary, as the owner of a company you will need to think through a number of other issues in overall compensation. You will be competing with companies of all shapes and sizes for the most skilled people in the workforce. Putting together a competitive compensation package means thinking beyond just the monetary side of compensation. For instance, although they may not be feasible in the earliest parts of the start-up phase, as quickly as possible you will want to consider things like health and dental plans and retirement savings programs like 401(k)s. Even from the start, you will need to figure out a holiday and vacation package that makes sense for your company.

Every organization is different, and it's important to align your benefits package with the types of people you intend to hire. If your business will rely on recent college graduates, something like company-sponsored life insurance will probably be unnecessary. However, if your staff will be older, married people who have families, life insurance and a solid family healthcare plan will be essential. The key is that all of these benefits are strategic in nature. Your goal in developing a compensation package is to attract and motivate the best talent in the most cost-effective way possible. You should never underestimate the effect that a thoughtful benefits plan can have on employee satisfaction and loyalty. There are few things as powerful as having a workforce that feels they work for a great company.

External Team Members

Although your core team is critical to your venture's success, you will leverage the team's efforts by building a strong **virtual team**—that is, all those who have a vested interest in your success, including professionals you contract for special needs, such as lawyers, accountants, and consultants. It also includes those who have invested in your business, especially if they have valuable expertise. For instance, you'll be well served if you secure angel investors who are successful entrepreneurs in your industry. You may also be able to gain help from those who haven't financially invested in your firm but are interested in helping new businesses succeed, perhaps by serving on advisory boards for new companies. Finally, at some point you'll likely pull together a board of directors, which is required by law if you are incorporated. Let's examine each of these outside team members in more detail.

Outside Investors

When you are considering bringing on outside investors, whether in the form of angel investors or venture capitalists, never underestimate the value these team members can bring with their experience and wisdom. For many angel investors in particular, the experience of working with a start-up is as much about the satisfaction of mentoring a young entrepreneur as it is about financial gain. Take, for example, the story of Norm Brodsky, the long-time entrepreneur and contributor to *Inc.* magazine. In describing his decision to invest in David Schneider's New York City restaurant, he said, "Yes, making money is important. I wouldn't go into a deal unless I thought I could get my capital back and earn a good return. But I don't really do this type of investing for the money anymore. I'm more interested in helping people get started in business. Whatever I make is a bonus on top of the fun I have being a part of it and the satisfaction I get from helping people like David succeed."

For an aspiring entrepreneur, finding an investor with that kind of an attitude is invaluable. As David Schneider put it, "I really liked the idea of having somebody I could go to who cared about this place as a business. … It's like he's always pushing people to better themselves. He wants you to move on, to expand, to grow."[49] In business, experience is the greatest competitive advantage, and an investor can bring that asset to a fledgling company. But Schneider's comments also point to another key benefit of having a strong investor on your side: You'll have someone to hold you accountable and keep you focused. Many entrepreneurs underestimate the challenge being your own boss can pose. When the going gets tough or decisions get complicated, it can be incredibly helpful to have someone prodding you forward. For all these reasons, choose carefully if you decide to raise capital through angel investors.

Lawyers

Every new venture will require legal advice. Although you may be able to incorporate on your own, other aspects of your venture will benefit from your attorney's guidance. As discussed earlier, your lawyer can draft an appropriate template for employee contracts. If your business is developing some intellectual property, you may wish to file a patent. The right attorney can help you search existing patents and decide which elements of your intellectual property are patentable. She will devise a suite of patents and then, if you deem it appropriate, help you patent your product in several important countries. Lawyers can also consult on the myriad unforeseen issues that are likely to arise, which is why it is so essential to choose your attorney carefully.

When making a decision to hire a lawyer, consider several factors. For instance, a smaller firm is likely to offer lower billing rates, a factor that can be very important to a start-up. However, small firms are often heavily dependent on a small handful of clients who make up the bulk of their business. For this reason, you may find that your company is a low priority for a small firm with several key accounts. In contrast, although a large firm may bill at a higher rate, it will almost always have someone available to answer your questions, and it will also offer the benefit of a large pool of lawyers with diverse areas of expertise to draw from. Because your legal issues may cover everything from employment law to intellectual property, a large firm isn't necessarily a bad choice. Although you may pay more, you may also find that a larger firm is more willing or able to set up a flexible payment plan.

In addition, when choosing your lawyer, it is essential that you find someone whom you like, who shows an appreciation for and interest in your company, and most important, who has deep knowledge of your industry. The last thing you want is to be paying several hundred dollars an hour to talk with someone who is distant or aloof. And as for hourly rates, yes, you should expect to pay a minimum of $150/hour—and likely much more than that depending on where you live. For this reason, it is critical that you do as much preparation and research as possible before you sit down with your attorney. Most firms bill in increments of as little as 10 minutes, so you need to use your time with an attorney as effectively and efficiently as possible. Also keep in mind that, although it is important to have a lawyer from the beginning to ensure that you avoid many of the classic mistakes, there is also a wide variety of free resources available to small businesses. These include everything from online templates for standard agreements and forms to nonprofit and government-sponsored law centers that can provide low-cost or pro bono advice. Although you should always turn to your lawyer for the final word, you can save your company a lot of money by using the available resources to get some of the legwork out of the way. Just remember that, as your company grows, your time will become more valuable, and at some point, spending hours doing your own research becomes counterproductive.

When John Earle first started his apparel company, Johnny Cupcakes, intellectual property was the least of his worries, but as his brand grew in popularity, counterfeiting and piracy become rampant. In an effort to bootstrap the company, CFO, John's mother Lorraine, a former law office manager, used her knowledge of the law to write cease-and-desist letters to over 200 counterfeiters. Lorraine used her legal connections to cost effectively trademark the Johnny Cupcakes logo and copyright designs. Lorraine explained, "People steal our name, our logo, our designs. In some countries, they're actually opening Johnny Cupcakes stores and selling our stuff."[50] Lorraine was able to use her past experience to save thousands of dollars on lawyer fees by doing the work herself and educating her son on legal matters during the process.

Accountants

It's often wise to hire an accountant to handle tax filings in the early years because you're likely to be too busy to do it yourself and too small to have an in-house person, such as a controller or CFO, to manage the process for you. Many of the same caveats about working with lawyers apply to accountants, although you may be well served by an accountant who is a sole proprietor. The nature of accountants' work is somewhat different from that of lawyers, and for this reason, you needn't work with a larger firm in your early years. Don't forget that an accountant is a trained business professional; beyond filing tax returns and keeping your filings up to date, an accountant can help you analyze the strengths and weaknesses of your company's financial performance. He may be able to help you find ways to improve cash flow, strengthen margins, and identify tax benefits that can save you money down the road. Furthermore, both lawyers and accountants represent another spoke in your network, as both groups frequently have a long list of business and professional contacts. These can include everything from potential partners and customers to angel investor networks and venture capital firms.

Board of Advisors

A board of advisors can be extremely beneficial to the early-stage company. Unlike a board of directors, a board of advisors has no fiduciary duty to shareholders. Instead, the goal is to offer a source of expert guidance and feedback to the lead entrepreneur. In choosing a board, you should look to enlist people with expertise in your field and a sincere interest in mentoring an emerging business. Good sources are your professors, current and former entrepreneurs, professional investors such as venture capitalists and angels, suppliers for your firm, and individuals who may have insight into your target customers. Beyond advice, this group can expand your personal network and provide leads to new customers or investors. In fact, board of advisor members will often become investors if your firm goes through a private placement.

One final note on boards of advisors relates to communication. Many first-time entrepreneurs struggle to strike the right balance between too much and too little communication. Keep in mind that, if you have developed a board of powerful advisors, they are busy individuals. Don't e-mail or phone them every time you have a question. Instead, accumulate questions and think about which ones are most critical to your firm and where the advisor can add the most value. Do some preliminary legwork to find alternative answers to these questions and options you might be inclined to pursue. If you are prepared, you will have a more productive conversation with your advisors, and they will be even more supportive of your future efforts.

The flip side to overcommunicating with advisors is touching base with them rarely—or only when you want help raising money. This type of communication suggests the entrepreneur is interested only in the advisor's network, but the advisor is less inclined to open up that network unless he has a strong understanding of the company's progress. Produce a monthly or bimonthly email newsletter that keeps all your important stakeholders, including your board of advisors, informed about the company's progress. This newsletter should be short and concise so that it will get read. More often than not, the newsletter will prompt an advisor to contact you with some useful input or connection to someone in her network. Properly managing your board of advisors will pay dividends, so don't neglect it.

Board of Directors

When incorporating a company, entrepreneurs must establish a board of directors whose purpose is to represent the interests of the equity holders. Thus, when you initially incorporate, the only shareholders might be you and your co-founders. Once you seek outside financing, it becomes important to fill out the board beyond the co-founders. Venture capitalists and more sophisticated angels often require representation on the board. A common board structure for the early-stage firm is five board members; these might include two insiders like the CEO and CFO, two members from the lead investors, and one outsider, who most often is selected with strong input from the investors. The outsider is often a person who has significant vertical market expertise and who can add value to the strategic operating decisions.

The board is in charge of governance and represents the shareholders. It meets quarterly to review the company's progress and its strategy going forward. The board will determine compensation for the company's officers and also oversee financial reporting. With the passage of the Sarbanes–Oxley Act, the responsibilities and potential liability of the board have greatly increased. Although the legislation applies only to public companies, more and more small businesses are finding it necessary to align with the act if they hope one day to sell to a public company or go public themselves. It's a voluntary choice to do so, but the act's standards are rapidly becoming the "best practices" for accounting and financial control at well-managed companies. This means that developing a clear set of expectations, ethical standards, and procedures for board members is essential. Furthermore, you'll want to ensure that your board has at least one or two members who can be considered independent, which means that they are not susceptible to potential conflicts of interest. Board members should be encouraged to act in the best interest of all the shareholders, not just the principal owner. We believe the entrepreneurial team should extend beyond the co-founders and early employees to include external individuals who can provide invaluable wisdom and input. Entrepreneurship is truly a team sport—the stronger your team, the stronger your bench, the more likely you'll not only survive but also thrive. The next section looks at some difficulties you might incur once the team is in place.

Keeping the Team Together

We've looked at the value of a well-functioning team. But not every team functions well, even if it's filled with superstars. Consider the Detroit Tigers, which had Major League Baseball's fourth-highest payroll ($200 million) in 2017.[51] The team finished in last place in the American League Central Division despite having seven-time all-star pitcher Justin Verlander and power players such as Miguel Cabrera, Jordan Zimmerman, and Justin Upton[52] Why has this happened? Common sense dictates that the team with the best talent should win, but a dysfunctional team often fails. Just before the 2017 season ended, the Tigers traded their underperforming star player Verlander to the Houston Astros. On his new team, Verlander went on to play in the 2017 World Series and was named MVP of the American League Championship Series after pitching seven shutout innings and several strikeouts.[53] How did Verlander go from underperforming to excelling in the span of a month? The key here is chemistry: Sometimes the whole really is greater than the sum of the parts. Consider the Oakland A's of Major League Baseball. Although as of the writing of this book they have not won the World Series since 1989, they have consistently achieved a winning record until 2014, despite having one of the lowest payrolls in the major leagues. In 2018, the Oakland A's made a comeback and won 97 games (the fourth most in all of baseball), and yet they spent 30% of what the winning Boston Red Sox spent on payroll.[54] The A's general manager, Billy Beane, argues that a manager can put together a winning combination as long as he understands the gaps in his team, works to fill those gaps, and focuses on finding players who match the team's culture and work ethic. Although we're not advocating the statistical construction of teams, we do believe that understanding and effectively directing your team toward its ultimate goal can make all the difference in the world.

You can hardly overestimate the importance of culture and fit. The key to building and growing a successful team is establishing a company culture and working to bring in team members who subscribe to that culture. Culture starts at day one in any new venture and evolves from the way the founders interact among themselves and with other early employees. Picture culture as analogous to duck imprinting. When a duckling is born, she follows the first thing she sees, which is usually her mother. Likewise, when a person joins a company, she quickly acculturates to the environment she is in—or leaves shortly thereafter.

Once established, a company culture is incredibly difficult to change. So decide what type of culture you want, and then work to create it. Company culture is an enigmatic and amorphous thing, and the ways in which it affects organizational performance are not completely understood. It often filters down from the very top of the company, and thus it reflects the values and skills of the CEO and other leaders. If you want a company with an open, trusting environment, then you need to foster an open and trusting relationship with your direct reports. If you lead with fear and intimidation, this approach will filter its way down to all levels of your organization. The bottom line is that you need to think through the culture you want to create, decide on one you are comfortable with, and work daily to communicate the values behind that culture. The most successful cultures are those rooted in core values and beliefs that are a part of the company's mission, vision, and mantra.

Keep in mind that not everyone will fit the culture of your company. For many first-time entrepreneurs, this represents a source of frustration and internal conflict, but it shouldn't. There are people who like buttoned-up, conservative work environments and people who like laid-back, laissez-faire workplaces. One person's "unprofessional" atmosphere makes another person's ideal company. Don't fight this, but do recognize the culture you are trying to create and seek to hire people who will feel comfortable in it.

As a company grows, it's common for the culture to evolve. The classic example is the loosely organized start-up culture where the pace of work is relentless, and as a result, a lot of misgivings are overlooked. Nine times out of 10, this culture will evolve toward a more structured "corporate" culture as the company gets bigger, and the chaos that was so critical to the early stage will begin to erode the company's success. Every start-up will see certain elements of its culture evolve and certain elements stay the same year after year. The most important point is to make the change deliberate and recognize the long-term commitment needed to instill it.

Even if a venture has a strong culture, problems with the team are inevitable. Just as the best cure is prevention, the best way to keep your team functioning well is to avoid some of the common pitfalls. We will take a look at some of the problems that most new-venture teams face and then examine ways to avoid them.

Burnout

We've all heard the stories of start-ups during which the team ate and slept in the office for weeks at a time. A diet of pizza and Red Bull is synonymous with the crazed hours of the classic launch phase. The atmosphere is relaxed but energized, and the people are highly motivated by the fast-paced environment and the thrill of being on the cutting edge of an emerging technology.

Although this approach works for many early-stage ventures, it's not for everyone, and it has its drawbacks. On top of the long hours, there's the uncertainty that your product will work as intended or that the market will respond to the product or service as you hoped. Every minor misstep seems to take on epic importance and increases the stress levels of your team. Moreover, your team members will notice that the balance between personal and professional life is out of whack, and they may start questioning whether this sustained effort is worth it. As these pressures increase, the risk of losing a critical team member mounts. It's important to manage and relieve these stresses as much as possible.

As the lead entrepreneur, you need to act as the coach of the team and keep the members focused on the end goal. This means that communication is critically important. Despite the ubiquity of texting in today's world, and although email is the standard business communication form these days, you need to see—and be seen by—your people! In the start-up phase, you should make a point of having daily face-to-face communication with every team member. Listen to each of them—not only about the progress of their assignments, but also about the stresses they may be feeling. Present them with regular updates on the overall progress of the venture, and give them realistic progress reports on how things are going. It is far more damaging to withhold negative information they will ultimately discover for themselves. If they understand that the venture is falling behind schedule or that the product isn't functioning quite as planned, they can be energized to correct these problems.

New ventures also have planned stress-relieving activities, or bonding experiences, such as the Friday happy hour or the lunchtime basketball game. Get away from your workspace and share some downtime with each other. The upside of these extracurricular activities is the strong bonds it helps the team build. A start-up can be like your college days, where you'll make some of your lifelong friends. Many new ventures also have stress relievers right in the workplace, such as foosball tables, dartboards, and other distractions so that individuals can break from their work for a few minutes and clear their minds. It's often a good idea to provide free soda, coffee, and snacks as well. These little perks are cost effective and build goodwill and camaraderie. Relieving stress will help keep your team strong and cohesive.

Family Pressure

If working long hours stresses your team members, it also stresses their families. Spouses and significant others complain to their partners about their never being home or their being too tired to pay attention to their families. Missing a child's ball games and school performances can create resentment. Stress at home can negatively affect performance and increase the risk of turnover. If spouses continually ask why their partners have left good-paying jobs for lower pay and the promise of a future payoff, your team members will question their own motives. So it's imperative that open communication occur on the home front as well.

Counsel your team members to set the expectations of their families even before they join your team. If a spouse is forewarned of the long hours, it minimizes the angst. It's also a good idea to include families in stress-relieving events on a regular basis. Company picnics are a nice way for spouses to connect with other spouses. In this way, they can develop an informal support group with people who are facing the same difficulties. In fact, some new ventures formalize these family support groups by organizing a few events that are spouse specific. It is important to remember and remind all involved that the long hours will subside and that, if the venture is successful, everyone will benefit.

Interpersonal Conflicts

In such a charged environment, interpersonal conflicts among team members are common. Resolve these disputes as quickly as possible, or they may escalate to the point where they become destructive. Lead entrepreneurs typically find that they spend as much time coaching and managing team issues as they do directly working on the business. If you find yourself in this situation, don't worry—this is a valuable and effective use of your time. If you can keep your team working together, you'll have more success than if you try to carry the burden all alone.

As the coach, you may be able to resolve some conflicts only by firing one of the team members. Although firing is a necessary part of running a company, you need to be prepared for the inevitable disruption it will cause (although it can be therapeutic to those who remain if it removes some of the stress that the fired individual brought to the company). Depending on the person's agreement with the company, his departure may require a buyout of equity and a lump-sum settlement. That's why firing is usually undertaken only if the person is not only prone to interpersonal conflicts but also underperforming in some way (either not skilled enough to do the jobs required or shirking his responsibilities). First try to resolve the conflict by mediating between the parties, and be sure not to appear to be favoring either one. It may be prudent to hire an outside expert who is perceived as a neutral party. Whatever resolution you agree on, make sure that it is implemented as planned.

CONCLUSION

Entrepreneurship is a team sport. The most critical task any lead entrepreneur undertakes is defining who should be on the team and then creating an environment in which that team can flourish. This chapter has identified what type of team members ventures might need, how to entice and compensate them, and how to build a strong, supportive culture. Maintaining a team requires ongoing effort, and many organizations find that team dynamics suffer when the firm experiences rapid growth. Chapter 13 revisits these issues and suggests ways that organizations can keep their entrepreneurial orientation.

YOUR OPPORTUNITY JOURNAL

Reflection Point	Your Thoughts...
1. What are your three strongest attributes?	
2. Talk to a close mentor and ask what he or she sees as your strengths. Do these match the attributes you identified in question 1?	
3. What skills do you need to develop prior to launch? What skills can you develop during the launch and early stages of your company? Create a plan to develop those skills.	
4. Create an organization chart for your venture. Show positions to be filled immediately and those to be filled later (along with the dates of filling those positions). Create a staffing plan based on your organization chart.	
5. Think about the types of employees you'd like to hire. What kind of values are you looking for? Remember, this is the point at which you create your company's culture.	

WEB EXERCISE

Scan Monster.com, Salary.com, and other job sites. Look at the postings for CEO and other key employees of early-stage companies in the industry that you are interested in pursuing. What skills are being sought? What level of previous experience is desired? How much are they offering for these key employees? Use this information to start creating your own staffing plan.

NOTES

1. http://www.facebook.com/press/info.php?founderbios.
2. https://www.newyorker.com/magazine/2011/07/11/a-womans-place-ken-auletta
3. https://www.statista.com/statistics/277229/facebooks-annual-revenue-and-net-income/
4. https://www.statista.com/statistics/264810/number-of-monthly-active-facebook-users-worldwide/
5. http://www.paulgraham.com/startupmistakes.html
6. Minniti, M., Bygrave, W., and Autio, E. *Global Entrepreneurship Monitor: 2005 Executive Report*. Wellesley, MA: Babson College and London Business School. 2006.
7. https://techcrunch.com/2011/05/28/what-makes-a-startup-successful-blackbox-report-aims-to-map-the-startup-genome/
8. https://csimarket.com/Industry/industry_Efficiency.php?ind=914
9. https://www.nada.org/2017NADAdata/ https://smallbusiness.chron.com/average-profit-margin-restaurant-13477.html
10. Lechler, T. Social Interaction: A Determinant of Entrepreneurial Team Success. *Small Business Economics*, 16: 263 – 278. 2001.
11. Ruef, M. Strong Ties, Weak Ties and Islands: Structural and Cultural Predictions of Entrepreneurial Team Success. *Industrial and Corporate Changes*, 11: 427 – 449. 2002.
12. Bird, B. *Entrepreneurial Behavior*. Glenview, IL: Scott Foresman. 1989.
13. Hofman, M. The Big Picture. *Inc.*, 25(11): 87 – 94. October 15, 2003.
14. http://www.entrepreneur.com/article/238138.
15. www.crunchbase.com/company/etsy.
16. www.nytimes.com/2007/12/16/magazine/16Crafts-t.html?_r=2&oref=slogin&ref=magazine&pagewanted=all.
17. www.businessinsider.com/etsy-now-profitable-gets-a-new-ceo-2009-12.
18. http://bits.blogs.nytimes.com/2012/07/18/one-on-one-chad-dickerson-ceo-of-etsy.
19. www.foodshouldtastegood.com/about-fstg/our-story/timeline.
20. www.foodshouldtastegood.com/about-fstg/in-the-news/2011.
21. www.generalmills.com/Media/News-Releases/Library/2012/February/food_taste_good_2_29.aspx.
22. http://www.blog.generalmills.com/2015/02/how-food-should-taste-good-got-its-start/.
23. Drucker, P. Managing Oneself. *Harvard Business Review*, 83(1): 100 – 105. 2005.
24. *HRfocus*, 82(9): 8 – 9. September 2005.

25. http://www.wsj.com/articles/why-introverts-make-great-entrepreneurs-144 0381699.
26. McFarland, K. The Psychology of Success. *Inc.*, 27(11): 158 – 159. November 15, 2005. http://www.wsj.com/articles/ why-introverts-make-great-entrepreneurs-1440381699.
27. Kuemmerle, W. A Test for the Faint Hearted. *Harvard Business Review*, 80(5): 122 – 126. 2002.
28. Ibid.
29. www.eventuring.org/eShip/appmanager/eVenturing/ShowDoc/eShipWebCacheRepository/Documents/FTNV-pp276-279.pdf.
30. Brief Profile of 2003 Inc. 500 Companies. *Inc.* 25(10). October 2003.
31. https://www.thebalancesmb.com/ben-and-jerry-s-the-men-behind-the-ice-cream-1200942
32. https://www.washingtonpost.com/business/on-small-business/when-we-were-small-ben-and-jerrys/2014/05/14/069b6cae-dac4-11e3-8009-71de85b9c527_story.html?noredirect=on&utm_term=.4fcd2b2f77a7
33. https://www.thebalancesmb.com/ben-and-jerry-s-the-men-behind-the-ice-cream-1200942
34. Ibid.
35. https://www.geekwire.com/2017/father-daughter-founding-team-landed-spot-techstars-automotive-startup/
36. Ibid.
37. https://www.geekwire.com/2018/seeva-raises-2m-hires-former-toyota-exec-help-self-driving-cars-navigate-tricky-weather/
38. Hoffman, Claire. The battle for facebook. *The Rolling Stone*. 2008. www.rollingstone.com/news/story/21129674/the_battle_for_facebook/print.
39. Presentation during 7th Annual Babson Forum on Entrepreneurship and Innovation, Babson College, Wellesley, MA. October 2, 2008.
40. Spirrison, J. B. Startups Ponder Equity Compensation Conundrum. *Private Equity Week*. October 4, 1999, pp. 1 – 2.
41. Robbins, S. Dividing Equity Between Founders and Investors: How to Figure Out Who Gets What Percentage of the Business When Investors Come on Board. *Entrepreneur*. October 13, 2003.
42. Beyster Institute. *Employee Ownership Plans—"Keys to Success."* www.beysterinstitute.org/about_employee_ ownership/keys_to.success.cfm.
43. Burlingham, B. The Boom in Employee Stock Ownership. *Inc.*, 22(11): 106 – 110. August 2000.
44. www.investopedia.com/articles/optioninvestor/09/expensing-esos.asp#axzz2Ex73uFMs.
45. Ibid.
46. https://www1.salary.com/MA/Boston/Information-Technology-Director-Salary.html
47. www.ebizmba.com/articles/job-Web sites.
48. https://www1.salary.com/MA/Boston/Chief-Information-Technology-Officer-Salary.html.
49. Burlingham, B. Touched by an Angel. *Inc.*, 19(10): 46 – 47. July 1997.
50. www.inc.com/magazine/20100501/my-son-the-entrepreneur.html.
51. https://www.cbssports.com/mlb/news/heres-every-mlb-teams-opening-day-payroll-for-2017/
52. https://www.forbes.com/sites/blakewilliams3012/2017/07/14/the-mlb-teams-that-are-struggling-despite-massive-payrolls/#79f8d82f7862
53. https://www.sbnation.com/mlb/2017/10/21/16515392/justin-verlander-alcs-mvp-astros-yankees
54. https://www.mlb.com/standings https://www.statista.com/statistics/236206/payroll-of-major-league-baseball-teams/.

Case Box, Inc.: Preserving Startup Culture in a Rapidly Growing Company[1]

The top executive team at Box was yet again discussing a continuing critical issue for the rapidly growing firm: how to preserve the culture and agility of a start-up while expanding to almost 1,000 employees at locations in San Francisco, London, and Paris as well as headquarters in Los Altos, California. The culture at headquarters was similar to that of other young start-ups in Silicon Valley: hard-working, rapid-acting, personally accountable, egalitarian, and collaborative with its own special characteristics. Co-founders Aaron Levie, 29, and Dylan Smith, 28, with Chief Operating Officer Dan Levin, 50, believed it critical to preserve the *secret sauce* behind their success. They talked about it frequently with each other and to company employees. They were determined not to let continued growth in a potentially huge market be crimped by becoming overly bureaucratic or harmed by failure to execute consistently and economically. They understood their close working relationship was unusual in a top team, especially one with the individual brilliance and industry visibility of Levie combined with the open, collaborative way all three worked together. This style permeated the company, yet they knew it might not easily scale. What would it take? (See Exhibit 7.1 for executive backgrounds.)

Exhibit 7.1 Background of Executives

Name	Role	Age	Joined	History	Link to Aaron
Aaron Levie	Co-founder/CEO, the visionary behind Box's product and platform strategy focused on incorporating the best of traditional content management with the most effective elements of social business software.	29	2005	Studied business at the Marshall School of Business at the University of Southern California before taking a leave of absence; created Box as a college business project with the goal of helping people easily access their information from any location. Box was launched from Aaron's dorm room in 2005 with the help of CFO Dylan Smith.	
Sam Ghods	Vice President of Technology, manages design and architecture of Box's application and technology stack.	28	2006	Attended University of Southern California, where he studied computer engineering and computer science for two years before joining Box. Learned much of the relevant coding from online learning: "70 % of what I learned was from the Internet."	Knew Aaron, Dylan, and Jeff from high school.
Dan Levin	COO	50	2010	Bachelor's in applications of computer graphics to statistical data analysis, Princeton University.	Consultant to Box then hired as COO to manage internal operations.
Dylan Smith	Chief Financial Officer and co-founder of Box, where he leads finance, investor relations, and other miscellaneous operations.	28	2005	Bachelor's in economics from Duke University. Prior to Box, Dylan spent his time earning Box's seed funding through various entrepreneurial endeavors (especially playing poker!).	Friends with Aaron since junior high.
Jeff Queisser	Vice President of Technical Operations, responsible for Box's core technology, architecture, and infrastructure.	28	2006	Became interested in computer programming at a young age, selling his first software at the age of 10, later formed Q-Squared, a successful IT consulting company based in Seattle. Attended Western Washington University before leaving to join Box.	"Originally from Seattle suburb. In fourth grade new kid on block, Aaron, around the corner. We became fast friends. Varied interests. He was magician, making good money on magic shows. I was the nerd (a plus). Learned Basic."

[1] This case was written by Allan R. Cohen. Copyright, Babson College, 2015.

Exhibit 7.1 (Continued)

Name	Role	Age	Joined	History	Link to Aaron
Evan Wittenberg	VP of People, leads a team that finds, develops, and retains the company's world-class talent while maintaining the unique culture.	45	2012	MBA with Honors from Wharton, BA with Distinction in Psychology and English Literature from Swarthmore College. Hewlett Packard's Chief Talent Officer responsible for a global workforce of 350,000 employees. Before HP, created and ran the Global Leadership Development function at Google. Previously, Director of the Graduate Leadership Program at the Wharton School.	Went to graduate school and worked at Google with Box's SVP of Marketing before being recruited.
Sam Schillace	Sr. VP Engineering, responsible for the engineering and QA teams.	45	2012	Co-founded Writely, which he sold to Google in 2006 to form the core of Google Docs. Sr. VP Engineering, Google, elsewhere. Bachelor's, master's degrees in mathematics from University of Michigan.	Close friend and colleague of Box COO Dan Levin; recruited from Google Ventures to lead Box Engineering.
Greg Strickland	Vice President of International.	34	2008	Was Box's VP of Business Operations, responsible for financial analysis, accounting, human resources, operations, strategic initiatives, and assisting with fund-raising. Bachelor's degree from University of California at Berkeley.	Early Box employee and self-described jack-of-all-trades, Strickland MC'd company's Friday lunch all-hands and led operations and expansion for Box in new offices and in international markets such as London.
Chris Yeh	Sr. VP Product and Platform.	44	2011	Came from Yahoo, where he was product lead for Yahoo! Groups, Delicious, and Tacit Software, Mercer Management Consulting. BS in Computer Science from University of Michigan and MBA Wharton.	Recruited from Yahoo! by Dan and Aaron to grow Box's developer community and platform strategy; eventually tapped to head both product and platform organizations.

Source: Company website and interviews.

Company Background

Box, Inc. was founded in 2005 to create software technology for business that would facilitate collaboration across multiple platforms with security. The company motto was *Simple, Secure Sharing from Anywhere*. CEO Aaron Levie stated publicly, "As we bring Box to more organizations, our mission remains the same: to make sharing, accessing, and managing content ridiculously easy."[2]

Levie and Smith had been friends since junior high school and had discussed various businesses. The idea of creating ways to collaborate from any device was the first that resonated with both of them. They knew their own problems with doing work, sharing files, and information and thought their concept could do a better job than anything that existed. Another friend, Jeff Queisser,[3] who was also in constant discussion about business ideas, described the history of their friendship.

[2] http://www.iposcoop.com/index.php?option=com_content&task=view&id=3605&Itemid=191, accessed February 2015. The formal description from the SEC S-1 amended registration document: "Box provides a cloud-based, mobile-optimized Enterprise Content Collaboration platform that enables organizations of all sizes to easily and securely manage their content and collaborate internally and externally. Our platform combines powerful, elegant and easy-to-use functionality that is designed for users with the security, scalability and administrative controls required by IT departments. We have built our platform to enable users to get their work done regardless of file format, application environment, operating system, device or location. Our mission is to make organizations more productive, competitive and collaborative by connecting people and their most important information."

[3] Jeff Queisser subsequently became vice president of technical operations at Box, responsible for core technology, architecture, and infrastructure.

I started a computer consulting business in the sixth grade. Aaron was a magician, and I was doing audiovisual at his magic shows. He and I were talking about business paths, and he was considering what domains to buy. They were all abject failures and flawed, but a good learning phase. Dylan was in the same school district, then Sam Ghods, now vice president of technology at Box, managing the design and architecture of Box's application and technology stack, moved into the neighborhood during high school. Aaron was applying to film school and convinced the four of us to join in writing and scoring his movie. It turned out to be like a test run for the four of us working together. We did it all and charged friends to see the movie. We earned the grand total of $15, but at least it wasn't a loss.

The four went to different colleges. Levie had rights to the name *Box.com* and was figuring out what to do with it. He decided to create a company and hired low-cost programmers abroad. With no notable competitors, people started paying him for service; there was no concept at the time of *freemium*[4] to get people interested.

Levie was stepping out of entrepreneurship classes to answer customer calls on his cell phone. Because the concept was attractive, he decided to drop out of school and convinced Smith to do so as well to handle finances. They moved to Berkeley and set up shop in the garage of Levie's uncle. Next they convinced Jeff Queisser and Sam Ghods to drop out and join them. These four became the core group of the business.[5]

Smith added more details.

The company was built over time, and we were having so much fun that we would rather work on Box than classes. We took a summer break and managed to raise money from Mark Cuban in October, then it all took off. We were about to do winter break from college, but in 24 hours we packed everything and went to the West Coast. Then we talked to our folks and the dean afterwards. We got paid subscriptions from day one in February 2005.

They found it a challenge to identify the right technical people. Through school friends, they located a firm abroad that had done similar work. Levie drove the programming, and Smith worked on a business model. Non-technical issues were the biggest challenge, as the team believed they were in a massive market and had to figure out how to make their technology known to others. They were certain theirs was easier to use than existing software. They wanted to determine how to be disruptive and get noticed.

Smith explained, "We decided to launch a free service, at the time a very innovative model, got it in front of many people." With money from Mark Cuban they could do it, then upsell, which separated them from the competition. They had a dedicated platform team and could build the ecosystem. Their philosophy was to gain vertical dominance. Platform openness became part of their value proposition because the IT environment was emerging rapidly, and they would be able to adapt to whatever was coming. Dropbox had a similar approach but was not working with enterprise-grade partners. The Box team thought it would be challenging for Dropbox to move this way given their DNA, the technology chosen, their partnerships, and Box's relationships with companies such as Netsuite, Oracle, and salesforce.com.

In retrospect, Smith saw things they would change if they could do it over.

As 19- to 20-year-olds trying to figure out how to do it, we were cautious. A couple of years in, there were about a dozen of us before we hired our first over 30-year-old, Karen Appleton, running our alliances and now business development. With the right attitudes and respect, age turned out not to be an issue, and our concerns were totally unfounded. We didn't have the experience per se, but it came naturally, instilling the culture we wanted, not consciously. We just hired really smart people, self-starters, and set them loose. We hired for non-negotiable personality traits and experiences—do they buy in, believe in always thinking creatively, and buy our direction? Had we done it earlier we would have avoided mistakes.

Smith acknowledged that they had to get rid of some without management experience and should have done so sooner. He thought problems were rarely a function of actual skills, but rather of not hiring to their cultural standards: "misfits" weren't proactive enough, or didn't work cross-functionally, or were not good communicators. He attributed Box senior executive success to his and Levie's natural talents, with important contributions from COO Dan Levin.

Aaron is a phenomenal leader, and I'm more interested in managing. We do well, stepping back to process what is going on. This allowed us to think about things. Bringing in Dan was a milestone to build a billion-dollar company. Aaron and I are totally gut, both voracious readers, especially early on when we didn't know exactly what we were doing. We reached out proactively for help. We hired smart people who we liked working with and went from there. Dan helped, determining a specific profile. Then we identified perfect candidates and would see if we could get them.

[4] *Freemium*, a combination of the words *free* and *premium*, was a concept developed in the 1980s for software. A version of a product was given away to build a user base, and better (premium) versions were made available for sale. The actual term was coined in 2006 or 2007.

[5] For more company history, see: http://techcrunch.com/2012/05/13/box-the-path-from-arringtons-backyard-to-a-billion-dollar-business/.

The Culture

As with all young companies, the emergent culture reflected the values and styles of the founders. Levie, the face of the company and highly visible in the tech community, was profiled often. For example, in an article accompanying his selection as entrepreneur of the year in 2013 by *Inc.* magazine, Eric Markowitz wrote:[6] "He possesses the sort of wisdom and focus you'd expect of an industry guru, but he acts with the 24/7 obsession of a scrappy start-up founder. Give him 10 minutes, and he will make you a believer. You talk with him for five minutes, and he says something funny and something smart and something insightful. He's a larger-than-life character."[7]

The rigorous hiring process that evolved from early mistakes, in which cultural fit was as important a criterion as specific knowledge and skills, led to a list of company values reflecting core beliefs of the co-founders and their first employees.

BOX VALUES

- **Believe your epic ideas are possible.**
- **We hire the best: trust each other.**
- **Blow our customer's minds in everything we do.**
- **Take risks. Fail fast. (Get Shit Done!)**
- **Bring your wacky self to work, every day.**
- **Think 10x.**
- **Make mom proud.**

Think big; trust and therefore collaborate; act quickly and learn from it; have fun while doing it—all were serious themes that played out repeatedly. Dan Levin believed it unique to have a company where people were anti-hierarchical, inclusive of youth and experience, speedy, and where they had fun and embodied operational excellence.[8]

Jeff Queisser filled in the history.

Because we were four friends, independently smart and motivated, we tried to stay objective and non-emotional, though there is heat sometimes. We spar, but in an intellectually productive way. We all lived together, so spent all our free time together. Aaron and Dylan would fight for an hour on what movie and dinner to go to. We made a bunch of hiring mistakes with people who didn't fit, not because they were hierarchical and stiff, but, for example, they wanted to be hippies and not work hard consistently. Eventually, trial and error led to a solid rubric for hiring the right people. We didn't appreciate the value of experience until Dan; we didn't get how valuable it could be to have someone who had done something before. We worked in a single communal office, so at least one of us was in every important conversation. When we grew to somewhere between 50 and 300 people and it got harder, we realized we liked what we had, so wrote down Box values, still going. We started to think how to preserve, transmit, and amplify the culture. We hired Greg Strickland, who had tried stand-up comedy on the side, created a weekly Friday company lunch where he would MC. He's very sarcastic and would publicly interview each new hire, "What do you think about peers, your manager?" It was awkward but a great equalizer, and we knew everyone who came in, which was a great unifying force. Then too many per week were being hired, and it got too big. We still do Friday lunch, but it's not so much fun.

Levie strongly believed the company style worked because of the unusual complementary relationships and style of working at the top. He focused on how to approach the market and stay competitive, Smith on finance and Levin on operations and organization.

The three of us are different but together. I have known Dylan 15 to 16 years, which is already great for decisions. There is always tension because of different perspectives and approaches, so decisions are balanced more than they would otherwise be. There is a deep level of trust with Dan and among the three of us. Top teams are driven by relationship; complementarity can work or be destructive. Dan happened to be someone we could really work well with. It is hard to do—we tried it before, but this one worked.

We were at 45 people when Dan came on; he is not heavy-handed, because we don't want a GE-like place, and he is sensitive to the right layers of process, timing, and structures. Dan makes sure the organization runs effectively. He runs the staff meeting, runs goal-setting, to move in an aligned and efficient way. That gives me time to focus on determining our competitive strengths, where

---

[6] *Inc.* magazine, "Don't Bet Against Aaron Levie," Eric Markowitz, December–January 2013.

[7] To get a sense of Levie's rapid and energetic style, go to http://www.inc.com/malachi-leopold/trep-life-building-box-aaron-levie.html. He talks about a number of themes in this case and shows the informality at Box headquarters. Some details, not all in the video, include: the large spiral slide that descends from the second floor into the lobby; the lack of private offices for anyone including executives; informal dress including Levie's trademark red sneakers worn with black suit and open collar; riding razor scooters; widespread availability of food and drink; free lunch daily; the company-designed videogame; the area for watching TV; playing speed chess—all are visible manifestations of the culture.

[8] For Levin comments on the culture: https://babson.mediaspace.kaltura.com/media/Culture+at+Box+%284+7%29/ 1_sx0typxf.

the market is moving, where we want to be, and what our best approach is. By not being bogged down, I can focus on external issues. I'm not skilled at facilitating management processes. Now we have leaders who can solve those things. I don't have to attempt to be good at an area that I'll likely never be good in, but it's covered.

We have to invest at least two hours per week on decisional alignment. There are 3% different conversations each time, only nuances, but they matter. Over a few months of a strategy, 1% difference cascades down to something very different. Unless there is absolute clarity and consistency, it gets worse. We aren't perfect at it, but we spend time on it. Even when we have a difference of opinion, we do not express that to others. We just have to review it and alter as needed.

Preserving the Culture through Growth

Box top management believed they had attracted good people and kept them enthusiastic about working there.[9] Key factors included the encouragement to dream big, the important and significant work, the opportunities for everyone to contribute, the presence of smart and trustworthy colleagues, and inspiring and accessible leadership. Growth, however, presented a new set of challenges.

The addition of more offices, especially in international locations, as well as the sheer growth of numbers, created challenges. Jeff Queisser described the complexities.

International is challenging. Our approach to starting the London office was to send Greg Strickland as a cultural reference point. Another Brit is leading sales there, and they make a great team. It was intentional to inject the Box culture. Will we be able to keep it up? Will we have the right Boxer? People treat different size organizations differently. Something changes, but we don't know at exactly what size. When there are 400 to 500 in HQ, and people don't know some of the others, they react differently. Fortunately, it hasn't blown up yet.[10] *Even being on multiple floors in the same building is a big difference, and now we have multiple office sites. We haven't yet done much investment in video conferencing, so we are not up to par for supporting growth.*

One thing we do is train our managers on the Box hiring bar. New managers take six months of kicking and screaming because we say no to particular hires they want. Aaron or Dylan have to approve every single offer. Even with 850, we hold it to only those who are spot-on with personality as well as tech ability. But we believe that one of best ways to screw up the company is hire the wrong people. We will bear long-term pain to not screw it up. It takes great discipline in an international company. The four of us, and Dan and Evan, and some old-timers, feel deep ownership on this. The belief in a very high hiring bar is correlated with tenure at Box.

The Juggling Act

Although Levie was extremely wary of becoming bureaucratic and ossified to remain responsive to changes in the market, he did not want to ignore the need for discipline and operational excellence. He believed both were possible and necessary for survival.

To keep everybody on the same page, you almost want to write down a decision statement: "This is the way we are going to approach this part of the market; until it is changed, that's what we will do." We look at the business for every quarter, what we want to accomplish, what's the most important work. A fixed process creates stasis when you don't review it frequently enough. If you lock in for a year, you get stasis.

Levie told MBA students at Stanford, "The more you have both of those things running simultaneously, where you can have the scale of a large company and the operational excellence of a GE but the start-up decision-making speed and agility of a small nimble company, there's nothing that prevents you from scaling up to 100,000 employees. It's just that most companies haven't thought about it. The problem is you need both."[11]

We're always thinking of new things, products, verticals, and so on. Most of the organization argues and laments that we too frequently change. Our challenge is that we don't invest enough in what we really care about because we do a lot of different things. That's one of the secrets in a tech industry: you have to plant a number of seeds because a portion of what you plant won't work (statistically), so have many different things, and invest as they mature. Say you have three to five investment areas, if only 30% work, you have one or two that work. If you have fewer investment areas and 30% work, you could have nothing. You have to put feelers out to see what unfolds, and you can't say in advance. You want to be in position to change

[9] In 2010, Box was named *One of the Best Places to Work* by San Francisco and Silicon Valley business journals and *Inc.* magazine.

[10] Approximate employee numbers at year-end 2013: Los Altos (HQ):700, including all engineering and product teams; London (EMEA HQ): 80; San Francisco: 100 (sales only); Tokyo: 6.

[11] From the video "At Full Speed: How Box's Aaron Levie Became Entrepreneur of the Year," Trep Life in *Inc.*, December 2013/January 2014.

rapidly. In our business, say an iPad comes out, if you have apps ready in three months, you can do well, otherwise, not. You can't stop for efficiency, yet you do have to manage costs and processes.[12]

As part of trying to manage this tension over rapid change and efficiency, Levie addressed hiring world-class people for areas in which the company did not have expertise. He used the example of sales.

Sales needs people who are world-class at building customer relationships. That is new to me, so we have to hire amazing people like Sam Schillace, our technical leader, who came from Google docs and is world-class. You are always hiring people better than yourself. As the saying goes, you hope to build a team you are almost unqualified to be part of. You need to amass the best talent so stop at nothing to get them.[13] *Once here, we don't always agree, which can be confusing because with all smart people, no one knows who is right. You try to bring credible arguments to the fight. We get in great dialog with interesting disagreements; the onus is on both sides to get the other side to agree with them. Sometimes we have to declare "we are going this way" because you have to move forward. It happens more when you have more people because there is less time for consensus, but as long as you are hearing all sides, you can make a better call. The goal is not consensus, but better decisions. We try to have a collaborative culture. It would be hypocritical if our products are designed to help sharing, and we don't do it.*

Smith was concerned about assuring that everyone stayed informed about the direction and decisions of the company, especially when it was necessary to invest in things that were not "awesome new features" or that did not grow the company directly. "We have to keep reminding people why we are doing basic systems work, paint the big picture, 'we have to do it anyway, we need your support.' The message is that we are one team. We try to reduce the scope of what we have to do as much as possible, make it clear, provide a timeline. All that helps."

Preventing silos from developing required conscious thought and better communications, when the team sought to encourage initiative and innovation. A team member described how they were developing communication mechanisms.

All-hands lunches, road shows, and a weekly executive staff meeting with about 20 regular members, mostly for communication. Dan points out that it isn't a meeting where we do much decision making. But without it, relevant information wouldn't cascade down through the organization. We talk about what the process is today, what it will be. We didn't think about it well before, so now we have had to be more thoughtful, cascade everything more consciously.

Now we have a month-long process with very specific goals and metrics, all to get everyone pointing in the right direction. And we make sure to have regular postmortem time, to keep learning.

Levin emphasized the continuing attention to growing talent from within. They used constant development to introduce large company processes not usually discussed in software companies, such as Six Sigma, but using language that fit the company. He talked about culture explicitly. Levin and Levie traveled often to other sites carrying the message and getting to know people, as well as providing easy access to themselves as top executives. Levin acknowledged that as they grew, "You have to write things down, simplify, and repeat."[14]

As part of his commitment to develop young leaders, Levin formulated several lessons that he tried to impart. Two he believed most important were: "Life is a team sport," and "You don't get anything done alone." He commented, "Situational leadership is critical, adapting your language, dress, style, and so on, to the situation is really important. I wish I had realized that earlier at 25 or 30 instead of 35 or older, so that I could have had more years of practice. I'm still learning to do it better."[15]

Continuing with the challenges of growth, Sam Ghods, one of the original four friends and now VP of technology, talked about the tension between allowing a great deal of autonomy to engineers, which was possible when the firm was small, and the desire to enforce standards and accountability as the firm grew larger. It was a struggle to maintain the right atmosphere and to keep smart, independent engineers engaged but not going off in their own directions. He had to dismiss a VP of engineering who was liked but isolated and secluded. The VP had created his own fiefdom and did not value aligning with the rest of the organization.

This created tension because he saw his role as protecting engineers from managers, instead of fostering open disagreement by putting things on the table and working them through.

---

[12] For a technical take on the need for simplicity, speed, and efficiency in a world moving toward mobile and cloud becoming a single platform, and how Box is organized for that: "Inside Box: How The Red-Hot Enterprise Start-Up Thinks and Works," Simon Bisson, *CITEworld*, February 10, 2014, http://www.citeworld.com/cloud/22958/inside-box?page=2.

[13] For more on the importance of and attention paid to hiring, see Dan Levin comments at: https://babson.mediaspace.kaltura.com/media/Hiring+at+Box+%283+7%29+/0_s5juqmgn.

[14] To hear Levin discuss spreading the culture: https://babson.mediaspace.kaltura.com/media/Preserving+the+Culture+Through+Growth+%285+7%29/1_yk9ka6la.

[15] To hear Levin discuss these lessons: https://babson.mediaspace.kaltura.com/media/Dan+Levin%27s+Advice+to+Young+Managers+%287+7%29/1_8fwkrcgl.

Evan Wittenberg, responsible for people development, thought constantly about how to reinforce what they wanted the culture to be. Ideas included

- Using Friday all-hands lunches to reinforce notions of accountability, such as trusting people to spend company money as if it were their own rather than imposing elaborate expense rules.
- Personalizing responses to individuals when there was an issue, rather than making new policies. "For example, we had one person who emailed how he influenced each sale. I took him aside to tell him that's not necessary, it is always a team accomplishment."
- Running a *hackathon*. Unlike at many companies, start with all Boxers invited, not just end with them. "The non-engineers working here really were tickled to be invited."
- Every day seek teachable opportunities. For example, ask new executives to review practices after a month when their perceptions are fresh, but after they have listened and observed for a while. Wittenberg described another example. "There was going to be a *rules of the refrigerator* document sent out because sometimes leftovers smelled. It was punitive/bureaucratic in tone, not collaborative. I said it needed an explanation, something like 'the problem is natural from being busy, so we will clear everything out at five on Friday.' It takes a lot of reinforcement to keep the culture right."

Dealing with Aaron Levie

As some may have expected, a forceful co-founder like Aaron Levie had a large impact on the culture. He consistently made, and was celebrated for, smart strategic choices in an evolving and rapidly changing technological climate, which he tried to reinforce while not automatically winning every argument.

Dylan Smith, longtime friend and co-founder, had the closest perspective. Smith had roomed with Levie during the start-up phase when they lived in his parents' attic, then in Smith's uncle's garage.

Aaron fires people up with vision, potential, disruption in our space. With way-high demands and expectations, impossible things he aspires to, fanatical focus, and overall energy, he is inspirational and gets people excited in all settings. For nuts and bolts he is rough around the edges, but overall someone who is driving the company in innovative space where technology is evolving so rapidly.

We have remained best friends, can have very honest direct conversations without worrying. Our vision is the same, but our thought process is very different. Big picture versus what is the risk and how can we make it less. We both had to evolve how we spend our time. What we see as our strengths is consistent with eight years ago. It's mostly clear who would do what. We have heard horror stories from other companies and partnerships.

It's the little things that are the hardest to resolve. The website name was one. It was very expensive to get the name. He was absolutely right, but I saw it as not mattering, while he thought the brand was important because it was easy to say and to type. We are very aligned on resource allocation; but when we argue, it's around organization and leadership decisions. I see certain gaps; he says, "But they do this so well" and does not see their deficiencies. When it comes down to brass tacks, he's more conflict-avoidant, sees positives in people. I push to replace the person when he or she is not aligned. The person may not be cancerous, but maybe we are missing an opportunity.

We have a regular standing meeting. Aaron, Dan, and I meet weekly to talk about the issues, and we also meet ad hoc. Sometimes we step back and take a day, tackle the top four to five open issues, mostly people and structural. For example, international issues, pricing, what should the organization look like. We don't have the wider team in those, though we get input, but it is the three of us driving.

Jeff Queisser, another long-time friend, had his own take on Levie and the pressure Levie imposed on the organization through his aspirations, as well as his belief that the market was vast and they had to compete on almost every front. Despite Box being focused on business adaptation, Levie insisted that to achieve viral spread, they needed to have the best possible consumer experience, which meant that using the product had to be very simple. There were several enterprise competitors such as suite vendors, sophisticated customers who wanted sophisticated things like data loss-prevention. Even if Box were under-resourced for these things, Levie wanted to do everything, and it was hard to convince him otherwise.

He has cumulative advantage; it's a delicate balance. I and others can be furious at Aaron because of his lack of technical sense because it leads to his taking suboptimal positions. Yet we wouldn't be where we are without similar decisions! He's very sharp and quick, can be verbally dominant. His gut is often very good, he has great business and market sense. He's not an engineer, so doesn't understand anything about the investment needed to have reliable and scalable products. That has driven some mediocre qualities in products, which creates a negative feedback cycle because we have to keep fixing bugs. The central fight with Aaron is over resource prioritization. Early on, he wanted continuously to make announcements for PR. That was annoying but in retrospect important.

So here's a start-up meta-lesson: You have to make a lot of decisions that are annoying, but can't do one at the exclusion of others. You have to do some halfway, in order to have it live, which is critical. You'll have to shore it up with extra hours and fixes, but that's needed in the early stages. That's the worst thing for tech-trained people. He's like an elephant charging through the savannah. It takes five people with blowguns to slow him down.

We hired Sam Schillace, founder of what became Google docs, a very successful serial entrepreneur, who sold six or seven companies. He's also sharp and quick verbally. He constantly hits Aaron about priority ranking, and a line below which we won't get priorities done next quarter. He provides constant verbal argument and points out trade-offs. We are forcing trade-off rules on Aaron because we work in a larger environment. Chris Yeh, leading our platform product strategy, is taking a more data-driven approach to Aaron: "Here are graphs showing what we can't ignore. Which are we going to do? We can't do all at once, can't suboptimize." It takes those two, Dan, me, the other Sam, to dent him. We have learned it is important to draw him out since he doesn't always by default explain why he takes a position. If we draw him out, we all benefit because he probably has a good idea not fully communicated. He responds to all this pounding defiantly. He's great at impassioned yelling. He's quick, has good logic. But we might use sideline email conversations, then a day or two later he internalizes the arguments and progress is made.

Ghods elaborated:

Aaron is one of most stubborn people I have ever met. He has an unshakeable will to do what he thinks is right. Because of it, we are pushed to our heights and miss some opportunities. He is relentless, nothing better when he is working with you, but if he is against your position, going by rote, it is very hard to work with him. If Aaron has decided it's important, you can talk 'til you are blue in the face, he will keep poking holes. The problem is reinforcement; when he gets vindicated (because he is smart, he often is right) he gets reinforced. He thinks if he presents a product vision and they don't get it, it's their problem.

Levie's response was complex:

I can go faster because I know what will happen next, but often there are mitigating factors to spoil the pattern. That's why I want to see all the data. I do second-guess myself. But I try to keep others from being affected. I convey a higher degree of conviction than is in my head. You can't study the high-tech industry as I love to do and not see many really smart people get it wrong. Serendipity has mattered; what if it doesn't work, what is my contingency plan, what if it goes wrong. You don't have to second-guess if betting on the market future. I try not to forget about luck, serendipity, and all that made for successful decisions, without delusions. I try to separate the right answer from previous data points that helped.

I don't see anyone holding back with me. Most of my time is spent fighting with people here! The first three months of a new person, I can get my way. Then they see a culture where people can push back, so they don't passively go along. It can be frustrating, but we get better decisions and execution. Most would say I like to micromanage, which I do, but we've gotten too big and it isn't scalable. What I really care about is to implement a process to stay attached to the ground. It is mostly through others, finding great leaders and checkpoints, and people on their team. I spend more time on independent projects than on leaders and execs. That's how I stay relevant. Many wouldn't say I add a lot, but I have the context of time and breadth, and I help connect the dots faster. I get a picture of the entire organization and make sure we are winning.

The Future of Box and the Executive Team: Go Public or Sell to a Larger Company?

The company now had more than 1,000 employees with offices in London, Tokyo, and Texas, in addition to headquarters in the Bay Area. Levie and Smith were still having a great time and thought they were poised to create a much larger enterprise.

Levie commented about Smith. "Dylan is adamant that Box is right to remain fiercely independent. We are focused on running a very large independent company. The nature of our platform means it makes more sense as an independent company. Cloud is such a massive market and we are just a small part of that. To sell would give away that upside for growth."[16] As Levie put it, "This is our life's work, we're having a blast, fun every day. As long as it is that way, here it is. If someday it gets huge and we are not learning a lot all the time, then.... Not to sell ourselves short, but we have been lucky. We think we can outperform the massive numbers being thrown at us to buy us out. We risk losing what we have built if we sell out."[17] In March 2014, Box publicly filed for an initial public offering (IPO) with the SEC. Soon after, the broader

[16] "Interview: CFO Dylan Smith," by Richard Crump, *Financial Director*, November 25, 2013.

[17] For example, Box turned down a buyout offer of $600 million from Citrix in 2012.

technology sector became volatile, and valuations for cloud-based companies on public markets came down from the record high multiples observed in 2013 and early 2014. Since then, Box had remained on file with the SEC, updating its S-1 with new financial results from the first quarter of its 2015 fiscal year, which showed continued revenue growth and improving operating margins. Box announced a $150 million investment from private firms Coatue and TPG Growth.[18] (See Exhibit 7.2 for recent financials.) At the time of the announcement and continuing to early 2015, the company remained consistent

Exhibit 7.2 Financials from 2011 to 3rd Quarter 2014

	Year Ended December 31, 2011	One Month Ended January 31, 2012	Year Ended January 31, 2013	Year Ended January 31, 2014	Three Months Ended April 30,	
					2013	2014
	(in thousands, except per share data)				(unaudited)	
Consolidated Statements of Operations Data:						
Revenue	$ 21,084	$ 3,376	$ 58,797	$ 124,192	$ 23,414	$ 45,330
Cost of revenue(1)	6,873	850	14,280	25,974	4,561	9,228
Gross profit	14,211	2,526	44,517	98,218	18,853	36,102
Operating expenses:						
Research and development(1)	14,396	1,915	28,996	45,967	9,439	14,898
Sales and marketing(1)	36,189	4,246	99,221	171,188	33,936	47,440
General and administrative(1)	13,480	1,125	25,429	39,843	8,261	11,546
Total operating expenses	64,065	7,286	153,646	256,998	51,636	73,884
Loss from operations	(49,854)	(4,760)	(109,129)	(158,780)	(32,783)	(37,782)
Remeasurement of redeemable convertible preferred stock warrant liability	(356)	(371)	(1,727)	(8,477)	(693)	267
Internet income (expense), net	(109)	27	(1,764)	(3,705)	(548)	(405)
Other income (expense), net	49	(8)	116	(26)	(9)	7
Loss before provision (benefit) for income taxes	(50,270)	(5,112)	(112,504)	(170,988)	(34,033)	38,447
Provision (benefit) for income taxes	1	15	59	(2,431)	6	64
Net loss	(50,271)	(5,127)	(112,563)	(168,557)	(34,039)	(38,511)
Accretion of redeemable	80	(9)	(226)	(341)	(85)	(43)

Source: Graph provided by the company based on company's SEC filing.

[18] "Box Raises $150 Million in Cash and Reports 2014 Sales Growth as It Crawls Toward IPO," *Forbes Magazine*, July 7, 2014. http://www.forbes.com/sites/alexkonrad/2014/07/07/box-raises-150-million-in-cash-and-reports-2014-sales-growth-as-it-crawls-toward-ipo/.

about its plans to go public without setting an exact date: "Our plan continues to be to go public when it makes the most sense for Box and the market. As always, investing in our customers, technology, and future growth remains our top priority."

The company continued working hard to build its business. On January 23, 2015, the IPO took place at an offering price of $14 per share, with an immediate first day price increase of greater than 60%.

Discussion Questions

1. Will Aaron be the next Bill Gates or flame out before Box can become profitable and really large?
2. What is the culture of the company?
3. What accounts for its being so open and freewheeling?
4. How does the culture reflect the four founders, their history together, their ages, the culture of Silicon Valley, etc.?

8 The Business Planning Process

Photo Credit: © Reproduced with permission of Gravyty

The team from Gravyty, an artificial intelligence (AI)-enabled startup that helps nonprofit organizations build more successful relationships with their supporters. Co-founders, CEO Adam Martel and CTO Rich Palmer, are seated second and third from the left, respectively.

This chapter was written by Andrew Zacharakis.

The most important aspect of writing the business plan is not the plan itself, but all the learning that goes on as you identify your concept and then research the concept, the industry, the competitors, and most important, your customers. Today, angels, VCs, and other potential investors are unlikely to want to see a full 40+ page document. They are more likely to ask you for an executive summary, a pitch deck of 10-12 slides and some in-depth financials. However, you cannot accurately construct a pitch deck, summary, or financials without doing all of the full research and analysis that would have gone into a longer business plan that someone might have asked for 20 years ago. And you will need one down the road especially when you are looking for significant investment. As such, the written plan has its place (as an articulation of all the learning you have achieved), but even a technically well-written plan does not necessarily ensure a successful new venture. *Inc.* magazine finds that few, if any, of the fastest-growing companies in the country have a business model exactly the same as the one in their original written business plan: Of those that wrote a formal business plan, 65% admitted that the existing business was significantly different from their original concept.[1] But following a formal process can help ensure that you don't miss any important gaps in your planning process. As General Dwight D. Eisenhower famously stated, "In preparing for battle I have always found that plans are useless, but planning is indispensable."[2]

This chapter takes the view that the *process* undertaken in developing a tight, well-written story is the most important thing. Furthermore, our research indicates that students who write a business plan, even if it is for an entrepreneurship class, are far more likely to become entrepreneurs than students who haven't written a business plan.[3] Business planning isn't just writing; it's research, it's talking to others, it's iterative, it's a *learning* process.

The purpose of business planning is to tell a story, the story of your business. Thorough business planning can establish that there is an opportunity worth exploiting and should then describe the details of how this will be accomplished. Although many question whether a business plan is necessary, research by Jianwen Liao and Bill Gartner finds that those entrepreneurs who write a plan are 2.6 times more likely to successfully launch your business.[4]

There is a common misperception that business planning is primarily used for raising capital. Although a good business plan assists in raising capital, **the primary purpose of the process is to help entrepreneurs gain a deeper understanding of the opportunity they are envisioning.** Many would-be entrepreneurs doggedly pursue ideas that will never be profitable because they lack a deep understanding of the business model. The relatively little time spent business planning can save thousands or even millions of dollars that might be wasted in a wild goose chase. For example, for a person who makes \$100,000 per year, spending 200 hours on a business planning process equates to a \$10,000 investment in time spent (\$50 per hour times 200 hours). However, launching a flawed business concept can quickly accelerate into millions in spent capital. Most entrepreneurial ventures raise enough money to survive two years, even if the business will ultimately fail. Assuming the only expense is the time value of the lead entrepreneur, a two-year investment equates to \$200,000, not to mention the lost opportunity cost and the likelihood that other employees were hired and paid and that other expenses were incurred. So do yourself a favor and spend the time and money up front.

The business planning *process* helps entrepreneurs shape their original vision into a better opportunity by raising critical questions, researching answers for those questions, and then answering them. For example, one question that every entrepreneur needs to answer is, "What is the customer's pain?" Conversations with customers and other trusted advisors assist in better targeting the product offering to what customers need and want. This pre-startup work saves untold effort and money that an entrepreneur might spend trying to reshape the product after the business has been launched. Although all businesses adjust their offerings based on customer feedback, business planning helps the entrepreneur to anticipate some of these adjustments in advance of the initial launch.

Perhaps the greatest benefit of business planning is that it allows the entrepreneur to articulate the business opportunity to various stakeholders in the most effective manner. Business planning provides the background information that enables the entrepreneur to communicate the upside potential to investors. Second, it provides the validation needed to convince potential employees to leave their current jobs for the uncertain future of a new venture. Finally, it can also help secure a strategic partner, key customer, or supplier. In short, business planning provides the entrepreneur with the deep understanding she needs to answer the critical questions that various stakeholders will ask. Completing a well-founded business plan gives the entrepreneur credibility in the eyes of various stakeholders.

Think of the business plan as a compilation of learning (both literally and figuratively). Start by making files on your computer devoted to different categories, and then start collecting information in each section. Write a synopsis for each of these sections that includes your interpretation of what the information means and how it implies that you should shape and reshape your concept. You can compile all this information however works best for you, but whatever method you choose to catalog it, the point is the same—you need a mechanism to start organizing your learning.

> *The key to understanding your business opportunity is to get out there and talk to people...people who sell, distribute, make and use similar products— most importantly, the customer. Writing a business plan without this groundwork leads to assumptions that may not hold water. There's not much room for error in your key assumptions and this field research helps validate those assumptions.*
>
> *Jim Poss, Founder and CEO*
> *BigBelly Solar* www.bigbellysolar.com

> *I think business planning is important in establishing an initial strategy and long term vision, however, a business plan is obsolete right after it is written and entrepreneurs have to evolve in real time. The greatest value of a business plan is the process of researching and articulating your idea/vision and the discipline that comes with this process.*
>
> *Gautam Gupta, Founder and CEO*
> *NatureBox* NatureBox.com

> *The business plan is relatively unimportant because the only thing you know for sure is that it WON'T be accurate with what actually happens. The planning, however, is hugely important. It helps identify the key assumptions that drive your business model, and the subsequent chain of assumptions you have built on top of the original assumptions. The more comprehensive the planning process, the better your ability to recognize and re-strategize the business going forward.*
>
> *Dan Hermann, Founder and CEO*
> *Lazy Bones* Mylazybones.com

> *A business plan is the persuasive yet concise story about where the company came from, what it has done, where it's going and how and with what resources it will get there. Basically the ever evolving story of the business. The reality is when you start a business all you are really doing is perpetually crafting a better and better story. The more research, the more concise, the more progress, the more customers, the better the story/business gets.*
>
> *Shane Eten, Founder and CEO*
> *BluCarbon* BluCarbon.com

The Planning Process

Business planning literally begins when you start thinking about your new venture. In Chapter 3, we highlighted the opportunity recognition process. That is the genesis of planning. It progresses from there when you start sharing your thoughts with potential cofounders over a cup of coffee or lunch. It moves on from that point when you share the idea with your significant other, friends, family, colleagues, and professors, among others. At each interaction, you are learning about aspects of your business opportunity. Do your friends think they would buy this product or service (potential customers)? Have they said things along the lines of "This is just like XYZ Company…" (potential competitor)? Have they informed you of potential suppliers or other people you might want to hire or at least talk to or learn from? All these bits and pieces of information are valuable learning that you should document and catalog.

Once you acquire a critical mass of learning, it's time to start organizing your information in a meaningful way. First, write a short summary (less than five pages) of your current vision. This provides a road map for you and others to follow as you embark on a more thorough planning process. Share this document with cofounders, family members, and trusted advisors. Ask for feedback on what else you should be thinking about. What gaps do the people who read this summary see? What questions do they ask, and how can you gain the learning necessary to answer those questions in a convincing and accurate manner? This feedback will provide a platform for you to attack each of the major areas important to launching and running a new venture.

I.	Cover
II.	Executive Summary
III.	Table of Contents
IV.	Industry, Customer, and Competitor Analysis
V.	Company and Product Description
VI.	Marketing Plan
VII.	Operations Plan
VIII.	Development Plan
IX.	Team
X.	Critical Risks
XI.	Offering
XII.	Financial Plan
XIII.	Appendices

FIGURE 8.1 Business Plan Outline.

Your planning process will focus on critical aspects of your business model; not coincidentally, these critical aspects map well to the typical format of a business plan (see Figure 8.1). Now that you have some feedback from your trusted advisors, you can begin attacking major sections of the plan. It really doesn't matter where you start, although it is often easiest to write the product/service description first. This is usually the most concrete component of the entrepreneur's vision. Wherever you begin, don't let the order of sections outlined in Figure 8.1 constrain you. If you want to start somewhere else besides product description, do so. As you work through the plan, you'll inevitably find that this is an iterative process. Every section of the plan interacts with the other sections, and as a result, you'll often be working on multiple sections simultaneously. Most important, keep in mind that this is *your* business planning process; this is your learning. You should follow whatever method feels most comfortable and effective.

Wisdom is realizing that the business plan is a "living document." Although your first draft will be polished, most business plans are obsolete the day they come off the presses. That means that entrepreneurs are continuously updating and revising their business plan—they recognize it is a learning process, not a finished product. You'll continue learning new things that can improve your business as long as you're involved with the business, and the day you stop learning how to improve it is the day that it will start its decline toward bankruptcy. So keep and file each major revision of your plan, and occasionally look back at earlier versions for the lessons you've learned. Remember, the importance of the business plan for you isn't the final product but the learning that you gain from writing the novel of your vision. The plan articulates your vision for the company, and it crystallizes that vision for you and your team. It also provides a history—a photo album, if you will—of the birth, growth, and maturity of your business. Although daunting, business planning can be exciting and creative, especially if you are working on it with your founding team. So now let us dig in and examine how to effectively conduct the business planning process.

The Story Model

One of the major goals of business planning is to attract various stakeholders and convince them of the potential of your business. Therefore, you need to keep in mind how these stakeholders will interpret your plan. The guiding principle is that you are writing a story, and all good stories have

Nike	*Just do it!*
McDonald's	*I'm lovin' it*
Facebook	*Facebook helps you connect and share with the people in your life*
Airbnb	*Belong Anywhere*
Amazon	*Earth's most customer centric company*
Uber	*Everyone's private driver*
TripAdvisor	*Know better. Book better. Go better.*
Spotify	*Music for everyone*
Go Pro	*Be a hero*
Dream Water	*Work Hard. Play Hard. Sleep Easy.*
Netflix	*See what's next.*

FIGURE 8.2 Taglines.

a theme—a unifying thread that ties the setting, characters, and plot together. If you think about the most successful businesses, they all have well-publicized themes. When you hear their taglines, you instantly gain insight into the businesses. For example, when you hear "the ultimate driving machine," most people think of BMW and driving high-performance cars. On top of that, they think of German engineering, which is the quality BMW wants to embody in the minds of its customers. Similarly, "Just do it" is intricately linked to Nike and the image of athletic excellence (see Figure 8.2).

A tagline is a sentence, or even a fragment of a sentence, that summarizes the essence of your business. It's the theme that every sentence, paragraph, page, and diagram in your business plan should adhere to—the unifying idea of your story. One useful tip is to put your tagline in a footer that runs on the bottom of every page. As you are writing, if the section doesn't build on, explain, or otherwise directly relate to the tagline, it most likely isn't a necessary component to the business plan. Rigorous adherence to the tagline facilitates writing a concise and coherent business plan. You might also want to put your tagline on your website, Twitter feed, business card, company letterhead, and other collateral material you develop for the business. It's a reminder to you and your team about what you are trying to accomplish as well as an effective marketing tactic that helps build your brand.

Now let's take another look at the major sections of the plan (refer back to Figure 8.1). Remember that, although there are variations, most planning processes will include these components. It is important to keep your plan as close to this format as possible because many stakeholders are accustomed to this format, and it facilitates spot reading. If you are seeking venture capital, for instance, you want to make quick reading possible because venture capitalists often spend as little as five minutes on a plan before rejecting it or putting it aside for further attention. If a venture capitalist becomes frustrated with an unfamiliar format, it is more likely that she will reject it rather than trying to pull out the pertinent information. Even if you aren't seeking venture capital, the common structure is easy for other investors and stakeholders to follow and understand. Furthermore, the highlighted business plan sections in Figure 8.1 provide a road map for questions that you need to consider as you prepare to launch your business.

The Business Plan

Although it's the business planning *process* that's important, it is easier to discuss that process by laying out what the final output, the business plan, might look like. We will progress through the sections in the order that they typically appear, but keep in mind that you can work on the sections in any order that you wish. Business planning is an iterative process.

The Cover

The cover of the plan should include the following information: company name, tagline, contact person, address, phone, email, date, disclaimer, and copy number. Most of the information is self-explanatory, but a few things should be pointed out. First, the contact person for a new venture should be the president or some other founding team member. Imagine the frustration of an excited potential investor who can't find out how to contact the entrepreneur to gain more information. More often than not, that plan will end up in the reject pile.

Second, business plans should have a disclaimer along these lines:

This business plan has been submitted on a confidential basis solely to selected, highly qualified investors. The recipient should not reproduce this plan or distribute it to others without permission.

Controlling distribution was, until recently, particularly important when seeking investment, especially if you did not want to violate Regulation D of the Securities and Exchange Commission, which specifies that you may solicit only qualified investors (high-net worth or high-income individuals). In April 2012, President Obama signed into law the Jumpstart Our Business Startups (JOBS) Act, intended to encourage funding of U.S. small businesses by easing various securities regulations. The JOBS Act directs the SEC to lift the ban on general solicitation and advertising of private placements in securities (i.e., investing in startups). This was previously prohibited to avoid the requirement to register with the SEC (i.e., go public). As of September 23, 2013, you are allowed to raise money by advertising the opportunity to the public,[5] and as of March 25, 2015, non-accredited investors may invest but still under certain limitations established to protect them from financial uncertainties.[6]

The cover should also have a line stating which number copy it is. For example, you will often see on the bottom right portion of the cover a line that says "Copy 1 of 5 copies." Entrepreneurs should keep a log of who has copies so that they can control for unexpected distribution. Finally, the cover should be eye-catching. If you have a product or prototype, a picture of it can draw the reader in. Likewise, a catchy tagline draws attention and encourages the reader to look further.

Executive Summary

This section is the most important part of the business plan. If you don't capture readers' attention in the executive summary, it is unlikely that they will read any other parts of the plan. This is just like a book's jacket notes. Most likely, the reader will buy the book only if she is impressed with the notes inside the cover. In the same way, you want to hit your readers with the most compelling aspects of your business opportunity right up front. Hook the reader. That means having the first sentence or paragraph highlight the potential of the opportunity. For example:

The current market for widgets is $50 million, growing at an annual rate of 20%. Moreover, the emergence of mobile applications is likely to accelerate this market's growth. Company XYZ is positioned to capture this wave with its proprietary technology: the secret formula VOOM.

This creates the right tone. The first sentence emphasizes that the potential opportunity is huge; the last sentence explains that Company XYZ has a competitive advantage that enables it to become a big player in this market. Too many plans start with "Company XYZ, incorporated in the state of Delaware, will develop and sell widgets." Ho-hum. This kind of opening is dull and uninspiring—at this point, who cares that the business is incorporated in Delaware (aren't they all?). Capture the reader's attention immediately or risk losing her altogether.

Once you have hooked the reader, you need to provide compelling information about each of the following subsections:

- Description of Opportunity
- Business Concept
- Industry Overview
- Target Market
- Competitive Advantage

- Business Model and Economics
- Team and Offering
- Financial Snapshot

Remember that you'll cover all these components in detail in the body of the plan. As such, we will explore them in greater detail as we progress through the sections. Given that, your goal in the executive summary is to touch on the most important or exciting points of each section. Keep it brief, and make it compelling.

Because the executive summary is the most important part of the finished plan, write it *after* you have gained a deep understanding of the business by working through all the other sections. Don't confuse the executive summary included in the plan with the short summary that we suggested you write as the very first step of the business plan process. As a result of your research, the two are likely to be significantly different. Don't recycle your initial summary. Rewrite it entirely based on the hard work you have done by going through the business planning process.

Table of Contents

Continuing the theme of making the document easy to read, a detailed table of contents is critical. It should include major sections, subsections, exhibits, and appendices. The table of contents provides the reader a road map to your plan (see Figure 8.3). Note that the table of contents is customized to the specific business, so it doesn't perfectly match the business plan outline presented earlier in Figure 8.1. Nonetheless, a look at Figure 8.3 shows that the company's business plan includes most of the elements highlighted in the business plan outline and that the order of information is basically the same as well.

FIGURE 8.3 **A Sample Table of Contents.**

Industry, Customer, and Competitor Analysis

Industry

The goal of this section is to illustrate the opportunity and how you intend to capture it. However, before you can develop your plot and illustrate a theme, you need to provide a setting or context for your story. Refer back to Chapters 2 and 3, where we described characteristics that create an attractive opportunity. In your plan, you'll need to delineate both the current market size and how much you expect it to grow in the future. In addition, you need to indicate what kind of market you're facing. History tells us that often the best opportunities are found in emerging markets—those that appear poised for rapid growth and that have the potential to change the way we live and work. For example, in the 1980s, the personal computer, disk drive, and computer hardware markets revolutionized our way of life. Many new companies were born and rode the wave of the emerging technology, including Apple, Microsoft, and Intel. In the 1990s, it was anything dealing with the Internet. eBay, Google, and Facebook have leveraged the Internet and changed the way we live. Mobility is the word today. Companies like Uber, Lyft, and Airbnb have introduced the sharing economy.

The mobile industry is fundamentally changing how consumers spend money, from the homes we buy and the doctors we visit to how we select entertainment and modes of travel, from what we eat and drink to how we communicate and get to work each day. Mobile does not simply change our purchasing behavior but also the purchasing options themselves. Five major platforms dominate—Apple, Google, Amazon, Microsoft, and Facebook, although it is Apple and Google that have the real power because they have built ecosystems around their platforms. Now that sharing information is just a thumb swipe away, customers are openly sharing more than ever before. Mobile is closing the divide for brands and advertisers between their advertisement and its impact on a subsequent purchase. The long-term race is to control the platform over which this information sharing occurs. Having this knowledge is quite simply the most valuable currency in today's commerce. In 2018, mobile technologies and services delivered $3.9 trillion, 4.6% of the world's GDP.[7] With 5G on the way and the Internet of Things (IoT) becoming a reality, these numbers are expected to climb higher in the coming years.

The sharing economy has created innovative new ways of consuming, by optimizing the use of services or products, connecting entire communities, and enhancing collaborative consumption. The LiquidSpace app links companies with extra office space and companies in the need of temporary space. Zilok.com facilitates the rent of an Xbox or a ladder through a peer-to-peer digital platform, and Airbnb allows you to lease your apartment to unknown people while you are on vacation. Price Waterhouse Cooper estimates that by 2025 the five main sectors of the industry will have revenues of around $335 billion.[8] Another market structure that tends to hold promise is a fragmented market where small, dispersed competitors compete on a regional basis. Many of the big names in retail revolutionized fragmented markets. For instance, category killers such as Walmart, Staples, and Home Depot consolidated fragmented markets by providing quality products at lower prices. These firms replaced the dispersed regional and local discount, office supply, and hardware stores.

Another key attribute to explore is industry economics. For example, do companies within the industry enjoy strong gross and net income margins? Higher margins allow for higher returns, which again leads to greater growth potential. This typically happens when the market is emerging and demand exceeds supply. So, again, you'll want to explore where the margins are today—and also where you expect them to go in the future.

You'll note that we keep referring to the future. A good market analysis will look at trends that are shaping the future. For instance, as the world continues to adopt wireless communication, more and more people are connected 24/7. What might this mean for your business? Another trend that has had tremendous ramifications on U.S. society is the life cycle of the baby boom generation. Over the last 50 years, business has responded to this generation's needs and wants. In the 1950s and 1960s, that meant building schools. In the 1970s and 1980s, it meant building houses and introducing family cars like the minivan. In the 1990s, it led to Internet concepts, as this group was more affluent and computer savvy than any generation before it. Today the baby boomers are in or approaching retirement. What opportunities does this trend portend? Identify the trends, both positive and negative, that will interact with your business.

You need to describe your overall market in terms of revenues, growth, and future trends that are pertinent. In this section, avoid discussing your concept, the proposed product or service you will offer. Instead, use dispassionate, arm's-length analysis of the market with the goal of highlighting a space or gap that is underserved. Thus, focus on how the market is segmented now and how it will be segmented into the future. After identifying the relevant market segments, identify the segment your product will target. Again, what are the important trends that will shape this segment in the future?

Customer

Once you've defined the market space you plan to enter, you'll examine the target customer in detail. As we discussed in Chapters 5 and 6, an accurate customer profile is essential to developing a product that customers truly want and marketing campaigns that they will actually respond to.

Define who the customer is by using demographic and psychographic information. The better the entrepreneur can define her specific customers, the more apt she is to deliver a product that these customers truly want. Although you may argue that everyone who is hungry is a restaurant's customer, such a vague definition makes it hard to market to the core customer. For instance, because I'm a middle-aged man, my eating habits will be different from what they were when I was 20-something. I will frequent different types of establishments and expect certain kinds of foods within a certain price range. I'm beyond fast food, for example. Thus, you'd have very different strategies to serve and reach me than you would to reach younger people. Unless you develop this deep understanding of your customer, your business is unlikely to succeed.

To help, companies often develop profiles of the different kinds of customers they target. For example, Apple has profiled its primary customer segments, which serve as an aid to help employees better understand their customers' needs. Their target customers come from households earning more than $60,000 annually, they have completed 4+ years of college study, one-third are between 18 and 34 years old, and one in five customers are self-employed. Having a clear understanding of your customer helps you design products and services that add value to your customer. For example, Apple's Handoff features, which allow an interaction between Apple devices such as starting to write an email on your iPhone and continue writing it on your laptop, strengthen the advantage of owning multiple Apple devices: 38 % of connected adults in the United States have at least one Apple device (i.e., a Mac, iPad, or iPhone), 14% have two devices, and 3% have three devices. This means that 17% of connected adults, or more importantly, 37% of Apple users, can take advantage of the Handoff feature between their devices, hence contributing to customer satisfaction, and brand loyalty.[9]

A venture capitalist recently said that the most impressive entrepreneur is the one who comes into his office and not only identifies who the customer is in terms of demographics and psychographics, but also identifies that customer by address, phone number, and email. You can even go one step further by including letters of interest or intent from key customers who express a willingness to buy, once your product or service is ready. When you understand who your customers are, you can assess what compels them to buy, how your company can sell to them (direct sales, retail, Internet), and how much it is going to cost to acquire and retain them as customers.

An exhibit describing customers in terms of the basic parameters and inserted into the text of your plan can be very powerful because it communicates a lot of data quickly.

Too often entrepreneurs figure that, if they love their product concept, so should everybody else. Although your needs and wants are the best place to start, you must recognize that they may not be the same as everyone else's. So to truly understand your customers, you need to talk to them. Early in your conceptualization of your product or service, go out and interview potential customers (the appendix at the end of Chapter 6 provides some questions that might be useful). Keep your questions open ended, and try not to direct the customer's answers. It is critical to *listen* at this stage rather than talking about your concept. After each customer interaction, go back and reevaluate your concept. Can you cost-effectively incorporate features that will make this product better fit the customer's need? After several individual conversations, run a focus group and then maybe a broader customer survey. At each step along the way, refine your concept and start to define the demographic and psychographic characteristics of your primary target audience. This process helps you create a better product that is more likely to gain customer acceptance than if you boldly (and blindly) charge ahead with your initial concept. As you get closer to launching, you'll likely have a beta customer use your product or service to further refine the concept. The key once again is that business planning is the *process*, not the output (written plan).

Competition

The competition analysis proceeds directly from the customer analysis, and you should complete it using a competitive profile matrix. You have already identified your market segment, profiled your customer, and described what he wants. Armed with this information, you can begin

	My Concept	Big-Box Stores	Amazon	History Channel Website	Museum Stores	Specialty Websites
History book selection	2	3	1	3	4	3
Display of artifacts	1	5	5	5	3	5
History-related gift items	1	5	4	2	1	2
Videos/DVDs	1	4	3	3	5	2
Price	3	2	1	2	3	3
Atmosphere	1	2	5	5	4	5
Employee knowledge	1	4	5	5	2	5
Ease of shopping for specific items	2	2	1	1	3	4
Location	4	1	1	1	5	3
Ease of browsing	1	2	3	3	2	4

FIGURE 8.4 **Competitive Profile Matrix.**

to research how your direct and indirect competitors are meeting those needs. The basis of comparison will be the different product features and attributes that each competitor uses to differentiate itself from the pack. A competitive profile matrix not only creates a powerful visual catch-point but also conveys information about your competitive advantage and is the basis for your company's strategy (see Figure 8.4).

The competitive profile matrix should be at the beginning of the section, followed by text describing the analysis and its implications. Figure 8.4 shows a sample competitive profile matrix for a new retail concept—a specialty store targeting the history enthusiast. Given the dominance of Amazon, you might think it's odd, quaint, or out-of-date to look at an opportunity for a bookstore or retail shop with a heavy emphasis on books. However, brick-and-mortar bookstores and niche bookstore like this example are on the rise as we move into third decade of the 21st century! The American Booksellers Association reports record growth in the opening of bookstores and retail shops with a heavy emphasis on books.[10] Their resurgence is just another example of Schumpeter's gales of creation destruction we explored in Chapter 1. Large bookstore chains such as Barnes & Noble and Border's put scores of independent bookstore out of business in the 1990s and early 2000s, but they got their comeuppance when Amazon put Border's out of business and crippled Barnes & Noble as we moved into the 2020s. Now as folks look to unplug and reconnect in physical spaces with real books they can touch and feel, opportunities abound for nascent booksellers again.

So, let's look again at the matrix in Figure 8.4. The entrepreneur rates each competitor (or competitor type) on various key success factors using a five-point scale (with 1 being strong on the attribute and 5 being weak). Often entrepreneurs include product attributes such as the product color, dimensions, specifications, but you should omit this unless you believe they are the main criteria customers will use to decide to buy your product over those of competitors. Instead, focus on the key success factors that often lead a customer to buy one product over another, such as price, quality, and/or speed. It is also a good idea to list your own concept in the matrix. Up until this point, your plan has been painting a picture of the industry and market. By including your concept in the matrix, you begin to shift the focus toward your company and the opportunity you believe it can capture. In Figure 8.4, we can see that the entrepreneur expects to do well on most attributes, except for price and location. In describing the matrix, the entrepreneur would explain why the business is weak on those attributes and why it is better on the rest. Understanding the strengths and weaknesses of the business concept helps the entrepreneur to define the company's strategy.

Gale Directory Library – Info Trac—Search for trade associations, consultants/ consulting firms, U.S. wholesalers and distributors, research centers, and an encyclopedia of American religions.

Factiva—Search the world's leading business and news publications, including *WSJ* & *Barron's.*

LexisNexis—Find brief information on thousands of U.S. and international companies.

Bloomberg—Integrates data, news, analytics, multimedia reports, email, and trading capabilities into a single platform.

Business Monitor International—Country risk, industry reports, and company coverage in global markets. Includes news, reports, and data.

Business Insights: Essentials—Easily find information on companies, industries, and more in the context of timely news, statistical data, and in-depth reports.

Capital IQ—Use this for complex financial statement and comparable analysis, financial modeling, sector analysis, and charting for companies worldwide.

Mergent Online—Find company financials, competitor, customer, and supplier information, recent analyst reports, and more on U.S. and global companies. Also includes industry reports and country snapshots.

Plunkett Research—Find analysis, research, statistics, and trade associations for major industries including top companies.

Thompson ONE—Company analyst reports, filings, estimates, M&A, new issue, IPO data.

FIGURE 8.5 Sample Sources for Information on Public/Private Companies.

Finding information about your competition can be easy if the company is public, harder if it is private, and very difficult if it is operating in "stealth" mode (it hasn't yet announced itself to the world). Most libraries have access to databases that contain a wealth of information about publicly traded companies (see Figure 8.5 for some sample sources), but privately held companies or "stealth ventures" represent a greater challenge.

The best way for savvy entrepreneurs to gather competitive information is through their network and trade shows. Who should be in the entrepreneur's network? First and foremost are the customers the entrepreneur hopes to sell to in the near future. Just as you are (or should be) talking to your potential customers, your existing competition is interacting with this group every day, and as a result, your customers are the best source of information about the "stealth" competition on the horizon. Although many entrepreneurs are fearful (verging on the brink of paranoia) that valuable information will fall into the wrong hands and lead to new competition that invalidates the current venture, the reality is that entrepreneurs who openly talk about their ideas with as many people as possible are far more likely to succeed. Take the risk. Talking allows entrepreneurs to get the kind of valuable feedback that can make the difference between success and failure in a venture.

Company and Product Description

The dispassionate analysis described in the previous section lays the foundation for describing your company and concept. In this section, you'll introduce the basic details of your company before moving on to a more detailed analysis of your marketing and operations plans.

You can begin by identifying the company name and where the business is incorporated. After that, you should provide a brief overview of the concept for the company and then highlight what the company has achieved to date. If you have reached any major milestones, be sure to list them, but don't worry if the business plan is your first step. Subsequent drafts will provide you with opportunities to showcase what you have achieved.

Once you have provided an introduction, take some time to communicate the product and its differentiating features. You can do this in writing, but keep in mind that graphic representations are visually powerful. See the graphics in the Gravyty executive summary and throughout the pitch deck at the end of this chapter. Some of their graphics easily show the reader important aspects of their technology, market, industry, and more. How can you highlight how your product fits into the customer value proposition? What is incorporated into your product, and what value-add do you deliver to the customer? Which of the customer's unmet wants and needs are fulfilled by your offering? In essence, you need to tell us why your product is better, cheaper, or faster and how that creates value for the customer. Your advantage may be a function of proprietary technology, patents, distribution, and/or design. In fact, the most powerful competitive advantages are derived from a bundle of factors because this makes them more difficult to copy.

Entrepreneurs also need to identify their market entry and growth strategies. Because most new ventures are resource constrained, especially for available capital, it is crucial that the lead entrepreneur establish the most effective way to enter the market. We discussed in Chapters 3 and 6 how to identify your core customer or primary target audience (PTA) based on an analysis of the market and customer sections. Focusing on a particular niche or subset of the overall market allows new ventures to effectively utilize scarce resources to reach those customers and prove the viability of their concept.

The business plan should also sell the entrepreneur's vision for the company's long-term growth potential. If the venture achieves success in its entry strategy, either it will generate internal cash flow that can be used to fuel continued growth, or it will be attractive enough to get further equity financing at improved valuations. The growth strategy should talk about the secondary and tertiary target audiences that the firm will pursue once it meets success with the core customer. For instance, technology companies might go from selling to users who want the best performance (early adopters) to users who want ease of use (mainstream market). Whatever the case, you should devote at least a paragraph or two to the firm's long-term growth strategy.

Marketing Plan

Up to this point, you've described your company's potential to successfully enter and grow in a marketplace. Now you need to devise the strategy that will allow it to reach its potential. The primary components of this section are descriptions of the target market strategy, product/service strategy, pricing strategy, distribution strategy, marketing communications strategy, sales strategy, and sales and marketing forecasts. Let's take a look at each of these subsections in turn.

Target Market Strategy

Every marketing plan needs some guiding principles. In targeting and positioning your product, you should lean heavily on the knowledge you gleaned from the customer analysis. For instance, product strategies often fall along a continuum whose endpoints are rational purchase and emotional purchase. For example, when a person buys a new car, the rational purchase might be a low-cost reliable option such as the Ford Focus. In contrast, some people see a car as an extension of their personality—and therefore might buy a BMW or an Audi because of the emotional benefits it delivers. Within every product space, there is room for products measured at different points along this continuum. You can also use this idea of a continuum to find other dimensions that help you classify your marketplace. These tools help entrepreneurs decide where their product fits or where they would like to position it, and once you have solidified your target market strategy, you can begin working on the other aspects of the marketing plan.

Product/Service Strategy

Building from the target market strategy, this section of the plan describes how you will differentiate your product from the competition. Discuss why the customer will switch to your product and how you will retain customers so that they don't switch to your competition in the future. You can create a powerful visual by using the attributes defined in your customer profile matrix to produce

FIGURE 8.6 Product Attribute Map.

a product attribute map. This tool is a great way to illustrate how your firm compares to the competition. In creating it, you should focus on the two most important attributes, putting one on the x-axis and the other on the y-axis. The map should show that you are clearly distinguishable from your competition on desirable attributes.

Figure 8.6 shows the competitive map for the retail concept that focuses on the history enthusiast. The two attributes on which it evaluates competitors are atmosphere (Is this a place where people will linger?) and focus (Does it have a broad topic focus, or is it specialized?). As you can see from Figure 8.6, our retail concept plans to have a high level of history specialization and atmosphere, which places it in the upper-right quadrant. From the product attribute map, it is easy to see how our retail concept will distinguish itself from the competition. The map implies that history specialization and atmosphere will attract history buffs and entice them to return time and again.

This section should also address what services you will provide the customer. What type of technical support will you provide? Will you offer warranties? What kind of product upgrades will be available and when? It is important to detail all these efforts because they will affect the pricing of the product. Many times entrepreneurs underestimate the costs of these services, which leads to a drain on cash and ultimately to bankruptcy.

Pricing Strategy

Pricing your product is challenging. Canvassing prevailing prices in the marketplace helps you determine what the perceived value for your product might be. If your product is of better quality and has lots of features, price it above market rates. We saw in Chapter 6 that a price-skimming strategy is best in the beginning, to gain a sense of what customers are willing to pay—that means pricing a bit higher than you believe the perceived value to be. It is always easier to reduce prices later than to raise them. Most important, if during the course of researching possible prices you find that you can't price your product well above what it will cost you to produce it, the business planning process will have saved you untold time and pain. You have two choices: redesign your concept or abandon it.

Remember to avoid "cost plus" pricing (also discussed in Chapter 6). First, it is difficult to accurately determine your actual cost, especially if this is a new venture with a limited history. New ventures consistently underestimate the true cost of developing their products. For example, how much did it really cost to write that software? The cost includes salaries and payroll taxes, computers and other assets, the overhead contribution, and more. Because most entrepreneurs underestimate these costs, they underprice their products. Second, we often hear entrepreneurs claim that they are offering a low price to penetrate and gain market share rapidly. One major problem with launching at a low price is that it may be difficult to raise the price later; it can send a signal of lower quality. In addition, demand at that price may overwhelm your ability to produce the product in sufficient volume, and it may unnecessarily strain cash flow.

Distribution Strategy

This section of your written plan identifies how your product will reach the customer. Because much of the cost of delivering a product is tied up in its distribution, your distribution strategy can define your company's fortune as much as or more than the product itself. Distribution strategy is thus more than an operational detail; it can be the basis of your company's competitive advantage. For example, Uber's former CEO Travis Kalanick once told CNN Money, "We're in the business of delivering cars in five minutes. And once you can deliver cars in five minutes, there's a lot of things you can deliver in five minutes."[11] Uber's whole business is based around controlling its partner drivers so that it can provide cars quickly. Uber has mastered its distribution strategy at least when it comes to delivering drivers, but more importantly, it has created a precedent for other companies. Apps like Shipster and Shyp will send a courier to wherever you are and deliver packages for you, and through Postmates App, you may order stuff like envelopes or an extension cord to be delivered to you within an hour.[12]

It's wise to examine how the customer currently acquires the product. If you're developing a new brand of dog food and your primary target customer buys dog food at Walmart, then you will probably need to include traditional retail outlets in your distribution plans. This is not to say that entrepreneurs are limited to a single-channel distribution strategy, just that to achieve maximum growth will probably require the use of common distribution techniques. Although it may be appealing to take retail outlets out of this chain, reeducating customers about a new buying process can be prohibitively expensive and challenging.

Once you determine the best distribution channel, the next question is whether you can access it. The Walmart example is a good one. A new startup in dog food may have difficulty getting shelf space at Walmart. A better entry strategy might focus on boutique pet stores to build brand recognition. Once your product is well known and in high demand, retail stores like Walmart will be much more likely to carry your brand. The key here is to identify appropriate channels and then assess how costly it is to access them.

Marketing Communications Strategy

Communicating effectively to your customer requires advertising and promotion, among other methods. Because these tools are expensive, resource-constrained entrepreneurs need to carefully select the appropriate strategies. What avenues most effectively reach your core customer? Your options include mass advertising, target advertising (e.g., Google Adwords), and public relations. Although mass advertising is often the most expensive approach, it is also one of the most effective tools for building a brand. In contrast, if you can identify your core customer by name, then direct mail may be more effective than mass media blitzes. Similarly, grassroots techniques such as public relations efforts geared toward mainstream media can be more cost-effective.

Bo Fishback, Eric Koester, and Ian Hunter are serial entrepreneurs and the cofounders of Zaarly, a private company focused on developing a proximity-based, real-time, buyer-powered market platform. They knew that their marketing strategy needed to generate demand before their app was released. They employed a multifaceted approach to accomplish this through social media posts, open/closed social media groups, online blogging, and features in media such as the *Huffington Post* to establish thought-leadership. They then were interviewed on FOX Business, Bloomberg, and *Inc.* magazine, which led to numerous other online articles in well-known media. Marketing in this way, they attracted enough attention that Meg Whitman became a board member, and they raised $14.1 million in funding. Launching in 2011, Zaarly's marketing campaign ensured they had customers on day 1, and after only 3.5 months, they had over 100,000 subscribers.

In contrast, The GAP launched the "Dress Normal" campaign to "promote a more coherent brand globally" and regain market share. The campaign ran through different advertising channels and presented celebrities "dressing normally." The idea of the campaign was that clothes that a person wears aren't important, but what they do defines who they are. This campaign failed to stem declining sales. Instead of previous campaigns that were aspirational (i.e., the clothes make the man or woman), the campaign ended up driving away customers, and sales fell significantly during the following months.[13] Your communications strategy can enhance or diminish the perception of your company. Plan carefully.

Promotional Tools	Budget over 1 Year
Print advertising	$ 5,000
Direct mail	3,000
In-store promotions	2,000
Tour group outreach	1,000
Public relations	1,000
Total	$ 12,000

FIGURE 8.7a Advertising Schedule.

Publication	Circulation	Ad Price for Quarter Page	Total Budget for Year 1
Lexington Minuteman newspaper	7,886	$500	$4,000
Boston magazine	1,400,000	$1,000	$1,000

FIGURE 8.7b Magazine Advertisements.

As you develop a multipronged advertising and promotion strategy, create detailed schedules that show which avenues you will pursue and the associated costs (see Figures 8.7a and 8.7b). These types of schedules serve many purposes, including providing accurate cost estimates, which will help in assessing how much capital you need to raise. They also build credibility in the eyes of potential investors by demonstrating that you understand the nuances of your market.

Sales Strategy

The section on sales strategy provides the backbone that supports all the subsections described so far. Specifically, it illustrates what kind and level of human capital you will devote to the effort. You should complete a careful analysis of how many salespeople and customer support reps you will need. Will these people be internal to the organization or outsourced? If they are internal, will there be a designated sales force, or will different members of the company serve in a sales capacity at different times? Again, a thoughtful presentation of the company's sales force builds credibility by demonstrating an understanding of how the business should operate.

Sales and Marketing Forecasts

Gauging the impact of sales efforts is difficult. Nonetheless, to build a compelling story, entrepreneurs need to show projections of revenues well into the future. How do you derive these numbers? There are two methods: the *comparable method* and the *build-up method*. After detailed investigation of the industry and the market, entrepreneurs know the competitive players and have a good understanding of their history. The **comparable method** models the sales forecast after what other companies have achieved and then adjusts these numbers for differences in things such as the age of the company and the variances in product attributes. In essence, the entrepreneur monitors a number of comparable competitors and then explains why her business varies from those models.

In the **build-up method**, the entrepreneur identifies all the possible revenue sources of the business and then estimates how much of each type of revenue the company can generate during a given period of time. For example, a bookstore generates revenues from books and artifacts. Thus, a bookstore owner would estimate the average sales price for each product category. Then he might estimate the number of people to come through the store on a daily basis and the percentage that would purchase each revenue source. From these numbers, he could create a sales forecast for a typical day, which could then be aggregated into larger blocks of time (months, quarters, or years). These rough estimates might then be further adjusted based on seasonality in the bookstore industry. In the end, the bookstore owner would have a workable model for sales forecasts.

The build-up technique is an imprecise method for the new startup with limited operating history, but it is critically important to assess the viability of the opportunity. It's so important, in fact, that you might want to use both the comparable and the build-up techniques to assess how well they converge. If the two methods are widely divergent, go back through and try to determine why. The knowledge you gain of your business model will help you better articulate the opportunity to stakeholders, and it will provide you with invaluable insights as you begin managing the business after its launch. Chapter 9 provides more details on how to derive these estimates.

Although we know for certain that these forecasts will never be 100% accurate, it is essential to minimize the degree of error. Detailed investigation of comparable companies can help you accomplish this goal, as can triangulating your comparable method results with your build-up method results. However, you go about building your forecast, always keep in mind that the smaller the error, the less likely your company will run out of cash. Beyond building credibility with your investors, rigorous estimates are also the single best tool for keeping your company out of financial trouble.

Operations Plan

The key in the operations plan section is to address how operations will add value for your customers. Here, you'll detail the production cycle and gauge its impact on working capital. For instance, when does your company pay for inputs? How long does it take to produce the product? When does the customer buy the product, and more importantly, when does the customer pay for the product? From the time you pay for your raw materials until you receive payment from your customers, you will be operating in a negative cash flow. The shorter that cycle, the more cash you have on hand and the less likely you are to need bank financing. It sounds counterintuitive, but many rapidly growing new companies run out of cash even though they have increasing sales and substantial operating profit. The reason is that they fail to properly finance the time their cash is tied up in the procurement, production, sales, and receivables cycle.

Operations Strategy

The first subsection of your operations strategy section provides a strategy overview. How does your business compare on the dimensions of cost, quality, timeliness, and flexibility? Emphasize those aspects that provide your venture with a comparative advantage. It is also appropriate to discuss the geographic location of production facilities and how this enhances your firm's competitive advantage. Your notes should cover such issues such as available labor, local regulations, transportation, infrastructure, and proximity to suppliers. In addition, the section should provide a description of the facilities, discuss whether you will buy or lease them, and explain how you will handle future growth (by renting an adjoining building, perhaps). As in all sections detailing strategy, support your plans with actual data.

Scope of Operations

What is the production process for your product or service? Creating a diagram makes it easier for you to see which production aspects to keep in-house and which to outsource (see Figure 8.8a). Considering that cash flow is king and that resource-constrained new ventures typically should minimize fixed expenses on production facilities, the general rule is to outsource as much

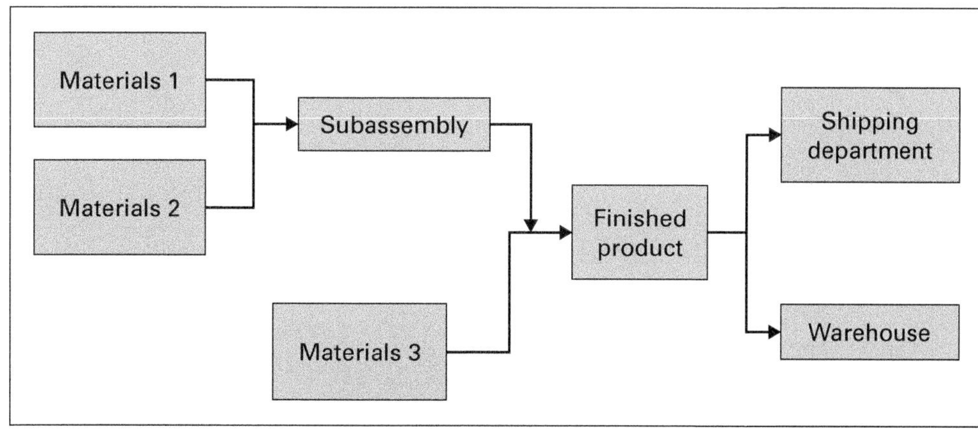

FIGURE 8.8a
Operations Flow.

production as possible. However, there is a major caveat to that rule: Your venture should control aspects of production that are central to your competitive advantage. Thus, if you are producing a new component with hardwired proprietary technology—let's say a voice recognition security door entry—it is wise to internally produce that hardwired component. The locking mechanism, on the other hand, can be outsourced to your specifications. Outsourcing the aspects that aren't proprietary reduces fixed costs for production equipment and facility expenditures, which means you have to raise less money and give up less equity.

The scope of operations section should also discuss partnerships with vendors, suppliers, and partners. Again, the diagram should illustrate the supplier and vendor relationships by category or by name (if the list isn't too long and you have already identified your suppliers).

The diagram helps you visualize the various relationships and ways to better manage or eliminate them. The operations diagram also helps identify staffing needs—for example, how many production workers you might need depending on the hours of operation and number of shifts.

Ongoing Operations

This section builds on the scope of operations section by providing details on day-to-day activities. For example, how many units will you produce in a day, and what kinds of inputs will you need? An operating cycle overview diagram graphically illustrates the impact of production on cash flow (see Figure 8.8b). As you complete this detail, you can start to establish performance parameters, which will help you to monitor and modify the production process into the future. If this plan is for your use only, you may choose to include such details as the specific job descriptions. However, for a business plan that will be shared with investors, you can get by with a much lower level of detail.

Development Plan

The development plan highlights the development strategy and also provides a detailed development time line. Many new ventures will require a significant level of effort and time to launch the product or service. This is the prologue of your story. For example, apps, new software

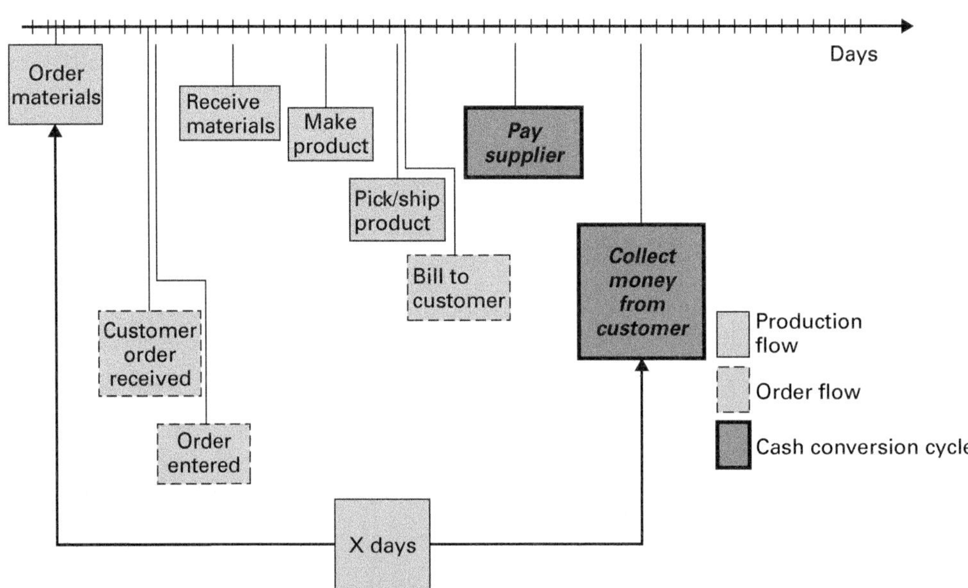

FIGURE 8.8b
Operating Cycle.
Source: Adapted from Professor Robert Eng,babson College

or hardware products often require months of development. Discuss what types of features you will develop and tie them to the firm's competitive advantage. This section should also discuss any patent, trademark, or copyright efforts you will undertake.

Development Strategy

What work remains to be completed? What factors need to come together for development to be successful? What risks to development does the firm face? For example, software development is notorious for taking longer and costing more than most companies originally imagined. Detailing the necessary work and what needs to happen for you to consider the work successful helps you understand and manage the risks involved. After you have laid out these details, you can assemble a development time line.

Development Time Line

A development time line is a schedule that you use to highlight major milestones and to monitor progress and make changes. It's often useful to illustrate time lines as Gantt charts. Figure 8.9 illustrates a typical Gantt chart for a new business launching a history-themed bookstore.

The time line helps you track major events, delegate responsibilities for project tasks, and schedule activities to best execute those events. In addition to plotting future milestones, it is a good idea to illustrate which development milestones you have already achieved as of the writing of the business plan. Finally, keep in mind that, as the old adage says, "Time is money." Every day your product is in development and not on the market, you lose a day's worth of sales. You will have to work hard to meet deadlines, especially in those industries where speed to market is critical.

Team

We mentioned in Chapter 2 that Georges Doriot would rather back a "grade-A man with a grade-B idea than a grade-B man with a grade-A idea." For this reason, the team section of the business plan is often the section that professional investors read right after the executive summary. This section is also critically important to the lead entrepreneur. It identifies the members responsible for key activities and conveys why they are exceptionally qualified to execute on those responsibilities. The section also helps you consider how well this group of individuals will work together. It is well established that ventures started by strong teams are much more likely to succeed than those led by weak teams.

Team Bios and Roles

Every story needs a cast of characters, and the best place to start is by identifying the key team members and their titles. Often the lead entrepreneur assumes a CEO role. However, if you are young and have limited business experience, it is usually more productive to state that the company will seek a qualified CEO as it grows. In these cases, the lead entrepreneur may assume the role of Chief Technology Officer (if she develops the technology) or Vice President of Business Development. However, don't let these options confine you. The key is to convince your investors that you have assembled the best team possible and that your team can execute on the brilliant concept you are proposing.

A simple, relatively flat organization chart is often useful to visualize what roles you have filled and what gaps remain. It also provides a road map for reading the bios that follow. The bios should demonstrate records of success. If you have previously started a business (even if it failed), highlight the company's *accomplishments*. If you have no previous entrepreneurial experience, discuss your achievements in your last job. For example, bios often contain a description

Activity	12	11	10	9	8	7	6	5	4	3	2	1	Opening Month
10–12 Months Prior to Opening													
1) Finalize business plan and financials													
2) Review plans with local bookstore/ specialty shop owners													
3) Fill in skill gaps with advisory board													
4) Determine exact location possibilities													
7–9 Months Prior to Opening													
5) Register rights to business name													
6) Seek funding from appropriate sources													
7) Update business plan per feedback from potential financiers													
8) Make initial contact with product vendors													
9) Contact POS/inventory vendors and store designers													
4–6 Months Prior to Opening													
10) Determine exact store design													
11) Finalize product vendors													
12) Confirm funding													
3 Months Prior to Opening													
13) Finalize store design plans													
14) Open vendor/bank accounts													
15) Place fixture orders													
16) Finalize marketing plan and implement to announce store opening events													
17) Submit merchandise orders with all vendors													
1 Month Prior to Opening													
18) Contact local media re placement in local newspapers and magazines													
19) Code merchandise category data in inventory management system													
20) Recruit and train staff													
21) Receive merchandise, fixtures, and complete setup of store													
Opening Month													
22) "Soft opening" of store to assess customer response, training, and system functioning													
Grand Opening of Store													

FIGURE 8.9 Gantt Chart.

of the number of people the entrepreneur previously managed and, more importantly, a measure of economic success, such as "grew division sales by 20-plus percent." The bio should demonstrate your leadership capabilities. Include the team's resumes as an appendix.

Advisory Boards, Board of Directors, Strategic Partners, External Members

Many entrepreneurs find that they are more attractive to investors if they have strong advisory boards. In building an advisory board, you want to create a team with diverse skills and experience. Industry experts provide legitimacy to your new business as well as strong technical advice. Other advisors should bring financial, legal, or management expertise. Thus, it is common to see lawyers, professors, accountants, and others who can assist the venture's growth on advisory boards. Moreover, if your firm has a strategic supplier or key customer, it may make sense to invite him onto your advisory board. Typically, these individuals are remunerated with a small equity stake and compensation for any organized meetings.

By law, most types of organization require a board of directors. Although members of the advisory board can also provide needed expertise, a board of directors is different from an advisory board. The directors' primary role is to oversee the company on behalf of the investors, and to that end, the board has the power to replace top executives if it feels doing so would be in the best interests of the company. Therefore, the business plan needs to briefly describe the size of the board, its role within the organization, and any current board members. Most major investors, such as venture capitalists, will require one or more board seats. Usually, the lead entrepreneur and one or more inside company members, such as the Chief Financial Officer or a Vice President, will also have board seats.

Strategic partners may not necessarily be on your advisory board or your board of directors, but they still provide credibility to your venture. For this reason, it makes sense to highlight their involvement in your company's success. It is also common to list external team members, such as the law firm and accounting firm that your venture uses. The key in this section is to demonstrate that your firm can successfully execute the concept. A strong team provides the foundation that can ensure your venture will implement the opportunity successfully.

Compensation and Ownership

A capstone to the team section should be a table listing key team members by role, compensation, and ownership equity. A brief description in the text should explain why the compensation is appropriate. Many entrepreneurs choose not to pay themselves in the early months. Although this strategy conserves cash flow, it would misrepresent the individual's worth to the organization. Therefore, the table should contain what salary the employee is due. If necessary, that salary can be deferred until a time when cash flow is strong. Another column that can be powerful shows what the person's current or most recent compensation was and what she will be paid in the new company. Highly qualified entrepreneurs taking a smaller salary than at their previous job make an impressive point. Although everyone understands that the entrepreneur's salary will increase as the company begins to grow, starting at a reduced salary sends the message that you and your team believe in the upside of your idea. Just be sure the description of the schedule underscores the plan to increase salaries in the future. In addition, it is a good idea to hold stock aside for future key hires and to establish a stock option pool for critical lower-level employees, such as software engineers. The plan should discuss such provisions.

Critical Risks

Every new venture faces a number of risks that may threaten its survival. Although the business plan, to this point, is creating a story of success, readers will identify and recognize a number of threats. The plan needs to acknowledge these potential risks; otherwise, investors will believe that the entrepreneur is naive or untrustworthy and may possibly withhold investment. How should you present these critical risks without scaring your investor or other stakeholders? Identify the risk and then state your contingency plan. Critical risks are critical assumptions—factors that need to happen if your venture is to succeed as currently planned. The critical assumptions vary from one company to another, but some common categories are market interest and growth potential, competitor actions and retaliation, time and cost of development, operating expenses, and availability and timing of financing.

Market Interest and Growth Potential

The biggest risk any new venture faces is that, once the product has been developed, no one will buy it. Although you can do a number of things to minimize this risk, such as market research, focus groups, and beta sites, it is difficult to gauge overall demand, and the growth of that demand, until your product hits the market. State this risk, but counter it with the tactics and contingencies the company will undertake. For example, sales risk can be reduced by mounting an effective advertising and marketing plan or by identifying not only a core customer but also secondary and tertiary target audiences that the company will seek if the core customer proves less interested.

Competitor Actions and Retaliation

Too many entrepreneurs believe either that direct competition doesn't exist or that it is sleepy and slow to react. Don't rely on this belief as a key assumption of your venture's success. Most entrepreneurs passionately believe that they are offering something new and wonderful that is clearly different from what is currently on the market. They go on to state that existing competition won't attack their niche in the near future. Acknowledge the risk that this assessment may be wrong. One counter to this threat is that the venture has room in its gross margins to operate at lower-than-anticipated price levels and the cash available to withstand and fight back against such attacks. You should also identify the strategies you will use to protect and reposition yourself, should an attack occur.

Time and Cost of Development

As mentioned in the development plan section, many factors can delay and add to the expense of developing your product. The business plan should identify the factors that may hinder development. For instance, there has been an acute shortage of skilled software engineers. You need to address how you will overcome the challenge of hiring and retaining the most qualified professionals, perhaps by outsourcing some development to the underemployed engineers in India. Compensation, equity participation, flexible hours, and other benefits that the firm could offer might also minimize the risk. Whatever your strategy, you need to demonstrate an understanding of the difficult task at hand and assure potential investors that you will be able to develop the product on time and on budget.

Operating Expenses

Operating expenses have a way of growing beyond expectations. Sales, administration, marketing, and interest expenses are some of the areas you need to monitor and manage. The business plan should highlight how you forecast your expenses (comparable companies and detailed analysis) and also lay out your contingency plans for unexpected developments. For instance, you may want to slow the hiring of support staff if development or other key tasks take longer than expected. Remember, cash is king, and your plan should illustrate how you will conserve cash when things don't go according to plan.

Availability and Timing of Financing

We can't stress enough how important cash flow is to the survival and flourishing of a new venture. One major risk that most new ventures face is that they will have difficulty obtaining needed financing, both equity and debt. If the current business plan is successful in attracting investors, cash flow will not be a problem in the short term. However, most ventures will need multiple rounds of financing. If the firm fails to make progress or meet key milestones, it may not be able to secure additional rounds of financing. This can put the entrepreneur in the uncomfortable position of having to accept unfavorable financing terms or, in the worst-case scenario, force the company into bankruptcy. Your contingency plans should identify viable alternative sources of capital and strategies to slow the "burn rate."[14]

A number of other risks might apply to your business. Acknowledge them and discuss how you can overcome them. Doing so generates confidence among your investors and helps you anticipate corrective actions that you may need to take.

Offering

Using your vision for the business and your estimates of the capital required to get there, you can develop a "sources and uses" schedule for the offering section of your business plan. The sources section details how much capital you need and the types of financing, such as equity investment and debt infusions. The uses section details how you'll spend the money. Typically, you should secure enough financing to last 12–18 months. If you take more capital than you need, you have to give up more equity. If you take less, you may run out of cash before reaching milestones that equate to higher valuations.

Financial Plan

Chapter 9 illustrates how to construct your pro forma financials, but you will also need a verbal description of these financials. We will defer discussion of this section until the next chapter.

Appendices

The appendices can include anything and everything that you think adds further validation to your concept but that doesn't fit or is too large to insert in the main parts of the plan. Common inclusions would be one-page resumes of key team members, articles that feature your venture, and technical specifications. If you already have customers, include a few excerpts of testimonials from them. Likewise, if you have favorable press coverage, include that as well. As a general rule, try to put all exhibits discussed in the written part of the plan on the same page on which you discuss them so the reader doesn't have to keep flipping back to the end of the plan to look at an exhibit. However, it is acceptable to put very large exhibits into an appendix.

Types of Plans

So far in this chapter, we have laid out the basic sections or areas you want to address in your business planning process. The earliest drafts should be organized on your computer so you can add and subtract as you gain a deeper understanding, but at some point, you may want to print a more formal-looking plan.

Business plans can take a number of forms depending on their purpose. Each form requires the same level of effort and leads to the same conclusions, but the final document is crafted differently depending on who uses it and when they use it. For instance, when you are introducing your concept to a potential investor, you might send a short, concise summary plan. As the investor's interest grows and she wants to more fully investigate the concept, she may ask for a more detailed plan. A business plan serves many more purposes than the needs of potential investors. Employees, strategic partners, financiers, and board members all may find use for a well-developed business plan. Most importantly, the entrepreneur herself gains immeasurably from the business planning process because it allows her not only to run the company better but also to clearly articulate her story to stakeholders, who may never read the plan. In sum, different consumers of the business plan require different presentation of the work.

Everything that you have gathered and organized in files on your computer is basically what we would call an *operational plan*. It is primarily for you and your team to guide the development, launch, and initial growth of the venture. There really is no length specification for this type of plan, but it's not unusual to exceed 80 pages. The biggest difference between an operational plan and the one you might present to a potential investor is the level of detail, which tends to be much greater in an operational plan. Remember, the creation of this document is where you really gain the deep understanding so important in discerning how to build and run the business.

If you need outside capital, a business plan geared toward equity investors or debt providers should be about 25–40 pages long. Recognize that professional equity investors, such as venture capitalists, and professional debt providers, such as bankers, will not read the entire plan from front to back. That being the case, produce the plan in a format that facilitates spot reading. The previous discussion highlighted sections that these readers might find useful. The key is to present a concise version of all the material you have produced in your planning process. Focus on what the investor values the most. Thus, operational details are often less important unless your competitive advantage derives from your operations. Our general guideline is that "less is more." For instance, we've found that 25-page business plans receive venture funding more often than 40-page plans (other things being equal).

You will need to create a pitch deck and some summary financials; and you may also want to produce an expanded executive summary. These plans are considerably shorter than an operational plan or the 25- to 40-page plan discussed earlier—typically, no more than 10 pages. The purpose of this plan is to provide an initial conception of the business to test initial reaction to the idea. It allows you to share your idea with confidants and receive feedback before investing significant time and effort on a longer business plan.

After you've completed the business planning process, rewrite the expanded executive summary. You can use this expanded summary to attract attention. For instance, send it to investors you have recently met to spur interest and a meeting. It is usually better to send an expanded executive summary than a full business plan because the investor will be more apt to read it. If the investor is interested, he will call you in for a meeting. If the meeting goes well, the investor often then asks for the full business plan.

Style Pointers for the Written Plan and Oral Presentation

Once you start writing plans for external consumption, the way you present the information becomes important. Not only do you need to capture the reader's attention with a well-researched opportunity, but also you need to present your case in a way that makes it easy and interesting to read. Too many business plans are text-laden, dense manifestos. Only the most diligent reader will wade through all that text. The key is to create visual catch-points.

Use a table of contents with numbered sections, as we described earlier in this chapter. Then use clearly marked headers and subheaders throughout the document. This allows the reader to jump to sections she is most interested in. Another way to draw the reader to important points is to use bulleted lists, diagrams, charts, and sidebars.[15] Your reader should be able to understand the venture opportunity by just looking at the visual catch-points of a plan. Work with your team and trusted advisors on ways to bring out the exciting elements of your story. The point is to make the document not only content rich but also visually attractive.

Some investors have no interest in a plan at all. Instead, they prefer to see an executive summary and slide deck, and they often read the slides instead of asking the entrepreneur to personally present those slides. We have already discussed executive summaries, so let's spend a few moments on the slide deck. You should be able to communicate your business opportunity in 10–12 slides, possibly along the following lines:

1. Cover page showing product picture, company name, and contact information
2. Opportunity description emphasizing customer problem or need that you hope to solve
3. Illustration of how your product or service solves the customer's problem
4. Some details (as needed) to better describe your product
5. Competition overview
6. Entry and growth strategy showing how you get into the market and then grow
7. Overview of your business model—how you will make money and how much it will cost to support those sales
8. Team description
9. Current status with time line
10. Summary including how much money you need and how it will be used

Contrast our suggestions above to the slide deck at the end of the chapter for Gravyty. Do the founders of Gravyty follow our guidelines? Can you understand the "story" of Gravyty as an early investor might by reading their slide deck? The key to creating a successful presentation is to maximize the use of your slides. For example, graphs, pictures, and other visuals are more powerful and compelling than texts and bulleted lists. Entrepreneurs who create bulleted lists often use them as cue cards during an oral presentation and either stare at the screen behind them as they talk or continually look back and forth between the screen and their audience. In either case, this behavior might prevent you from creating a personal connection with your audience.

This connection is important because it conveys that you have confidence in your plan and that you have a strong command of the concept. A second problem with bulleted lists is that those in your audience will tend to read them, and their attention will be focused on the slide and not on what you are saying. Again, you want to create a strong personal connection with your audience. You should be able to use graphics to communicate the key points. Doing so will better engage your audience and make them more inclined to view your opportunity favorably.

CONCLUSION

The business plan is more than just a document; it is a process, a story. Although the finished product is often a written plan, the deep thinking and fact-based analysis that go into that document provide the entrepreneur the keen insights needed to marshal resources and direct growth. The whole process can be painful, but it almost always maximizes revenue and minimizes costs. The reason is that the process allows the entrepreneur to better anticipate instead of react.

Business planning also provides talking points so that entrepreneurs can get feedback from a number of experts, including investors, vendors, and customers. Think of business planning as one of your first steps on the journey to entrepreneurial success. Also remember that business planning is a process and not a product. It is iterative, and in some sense, it never ends. As your venture grows, you will want to come back and revisit earlier drafts, create new drafts, and so on for the entire life of your business. Keep your business plan files easily accessible (on a secure cloud site) and close by (on your computer or tablet), and continue to add to and revise it often. It is the depository of all the learning that you have achieved as well as your plans for the future. Although preparing the first draft of your plan is tough, the rewards are many. Enjoy the journey.

YOUR OPPORTUNITY JOURNAL

Reflection Point	Your Thoughts...
1. What data have you gathered about your opportunity?	
a. What do these data suggest as far as reshaping your opportunity?	
b. What new questions do they raise, and who should you talk to in order to answer these questions?	
2. Who have you shared your vision with?	
a. Who have they referred you to?	
b. What new learning have you gained from these conversations?	
3. What is your "tagline"?	
4. Does your executive summary have a compelling "hook"?	
5. Does your business planning process tie together well? Do you have a compelling, articulate story?	

WEB EXERCISE

Scan the Internet for business plan preparation sites. What kinds of templates are available? Do these make it easier to write a plan? What is the downside, if any, of using these templates? What are the benefits? Find some sample plans online. These plans are often advertised as superior to "typical" plans. Are they better? What makes them better?

NOTES

1. Bartlett, S. *Seat of Your Pants. Inc.*, October 2002.
2. *The Quotations Page*. www.quotationspage.com/quote/36892.html.
3. Lange, J., Bygrave, W., and Evans, T. *Do Business Plan Competitions Produce Winning Businesses?* Paper presented at 2004 Babson Kauffman Entrepreneurship Research Conference, Glasgow, Scotland.
4. Liao, J., and Gartner, W. The Effects of Pre-venture Plan Timing and Perceived Environmental Uncertainty on the Persistence of Emerging Firms. *Small Business Economics*, 27(1): 23–40. 2006.
5. Murphy, Elizabeth. Eliminating the Prohibitions Against General Solicitation and General Advertising in Rule 506 and Rule 144a Offerings. Final Rule. July 10, 2013. https://www.sec.gov/rules/final/2013/33-9415.pdf.
6. Fields, Brent. *Amendments for Small and Additional Issues Exemptions under the Securities Act*, Regulation A. Final Rules. March 25, 2015. http://www.sec.gov/rules/final/2015/33-9741.pdf.
7. The Mobile Economy 2019 Copyright 2019 GSM Association
8. Matzler, Kurt, Viktoria Veider, and Wolfgang Kathan. "Adapting to the Sharing Economy." *MIT Sloan Management Review*, 56.2 (2015): 71–7. *Pro-Quest*. Web. September 2, 2015.
9. By Metafacts. "Apple's Girds Up Its Legs with Handoff." November 3, 2014. http://technologyuser.com/2014/11/03/apple-girds-up-its-legs-with-handoff/.
10. https://www.bookweb.org/for-the-record.
11. Andel, Tom. "Uber Experiments with Parcel Delivery." *Industry Week* (2014), *ProQuest*. Web. 9 July 2015.
12. Alsever, J. "Yes, There's an Uber for That." *Fortune* [serial online]. *June 15*, 2015; 171(8):62. Available from: Business Source Alumni Edition, Ipswich, MA. Accessed July 9, 2015.
13. O'Reilly, L. "The Gap's Sales Go into a 3-Month Slide Following Its 'Dress Normal' Ad Campaign Failure." December 5, 2014. *Business Insider*. Read more: http://www.businessinsider.com/gap-november-sales-down-4-percent-2014-12#ixzz3fROcLXES.
14. *Burn rate* is how much more cash the company is expending each month than earning in revenue.
15. A running sidebar, a visual device positioned on the right side of the page, periodically highlights some of the key points in the plan. Don't overload the sidebar, but one or two items per page can draw attention to highlights that maintain reader interest.

Case — Gravyty: The Art + Science of Better Nonprofit Fundraising[1]

Discussion Questions

Gravyty, co-founded by Adam Martel and Rich Palmer, helps nonprofit organizations build more relationships with their supporters through artificial intelligence (AI)-enabled tools that prioritize donors and optimize the sequence of actions to lead to bigger gifts.

1. Examine the executive summary (following pages 244–245) including the competition overview chart. What do you think is done well in the summary? How could it be improved?
2. Now take a look at the deck that begins after executive summary. What are the three strongest aspects of their presentation deck?
3. Is there anything missing from the deck? What is not clear or what is hard to understand?
4. Are there more actions and more learning that Adam and Rich need to do before they launch?
5. If Adam and Rich are asked by early investors to provide a detailed business plan, what parts of this deck need to be fortified and elaborated?

[1] This case was created by Rich Palmer and Andrew Corbett.

GRAVYTY Art+Science of Better Nonprofit Fundraising

Quick Facts

About

Gravyty helps nonprofit organizations raise more money by increasing their fundraisers' efficiency with actionable data analytics and portfolio optimization tools. It gives fundraisers the ability to maximize their time building relationships with the right donors at the right time.

Founding Team

Adam Martel
CEO | Professional fundraiser, financial analyst, experience with three startups, team building expert

Rich Palmer
CTO | Product developer, software engineer, big data analyst (RelSci, CapitalIQ, athenahealth)

Advisory Board

6 members from Babson College, Rexer Analytics, Bloomerang, and more.

Customer Board

7 members from Tufts, Boston Conservatory, Yeshiva, Emmanuel, MIT CSAIL, Franklin College, and more.

Competition

Direct Advizor Solutions, Pursuant, Reeher
Indirect Blackbaud, Evertrue, Bloomerang, Abila, DonorPerfect

Seed Round

$500k; $320k invested; $2.25M pre-money valuation; led by NXT Ventures

Contact
www.gravyty.com
hello@gravyty.com

Fundraisers Need Better Tools

Nonprofit organizations (NPOs) need revenue from individual and corporate donations to grow every year. They rely on professional fundraisers as the primary source of their donations; yet, they are ill-equipped to address these growing expectations. With primitive tools, limited data analytics skills, 6-month onboarding, and painful migrations - they need innovation.

Better Tech for People-People

By nature, the fundraising profession attracts gregarious and social people. By combining data analytics and visualization, predictive modeling, and portfolio productivity, we offer the first cloud-based platform that uses big data sources to enable fundraisers to better focus on donors and take advantage of data analytics without needing a technical background.

Strong Integrated Solutions

We aren't replacing CRMs - we are augmenting them. Pulling data from public, private, and behavioral sources allows our algorithms to predict with high accuracy who is going to make the next big gift.

While our solution is valuable to 600k donation-driven NPOs, we are initially targeting higher education, hospitals, arts, and medical affinity organizations. Our cloud-based and secure SaaS product is $250/mo per user.

Milestones and R&D

- Live & Selling Product
- NPO Clients: 11
- Pipeline: 71 clients; 200+ users
- 2 Hires: 1 full-time, 1 part-time
- Negotiating a license deal with an established nonprofit tech company

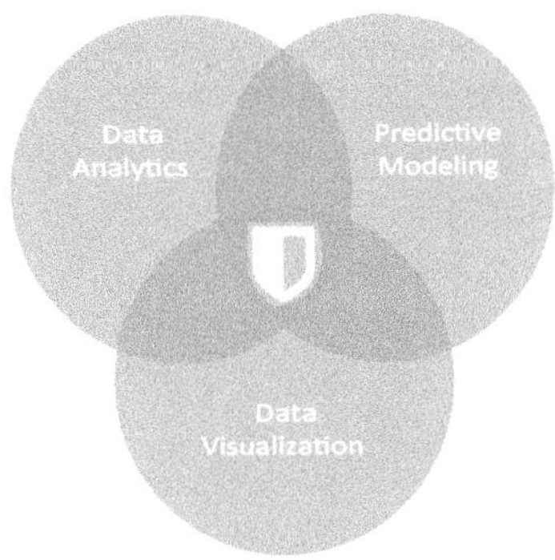

Growing & Dynamic Market

There are 1.5M NPOs in the US that raised over $350B in 2014. This was a 5% increase over the year before. NPOs spend $114k per year on technology to enable their operations – which is a $58B estimated market.

Additionally, NPOs have publicly stated that they want more technology solutions and are willing to pay. We believe there is an opportunity to capitalize on this soft market by increasing fundraiser efficiency so they can address a larger portion of their organization's donor pool without increasing staff.

of donations come from 10% of donors

total spent on NPO technology in 2014

Our Impact

Through our tools, customers have been achieving wonderful things. Select results include:

92%	Faster Onboarding
60%	More Donations
14.3%	Increased Efficiency

Market & Competition Overview

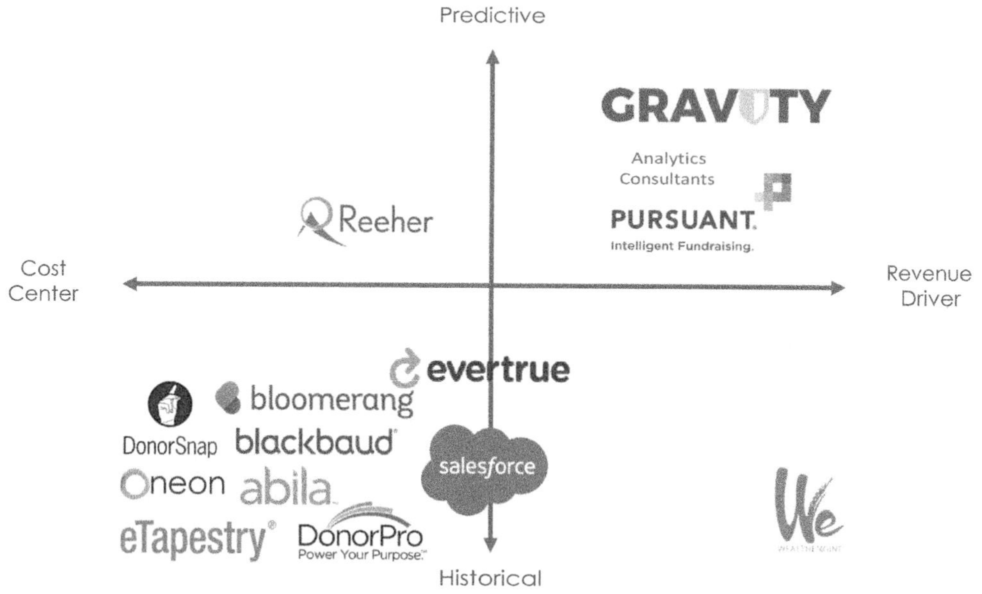

Predictive

GRAVYTY

Analytics Consultants

PURSUANT. Intelligent Fundraising.

Reeher

Cost Center

Revenue Driver

evertrue

bloomerang

DonorSnap

blackbaud

salesforce

Oneon abila

eTapestry

DonorPro Power Your Purpose.

Historical

Logos are for informational purposes only and are not authorized, sponsored by, or associated with the trademark owner.

GRAVYTY

Superior nonprofit fundraising through actionable predictive intelligence.

www.gravyty.com
hello@gravyty.com

The missions of
life-changing nonprofits

are being financed with

Sticky Notes & Spreadsheets

Staggering Inefficiencies

Attrition Epidemics

Blind Luck

There is no efficient, actionable way for fundraisers to leverage data to engage high potential donors.

CRMs are difficult to use and backwards looking

Fundraisers turnover every 12–18 months

A belief that *more* data equals effectiveness

Expensive and stagnant consultants

Hidden Truth

of
Donors

Donation
Amount

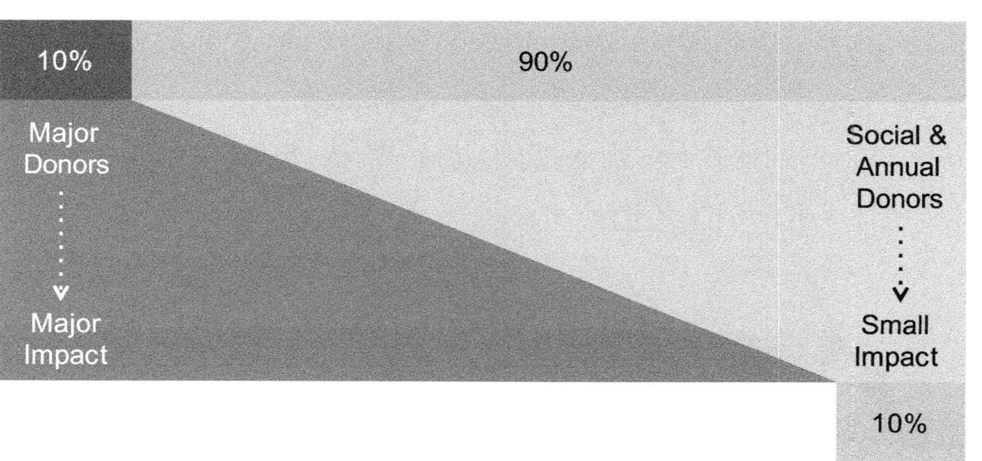

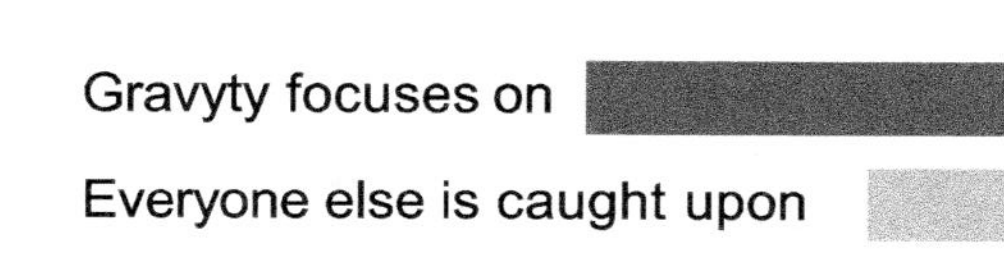

Gravyty Engine

Donor and Lead Management Predictive Intelligence

Result of analysis on 150,000 major donors at nonprofits spanning multiple sectors and over 29 years of giving history.

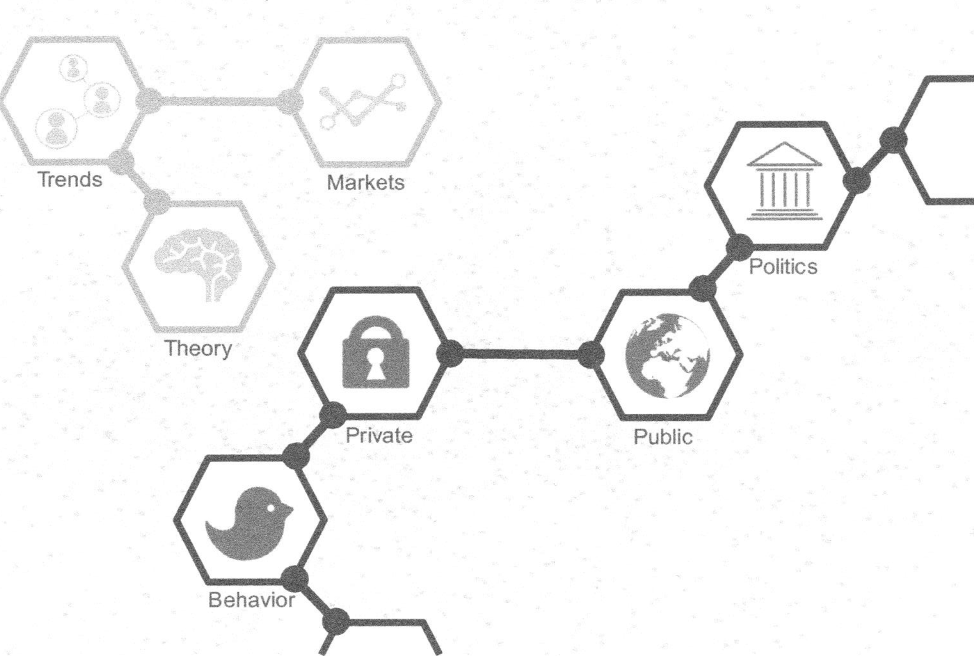

Fundraising 1.0

Guts, Grit, and Good Luck

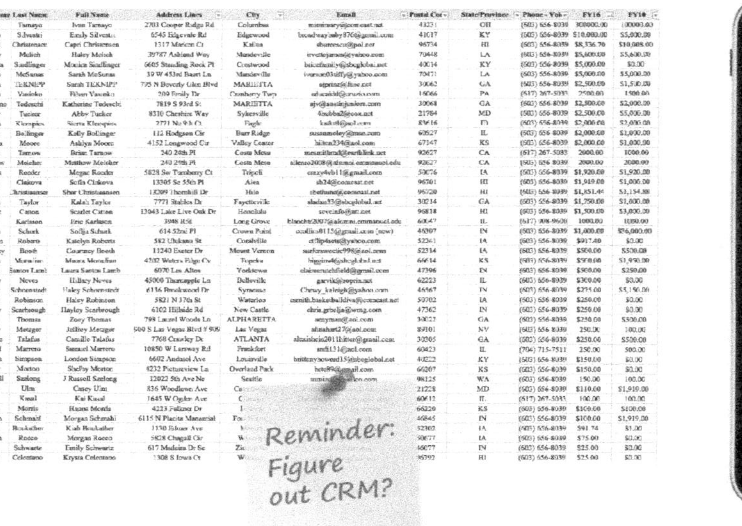

Fundraising 2.0

Data-driven, Adaptable, Focused

GRAVYTY

Customer Value Proposition

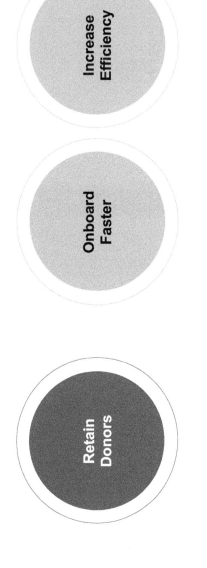

Outcome &
Donation Amounts

Productivity &
Enterprise Management

Big Market With A Focused Start

Based on Average Tech Spend

Segment
601k NPOs
$58B

Target
512k NPOs
$49B

Initial
240k NPOs
$23B

Initial Market

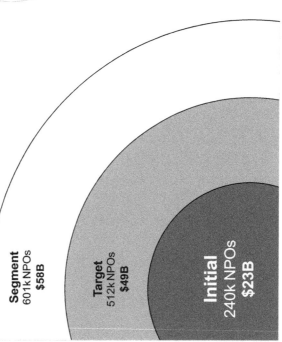

Higher Ed
Hospitals
Medical Affinity
Arts & Culture
Religion

Pilot Customers

4

Higher Ed ($4M – 20M)
Medical Affinity ($1M)

250,000+
Donors Analyzed

4
Avg Users

Upcoming / Prospects

10

Higher Ed ($2M – 700M)
Hospitals ($800M)
Religious ($25M)

Pipeline

50

Nonprofits across Higher Ed, Hospitals, Medical Affinity, Arts & Culture, & Religious

Initial Results With Our Platform

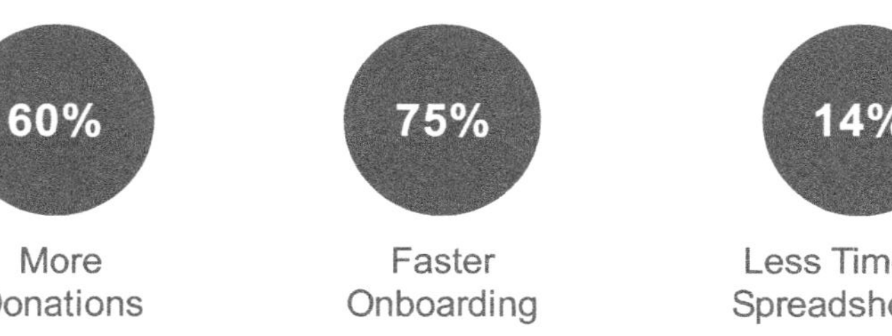

"Gravyty helps me allocate my scarcest resource – time."

Sam Sanker,
Associate Director, Tufts

"Gravyty will change the way nonprofit organizations approach and execute their daily fundraising responsibilities."

Deb Girard
Executive Director, Melanoma Foundation

"I believe their product will revolutionize how fundraisers strategize, create their pipelines and manage their prospects."

Carmina Portillo
Director of Institutional Advancement, Yeshiva University

SXSW

Founder's Guide

VENTUREFIZZ

NETWORKWORLD

Sales Strategy

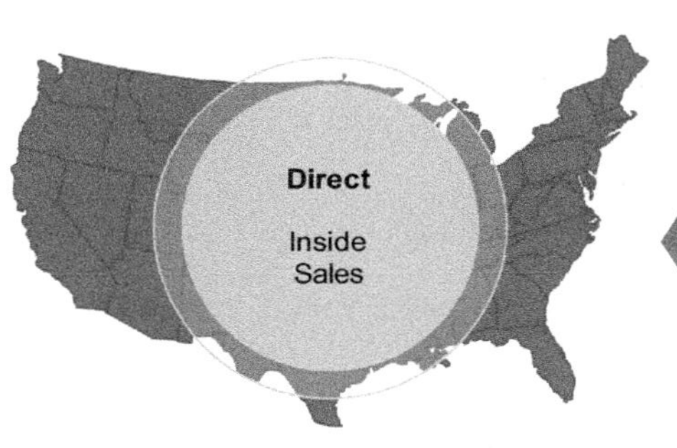

Top Down Through Boards

100% Remote

Warm Leads

Marketing Methods

Industry Consultants
NPO Clients Referral Fees

Strategic Partners
Revenue Sharing

Inbound Marketing

Targeted PR

Conferences (CASE, AFP)

We Are Not a CRM or Crowdfunding Platform

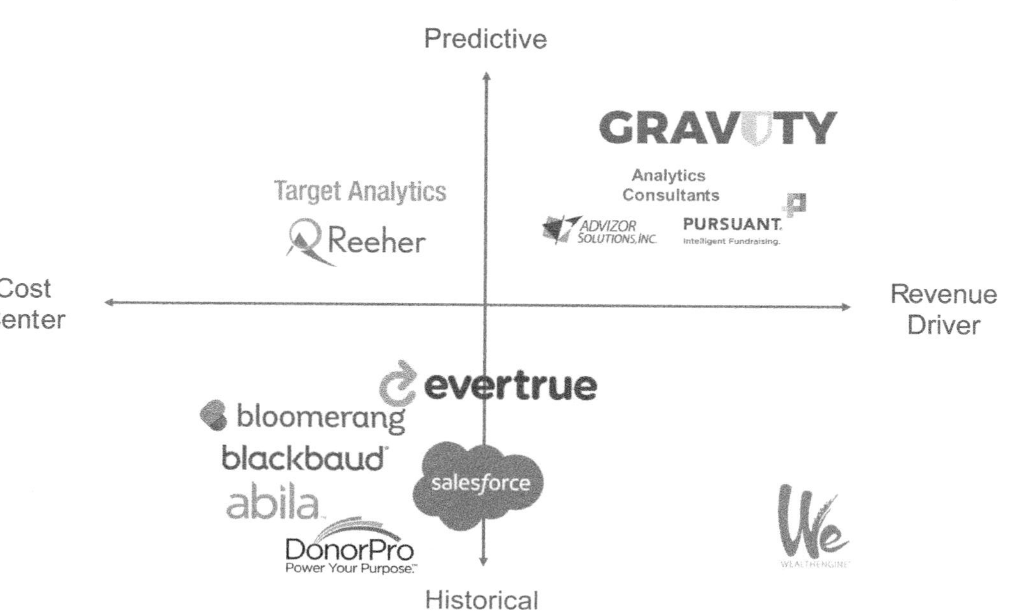

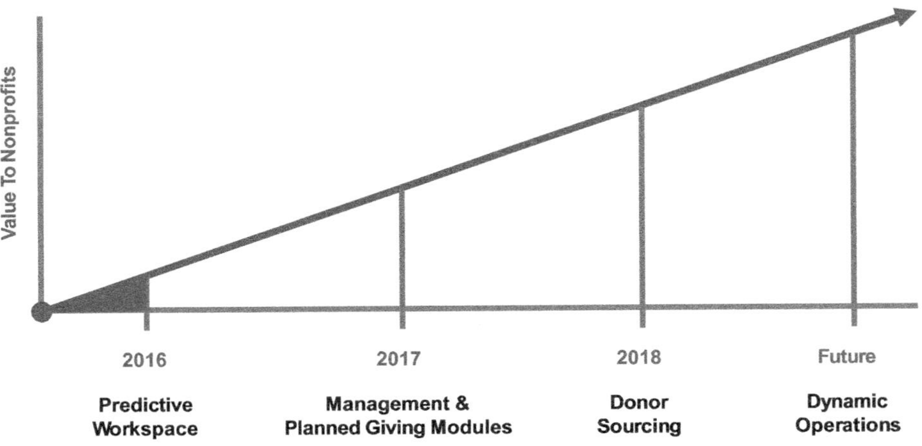
Product Roadmap
Become the most trusted and valuable development solution.
Value To Nonprofits
2016
Predictive Workspace
2017
Management & Planned Giving Modules
2018
Donor Sourcing
Future
Dynamic Operations
Key Focus Areas

Business Model + Simplified Financials

$1,400		5		5 year		$250/mo		$60k-75k
CAC	••	Users/NPO	••	lifetime	••	per user	••	LTV

	Annual		
	2016	2017	2018
Revenue	$242,207	$2,762,407	$10,870,124
Costs	$303,488	$2,458,185	$7,587,395
EBITDA	$(61,281)	$304,222	$3,282,729

	Headcount		
Product	1	7	10
Sales & Support	2	11	16
Operations	-	4	4
Founders	2	2	2
Total	5	24	32

Founding Team

Seasoned Fundraiser
Financial Analyst
Merrimack & Babson

STATE STREET

Adam Martel
CEO

Rich Palmer
CTO & COO

Product Designer
& Developer
RPI & Babson

REL SCI

athenahealth

Key Advisors

Karl Rexer, PhD
Founder
Rexer Analytics

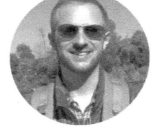

Andrew Corbett
Chair, Entrepreneurship Division
Babson College

Carmina Portillo
Dir of Institutional Advancement
Yeshiva University

Lori Sterling
Fmr. Dir. Advancement Services
Babson College

Jay Love
CEO, Bloomerang
Founder, eTapestry

William F Markey Jr
Managing Director
Armstrong Franklin

Exit Potential

CRMs / Nonprofit Tech

blackbaud	$3B Public Co; 8,000 NPOs $17.5M to $293.9M Acquisitions
abila	$70M revenue 6,000 NPOs
bloomerang	CEO is key Gravyty advisor with 6 profitable exits

Providers with NPO Customers

salesforce.org	$50B Public Co 20,000 NPOs
HubSpot	$1.5B Public Co 4,000 NPOs; 5 Acquisitions
Constant Contact	$1.1B Public Co 16,000 NPOs; 7 Acquisitions

Acquisition Rationale

Innovation •• Movement along value chain •• Customer adoption •• Stickiness
Fear of CRM competition •• Predictive analytics demand from customers •• Acqui-hire

Outcome

Revenue Multiple

3-5

Time Horizon (Years)

Funding & Milestones

Raising up to $500k

Angels, Angel Groups, FFF (Accredited), Accelerators, Strategic Partners

Next Round

Est. $1M; Q1 2017

$125k
Closed

$200k
In Talks/Prospect

Use of Proceeds

$0 - $250k

$251-$500k

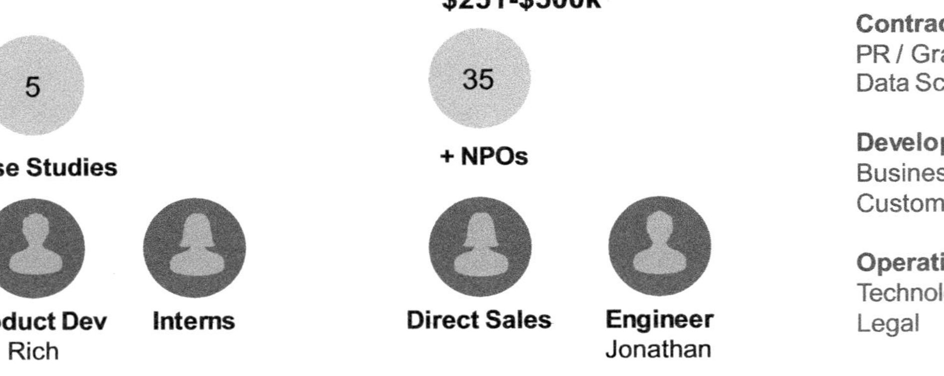

Contracts
PR / Graphics
Data Science

Development
Business &
Customer

Operations
Technology &
Legal

Thank You

gravyty.com

hello@gravyty.com

Appendices

Attributions

NounProject.com Artists

- Creative Stall
- Lorena Salagre
- PJ Souders
- Oliviu Stoian
- Cristiano Zoucas
- Design Initiative
- Yi Chen
- Okan Benn
- Alex Fuller
- Nayeli Zimmermann
- Mister Pixel
- Darlena Tran
- Mattjis de Block
- Mark Shorter
- Eric Bird
- Ralf Schmitzer
- Shimaru
- Alex Auda Samora
- Edward Boatman
- Lemon Liu
- Gregor Cresnar
- Andrew Fortnum
- Mattjis de Block

Value To User

	GRAVITY	Consultants Analytics, Reher, Pursuant	CRMs Blackbaud, Abila
Ease of Use	Quick onboarding and user adoption; Useful immediately	Long customization process; Difficult to change	Steep learning curve; UI cluttered; painful migrations
Costs	Automated/easy Implementation; No migration	Expensive fees; Implementation fees; 3-4 Rotations	Consulting fees; Implementation fees; Dedicated staff
Benefits	Increased efficiency, donations, and confidence; Daily results	Customizable; Thorough data; Safe choice "IBM"	Stable and scalable repository for reporting; Established businesses
	$250 per user/mo	**$30,000-50,000+** per year	**$49-800+** per user/mo

Key Risks	Addressed By
A large player moves into our space.	Innovation through acquisition; Premium pricing; Formation of partner programs; First-mover
How do I know that this prediction works?	Case study programs; Testimonials; Land-and-expand trial; Analytics PhD advisor
Long sales cycle and expensive staff.	Top down sales; Remote sales; Robust pipeline; Partner referral program; API = scale potential; Consultants = no fee; Commission-based staff

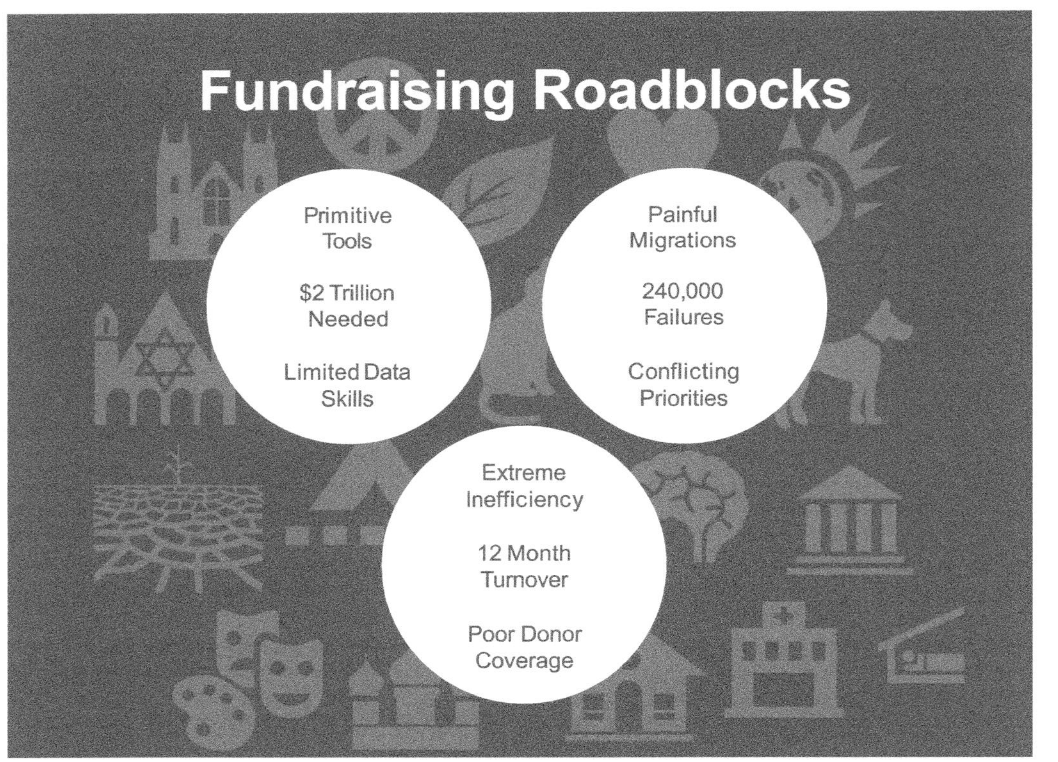
Fundraising Roadblocks
Primitive Tools
$2 Trillion Needed
Limited Data Skills
Painful Migrations
240,000 Failures
Conflicting Priorities
Extreme Inefficiency
12 Month Turnover
Poor Donor Coverage

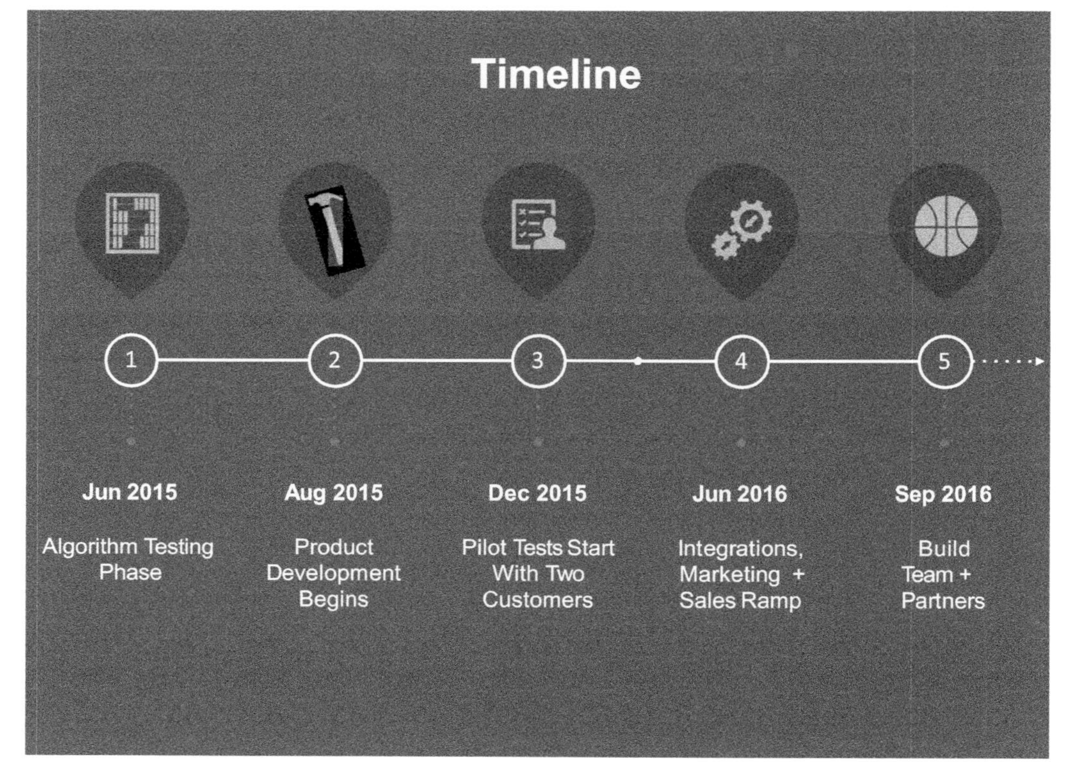
Timeline
1
2
3
4
5
Jun 2015
Algorithm Testing Phase
Aug 2015
Product Development Begins
Dec 2015
Pilot Tests Start With Two Customers
Jun 2016
Integrations, Marketing + Sales Ramp
Sep 2016
Build Team + Partners

Concerns At A Typical Nonprofit

VPs & Executive Directors
"Are we meeting our goals efficiently?"

Fundraisers
"Are we engaging donors and hitting our targets in the right way?"

Research & Data
"Is this the right set of donors to target?"

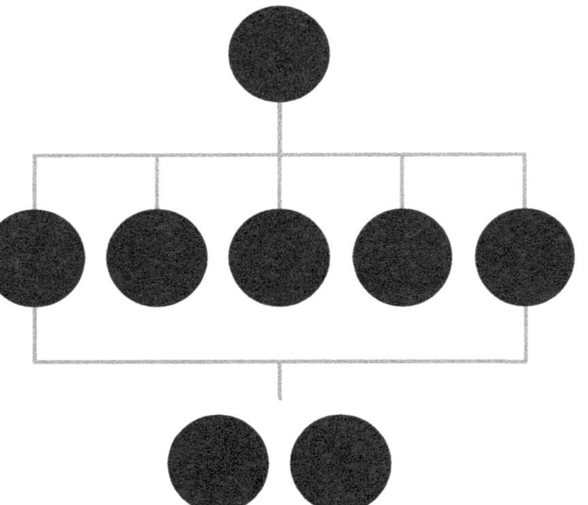

Value Proposition for VPs

Expand capabilities of existing team and cover 10%+ without hiring more people.

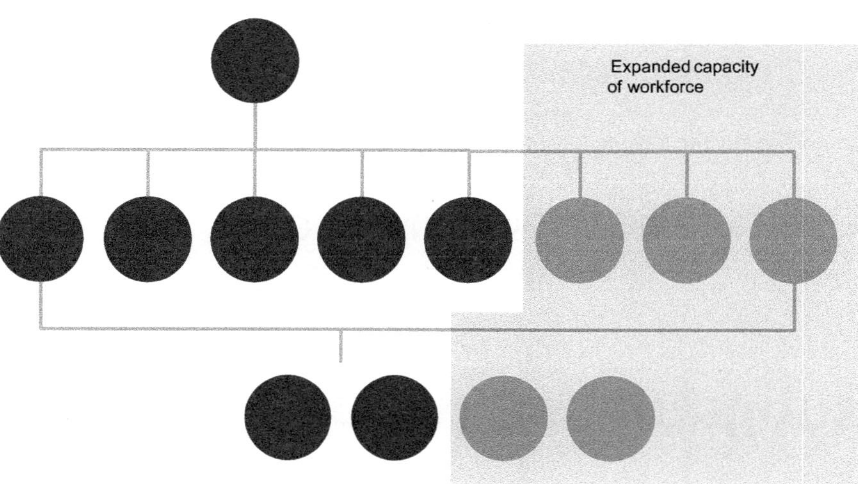

Select Financial Assumptions

$250	Per seat, per month
2.5%	NPO Count - Growth Rate – Net
8%	R&D (% of Revenue)
30%	SG&A (% of Revenue)
75%	Retention Rate
$114k	Average Technology Budget at NPO

Organization Seats

3 (Small); 5 (Med); 10 (Large)

Case Study

In 2014, a nonprofit raised $17.3M from 2,400 donors.

The top 136 donors gave $15.5M. The remainder gave $1.8M. The nonprofit has 15 professional fundraisers and many volunteers.

Case Study

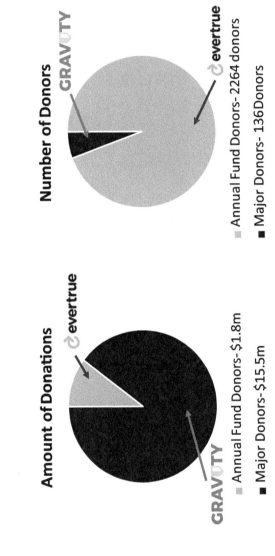

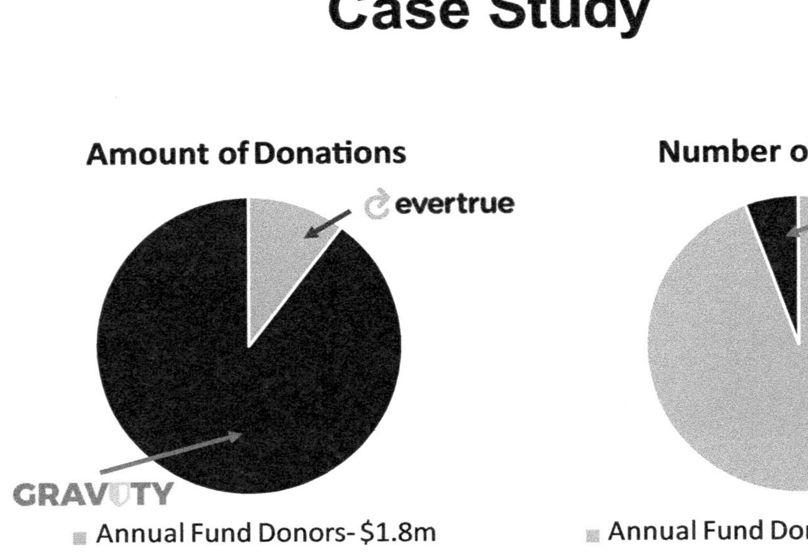
Amount of Donations
evertrue
GRAVITY
Annual Fund Donors- $1.8m
Major Donors- $15.5m
Number of Donors
GRAVITY
evertrue
Annual Fund Donors- 2264 donors
Major Donors- 136Donors

Building Your Pro Forma

9

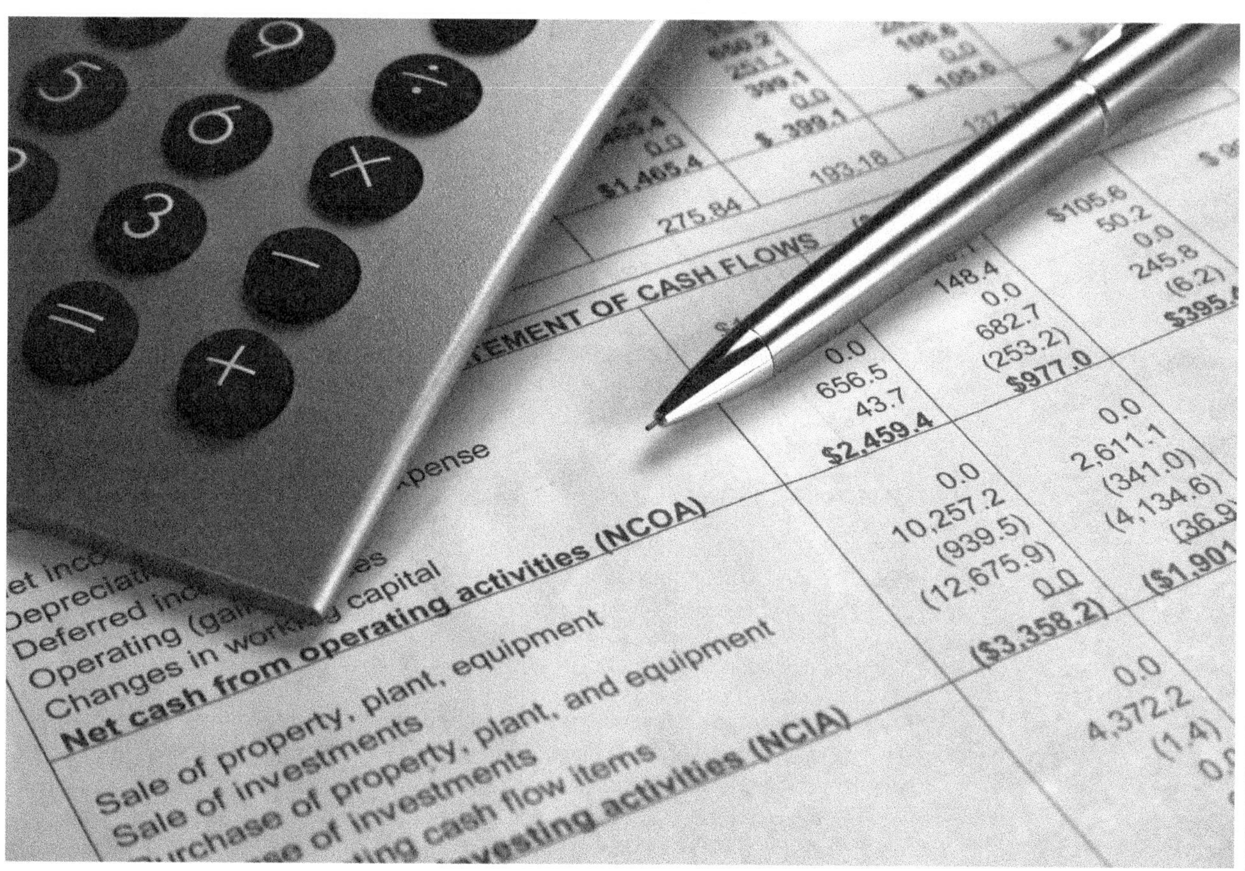

Photo Credit: lvsigns/Getty Images

Financial Statements.

This chapter was written by Andrew Zacharakis.

Financial Statements

Many entrepreneurs are intimidated by numbers, even after they've gone through the business planning process. They understand their concept, and they even have a good sense of the business model, but ask them to put together pro forma financials or read an income statement, and they have a panic attack.

You might feel that building your financials or understanding them isn't that important because you can always hire an accountant. Although an accountant is a useful advisor, in the pre-launch stage, the lead entrepreneur needs to understand the numbers inside and out. After all, the lead entrepreneur is the person who will be articulating her vision to potential employees, vendors, customers, and investors. If the entrepreneur is easily stumped by simple questions of profitability or costs, potential employees, customers, and other parties important to the new venture's success will lose confidence in the lead entrepreneur's ability to execute on the concept. Financial statements serve to bridge the entrepreneur's great idea and what that idea really means in terms of dollars and cents. So, although it can be painful, learn the numbers behind your business. The rewards of gaining this deep insight are often the difference between success and failure.

If for no other reason, the lead entrepreneur needs to understand the numbers so she can decide whether this business has the potential to provide her with a good living. It is too easy to get caught in a trap where a new venture is slowly draining away your investment or where you are working, in real terms, for less than the minimum wage.[1] The goal of this chapter is to give you an introduction to entrepreneurial financial planning. Unlike in existing businesses, which have an operating history, entrepreneurs must develop their financials from scratch. There are no previous trends in revenue and costs that you can use as a basis to project future revenues and costs. Yet the failure to come up with solid projections may cost you your initial investment as well as that of your investors. This chapter will help you generate sound projections.

Common Mistakes

In preparing this chapter, we sent an e-mail to several acquaintances who are professional equity investors (either angels or venture capitalists). We asked them, "What are the most common mistakes you see when you review an entrepreneur's business proposal?" We wanted to know what "red flags" made them hesitant to believe that the business could survive and succeed. Here are the six mistakes they consistently cited.

1. **Not understanding the revenue drivers.** Entrepreneurs need to know what the leverage points are that drive revenues. They need to understand how many customers are likely to see the product, how many of those who see it will buy it, and how much, on average, they will buy each time. Although every entrepreneur claims his estimates are "conservative," 99% of the time entrepreneurs are overly optimistic in their projections. So avoid the "conservative" adjective; it strikes most sophisticated investors as naive.

2. **Underestimating costs.** If you were to graph the revenue and cost projections of entrepreneurs over time, you would often see revenues growing in a "hockey stick" fashion, while costs slowly progress upward (see Figure 9.1). We often see revenue projections of $15 million after five years on costs of only $5 million. That is unbelievable. When we dig into those numbers, we often see that the firm has only five employees in year 5. That assumes revenues per employee of $3 million, which is nearly impossible. Often entrepreneurs underestimate how much infrastructure they need in the way of employees and physical assets to achieve that level of sales. Entrepreneurs also underestimate the cost of marketing expenditures to acquire and retain customers. Poor projections lead to cash crunches and ultimately to failure.

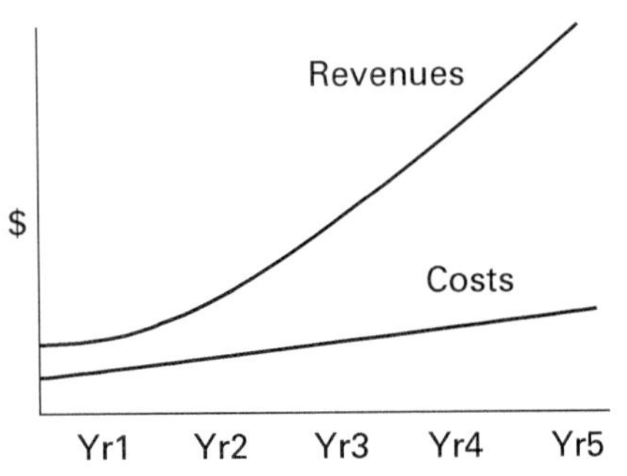

FIGURE 9.1 Hockey Stick Sales Growth.

3. **Underestimating time to generate revenues.** Pro forma financials often show sales occurring immediately. Typically, a business will incur costs for many months before it can generate revenue. For instance, if you are opening a restaurant, you will incur rent, inventory, and labor costs, among others, before you generate a dime in revenue. Another "red flag" is how quickly revenues will ramp up. Often projections show the business at full capacity within the first year. That is rarely realistic.

4. **Lack of comparables.** Investors typically think about the entrepreneur's concept from their knowledge of similar businesses. They will compare your gross margins, net income margins, and other metrics to industry standards and selected benchmark companies. Yet many entrepreneurs' projections have ratios that far exceed industry standards, and when questioned about this above-average performance, they can't explain it. You need to understand your business model in relation to the industry and be able to explain any differences.

5. **Top-down versus bottom-up forecasting.** Investors often hear entrepreneurs claim that their revenues represent 3% of the market after year 3. The implication is that it is easy to get that 3%. Investors know that, although it doesn't sound like much, the trick is how you get to that 3%. They want to see the process—the cost of acquiring, serving, and retaining the customer. Investors won't believe that you can get 3% without causing competitors to take notice and action.

6. **Underestimating time to secure financing.** The last pet peeve of investors is that entrepreneurs assume financing will close quickly. Whether entrepreneurs want to raise $25,000 or $1 million, they project it will happen in the next month. In reality, it often takes as long as six months to close a round of financing. Fred Adler, famed venture capitalist who invested in Data General, used to hand out T-shirts that said, "Happiness is a positive cash flow." Yet, if entrepreneurs are too optimistic about how quickly they can close a round of financing, they will quickly have negative cash flow, which often means they are out of business.

Understanding these pitfalls will help you generate realistic financials and, more important, enable you to convincingly articulate your business model so that you can sell your vision to employees, customers, vendors, and investors. Before we move on, here is a quick overview of financial statements.

Financial Statement Overview

You'll need to master three standard financial statements to properly project and manage your business into the future: the income statement, the statement of cash flows, and the balance sheet. Most people first want to know why there are three statements. The reason is simple: Each one provides a slightly different view of the company. Any one alone is only part of the picture. Together they provide a detailed description of the economics of your company.

The first of these statements, the **income statement**, describes how well a company conducted its business over a recent period of time—typically, a quarter (three months) or a year. This indicator of overall performance begins with the company's revenues on the top line. From that accounting of sales, subtract the company's expenses. These include

- Cost of the products that the company actually sold
- Selling, marketing, and administrative costs
- Depreciation—the estimated cost of using your property, plant, and equipment
- Interest on debts
- Taxes on profits

The bottom line of the statement (literally) is the company's profits—called *net income*. It is important to realize that the income statement represents a measurement of business performance. It is *not* a description of actual flows of money.

A company needs cash to conduct business. Without it, there is no business. The second financial statement, the **statement of cash flows**, monitors this crucial account. As the name implies, the statement of cash flows concerns itself exclusively with transactions that involve cash. It is not uncommon to have strong positive earnings on the income statement and a negative statement of cash flows—less cash at the end of the period than at the beginning. Just because you shipped a product does not necessarily mean you received the cash for it yet. Likewise, you might have purchased something like inventory or a piece of equipment that will not show up on your income statement until it is consumed or depreciated. Many noncash transactions are represented in the income statement.

What is curious (and sometimes confusing to those who have never worked with financial statements before) is the way the statement of cash flows is constructed. It starts with the bottom line (profits) of the income statement and works backward, removing all the noncash transactions. For example, since the income statement subtracted depreciation (the value of using your plant and equipment), the statement of cash flows adds it back in because you don't actually pay any depreciation expense to anybody. Similarly, the cash-flow statement needs to include things that you paid for but did not use that period. For example, you might have paid for inventory that has not yet sold, or you might have bought a piece of equipment that you will depreciate over time, so you would need to put those items on the cash flow statement. After all these adjustments, you are left with a representation of transactions that are exclusively cash.

The **balance sheet** enumerates all the company's assets, liabilities, and shareholder equity. **Assets** are all the things the company has that are expected to generate value over time—things like inventory, buildings, and equipment; accounts receivable (money that your customers still owe you); and cash. **Liabilities** represent all the money the company expects to pay eventually. These include accounts payable (money the company owes its suppliers), debt, and unpaid taxes. **Shareholder equity** is the money that shareholders have paid into the company as well as the company's earnings so far. Where the income statement describes a process or flow, the balance sheet is a snapshot of accounts at a specific point in time.

All your assets come from a liability or shareholder equity. Therefore, the sum of the asset accounts must equal the sum of the liabilities and shareholder equity account.

$$\text{Assets} = \text{Liabilities} + \text{Shareholder Equity}$$

The assets are shown on the left side of the balance sheet, with the liabilities and shareholder equity on the right. The balance sheet *always* balances. If your balance sheet does not balance, you have made a mistake.

This is, of course, only a partial treatment of financial statements, but it should be enough for you to understand this chapter. We strongly recommend reading John and Tage Tracy's excellent book, *How to Read a Financial Report*.[2] It is a simple, short, and easy way for novices to quickly learn the basics. The remainder of this chapter will step you through a process to generate your financials.

Building Your Pro Forma Financial Statements

Figure 9.2 previews the points we will cover. Think of this as a checklist in developing your financials. Rigorously completing each step will lead to better financial projections and decisions. Underlying these steps are two methods: the **build-up method** and the **comparable method**. Our advice is to go through all the steps in an iterative fashion so that you not only know the numbers but also "own the numbers."

Build-Up Method

1. Identify all your sources of revenues
2. Determine your revenues for a "typical day"
3. Understand your revenue drivers
   a. How many customers you will serve
   b. How much product they will buy
   c. How much they will pay for each product
   d. How often they will buy
4. Validate driver assumptions
   a. Primary research (talk to customers, attend trade shows, etc.)
   b. Secondary research (industry reports, company reports, etc.)
5. Recombine. Multiply the typical day by the number of days in a year
6. Determine Cost of Goods Sold (COGS) for a typical day
7. Recombine. Multiply COGS by number of days in a year
8. Determine operating expenses by most appropriate time frame
9. Refine operating costs
10. Create preliminary income statement

Comparable Method

11. Compare revenue projections to industry metrics
12. Run scenario analysis
13. Compare common-sized cost percentages to industry averages

Building Integrated Financial Statements

14. Derive monthly income statements for first two years, yearly statements for years 3–5
15. Create balance sheet (yearly for years 1–5)
16. Create cash-flow statement (monthly for years 1 and 2, yearly for years 3–5)

Final Steps

17. Write a two- to three-page description of financial statements

FIGURE 9.2 Financial Construction Checklist.

Build-Up Method

Scientific findings suggest that people make better decisions by decomposing problems into smaller decisions. If you think about the business planning process, you are going through a series of questions that help you answer the big question: Is this an attractive opportunity? Thus, you evaluate the industry, the competition, the customer, and so forth. Based on that analysis, you decide whether to launch the business. Constructing pro forma financials is part of this process. In the build-up method, you look at the revenue you might generate in a typical day. You then multiple that day times the number of days you're open in a year to come up with your yearly revenue. You then do a similar exercise for costs. Doing your revenues and costs on a daily basis helps you come up with more realistic annual projections.

The place to start is the income statement; the other two statements are in part derived from the income statement. First, identify all your revenue sources (usually the various product offerings).

Second, identify all your costs. Once you have the business broken down into its component parts, the next step is to think about how much revenue you can generate in a year, but we can decompose this estimate as well.

Revenue Projections

Instead of visualizing what you will sell in a month or a year, break it down into a typical day. For example, recall from the last chapter that physical bookstores are on the rise again with folks launching new brick-and-mortar independent stores filling the opportunity created by Amazon's decimation of the large, big box bookstores that were prevalent in the 1990s. If you were starting some form of a retail bookstore, you would estimate how many customers you might serve in a particular day and how much they would spend per visit based on the types of books and ancillary items they would buy. Figure 9.3 illustrates the process for our niche history bookstore. First, it details the product mix and the average price for each item—books, maps, and other ancillary products. Second, it estimates the traffic that the store will draw on a typical day. It lists the assumptions at the bottom of the schedule. Then it estimates how many people will come into the store to buy an item and how many items they will buy. The last column gives total revenue per day by product category.

Figure 9.3 highlights critical revenue assumptions, or what we might call *revenue drivers*. Simply put, going through this exercise tells you how you will make money. It also helps you understand how you might be able to make more money. In other words, what revenue drivers can you influence? A retail shop might be able to increase its daily sales by increasing the traffic coming into the store through advertising or by increasing the number of people who buy and how much they buy through up-selling—"Can I get you anything else today?" Although this thought exercise is invaluable, your estimates are only as good as your assumptions.

How do you strengthen your assumptions? How do you validate the traffic level, the percentage of customers who buy, and so forth? The answer is through research. The first place to start is by talking to people who know the business. Talk to bookstore owners, book vendors, real estate leasing agents, and others in the industry. A good way to interact with these participants is at industry trade shows. The next thing to do is to visit a number of bookstores and count how many people come in, what portion buy, and how much they spend. Although you might feel

Product/Service Description	Price	Units Sold/Day	Total Revenue
1. Books	$20	75 visitors*75%*1.5 books	$1,687.50
2. DVDs	$30	75 visitors*15%*1 DVD	337.50
3. Maps	$50	75 visitors*10%*1 map	375.00
4. Ancillary Items	$100	75 visitors*5%*1 globe	375.00
5. Other (Postcards, Magazines, etc.)	$5	75 visitors*20%*2 items	150.00
Totals			$2,925.00

Assumptions:
Traffic—75 visitors a day

- Books—75% of visitors will buy 1.5 books each
- DVDs—15% of visitors will buy 1 DVD each
- Maps—10% of visitors will buy 1 map each
- Ancillary Items—5% of visitors will buy 1 ancillary item each
- Other—20% of visitors will buy 2 misc. items
- 50% of sales will happen during the holiday season
- 30% of sales will happen during summer tourist season (May through September)

FIGURE 9.3
Revenue Worksheet.

conspicuous, there are ways to do this field research without drawing attention to yourself or interfering in the store's business. For example, you might go sit outside a bookstore and watch how many people who walk by enter the store and how many people come out of the store with a package. Finally, talk to your expected customers—avid readers in this example. Find out how often they buy history books. Ask them how much they spend on these items a month and where they currently buy them. By going through several iterations of primary research, you will sharpen your estimates.

In addition to conducting the research yourself, you can seek out secondary sources such as industry reports and Web sites. For example, there are lots of excellent resources on retail bookstore operations that can be found at the website for the American Booksellers Association (https://www.bookweb.org/) including an entire section of education materials for current and aspiring bookstore owners.[3] The ABA also publishes its annual *ABACUS Survey*, which provides detailed information on all sorts of financial metrics in the industry such as sales data on new and used books and operating costs.

Once you are comfortable that your assumptions are sound, you can then multiply the typical day by the number of days of operation in the year to arrive at yearly revenue estimates. This is a first cut. Clearly, a typical day varies by the time of the year. People do much of their shopping around the December holiday season. Therefore, most pro forma projections for new companies typically show monthly income figures for the first two years. This allows the entrepreneur to manage seasonality and other factors that might make sales uneven for the business.

Cost of Goods Sold

Once you have your revenue projections, you next consider costs. An income statement has two categories of costs—cost of goods sold and operating expenses. **Cost of goods sold (COGS)** is the direct costs of the items sold. For a bookstore, COGS is the cost of inventory that is sold in that period. As a first cut, you might assume that COGS for a retail outlet would be around 50% (assumes a 100% markup). Because sales from Figure 9.3 were approximately $3,000 per day, COGS would be around $1,500.

As with revenue assumptions, you need to sharpen your COGS assumptions. Use a schedule similar to that in Figure 9.3 to refine COGS by product (see Figure 9.4). After some investigation at Google.com/Finance, you find that the gross margin on books is only 22% for Barnes & Noble. On other items you might sell, other companies' gross margins (for TransWorld Entertainment) are around 40%. Although these margins are lower than first estimated, these companies have a different business model—high volume, lower margins. Where will your bookstore operate? If

Product/Service Description	Price	Gross Margin	Revenue	COGS
1. Books	$20	40%	$1,687.50	$1,012.50
2. Videos	$30	50%	337.50	168.75
3. Maps	$50	50%	375.00	187.50
4. Ancillary Items	$100	50%	375.00	187.50
5. Other (Postcards, Magazines, etc.)	$5	50%	150.00	75.00
Totals			$2,925.00	$1,631.25
Total Revenue	$2,925.00			
COGS	1,631.25			
Gross Profit	$1,293.75			
Gross Profit Margin	44%			

FIGURE 9.4
Cost of Goods Worksheet.

it is high volume, your margins should be similar to these companies' margins. If you choose to offer a premium shopping experience, meaning a highly knowledgeable sales staff and unique historical artifacts, you would likely achieve higher margins. Remember that your financials need to mirror the story you related in your business plan—be consistent. Figure 9.4 shows the price per item, the gross margin (revenue minus COGS) per item, and the revenue per item (from Figure 9.3) and then calculates COGS in dollar terms [revenue times (1 – COGS)]. Because the gross margins for items differ, the overall gross margin is 44%.

Operating Expenses

In addition to direct expenses, businesses incur operating expenses, such as marketing, salaries and general administration (SG&A), rent, interest expenses, and so forth. The build-up method forecasts those expenses on a daily, monthly, or yearly basis as appropriate (see Figure 9.5). For example, you might get rental space for your store at $30 per square foot per year depending on location. You might need about 3,000 square feet, so your yearly rent would be $90,000 (put in the yearly expense column). You'll pay your rent on a monthly basis, so you would show a rent expense of $7,500 in the month-to-month income statement. At this point, however, you are just trying to get a sense of the overall business model and gauge whether this business can be profitable; showing it on a yearly basis is sufficient.

Based on the first cut, your bookstore is projecting operating expenses of approximately $315,000 per year. However, the "devil is in the details," as they say, and one problem area

Expense	Daily	Monthly	Yearly	Total
Store Rent			90,000	$90,000
Manager Salary			60,000	$60,000
Assistant Manager			40,000	$40,000
Hourly Employees	176			$63,360
Benefits	21		12,000	$19,603
Bank Charges			10,530	$10,530
Marketing/Advertising		1,000		$12,000
Utilities		333		$4,000
Travel			1,000	$1,000
Dues			1,000	$1,000
Depreciation		833		$10,000
Misc.			4,000	$4,000
				$0
Totals				$315,493

Assumptions:

- Rent—3,000 sq. ft. at $30/sq. ft. = $90,000
- Hire 1 manager at $60,000/year
- Hire 1 assistant manager at $40,000/year
- Store is open from 9 a.m. to 7 p.m. daily, so 10 hours per day Need 2 clerks when open and 1 clerk an hour before and after open 2 clerks × 10 hours × $8/hour + 1 clerk × 2 hours × $8/hour Benefits are 12% of wages and salaries
- Bank charges about 1% of sales Advertising—$1,000/ month Travel—$1,000/year to attend trade shows Dues—$1,000/year for trade association
- Depreciation—$100,000 of leasehold improvements and equipment, depreciated over 10 years using the straight-line method

FIGURE 9.5 **Operating Expenses Worksheet.**

is accurately projecting operating costs, especially labor costs. Constructing a headcount schedule is an important step in refining your labor projections (see Figure 9.6). Although the store is open on average 10 hours per day, you can see from the headcount table that Sunday is a shorter day and that the store is open 11 hours on the other days. The store operates with a minimum of two employees at all times (including either the store manager or the assistant store manager). During busier shifts, the number of employees reaches a peak of six people (afternoon shift on Saturday, including both managers). Looking at the calculation below the table, you see that the new wage expense is about $66,000, a bit higher than the first estimate. This process of examining and reexamining your assumptions over and over is what leads to compelling financials.

Just as you refine the hourly wage expense, you need to also refine other expenses. For example, marketing expenses are projected to be $12,000. Create a detailed schedule of how you plan on spending those advertising dollars. If you refer back to the last chapter, Figure 8.7a has a schedule of detailed expenses. This illustrates another point: *Financial analysis is really just the mathematical expression of your overall business strategy*. Everything you write about in your business plan has revenue or cost implications. As investors view pitch decks and read executive summaries and business plans, they build a mental picture of the financial statements, especially the income statement. If the written plan and the financials are

	Mon.	Tues.	Wed.	Thurs.	Fri.	Sat.	Sun.	Total
Store Hours	10:00 – 9:00	10:00 – 9:00	10:00 – 9:00	10:00 – 9:00	10:00 – 9:00	11:00 – 5:00		
Hours Open	11	11	11	11	11	11	6	72
Shift 1	9:30 – 1:30	9:30 – 1:30	9:30 – 1:30	9:30 – 1:30	9:30 – 1:30	9:30 – 1:30	10.00 – 2:00	
Shift 2	1:30 – 5.30	1:30 – 5.30	1:30 – 5.30	1:30 – 5.30	1:30 – 5.30	1:30 – 5.30	1:00 – 5:00	
Shift 3	5:30 – 9:30	5:30 – 9:30	5:30 – 9:30	5:30 – 9:30	5:30 – 9:30	5:30 – 9:30		
Shift 1 Hrs.	4	4	4	4	4	4	4	
Shift 2 Hrs.	4	4	4	4	4	4	4	
Shift 3 Hrs.	4	4	4	4	4	4	0	
Total Shift Hours	12	12	12	12	12	12	8	80
Staff Headcount								
Shift 1	2	2	1	2	1	4	3	
Shift 2	1	1	0	1	1	4	4	
Shift 3	1	1	1	2	4	4	0	
Total Staff	4	4	2	5	6	12	7	40
Shift 1	8	8	4	8	4	16	12	
Shift 2	4	4	0	4	4	16	16	
Shift 3	4	4	4	8	16	16	0	
	16	16	8	20	24	48	28	160
Mgr.	0	0	8	8	8	8	8	40
Asst. Mgr.	8	8	8	0	8	8	0	40

Total hourly employee hours/week = 160	
Hourly rate $8/hour	8
Total wages per week	$1,280
Total wages per year	$66,560

FIGURE 9.6 Headcount Table.

tightly correlated, investors have much greater confidence that the entrepreneur knows what she is doing.

Preliminary Income Statement

Once you have forecasted revenues and expenses, you put them together in an income statement (Figure 9.7). Figure 9.3 forecasted average daily sales of almost $3,000. You need to annualize that figure. You can expect the store to be open, on average, 360 days per year (assuming that the store might be closed for a few days such as Christmas and Thanksgiving). Note that the first line is called Total Revenues and then shows the detail that creates that total revenues line by itemizing the different revenue categories. COGS is handled in the same manner as revenues; you multiply the typical day by 360 days to get the annual total.

After adjusting the hourly wages per the headcount table (which also means adjusting employee benefits), take the operating expenses worksheet (see Figure 9.5) and put it into the income statement. If you believe that you can secure debt financing, put in an interest expense. However, for the initial forecasts, you may not yet know how much debt financing you'll need or can secure to launch the business, so leave out the interest expense until you derive a reasonable estimate. Next compute taxes. Make sure to account for federal, state, and city taxes as applicable. Note that the right column calculates the expense percentage of total revenues. This is called a *common-sized income statement*. Although you have been rigorous in building up your statement, you can further validate it by comparing your common-sized income statement to the industry standards, which is where you start using the comparable method.

Total Revenues	**$1,053,000**	**100%**
Historical Books	607,500	
Videos	121,500	
Maps	135,000	
Ancillary Items	135,000	
Other	54,000	
Total COGS	**$587,250**	**55.8%**
Historical Books	364,500	
Videos	60,750	
Maps	67,500	
Ancillary Items	67,500	
Other	27,000	
Gross Profit	**$465,750**	**44.2%**
Operating Expenses	90,000	
Store Rent		
Manager Salary	60,000	
Assistant Manager	40,000	
Hourly Employees	66,560	
Benefits	19,987	
Bank Charges	10,530	
Marketing/Advertising	12,000	
Utilities	4,000	
Travel	1,000	
Dues	1,000	
Depreciation	10,000	
Misc.	4,000	
Total Operating Expenses	**$319,077**	**30.3%**
Earnings from Operations	**$146,673**	**13.9%**
Taxes	**$58,669**	**5.6%**
Net Earnings	**$88,004**	**8.4%**

FIGURE 9.7 Income Statement.

Comparable Method

How can you tell whether your projections are reasonable? In the **comparable method**, you look at how your company compares to industry averages and benchmark companies. The first thing to do is gauge whether your revenue projections make sense and then see whether your cost structure is reasonable. Comparables help you validate your projections. For instance, a good metric for revenue in retail is sales per square foot. The bookstore is projecting sales of $1 million in 3,000 square feet, which equates to $351 per square foot. Secondary research into the average per bookstore[4] and also into what one or two specific bookstores achieve is a good place to start.[5] For example, $351 is in line with independent bookstores ($350/square foot) but higher than Barnes & Noble ($247/square foot[6]).

The projections seem reasonable considering that you will be selling certain items like maps, which have a much higher ticket price than books, but there are a couple of caveats to this estimate. First, it is likely to take a new bookstore some time to achieve this level of sales. In other words, the income statement that has been derived might be more appropriate for the second or third year of operation. At that point, the bookstore will have built up a clientele and achieved some name recognition.

Second, you should run some scenario analyses. Does this business model still work if your bookstore only achieves Barnes & Noble's sales per square foot ($247)? Also run a few other scenarios related to higher foot traffic, recession, outbreak of war (sales of books on Islam increased with the rise of ISIS and escalating tensions in the Middle East), and other contingencies. Having some validated metrics, such as sales per square foot, helps you run different scenarios and make sound decisions about whether to launch a venture in the first place and then about how to adjust your business model so that the venture has the greatest potential to succeed.

Other metrics that are easily obtainable for this type of establishment include *sales per customer* or *average ticket price*. Figure 9.3 shows expected sales of $2,925 per day from 75 unique store visitors. That translates into an average transaction per visitor of $39. However, not every visitor will buy; many people will just come in and browse. Figure 9.3 assumed that 75% of visitors would buy a book and a lower percentage would buy other items. If that percentage holds true, 56 people will actually purchase something each day. Thus, the average receipt is $52. This average ticket price is considerably higher than Barnes & Noble's rate of $27.

As with all your assumptions, you have to gauge whether a higher ticket price is reasonable. An entrepreneur might reason that the bookstore isn't discounting its books and is also selling higher-priced ancillary goods. Run scenario analyses again to see whether your bookstore survives if its average ticket price is closer to Barnes & Noble's. In other words, see what happens to the model overall when you change one of the assumptions—in this case, the average selling price.

After you're comfortable with the revenue estimate, you next need to validate the costs. The best way is to compare your common-sized income statement with the industry averages or some benchmark companies. It is unlikely that your income statement will exactly match the industry averages, but you need to be able to explain and understand the differences. Figure 9.8 looks at the common-sized income statements for your store and for Barnes & Noble. The first discrepancy appears in the COGS. Your store projects a COGS of 56% of revenue, whereas Barnes & Noble is projecting 71%. Why would Barnes & Noble's COGS be so much higher? On further investigation, you find that Barnes & Noble includes occupancy costs like rent and utilities in their COGS. If you add your store's $90,000 rent plus $4,000 in utilities into COGS, COGS becomes 65% of revenue, which is still lower than Barnes & Noble's. However, a COGS of 65% is in line with the specialty retail industry rate of 62%.[7] The reasoning for this discrepancy is similar to that for the higher ticket price. Your specialty bookstore's COGS is likely lower than Barnes & Noble's because it is not a discount bookseller (meaning it earns higher margins on every book sold than does Barnes & Noble). You also plan to sell other retail items that generate higher margins.

Because the gross profit margin is the inverse of COGS—revenue minus COGS—the explanation provided for COGS also holds for the gross margin. Barnes & Noble's gross margin is 29% versus 35% for your specialty bookstore (with rent included in COGS).

When you compare operating expenses for the two companies, you can see that your bookstore is projecting operating expenses to be 30% of revenue versus 29% for Barnes & Noble. However, we must once again adjust for the occupancy expense because you include occupancy in operating expenses, whereas Barnes & Noble includes it in COGS. With that adjustment, your operating expenses are about 21% of revenue, somewhat less than Barnes & Noble. We would want to investigate to see if we are underestimating the number of employees we will need. Or whether we paying lower rent because we aren't in a high-profile location. The key is to determine if lower costs are reasonable or not.

Based on the comparable analysis, it appears that your projections are reasonable. Your earnings from operations are higher (13.9%) than Barnes & Noble's (0.5%) and the independent book

	Our Specialty Bookstore		Barnes & Noble (FY2014) (in millions)		Industry Average
Total Revenues	**$1,053,000**	**100%**	**$6,381**	**100%**	**100%**
Historical Books	607,500				
Videos	121,500				
Maps	135,000				
Globes	135,000				
Other	54,000				
Total COGS	**$587,250**	**55.8%**	**$4,523**	**70.9%**	**62.2%**
Historical Books	364,500				
Videos	160,750				
Maps	67,500				
Globes	67,500				
Other	27,000				
Gross Profit	**$465,750**	**44.2%**	**$1,858**	**29.1%**	**37.8%**
Operating Expenses	90,000				
Store rent					
Manager Salary	60,000				
Assistant Manager	40,000				
Hourly Employees	66,560				
Benefits	19,987				
Bank Charges	10,530				
Marketing/Advertising	12,000				
Utilities	4,000				
Travel	1,000				
Dues	1,000				
Depreciation	10,000				
Misc	4,000				
Total Operating	**$319,077**	**30.3%**	**$1,824**	**28.6%**	**33.9%**
Expenses Earnings from	**$146,673**	**13.9%**	**$34.2**	**0.54%**	**3.9%**
Operations Taxes and others*	**$58,669**		**$81**		
Net Earnings	**$88,004**	**8.4%**	**$(47)**	**–0.74%**	

FIGURE 9.8
Comparable Analysis.

store average (3.9%), but that may be explained by the higher gross margins and the fact that you haven't yet included any interest expenses. For example, if you use debt financing for any of your startup expenses, such as leasehold improvements, you will have an interest expense that would reduce your net income margin to be more in line with the comparable companies.

This exercise has primarily used benchmark companies, but industry averages also provide useful comparable information. Bizminer.com is an excellent source to use as a starting point in building financial statements relevant to your industry. Specifically, Bizminer and other sources help entrepreneurs build income statements by providing industry averages for cost of goods sold, salary expenses, interest expenses, and other costs. Again, your firm will differ from these industry averages, but by going through scenario analyses and understanding your business model, you should be able to explain why your firm differs.

Building Integrated Financial Statements

Once you have a baseline income statement, the next step is to construct monthly income and cash-flow statements for two years (followed by years 3 through 5 on a yearly basis) and a yearly balance sheet for all five years. Five years is standard because it usually takes new firms some time to build sales and operate efficiently. Five years also gives the entrepreneur a sense of whether her investment of time and energy will pay off. Can the business not only survive but also provide the kind of financial return to make the opportunity costs of leaving an existing job worthwhile?

The income statement, cash-flow statement, and balance sheet are the core statements for managing any business. Changes in one statement affect all others. Understanding how these changes affect your business can mean the difference between survival and failure. Many entrepreneurs will find their businesses on the verge of failure, even if they are profitable, because they fail to understand how the income statement is related to the cash-flow statement and balance sheet. How is that possible, you might ask?

Entrepreneurs need to finance rapid growth. For example, a bookstore needs to buy inventory in advance of selling to its customers. The owner needs to ensure that he has enough books and other products on hand so that he doesn't lose a sale because a customer is frustrated that the book isn't in stock. (Americans are notorious for wanting instant gratification.) Yet having inventory on hand drains cash. If the bookstore expects sales of $500,000 in December, then it must have $280,000 worth of inventory at the end of November ($500,000 × 56%—the average COGS). How does the bookstore pay for this? Internal cash flow? Vendor financing? Equity? Having strong pro forma financials helps the entrepreneur anticipate these needs far enough in advance to arrange the appropriate financing.

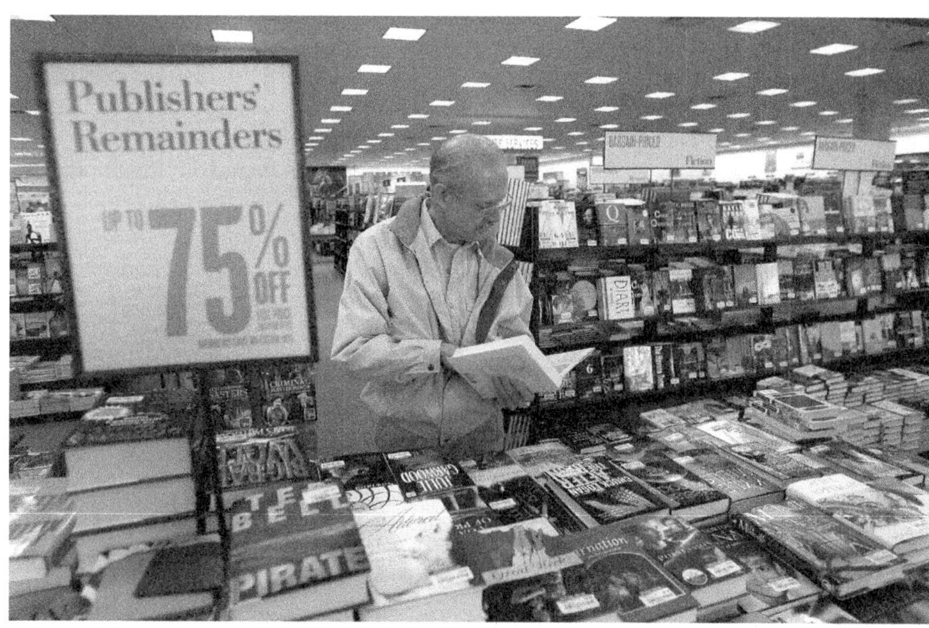

Photo Credit: Tim Boyle/Getty Images

Tom Iverson shops for sale books at a Barnes & Noble book store in Arlington Heights, Illinois.

The bookstore example illustrates why a new business wants to show the income and cash-flow statements on a monthly basis for the first two years; there are likely to be seasonal fluctuations in demand for which you need to anticipate and plan. Moreover, the first two years are the most vulnerable period in a new venture's life. It takes time to build up your clientele (during which you earn lower revenues), learn how to efficiently operate (during which you have higher costs), develop a track record so you can secure vendor financing (remember the cash-flow implications), and understand seasonality (which will make demand vary). For instance, monthly projections allow the entrepreneur to anticipate and understand any seasonality that might happen in the business. In addition to the financing issue discussed previously, seasonality affects other key operations and decisions. For example, your bookstore will need to hire more salespeople during the holiday season. Integrated financials can help the entrepreneur plan for that hiring increase.

In sum, it is critical to show the first two years of pro forma projections on a monthly basis because this is when a company is most vulnerable to failure. Monthly forecasts help you understand these issues and prepare for them. For years 3 through 5, yearly projections are sufficient because the further out one goes, the less accurate the projections become. Nevertheless, your longer-term projections communicate your vision of the upside potential of your opportunity. The exercise of going through the projection process is more important than the accuracy of the projections. The process helps you gain a deeper understanding of the business and whether you should pursue the opportunity.

As the bookstore example indicates, changes in one statement affect other statements. Figure 9.9 formally shows how the pro forma financials are integrated. You can see that the income statement drives the balance sheet, which drives the cash-flow statement (although the cash from financing and uses of cash from the cash-flow statement feed back into the balance sheet). We'll briefly touch on how to move from our base income statement to a full set of pro forma financial projections, but going into a step-by-step process is beyond the scope of this chapter.

Income Statement

The base income statement generated shows the level of operations that might be achievable in year 3 or 4. Thus, you need to make a number of adjustments to generate the other years. First, you need to create monthly statements for the first two years. That means you need to understand the seasonality of your business and the sales cycle. One mistake that many entrepreneurs make is showing revenues from the first day they launch the business. Remember that most new businesses incur expenses well in advance of generating revenue. In thinking about the bookstore, you would consider the business launched soon after the first round of financing has closed. At this point, the entrepreneur can start spending money to establish the business. For instance, he might sign a lease, contract for equipment, and so forth. Show those expenses as incurred. Thus, show expenses for three months (the time to build out the store before opening) before you show your first revenue.

The next consideration in generating your monthly forecasts is seasonality. Revenues in retail are not evenly spread across the 12 months. Figure 9.10 estimates how sales might be spread for a retail operation. The make-or-break time is the holiday season, and you see sales jumping dramatically in November and December. Another important spike might be the tourist season (if you were to locate your store in Boston, demand might jump if you focused on Revolutionary War and colonial goods). Based on these projections, it makes sense to lease and build out the retail space in the January to March time frame when sales levels are expected to be low.

Another consideration is how long it will take your new business to build its clientele and ramp up its revenues. You are projecting sales of $350 per square foot once you hit your optimal operating position. In the first year of operation, that number might be significantly lower—say, $200 per square foot, which is well below the Barnes & Noble average of $247 and the independent bookstore average of $350. In year 2, a reasonable estimate might be that average sales per square foot hit $250, and finally in year 3, you might hit the independent bookstore average of $350. And as you've seen, the business is not generating sales for the first

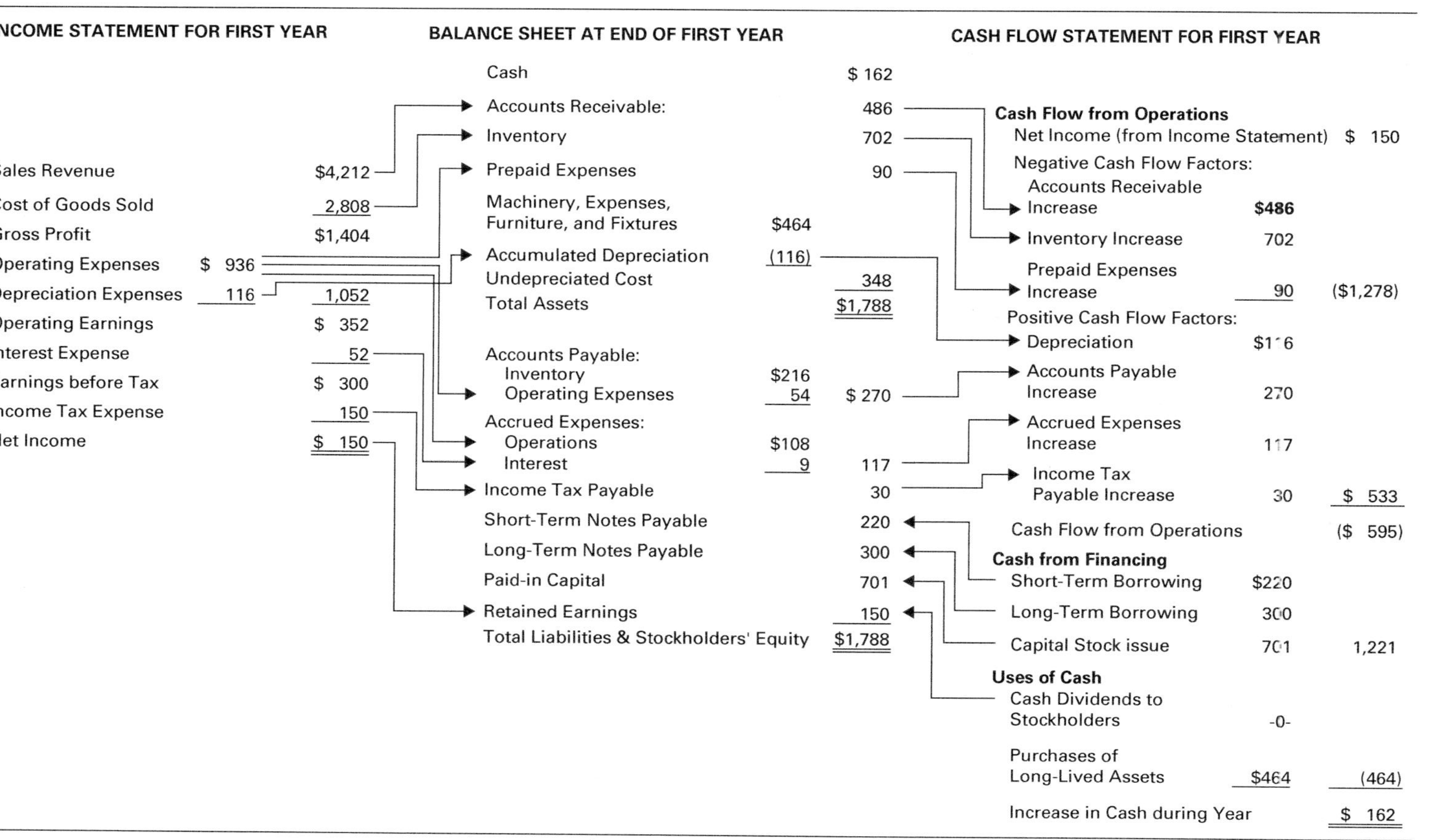
EXHIBIT D-MASTER EXHIBIT
(Dollar amounts in thousands)

INCOME STATEMENT FOR FIRST YEAR

Sales Revenue		$4,212
Cost of Goods Sold		2,808
Gross Profit		$1,404
Operating Expenses	$ 936	
Depreciation Expenses	116	1,052
Operating Earnings		$ 352
Interest Expense		52
Earnings before Tax		$ 300
Income Tax Expense		150
Net Income		$ 150

BALANCE SHEET AT END OF FIRST YEAR

Cash		$ 162
Accounts Receivable:		486
Inventory		702
Prepaid Expenses		90
Machinery, Expenses, Furniture, and Fixtures	$464	
Accumulated Depreciation	(116)	
Undepreciated Cost		348
Total Assets		$1,788
Accounts Payable:		
Inventory	$216	
Operating Expenses	54	$ 270
Accrued Expenses:		
Operations	$108	
Interest	9	117
Income Tax Payable		30
Short-Term Notes Payable		220
Long-Term Notes Payable		300
Paid-in Capital		701
Retained Earnings		150
Total Liabilities & Stockholders' Equity		$1,788

CASH FLOW STATEMENT FOR FIRST YEAR

Cash Flow from Operations		
Net Income (from Income Statement)		$ 150
Negative Cash Flow Factors:		
Accounts Receivable Increase	**$486**	
Inventory Increase	702	
Prepaid Expenses Increase	90	($1,278)
Positive Cash Flow Factors:		
Depreciation	$116	
Accounts Payable Increase	270	
Accrued Expenses Increase	117	
Income Tax Payable Increase	30	$ 533
Cash Flow from Operations		($ 595)
Cash from Financing		
Short-Term Borrowing	$220	
Long-Term Borrowing	300	
Capital Stock issue	701	1,221
Uses of Cash		
Cash Dividends to Stockholders	-0-	
Purchases of Long-Lived Assets	$464	(464)
Increase in Cash during Year		$ 162

Source: Reprint of Exhibit D from *How to Read a Financial Report*, Second Edition, by John Tracy. New York: John Wiley & Sons, 1983.

FIGURE 9.9 Interrelated Financial Statements.

	(000)												
	Jan. 3%	Feb. 2%	Mar. 3%	Apr. 4%	May 6%	June 7%	July 9%	Aug. 8%	Sept. 5%	Oct. 3%	Nov. 10%	Dec. 40%	Year 100%
Year 1				$24.0	$36.0	$42.0	$54.0	$48.0	$30.0	$18.0	$60.0	$240.0	$552.0
Year 2	$22.5	$15.0	$22.5	$30.0	$45.0	$52.5	$67.5	$60.0	$37.5	$22.5	$75.0	$300.0	$750.0
Year 3	$31.5	$21.0	$31.5	$42.0	$63.0	$73.5	$94.5	$84.0	$52.5	$31.5	$105.0	$420.0	$1,050.0

FIGURE 9.10 Seasonality Projections.

three months of year 1 due to the time it takes to build out the store, so you need to adjust the sales accordingly.

Balance Sheet

The *balance sheet* can be the most difficult to integrate into your other financial statements. For pro forma projections, yearly balance sheets are sufficient. Again, going into great detail is beyond the scope of this chapter, but there are a few items that often cause confusion.

First, will your business sell on credit? If so, it will record accounts receivable. Figure 9.9 shows how your sales from the income statement drive your accounts receivable on the balance sheet (some portion of those sales), which then drive an accounts receivable increase on the cash-flow statement. Although you record the sale when the customer takes possession, you may not actually receive payment until some point in the future. Recording the sale has a positive impact on your profitability but does not affect your cash flow until the customer actually pays. If your business is buying equipment, land, or a plant or is adding leasehold improvements, you will have an asset of plant and equipment. A common error is to show this as a capital expense, meaning that it appears in full on your income statement the moment you contract for the work. This assumes you will fully use that equipment within the year (or whatever length your income statement covers). To accurately reflect the acquisition of the asset, instead show the full outflow of money as it occurs on your cash-flow statement and then depreciate the cost per year of life of the asset on your income statement. You would also have an accumulated depreciation line item on your balance sheet showing how much of the asset has been used up. Referring back to Figure 9.5, you see the bookstore is projecting leasehold improvements of $100,000, which it expects to use up over 10 years ($10,000 per year or $833 per month).

Accounts payable acts in a manner similar to accounts receivable, except that it is a loan to your company from a supplier (see Figure 9.9). Once the new store is able to secure vendor financing on inventory, for example, it will show the COGS as it sells its books, but it may not have to pay the publisher until later (assuming that the book is a fairly fast-moving item). So the expense would show up on your income statement but not on your cash-flow statement—until you paid for it. Until then, it is held in accounts payable on the balance sheet.

The final problem area is retained earnings. Entrepreneurs know that the balance sheet should *balance*. A common error is to use the retained earnings line to make the balance sheet balance. Retained earnings is actually

Previous Retained Earnings + Current Period Net Income − Dividends Paid during the Current Period

If you find that your balance sheet isn't balancing, the problem is often in how you have calculated accounts receivable or accounts payable. Balancing the balance sheet is the most frustrating aspect of building your pro forma financial statements. Yet hardwiring the retained earnings will ultimately lead to other errors, so work through the balancing problem as diligently as possible.

Cash-Flow Statement

If you have constructed your financial statements accurately, the **cash-flow statement** identifies when and how much financing you need. You might want to leave the financing assumptions empty until after you see how much the cash-flow statement implies you need (see Figure 9.11). One of the many benefits of this process is that it will help you determine exactly how much you need to protect you from giving up too much equity or acquiring too much (or not enough) debt. The bookstore cash-flow statement shows some major outlays as the store is gearing up for operation, such as inventory acquisition and equipment purchases. You can also see from the cash-flow statement that the business is incurring some expenses prior to generating revenue [($17,000) listed as net earnings]. This net earnings loss is reflected on the company's monthly income statement and is primarily attributable to wage expenses to hire and train staff.

You can see that in the first six months, the cash position hits a low of just over –$316,000. This is how much money you need to raise to launch the business. For a new venture, most of the money will likely be in the form of equity from the entrepreneur, friends, and family. However, the entrepreneur may be able to secure some debt financing against his equipment (which would

	Month 1	Month 2	Month 3	Month 4	Month 5	Month 6
OPERATING ACTIVITIES						
Net Earnings	(17,000)	(12,882)	(2,244)	(7,079)	(1,277)	8,394
Depreciation	1,115	1,115	1,115	1,115	1,115	1,115
Working Capital Changes						
(Increase)/Decrease Accounts Receivable	0	(64)	(88)	40	(48)	(80)
(Increase)/Decrease Inventories	(104,562)	(19,605)	32,676	(39,211)	(65,351)	71,886
(Increase)/Decrease Other Current Assets	0	(230)	(316)	144	(172)	(287)
Increase/(Decrease) Accts Pay & Accrd Expenses	0	3,215	4,421	(2,010)	2,411	4,019
Increase/(Decrease) Other Current Liab	0	3,445	4,737	(2,153)	2,584	4,306
Net Cash Provided/(Used) by Operating Activities	(120,446)	(25,005)	40,301	(49,154)	(60,737)	89,354
INVESTING ACTIVITIES						
Property & Equipment	(101,000)	0	0	0	0	0
Other Net Cash Used in Investing Activities	(101,000)	0	0	0	0	0
FINANCING ACTIVITIES						
Increase/(Decrease) Short-Term Debt						0
Increase/(Decrease) Curr. Portion LTD						0
Increase/(Decrease) Long-Term Debt						0
Increase/(Decrease) Common Stock						0
Increase/(Decrease) Preferred Stock						0
Dividends Declared						0
Net Cash Provided/(Used) by Financing	0	0	0	0	0	0
INCREASE/(DECREASE) IN CASH	(221,446)	(25,005)	40,301	(49,154)	(60,737)	89,354
CASH AT BEGINNING OF PERIOD	0	(221,446)	(246,451)	(206,150)	(255,304)	(316,041)
CASH AT END OF PERIOD	(221,446)	(246,451)	(206,150)	(255,304)	(316,041)	(226,687)

FIGURE 9.11 Cash-flow Statement.

act as collateral if the business should fail). In any event, once you recognize your financing needs, you can devise a strategy to raise the money necessary to start the business. To provide some buffer against poor estimates, you might raise $350,000. This amount would show up on both the cash-flow statement and the balance sheet.

Putting It All Together

Once you have completed the financial spreadsheets, write a two- to three-page explanation to precede them. Although you understand all the assumptions and comparables that went into building the financial forecast, the reader needs the background spelled out. Describing the financials is also a good exercise in articulation. If your reader understands the financials and believes the assumptions are valid, you have passed an important test. If not, work with the reader to understand her concerns. Continual iterations strengthen your financials and should give you further confidence in the viability of your business model.

This section of the business plan should include a description of the key drivers that affect your revenues and costs so that the reader can follow your pro forma financials. This description is typically broken down into four main sections. First, the "overview" paragraph briefly introduces the business model.

The first subsection should discuss the income statement. Talk about the factors that drive revenue, such as store traffic, percentage of store visitors that buy, average ticket price, and so forth. It is also important to talk about seasonality and other factors that might cause uneven sales growth. Then discuss the expense categories, paying attention to the cost of goods sold and major operating expense categories, such as rent, interest expense, and so forth. Based on your description, the reader should be able to look at the actual financials and understand what is going on. The key focus here is to help the reader follow your financials; you don't need to provide the level of detail that an accountant might if he were auditing your company. The next subsection should discuss the cash-flow statement. Here, you focus on major infusions of cash, such as equity investments and loan disbursements. It is also good to describe the nature of your accounts receivable and accounts payable. How long, for instance, before your receivables convert to cash? If you are spending money on leasehold improvements, plant and equipment, and other items that can be depreciated, you should mention them here. Typically, the discussion of the cash-flow statement is quite a bit shorter than the discussion of the income statement.

The final subsection discusses the balance sheet. Here, you would talk about major asset categories, such as the amount of inventory on hand and any liabilities that aren't clear from the previous discussion.

CONCLUSION

Going through these exercises allows you to construct a realistic set of pro forma financials. It's a challenge, but understanding your numbers "cold" enables you to articulate your business to all stakeholders, so you can build momentum toward the ultimate launch of your business. Just as we said in the previous chapter that the business plan is a living document, so, too, are the financial statements a set of living documents. They are obsolete immediately after they come off the printer. As you start your launch process, you can further refine your numbers, putting in actual revenues and expenses as they occur and adjusting projections based on current activity. Once the business is operating, the nature of your financial statements changes. They not only help you to assess the viability of your business model but also help you to gauge actual performance and adjust your operations based on that experience.

Although most entrepreneurs tell us that drafting the financials induces some pain, they also concede that going through the process is gratifying and rewarding. They learn to master new management skills, build their business, and protect their investment. So dig in.

YOUR OPPORTUNITY JOURNAL

Reflection Point	Your Thoughts...
1. What are your revenue sources? How can you influence these revenues (what are your drivers)?	
2. Identify some companies that you can benchmark. What are their revenue sources? How do they drive revenue?	
3. Refine your projections. Who can you talk to that is knowledgeable about your business (customers, vendors, competitors)? What secondary sources can you find (BizMiner.com, Google.com/finance)?	
4. Compare your common-sized financials to those of your benchmark company. Can you validate or explain differences between you and the benchmark company?	
5. Are there other metrics you can use (sales per employee or sales per square foot) to verify your projections?	
6. What happens to the viability of your business when you run some scenario analyses based on the different metrics you've identified?	

WEB EXERCISE

Look for some comparison metrics (the *Bizminer* site www.bizminer.com is useful, but see if you can find others). How do your sales per employee figures match the benchmark reports?

How does your pro forma balance sheet match up to some of the presented ratios? Can you explain any differences?

NOTES

1. By minimum wage, we mean that the money the entrepreneur can take out of the business is less on an hourly basis than the minimum wage.
2. Tracy, John & Tracy, Tage. *How to Read a Financial Report: Wringing Vital Signs Out of the Numbers*. Eighth edition. Hoboken, NJ: John Wiley & Sons, Inc. 2014.
3. https://www.bookweb.org/education?field_education_tags_tid%5B%5D=547
4. 1999 ABACUS Financial Survey. Annual Survey conducted by the American Book-sellers Association. http://bookweb.org.
5. Look for publicly traded companies on your favorite database, such as http://SEC.gov.
6. Barnes & Noble retail sales divided by total square footage of retail stores, Barnes & Noble 214 Annual Report, pp. 5 and 10.
7. http://bizstats.com/corporation-industry-financials/retail-trade-44/sporting-goods-hobby-book-music-stores-451/show.

Case | Gravyty: Understanding Your Market and Building Realistic Proformas[1]

Basis of Presentations

This plan contains 18 months of projections. While we believe that the assumptions underlying the projections are reasonable, there can be no assurance that these results can be realized, the nature of the underlying assumption will stay the same, or that actual results will meet expectations.

Top-Down vs. Bottom-Up Financials

Gravyty believes that "bottom-up" financial analysis is the best approach to business planning. This is in contrast to "top-down" analysis, which states the percentage of a given total addressable market (TAM) an entrepreneur thinks can be captured. Bottom up financials allow us to think client-by-client, month-by-month about the strategies and personnel necessary to build the business.

Nonprofits in the United States are required to file a Form 990 with the Internal Revenue Service (IRS) in order to maintain their status. Within the Form 990, is a National Taxonomy of Exempt Entities (NTEE) code, which is used by the IRS to classify these organizations into 24 different groups. Management has chosen to focus initially on those segments in the chart below for their bottom up approach based on size of the market, access to early adopters, and the initial perceived need based on the value proposition.

		Estimated Organizations				
		50%	*40%*	*10%*	Based on Average	Distributed
Number of Organizations Filing Form 990	**# of NPOs**	**Small**	**Medium**	**Large**	**Technology Spend**	**Technology Spend**
Philanthropy, Voluntarism & Grantmaking Foundations	89,194	44,597	35,678	8,919	$ 10,207,628,942	$ 8,676,484,600.70
Education	80,065	40,033	32,026	8,007	$ 9,162,878,795	$ 7,788,446,976
Recreation & Sports	49,765	24,883	19,906	4,977	$ 5,695,255,895	$ 4,840,967,511
Community Improvement & Capacity Building	49,132	24,566	19,653	4,913	$ 5,622,813,476	$ 4,779,391,455
Human Services	46,843	23,422	18,737	4,684	$ 5,360,853,449	$ 4,556,725,432
Arts, Culture & Humanities	45,409	22,705	18,164	4,541	$ 5,196,742,187	$ 4,417,230,859
Religion-Related	30,554	15,277	12,222	3,055	$ 3,496,691,422	$ 2,972,187,709
Health Care	27,422	13,711	10,969	2,742	$ 3,138,255,946	$ 2,667,517,554
Housing & Shelter	21,852	10,926	8,741	2,185	$ 2,500,808,436	$ 2,125,687,171
Public & Societal Benefit	20,410	10,205	8,164	2,041	$ 2,335,781,630	$ 1,985,414,386
Mutual & Membership Benefit	19,691	9,846	7,876	1,969	$ 2,253,497,113	$ 1,915,472,546
Employment	16,902	8,451	6,761	1,690	$ 1,934,315,586	$ 1,644,168,248

Customer Acquisition

Given the high touch nature of the business, we chose to control early growth to maximize learning over revenue. Given our domain expertise, we had several existing connections to organizations who would be beta testers and potential early clients. However, we decided that we would only believe we were onto something when the first "stranger" bought for "full price." This means a customer would buy their services based on the merits of the value proposition and realization, rather than as a favor.

When thinking about customer acquisition, we want to plan carefully around personnel numbers. Since our intention is to raise outside capital for the business, we tested for a breaking point. Could a customer success manager handle 25, 50, 75, or 100+ customers before quality or morale is impacted? We also believe that after an early investment in R&D, the business would scale based on an inside and outside sales team.

[1] This case was written by Rich Palmer and Andrew Corbett.

High Level Assumptions				
Monthly	**Year 1**	**Year 2**	**Year 3**	**Year 4**
Acquisition Growth Rate (20% Reduction)	20%	16%	13%	10%
Churn Rate (20% Increase)	1%	1%	1%	2%

Paying Customers Aquired by NPO Type																			Annual & Semi-Annual		
Organizations	**Jan-16**	**Feb-16**	**Mar-16**	**Apr-16**	**May-16**	**Jun-16**	**Jul-16**	**Aug-16**	**Sep-16**	**Oct-16**	**Nov-16**	**Dec-16**	**Jan-17**	**Feb-17**	**Mar-17**	**Apr-17**	**May-17**	**Jun-17**	**Q3 + Q4 2017**	**2018**	**2019**
Philanthropy, Voluntarism & Grantmaking Foundations			1	2	3	4	5	6	8	10	12	15	18	21	25	29	34	40	98	416	1,341
Education			1	2	3	4	5	6	8	10	12	15	18	21	25	29	34	40	98	416	1,341
Arts, Culture & Humanities			1	2	3	4	5	6	8	10	12	15	18	21	25	29	34	40	98	416	1,341
Religion-Related			1	2	3	4	5	6	8	10	12	15	18	21	25	29	34	40	98	416	1,341
Health Care				1	2	3	4	5	6	8	10	12	14	17	20	24	28	33	81	344	1,109
Environment					1	2	3	4	5	6	8	10	12	14	17	20	24	28	69	293	944
Science & Technology			1	2	3	4	5	6	8	10	12	15	18	21	25	29	34	40	98	416	1,341
Medical Research			1	2	3	4	5	6	8	10	12	15	18	21	25	29	34	40	98	416	1,341
Subtotal Customers Aquired	-	-	6	13	21	29	37	45	59	74	90	112	134	157	187	218	256	301	738	3,133	10,099
Churn	-	-	-	-	-	-	-	-	-	-	-	1	1	1	2	2	3	3	8	45	174
Net Customers	-	-	6	13	21	29	37	45	59	74	90	111	133	156	185	216	253	298	730	3,088	9,925

Headcount Requirements

Headcount Needs Per X Organizations - Growth Team	
Type	**1 Per**
Sales	30
Development	200
Customer Success	75

Head Count Needs																			Annual & Semi-Annual		
Founding Team	**Jan-16**	**Feb-16**	**Mar-16**	**Apr-16**	**May-16**	**Jun-16**	**Jul-16**	**Aug-16**	**Sep-16**	**Oct-16**	**Nov-16**	**Dec-16**	**Jan-17**	**Feb-17**	**Mar-17**	**Apr-17**	**May-17**	**Jun-17**	**Q3 + Q4 2017**	**2018**	**2019**
Management Team	2	-	-	-	-	-	-	-	-	-	-	-	-	-	-	-	-	-	-	-	-
Initial Development Team	1	-	1	-	-	-	-	-	-	-	-	-	-	-	-	-	-	-	-	-	-
Growth Team																					
Sales	-	-	-	-	-	-	1	1	1	2	3	3	4	5	6	7	8	9	24	102	330
New Hires	-	-	-	-	-	-	1	-	-	1	1	-	1	1	1	1	1	1	15	78	228
Development	-	-	-	-	-	-	-	-	-	-	-	-	-	-	-	1	1	1	3	15	49
New Hires	-	-	-	-	-	-	-	-	-	-	-	-	-	-	-	1	-	-	2	12	34
Customer Success	-	-	-	-	-	-	-	-	-	-	1	1	1	2	2	2	3	3	9	41	132
New Hires	-	-	-	-	-	-	-	-	-	-	1	-	-	1	-	-	1	-	6	32	91
Hiring	-	-	1	-	-	-	1	-	-	1	2	-	1	2	1	2	2	1	23	122	353
Total Headcount	3	3	4	4	4	4	5	5	5	6	8	8	9	11	12	14	16	17	40	162	515

Headcount

Based on our customer acquisition schedule and the headcount needs to support these customers, we put together an estimated cost schedule for salaries to bring into the Income Statement. Initially, these would be the main costs for the business, so it was important to keep them in check to extend runway of initial capital investments.

Cost Assumptions

We model both variable and fixed costs for the business. These were often aggregate percentage numbers that were used to simplify some complexity within the financial model—so long as they could find rule-of-thumb numbers or reasonable comparables.

We used a learning curve as a means to quantify efficiency. Through time, we believe we will get better and faster at various processes, which will bring down costs.

We also believe that R&D as a percentage of Revenue will be on the lower end because most of the "R&D" costs will be tied up in Developer salaries. Similarly, we believe that SG&A percentages will be on the lower end of comparable companies due to initial sales/advertising efforts focused on the existing networks of the founding team and the word-of-mouth nature of product adoption within nonprofit sector.

Income Statement Assumptions

As with many sectors of the economy, the nonprofit industry is comprised of small, medium, and large organizations. There are about 1.5M nonprofits in the United States and 10M nonprofits globally. The distribution of these organization is a hierarchy, with the greatest number of nonprofits in the "small" category, and the large amount of assets under management (AUM) consolidated in "large" organizations. Small organizations are often nimbler in their ability to try new products, but their budgets are smaller, and they may lack sophistication. Large organizations have bigger budgets, but the sales cycles may be slower due to larger implementations and more layers of sign off before committing to purchase decisions.

Annual Salary Per Employee Type		
Management Salaries	**Salary**	**Growth**
Founder 1	$ 70,000	10%
Founder 2	$ 70,000	
Engineering Salaries	**Salary**	**Growth**
Developer	$ 50,000	10%
Operations Salary	**Salary**	**Growth**
Customer Success	$ 65,000	3%
Sales Salaries	**Salary**	**Growth**
Sales Executive	$ 100,000	8%

Headcount & Salaries

	Jan-16	Feb-16	Mar-16	Apr-16	May-16	Jun-16	Jul-16	Aug-16	Sep-16	Oct-16	Nov-16	Dec-16	Jan-17	Feb-17	Mar-17	Apr-17	May-17	Jun-17	Q3 + Q4 2017	2018	2019
Head Count Needs																				Annual & Semi-Annual	
Founding Team																					
Founder 1	$ -	$ -	$ -	$ -	$ -	$ 5,833	$ 5,833	$ 5,833	$ 5,833	$ 5,833	$ 5,833	$ 5,833	$ 6,417	$ 6,417	$ 6,417	$ 6,417	$ 6,417	$ 6,417	$ 38,500	$ 84,700	$ 93,170
Founder 2	$ -	$ -	$ -	$ -	$ -	$ 5,833	$ 5,833	$ 5,833	$ 5,833	$ 5,833	$ 5,833	$ 5,833	$ 6,417	$ 6,417	$ 6,417	$ 6,417	$ 6,417	$ 6,417	$ 38,500	$ 84,700	$ 93,170
Subtotal	$ -	$ -	$ -	$ -	$ -	$ 11,667	$ 11,667	$ 11,667	$ 11,667	$ 11,667	$ 11,667	$ 11,667	$ 12,833	$ 12,833	$ 12,833	$ 12,833	$ 12,833	$ 12,833	$ 77,000	$ 169,400	$ 186,340
Engineering																					
Initial Team	$ 4,167	$ 4,167	$ 8,333	$ 8,333	$ 8,333	$ 8,333	$ 8,333	$ 8,333	$ 8,333	$ 8,333	$ 8,333	$ 8,333	$ 9,167	$ 9,167	$ 9,167	$ 9,167	$ 9,167	$ 9,167	$ 55,000	$ 121,000	$ 133,100
Growth Team														$ -	$ -	$ 4,167	$ 4,167	$ 4,167	$ 165,000	$ 907,500	$ 3,260,950
Subtotal	$ 4,167	$ 4,167	$ 8,333	$ 8,333	$ 8,333	$ 8,333	$ 8,333	$ 8,333	$ 8,333	$ 8,333	$ 8,333	$ 8,333	$ 9,167	$ 9,167	$ 9,167	$ 13,333	$ 13,333	$ 13,333	$ 220,000	$ 1,028,500	$ 3,394,050
Sales																					
Sales Executive	$ -	$ -	$ -	$ -	$ -	$ -	$ 8,333	$ 8,333	$ 8,333	$ 16,667	$ 25,000	$ 25,000	$ 36,000	$ 45,000	$ 54,000	$ 63,000	$ 72,000	$ 81,000	$ 1,296,000	$ 11,897,280	$ 41,570,496
Subtotal	$ -	$ -	$ -	$ -	$ -	$ -	$ 8,333	$ 8,333	$ 8,333	$ 16,667	$ 25,000	$ 25,000	$ 36,000	$ 45,000	$ 54,000	$ 63,000	$ 72,000	$ 81,000	$ 1,296,000	$ 11,897,280	$ 41,570,496
Operations																					
Customer Success	$ -	$ -	$ -	$ -	$ -	$ -	$ -	$ -	$ -	$ -	$ 5,417	$ 5,417	$ 5,579	$ 11,158	$ 11,158	$ 11,158	$ 16,738	$ 16,738	$ 301,275	$ 2,827,299	$ 9,375,598
Subtotal	$ -	$ -	$ -	$ -	$ -	$ -	$ -	$ -	$ -	$ -	$ 5,417	$ 5,417	$ 5,579	$ 11,158	$ 11,158	$ 11,158	$ 16,738	$ 16,738	$ 301,275	$ 2,827,299	$ 9,375,598
Total Salaries	$ 4,167	$ 4,167	$ 8,333	$ 8,333	$ 8,333	$ 20,000	$ 28,333	$ 28,333	$ 28,333	$ 36,667	$ 50,417	$ 50,417	$ 63,579	$ 78,158	$ 87,158	$ 100,325	$ 114,904	$ 123,904	$ 1,894,275	$ 15,922,479	$ 54,526,484

Cost Assumptions																			Annual & Semi-Annual		
	Jan-16	Feb-16	Mar-16	Apr-16	May-16	Jun-16	Jul-16	Aug-16	Sep-16	Oct-16	Nov-16	Dec-16	Jan-17	Feb-17	Mar-17	Apr-17	May-17	Jun-17	Q3 + Q4 2017	2018	2019
Select Variable Costs																					
Monthly (% of Revenue) (excl Payroll)																					
Payroll Tax & Benefits	15%	15%	15%	15%	15%	15%	15%	15%	15%	15%	15%	15%	15%	15%	15%	15%	15%	15%	15%	15%	15%
Hosting, Storage, R&D	6%	6%	6%	6%	6%	6%	6%	6%	6%	6%	6%	6%	6%	6%	6%	6%	6%	6%	6%	6%	6%
Technology Operations	2%	2%	2%	2%	2%	2%	2%	2%	2%	2%	2%	2%	2%	2%	2%	2%	2%	2%	2%	2%	2%
Total Select Variable Costs	23%	23%	23%	23%	23%	23%	23%	23%	23%	23%	23%	23%	23%	23%	23%	23%	23%	23%	23%	23%	23%
Fixed Costs																					
Monthly																					
Office Cost	$ -	$ -	$ -	$ -	$ -	$ 500	$ 500	$ 500	$ 500	$ 500	$ 500	$ 500	$ 500	$ 500	$ 500	$ 500	$ 500	$ 500	$ 3,000	$ 48,000	$ 120,000
Annual																					
Franchise Tax	$ 800												$ 800							$ 800	$ 800
Liability Insurance	$ 600												$ 600							$ 600	$ 600
Accountant Fees		$ 2,000												$ 2,000						$ 5,000	$ 10,000
Fixed One-Time																					
Setting Up Office						$ 5,000														$ 10,000	$ 20,000
Legal Fees for C Corp	$ 1,000																				
Total Fixed Costs	$ 2,400	$ 2,000	$ -	$ -	$ -	$ 5,500	$ 500	$ 500	$ 500	$ 500	$ 500	$ 500	$ 1,900	$ 2,500	$ 500	$ 500	$ 500	$ 500	$ 3,000	$ 64,400	$ 151,400
Learning Curve																					
Learning Curve Adjustment	100%	99%	97%	96%	94%	93%	91%	90%	89%	87%	86%	85%	83%	82%	81%	80%	79%	77%	71%	59%	49%
Other Costs																					
Monthly																					
Income Taxes	35%	35%	35%	35%	35%	35%	35%	35%	35%	35%	35%	35%	35%	35%	35%	35%	35%	35%	35%	35%	35%

Comparable Numbers

Blackbaud	2014	2013	2012	2011	Growth
Revenue	564.42	503.82	447.42	370.87	
Cost of Revenue	273.44	232.66	202.46	157.19	
% of Revenue	48%	46%	45%	42%	5%
Gross Profit	290.98	271.16	244.96	213.68	
% of Revenue	52%	48%	43%	38%	11%
SG&A	165.64	147.93	158.35	112.29	
% of Revenue	29%	26%	28%	20%	15%
R&D	77.18	65.64	64.69	47.67	
% of Revenue	14%	12%	11%	8%	18%
Total Operating Expense	519.05	452.27	427.98	319.94	
% of Revenue	92%	80%	76%	57%	18%

Comp Set

November 2015 LTM	Total Revenue	Cost Of Revenues	% COGS	Gross Profit	R&D	% R&D	SG&A	% SGA	Total Operating Expenses	% OpEx	Net Income	% Net Profit	CapEx	% CapEx
Blackbaud Inc. (NasdaqGS:BLKB)	614.9	296.7	48%	52%	84.9	14%	184.1	30%	567.4	92%	24.1	4%	20.2	3%
Intuit Inc. (NasdaqGS:INTU)	4,192.00	695	17%	83%	798	19%	1,771.00	42%	3,306.00	79%	365	9%	142	3%
MicroStrategy Inc. (NasdaqGS:MSTR)	535.2	109.3	20%	80%	61.9	12%	239.2	45%	410.5	77%	89.5	17%	3.9	1%
Paycom Software, Inc. (NYSE:PAYC)	203.6	29.4	14%	86%	7.57	4%	124.8	61%	170.6	84%	18.3	9%	12.5	6%

Revenue	Jan-16	Feb-16	Mar-16	Apr-16	42,521	42,551	42,582	42,613	42,643	42,674	42,704	42,735	42,766	42,794	42,825	42,855	42,886	42,916	Q3 + Q4 2017	2,018	2,019
																			Annual & Semi-Annual		
Revenue																					
Net Clients	0	0	6	13	$ 21	$ 29	$ 37	$ 45	$ 59	$ 74	$ 90	$ 111	$ 133	$ 156	$ 185	$ 216	$ 253	$ 298	$ 730	$ 3,088	$ 9,925
% Small	50%	50%	49%	48%	$ 0	$ 0	$ 0	$ 0	$ 0	$ 0	$ 0	$ 0	$ 0	$ 0	$ 0	$ 0	$ 0	$ 0	[illegible]	[illegible]	[illegible]
% Medium	50%	51%	51%	52%	$ 1	$ 1	$ 1	$ 1	$ 1	$ 1	$ 1	$ 1	$ 1	$ 1	$ 1	$ 1	$ 1	$ 1	[illegible]	[illegible]	[illegible]
% Large	0%	0%	0%	0%	$ -	$ -	$ -	$ -	$ -	$ 0	$ 0	$ 0	$ 0	$ 0	$ 0	$ 0	$ 0	$ 0	[illegible]	[illegible]	[illegible]
Clients By Size																					
Small	0	0	3	6	$ 10	$ 14	$ 17	$ 21	$ 27	$ 26	$ 30	$ 36	$ 40	$ 44	$ 49	$ 52	$ 55	$ 58	$ 12[illegible]	$ 422	$ 1,038
Medium	0	0	3	7	$ 11	$ 15	$ 20	$ 24	$ 32	$ 40	$ 50	$ 62	$ 75	$ 89	$ 106	$ 125	$ 148	$ 176	$ 43[illegible]	$ 1,865	$ 6,055
Large	0	0	0	0	$ -	$ -	$ -	$ -	$ -	$ 7	$ 10	$ 13	$ 18	$ 23	$ 30	$ 38	$ 49	$ 64	$ 17[illegible]	$ 801	$ 2,832
Net Clients	0	0	6	13	$ 21	$ 29	$ 37	$ 45	$ 59	$ 74	$ 90	$ 111	$ 133	$ 156	$ 185	$ 216	$ 253	$ 298	$ 730	$ 3,088	$ 9,925
Users By Size																					
Small	-	-	6	13	$ 20	$ 28	$ 35	$ 42	$ 54	$ 52	$ 61	$ 71	$ 81	$ 89	$ 98	$ 105	$ 111	$ 115	$ 24[illegible]	$ 843	$ 2,076
Medium	-	-	12	27	$ 44	$ 61	$ 79	$ 96	$ 128	$ 162	$ 199	$ 248	$ 300	$ 355	$ 425	$ 502	$ 593	$ 706	$ 1,746	$ 7,461	$ 24,221
Large	-	-	-	-	$ -	$ -	$ -	$ -	$ -	$ 74	$ 99	$ 134	$ 177	$ 228	$ 298	$ 383	$ 493	$ 639	$ 1,72[illegible]	$ 8,009	$ 28,317
Net Users	-	-	18	39	$ 64	$ 88	$ 113	$ 138	$ 182	$ 288	$ 359	$ 453	$ 557	$ 672	$ 821	$ 989	$ 1,197	$ 1,460	$ 3,713	$ 16,314	$ 54,614
Revenue by Size																					
Small	$ -	$ -	$ -	$ -	$ 294	$ 630	$ 1,007	$ 1,376	$ 1,736	$ 2,088	$ 2,706	$ 2,613	$ 3,039	$ 3,565	$ 4,036	$ 4,439	$ 4,888	$ 5,235	$ 84,06[illegible]	$ 506,079	$ 1,245,706
Medium	$ -	$ -	$ -	$ -	$ 2,448	$ 5,358	$ 8,741	$ 12,192	$ 15,710	$ 19,298	$ 25,555	$ 32,373	$ 39,766	$ 49,536	$ 59,947	$ 71,017	$ 85,061	$ 100,308	$ 2,355,48[illegible]	$ 17,907,074	$ 58,129,854
Large	$ -	$ -	$ -	$ -	$ -	$ -	$ -	$ -	$ -	$ -	$ -	$ 29,600	$ 39,600	$ 53,724	$ 70,809	$ 91,360	$ 119,178	$ 153,063	$ 4,583,85[illegible]	$ 38,445,488	$ 135,922,480
Gross Revenue	$ -	$ -	$ -	$ -	$ 2,742	$ 5,988	$ 9,748	$ 13,568	$ 17,447	$ 21,386	$ 28,261	$ 64,586	$ 82,406	$ 106,825	$ 134,793	$ 166,816	$ 209,127	$ 258,606	$ 7,023,40[illegible]	$ 56,858,641	$ 195,298,040

Income Statement	Jan-16	Feb-16	Mar-16	Apr-16	42,521	42,551	42,582	42,613	42,643	42,674	42,704	42,735	42,766	42,794	42,825	42,855	42,886	42,916	Q3 + Q4 201[illegible]	2,018	2,019
																			Annual & Semi-Annual		
Gross Profit																					
Revenue	$ -	$ -	$ -	$ -	$ 2,742	$ 5,988	$ 9,748	$ 13,568	$ 17,447	$ 21,386	$ 28,261	$ 64,586	$ 82,406	$ 106,825	$ 134,793	$ 166,816	$ 209,127	$ 258,606	$ 7,023,40[illegible]	$ 56,858,641	$ 195,298,040
Cost of Goods Sold																					
Hosting, Storage, R&D	$ 12.91	$ 26	$ 51.63	$ 103	$ 207	$ 444	$ 712	$ 976	$ 1,237	$ 1,493	$ 1,944	$ 4,376	$ 5,499	$ 7,022	$ 8,727	$ 10,638	$ 13,136	$ 16,001	$ 396,89[illegible]	$ 2,680,122	$ 7,678,753
Total Cost of Goods Sold	$ 13	$ 26	$ 52	$ 103	$ 207	$ 444	$ 712	$ 976	$ 1,237	$ 1,493	$ 1,944	$ 4,376	$ 5,499	$ 7,022	$ 8,727	$ 10,638	$ 13,136	$ 16,001	$ 396,89[illegible]	$ 2,680,122	$ 7,678,753
Gross Profit	-$ 13	-$ 26	-$ 52	-$ 103	$ 2,536	$ 5,544	$ 9,036	$ 12,591	$ 16,210	$ 19,893	$ 26,317	$ 60,211	$ 76,907	$ 99,803	$ 126,066	$ 156,177	$ 195,990	$ 242,605	$ 6,626,51[illegible]	$ 54,178,519	$ 187,619,287
Operating Expenses																					
Sales & Marketing																					
SG&A	$ -	$ -	$ -	$ -	$ 774	$ 1,666	$ 2,671	$ 3,662	$ 4,638	$ 5,600	$ 7,289	$ 16,408	$ 20,621	$ 26,331	$ 32,726	$ 39,893	$ 49,262	$ 60,003	$ 457,67[illegible]	$ 915,347	$ 1,830,693
Subtotal	$ -	$ -	$ -	$ -	$ 774	$ 1,666	$ 2,671	$ 3,662	$ 4,638	$ 5,600	$ 7,289	$ 16,408	$ 20,621	$ 26,331	$ 32,726	$ 39,893	$ 49,262	$ 60,003	$ 457,67[illegible]	$ 915,347	$ 1,830,693
Operations																					
Salaries	$ 4,167	$ 4,167	$ 8,333	$ 8,333	$ 8,333	$ 20,000	$ 28,333	$ 28,333	$ 28,333	$ 36,667	$ 50,417	$ 50,417	$ 63,579	$ 78,158	$ 87,158	$ 100,325	$ 114,904	$ 123,904	$ 1,894,27[illegible]	$ 15,922,479	$ 54,526,484
Payroll Tax & Benefits	$ 625	$ 625	$ 1,250	$ 1,250	$ 1,250	$ 3,000	$ 4,250	$ 4,250	$ 4,250	$ 5,500	$ 7,563	$ 7,563	$ 9,537	$ 11,724	$ 13,074	$ 15,049	$ 17,236	$ 18,586	$ 284,14[illegible]	$ 2,388,372	$ 8,178,973
Technology Operations	$ 55	$ 55	$ 55	$ 55	$ 55	$ 120	$ 195	$ 271	$ 349	$ 428	$ 565	$ 1,292	$ 1,648	$ 2,136	$ 2,696	$ 3,336	$ 4,183	$ 5,172	$ 140,46[illegible]	$ 1,137,173	$ 3,905,961
Subtotal	$ 4,847	$ 4,847	$ 9,638	$ 9,638	$ 9,638	$ 23,120	$ 32,778	$ 32,855	$ 32,932	$ 42,594	$ 58,544	$ 59,271	$ 74,764	$ 92,019	$ 102,928	$ 118,710	$ 136,322	$ 147,662	$ 2,318,88[illegible]	$ 19,448,023	$ 66,611,417
Total Variable Cost	$ 4,847	$ 4,847	$ 9,638	$ 9,638	$ 10,413	$ 24,785	$ 35,449	$ 36,516	$ 37,570	$ 48,194	$ 65,833	$ 75,679	$ 95,385	$ 118,349	$ 135,654	$ 158,604	$ 185,584	$ 207,665	$ 2,776,55[illegible]	$ 20,363,370	$ 68,442,110
Total Fixed Costs	$ 2,400	$ 2,000	$ -	$ -	$ -	$ 5,500	$ 500	$ 500	$ 500	$ 500	$ 500	$ 500	$ 1,900	$ 2,500	$ 500	$ 500	$ 500	$ 500	$ 3,000	$ 64,400	$ 151,400
Total Operating Expenses	$ 7,247	$ 6,847	$ 9,638	$ 9,638	$ 10,413	$ 30,285	$ 35,949	$ 37,016	$ 38,070	$ 48,694	$ 66,333	$ 76,179	$ 97,285	$ 120,849	$ 136,154	$ 159,104	$ 186,084	$ 208,165	$ 2,779,55[illegible]	$ 20,427,770	$ 68,593,510
Cummulative Operating Expenses		$ 14,093	$ 16,485	$ 19,277	$ 20,051	$ 40,698	$ 66,235	$ 72,966	$ 75,087	$ 86,764	$ 115,028	$ 142,513	$ 173,464	$ 218,135	$ 257,003	$ 295,258	$ 345,188	$ 394,249	$ 2,587,72[illegible]	$ 23,207,327	$ 89,021,280
Net Income Before Taxes	-$ 7,260	-$ 6,872	-$ 9,690	-$ 9,742	-$ 7,877	-$ 24,742	-$ 26,913	-$ 24,425	-$ 21,860	-$ 28,801	-$ 40,016	-$ 15,968	-$ 20,379	-$ 21,046	-$ 10,088	-$ 2,926	$ 9,906	$ 34,439	$ 3,846,95[illegible]	$ 33,750,749	$ 119,025,777
Provision for Income Taxes	$ -	$ -	$ -	$ -	$ -	$ -	$ -	$ -	$ -	$ -	$ -	$ -	$ -	$ -	$ -	$ -	$ 3,467	$ 12,054	$ 1,346,43[illegible]	$ 11,812,762	$ 41,659,022
Net Income	-$ 7,260	-$ 6,872	-$ 9,690	-$ 9,742	-$ 7,877	-$ 24,742	-$ 26,913	-$ 24,425	-$ 21,860	-$ 28,801	-$ 40,016	-$ 15,968	-$ 20,379	-$ 21,046	-$ 10,088	-$ 2,926	$ 6,439	$ 22,386	$ 2,500,52[illegible]	$ 21,937,987	$ 77,366,755

Valuation

The idea of valuation, especially at the earliest stage is more "art" than "science." As such, we want to approach the question of valuation from several different angles.

- **Frameworks.** Two high-level approaches in the Risk Factor Summation Model as well as the Berkus Method for early-stage valuations. By nature, these are directionally correct rather than specific.
- **Comparables.** A look at public information about venture capital deals that had been done within the industry and our city.
- **Discounted Cash Flow (DCF).** A DCF analysis to see if there would be interesting insights gleaned.

We are seeking $500k in funding and believe that an early sale of 20% of the business would leave ample upside potential while giving enough runway to gain significant traction.

As all entrepreneurs do, we also calculate what a potential exit would look like, and model valuation based off both Revenue and Net Income multiples achieved by the end of 2019.

Risk Factor Summation Method		
Risk Factors	Rank	Value
Management	2	$ 500,000
Stage of Business	0	$ -
Political	2	$ 500,000
Manufacturing	2	$ 500,000
Sales	-1	-$ 250,000
Funding/Capital Raising	-1	-$ 250,000
Competition	0	$ -
Technology	-1	-$ 250,000
Litigation	2	$ 500,000
International	2	$ 500,000
Reputation	1	$ 250,000
Potential Lucrative Exit	2	$ 500,000
		$ 2,500,000

Berkus Method		
Risk Factors	Rank	Value
Sound Idea	1	$ 500,000
Prototype	1	$ 500,000
Quality Management Team	1	$ 500,000
Strategic Relationships	1	$ 500,000
Product Rollout or Sales	0	$ -
		$ 2,000,000

Angel List Valuation Comps	
Boston	Value
75th Percentile	$ 3,000,000
Mean	$ 4,200,000
25th Percentile	$ 5,000,000
Big Data	
75th Percentile	$ 3,000,000
Mean	$ 4,500,000
25th Percentile	$ 6,000,000
Predictive Analytics	
75th Percentile	$ 3,000,000
Mean	$ 4,200,000
25th Percentile	$ 5,000,000
Enterprise 2.0	
75th Percentile	$ 3,000,000
Mean	$ 4,100,000
25th Percentile	$ 8,000,000
Business Productivity	
75th Percentile	$ 2,000,000
Mean	$ 3,800,000
25th Percentile	$ 6,000,000
Average	
75th Percentile	$ 2,800,000
Mean	$ 4,160,000
25th Percentile	$ 6,000,000
Overall Average	**$ 2,886,667**

Discussion Questions

1. What questions would investors likely have?
2. How well does the Executive Summary (see Chapter 8) tie back to the financial projections of the business? Is there anything from the Financials that should have been included in the Executive Summary to paint a clearer picture of the business?
3. Given the different segments of this market listed on the first chart, what questions would you ask to figure out which market(s) to focus on launching in first?
4. Do the assumptions for headcount pass the "common sense" check? For example, does it make sense to have one customer success person per 75 customers? Would you wait 11 months to make this hire as the company is suggesting?
5. Given the founding team of 3, what strategies might the team use to hire 6 people within the first year (1 Developer, 1 Customer Success, 4 Sales)?
6. What are the differences between the risk factor summation method, Berkus method, and Angel List comparable valuation methods? How much should this business be valued at?
7. Why are there big deviations within valuations for some of the comparables? What do you think contributes to that? What is within the entrepreneur's control to influence these valuations?
8. Gravyty is looking to raise $500,000 at a $2.25M pre-money valuation. Does this seem appropriate? Why or why not?

10 Raising Money for Starting and Growing a Business

Photo Credit: © Jamel Toppin/The Forbes Collection/Contour RA/Getty Images

AirBnB founders Nathan Blecharczyk, Brian Chesky, and Joe Gebbia.

A new business searching for capital has no track record to present to potential investors and lenders. All it has is a plan—sometimes written, sometimes not—that projects its future performance. This means that it is very difficult to raise debt financing from conventional banks because they require as many as three years of actual—not projected—financial statements

This chapter was written by William D. Bygrave.

and assets that adequately cover the loan. Thus almost every new business raises its initial money from the founders themselves and what we call informal investors: family, friends, neighbors, work colleagues, and strangers; a few raise it from lending institutions, primarily banks; and a miniscule number raise it from venture capitalists, who are sometimes called *formal investors*.

Bootstrapping New Ventures

Most entrepreneurs start by bootstrapping their business. Bootstrapping is starting your business with the resources at hand without seeking outside capital. Founders basically self-fund and conserve spending by working out of their home, using existing equipment and computers, and not paying themselves or co-founders any salary. Once entrepreneurs gain some traction, such as developing a rudimentary prototype, they have evidence that the business might be possible and can seek outside financing. Steve Jobs and Steve Wozniak developed their first computer, Apple I, in a parent's garage and funded it with $1,300 raised by selling Jobs's Volkswagen and Wozniak's calculator. They then found an angel investor, Armas Markkula, Jr., who had recently retired from Intel a wealthy man. Markkula personally invested $91,000 and secured a line of credit from Bank of America. Sergey Brin and Larry Page maxed out their credit cards to buy the terabyte of storage that they needed to start Google in Larry's dorm room. Then they raised $100,000 from Andy Bechtolsheim, one of the founders of Sun Microsystems, plus approximately $900,000 from family, friends, and acquaintances. Both Apple and Google subsequently raised venture capital and then went public.

Joe Gebbia, Brian Chesky, and Nathan Blecharcyk also relied on creative bootstrapping to launch Airbnb. In 2007, after launching in SXSW and only getting two bookings, they had to come up with ideas to self-fund their new venture. The co-founders leveraged their design skills and created two cereal brands, "Obama's O's" and "Cap'n McCain." They thought of it as a public relationship strategy, but ended up making over $30,000. In 2009, they received $20,000 of funding from Paul Graham, which later led to a venture capital round of $600,000. As of 2018, the company has raised $3 billion and is valued at more than $31 billion, with $2.6 billion in revenue.[1,2,3]

Before you turn to outside equity investors for start-up money, you should look at all the possibilities of getting funding from other external sources. Sources might include the following:

- Services at reduced rates (some accounting and laws firms offer reduced fees to start-up companies as a way of getting new clients)
- Vendor financing (getting favorable payment terms from suppliers)
- Customer financing (getting down payments in advance of delivering goods or services)
- Reduced rent from a landlord
- An incubator that offers rent and services below market rates
- Leased instead of purchased equipment
- Government programs such as the Small Business Innovation Research awards for technology companies

There is a pattern in the initial funding of Apple, Google, and Airbnb that is repeated over and over in almost every start-up. The company bootstraps, raises money from the **Four Fs** (founders, family, friends, and fools) and then if all is going well, seeks outside capital. First, the founders themselves dip into their own pockets for the initial capital; next they turn to family, friends, and foolhardy investors (business angels). If their companies grow rapidly and show the potential to be superstars, they raise venture capital and have an initial public offering (IPO) or are acquired by a bigger company. The money from family and friends might be a loan or equity or a combination of both, but when it is raised from business angels, venture capitalists, or with an IPO, it will be equity. The following sections will step through the capital raising proccss.

Informal Investors

Self-funding by entrepreneurs, along with funding from informal investors, is the lifeblood of an entrepreneurial society. One of the most noteworthy findings of the Global Entrepreneurship Monitor (GEM) studies is the amount and extent of funding by the Four Fs. The prevalence rate of informal investors among the adult population of all the GEM nations combined is 5.7%,[4] and the total sum of money they provide to fund entrepreneurship is equal to 1.2% of the combined gross domestic product (GDP) of those nations. The entrepreneurs themselves provide 65.8% of the start-up capital for their new ventures; assuming that the remainder of the funding comes from informal investors, the funding from entrepreneurs and informal investors combined amounts to 3.5% of the GDP of all the GEM nations.

Half of all informal investors in the United States expect to get their money back in two years or sooner, according to the GEM study. This suggests that they regard their money as a short-term loan instead of a long-term equity investment. We are using the term *investment* loosely in this context because it may be more like a loan rather than a formal investment. Whether it is a loan or an equity investment, the downside financial risk in the worst case is the same because if the business fails, the informal investors will lose all their money. It is important to make clear to informal investors what the risks are. If you have a business plan, you should give them a copy and ask them to read it. But assume that they probably will not read it thoroughly; hence, you should make sure you have discussed the risks with them. A guiding principle when dealing with family and friends is not to take their money unless they assure you they can afford to lose their entire investment without seriously hurting their standard of living. It may be tempting to borrow from relatives and friends because the interest rate is favorable and the terms of the loan are not as strict as they would be from a bank, but if things go wrong, your relationship might be seriously impaired, perhaps even ended.

How should you treat money that a relative or friend puts into your business in the early days? At the beginning, the business has no operating experience, and it is very uncertain what the outcome will be. Thus, it is extremely difficult—maybe impossible—to place a valuation on the fledgling venture. It is probably better to treat money from friends and family as a loan rather than as an equity investment. As in any loan, you should pay interest, but to conserve cash flow in the first year or two, make the interest payable in a lump sum at the end of the loan rather than in monthly installments. You should give the loan holders the option of converting the loan into equity during the life of the loan. In that way, they can share in the upside if your company turns out to have star potential, with the possibility of substantial capital gains for the investors.

When you are dealing with relatively small amounts of money from relatives and friends—especially close family such as parents, brothers, and sisters—you may not need a formal loan agreement, particularly if you ask for money when you are under pressure because your business is out of cash. But at a minimum, you should record the loan in writing, with perhaps nothing more than a letter or a note. If you want something more formal, Lending Karma and similar peer-to-peer platforms sets up loan agreements for small businesses with informal investors.[5] A documented loan agreement could be

Photo Credit: Peter Kramer/Getty Images

Author Alice Walker (L), Producer Scott Sanders, TV Personality Oprah Winfrey and actor LaChanze at the curtain call for *The Color Purple* at the Broadway Theater on December 1, 2005, in New York City.

Angels on Broadway: The Color Purple[8]

The term *angel* was first used in a financial context to describe individual investors who put up money to produce new plays and musicals in the theater. Putting together a new theatrical production is not unlike starting up a high-potential business. It costs between $10 and $12 million to produce a Broadway musical. Occasionally, a show is a gigantic success, for example, *Hamilton*, but more often than not it either fails or is mediocre. Seventy-five percent of Broadway shows fail.[9] It is said that you can make a killing on Broadway, but you can't make a living—in contrast to Wall Street, where you can make a steady living with an occasional killing.

The musical version of *The Color Purple* opened on Broadway in December 2005—eight years after producer Scott Sanders first recognized the opportunity of producing a musical stage version of Stephen Spielberg's 1985 movie, in which Oprah Winfrey was one of the stars. Oprah called it one of the greatest experiences of her life. After Sanders persuaded the author, Alice Walker, to allow him to produce a musical based on her 1982 Pulitzer Prize—winning novel, Walker wrote to Oprah in 1997 and asked her "to do a little angel work for the show." But there was no response from Oprah until July 2005.

In the meantime, Sanders had raised almost all the $11 million needed to put the show on Broadway. He put in some of his own money; then in 2002 he raised $2 million from AEG Live—a strategic partner—with a commitment for another $2 million of follow-on investment. With the initial $2 million, he produced a month-long trial run of *The Color Purple* in Atlanta to sold-out audiences and standing ovations in 2004. This attracted Roy Furman, a Wall Street financier and frequent Broadway angel, who had worked with Sanders in the past. Furman agreed to raise half the $11 million that Sanders needed and made a seven-figure investment himself. Furman took an active interest in the production, attending rehearsals and management meetings. Then when the show was fully financed, Oprah called. She agreed to allow Sanders to put, "Oprah Winfrey presents *The Color Purple*" on the theater marquee. To make room for Oprah to invest $1 million, other investors' commitments were trimmed. Oprah also offered to feature a couple of songs from the musical on her hugely successful TV show. A book endorsement by Oprah almost guaranteed a place on the best-sellers list; Sanders and Furman hoped that by featuring *The Color Purple* on her show, Oprah would help to make it a Broadway hit.

Sanders and Furman estimated that if the average audience was 75% of full capacity in the 1,718-seat Broadway Theatre, *The Color Purple* would pay back the original investment in 12 months. Five months after its opening, *The Color Purple* was grossing more than $1 million a week, making it one of the top five shows on Broadway. The show recouped its investment within the first year and grossed more than $100 million before it closed on Broadway in 2008.[10]

important if you subsequently start dealing with professional investors such as sophisticated business angels and venture capitalists.

Business Angels

Business angels fund many more entrepreneurial firms than venture capitalists do.[6] Angels invest in seed-stage and very early-stage companies that are not yet mature enough for formal venture capital or companies that need financing in amounts too small to justify the venture capitalist's costs, including evaluation, due diligence, and legal fees.

We do not know how many wealthy persons are business angels, but we do know that Securities and Exchange Commission (SEC) Rule 501 defines an "accredited investor" as a person with a net worth of at least $1 million, or annual income of at least $200,000 in the most recent two years, or combined income with a spouse of $300,000 during those years. According to the SEC, the pool of accredited investors that fit the profile is approximately 12 million households as of 2016.[7] So that is the number of business angels qualified to invest in private offerings governed by SEC rules.

Searching for Business Angels

Most nascent entrepreneurs do not know anyone who is a business angel, so how should they search for one? The good news is that today there are "formal" angel groups, which are angels who have joined together to seek and invest in young companies. Most of them are wealthy entrepreneurs; some are still running their businesses, while others are retired. Angel investor groups have been around for many years, but they started to proliferate in the late 1990s when it seemed as if everyone was trying to make a fortune by getting in early on investments in Internet-related start-ups.

Angel groups have different ways of selecting potential companies to invest in. A few groups consider only opportunities that are referred to them, but most welcome unsolicited business plans from entrepreneurs. They evaluate the plans and invite the entrepreneurs with the most promising ones to make a presentation to the group at one of their periodic (usually monthly) meetings. A few of those presentations eventually result in investments by some of the angels in the group. Some groups charge the entrepreneurs a fee to make a presentation, and a few even require a fee when an entrepreneur submits a business plan. The size of each investment ranges from less than $100,000 to as much as $2 million—and in a few instances, considerably more.

As important as angel groups have become, they comprise only a few thousand investors compared with hundreds of thousands of business angels who invest on their own. Entrepreneurs are much more likely to raise money from angels who invest individually rather than in packs. Unfortunately, individual business angels are very hard to find. Searching for them requires extensive networking. But according to the late Bill Wetzel, pioneering researcher on angel financing, "Once you find one angel investor, you have probably found another half dozen."[11] Consider how other entrepreneurs found business angels. Steve Jobs and Stephen Wozniak found Armas Markkula through an introduction by a venture capitalist who looked at Apple and decided it was too early for him to invest. Sergey Brin and Larry Page were introduced to Andy Bechtolsheim by a Stanford University faculty member. Today, entrepreneurs have platforms such as Y Combinator or AngelList that provide access to angel investors. Companies like Airbnb and Dropbox went through an application process to ultimately raise seed capital. When a leader in an industry related to the one the new company is entering becomes a business angel, it sends an important signal to other potential investors. For instance, once Andy Bechtolsheim had invested in Google, Brin and Page soon put together $1 million of funding.

Types of Business Angels

Business angels range from silent investors who sit back and wait patiently for results, to others who want to be involved in the operations of the company, as a part-time consultant or as a full-time partner. Richard Bendis classifies business angels in the following categories: entrepreneurial, corporate, professional, enthusiast, and micromanagement.[12]

Entrepreneurial angels have started their own businesses and are looking to invest in new businesses. Some have realized substantial capital gains by taking their companies public or merging them with other companies. Others are still running their businesses full-time and have sufficient income to be business angels. In general, entrepreneurial angels are the most valuable to the new venture because they are usually knowledgeable about the industry, and just as important, they have built substantial businesses from the ground up and so understand the challenges that entrepreneurs face. They can be invaluable advisors and mentors.

Corporate angels are managers of larger corporations who invest from their savings and current income. Some are looking to invest in a start-up and become part of the full-time management team. Corporate angels who have built their careers in big, multinational corporations can be a problem for a neophyte entrepreneur because they know a lot about managing companies with vast resources but have never worked in a small company with very limited resources. Here is an example of what might go wrong: A fish-importing wholesaler was started and run by two young men. The company grew fast, but it ran out of working capital. Two angels, one of them a marketing executive with a huge multinational food company, invested $500,000 on condition that the young company hire the marketing executive as its marketing/sales vice president. Very soon there was a clash of cultures. The founders continued to work 12-hour days, while the new vice president was traveling first class and staying in fancy hotels when he made sales trips. Within a year, the business angels took control of the company. The two founders left, and a year later it closed its doors.

Professional angels are doctors, dentists, lawyers, accountants, consultants, and even professors who have substantial savings and incomes and invest some of their money in start-ups. Generally, they are silent partners, although a few of them, especially consultants, expect to be retained by the company as paid advisors. Ashton Kutcher is a famous actor and successful investor. In 2011, he created a Venture Fund named A Grade Investments. He mostly invests in technology companies and has funded success stories such as Spotify, Airbnb, Foursquare, Uber, and Fab, among others. The fund has invested in more than 60 companies in only 7 years and has had 10 successful exits. In 2010, *Time* magazine named Kutcher one of the Top 100 Most Influential People, and his company, Katalyst, has been recognized as one of the Top 10 most Innovative Companies.[13]

Enthusiast angels are retired or semiretired entrepreneurs and executives who are wealthy enough to invest in start-ups as a hobby. It is a way for them to stay involved in business without any day-to-day responsibilities. They are usually passive investors who invest relatively small amounts in several companies.

Micromanagement angels are entrepreneurs who have been successful with their own companies and have strong views on how the companies they invest in should be run. They want to be a director or a member of the board of advisors and get regular updates on the operations of the company. They do not hesitate to intervene in the running of the business if it does not perform as expected.

There is no ideal type of business angel. And in general, most entrepreneurs cannot pick and choose because it is so hard to find business angels who are prepared to invest. But just as a wise angel will carefully investigate the entrepreneur before investing, likewise a smart entrepreneur will find out as much as possible about a potential business angel. There is probably no better source of information than other entrepreneurs in whom the angel has previously invested. Ask the business angel whether he or she has invested in other entrepreneurs and whether you may talk with them.

Putting Together a Round of Angel Investment

If you're raising a round of investment from business angels, you'll need a lawyer knowledgeable in this area because there are various SEC rules that you need to comply with. Most private placements by start-up entrepreneurs are made under Regulation D, Rule 504, dealing with offerings up to $1 million; fewer are made under Rule 505, dealing with offerings up to $5 million.

The first thing you'll want to do is place a value on your start-up. Valuation of a seed-stage company is more art than science. It's also very subjective, with entrepreneurs placing a substantially higher value than business angels. Informed business angels will determine the value based on similar deals made by other angels and venture capital firms. The comparable-market valuation method will provide a back-of-the-envelope estimate to see whether the company has a chance of meeting the business angel's required return.

In general, business angels are satisfied with a lower return than venture capitalists are because, unlike venture capitalists, they have only minimal operating costs and they do not have to pay themselves carried interest on any capital gains. To produce a return of 25% for their investors, venture capitalists need to get a return of 35% or more from their investment portfolio. According to the Center of Venture Research, angel investors expect a 26% average annual return with a payback time between five and seven years. One-third of their investments result in substantial capital loss. The average equity received in 2017 was 12.2% at valuations of $3.2 million. The split between stages was: 41% seed and start-up, 41% early, and 18% expansion.[14]

Although financial returns are very important to business angels, they also invest for nonfinancial reasons. These include a desire to give back and mentor budding entrepreneurs, to be involved in start-ups without total immersion, to have fun, to be part of a network of other business angels, to stay abreast of new commercial developments, to be involved with the development of products and services that benefit society, and to invest in entrepreneurs without the pressure of being a full-time venture capitalist.[15]

Most angel investments are for preferred stock convertible into common stock on a one-to-one ratio. Preferred stock gives investors priority rights over founders' common stock, which relates to liquidation and voting. The potential problem with convertible preferred stock is that it sets a valuation on the stock at the first round. If that valuation turns out to be higher than the venture capitalist's valuation at the second round, negotiations between the venture capitalist and the entrepreneur will be difficult. The shortfall might even be a deal breaker.

Some seed-stage companies that expect to get venture capital investment in later rounds of financing use convertible debt rather than convertible preferred stock. **Convertible debt** is a bridge loan that converts to equity at the next round of investment, assuming that it is an equity round. Convertible debt securities allow the next-round investors, who are usually venture capitalists, to set the value of the company and provide the first-round angel investors with a discount. Business angels would like to get a 30% discount, but actual discounts range from 10% to 30%. Convertible debt has the advantage over convertible preferred stock because it reduces or eliminates squabbling over the valuation between venture capitalists and the entrepreneur on behalf of the angels.

The major conditions of a proposed deal are spelled out in a term sheet. Venture Deals, an online resource maintained by the managing directors of The Foundry Group, offers a sample Series A Term Sheet and other standard forms. For insight into what terms most benefit founders, Y Combinator founder Sam Altman put together an ideal "founder-friendly" term sheet and explained his logic[16]

Amount of Capital Needed to Start a Business

The amount of capital that entrepreneurs need to start their ventures depends, among other things, on the type of business, the ambitions of the entrepreneur, the location of the business, and the country where it is started. According to the GEM Report, the median level of funding required to start a business is $17,500, with entrepreneurs providing 57% of the funding. The amount needed to start a business is highest in extractive industry at $347,000, because of the large investment in capital equipment necessary for extracting raw materials such as oil and gas. Meanwhile, start-ups in the business services sector required an average of $20,000 and the lowest amount of funding was required by consumer-oriented businesses, which needed only $11,216. The businesses that need the most start-up capital are those created with the intent to grow and hire employees. For example, nascent businesses that expect to create six or more jobs in five years require an average of $50,000 in start-up money. Business started by men require more capital than those started by women ($20,000 vs. $10,000); a partial explanation is that women are more likely than men to start necessity-pushed businesses, which are more likely to be consumer-oriented and less likely to be business services.[17]

Financial Returns on Informal Investment

What financial return do informal investors expect? The median expected payback time, as you can see in Figure 10.1, is two years, and the median amount returned is one times the original investment. In other words, there is a negative or zero return on investment for half the informal investments. It seems that altruism is involved to some extent in an informal investment in a relative's or a friend's new business.[18] Put differently, investments in close family are often made more for love, not money.

The amount invested by strangers is the highest. What's more, the median return expected by strangers is 1.5 times the original investment, compared with just 1 for relatives and friends. The most likely reason is that investments by strangers are made in a more detached and businesslike manner than are investments by relatives and friends.

There is a big variation in the return expected by informal investors: 34% expect that they will not receive any of their investment back, whereas 5% expect to receive 20 or more times the original investment. Likewise, there is a big variation in the payback time: 17% expect to get their return in six months, whereas 2% expect to get it back in 20 years or longer.

Relationship: Investor– Investee	Percent Total	Mean Amount Invested US$	Median Payback Time	Median X Return
Close family	49.4%	23,190	2 years	1 x
Other relative	9.4%	12,345	2 years	1 x
Work colleague	7.9%	39,032	2 years	1 x
Friend, neighbor	26.4%	15,548	2 years	1 x
Stranger	6.9%	67,672	2 – 5 years	1.5 x
	100.0%	24,202	2 years	1 x

FIGURE 10.1 **Relationship of Informal Investor to Investee.**

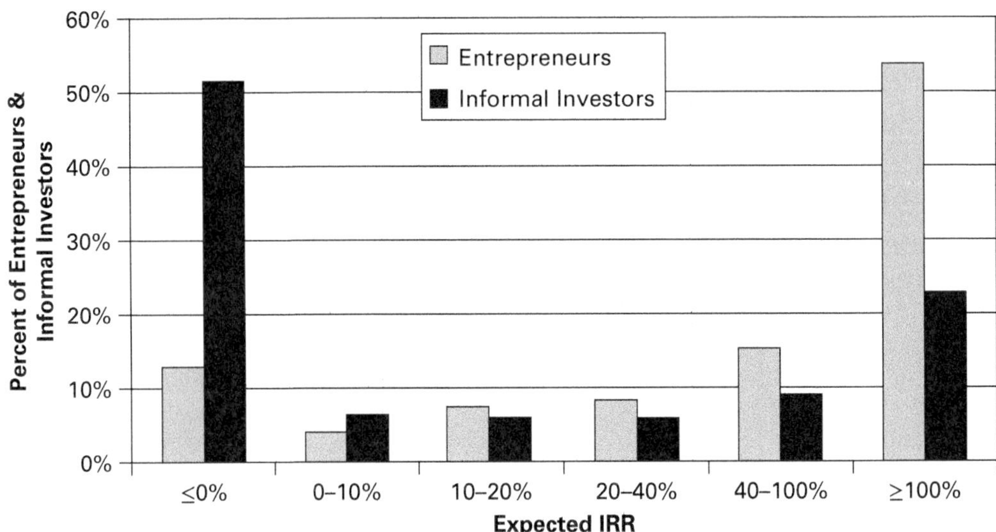

FIGURE 10.2 Expected IRR for Entrepreneurs and Informal Investors.

Entrepreneurs are much more optimistic about the return on the money that they themselves put into their own ventures: 74% expect the payback time to be two years or sooner, and their median expected return is 2 times their original investment, whereas 15% expect 20 or more times that investment.

The expected **internal rate of return or IRR** (compound annual return on investment) is calculated from the expected payback time and the times return for informal investors and entrepreneurs who reported both (see Figure 10.2). The returns expected by entrepreneurs are almost the reverse of those expected by informal investors: 51% of informal investors expect a negative or zero return, and only 22% expect a return of 100% or more; by contrast, only 13% of entrepreneurs expect a negative or zero return, but a whopping 53% expect a return of 100% or more.

Crowdfunding

As an activity, crowdfunding dates back to 1713 when Alexander Pope united subscribers to fund the translation of Homer's *Iliad* into English. He promised to include the 750 donors' names in the book in exchange for two gold guineas.[19] The Internet has modernized crowdfunding by connecting people in search of funds with the general public. Crowdfunding is generally defined as the collective "*crowd pooling funds*" to support a specific project or organization.[20] There are four common types of crowdfunding.

- Rewards—donors receive some kind of reward in exchange for the capital, often a promise of the product that their capital helps fund.
- Donation—most common with non-profit organizations and natural disasters. This is a way to donate to a cause.
- Lending—on this platform, the crowd lends money to an individual or company with the expectation that the principal and interest will be paid back at a point in time.
- Equity—Entrepreneurs exchange equity in return for funding, just like they would with an angel or venture capitalist. The most one person can invest in all crowdfunded securities combined in one year is: The greater of $2,000 or 5% of annual income or net worth (excluding a home) if the person's annual gross income or net worth is less than $100,000, or 10% of annual income or net worth, up to $100,000, if the person's income or net worth is at least $100,000.[21]

Crowdfunding serves as an alternative source of capital to support a wide range of ideas and ventures. An entity or individual raising funds through crowdfunding typically seeks small individual contributions from a large number of people.[22] A crowdfunding campaign generally has a specified target amount to be raised, or goal, and an identified use of those funds. Individuals interested in the crowdfunding campaign—members of the "crowd"—may share information about the project, cause, idea or business with each other and use the information to decide whether or not to fund the campaign based on the collective "wisdom of the crowd."[23] Crowdfunding has been used to fund a variety of projects including artistic endeavors, technology start-ups, comic writers, dance shows, film production, photography, and food businesses, among others. In 2018, crowdfunding campaigns in North America raised over $17.2 billion.[24] In May 2016, the SEC began to allow companies to participate in "equity crowdfunding" by offering and selling securities through Internet crowdfunding campaigns. In the first year, 326 companies raised $30 million dollars in equity.[25]

It is common for entrepreneurs in rewards crowdfunding to offer their donors non-monetary goods in return for their donation. For example, a donor's name in the film's credits or tickets for the launch of the supported movie production. Some other entrepreneurs raise donations for social causes where the reward is personal satisfaction for the donors. In lending and equity, subscribers receive interest on their loan or a percentage of ownership of the company.[26]

The most popular platforms are Kickstarter and Indiegogo. From the time of its launch in 2009 through the end of 2018, Kickstarter has hosted and facilitated the launch of over 431,000 entrepreneurial projects. Of these projects, just under 40% reached their fundraising goal. In total, $3.65 billion has been pledged by "backers" to fund successful Kickstarter projects.[27] Crowdfunding platforms are popular among entrepreneurs as they learn about the market by receiving direct feedback from the masses without spending a lot of money. These platforms directly connect creators to consumers and possible investors while promoting and advertising their products. Among the most successful and unique crowdfunding campaigns have been the "*Pebble Time*" Smartwatch[28] and "*The Coolest Cooler*"[29] via Kickstarter, along with "*Jibo, the World's First Family Robot*"[30] and "*Flow Hive*"[31] via Indiegogo. The JOBS Act and its amendment, the Crowdfund Act, enables start-ups and small and mid-sized businesses to use SEC-approved crowdfunding portals to raise money from anyone online. The crowdfunding provision creates an exemption that will let a company sell up to $1 million in unregistered stock every 12 months to an unlimited number of investors who need not be accredited.

One success story of crowdfunding is Flow Hive, an innovative beekeeping hive kit that drains its honeycombs without disturbing the worker bees (harvesting honey usually involves breaking open a hive and potentially killing its bees). The product was launched by third-generation beekeeper Cedar Anderson, and his father Stuart. Cedar was inspired to redesign the traditional beehive because he felt bad about crushing bees while harvesting honey, and didn't like being stung. The father-son team worked on prototypes for years and eventually secured a patent. They decided to use IndieGoGo to raise $70,000 in production funds. The project was launched in February 2015, and in less than two months, the project had become the highest funded Indie-GoGo project outside of the United States in history, raising over $12.2 million and receiving 20,000 pre-orders. Using IndieGoGo "In Demand" feature, which allows successful campaigns to continue raising funds, Flow Hive raised an additional $2.7 million for a total of $14.9 million. Flow Hive is now a registered B-Corporation, and Stuart Anderson says he is grateful to work with his son and promote "a better, more sustainable world."[32]

Venture Capital

By far the rarest source of capital for nascent entrepreneurs is venture capital.[33] In fact, nascent companies with venture capital in hand before they open their doors for business are so rare that even in the United States—which has almost two-thirds of the total of classic venture capital[34] in the entire world—far fewer than one in 10,000 new ventures gets its initial financing from venture capitalists. In general, venture capital is invested in companies that are already in business rather than in nascent companies with products or services that are still on paper. For example, out of 7,750 U.S. businesses in which $69.1 billion of venture capital was invested in 2016, only 2,340 received venture capital for the first time, and of those, seed-stage companies accounted for less than 10% of the capital invested into the venture ecosystem. From 1970 through 2014, the venture capital industry invested $635 billion in 49,500 companies at all stages of development.[35] It is estimated that over the same period, informal investors provided more than a trillion dollars to more than 10 million nascent and baby businesses.

Classic Venture Capital

Although classic venture capitalists finance very few companies, some of the ones that they do finance play a very important—many say a crucial—role in the development of knowledge-based industries, such as biotechnology; medical instruments and devices; computer hardware, software, and services; telecommunications hardware and software; Internet technology and services; electronics; semiconductors; nanotechnology; and clean technology (cleantech). Venture capitalists like to claim that the companies they invest in have the potential to change the way in which people work, live, and play. And, indeed, an elite few have done just that worldwide; some famous examples are Intel, Apple, Microsoft, Federal Express, Cisco, Genentech, Amazon, eBay, Google, Facebook, Twitter, Airbnb, and Uber.

It's not by chance that almost all the venture-capital-backed companies with global brand names are American; rather, it is because the United States is the predominant nation with respect to classic venture capital investments. In 2018, 48% of all the classic venture capital invested globally was invested in the United States representing $99.5 in investments.[36]

Photo Credit: Georges F. Doriot, ca. 1955. HBS Archives Photograph Collection: Faculty and Staff. Baker Library, Harvard Business School (olvwork377916).

Georges Doriot (1899–1987) founded the venture capital industry when he started American Research and Development in Boston in 1946. His venture capital firm made many seed-stage investments, the most famous of which was $70,000 for 77% of the start-up equity of Digital Equipment Corporation. (1979 photo)

Mechanism of Venture Capital Investing

The formal venture capital industry was born in Massachusetts at the end of World War II when a group of investors inspired by General Georges Doriot, a legendary professor at the Harvard Business School, put together the first venture capital fund, American Research and Development. They did so because they were concerned that the commercial potential of technical advances made by scientists and engineers at the Massachusetts Institute of Technology during World War II would be lost unless funding was available to commercialize them. The fledgling venture capital industry grew and evolved; eventually, the most common form of organization for U.S. venture capital funds became the limited partnership.

The mechanism of venture capital investing is shown in Figure 10.3.[37] At the center of the process are the general partners of venture capital funds, which are limited partnerships with a 10-year life that is sometimes extended. The general partners of venture capital funds raise money from limited partners. In return for managing the partnership, the general partners receive an annual fee of 2% to 3% of the principal that has been paid into the fund. The general partners then invest money in portfolio companies in exchange for equity. If all goes well, the investment in the portfolio companies grows, and the equity is eventually harvested, usually

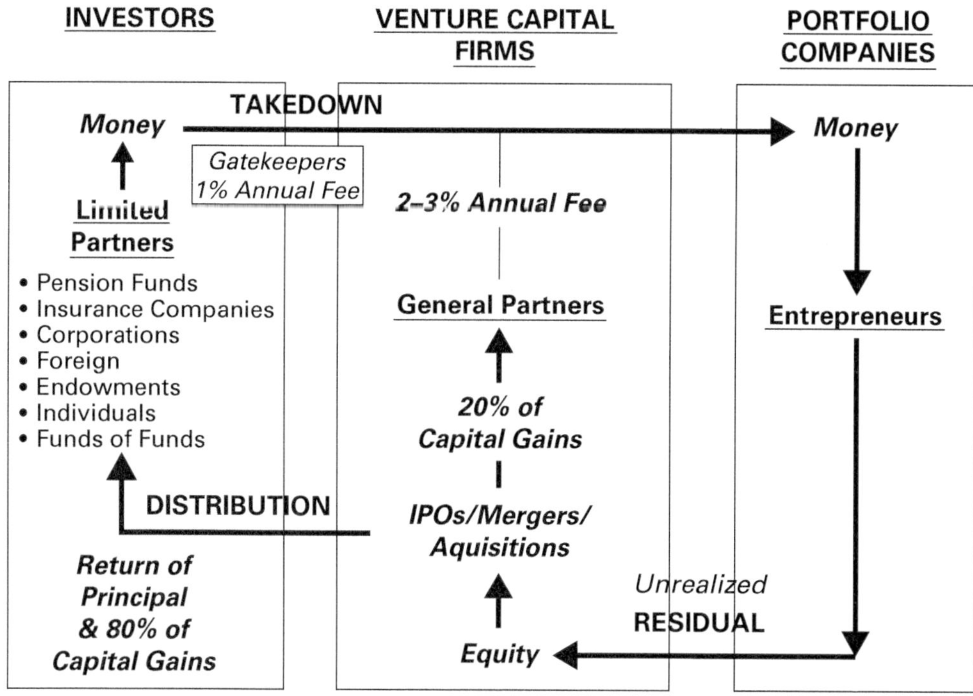

FIGURE 10.3 Flow of Venture Capital.

with an IPO or a trade sale to a bigger company. The capital gain on the harvest is shared 80%–20% between the limited partners and the general partners once the limited partners have received back all the principal they put into the limited partnership. The general partners' share is called the *carried interest*, which is usually 20%. Sometimes gatekeepers (formally called *investment advisors*) are employed by limited partners to advise them on what venture capital funds they should invest in and to watch over an investment once it has been made. The gatekeeper's fee is approximately 1% of the capital invested.

Historically, the biggest portion of the money invested by limited partners came from pension funds—in both the public and the private sectors—with the balance coming from funds of funds, endowments, foundations, insurance companies, banks, and individuals.

Kleiner Perkins: A Legendary Venture Capital Firm

Eugene Kleiner and Tom Perkins formed their venture capital firm, then known as Kleiner Perkins, in 1972. Kleiner was one of the founders of Fairchild Semiconductor, and Perkins was a rising star at Hewlett-Packard. Headquartered on Sand Hill Road in the heart of Silicon Valley, it is probably the most successful venture capital firm ever. Since 1972 it has invested in more than 400 companies, among them Nest, Twitter, Coursera, Snapchat, Square, Slack, Spotify, and Uber.[38]

In 2016, Kleiner Perkins raised a $1 billion for its KPCB Digital Growth Fund III and $400 million early-stage fund, KPCB XVII.[39] The limited partner investors in the 15th fund since 1972 are largely the same ones that have invested in KPCB funds over the last 25 years or so. This family of funds has been so successful that it is virtually impossible for new limited partners to invest because the general partners can raise all the money they need from the limited partners who invested in previous funds. The $1 billion fund was devoted to large, late-stage private companies focused on growth, while the $400 million fund was to be invested by the general partners over three years in smaller, early-stage companies.

As we've mentioned, each venture capital partnership (called a *venture capital fund*) has a 10-year life. If a venture capital fund is successful, measured by the financial return to the limited partners, the general partners usually raise another fund four to six years after the first fund. This, in essence, means that successful venture capital firms generally have two to four active funds at a time because each fund has a life of 10 years.

Financial Returns on Venture Capital

A rule of thumb for a successful venture capital fund is that, for every 10 investments in its portfolio, two are big successes that produce excellent financial returns; two are outright failures in which the total investment is written off; three are walking wounded, which in venture capital jargon means that they are not successful enough to be harvested but are probably worth another round of venture capital to try to get them into harvestable condition; and three are living dead, meaning that they may be viable companies but have no prospect of growing big enough to produce a satisfactory return on the venture capital invested in them.

Approximately 35% IPOs between 1980 and 2015 were venture capital backed.[40] Of the others that were harvested, mergers and acquisitions were the most common exit. In comparatively rare instances, the company's managers bought back the venture capitalist's investment.

The highest return on a venture capital investment is produced when the company has an IPO or is sold to or merged with another company (also called a *trade sale)* for a substantial capital gain. In general, however, trade sales do not produce nearly as big a capital gain as IPOs do because most trade sales involve venture-capital-backed companies that aren't successful enough to have an IPO. For instance, one way of harvesting the walking wounded and living dead is to sell them to other companies for a modest capital gain—or in some cases, a loss. The median post-IPO valuation of venture-capital-backed companies that went public in in 2017 was $411 million compared with a median valuation of $91 million for those that were exited through mergers and acquisitions.[41]

The overall IRR to limited partners of classic venture capital funds, over the entire period since 1946 when the first fund was formed, has been in the mid-teens. But during those six decades, there have been periods when the returns have been higher or lower. When the IPO market is booming, the returns on venture capital are high, and vice versa. The returns of U.S. venture capital are shown in Figure 10.4. Over the 20-year horizon, seed and early-stage funds outperformed balanced and expansion and later-stage ones. This is what we might have expected because the earlier the stage of investment, the greater the risk, and hence, the return should be higher to compensate for the risk. The seed and early-stage risk premium was spectacular for the 20-year horizon (68.55% versus 9.02% for expansion and later-stage funds) because the 20-year horizon includes the years 1999 and 2000, which

	Investment Horizon IRR (%) through December 31, 2014				
Fund Type	**1 Year**	**3 Years**	**5 Years**	**10 Years**	**20 Years**
Seed/Early Stage	11.83	8.66	16.14	9.46	68.55
Later/Expansion Stage	10.28	6.19	12.75	8.80	9.02
Multistage	10.08	7.54	14.72	8.43	9.07
All Venture Funds	11.08	8.03	15.30	9.04	22.90
NASDAQ	28.24	13.38	17.98	10.04	7.68
S&P 500	21.83	11.41	15.79	8.50	7.20

Source: Cambridge Associates LLC. U.S. Venture Capital IndexR and Selected Benchmark Statistics, 2017.

FIGURE 10.4 Venture Capital IRRs and NASDAQ and S&P 500 Returns.

were the peak of the Internet bubble, when year-to-year returns on all venture capital funds were 62.5% and 37.6%, with returns on seed and early-stage funds being far higher. However, the 10 year returns on seed and early-stage funds performed similarly to expansion and later-stage funds; but more recently, seed and early-stage funds outperformed expansion and later-stage funds.

Dealing with Venture Capitalists

The first big challenge for an entrepreneur is reaching a venture capitalist. It is easy to get names and contact information for almost every venture capital firm from the Internet. However, venture capital firms pay much more attention to entrepreneurs who are referred to them than to unsolicited business plans that arrive by mail or e-mail. Entrepreneurs are referred to venture capitalists by accountants, lawyers, bankers, other entrepreneurs, consultants, professors, business angels, and anyone else in contact with venture capitalists. But most of them are reluctant to recommend an entrepreneur to a venture capitalist unless they are confident that the entrepreneur is a good candidate for venture capital.

Entrepreneurs should be wary of "finders" who offer to raise venture capital for the entrepreneur. Most venture capitalists do not like dealing with finders because they charge the company a fee based on the amount of money raised—a fee that comes out of the money venture capitalists invest in the company. What's more, it's the entrepreneur, not the finder, who has to deal with the venture capitalists.

If the entrepreneur is fortunate enough to find a venture capitalist who would like to learn more about the new business, a meeting will take place at either the company's or the venture capital firm's office. The first meeting is usually an informal discussion of the business with one of the partners of the venture capital firm. If the partner decides to pursue the opportunity, he or she will discuss it with more of the partners; if they like the opportunity, they will invite the entrepreneur to make a formal presentation to several partners in the firm. This meeting is the crucial one, so it is important to make as good a presentation as possible. Not only are the venture capital partners assessing the company and its product or service, but also they are carefully scrutinizing the entrepreneur and other team members to see whether they have the right stuff to build a company that can go public.

If the venture capital partners like what they see and hear at this meeting, the firm will pursue the entrepreneur with the intent to invest and will begin its due diligence on the entrepreneur, other team members, and the company. Entrepreneurs who get to this stage will be evaluated as never before in their lives. It is not unusual for a venture capital firm to check dozens of references on the entrepreneur. Any suggestion of dubious conduct by the entrepreneur will be investigated. After all, the entrepreneur is asking the venture capital firm to trust him or her with several million dollars that in most cases is not secured by any collateral. All entrepreneurs should get a copy of their credit reports and be prepared to explain any delinquencies.

Entrepreneurs who get to this stage may be wondering whether the venture capital firm is the right one for them and be tempted to approach other venture capital firms to see what they might offer. But instead, they should conduct due diligence on the venture capital firm. Ask for a list of the entrepreneurs the firm has invested in and permission to speak with them. Here are some things to look for.

Value Added. The best venture capitalists bring more than money to their portfolio companies.[43] They bring what they call *value added*, which includes help with recruiting key members of management, strategic advice, industry contacts, and professional contacts such as accountants, lawyers, entrepreneurs, consultants, other venture capitalists, commercial bankers, and investment bankers.

Venture Capital is "Relationship" Capital

Brook Byers and Ray Lane talking about how Kleiner Perkins Caufield & Byers helps entrepreneurs:[42]

Brook Byers (referring to Kleiner Perkins Caufield & Byers's network): It's not keiretsu, it's relationship capital.

Ray Lane: Whether you call it a network, a Rolodex, keiretsu, or whatever, it is something that entrepreneurs crave, because they're looking for help. As Brook said, money is not a differentiator in our business, but they're looking for help. Either you have knowledge in their domain, and you can help them get from start-up to a company that actually gets something in the market, or you help them scale through relationships. In this world, at least in the enterprise world, it helps to know somebody.

Patience. Some venture capital firms, especially newer ones with relatively inexperienced partners, are more likely to get impatient when a portfolio company fails to meet expectations. Studies of venture-capital-backed companies that have not yet gone public or been acquired find that approximately 50% to 60% of them have changed CEOs at some time after the first round of venture capital;[44] only 18% of those that have had IPOs have changed CEOs.[45] Another indication of lack of patience is a venture capital firm quick to invoke covenants in the investment agreement, which contains a couple of hundred pages. There are all manner of covenants in those agreements, and it is not unusual for a company to violate one or perhaps more. An experienced venture capitalist will usually waive a covenant unless the violation is so severe that it jeopardizes the viability of the company.

Deep Pockets. Will the firm have enough money to invest in follow-on rounds of venture capital if the company needs them? Venture capital firms that have been in business for a long time have established a reputation of producing good returns for their limited partners, so they are able to raise new funds from time to time. In contrast, a young venture capital firm with only one small fund without a proven track record of producing satisfactory returns for its limited partners will have difficulty raising a second fund.

Board of Directors. Does the venture capitalist sit on the board and regularly attend meetings? How often does the board meet? And how many other boards does the venture capitalist serve on? A rule of thumb is that a venture capitalist should not be on more than half a dozen boards of portfolio companies.

Accessibility. Is the venture capitalist readily available when the entrepreneur needs advice? Conversely, does the venture capitalist interfere too much in the day-to-day running of the company?

Negotiating the Deal

The valuation of the company is probably the biggest issue to be negotiated (discussed a bit later in the chapter). Generally, the entrepreneur's valuation is higher than the venture capitalist's. Entrepreneurs can make valuations of the company based on computations; they can also talk to other entrepreneurs who have recently received venture capital. In general, venture capitalists have more information about pricing than entrepreneurs do because they know the valuations of similar deals that have been recently completed, and those will be the basis for the valuation. Once a valuation is determined, a term sheet is presented.

A *term sheet* listing the main conditions of the deal. (You can find samples on the Web.[46]) The term sheet will specify how much money the venture capital firm is investing, how much stock it is getting, a detailed listing of all the stock issued or reserved for stock options *before* the venture capital is invested—and *after*. The venture capitalists will in almost every case get convertible preferred stock. The rights of the preferred stock will be spelled out; they will include dividend provisions, liquidation preferences, conversion rights (usually one share of preferred stock converts to one share of common stock), antidilution provisions, voting rights, and protective provisions.

The term sheet will also have clauses covering information rights, such as a requirement for the company to supply timely unaudited quarterly and audited annual financial statements, board membership, a description of how the venture capital will be used, employment agreements, stock registration rights, and terms under which management can sell stock privately. It will also specify the date when the deal will close.

Term sheet provisions are subject to negotiation. But the sheet will contain a date and time when the venture capitalist's offer will expire unless the entrepreneur has accepted the offer in writing.

Valuation

Once you've decided to raise outside capital, you need to determine how much your company is worth so you can decide how much equity you need to sell to raise the needed capital. There are four basic ways of valuing a business:

- Earnings capitalization valuation
- Present value of future cash flows
- Market-comparable valuation
- Asset-based valuation

No single method is ideal because the value of a business depends among other things on the following:

- Opportunity
- Risk
- Purchaser's financial resources
- Future strategies for the company
- Time horizon of the analysis
- Alternative investments
- Future harvest

The valuation of a small, privately held corporation is difficult and uncertain. It is not public, so its equity, unlike that of a public company, has very limited liquidity or probably none at all; hence, there is no way to place a value on its equity based on the share price of its stock. What's more, if it is an existing company rather than a start-up, its accounting practices may be quirky. For instance, the principals' salaries may be set more by tax considerations than by market value. There may be unusual perquisites for the principals. The assets such as inventory, machinery, equipment, and real estate may be undervalued or overvalued. Goodwill is often worthless. There might be unusual liabilities or even unrecognized liabilities. Perhaps the principals have deferred compensation. Is it a subchapter S or limited liability corporation or a partnership? If so, tax considerations might dominate the accounting.

When valuing any business, especially a start-up company with no financial history, we must not let finance theory dominate over practical rule-of-thumb valuations. In practice, there is so much uncertainty and imprecision in the financial projections that elaborate computations are not justified; indeed, they can sometimes lead to a false sense of exactness.

The engine that drives enterprise is not thrift, but profit.

—John Maynard Keynes

The following sections describe the four methods to determine the valuation.

Earnings Capitalization Valuation

We can compute the value of a company with the earnings capitalization method as follows: Company Value = Net Income / Capitalization Rate

This method is precise when net income is steady and very predictable but not useful when valuing a company, particularly a start-up, whose net income is very uncertain. Even for an existing small business, the method is fraught with problems: For example, should the net income be that for the most recent year, or next year's expected income, or the average income for the last five years, or…? Hence, we seldom use the earnings capitalization method for valuing small, privately held businesses.

Present Value of Future Cash Flows

The present value of a company is the present value of the future free cash flows, plus the residual (terminal) value of the firm:

$$PV = \sum_{t=1}^{N} (FCF_t)/(1+K)t + (RV_N)/(1+K)N$$

where K is the cost of capital, FCF_t is the free cash flow in year t, N is the number of years, and RV_N is the residual value in year N.

$$\begin{aligned} \text{Free Cash Flow} = {} & \text{Operating Income} \\ & - \text{Interest} \\ & - \text{Taxes on Operating Income} \\ & + \text{Depreciation \& Other Noncash Charges} \\ & - \text{Increase in Net Working Capital} \\ & - \text{Capital Expenditures}(\text{Replacement \& Growth}) \\ & - \text{Principal Repayments} \end{aligned}$$

Free cash flow is cash in excess of what a firm needs to maintain its optimum rate of growth. A rapidly growing, high-potential firm will not generate any free cash flow in its first few years. In fact, entrepreneurs and investors want to use excess cash to grow faster. Therefore, we determine the value of such a firm entirely by its residual value.

Market-Comparable Valuation (Multiple of Earnings)

This valuation method is the company's net income (NI) multiplied by a ratio of the market valuation to net income (P/E) of a comparable public company, or preferably the average for a number of similar public companies. Ideally, the comparable companies should be in the same industry segment as the company that we are valuing. If the company is private, we usually discount its valuation because its shares are not liquid.

$$\text{Total Equity Valuation} = NI \times P/E$$

For a public company, the total equity valuation is the same as the market capitalization. If we substitute net income per share (earnings per share or EPS) for total net income in this formula, we have the price per share instead of market capitalization.

Variations on this method use earnings before interest, taxes, depreciation, and amortization (EBITDA) multiplied by the ratio of price per share to EBITDA per share of comparable companies, or simply the operating income (EBIT) multiplied by the ratio of price per share to EBIT per share.

The NI × P/E method is the most common technique for valuing rapidly growing companies that are seeking investment from professional investors such as venture capitalists or that are going public. For a fast-growing company with no free cash flow, NI × P/E is the same as the residual value, RV_N, in the equation in the previous section.

Asset-Based Valuation

There are three basic variations on the asset-based method:

- Modified (adjusted) book value
- Replacement value
- Liquidation value

Modified book value is appropriate for an established company that is stable or growing slowly. In this case, the value of the company is its book value, which is paid-in equity plus retained earnings or, looked at another way, assets minus liabilities. The problem with taking the book value on the existing balance sheet is that it assumes that accounting records accurately reflect the economic value of the assets and the liabilities. Unfortunately, the accounting of most businesses distorts the economic value of an organization—none more so than private, closely held companies. Hence, we must make adjustments to assets and liabilities before we can determine an accurate value. The major weakness of the modified book value is that it reflects the past instead of the future. It is static, not dynamic, because it is based on existing assets and liabilities rather than future earnings.

Replacement value is appropriate when someone is considering whether to set up a similar business from scratch or to buy an existing business.

Liquidation value is appropriate for a business that has ceased to be a going concern. It might be in bankruptcy, or it might simply be a business for sale that no one is willing to buy as a going concern. Just as the name implies, the valuation of the business is what someone is willing to pay for the assets.

Example of Market-Comparable Valuation

Here is a simplified illustration of market-comparable valuation, which is the most commonly used method for valuing a potential superstar company that is trying to raise venture capital:

> *Bug-Free Web Software (BFWS), a 12-month-old Internet software company, has successfully beta-tested its product and is seeking $4 million of venture capital to go into full-scale production and distribution. BFWS is forecasting sales revenue of $50 million with net income of $5 million in five years. What percentage of the equity will the venture capitalists require?*

To value this company and estimate the amount of equity that the venture capitalists will need to get their required rate of return (internal rate of return or IRR), we need the following:

1. Future earnings (NI)
2. Comparable price-to-earnings ratio (P/E)
3. Amount being invested (at time 0) (INV_0)

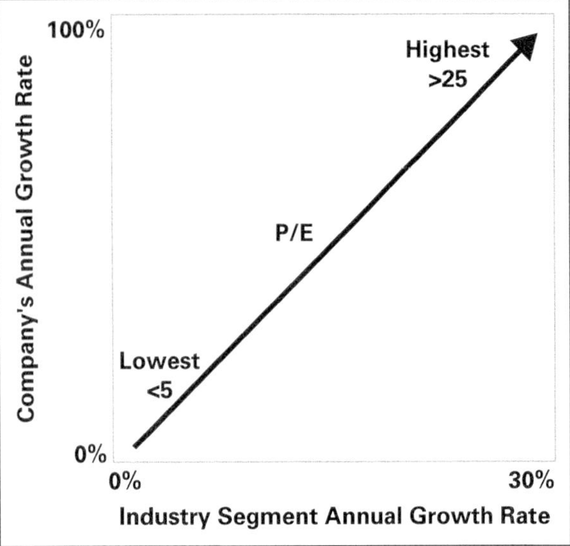

FIGURE 10.5 Price to Earnings.

4. Risk-adjusted cost of capital (IRR)
5. Number of years before the investment will be harvested (N)

BFWS's financial projections forecast that the net income in five years will be \$5 million, so NI is \$5 million and N is 5 years. What is the P/E? The P/E will be the average for public companies that are comparable to BFWS. In general, P/E ratios are determined by the rate of growth of a company and of the industry segment the company is in. This is illustrated in Figure 10.5.

In the bottom left corner are companies in slow-growing industries; they grow at approximately the same rate as the industry—for example, automobile manufacturers. If the company is growing faster than the overall industry, its P/E should be higher than the industry average, and if it is growing slower, its P/E should be lower than average (of course, if a company is losing money, its NI is negative, so it does not have a positive P/E ratio, in which case you might use a multiple of revenues). In the upper right corner are rapidly growing companies in high-growth industry segments, which is where BFWS expects to be. P/E ratios for superstar software/Internet companies in the top right corner are sometimes much higher than 25, but when valuing a very young company such as BFWS with no history of sales and income, venture capitalists will be conservative and use a P/E of approximately 20.

Using BFWS's financial projections, the future value of the company in five years will be as follows:

$$FV_5 = NI_5 \times (P/E)_5$$
$$FV_5 = NI_5 \times (P/E)_5 = \$5\text{million} \times 20 = \$100\text{million}$$

Company Stage	Expected Annual Return (IRR)
Seed	80%
Start-up	60%
First-stage	50%
Second-stage	40%
Third-stage/Mezzanine	30%
Bridge	25%

FIGURE 10.6 Expected IRR of Investors by Stage of Investment.

We now want to calculate the percentage of the equity that the venture capitalists will need to get their required IRR. The expected return depends on the risk involved. In general, the younger the company, the greater the risk. Figure 10.6 shows the expected IRR for the various stages of a company in which the investment is being made.

A *seed-stage* company is one with not much more than a concept; a *start-up* company is one that is already in business and is developing a prototype but has not sold it in significant commercial quantities; a *first-stage* company has developed and market-tested a product and needs capital to initiate full-scale production. *Second-stage* and *third-stage/mezzanine* financing fuels growing companies; *bridge* financing may be needed to support a company while it is between rounds of financing, often while it waits to go public.

Holding Period	Future Value, $million				
Years	20	40	60	80	100
2	51%	26%	17%	13%	10%
3	82%	41%	27%	20%	16%
4	NA	66%	44%	33%	26%
5	NA	NA	70%	52%	42%
6	NA	NA	NA	84%	67%
7	NA	NA	NA	NA	NA
8	NA	NA	NA	NA	NA

FIGURE 10.7 Percentage of Equity to Produce a 60% IRR on a \$4 Million Investment.

BFWS has a prototype that has successfully passed its beta test and now wants to go into full-scale production, so it is classified as being at the start-up stage, where the expected IRR is 60%. Now we need to find out what percentage of BFWS's equity the venture capitalists will need to meet a 60% return. Figure 10.7 shows the percentage of the equity needed to produce a return of 60% on a \$4 million investment for various future values (from \$20 million to \$100 million) and holding periods (from two to eight years).

The future value of BFWS is expected to be \$100 million in five years; hence, the venture capitalist will require 42% of BWFS's equity.

The market-comparable valuation formula is as follows:

$$Percentage\,of\,Equity = \frac{\mathrm{INV_0} \times (1 + \mathrm{IRR}/100)^{\mathrm{N}} \times 100}{\mathrm{NI_N} \times (\mathrm{P/E})_{\mathrm{N}}}$$

Applying this formula to BFWS:

$$Percentage\,of\,Equity = \frac{4{,}000{,}000 \times (1 + 60/100)^5 \times 100 = 42\%}{5{,}000{,}000 \times 20}$$

There is a lot of uncertainty in this computation: Will BFWS achieve the net income it has forecasted? If so, will it reach it in five years, or longer? Will the price-to-earnings ratio for comparable public companies be 20, or higher? Or will it be lower? Will the window for floating IPOs be open in five years, or will it be shut and delay BFWS's IPO? Any of these contingencies will affect the IRR when the venture capitalists harvest their investment in BFWS. Occasionally, a venture-capital-backed company does better than expected. However, more often than not it does not meet its financial forecast; consequently, the actual IRR is usually less than expected.

Asset-Based Valuation Example

Most companies are ordinary rather than glamorous superstars. In this section, we'll examine how to value an ordinary company that does not have the potential to attract venture capital or go public.

Suppose you want to become an entrepreneur by buying out an ordinary business—let's call it XYZ Corporation—that is well established in an industry that is growing about as fast as the overall economy and is an average performer. You will probably hope to buy it for its *modified book value*. The balance sheet for XYZ Corporation is shown in Figure 10.8. It lists the assets and liabilities as they are reported on the latest financial statements. The reported book value (total shareholder equity) is \$5,159,000. In the second column are the adjustments that the accountants make to bring the assets and liabilities to actual market value; the footnotes explain the adjustments. The third column shows the restated numbers, which are the reported values (column 1) plus the adjustments (column 2). The restated book value is \$6,309,000. That is probably what the seller will ask for the company.

Here are the critical questions the buyer should ask before buying an existing business:

- What is the growth rate of the industry?
- By how much is the company's growth rate above or below the industry average?
- What adjustments need to be made to the income and cash-flow statements and the balance sheet to reflect how the new owners will operate the business?
- How do the adjusted earnings and cash flows compare with industry averages?
- How does the balance sheet compare within industry averages (especially debt to equity)?
- How is the purchase being financed, and how will that change the income and cash-flow statements and balance sheet?
- How will the new owner's strategies affect the company's future performance?

Assets	As Reported	Adjustments	Restated	Liabilities	As Reported	Adjustments	Restated
Cash	1,500		1,500				
Accounts Receivable (net) (1)	3,300	(100)	3,200	Capitalized Leases	500		500
Inventory (2)	3.419	450	3,869	Long-Term Debt	600		600
TOTAL CURRENT ASSETS	8,219	350	8,569	TOTAL LIABILITIES	4,860	100	4,960
Land and Buildings (3)	1,000	750	1,750				
Machinery & Equipment (4)	750	200	950	SHAREHOLDER EQUITY			
Other Assets (5)	50	(50)	0	Capital Stock	500		500
TOTAL ASSETS	10,019	1,250	11,269	Retained Earnings (7)	4,659	1,150	5,809
Liabilities							
Accounts Payable	1,700		1,700	TOTAL SHAREHOLDER EQUITY	5,159	1,150	6,309
Short-Term Debt	1,410		1,410				
Accruals (6)	650	100	750				
TOTAL CURRENT LIABILITIES	3,760	100	3,860	TOTAL LIABILITIES & SHAREHOLDER EQUITY	10,019	1,250	11,269

RESTATEMENT NOTES:

1. Deduct $100 K for uncollectible receivables
2. LIFO reserve adjustment of inventory to fair market value
3. MAI appraisal of land & building reflect value of $950 K
4. Machinery & equipment appraisal reflects current market value of $950 K
5. Other assets were principally goodwill from expired patents—deduct
6. Investigation found accruals unrecorded of an additional $100 K
7. The net pretax effect of change in (1) through (6)

FIGURE 10.8 **XYZ Balance Sheet Adjusted to Reflect Fair Market Value of Assets and Liabilities ($000s).**

When these questions have been answered, the buyer should make five-year pro forma financial statements and do some sensitivity analysis of the critical factors such as sales revenue, cost of sales, and interest and repayment of both the old debt the buyer takes over and any new debt added to help finance the purchase of the business.

Harvesting Investments

When business angels or venture capitalists put money into a business, there has to be a way they can realize their investments at a future date. This is called the exit or harvest for the investor. There are three ways to exit an investment: an initial public offering, an acquisition, and a buyback of the investor's stock by the company itself. Most investors prefer an IPO because it produces the highest valuation in most cases—but not in every case. An acquisition is the second choice. And a buyback is a distant third because in almost every instance it produces a mediocre return.

One of the questions neophyte entrepreneurs seeking external equity financing most often ask is, "Can I buy back the investors' equity?" The answer is, "In principle yes, but in practice it is extremely unlikely." Buybacks are rare because a successful and rapidly growing company needs all the cash it can get just to keep on its growth trajectory. It has no free cash to buy out its external investors. A firm doing a buyback is more likely to be one of the living dead for which an IPO or acquisition is not feasible, but somehow the company arranges a refinancing in which it buys back the stock owned by the original investors. Sometimes a venture capital agreement includes a redemption (buyback) clause that allows the venture capital firm to exit its investment by selling it back to the company at a premium if an IPO or acquisition does not occur within a specified time period.

Initial Public Offering

Only a miniscule number of companies raise money with a firm commitment IPO.[47] Over the period 2013–2017, 338 venture-capital-backed companies went public, which averages out at only 68 IPOs per year.[48]

Without doubt, IPOs are glamorous and generally yield the biggest returns for the pre-IPO investors, but in the long run, they're not always satisfactory for the entrepreneurs and the management team, for a variety of reasons. Granted, many entrepreneurs, such as Bill Gates (Microsoft), Larry Ellison (Oracle), Robert Noyce and Gordon Moore (Intel), Bernie Marcus and Arthur Blank (Home Depot), Sergey Brin and Larry Page (Google), Jeff Bezos (Amazon), and Mark Zuckerberg (Facebook), took their companies public and never looked back, but that is not always the case.

Dell was facing tough times competing with new devices. In 2013, International Data Corporation (IDC) predicted that for the very first time, tablets would outsell PCs as consumers shifted to more portable devices. Constant pressure from Wall Street did not allow Michael Dell to revive the company. So, in February 2012, he proposed that his investors take Dell private by buying back shares at $13.65 per share. There were some other bidders in the middle trying to take over the company. Blackstone raised the bid to $14.25 in March, and soon afterward Carl Icahn offered $15 per share.

Michael Dell was about to lose control of his company, so he raised his bid to $13.75 per share and through a special dividend convinced the shareholders to vote in his favor.[49]

Pros and Cons of an IPO

The following are the upsides of going public.

Financing. The principal reason for a public offering is to raise a substantial amount of money that does not have to be repaid. For example, the average amount of money raised by the 338 venture-capital-backed companies that floated IPOs during the period 2013–2017 was $111 million. In 2017, 1,624 companies went public globally, up 49% versus 2016. The total money raised was nearly $249 billion globally, resulting in average $200 million for each company. The year 2014 was atypical, as it included Alibaba's blockbuster offering of almost $25 billion.[50]

Follow-On Financing. A public company can raise more capital by issuing additional stock in a secondary offering.

Realizing Prior Investments. Once a company is public, shareholders prior to the IPO know the value of their investment. What's more, their stock is liquid and can be sold on the stock market after the **lockup period** is over. The lockup period is a length of time after the IPO date (usually 180 days) when the prior shareholders are not permitted to sell any of their stock.

Prestige and Visibility. A public company is more visible and has more prestige. This sometimes helps the company with marketing and selling its products, outsourcing, hiring employees, and banking.

Compensation for Employees. Stock options presently held by employees or granted in the future have a known value.

Acquiring Other Companies. A public company can use its shares to acquire other companies. And here are the downsides of going public.

High Expenses. Expenses associated with going public are substantial. They include legal and accounting fees, printing costs, and registration fees. On average, companies spend anywhere from $7.3 million for IPOs less than $100 million to $27million for IPOs from $250 to $500 million.[51] Those expenses are not recoverable if the company does not actually go public, which happens to about half the companies that embark on the IPO process and fail to complete it. If the company does go public, the underwriter's commission takes between 4% and 7% of the money raised.

Public Fishbowl. When a company goes public, SEC regulations require that it disclose a great deal of information about itself that until then has been private and known only to insiders. That information includes compensation of officers and directors, employee stock option plans, significant contracts such as lease and consulting agreements, details about operations including business strategies, sales, cost of sales, gross profits, net income, debt, and future plans. The IPO prospectus and other documents that have to be filed with the SEC are in the public domain; they are a gold mine for competitors and others that want to pry into the company's affairs. When Alibaba went public, it had to reveal their numbers and current position in both Chinese and international markets. With increasing competition, it is clear that the company will try to move to new markets. This signals competitors like Amazon to strengthen and raise barriers for Alibaba to enter markets where Amazon currently dominates, like the United States.[52]

Short-Term Time Horizon. After an IPO, shareholders and financial researchers expect ever-increasing performance quarter by quarter. This expectation forces management to focus on maximizing short-term performance rather than on achieving long-term goals.

Post-IPO Compliance Costs. To meet SEC regulations, a public company incurs accounting costs it never had when it was private. Those can amount to $100,000 or more annually.

Management's Time. After an IPO, the CEO and the CFO have to spend time on public relations with the research analysts, financial journalists, institutional investors, other stockholders, and market makers—so named because they make a market for the company's stock. This is a distraction from their main job, which is running the company for optimal performance. Some public companies have executives whose main job is dealing with investor relations.

Takeover Target. A public company sometimes becomes the target of an unwelcome takeover by another company.

Employee Disenchantment. A rising stock price boosts the morale of employees with stock or stock options, but when it is sinking, it can be demoralizing—especially when an employee's options go "underwater" (the stock price falls below the options price). Underwater options can make it difficult to motivate and retain key employees.

The Process of Going Public

Before a company can have an IPO, it must file a registration statement with the SEC to ensure that the prospectus discloses everything the public needs to know before deciding whether to buy its shares. The IPO cannot go forward until the SEC has approved the registration statement. A delay sometimes wreaks havoc on a company's finances if the IPO window closes suddenly.

Entrepreneurs with serious aspirations to take their companies public should be farsighted and run their companies from the beginning as if they will have a future IPO. In practice, this means their accounting and law firms should be well-known national firms with lots of clients who have had IPOs. Of course, this is more expensive than starting out with small, local firms, but it will pay off in the long run if there is an IPO or acquisition by a public company.

When a company decides it's time to go public, the first step is to select an investment banker. This is where professional advisors such as accounting firms, law firms, and venture capitalists are valuable. Studies have shown that companies backed by leading venture capital firms and taken public by leading underwriters have the highest market capitalizations.[53] Leading investment bankers are not shy. They aggressively pursue companies that they would like to take public. Banks compete for a company's IPO in what's called a *beauty contest* or *bake-off*. They present their credentials to the company's CEO and board of directors and place a preliminary valuation on the company using the market-comparable (NI × P/E) method. The company usually selects the underwriter that has had the most success with IPOs in the same industry during the previous few years. If the company selects more than one underwriter, the bank managing the IPO is the *lead underwriter*, and the other banks are called the *syndicate*.

As soon as the underwriter has been selected, the IPO process begins in earnest with an "all-hands" meeting in which the key players—including the lead underwriter, accounting and law firms, and company executives—decide what they will do and when. They then prepare the prospectus with all the information the SEC deems the public needs to know before investing. This document includes details of the offering, what the company plans to do with the proceeds, the company's financial history and its future strategy, information about company management, and the company's industry niche, especially its competition. Risks are spelled out in detail. The preliminary prospectus is colloquially called the *red herring* because on the front page is a notice printed in red stating that some information is subject to change—in particular, the price per share and the number of shares to be offered. After filing the preliminary prospectus with the SEC, the company waits for the SEC, the National Association of Securities Dealers (NASD), and perhaps state securities organizations to review the documents for any omissions or problems that it must correct before the IPO can proceed. A *quiet period* lasts from the moment the company files the preliminary prospectus with the SEC until 25 days after the IPO. During this time, the company is forbidden to distribute any information about itself that is not contained in its prospectus.

Once the preliminary prospectus has been approved, the lead underwriter and the CEO embark on a whirlwind tour of leading financial centers such as New York, San Francisco, Los Angeles, Chicago, Boston, and perhaps overseas centers such as London, Paris, Frankfurt, Hong Kong, and Tokyo. The purpose of the tour, or "road show," is to promote the upcoming IPO and gauge the level of interest from potential investors. During the road show and immediately after, the underwriter builds a book of investors who say they want to buy the stock. The underwriter and the company meet the day before the IPO and use the order book to set the price of the stock and the size of the offering. The more the stock is oversubscribed, the higher the price will be. The underwriter commits to deliver the agreed-upon proceeds to the company regardless of whether it sells all the stock at the offering price. This commitment creates tension between the company, which is pushing for a high price, and the underwriter, which wants to set a price that will enable it to sell all the stock at the offering price. Once the price had been set, the company distributes stock to the banks in the syndicate, which then allocate it to their clients.

The underwriter hopes the price at the end of the first day's trading will be about 15% higher than the offering price; this is known as the *first-day pop*. The number of shares in the offering multiplied by the pop is known as *money left on the table*; it is the additional amount of money the company would have received if the offering price had been the same as the first day's closing price (academic researchers refer to it as *underpricing*). For example, Google closed up 17%, GoPro 30%, and Alibaba 38%. However, not all IPOs have that first day pop, Facebook opened at $38/share and closed basically flat at $38.23.

BFWS Goes Public

Let's return to our example. Two years after raising its second round of venture capital and five years after it was founded, the IPO window for software companies is open, so BFWS decides to go public. It has exceeded its forecasts and has revenue of $75 million, with net income of $8.33 million. Revenue is growing at 50% per year. It wants to raise $50 million gross with an IPO. Based on the prevailing industry P/E ratio of 30, the investment bank values the company post-IPO at $250 million ($8.33 million × 30). To raise $50 million, BFWS will have to sell 20% of its equity (50/250 × 100). That leaves the existing stockholders with 80% of the company.

Everyone should be happy with the return on their investments. At the IPO price, the $4 million of first-round venture capital is worth $64.8 million (16.2 × return and IRR of 100%), and the $6 million of second-round venture capital is worth $38.1 million (6.3 × return and IRR of 152%). The founders and the original investors hold stock worth $72.9 million, and the stock option pool is worth $24.3 million. The original founders and stockholders own 29.1% of BFWS, the venture capitalists 41.1%, the stock option pool 9.7%, and the public 20%. And the company receives the proceeds of $50 million minus the underwriters' 7% commission; that is $46.5 million.

Selling the Company

By far the most common way for investors to realize their investment, if a company has done well and chooses not to go public, is to sell the business to another company. A company is usually bought by a bigger company for strategic reasons, such as when a big pharmaceutical company buys out a young biotech company that has developed a promising drug but lacks the resources and experience to take it through the Food and Drug Administration (FDA) approval process or to market it, once it receives FDA approval.

A Strategic Acquisition: Food Should Taste Good

Pete Lescoe created Food Should Taste Good, Inc. in 2006. His goal was to create a unique snack with great taste using real ingredients and sophisticated flavor. As a food lover, he had been working in restaurants and grocery stores. Over this professional development, he learned that food tasted better when made with real ingredients. This drove Pete to start his own company dedicated to making wholesome snacks.[54]

The brand name speaks for itself. Food Should Taste Good chips are made from high-quality ingredients. They offer gluten free, cholesterol free, and zero grams of trans fats. They are also kosher certified, and many products are certified vegan. The first flavors, launched in January 2006, were multigrain and jalapeño chips, the former for wholesome and the latter for spicy lovers. But it was not until September that year when they finally earned space on grocery shelves. They continued to innovate in the snack market, creating mini tortilla shapes and launching new flavors: olive, chocolate, sweet potato, cinnamon, potato and chive, and kettle corn, among others. By 2010, the company had revenues of $49.4 million with a three-year growth of 562%.[55] In early 2012, General Mills acquired Food Should Taste Good and with more than 14 products in the natural and organic segment, generated sales of about $330 million in fiscal year 2014.[56]

Why Be Acquired?

The acquisition of Food Should Taste Good by General Mills is a very good example of what the seller and the acquirer are seeking from a strategic acquisition. The following are the advantages and disadvantages of an acquisition from the perspective of the seller.

Management. By selling the company rather than going public, the managers can stay focused on what they do best—continuing to build the company—rather than having to spend a lot of time on public relations with the financial community. Also, they probably will not be as driven by quarter-by-quarter results as they would be if the company were public. For example, Food Should Taste Good will have a relatively small effect on General Mills' net income; it can probably focus on rapid sales growth rather than optimizing quarterly profits for the next few years.

Founder and CEO. Selling a company the entrepreneur has built from nothing into a thriving enterprise can be traumatic. Edward Marram (co-author of Chapter 13 of this book) sold his company, Geo-Centers, in 2005. He said his head told him that it was the right thing to do, but his heart told him not to do it. After all, he was selling a company he started from nothing in 1975 and built into an organization with 1,100 employees. When a company is private, the CEO reports only to a board of directors, but when it is acquired, he or she has to report to a boss; if the acquirer is a big company, that boss may report to a boss. It can be very frustrating for the CEO/founder who has been making all the important decisions to find that his or her ideas have to be approved by a hierarchy before they can be implemented.

Company. General Mills has very deep pockets; it will be able to provide capital to Food Should Taste Good if it needs it.

Investors. Acquisitions are often paid for in cash rather than stock. Thus, investors get cash immediately after the deal is completed, unlike in a public offering, when pre-IPO investors have stock they cannot sell for 180 days, meaning they face the risk that the stock will go down before they can sell it. Of course, if the company is bought with the acquirer's stock instead of cash and if there are restrictions on the sale of the stock, there is still a risk that the stock price will go down before the investors can sell it.

Entrepreneur and Employee Stock. If it is a cash transaction, the entrepreneurs and employees get cash immediately. The potential disadvantage is that they no longer hold stock, so they have no upside potential if the company continues to do well. True, there is usually an *earn-out*, which is additional compensation to be paid in a few years if the company meets targets specified at the time of the acquisition.

Employment Agreement. Key employees will have an employment agreement that forbids them to compete with the company for a specific number of years—usually no more than two—if they leave. That will probably be the same agreement they had with the company before it was acquired. However, the CEO and top management will almost certainly be required to sign new noncompete agreements as part of their employment contracts with the acquirer.

Culture. Initially, the acquirer will not interfere in the management of the purchased company, but eventually it will probably want to put in its own management system and maybe its own executives in a few key positions. When it does that, there is a risk there will be a clash of cultures.

Expenses and Commissions. The expenses and investment banker's commission are substantially lower for an acquisition than for an IPO.

CONCLUSION

Financing is a necessary but not a sufficient ingredient for an entrepreneurial society. It goes hand in hand with entrepreneurs and opportunities in an environment that encourages entrepreneurship.

Grassroots financing from the entrepreneurs themselves and informal investors is a crucial ingredient for an entrepreneurial society. Close family members and friends and neighbors are by far the two biggest sources of informal capital for start-ups. Hence, entrepreneurs should look to family and friends for their initial seed capital to augment their own investments in their start-ups. Many entrepreneurs waste a lot of valuable time by prematurely seeking seed capital from business angels and even from formal venture capitalists—searches that come up empty-handed almost every time. Entrepreneurs must also understand that they themselves will have to put up about two-thirds of the initial capital needed to launch their ventures.

When an entrepreneur accepts money from a financially sophisticated investor such as a business angel or a venture capitalist, there has to be a future harvest when the investment can be realized. Generally, that harvest occurs when the company is acquired; occasionally, it happens when the company goes public. The harvest is primarily for the investors rather than the entrepreneurs. If entrepreneurs are not careful, they can give would-be investors the impression that they themselves are planning to exit the company at the harvest. That is not what professional investors like to hear. They want to invest in entrepreneurs whose vision is to build a business and continue building it after the harvest, not in entrepreneurs who are in it to get rich quick. Remember that Bill Gates made almost all his huge fortune by the appreciation of Microsoft's stock after its IPO; so did Microsoft employees and investors who held onto their stock for many years after the IPO.

YOUR OPPORTUNITY JOURNAL

Reflection Point	Your Thoughts...
1. How much equity financing do you need to get your business launched? When do you need it?	
2. Where will you get your initial financing? How much money can you invest from your personal resources (savings, second mortgage, etc.)?	
3. Create a strategy for other equity financing. Build a list, and rank-order Four F funding sources. Estimate how much each of these investors might be able and willing to invest.	
4. Do you think your business has the potential to raise formal venture capital (high-tech, high-innovation, high-growth prospects, first-rate management team, etc.)? If so, when might you be ready for venture capital? How much would you raise?	
5. What valuation method makes the most sense for your company? What comparable companies can you refer to as you prepare your valuation?	
6. Imagine your harvest. What companies might likely acquire you? How can you prepare for that future acquisition?	
7. Is there a possibility that your company could go public (high-growth industry)? What do you need to do to prepare for that?	

WEB EXERCISE

What can you learn about equity financing on the Web? Search for some investor/entrepreneur matching sites (e.g., www.angelinvestmentnetwork.us). Look at some crowdfunding sites (www.kickstarter.com). Do you think these services are effective? Would they work for your business? What can you learn about venture capital on the Web? Look at http://www.pwcmoneytree.com/. What regions and sectors are receiving the most money? Which venture capital funds are the most active? Are they investing in your sector?

NOTES

1. http://www.telegraph.co.uk/technology/news/9525267/Airbnb-The-story-behind-the-1.3bn-room-letting-website.html.
2. http://notes.fundersandfounders.com/post/82297315548/how-airbnb-started.
3. https://www.forbes.com/sites/bizcarson/2018/10/03/old-unicorn-new-tricks-airbnb-has-a-sky-high-valuation-heres-its-audacious-plan-to-earn-it/#55ac699e6fa3
4. GEM 2007 – 2014 NES Global Key Indicators (Excel Format). 2014. Retrieved from: http://www.gemconsortium.org/data/sets.
5. http://www.lendingkarma.com/
6. Sohl, Jeffrey. *The Angel Investor Market in 2008: A Down Year in Investment Dollars but Not in Deals*. Center for Venture Research. March 26, 2009. www.wsbe. unh.edu/files/2008_Analysis_Report_ Final.pdf. National Venture Capital Association/PricewaterhouseCoopers. *MoneyTree Report™*. October 20, 2009. www.nvca.org/index.php?option=com_docman&task=doc_download&gid=496&ItemId=93.
7. https://seekingalpha.com/article/4121810-many-accredited-investors-america
8. Excerpted from The Making of *The Color Purple*, *Business Week*. November 21, 2005, pp. 105 – 112.

9. Seitz, Patrick. What's a Dream Team's DNA? Businesses Could Learn Some Team Dynamics from Broadway, Scientists. *Investor's Business Daily*, June 6, 2005.
10. www.playbill.com/news/article/114543-Broadways-The-Color-Purple-Will-Close-Feb24.
11. http://activecapital.org.
12. Cited in David R. Evanson and Art Berof. Heaven Sent: Seeking an Angel Investor? Here's How to Find a Match Made in Heaven. *Entrepreneur*. January 1998.
13. https://www.crunchbase.com/search/organizations/field/people/num_exits/ashton-kutcher
14. Jeffrey Sohl, "The Angel Market in 2017: Angels Remain Bullish for Seed and Start-Up Investing", Center for Venture Research, May 17, 2018. https://paulcollege.unh.edu/sites/default/files/resource/files/2017-analysis-report.pdf
15. *Venture Support Systems Project: Angel Investors*. Release 1.1. Cambridge, MA: MIT Entrepreneurship Center, February 2000.
16. https://www.venturedeals.com/resources; http://blog.samaltman.com/a-founder-friendly-term-sheet
17. https://www.gemconsortium.org/report/49562
18. Bygrave, W. and Bosma, N. Investor Altruism: Financial returns from informal investments in businesses owned by relatives, friends, and strangers. In Minniti, M., ed., *The Dynamics of Entrepreneurship*. Oxford, UK: Oxford University Press. 2011.
19. https://www.kickstarter.com/blog/kickstarter-before-kickstarter.
20. Dresner, S. (2014) Bloomberg Financial: *Crowdfunding: A Guide to Raising Capital on the Internet*. Somerset, NJ: John Wiley & Sons, Incorporated. 2014.
21. https://www.gpo.gov/fdsys/pkg/FR-2015-11-16/pdf/2015-28220.pdf.
22. Dresner, S. 2014.
23. Ibid.
24. https://blog.fundly.com/crowdfunding-statistics/#regional.
25. https://www.sba.gov/sites/default/files/advocacy/Crowdfunding_Issue_Brief_2018.pdf
26. Ibid.
27. https://www.kickstarter.com/help/stats, 1.26.19
28. https://www.kickstarter.com/projects/getpebble/pebble-time-awesome-smartwatch-no-compromises
29. https://www.kickstarter.com/projects/ryangrepper/coolest-cooler-21st-century-cooler-thats-actually/description.
30. https://www.indiegogo.com/projects/jibo-the-world-s-first-social-robot-for-the-home#/story.
31. https://www.indiegogo.com/projects/flow-hive-honey-on-tap-directly-from-your-beehive#/
32. https://www.wsj.com/articles/the-10-biggest-crowdfunding-campaigns-where-are-they-now-1525140660 https://www.honeyflow.com/about/about-flow/flow-story/p/122
33. Venture capital data were obtained from the following sources: National Venture Capital Association Yearbooks, European Venture Capital Association Year books, Australian Venture Capital Association, Canadian Venture Capital Association, IVC Research Center (Israel), and South African Venture Capital and Private Equity Association.
34. Classic venture capital is money invested in seed-, early-, startup-, and expansion-stage companies. Pearce, B. *Venture Capital Insights 4Q14*. Ernst & Young. January 2015.
35. National Venture Capital Association Yearbook 2017. March 2017.
36. https://www.pwc.com/us/en/moneytree-report/moneytree-report-q4-2018.pdf
37. Bygrave, W. D. *Venture Capital Investing: A Resource Exchange Perspective. Dissertation*, Boston University, 1989.
38. Source from: http://www.kpcb.com/companies.
39. Sourced from: https://www.afr.com/technology/kleiner-perkins-raises-14-billion-to-back-startups-20160630-gpvmw3
40. https://site.warrington.ufl.edu/ritter/files/2016/02/Initial-Public-Offerings-VC-backed-IPO-Statistics-Through-2015-2016-01-06.pdf
41. Franklin, B. NVCA 2018 Yearbook, *National Venture Capital Association*. Mar. 2018. P30-31
42. http://www.siliconbeat.com/entries/2004/11/"www.siliconbeat.com/entries/2004/11/13/qa with kleiner perkins caufield byers.html."
43. Rosenstein, J., Bruno, A. V., Bygrave, W. D., and Taylor, N. T. CEO Appraisal of Their Boards in Venture Capital Portfolios. *Journal of Business Venturing*, 8(2): 99 – 113. 1993.
44. Rosenstein, J., Bruno, A. V., Bygrave, W. D., and Taylor, N. T. How Much Do CEOs Value the Advice of Venture Capitalists on Their Boards? *Frontiers of Entrepreneurship Research*, 1990. Wellesley, MA: Babson College. 1990. Bygrave, W. D., Marram, E., and Scherzer, T. *Boards of Directors of Venture-Capital-Backed Companies*. Presentation at Babson-Kauffman Entrepreneurship Research Conference, Boulder, Colorado, June 2002. Summary published in *Frontiers of Entrepreneurship 2002*. Wellesley, MA: Babson College, 2002.
45. Bygrave, W. D., Johnstone, G., Lewis, J., and Ullman, R. Venture Capitalists' Criteria for Selecting High-Tech Investments: Prescriptive Wisdom Compared with Actuality. *Frontiers of Entrepreneurship Research* 1998. Wellesley, MA: Babson College, 1998. www.babson.edu/entrep/fer/papers98/XX/XX_A/XX_A.html.
46. https://fundingsage.com/holy-grail-entrepreneurship-term-sheet-part-1/
47. In a firm commitment IPO, an under-writer guarantees to raise a certain amount of money for a company; in contrast, with a best efforts offering, an underwriter does its best to sell as many of the shares as it can at the offering price. Firm commitment offerings are far superior to best efforts offerings. All IPOs that are listed on the NASDAQ, the New York Stock Exchange, and the American Stock Exchange are firm commitment offerings. The statistics given in this book refer to firm commitment offerings.
48. Franklin, B. 2018 Yearbook, *National Venture Capital Association*. March 2018. "Global IPO market climbs to 10-year high in 2017." *EY*. Dec. 2017. https://www.ey.com/Publication/vwLUAssets/ey-global-ipo-market-climbs-to-10-year-high-in-2017/$FILE/ey-global-ipo-market-climbs-to-10-year-high-in-2017.pdf http://

fortune.com/2015/01/05/ipos-raised-249-billion-in-2014-and-the-fund raising-frenzy-could-continue/; http://www.businessinsider.com/2014-us-ipo-record-year-2014-12.

49. http://www.theguardian.com/technology/2013/sep/12/michael-dell-buys-back-pc-company-founded.

50. Franklin, B. 2018 Yearbook, *National Venture Capital Association*. March 2018. "Global IPO market climbs to 10-year high in 2017." *EY*. Dec. 2017. https://www.ey.com/Publication/vwLUAssets/ey-global-ipo-market-climbs-to-10-year-high-in-2017/$FILE/ey-global-ipo-market-climbs-to-10-year-high-in-2017.pdf http://fortune.com/2015/01/05/ipos-raised-249-billion-in-2014-and-the-fund raising-frenzy-could-continue/; http://www.businessinsider.com/2014-us-ipo-record-year-2014-12.

51. https://www.pwc.com/us/en/deals/publications/assets/cost-of-an-ipo.pdf

52. http://www.forbes.com/sites/joel backaler/2014/09/07/after-alibabas-ipo-key-questions-about-its-international-expansion/

53. Bygrave, W. D., and Timmons, J. *Venture Capital at the Crossroads*. Boston: Harvard Business School Press, 1992.

54. http://www.foodshouldtastegood.com/about-fstg/timeline.

55. http://www.wsj.com/articles/general-mills-to-buy-natural-foods-company-annies-1410210721.

56. http://www.foodbusinessnews.net/articles/news_home/Business_News/2014/04/Inside_General_Mills_natural_a.aspx?ID={628E40CD-FB84-4111-86E9-7F14197BCF62}

Case MetaCarta: Growing a Company, Do We Take the VC Money?[1]

Doug Brenhouse leaned back in his office chair and took a moment to himself away from the turmoil involved with the biggest decision of his professional life. Should he and his two co-founders, John Frank and Erik Rauch, accept the funding and terms that Sevin Rosen and its syndicate of three other VC firms had on the table? Three years after creating MetaCarta, a software start-up building a product that converts unstructured textual information into maps (geographic search versus the text searches of Google), the team needed money, but who should they take money from, and what were the implications of those investors? The current deal, if accepted, would dramatically change both the ownership structure and the day-to-day control of the company. Doug wondered if the team was ready to relinquish so much control over the growth of their firm.

Doug's History

Doug Brenhouse's background was a combination of entrepreneurship and engineering. In his family, owning a small business was "the norm." His father was a partner in a wood products manufacturing company. Two of Doug's uncles owned a women's clothing store chain, and the other was an independent home builder. One of his aunts was an independent insurance agent, and many of his friends' parents also had businesses of their own. With entrepreneurs to his left and right, Doug considered that he too would eventually pursue his entrepreneurial ambitions. It was just a question of when the time would be right.

In 1996, Doug earned a bachelor's degree in mechanical engineering with a minor in management from McGill University. After graduation, he joined Active Control Experts, Inc., a small company that designed piezoelectric actuators in Cambridge, Massachusetts. The company used specialized ceramics that produce an electric current when physical force is exerted onto them. The technology applied to vibration dampening in aviation, sound production in speakers, and physical shock absorption in sporting goods, such as skis[2] and mountain bikes.[3] The company had been founded only four years earlier and retained its start-up culture. In 1997, *Inc.* magazine named Active Control Experts the 79th fastest growing private company in America.[4] Doug learned a lot working for an early-stage entrepreneurial company and thought that this experience was preparing him for his own venture. After three years with the company, Doug wanted to explore the option of founding his own company.

In 1999, Doug enrolled in Babson College's MBA program. As he was about to enter his second year, Babson created a new program where students could apply their studies directly to launching a new venture. Doug stated, "Babson was a natural fit. In addition to the standard business education, I was able to walk the path of the first seven months of a business while actually starting one." Doug spent the early part of the program trying to figure out what kind of business to start. Doug looked at a variety of opportunities. Doug recalled:

> *One of the best places to see what kind of opportunities were emerging was the MIT 50 k Business Plan Competition. There was a social mixer at the beginning of the year. Everyone was gathering around big dishes of food. It was almost like speed dating, just trying to meet as many people as you could. Here, I met my business plan competition team [John Frank and Erik Raush]. John was a very charismatic guy. It seemed like [his idea] was more than just putting together some students for a business plan competition. I could sense that John was going to launch this business regardless of the outcome of the 50k.*[5]

Pattie Maes,[6] Founder and Director of MIT Media Lab's Fluid Interface Group, had advised John to go find a partner with business expertise. Serendipitously, John and Doug had come to the MIT 50k looking for the same thing; someone with complementary skills to partner with. Through this introductory social event, the three-member founding team was established.

Erik's and John's Backgrounds

Erik Rauch was a brilliant scholar and somewhat eccentric. He had a peculiar hobby of recording in his journal places with odd names, such as Hopeulikit, Georgia, and North Pole, Arkansas. His fascination with places and maps helped him see the potential that would eventually be MetaCarta. He enrolled in Yale University in 1992, earning the Morton B. Ryerson Scholarship. During his time there, he excelled at computer science and related mathematics. Erik was a research assistant in both Yale's Mathematics and Computer Science Departments. His work included writing an algorithm for floating-point variable optimization and using computer programming for fractal geometry

---

[1] This case was written by Andrew Zacharakis and Brian Zinn with support from The John H. Muller, Jr. Chair in Entrepreneurship at Babson College.

[2] BUSINESSWIRE, "ACX Technology Enables World's first Electric Snowboard," November 3, 1997.

[3] Sally McGrane, "Maybe an Electric Ski Would Help," *New York Times*, December 3, 1998. http://tech2.nytimes.com/mem/technology/techreview.html?res = 9B0DEFD6153BF930A35751C1A96E958260

[4] www.inc.com/inc5000/2007/company-profile.html?id = 1998079.

[5] Doug Brenhouse, interviewed by authors, Wellesley, MA, February 4, 2011. All quotes in case are from this interview.

[6] http://en.wikipedia.org/wiki/Pattie_Maes.

simulation. Erik graduated from Yale in 1996. He went on to work in the Theoretical Physics Department at IBM's T. J. Watson Research Center and to study graduate-level computer science at Stanford University, before beginning his work toward a PhD in artificial intelligence at MIT.

John Frank began his pursuit of scientific expertise at Yale University, earning his bachelor's degree in physics in 1999. While at Yale, he completed an internship with IDEO, a renowned design and innovation consulting firm. He was also the Team Director of "Team Lux—Yale Undergraduates Racing with the Sun." This was a student-led team that built and raced a solar-powered vehicle in the 1,250 mile Sunrayce 97 competition, finishing ninth out of 56 teams. After graduating from Yale, John began his doctoral studies in physics at MIT. At MIT, he first conceived of the software applications that would shape the next 10 years of his life and also enlisted Erik's help to build the software.

John's Idea

John Frank encountered a problem for a class he was taking at MIT. He was doing a project on how trees affected rainfall in the South Pacific. To conduct this research, he had to compare the vegetation on an island to a variety of other climatic features of each geographic area he examined. He needed to locate all the weather station information on each island and no matter what Internet search he tried to construct, he couldn't get access to all of the data he needed. John thought, wouldn't it be great if I could take a map, put it on top of the island and use that as the filter? Then I could find everything about this geography and get back the information that I need, and I would not have to know the names of all the different knolls and hills and stations that people refer to when they write about that location.

Traditional search engines can use specific text, such as the name of a city or river, to relate locations with other search terms. John wanted to create software that could search through online information and unstructured documents and identify which specific geographic location that document is referring to. This would include associating a mention of the "Potomac River" with the states that it runs through, as well as recognizing that a reference to "approximately 200 miles northeast of New York City" should most likely be connected with the area near Boston, Massachusetts. In other words, this search engine would build maps based on textual data. The initial program they developed was able to produce locations on a map based on search terms. For example, if you wanted to search wine, a map would be generated that showed all the locations related to wine. You could even search in different languages. The maps[7] below illustrate different results based on a search term.

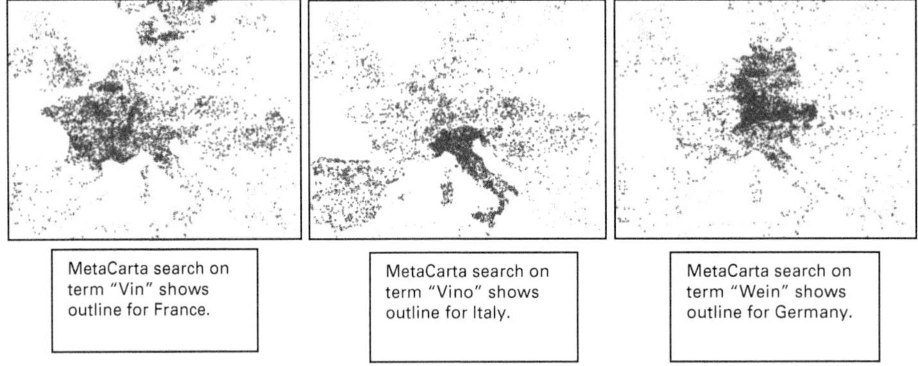

MetaCarta search on term "Vin" shows outline for France.

MetaCarta search on term "Vino" shows outline for Italy.

MetaCarta search on term "Wein" shows outline for Germany.

John possessed solid programming skills, but he needed someone with superior expertise to develop his concept into potentially revolutionary software. He brought his idea to Erik Rauch. John and Erik had known each other from their time at Yale. Knowing Erik's experience with doctoral-level artificial intelligence programming, John enlisted his help.

Forming a Founding Team

Doug, John, and Erik understood that their collective ability to work together was crucial to the success of the venture. According to Doug:

It is very much like getting married. You have to "date" for a while and really like the person that you are going to "marry." We ended up "dating" for four months or so before deciding that the business was worth pursuing and incorporating. We spent a lot of time together. Both socially and working on the business. Both were equally important. We got to know each other's friends and family pretty quickly. On the "work" side, it was like feeling around in the dark. We were doing a lot of research into what

[7] http://en.wikipedia.org/wiki/Erik_Rauch.

business models might make sense, what other companies were doing, how we packaged what we had and pitched it to investor—there was a lot of trial and error, and we got to see how we each dealt with different situations, where each other's strengths and weaknesses were, and as it turned out, we complemented each other incredibly well.

Things were moving fast. The trio incorporated MetaCarta in January and started to raise money. This violated the MIT 50k rules, and the team was initially disqualified until one of MetaCarta's advisors convinced the 50k committee to let the team compete. Unfortunately, Doug and his partners did not win, but the competition was another opportunity for the three students to test their "fit" as a team. With John and Erik providing the technical expertise and Doug articulating the business proposition, the team chemistry was strong and Doug knew this was the opportunity he was looking for.

Dynamics of the Founding Team

All three of the founding members shared science and engineering backgrounds. From this common foundation, their skills branched out in different directions:

[We had] very complementary skills. Erik was very technical. Big brain, it made sense for him to be pursuing a PhD in Artificial Intelligence. John spanned the gamut: very capable, very good at explaining technology. His father was a CEO of a variety of businesses. Besides good DNA, I think that he picked up a lot at the dinner table about how to be charismatic and how to run a business. My skills, though I have an engineering background, were much more on the business side, running and managing the business.

The MetaCarta founders needed to decide how to structure their fledgling team before attempting to develop the idea into a business. They anticipated the need for help from more experienced executives in later stages. Their initial titles reflected that expectation:

We all fit into our roles extremely well. We intentionally took on roles where we expected "C" level [hires] to come on. We had these grand visions of growth of the company. I took a VP role and John took the President role thinking that a CEO and a COO would [join at a later date]. Erik was initially Chief Scientist. He was continuing his PhD studies and was part-time.

Dividing the Equity

John, Doug, and Erik arranged a division of equity in the company before they had a concrete valuation of the business. If they had waited until after starting the process of seeking financing to decide how to share ownership among the founders, it could have been a much more complicated decision. By agreeing soon after their initial formation of the company simplified the decision because factors such as the influence of the investors, the complexity of proposed investment deal terms, and changing priorities of all the involved parties did not confuse the decision.

We all recognized our equity positions were reliant on the value over time and not their immediate worth. We all had the mind-set of vesting [the equity] over a period of three years. We realized that if the team dynamics didn't work, for whatever reason, there would be enough equity to entice [a new hire] to fill the role.

The Business Model

MetaCarta's original business model was to allow free access to its search product online. The company would monetize its service through Internet advertising.

This was 2000. The dot-com boom was well underway. Internet advertising was tremendous and what made the most sense was that you could create a geographic search engine. Then folks who advertise on the Internet, like McDonalds or Nike, might be willing to pay more for their advertisement on a map that was driving real purchasers into their physical stores. The story was resonating with early investors, and we raised $100,000. Everything was going as planned, but then came the dot-com bust, and the stock market fell apart practically overnight, and there was [no longer the same level of] Internet advertising dollars. So the idea of selling Internet advertising at a premium disappeared. We thought, "Now, what should we do?" We thought hard and long and changed the business model.

Instead of providing a free search engine to the public, the MetaCarta team thought the capability would be useful as an enterprise search engine...government agencies, *Fortune* 500 companies...although the new business model did not target as large of a market, the core customer was clear, and the value proposition meant that the customer should be willing to pay for the product.

Difficulty Raising Capital

Now the team had to raise money based on this different business model. Getting money on the new business model was difficult. The angel investor community and venture capital firms had recently been shaken by the stock market crash, resulting in a plunge in early-stage investing. The following chart shows total dollars invested per year by venture capitalists (VCs) and angels. As can be seen, 2001–2003 was not a strong period relative to the recent past to raise capital. The team's new mantra became, "There is no bad time to start a business," but Doug wondered if they were deluding themselves.

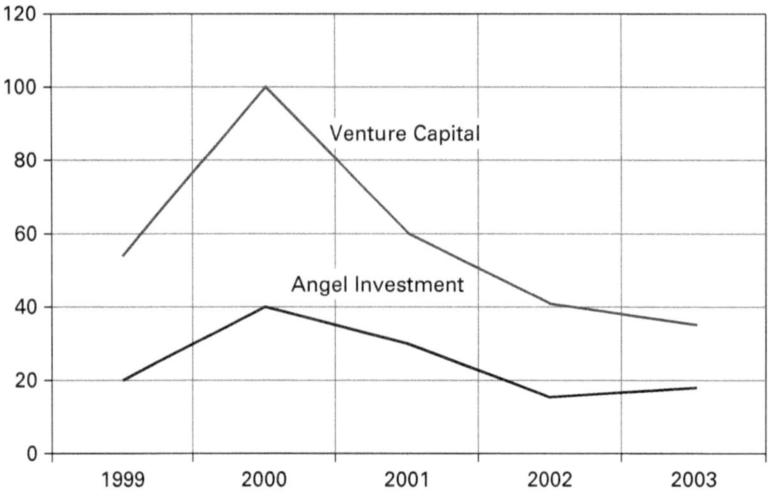

Angel Data From Jeffrey Sohl, University of New Hampshire, Center For Venture Research. Venture Capital Data From Thomson One Banker (New York, Ny): Thomson Financial.

MetaCarta needed capital at precisely the time when it was most difficult for a software company to find funding.

It was incredibly hard work. We talked to everybody that we possibly could. It was all about getting to the next conversation and not getting discouraged. This was a time where the Internet bubble had crashed. A bunch of folks were sitting around not interested in spending their money on technology, but still wanted to get together [for angel investor meetings] for social reasons. We went and pitched, and some of the guys were asleep. They would ask questions that were intended, it seemed, to derail the opportunity. There was lots of criticism and very little [of it] was constructive. We would go to talk to people, and they would look you in the eye and say, "We just don't get it. We think that you guys are idiots. This doesn't make any sense to me."

I remember that we went to one local VC firm, and we pitched to them. We were explaining one of our potential markets, oil and gas, to them and why [that was so attractive]. We already had Chevron interested as an investor and potential customer. The venture capital folks asked, "Why do people in the oil and gas industry need to read documents?" This person at a prominent venture capital firm in Boston just could not comprehend why this technology would be important.

Alternative Financing: DARPA

In October 1957, the Soviet Union launched Sputnik, the first human-built object to orbit the Earth. Military experts at the time believed that the technology that launched Sputnik was the first step in developing intercontinental nuclear missiles.[8] The United States hoped to launch a satellite of its own within six months, albeit one far smaller than Sputnik. In addition to the U.S. satellite project, the federal government created DARPA (Defense Advanced Research Projects Agency). This agency's mission was to provide research and funding to develop technologies that could be used by the U.S. military and, in some cases, the public as well.

Because of the difficulty in securing conventional financing, MetaCarta explored an unconventional funding source: DARPA. Doug and his team were successful in securing $500,000 in funding.

DARPA funding was a big step for us. It allowed us to move out of John's living room and into an office and add a few talented people to the team. We also started taking small salaries for ourselves.

[8] Jorden, William J. Soviet Fires Earth Satellite into Space; It Is Circling the Globe at 18,000˜M.P.H.; Sphere Tracked in 4 Crossings Over U.S. *New York Times*. Oct 5, 1957. www.trumanlibrary.org/museum/sputnik1.htm.

Getting the DARPA money was a big boost to the team. Not only could they pay themselves and hire more talent, but the DARPA money came in the form of a grant. No dilution. Furthermore, DARPA provided credibility to the team and their project. John and Doug soon realized that although this infusion was welcome, they needed more. The company was continuing to grow quickly and that required additional financing.

Angels

Although the angel investment community had still not recovered, John and Doug decided to go back to solicit angel investment.

> *We ended up raising money from family, friends, and business connections. We also got introductions to local software luminaries in the Boston area, some from MIT, and some from different angel groups in town. Pitching to angels was starting to wear on us. We often left those meetings asking ourselves, "Why did we do this again? Right, because this is what we do." At the end of the day, we ended up meeting some great people in Boston, who introduced us to some other great people. As we managed to pick up one, then two, then four, then eight, we managed to bring together a great group of investors in Boston. The same was true for New York. We ended up hooking up with three partners from Goldman Sachs. One introduced us to another, who introduced us to [the third]. We had a contingent in Boston and a contingent in New York. They were great to work with.*

Valuing the company at such an early stage presented a challenge for the founding team. Even after identifying interested investors, terms of the deal would shape the company's future. If John, Doug, and Erik demanded too high a valuation, some investors would lose interest. Too low of a valuation would lead to an erosion of their founders' equity as financing rounds progressed. Once the first investor in a particular round would come to an agreement with the founders on the terms of the deal, the other potential investors interested in the round would be faced with a "take it or leave it" ultimatum. Furthermore, most early-stage investors, including both angel investors and venture capitalists, write clauses into their investment contracts that prevent such dilution, often at the expense of the founders.

MetaCarta and the angel investors reached a compromise that is common for early-stage investments: convertible debt. In the fourth quarter of 2001, the investors contributed \$1 million with an 8% accruing interest rate.

> *The debt was convertible at a discount to the next round or at a fixed valuation, which was \$4 million in eighteen months. We figured that if we made it to that date, then we would be successful enough to be worth this valuation. The first money we raised was in the fourth quarter of 2001. It converted in 2003.*

Therefore, if MetaCarta did not raise any additional capital before November 1, 2003, then the company would be valued at \$4 million before the angel investment of \$1 million of debt was converted to equity. With the \$4 million "pre-money" valuation (value before the additional equity investment is added) and the original \$1 million, the company's post-money valuation would be \$5 million at the conversion. This would give the angel investors 20% ownership of the company, if MetaCarta did not raise a venture capital round of investment before that conversion.

The second qualifying event in the contract was a venture capital round of funding. If MetaCarta were to raise a venture capital round of financing, then the \$1 million initial investment plus any accrued interest would convert to stock at a 20% discount to the price paid by the venture capitalists. Convertible debt allows the next round of investors to set the price and the valuation, but makes sure that the first investors receive a benefit for taking the increased risk of investing earlier.

Going Back for More

Although the company had sold their product to several government customers at this point, like many start-ups, the cash burn rate was faster than expected. Product development was proceeding briskly but to keep on track, MetaCarta needed more money. In the second quarter of 2002, MetaCarta founders approached the task of finding more growth capital from two directions. First, they contacted the company's existing angel investors. These individuals had not been anticipating the next round of financing until 2003. Nonetheless, the MetaCarta executive team had found its angel investors primarily from successful professionals from the software and technology communities in Boston and New York. Not only were these investors more open to initial investment in a software start-up, but given the company's success to date, the experienced investors understood the requirements to keep MetaCarta growing. Whereas investors who were only familiar with more traditional businesses may have balked at the idea of MetaCarta asking for additional angel funding, the technology-minded financiers of this company did not shy away. The company raised a second angel round in 2002 from its original investors.

The second direction for raising capital was much more arduous. In-Q-Tel is the venture arm of the U.S. Central Intelligence Agency. Based on MetaCarta's product's potential for government use, the founders approached In-Q-Tel.

> *In-Q-Tel is a very interesting source of capital. They are the venture arm of the U.S. Central Intelligence Agency (CIA). They were very prestigious in that the government customer base that we were focusing on views companies that receive money from In-Q-Tel as vetted technologies. From a technology perspective, having due diligence done by them was second to none. So, we spent a long time talking with them, showing them what we had, and convincing them to take a look. They took a look and they liked what they saw. Once we got their seal of approval that the technology that we had was exceptional, they agreed to invest. There was a bunch of nuances around what they received for their investment.... We structured the deal such that it was very good for both of us....*
>
> *The company was now two years old, In-Q-Tel had come in in a significant way, we had the DARPA funding, the angel backing, and customers that were really positive on us.*
>
> *In-Q-Tel's backing was really important. We were able to "wave that flag." We were able to say that we had hit all these milestones that we had said that we were going to hit. We were able to walk into any meeting and say that we had taken money from In-Q-Tel and that they had already vetted the technology. Here is the name of the person to go talk to. He was part of the CIA. It was the best possible seal of approval. It was a lot of work to get it. We had been pursuing them for long time. It was early 2001 when we started [talking to In-Q-Tel] and took us a year and a half until they invested. And we were actively pursuing them for that whole time.*

And More Money

Although happy about the product development and growth in customers, Doug could not believe how fast they were burning capital. Alas, another year later and MetaCarta was in need of more capital. Based on the success of previous fundraising and the increasing traction with customers, several venture capital firms expressed interest, but the fundraising environment in 2003 was still tight. Sevin Rosen Funds, one of the leading VC firms in the country with such notable investments as Compaq, Ciena, and Electronic Arts, was very interested. Considering that Sevin Rosen was in Texas and the Silicon Valley, Kevin Jacques, a venture partner at Sevin Rosen, enlisted a Boston firm to also participate, Solstice Capital. After several months, Kevin Jacques put an offer on the table. Sevin Rosen and a syndicate of other venture firms would invest $6.5 million into MetaCarta at a pre-money valuation of $6.5 million. Doug, John, and Erik realized that would require 50% of the equity and give the investors the majority of the shares. The venture syndicate also wanted to include an option pool to entice future hires and reward strong performance from the existing employees. While Doug, John, and Erik agreed that an option pool was necessary and understood that they too would be eligible for option grants, they also realized that this would further dilute their current equity. As is common, the VCs wanted the shares to come out of the founders' and earlier round investors' stakes. Doug recounted:

> *The $6.5 pre-money valuation resulted in a cram down to the angels, which was unfortunate. We were upset that our early backers were being offered a lower share price than they paid. Also, we as founders were struggling with the amount of dilution, grappling with the notion that although the piece may have been smaller, the potential size of the pie was now much bigger.*

The following table shows MetaCarta's capitalization over time, assuming they would take the Sevin Rosen money. The co-founders debated. *Should we take the money? The impact on our ownership and that of the previous investors is pretty severe.* They also questioned whether the short-term hit on the value of the investors and on themselves would be erased by the growth that the new capital would enable. MetaCarta could seek different venture capital sources, but the process between the initial meeting and closing the deal was likely to take months, and the outcome might very well be the same, especially if economic conditions worsened. What should they do? The co-founders decided to sleep on it and decide in the morning.

MetaCarta Capitalization Table

	Date Capital	Invest/ Share	Price	Share	Value	Pre-money	Post Money	
Preround Financing								
Founders						100%	100%	
DARPA	2001	$500		0	$0	0%	0%	Grant, no equity implications.
Angel, First Investment	2001	$1,000		0	$0	0%	0%	Convertible debt
Total		**$1,500**		**0**	**$0**	**100%**	**100%**	
Series A								
Founders			$0.64	6,250	$4,000	100%	63%	
Angel, First Investment			$0.51	2,109	$1,030		21%	Converted to equity at 20% discount. Note principal plus interest (8%) buys equity at 80% discount off share price
Angel, Second Investment Plus In-Q-Tel	2002	$1,000	$0.64	$1.563	$1,000		16%	
Total		**$1,000**		**9,922**	**6,080**		**100%**	
Series B (proposed)								
Founders			$0.33	6,250	$2,063	63%	16%	
Angel, First Investment			$0.33	62,109	$696	21%	5%	
Angel, Second Investment			$0.33	1,563	$516	16%	4%	
Option Pool			$0.33	9,775	$3,226		25%	
Sevin Rosen and Other VCs	2003	$6,500	$0.33	19,697	$6,500		50%	
Total		**$6,500**		**39,394**	**$13,000**	**100%**	**100%**	

Discussion Questions

1. Why has this deal attracted venture capital?
2. Should MetaCarta take the Sevin Rosen offer?
3. How was the valuation determined? Is there anything MetaCarta could do to improve the valuation?
4. What would you, as an angel investor think about the current terms? What, if anything can you do about it?

11 Debt and Other Forms of Financing

Photo Credit: M4OS Photos/Alamy Stock Photo

The success of Wayfair, the e-commerce home goods reseller, was not only due to their clever target marketing and web analytics, but from a business model that relied upon an efficient cash conversion cycle.

This chapter was written by Joel Shulman.

Entrepreneurs at small, growing firms, unlike finance treasurers at most *Fortune* 500 companies, do not have easy access to a variety of inexpensive funding sources. In the entire world, only a handful of very large firms have access to funding sources such as asset-backed debt securitizations, A-1 commercial paper ratings, and below-prime lending rates. Most financial managers of small- to medium-sized firms are constantly concerned about meeting cash-flow obligations to suppliers and employees and maintaining solid financial relationships with creditors and shareholders. Their problems are exacerbated by issues concerning growth, control, and survival. Moreover, the difficulty of attracting adequate funds exists even when firms are growing rapidly and bringing in profits.

This chapter describes various financing options for entrepreneurs and identifies potential financing pitfalls and solutions. We also discuss how these issues are influenced by the type of industry and the life cycle of the firm and how to plan accordingly.

Getting Access to Funds—Start with Internal Sources

Entrepreneurs requiring initial start-up capital, funds used for growth, and working capital generally seek funds from *internal* sources. Managers or owners of large, mature firms, in contrast, have access to profits from operations as well as funds from external sources.

We distinguish internal from external funds because internal funding sources do not require external analysts or investors to independently appraise the worthiness of the capital investments before releasing funds. External investors and lenders also don't share the entrepreneur's vision, so they may view the potential risk/return trade-off in a different vein and demand a relatively certain return on their investment after the firm has an established financial track record.

Figure 11.1 shows a listing of funding sources and approximately when a firm would use each. In the embryonic stages of a firm's existence, as we've discussed, much of the funding comes from the entrepreneur's own pocket, including personal savings accounts, credit cards, home equity lines, and other assets such as personal computers, in-home offices, furniture, and automobiles.

Soon after entrepreneurs begin tapping their personal fund sources, they may also solicit funds from relatives, friends, and banks. Entrepreneurs would generally prefer to use other people's money (OPM) rather than their own because if their personal investment turns sour, they still have a nest egg to feed themselves and their families. The need to protect a nest egg may be particularly acute if the entrepreneur leaves a viable job to pursue an entrepreneurial dream on a full-time basis. The costs to the entrepreneur in this case include the following:

- The opportunity cost of income from the prior job
- The forgone interest on the initial investment
- The potential difficulty of being rehired by a former employer (or others) if the idea does not succeed

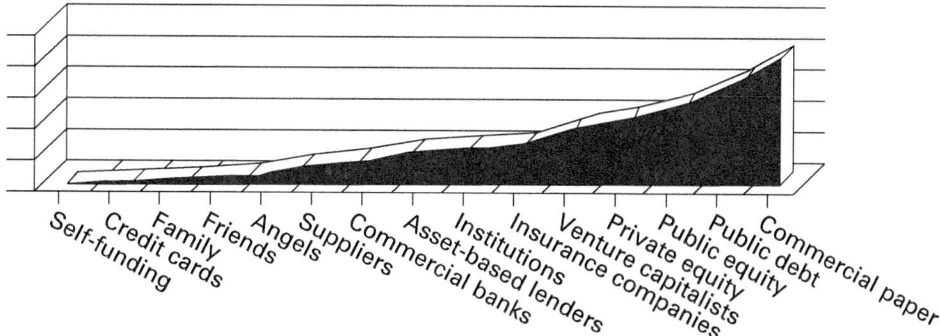

FIGURE 11.1 **Sources of Outside Funding: Levels of Funding and Firm Maturity.**

Add to this the embarrassment of having to beg for a new job while paying off old debts, and the prospective entrepreneur quickly realizes that the total cost of engaging in a new venture is very high. Family and friends may volunteer to fund the entrepreneur's project in the early stages and often will do so without a formal repayment schedule or specified interest cost. However, the funds are far from free. Total costs—including nonfinancial indirect costs, such as family pressure, internal monitoring, and strained relations—are probably extremely high. Moreover, family and friends make poor financial intermediaries because they have limited financial resources, different repayment expectations, and narrow loan diversification. This will contribute to the entrepreneur's desire to get outside funding from a traditional source as soon as possible. The question is, "Where can you go before a bank will give you money?"

Start with Credit Cards and Home Equity Lines

Entrepreneurs who require an immediate infusion of cash often don't have the luxury of time to await the decision of a prospective equity investor or credit lender. They're prone to tapping their personal credit cards for business purchases or borrowing against a low-interest-bearing home equity line of credit. According to a Federal Reserve report,[1] at the end of 2018, consumers had personal credit outstanding over $4 trillion, with approximately a quarter of that applied to revolving credit (credit cards). Nonrevolving credit includes personal credit associated with loans for automobiles and vacations but does not include home equity lines. This credit, which is derived from commercial banks, finance companies, credit unions, and savings institutions, is for personal consumption. Presumably, entrepreneurs have applied some of it to their businesses. Many banks set up credit cards for either personal or business use. And "points" systems that provide credit toward frequent-flyer miles or future purchases may give consumers an economic incentive to maximize their use of credit cards, whether for personal or business purposes. Home equity lines of credit (HELOCs) are another important way in which consumers provide funding for their businesses. Several studies have shown that many entrepreneurs use HELOCs to raise capital. For example, a Rasmussen Report found 30% of respondents use home loans for funding. And another study by the Small Business Research Board found 54% of entrepreneurs use home equity.[2]

Laugh at Your Own Risk

Back in 2000, Adam Lowry and Eric Ryan did not plan on going into the comedy business, but they seemed to make everyone laugh. They both lived in the Bay Area, the Internet start-up capital of the world. Yet potential investors thought they were crazy for trying to start up their company called Method, a household products company that would sell soap and cleaning supplies from environmentally friendly ingredients in cool packaging. They pooled together $100,000 in personal savings to start. By the spring of 2001, Lowry and Ryan had hired Alastair Dorward as CEO. And they were $300,000 in debt, split among the three partners' credit cards. By this time, the tech bubble had burst, and all of a sudden venture capitalists were no longer laughing at their idea. In late 2001, the partners received a term sheet for $1 million. To celebrate, the partners took their investors, lawyers, and accountants out to dinner. The three entrepreneurs' credit cards were all declined. Thank goodness Lowry knew the owner of the restaurant. Lowry said, "We convinced him we were good for it—that the guy over there was about to give us a million bucks."[3] In 2012, Method was acquired by Belgian firm, Ecover, making the world's largest "green-cleaning company." In 2018, with over $200 million in sales, the company was bought by SC Johnson.[4]

Cash Conversion Cycle

One of the most important considerations in setting up a business is deciding when to pay the bills.

The business operating cycle for a traditional manufacturer begins with the purchase of raw materials and ends with collections from the customer. It includes three key components: the inventory cycle, the accounts receivable cycle, and the accounts payable cycle. The **inventory cycle** begins with the purchase of the raw materials, includes the work-in-process period, and ends with the sale of the finished goods. The **accounts receivable cycle** then begins with the sale and concludes with the collection of the receivable. During this operating cycle, the business generally receives some credit from suppliers.

The **accounts payable cycle** begins with the purchase of the raw materials or finished goods, but it ends with the payment to the supplier. The vast majority of organizations, particularly manufacturing operations, experience a gap between the time when they have to pay suppliers and the time when they receive payment from customers. This gap is known as the **cash conversion cycle (CCC)**. For most companies, the credit provided by suppliers ends long before the accounts receivables are paid. This means that, as companies grow sales levels, they need to get external financing to fund working capital needs. One of the primary causes of bankruptcy is the inability to finance operations, shutting down potentially successful ventures. Some companies generate payments from customers before they need to pay their suppliers. Their cash conversion cycle is negative, although from a cash-flow perspective it is very positive. Your industry's typical cash conversion cycle is one of the most important things you should find out about your overall financing scheme. It makes a big difference to your chances for success and growth—if you are fortunate enough to receive payments before providing the service or paying your supplier.

Negative Cash Conversion Cycle

Niraj Shah and Steve Conine, two college friends, founded an e-commerce store in 2002 that has had many names, but today is company most everyone knows: Wayfair.com. The key to their success is not only their mastering of Web analytics and target marketing, but also the business advantage behind their business's cash conversion cycle.

This two engineers created a conglomerate of sites like simplydogbeds.com for people searching for dog beds, or everycuckooclock.com for people that wanted to buy cuckoo clocks. This way, they would help customers find their way to the e-commerce powerhouse that today sells millions of different home items. But the brilliance of the business also relies on its efficient cash conversion cycle. Around 90% of the objects they sell are stored by the suppliers, which means they have very little inventory. This model allowed them to grow sales into the hundreds of millions without raising a single dime. Today, Wayfair has over 12,000 employees and over surpassed $4 billion in sales in 2017.[5]

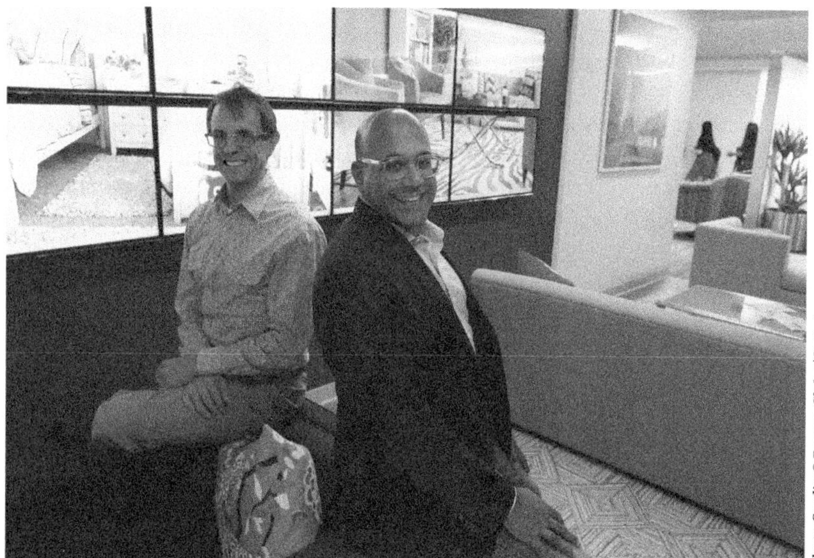

Photo Credit: © Boston Globe/Getty Images

Steve Conine and Niraj Shah, the founders of Wayfair, were able to grow their multi-million dollar company without raising capital.

Working Capital: Getting Cash from Receivables and Inventories

The timing of collection of accounts receivable and payment of accounts payable is a key determinant in whether a firm is cash rich or cash poor. For example, an increase in net working capital (i.e., current assets minus current liabilities) doesn't necessarily translate into an increase in liquidity. One reason is that increases in net working capital often result from increases in operating assets, net of increases in operating liabilities. These operating assets, such as accounts receivable or inventory, are usually tied up in operations, and firms don't commonly liquidate them (prematurely) to pay bills, typically paying with liquid financial assets, such as cash and marketable securities, instead. Thus, we can use only liquid financial assets to assess a firm's liquidity.

Further, corporate insolvency usually results when the firm fails to service debt obligations or callable liabilities on time. We can estimate corporate liquidity fairly accurately by taking the difference between liquid financial assets and callable liabilities, referred to as the *net liquid balance*. The net liquid balance is actually a part of net working capital. *Net working capital* is easy to calculate in one of two ways:

- take the difference between current assets and current liabilities (as described earlier), or
- take the difference between long-term liabilities, including equities, and long-term assets (such as fixed assets).

The first formula is often misinterpreted to be the difference between two liquid components, whereas the second definition suggests that the residual of long-term liabilities minus long-term assets is used to finance current assets, some of which may be liquid. The second definition also enables us to analyze the current assets and liabilities as consisting of both liquid financial/callable components and operating components.

Net working capital is actually the sum of the working capital requirements balance. This suggests that only a part of net working capital is liquid. Clearly, as a small firm grows, current operating assets will increase. If current operating liabilities don't increase at the same rate as the increase in current operating assets (which is true when an entrepreneur pays suppliers before receiving payment from customers), then the entrepreneur will find that the firm's net liquid balance will decrease (assuming the firm does not increase its long-term funding arrangements). This may be true even though the firm is generating paper profits. As long as the increase in working capital requirements *exceeds* the increase in profits, then the firm will find itself reducing its liquidity levels.

This highlights one of the fundamental weaknesses of the traditional liquidity ratios, such as the current ratio or quick ratio. These ratios include both liquid financial assets and operating assets in their formulas. Because operating assets are tied up in operations, including these assets in a liquidity ratio is not very useful from an ongoing-concern perspective. Note the difference between a liquidity perspective and a liquidation perspective. A liquidation perspective assumes that in the event of a crisis, the firm may sell assets off to meet financial obligations, whereas a liquidity perspective assumes that the firm meets its financial obligations without impairing the viability of future operations. From an ongoing perspective, a new ratio—*net liquid balance* to *total assets*—may be more indicative of liquidity than either the current ratio or the quick ratio.

Using Accounts Receivable as Working Capital

Accounts receivable—that is, the money owed to the company as a result of sales made on credit for which payment has not yet been received—are a major element in working capital for most companies. And they are one of the reasons we can assert that *working capital* is not the same as *available cash* and that the timing of short-term flows is vitally important.

If a company is selling a major part of its output on credit and giving 30 days' credit, its accounts receivable will be about equal to sales of 30 days—that is, to one-twelfth of its annual sales—if sales are reasonably stable over the year. And if the company's collection policies are so liberal or ineffective that in practice customers are paying an average of, say, 45 days after they are billed, accounts receivable are no less than one-eighth of annual sales. Investment in accounts receivable is a use of funds. The company has to finance the credit it is giving to its customers by allowing its money to be tied up in this way instead of being available for investment in productive uses. Therefore, accounts receivable, like cash, have an opportunity cost.

The magnitude of a company's accounts receivable obviously depends on a number of factors:

- The level and the pattern of sales
- The breakdown between cash and credit sales
- The nominal credit terms offered
- The way these credit terms are enforced through a collection policy

We'll discuss each of these factors in detail in the following sections.

The Sales Pattern

The basis of all receivables and collections is clearly *actual net sales*—that is, sales sold minus any returns. From actual sales come the assumptions about receipts from future cash sales and collections of future credit sales. These are the key inputs in forecasting cash flow, as discussed later in this chapter. Techniques for forecasting future sales fall into two broad groups:

- Techniques that use external or economic information
- Techniques that are based on internal or historical data from the company's own past sales

Most managers are more familiar with the techniques in the second group than they are with economic forecasting. The methods for forecasting from historical data range from the very simple (such as a straightforward moving average) to fairly sophisticated models. For instance, variations on exponential smoothing make it possible to take into account both long-term trends in the company's sales and seasonal variations. Simply put, although the more sophisticated techniques are useful, no forecasting method based *only* on historical sales data is completely satisfactory. You cannot be sure that either total industry sales or the company's share of the sales will be the same as they have been; you must consider a variety of external factors.

Methods of forecasting environmental change also fall into two broad groups. One group is primarily concerned with *forecasting the future performance of the economy as a whole*, particularly future levels of the gross national product (GNP) and the national income. These *GNP models*, as they are called, are highly complex, computer-based models. Their construction may be beyond the capabilities of most entrepreneurs, but you can easily purchase their output. The other group is more concerned with *forecasting sales for individual industries and products*. One way to do this is to identify economic time series to use as leading indicators to signal changes in the variable being forecast. Again, this technique is best wielded by an experienced economist with a computer. The important point for the entrepreneur is that forecasting techniques are becoming progressively less of an art and more of a science.

Cash versus Credit Sales

The relative proportions of cash sales and credit sales may make an important difference to expected cash flows. Unfortunately, this is a variable over which most entrepreneurs have little control. For example, a company in retail sales can certainly take steps to increase its cash sales, either by banning credit entirely or by offering a discount on cash sales. But a company selling primarily to other corporate organizations—other manufacturing companies, wholesalers, distributors, or retail chains—has few cash sales. Its best hope is to set its credit terms to encourage prompt payment, but the sales will still be credit sales, not cash sales.

Credit Policies

Credit policies boil down to two general questions:

- To whom should we give credit?
- How much credit should we give?

These two questions are closely interconnected. The business needs to evaluate most potential credit sales on their own merits, and this is costly and time consuming. In fact, the salaries and overhead of the credit analysts are likely to be the largest single item in the cost of giving credit to customers.

How much freedom a company has in setting the terms on which it will grant credit depends very much on its *competitive position*. For example, an organization in a monopolistic position has considerably more flexibility than does one that faces aggressive competition. But real monopolies are rare. Most companies approach such a position only during very short periods, after they have introduced radically new products and before their competitors have had time to introduce similar ones. A company in such a position may be tempted to take advantage of it through product price, but it is likely to tighten up its credit policy as well. The advantage of restricting credit will be fairly short-lived, but the damage to customer relations could continue for a long time.

Nevertheless, economic factors do play an important part in credit policy. The key issue is *elasticity of demand* for the entrepreneur's product (we assume that the credit terms are a component of the overall price as the customer sees it and that customers will resist a reduction in credit, just as they will resist a price increase). If demand for a product is *inelastic*—that is, if an increase in price or a restriction in the terms of credit will produce a relatively small drop in demand, with the result that net sales revenues actually increase—then there is some potential flexibility in the terms of sale. Even here, however, it will be the industry as a whole that enjoys this flexibility; individual companies will probably have to accept general industry practice. If demand for a product is *elastic*, on the other hand, there will be little room to change the terms of the sale at either the company or the industry level.

Finally, a company operating below full capacity or below its optimal output may well be tempted to offer unusually generous credit terms to stimulate demand. The key question then is whether the cost of the additional funds tied up in accounts receivable will be more than offset by the additional sales and reduced operating costs. Alternatively, a company working at full capacity, with its product back-ordered, is in a position to tighten up on its credit policies to reduce its investment in receivables.

Setting Credit Terms

The terms of credit include both the *length of time* given before payment is due and the *discount* given for prompt payment. Terms expressed as "2/10, net 30" mean that payment is due within 30 days (from the date of the invoice) and that the payer can deduct 2% from the bill if he makes the payment in 10 or fewer days. Some companies, on the other hand, set their net terms as payment by the end of the month following the month in which the sale is invoiced. Obviously, this latter policy is considerably more generous than "net 30" and is likely to result in a much larger investment in receivables.

An entrepreneur's failure to take advantage of cash discounts available on its accounts payable may be a very expensive mistake, equivalent to borrowing short-term funds at 36%. Is it an equally serious mistake for a company to offer the same terms to its customers? The answer is that it depends on whether giving a cash discount really does speed up collections and whether the *opportunity cost* of the funds that would otherwise have been locked up in receivables justifies the reduction in net sales revenues.

For example, assume that an entrepreneur's terms are 2/10, net 30 and that 25% of its customers actually take advantage of this discount. Annual sales are $36 million, of which $9 million are discounted, and the company recognizes profits when the sales are made. The discount's cost, therefore, is 2% of $9 million, or $180,000. Assuming that 25% of the customers pay in 10 days and the rest pay in 30, the average collection period (including both discount and non-discount sales) is 25 days, giving average accounts receivable of $2.5 million, as shown in the following equation:

$$\$36{,}000{,}000 / (360 / 25) = \$2{,}500{,}000$$

If the company did not give a discount, none of its customers would pay within 10 days, and the average collection period would fall from 25 to 30. In that case, average accounts receivable would be $3 million:

$$\$36{,}000{,}000 / (360 / 30) = \$3{,}000{,}000$$

The question is, then, whether the added return the company makes on the $500,000 by which the discount policy has reduced the average accounts receivable exceeds $180,000, the cost of the discount policy. As this represents a return on investment of more than 36%, the answer is probably no.

A change in the net terms, however, is likely to make a greater difference to the average accounts receivable balance than giving or withholding a discount for prompt payment. Even if you give terms of 2/10, net 30, you can assume that a relatively small percentage of customers will take advantage of the discount. But if you change the net terms from 30 days to 45, doubtless a high percentage of customers *will* take advantage. Going back to the previous example and assuming that 25% of customers pay within 10 days and the rest at the end of 45 days, the average payment period now is approximately 36 days [(10 × .25) + (45 × .75)], and the average accounts receivable is $3.6 million, as shown:

$$\$36{,}000{,}000 / (360 / 36) = \$3{,}600{,}000$$

In this example, we assumed that, if the net terms are set at 30 or 45 days, everyone who does not take advantage of the discount for prompt payment will pay by the end of the net period. This is unrealistic. Many entrepreneurs and the companies they do business with make a practice of reducing their requirements for funds by paying all their bills late. True, the most commonly offered terms are 2/10, net 30, but a survey revealed that the actual experience of U.S. companies is that their average receivables run between 45 and 50 days. A company's accounts receivable depend not only on the terms of credit offered but also on how well those terms are enforced through the company's collection policy.

Collection Policies

Some of a company's accounts receivable will be paid sometime after the theoretical time limit has expired. Others will never be paid at all and will have to be written off as bad debts. Neither of these variables is completely within the company's control, but both can be controlled to some extent.

The collection techniques of companies selling directly to the ultimate consumer are often highly standardized and even automated. The firms store master records of customers in computer data files and periodically search for overdue accounts. Each customer whose account has been outstanding for more than the net terms receives a series of increasingly stronger letters asking for payment. A system like this provides little opportunity to match the collection technique to the particular customer and situation. The average amount owed is probably small, however, and more individualized techniques are hard to justify in such circumstances.

When an entrepreneur's firm sells primarily in the industrial market and its customers are businesses, it will look at each individual case and determine how best to collect. If the other company is able to pay, the entrepreneur should rigorously attempt to secure payment before the situation becomes any worse. The methods include the following:

- Refusing any further orders or supplying only for cash
- Threatening legal action
- Actually undertaking legal proceedings, using a specialized collection agency

If the other company is already in serious financial trouble, however, an all-out collection attempt may simply force the customer into insolvency, followed by liquidation or reorganization. The wisest approach in this case may be to continue to give credit, or at least not to try to collect existing receivables, in the hope of keeping the other company in business. But if your company is one of a number of creditors, you gain nothing by being generous unless the other creditors are willing to do the same. Otherwise, you are simply subordinating your claims to those of others and increasing the chance that the debt will never be paid at all.

It's safe to say that collection procedures are expensive and therefore are justifiable *only when the expected results exceed the cost.* Collection operations are, in fact, an excellent demonstration of the economists' law of diminishing returns. For a given volume of overdue accounts, the first few thousand dollars spent on collection will probably produce worthwhile results. But further expenditure is likely to yield less and less return.

How much should you be willing to spend on collection? The answer depends on the reduction you expect in accounts receivable and the return you'd expect if these additional funds were available for reinvestment in productive operations. Assume that you can reduce overdue accounts receivable $250,000 by hiring an assistant for $25,000. To cover the assistant's salary, you need to earn at least a 10% return on the funds released from accounts receivable. This represents a fairly reasonable rate of return and should be attainable. However, consider all the other nonwage costs of hiring an assistant, including FICA taxes, health care, and benefits, which could easily push the costs of the assistant up another $10,000, or 40%. Whenever you consider reducing excess receivables, examine the size and scope of the collection attempts and judge whether the costs justify the expenditure.

Setting Credit Limits for Individual Accounts

Another method of reducing overdue accounts and limiting bad debts is setting limits to the credit allowed on individual accounts. Again, as in collections, entrepreneurs need to distinguish between *sales to individual consumers* and *sales to corporate buyers.* An entrepreneur selling directly to consumers clearly cannot afford to undertake a thorough credit investigation of each one (unless the product being sold is a very expensive item, such as a boat or an automobile) and will set fairly arbitrary limits on the basis of limited information. But if the customers are business organizations, the setting of credit limits requires more thorough analysis, especially when the firm adds a new customer to its files and when it suspects an existing customer's circumstances have deteriorated.

Dun & Bradstreet offers resources and business reports through its website (www.dnb.com). You can check others' business credit ratings and your own business credit information. These ratings range from "high" to "limited" and include an estimate of the company's financial strength, usually based on net worth. If more detail is needed, Dun & Bradstreet and other agencies sell reports that include information about a company's principal officers, any past bankruptcies, and, most important, the company's credit history in relationship to its existing suppliers.

There are a number of other sources of information:

- Some industry associations operate credit advisory services for the benefit of their members.
- Companies selling directly to the consumer can get information from local credit bureaus.
- Commercial banks are also a useful source of credit information. An entrepreneur considering an extension of credit to a customer can ask her bank to carry out a credit investigation, which the bank will do by approaching the customer's bank for information about the customer.

You can cut short much of the work of appraising the creditworthiness of new customers by using external sources of information, but monitoring accounts receivable and deciding whether to increase credit limits or ban further credit represent a continuing task for your own staff. The decisions are often difficult. No company likes to turn down orders. Once again, you face a trade-off: the potential profit on the sale versus the cost of financing increased receivables and the probability of bad debt. Because the cost of the latter far exceeds the cost of the former, most entrepreneurs are very careful about granting credit.

The two major determinants of the credit decision are the character of the individual creditor or management of the creditor firm and the capacity of the firm to repay the loan. Entrepreneurs will find that the same simple set of guidelines they use in extending credit to customers is what banks use in extending credit to entrepreneurs. They're known as the Five Cs of credit:

- *Character* refers to the customer's integrity and willingness to repay the financial obligation.
- *Capacity* addresses the borrower's cash flow and ability to repay the debt from ongoing business operations.
- *Capital* is the borrower's financial net worth; consequently, a wealthy borrower may be a desirable customer even if his or her annual cash flows are relatively low.
- *Collateral* refers to the resale value of the product in the event repossession becomes necessary.
- *Conditions* refer to national or international economic, industrial, and firm-specific prospects during the time period of the credit.

The credit-granting decision is only part of the entrepreneur's concern. Another important task is monitoring accounts receivable balances. Because receivables tied up in operations may represent a large opportunity cost, either in lost investment returns or in greater borrowing balances, entrepreneurs are careful not to let the accounts receivable balances get too large.

Although the opportunity costs for accounts receivable may be quite large, the largest current asset balances are usually in inventories. As the entrepreneur's business grows, inventory balances rise, and resulting operating cash flows decline. You need to monitor both accounts receivable and inventories and keep the levels as low as possible without interfering with profitable sales. This is especially true if you have a shortage of capital or credit limitations.

Inventory

Inventory represents the most important current asset of most manufacturing and trading companies, yet money invested in inventory doesn't earn a return. In fact, it costs money to maintain inventories. Some inventory will be devalued or become a total loss because it deteriorates or becomes obsolete before it can be used or sold. These costs can easily add up to 20% or more of the inventory value annually. Because the money tied up in inventory might otherwise be invested profitably, the real costs plus the opportunity costs of carrying inventory may add up to 30%, 40%, or even more. As with accounts receivable, the dollar amount of inventory depends on when the entrepreneur chooses to recognize profit: Is it at the time of production or the time of sale? A strong argument can be made for valuing inventories at cost or market, whichever is lower. Given uncertainty about how much cash flow the inventory will actually generate, a conservative approach to valuation is best.

Entrepreneurs usually also want to keep inventory levels as low as possible, not only to reduce the inventory carry charges such as storage costs and insurance but also to ensure that as little capital as possible is tied up in inventory.

But carrying too little inventory also incurs heavy costs. These include the following:

- The costs of too frequent reordering
- The loss of quantity discounts
- The loss of customer goodwill or plant efficiency due to items being unavailable when needed

You'll want to weigh these costs against those of carrying excessive inventory to be able to judge the optimal level of inventory.

The control of investment in inventories is particularly important to the *management of working capital*. Inventories are likely to represent your largest current investment and to be the least liquid of your current assets. Marketable securities can be turned into cash in a matter of hours, and most accounts receivable will usually be collected within the next 30 days. But three months' supply of inventory will take three months to turn into cash, if forecasts of demand or usage prove accurate. If your forecasts were optimistic, you might need even more time. The alternative—an immediate forced sale—is hardly attractive. You can sell marketable securities for their market value and sell, or factor, receivables for something like 80% of their face value. But inventories, other than some raw materials for which a ready market always exists, traditionally sell for little more than 10% of their acquisition cost in a forced sale. Thus, controlling a company's investment in inventory is of critical importance to managing your working capital.

One Company's Old Inventory Is Another's Treasure

Today, Patrick Byrne's company brings in over $1 billion in sale every year, but he could not raise money from any of the 50 venture capital firms to which he pitched his idea. In fact, his investment banker closed 181 out of 182 deals in 1999, and Overstock.com was the only deal that did not receive an investment. Byrne then got his break when a company named Miadora.com, an online jewelry e-tailer that received over $51 million in venture capital, was about to go bankrupt. The venture capitalists needed someone to purchase and liquidate the inventory fast. Overstock.com was officially born. Over the next few months, Overstock.com liquidated 18 different companies, all backed by venture capitalists. And Byrne finally received some venture capital backing himself.[6]

Overstock.com grew from $1.8 million in revenue in 1999 to over $1.7 billion by 2018.

Sources of Short-Term Cash: More Payables, Less Receivables

Entrepreneurs usually don't have all the cash they need all the time. Very often an entrepreneurial firm needs to build up its inventory, thus reducing cash levels. Or an entrepreneur's customers may place unusually large orders, thus increasing accounts receivable financing or reducing company cash levels. This section describes the many ways entrepreneurs obtain additional short-term cash to restore their cash balances to the required levels.

As a rule, entrepreneurs look for short-term cash at the lowest possible rates. For example, an entrepreneur faced with a cash shortage might look first to her company's suppliers because they extend credit to the company by collecting for goods and services after supplying them. The entrepreneur can enlarge this credit by paying bills more slowly—and also obtain additional cash by collecting from her customers more quickly.

Cash from Short-Term Bank Loans

Although supplier financing is convenient, it is often cheaper to pursue bank financing if possible. Entrepreneurs faced with a severe cash shortage may also try to convert into cash two of their working capital assets: accounts receivable and inventory. An entrepreneur may pledge her accounts receivable to a finance company in exchange for a loan, or she may sell them to a factoring company for cash. Similarly, an entrepreneur may pledge her inventory (often using a warehousing system) in exchange for a loan.

Cash from Trade Credit

Trade credit is one important and often low-cost source of cash. Nearly all entrepreneurs make use of trade credit to some degree by not paying suppliers immediately for goods and services. Instead, companies bill the entrepreneur, and the entrepreneur pays in 10 days, 30 days, or more. From the time the supplier first provides the goods or services to the time the customer finally pays for them, the supplier has, in effect, loaned the entrepreneur money. The sum of all these loans (bills) represents an entrepreneur's trade credit. By paying bills more slowly, an entrepreneur can increase the amount of these loans from his suppliers.

One way to take more time to pay bills (or stretch payables) is to stop taking discounts. For example, if your company normally takes advantage of all prompt-payment discounts, such as 2% for payment within 10 days, you can increase your company's cash by passing up the discount and paying the bill in the expected 30 days. Of course, this is an expensive source of cash. If you lose a 2% discount and have the use of the funds for 20 more days, you've paid approximately 36% interest (annual rate) for using the money.

In practice, though, the interest cost wouldn't really be 36% because, by forgoing discounts and aggressively stretching payables, you wouldn't pay the bill in 30 days. Instead, you might try to pay it in 60 days. Now the equivalent interest rate is only about 15% (50 days' extra use of the money for 2%).

This brings up the subject of late payments. Many entrepreneurs don't consider 30 days (or any other stated terms) a real deadline. Instead, they try to determine the exact point at which further delay of payment will bring a penalty. For example, if a company pays too slowly, the supplier may take one of the following actions:

- Require payment in full on future orders
- Report the company to a credit bureau, which would damage the company's credit rating with all suppliers
- Bring legal action against the company

Many cash managers believe, however, that as long as they can pay company bills just before incurring any of these penalties, they maximize their company's cash at little or no cost. The *hidden costs* of this approach include such risks as a damaged reputation, a lower credit limit from suppliers, higher prices from suppliers to compensate for delayed payment, and the risk of exceeding the supplier's final deadline and incurring a penalty.

Cash Obtained by Negotiating with Suppliers

If an entrepreneur wants more credit and would like to stretch out her payables, very often she can negotiate with her suppliers for more generous credit terms, at least temporarily. If she and her supplier agree on longer credit terms (say, 60 or 90 days), she can get the extra trade credits she needs without jeopardizing her supplier relations or credit ratings. One way suppliers compete is through credit terms, and you can use that fact to your advantage.

Some suppliers use generous terms of trade credit as a form of sales promotion that may well be more effective than an intensive advertising campaign or a high-pressure sales team. The credit may be a simple extension of the discount or net terms, or it may take a modified form such as an inventory loan.

Cash Available Because of Seasonal Business Credit Terms

If the entrepreneur is in a highly seasonal business, as many types of retailers are, he will find large differences in credit terms in different seasons. For example, as a retailer, he might be very short of cash in the fall as he builds up inventory for the holiday selling season. Many suppliers will understand this and willingly extend their normal 30-day terms.

Furthermore, some suppliers will offer exceedingly generous credit terms to smooth out their own manufacturing cycle. Consider a game manufacturer that sells half its annual production in the few months before Christmas. Rather than producing and shipping most of the games in the late summer, this manufacturer would much rather spread out its production and shipping schedule over most of the year. To accomplish this, the manufacturer may offer seasonal dating to its retail store customers. **Seasonal dating** provides longer credit terms on orders placed in off-peak periods. For example, the game manufacturer might offer 120-day terms on May orders, 90-day terms on June orders, and so on. This will encourage customers to order early, and it will allow the game manufacturer to spread out production over more of the year.

Advantages of Trade Credit

Trade credit has two important advantages that justify its extensive use. The first advantage is convenience and ready availability; because it is not negotiated, it requires no great expenditure of executive time and no legal expenses. If a supplier accepts a company as a customer, it automatically extends the usual credit terms even though it may set the maximum line of credit low at first.

The second advantage (closely related to the first) is that the *credit available from this source automatically grows as the company grows*. Accounts payable are known as a spontaneous source of financing. As sales expand, production schedules increase, which in turn means that larger quantities of materials and supplies must be bought. In the absence of limits on credit, the additional credit becomes available automatically simply because the firm has placed orders for the extra material. Of course, if the manufacturing process is long and the company reaches the deadline for the supplier's payment before selling the goods, it may need some additional source of credit. But the amount needed will be much less than if no trade credit had been available.

Cash Obtained by Tightening Up Accounts Receivable Collections

Rapidly growing accounts receivable tie up a company's money and can cause a cash squeeze. However, these same accounts receivable become cash when collected. Some techniques—such as lockboxes and wire transfers—enable firms to collect receivables quickly and regularly. But how can the firm increase the rate of collection temporarily during a cash shortage?

The most effective way is simply to *ask for the money*. If the entrepreneur just sends a bill every month and shows the amount past due, the customer may not feel a great pressure to pay quickly. But if the entrepreneur asks for the money, with a handwritten note on the statement of account, a phone call, or a formal letter, the customer will usually pay more quickly. Of course, more aggressive collection techniques also have costs, such as the loss of customer goodwill, the scaring away of new customers, the loss of old customers to more lenient suppliers, and the generation of industry rumors that the company is short of cash and may be a poor credit risk.

The entrepreneur can also *change his sales terms* to collect cash more quickly. Options include the following:

1. *Introduce, increase, or eliminate discounts.* A company can initiate a discount for prompt payment (e.g., a 2% discount for payment within 10 days). Similarly, a company with an existing discount may increase the discount (e.g., increase the discount from 1% to 2%). Finally, a company can eliminate the discount altogether and simply demand cash immediately or upon delivery (COD). Companies will have difficulty instituting these measures if competitors offer significantly more lenient credit terms.
2. *Emphasize cash sales.* Some entrepreneurs, particularly those selling directly to consumers, may be able to increase their percentage of cash sales.
3. *Accept credit cards.* Sales made on bank credit cards or on travel or entertainment cards are convertible within a couple of days into cash. The credit card companies charge 3% to 7% of the amount of the sale for this service.

Obtaining Bank Loans Through Accounts Receivable Financing

One approach to free up working capital funds is to convert accounts receivable into cash more quickly through aggressive collection techniques. However, if you fear aggressive collection may offend customers and cause them to take their business to competitors, you may decide to convert accounts receivable to cash through a financing company, using either pledging or factoring. The following sections describe both methods. In practice, finance companies and banks offer many variations on them.

Pledging

Pledging means using accounts receivable as collateral for a loan from a finance company or bank. The finance company then gives money to the borrower, and as the borrower's customers pay their bills, the borrower repays the loan to the finance company. With this form of accounts receivable financing, the borrower's customers are not notified that their bills are being used as collateral for a loan. Therefore, pledging is called *non-notification financing*. Furthermore, if customers do not pay their bills, the borrower (rather than the finance company) must absorb the loss. Thus, if the customer defaults, the lender has the right of recourse to the borrower.

A finance company will not usually lend the full face value of the accounts receivable pledged. Typically, a company can borrow 75% to 90% of the face value of its accounts receivable if it has a good credit rating and its customers have excellent credit ratings. Companies with lower credit ratings can generally borrow 60% to 75% of the face value of their receivables. Pledging receivables is not a cheap source of credit. It's used mostly by smaller companies that have no other source of funds open to them.

Pledging with Notification

Another form of pledging is called **pledging with notification**, in which the borrower instructs its customers to pay their bills directly to the lender (often a bank). As checks from customers arrive, the bank deposits them in a special account and notifies the borrower that money has arrived. Here, the lender controls the receivables more closely and does not have to worry that the borrower may collect pledged accounts receivable and then not notify it. The company loses under this system, however, because it must notify its customers that it has pledged its accounts receivable, which can reduce its credit rating.

Factoring

Factoring is selling accounts receivable at a discount to a finance company known as the *factor*. The factor takes over credit checking and collection. If the factor rejects a potential customer as an unacceptable credit risk, the company must either turn down the order or insist on cash payment.

The fees that factors charge vary widely. They include the following:

- An interest charge, usually expressed on a daily basis for the time the bill is outstanding
- A collection fee, usually in the range of an additional 6% to 10% (on an annual basis)
- A credit-checking charge, either a percentage of the invoice or a flat dollar amount

The factor keeps a hold-back amount to more than cover these various fees and charges, deducts the total from the hold-back amount, and sends the remainder to the company.

Recourse

Factoring may be with or without recourse. *Factoring without recourse* means that, if the customer doesn't pay its bill (it is a true deadbeat), the factor must absorb the loss. *Factoring with recourse*, on the other hand, means that, if the customer doesn't pay the bill within a pre-negotiated time (e.g., 90 days), the factor collects from the selling company. The company must then try to collect from the customer directly.

Naturally, a factor charges extra for factoring without recourse, typically 6% to 12% (on an annual basis) added to the interest rate it charges the selling company. For factoring without recourse, factors generally come out ahead because they minimize bad-debt expense by carefully checking each customer's credit. Nevertheless, the selling company might prefer factoring without recourse for two reasons:

- The company does not have to worry that any bills will be returned. In this way, factoring without recourse is a form of insurance.
- The factor expresses the extra charge for factoring without recourse as part of the daily interest rate. This daily interest rate may look very small.

Most factoring is done with notification. This means the customer company is notified and instructed to pay its bill directly to the factor. When factoring is without notification, the customer sends payment either directly to the supplier or to a post office box. In general, factoring is more expensive than pledging. On the other hand, factors provide services, such as credit checking and credit collection, that a company would otherwise have to carry out itself. For a small company, using a factor is often less expensive than providing the same services for itself.

Obtaining Loans against Inventory

An entrepreneur's inventory is an asset that can serve as collateral for a loan, providing needed cash without jeopardizing access to the inventory. There are four basic ways to use inventory as security for a loan, depending on how closely the lender controls the physical inventory:

1. *Chattel mortgage*, in which specific inventory is used to secure the loan.
2. *Floating (or blanket) lien*, in which the loan is secured by all the borrower's inventory.
3. *Field warehousing*, in which the lender physically separates and guards the pledged inventory right on the borrower's premises.
4. *Public warehousing*, in which the lender transfers the pledged inventory to a separate warehouse.

Obtaining "Financing" from Customer Prepayments

Some companies are actually financed by their customers. This situation typically occurs on large, complex, long-term projects undertaken by defense contractors, building contractors, ship builders, and management consulting firms. These companies typically divide their large projects into a series of stages and require payment as they complete each stage. This significantly reduces the cash they require, compared with firms that finance an entire project themselves and receive payment on completion. In some companies, customers pay in advance for everything they buy. Many mail-order operations are financed this way.

Choosing the Right Mix of Short-Term Financing

The entrepreneur attempts to secure the required short-term funds at the lowest cost. The lowest cost usually results from some combination of trade credit, unsecured and secured bank loans, accounts receivable financing, and inventory financing. Although it is virtually impossible to evaluate every possible combination of short-term financing, entrepreneurs can use their experience and subjective opinion to put together a short-term financing package that will have a reasonable cost. At the same time, the entrepreneur must be aware of future requirements and the impact that using certain sources today may have on the availability of short-term funds in the future. In selecting the best financing package, the entrepreneur should consider the following factors:

- The firm's current situation and requirements
- The current and future costs of the alternatives
- The firm's future situation and requirements

For small firms, the options may be somewhat limited, and the total short-term financing package may be less important. On the other hand, larger firms may face myriad possibilities. Clearly, the short-term borrowing decision can become quite complex, but choosing the right combination of options can be of significant financial value to the entrepreneur's firm.

Traditional Bank Lending: Short-Term Bank Loans

After an entrepreneur has fully used her trade credit and collected her receivables as quickly as competitively possible, she may turn to a bank for a short-term loan. The most common bank loan is a *short-term, unsecured loan* made for 90 days. Standard variations include loans made for periods of 30 days to a year and loans requiring collateral. Interest charges on these loans typically vary from the prime rate (the amount a bank charges its largest and financially strongest customers) to about 3% above prime.

Commercial banks are the most important suppliers of debt capital to small firms, supplying more than 80% of lending in the credit line market and more than 50% in other markets, such as commercial mortgages and vehicle, equipment, and other loans. After banks tightened their standards for loans of all kinds in the wake of the 2008 banking crash, it has been more difficult for small businesses, but the U.S. Small Business Association helps facilitate more than $30 billion to small businesses ever year, and there are other ways to smartly "manage" your cash needs.[7]

Very often, an entrepreneur doesn't immediately need money but can forecast that she will have a definite need in, say, six months. The entrepreneur will not want to borrow the required money now and pay unnecessary interest for the next six months. Instead, she will formally apply to her bank for a *line of credit*, which is an assurance by the bank that, as long as the company remains financially healthy, the bank will lend the company money (up to a specified limit) whenever the company needs it. Banks usually review a company's credit line each year. A line of credit is not a guarantee that the bank will make a loan in the future. Instead, when the company actually needs the money, the bank will examine the company's current financial statements to make sure that actual results coincide with earlier plans.

Banks also grant *guaranteed lines of credit*, under which they guarantee to supply funds up to a specified limit regardless of circumstances. This relieves the company of any worries that money may not be available when it's needed. Banks usually charge extra for this guarantee, typically 1% a year on the unused amount of the guaranteed line of credit. For example, if the bank guarantees a credit line of $1 million and the company borrows only $300,000, the company will have to pay a commitment fee of perhaps $7,000 for the $700,000 it did not borrow.

In return for granting lines of credit, banks usually require that an entrepreneur maintain a *compensating balance* (i.e., keep a specified amount in its checking account without interest). For example, if an entrepreneur receives a $1 million line of credit with the requirement that she maintain a 15% compensating balance, the entrepreneur must keep at least $150,000 in her demand account with that bank all year. The bank, of course, does not have to pay interest on this demand account money, so the use of this money compensates it for standing ready to grant up to $1 million in loans for a year. Of course, when the bank actually makes loans, it charges the negotiated rate of interest.

Maturity of Loans

The most common time period, or maturity, for short-term bank loans is 90 days; however, an entrepreneur can negotiate maturities of 30 days to one year. Banks often prefer 90-day maturities, even when the entrepreneur will clearly need the money for longer than 90 days, because the three-month maturity gives the bank a chance to check the entrepreneur's financial statements regularly. If the entrepreneur's position has deteriorated, the bank may refuse to renew the loan and thus avoid a future loss.

Entrepreneurs, on the other hand, prefer maturities that closely match the time they expect to need the money. A longer maturity (rather than a series of short, constantly renewed loans) eliminates the possibility that the bank will refuse to extend a short-term loan because of a temporary weakness in the entrepreneur's operations.

Interest Rates

The rates of interest charged by commercial banks vary in two ways:

1. The general level of interest rates varies over time.
2. At any given time, different rates are charged to different borrowers.

The base rate for most commercial banks traditionally has been the *prime rate*, which is the rate commercial banks charge their very best business customers for short-term borrowing. This is the rate that makes the news every time it changes. Congress and the business community speculate about the prime's influence on economic activity because historically it has been the baseline for loan pricing in most loan agreements. "Prime plus two" or "2% above prime" was a normal statement of the interest rate on many loan contracts. However, as the banking industry has begun to price its loans and services more aggressively, the prime is becoming less important and compensating balances less popular.

The current trend in loan pricing is *to price the loan at a rate above the marginal cost of funds* as typically reflected by the interest rates on certificates of deposit. The bank then adds an interest rate margin to the cost of funds, and the result is the rate charged to the borrower. This rate changes daily in line with the changes in money market rates offered by the bank. As liability management becomes more of a way of life for bankers, the pricing of loans will become a function of the amount of competition, both domestic and international, that the banker faces in securing loanable funds. As a result of this competition for corporate customers and enhanced competition from the commercial paper market, large, financially stable corporations are often able to borrow at a rate below prime.

The interest borrowers pay depends on several factors:

- The dollar amount of the loan
- The length of time involved
- The nominal annual rate of interest
- The repayment schedule
- The method used to calculate the interest

The various methods used to calculate interest are all variations of the simple interest calculation. *Simple interest* is calculated on the amount borrowed for the length of time the loan is outstanding. For example, if you borrow $1 million at 10% and repay in one payment at the end of one year, the simple interest is $1 million times 0.10, or $100,000. In the *add-in interest* method, the lender calculates interest on the full amount of the original principal and immediately adds it to the original principal, calculating payments by dividing principal plus interest by the number of payments to be made. If there is only one payment, this method is identical to simple interest. However, with two or more payments, this method results in an effective rate of interest greater than the nominal rate. Continuing with the add-in interest example, if you repaid the $1 million loan in two six-month installments of $550,000 each, the effective rate is higher than 10% because you don't have the use of the funds for the entire year.

The *bank discount method* is common in short-term business loans. Generally, there are no immediate payments, and the life of the loan is usually one year or less. Interest is calculated on the amount of the loan, and the borrower receives the difference between the amount to be paid back and the amount of interest. In our example, the lender subtracts the interest amount of $100,000 from the $1 million, and you have the use of $900,000 for one year. If you divide the interest payment by the amount of money you actually used ($100,000 divided by $900,000), the effective rate is 11.1%.

If the loan were to require a compensating balance of 10%, you have the use of the loan amount less the compensating balance requirement. The effective rate of interest in this case would be 12.5% minus the interest amount of $100,000 divided by the funds available, which is $800,000 ($1,000,000 minus $100,000 interest and minus a compensating balance of $100,000). The effective interest cost on a *revolving credit* agreement includes both interest costs and the commitment fee. For example, assume the TBA Corporation has a $1 million revolving credit agreement with a bank. Interest on the borrowed funds is 10% per annum. TBA must pay a commitment fee of 1% on the unused portion of the credit line. If the firm borrows $500,000, the effective annual interest rate is 11% [(0.1 × $500, 000) + (0.01 × $500, 000) divided by $500,000].

Because many factors influence the effective rate of a loan, when evaluating borrowing costs, use only *the effective annual rate* as a standard of comparison to ensure that you compare the actual costs of borrowing.

Collateral

To reduce their risks in making loans, banks may require collateral from entrepreneurs. Collateral may be any asset that has value. If the entrepreneur does not repay the loan, the bank owns the collateral and may sell it to recover the amount of the loan.

Typical collateral includes both specific high-value items owned by the company (such as buildings, computer equipment, or large machinery) and all items of a particular type (such as all raw materials or all inventories). Banks use blanket liens as collateral when individual items are of low value, but the collective value of all items is large enough to serve as collateral.

The highest level of risk comes in making loans to small companies, so it's not surprising that a high proportion of loans made to small companies—probably 75%—are secured. Larger companies present less risk and have stronger bargaining positions; only about 30% of loans made to companies in this class are secured.

One aspect of protection that most banks require is *key person insurance* on the principal officers of the company taking out the loan. Because the repayment of the loan usually depends on the entrepreneur's or managers' running the company in a profitable manner, if something should happen to them, there may be some question about the safety of the loan. If the officer or officers die, the proceeds of the key person policy are paid to the bank in settlement of the loan.

When making loans to very small companies, banks often require that the owners and top managers personally sign for the loan. Then, if the company does not repay the loan, the bank can claim the signer's personal assets, such as houses, automobiles, and stock investments.

Applying for a Bank Loan

To maximize the chances of success in applying for a bank loan, make personal visits to the bank, and make quarterly delivery of income statements, balance sheets, and cash-flow statements to sustain good relationships.

You'll need to conduct the actual process of obtaining bank credit (whether a line of credit or an actual loan) on a personal basis with the bank's loan officer. The loan officer will be interested in knowing the following information:

- How much money the company needs
- How the company will use this money
- How the company will repay the bank
- When the company will repay the bank

You should be able to fully answer these questions and support your response with past results and realistic forecasts.

Restrictive Covenants

Bank term loans are negotiated credit, granted after formal negotiations take place between borrower and lender. As part of the conditions, the bank usually seeks to set various restrictions, or **covenants**, on the borrower's activities during the life of the loan. These restrictions are tailored to the individual borrower's situation and needs; thus, it is difficult to generalize about them. This section introduces some of the more widely used covenants and their implications. All are (at least to some degree) negotiable; it is wise for the financial executive to carefully review the loan contract and try to moderate any overly restrictive clause a bank may request.

The restrictive covenants in a loan agreement may be

- *General provisions* found in most loan agreements and designed to force the borrower to preserve liquidity and limit cash outflows
- *Routine provisions* found in most loan agreements and normally not subject to modification during the loan period
- *Specific provisions* used according to the situation to achieve a desired total level of protection

Let's look at each in more detail.

General Provisions

The most common of all general provisions is a requirement relating to the *maintenance of working capital*. This may simply be a provision to keep net working capital at or above a specified level. And if the company is expected to grow fairly rapidly, the required working capital may be set on an increasing scale. For example, the bank may stipulate that working capital is to be maintained above $500,000 during the first 12 months of the loan, above $600,000 during the second, above $750,000 during the third, and so on. If the borrower's business is highly seasonal, the requirement for working capital may have to be modified to reflect these seasonal variations.

The provision covering working capital is often set in terms of the borrower's current ratio—current assets divided by current liabilities—which must be kept above, for example, 3 to 1 or 3.5 to 1. The actual figure is based on the bank's judgment and whatever is considered a safe figure for that particular industry. Working capital covenants are easy to understand and very widely used. Unfortunately, they are often of rather doubtful value. As we discussed earlier in this chapter, a company may have a large net working capital and still be short of cash.

Another widely used covenant is *a limit on the borrower's expenditures for capital investment*. The bank may have made the loan to provide the borrower with additional working capital and does not wish to see the funds sunk into capital equipment instead. The covenant may take the form of a simple dollar limit on the investment in capital equipment in any period. Or the borrower may be allowed to invest up to, but not more than, the extent of the current depreciation expense. This provision may prove to be a serious restriction on a rapidly growing company. And clearly, any company will find such a covenant damaging if the maximum expenditure is set below the figure needed to maintain productive capacity at an adequate and competitive level.

Most term loan agreements include *covenants to prevent the borrower from selling or mortgaging capital assets without the lender's permission*. This may be extended to cover current assets other than the normal sale of finished goods, in which case the borrower is prohibited from factoring accounts receivable, selling any part of the raw material inventory, or assigning inventory to a warehouse finance company without the bank's express permission.

Limitations on additional long-term debt are also common. The borrower is often theoretically forbidden to undertake any long-term debt during the life of the term loan, although in practice the bank usually allows new debt funds to be used in moderation as the company grows. The bank may extend the provision to prevent the borrower from entering into any long-term leases without authorization.

One type of covenant that clearly recognizes the importance of cash flows to a growing company is a *prohibition of or limit to the payment of cash dividends*. Again, if dividends are not completely prohibited, they may be either limited to a set dollar figure or based on a set percentage of net earnings. The latter approach is obviously the less restrictive.

Routine Provisions

The second category of restrictive covenants includes routine provisions found in most loan agreements that usually are not variable. The loan agreement ordinarily includes the following requirements:

- The borrower must furnish the bank with periodic financial statements and maintain adequate property insurance.
- The borrower agrees not to sell a significant portion of its assets. A provision forbidding the pledging of the borrower's assets is also included in most loan agreements. This provision is often termed a *negative pledge clause*.

- The borrower is restricted from entering into any new leasing agreements that might endanger the ability to repay the loan.
- The borrower is restricted from acquiring other firms unless prior approval has been obtained from the lender.

Specific Provisions

Finally, a number of restrictions relate more to the borrowing company's management than to its financial performance. For example:

- Key executives may be required to sign employment contracts or take out substantial life insurance.
- The bank may require the right to be consulted before any changes are made in the company's top management.
- Some covenants prevent increases in top management salaries or other compensation.

Restrictive covenants are very important in term loans. If any covenant is breached, the bank has the right to take legal action to recover its loan, probably forcing the company into insolvency. On the other hand, covenants may protect the borrowing company as well as the lender, in that their intention is to make it impossible for the borrower to get into serious financial trouble without first infringing one or more restrictions, thus giving the bank a right to step in and apply a guiding hand. A bank is very reluctant to force any client into liquidation.

Equipment Financing

Capital equipment is often financed by intermediate-term funds. These may be straightforward term loans, usually secured by the equipment itself. Both banks and finance companies make equipment loans of this type. The nonbank companies charge considerably higher interest rates; they are used primarily by smaller companies that find themselves unable to qualify for bank term loans. As with other types of secured loans, the lender will evaluate the quality of the collateral and advance a percentage of the market value. In determining the repayment schedule, the lender ensures that the value of the equipment exceeds the loan balance. In addition, the loan repayment schedule is often made to coincide with the depreciation schedule of the equipment.

One further form of equipment financing is the *conditional sales contract*, which normally covers between two and five years. The buyer agrees to buy a piece of equipment by installment payments over a period of years. During this time, the buyer has the use of the equipment, but the seller retains title until the payments have been completed. Companies unable to find credit from any other source may be able to buy equipment on these terms. The lender's risk is small because it can repossess the equipment at any time if the borrower misses an installment. Equipment distributors who sell equipment under conditional sales contracts often sell the contract to a bank or finance company, in which case the transaction becomes an interesting combination of equipment financing for the buyer and receivables financing for the seller.

The credit available under a conditional sales contract is less than the full purchase price of the equipment. Typically, the buyer is expected to make an immediate down payment of 25% to 33% of the full cash price, and only the balance is financed. The cost of the credit given may be quite high. Equipment that is highly specialized or subject to rapid obsolescence represents a greater risk to the lender than widely used standard equipment, and the interest charged on the sale of such specialized equipment to a small company may exceed 15% to 20%.

Obtaining Early Financing from External Sources

It's almost impossible for a brand-new company to get a conventional bank loan because it has no trading history and usually no assets to secure the loan. Even after a young company is up and running, it is still difficult to get a bank loan. Many entrepreneurs overlook the possibility of getting an SBA-guaranteed loan.

SBA-Guaranteed Loans[8]

The U.S. Small Business Administration (SBA) administers three separate loan programs. The SBA sets the guidelines for the loans, whereas its partners (lenders, community development organizations, and micro-lending institutions) make the loans to small businesses. The SBA does not make direct loans but works with thousands of lenders and other intermediaries. The SBA guarantees these loans, thereby eliminating some of the risk to the lending partners. The SBA guarantees 85% of a loan under $150,000 and up to 75% of a loan greater than that figure, but their maximum exposure amount is $3,750,000. Interest rates on SBA-guaranteed loans are negotiated between the borrower and the bank, but they are subject to SBA maximums and generally cannot exceed 2.75% over the prime rate for loans greater than $50,000. The bank has to pay a one-time guarantee fee of 0.25% to 3.75% of the principal; that fee is usually passed on to the borrower.

To qualify for SBA loan assistance, a company must be operated for profit and fall within size standards. It cannot be a business engaged in the creation or distribution of ideas or opinions, such as newspapers, magazines, and academic schools, or in speculation or investment in rental real estate. SBA-guaranteed loans can be used for the following purposes:

- Expand or renovate facilities
- Purchase machinery, equipment, fixtures, and leasehold improvements
- Finance receivables and augment working capital
- Refinance existing debt (for compelling credit reasons of benefit to the borrower)
- Provide seasonal lines of credit
- Construct commercial buildings
- Purchase land or buildings

Applying for an SBA Loan

The bank will require your company to have adequate paid-in equity, which usually means that the owners have invested sufficient money in the company that the debt-to-equity ratio will be no more than 4:1. Put another way, if you are seeking a $100,000 loan, your paid-in equity must be at least $20,000. For a start-up company, the bank will also expect that the paid-in equity will be cash. Another important condition is that everyone who owns 20% or more of the company must provide personal guarantees.

You'll have a better chance of getting a loan in a timely manner from a bank that processes lots of SBA loans rather than one that processes only a few. Visit the SBA website to get all of the details about the program, find the right loan for you, and learn about the loan matching process (https://www.sba.gov/funding-programs/loans).

Once you've selected a bank:

- Prepare a current business balance sheet listing all assets and liabilities and the net worth. Start-up businesses should prepare an estimated balance sheet including the amount invested by the owner and others.
- Prepare a profit-and-loss statement for the current period and the most recent three fiscal years. Start-up businesses should prepare a detailed projection of earnings and expenses for at least the first year of operation.
- Prepare a personal financial statement of the proprietor and each partner or stockholder owning 20% or more of the business.
- List collateral to be offered as security for the loan.
- List any existing liens.
- State the amount of the requested loan and the purposes for which it is intended.

If your loan request is refused, contact the local SBA office regarding other loans that may be available from the SBA.

SBA National Small Business Person of the Year, 2018[9]

Rebecca Fyffe is a trailblazer in many ways and an inspiration to any entrepreneur. At just 25 years old, Fyffe took charge of Illinois-based Landmark Pest Management, and used technology, innovation, and a smart approach to financing to grow her business and in a decade and a half become the businessperson of the year.

"Rebecca took over a struggling business in 2001 when she was 25 years old, one of only a few women in the industry and the youngest pest control company CEO in the country," Linda McMahon, Administrator of the U.S. Small Business said. "Since then, her company has prospered under her leadership, growing from 18 to 70 full-time employees with substantial revenue growth."

Fyffe and Landmark's uses a science-based approach to pest control featuring many methods developed by the company via field trials and in-house innovations. And, she could do so because she found the funding that worked for her. Fyffe used the SBA-backed Women's Development Center, to secure the "right" loan: an SBA-backed 7(a) loan that gave her the capital she needed to properly grow her firm. A firm that she intends to continue grow to a multistate powerhouse.

CONCLUSION

Working capital is often misinterpreted as being synonymous with *firm liquidity*. In fact, only a part of net working capital is liquid; the balance of net working capital is tied up in firm operations. *Liquidity* is largely a function of a firm's growth and the timing of receipts and payments. In situations where payments are made to suppliers before customers pay, growth in sales generally results in lower liquidity.

Preparing a cash-flow forecast assists entrepreneurs in assessing the timing and maturity of funding needs. With a cash-flow forecast, the entrepreneur can more easily determine the type of funding to procure and the small, growing firm's ability to grow with available funds. This includes efficiencies in accounts receivable, inventories, payables, and accruals. To the extent that entrepreneurs can successfully negotiate with customers and suppliers, they will be able to manage future growth. However, small firms are rarely afforded the benefits associated with growth funded exclusively through internal cash generation. The more common occurrence includes external debt sources, leasing, cash innovations, and governmental programs for small firms. Such is the fate of the small business entrepreneur. Early growth stages result in large funding requirements and huge risks for those who can't meet payroll and supplier demands. However, once an entrepreneur has negotiated for a level of funds from external sources, including bank financing, privately placed debt, leasing options, and other financing innovations, that entrepreneur has a better chance for long-term corporate survival.

YOUR OPPORTUNITY JOURNAL

Reflection Point	Your Thoughts...
1. What sources of capital do you have? Are you willing to take on a home equity loan? Use your personal credit cards? How much of a "nest egg" do you need to feel comfortable pursuing a new venture?	
2. What do you expect your cash conversion cycle to be? Is there a way to improve it? What accounts receivable terms are common in your industry? How should you manage accounts receivable?	
3. How much inventory does your business need to carry to avoid stock-outs? What terms can you get on inventory (accounts payable)?	
4. Can you finance your accounts receivable? What means (bank loans, factoring, etc.) are most available to you? Can you get loans on your inventory?	
5. What short-term loans are needed for your business (e.g., line of credit)? When will you be bank creditworthy?	

WEB EXERCISE

Visit the SBA website (www.sba.gov). The website has useful information on a number of start-up issues. Take a look at the SBA loan programs. What steps do you need to undertake to qualify for these programs?

NOTES

1. https://www.federalreserve.gov/releases/g19/current/
2. *Financial Services for Small Businesses in the U.S.* Rockville, MD: Packaged Facts, March 2008, p. 272.
3. Excerpted from R. McCarthy, N. Heintz, and B. Burlingham. Starting Up in a Down Economy. *Inc.* May 1, 2008. www.inc.com/magazine/20080501/starting-up-in-a-down-economy.html.
4. https://beautymatter.com/2017/09/sc-johnson-scoops-up-ecover-and-method/
5. https://www.statista.com/statistics/660826/wayfair-emplyoees/
6. O'Malley, T. 50 VCs Say No and I Still Did It. *American Venture*, p. 36. December 2005.
7. https://www.sba.gov/about-sba/sba-newsroom/press-releases-media-advisories/sba-lending-activity-fy17-shows-consistent-growth
8. Excerpted from the SBA website. www.sba.gov.
9. From the SBA press release: https://www.sba.gov/node/1619694

Case FEED Resource Recovery[1]

It was the spring, and Shane Eten had just won a $20,000 sustainability award at the highly competitive Rice University Business Plan Competition. Shane was already thinking about how he would use the $20,000. This wasn't the first time his idea, Feed Resource Recovery (**feed**), had won or placed well in a business plan competition—he'd finished second at the Babson College, second at the University of Colorado, and second at the UC–Berkeley competitions. Although the prize money and services in kind were helpful, Shane knew that he couldn't successfully launch his business on prize money alone. Shane estimated that he would need $150,000–$250,000 to build the anaerobic digester prototype and much more money after that to scale production and sell the system across the country. Where would he get the money?

Based on his success in the business plan competitions and through strong personal networking, Shane had talked to several venture capitalists, and they all expressed strong interest in the business. Potential investors seemed to be coming out of the woodwork, but still Shane was uneasy. How much of the company would he have to give up if he was going to secure their investments? Even from his preliminary conversations with the venture capitalists, he knew that the valuation[2] of the company was only going to be part of the problem. He was discouraged by the grim prospect of having to jump through hoops, answering the venture capitalists' endless list of questions. He figured it would take at least six months of battling back and forth over equity and shares during which time the venture capitalists would be looking over his shoulder, and all this before a prototype was ever built. Furthermore, several of the venture capitalists were saying, "This is a great idea, come back when you have a prototype built," so Shane wasn't even sure if they were really interested or just talking. But what other choice did he have? How could he raise the substantial amount of funding that he would require to assemble a team and build a working prototype? And how could he accomplish all of this without giving up all rights to his idea? The task was daunting, and the answers were scarce.

From Athlete to Entrepreneur: The History of Shane Eten

Shane Eten was born in Philadelphia and lived in a number of places while his father attended medical school. The family eventually settled in Cape Cod, Massachusetts, where his father and mother started a family-owned medical practice. Living near the sea inspired Shane's father.

> *My father built a sailboat in our back yard. He started when I was in sixth grade. He told me he was going to build a sailboat and sail it around the world. He was probably a little crazy, but he actually built a thirty-six foot trimaran.*[3]

For as long as Shane could remember, his father had a dream of building the sailboat. He would wake Shane up early in the morning on weekends and make him help work on the boat, sometimes working 12-hour days. After several years of effort, they successfully launched it and saw it sail.

> *Although at the time I really hated working on that boat, looking back I realize that it was a very important part of my childhood because it taught me the importance of hard work and taking a dream you have and making it reality.*

Like many boys, Shane was more interested in playing sports than school. He always enjoyed the team aspect and the competitive nature that came with athletics. His goal was to play Division I basketball in college. Hampered by knee injuries but still wanting to pursue his dream of playing college basketball, Shane chose to attend Trinity College, a Division III school, and play ball there. Unfortunately, his knees never fully recovered from a series of knee surgeries, so Shane never had a chance to play in college.

At Trinity, Shane majored in psychology. Although he enjoyed studying psychology, Shane didn't want to pursue a career in the field, but he didn't know exactly what he wanted.

> *I really didn't enjoy school and to continue down the psychology career path would require me going back to school almost immediately. I like getting out there and getting my hands dirty with real work. In the field of psychology, I would have been doing a lot of research and theoretical education-based work. I wasn't ready for that. I wanted to get out in the world and make something happen.*

After graduating from Trinity, Shane went on many interviews and eventually found a job working for an up-and-coming computer company, Angstrom Microsystems. Angstrom Microsystems built supercomputers from off-the-shelf components and Linux software. Shane loved working for this fast-growing entrepreneurial company because his job was never the same day-to-day. He had the opportunity to work with many different aspects of the business. His original job was working with

[1] This case was prepared by Reuben Zacharakis-Jutz under the direction of Professor Andrew Zacharakis. Funding provided by the John H. Muller Chair in Entrepreneurship.

[2] The valuation of a company is broken into two parts. The pre-money valuation is how much the company is deemed to be worth prior to the investment. The post-money valuation is the pre-money valuation plus the investment. The percentage of equity that the investor receives is the investment/post-money valuation. The percentage that the entrepreneur retains is the pre-money valuation/post-money valuation.

[3] A trimaran is a fast pleasure sailboat with three parallel hulls.

vendors. Then he moved his way up to product development, and finally he settled in customer account management. While Shane was with Angstrom, the company grew from $500,000 to $15 million in sales in his first eight months. With the hands-on experience he gained and the opportunity of being able to see how so many aspects of a company worked, Shane realized:

> *Entrepreneurship is fun and, most importantly, competitive. There's a real science to starting a company. It was at this time that I first started thinking about building my own company.*

Unfortunately, Angstrom's success was short-lived as the market took a turn for the worse when one of Angstrom's largest customers stopped growing. The CFO of Angstrom left for a position at a candle company. He called Shane and convinced him to come along for the ride. The position that Shane had been offered was 180 degrees different from his job at Angstrom and an opportunity to test his abilities in a new way. Although Shane liked the tech industry, he decided to give it a shot. So at age 24 he started as a manager of a candle manufacturing plant.

> *It was a drastic change. Laurence Candle Company was a 60-year-old, third-generation company, and I was managing people mostly older than me—some who had been working there for 30 years.*

He was forced to get on the floor and get dirty learning the process of making candles.

The Laurence Candle Company was struggling because its product was very similar to another established brand, Yankee Candle. The company needed new ideas so Shane raised his hand and asked if they would give him a shot at designing a new line of candles. After doing a bunch of market research and going to trade shows to see what was out there, he launched a new line of candles made from a new type of wax made out of soy. Soy wax was environmentally friendly because the wax was made from an all-natural crop; it was considered renewable and therefore sustainable. The soy wax candle line took off. Not only was soy cheaper than traditional paraffin wax, but also it could be sold as all-natural for 30%–40% more than traditional candles. Sales jumped instantly. It saved the company.

> *There was a new consumer emerging at this time, and if you could say that it was all-natural, then you could say that it was sustainable or noble. This new brand of customer was willing to pay a premium for environmentally friendly products.*

Shane put in 60- to 70-hour workweeks developing the line of soy candles. He also started research on adding biodegradable plastic wrappers to the candles. It was at this point that Shane knew if he was going to put in this much time and effort toward an idea, the next time it would be for himself and his own company.

Working for small companies, Shane had learned a lot about how the business world worked, but he knew that he needed a stronger foundation in accounting and working with numbers. If he was going to be successful in starting and managing his own ventures, he was going to have to go back for an MBA. At 28 years of age, he decided it was time to go back to school. Soon after he applied, Shane was accepted to Babson College.

The CleanTech Industry

Shane entered Babson with a goal of finding an idea to launch his own business. He was intrigued with opportunities in the Clean Technology space, especially around combating global warming. Investment and growth in the CleanTech industry exploded in 2007, passing the record set in 2006 in the first three quarters.[4] Exhibit 11.1 shows an explosive upward investment trend.[5]

The increased growth and investment in the CleanTech industry has been brought on not only by the large price increases in gas and other fossil fuels but also by the raised awareness of global warming by prominent figures such as former Vice President Al Gore. Gore's work with the United Nations Intergovernmental Panel on Climate Change, his winning the Nobel Peace Prize, and his involvement in the Academy Award–winning documentary *An Inconvenient Truth* have brought to light the serious issues of climate change and global warming. These works have also brought legitimacy and an increased interest in the CleanTech industry.

> *Taken at face value, the surprisingly entertaining An Inconvenient Truth provides an idealistic, persuasive, and compelling dissection of the perils of global warming. Frightening and timely, the smartly organized documentary is an urgent plea for responsibility and action as well as an impassioned call to heed the ominous warnings of science.*[6]

Gore's words resonated with Shane. As Gore stated:

> *But along with the danger we face from global warming, this crisis also brings unprecedented opportunities. What are the*

---

[4] November 28, 2007. *CleanTech Venture Investments by US Firms Break Record in 2007.* National Venture Capital Association (NVCA). Thompson Financial Press Release. Retrieved January 30, 2008, from http://nvca.org/pdf/CleanTechInterimPR.pdf.

[5] Ibid.

[6] Ogle, C. June 9, 2006. Seeing Entertaining Documentary Makes You Want to Save the World. *Miami Herald* online movie review. Retrieved January 30, 2008, from http://ae.miami.com/entertainment/ui/miami/movie.html?id=616935&reviewId=20952.

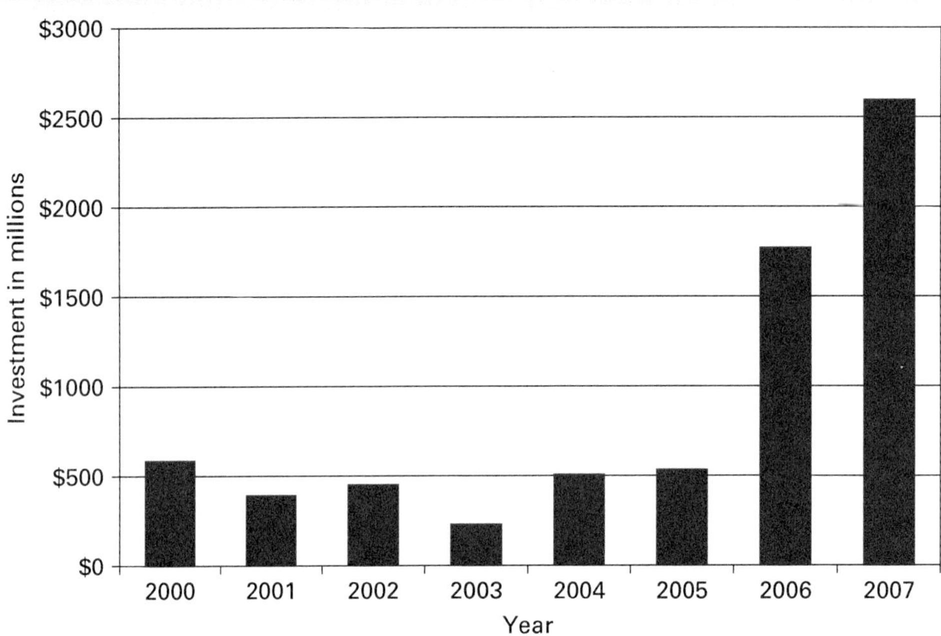

EXHIBIT 11.1 **Annual CleanTech Investment.**
Source: National Venture Capital Association.

> *opportunities such a crisis also offers? They include not just new jobs and new profits, although there will be plenty of both, we can build clean engines, we can harness the sun and the wind; we can stop wasting energy; we can use our planet's plentiful coal resources without heating the planet.*
>
> *The procrastinators and deniers would have us believe this will be expensive. But in recent years, dozens of companies have cut emissions of heat-trapping gases while saving money. Some of the world's largest companies are moving aggressively to capture the enormous economic opportunities offered by a clean energy future.*
>
> *But there's something even more precious to be gained if we do the right thing. The climate crisis also offers us the chance to experience what very few generations in history have had the privilege of knowing: a generational mission; the exhilaration of a compelling moral purpose; a shared and unifying cause; the thrill of being forced by circumstances to put aside the pettiness and conflict that so often stifle the restless human need for transcendence; the opportunity to rise.*[7]

Consumers and the public in general are expecting companies to be more ecofriendly; they want to see real efforts made toward carbon reduction and recycling. This has encouraged companies to race toward new technologies to capture a piece of this new market. One example of the efforts that mainstream companies are making is Google's recent pledge to become a carbon neutral company.

> *Google today announced a new strategic initiative to develop electricity from renewable energy sources that will be cheaper than electricity produced from coal. The newly created initiative, known as RE < C, will focus initially on advanced solar thermal power, wind power technologies, enhanced geothermal systems and other potential breakthrough technologies. RE < C is hiring engineers and energy experts to lead its research and development work, which will begin with a significant effort on solar thermal technology, and will also investigate enhanced geothermal systems and other areas. Google expects to spend tens of millions on research and development and related investments in renewable energy. As part of its capital planning process, the company also anticipates investing hundreds of millions of dollars in breakthrough renewable energy projects which generate positive returns.*[8]

Another example is Walmart. Although Walmart has faced much criticism for its energy consumption and pollution

[7] Excerpt from Gore, A. 2006. *An Inconvenient Truth: The Planetary Emergency of Global Warming and What We Can Do About It.* Paramount Classics.

[8] Fuller, J. November 27, 2007. *Google's Goal: Renewable Energy Cheaper than Coal Creates Renewable Energy R&D Group and Supports Breakthrough Technologies.* Google Press Center, Mountain View, CA. Retrieved January 30, 2008, from www.google.com/intl/en/press/pressrel/20071127_green.html.

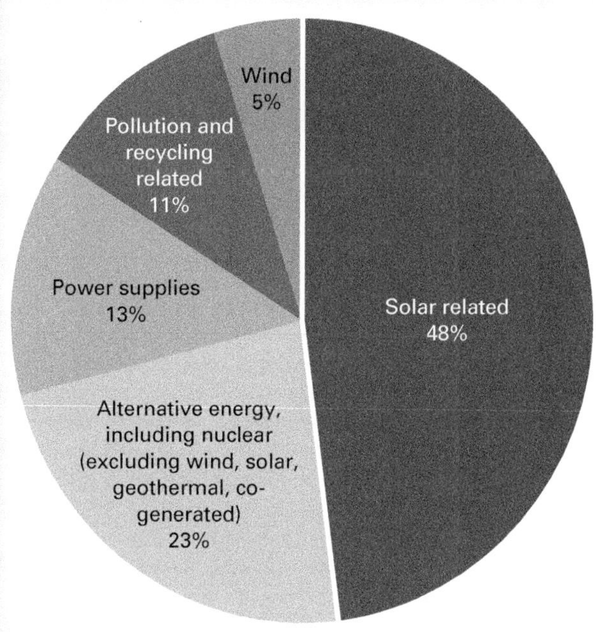

EXHIBIT 11.2 **U.S. CleanTech Investment by Industry.**
Source: National Venture Capital Association.

practices, the company has invested large amounts of money in green technologies. For example, Walmart installed solar power in 22 of its super centers, which accounts for roughly 1% of the U.S. super centers. Walmart has also made other green commitments promising to decrease its carbon footprint. It has pledged to eventually run off 100% of renewable energy sources. In the short run, company officials say they will adapt old stores to be 25% more efficient and new stores 30% more efficient.[9]

The increased interest in clean technology has attracted many investors. Exhibit 11.2 shows the distribution of investment in the CleanTech industry by subcategory.[10]

With the wealth of interest by angel investors and venture capitalists alike, many new companies have hit the ground running and have found success. This explains the high interest that Shane has received from these investors. The CleanTech Venture Network estimated that over 240 CleanTech companies could be positioned for a liquidity event between 2007 and 2009.[11] A small niche within the CleanTech sector known as waste conversion technologies is beginning to catch on. One such example is Converted Organics Inc. Converted Organics, based in Boston, is a development-stage company dedicated to producing a valuable all-natural, organic soil additive through food waste recycling. Started in 2003, Converted Organics Inc. is a five-employee operation that has just recently gone public raising $9.9 million in an IPO and has a market capitalization of $14.3 million.[17] Other examples of recent transactions involving waste conversion providers are noted in Exhibit 11.3.

- **BlueFire Ethanol, Inc.** is established to deploy the commercially ready, patented, and proven Arkenol Technology Process for the profitable conversion of cellulosic ("Green Waste") waste materials to ethanol. They acquired a $15,000,000 investment from Quercus Trust.[12]
- **Disenco Energy PLC**, a UK-based developer of a revolutionary home power generating unit known as the Disenco Home Power Plant, closed their initial IPO for $2,750,000.[13]
- **Oakleaf** merged with Greenleaf, which rents stationary compactors, containers, balers, and other waste management and recycling equipment to commercial businesses and haulers.[14]
- Scotts paid $20 million last year for **Rod McLellan Co.**, which focuses on naturally derived fertilizers.[15]
- The Carlyle Group acquired residuals recycler **Synagro Technologies** for about $447.5 million in cash, including the assumption of ~$310 million in debt. Synagro operates at over 1,000 wastewater treatment plants throughout the country, providing operations and residuals management services. Many of these wastewater treatment plants employ anaerobic digestion. The company is using this experience to expand into the agribusiness market with its first operational facility, which was designed and built in Chino, California. This digester is designed for 225 wet tons of fresh cow manure per day. It employs dewatering and onsite cogeneration using Capstone Micro turbines.[16]

EXHIBIT 11.3 **Sample Investments into CleanTech Companies.**

Roots of Feed Idea

At Babson, the entrepreneurship professors stress the importance of opportunity and an entrepreneur's fit to that opportunity. So Shane thought he should leverage his past experience

[9] Walmart. *Environmental Overview.* Retrieved January 30, 2008, from www.walmartstores.com/GlobalWMStoresWeb/navigate.do?catg=345.

[10] NVCA 2007.

[11] Parker, N. February 14, 2007. CleanTech Is Ripe for Growth. *Israel Venture Capital & Private Equity Journal (IVCJ).* Retrieved January 30, 2008, from www.altassets.com/casefor/sectors/2007/nz9921.php.

[12] January 8, 2008. *BlueFire Ethanol Closes $15.5 Million in Financing.* BlueFire Press Release. Retrieved January 30, 2008, from http://bluefireethanol.com/pr/45/.

[13] February 26, 2007. *Disenco Energy PLC Closes IPO for US$2,750,000 and Lists on the TSX Venture Exchange.* PR Newswire Europe Ltd. Retrieved January 30, 2008, from www.prnewswire.co.uk/cgi/news/release?id=191571.

[14] July 26, 2004. *Greenleaf Compaction, Inc. Has Merged with Oakleaf Waste Management.* Oakleaf News Releases. Retrieved January 30, 2008, from www.oakleafwaste.com/oakleaf/news/releases/2004/072604_2.asp.

[15] Lambert, E. September 4, 2006. *Organic Miracle Needed.* Retrieved January 30, 2008, from www.forbes.com/forbes/2006/0904/066.html.

[16] January 29, 2007. *The Carlyle Group to Acquire Synagro Technologies for $5.76 per Share.* Carlyle Group News. Retrieved January 30, 2008, from www.carlyle.com/News/NewsArchive/2007/item7052.html.

[17] Van der Pool, L. March 16, 2007. Spurned by VCs, Waste Conversion Startup Goes Public. *Boston Journal Online.* Retrieved January 30, 2008, from www.bizjournals.com/boston/stories/2007/03/19/story8.html.

and start his own candle line. However, copyright laws and low profit margins discouraged him. Next, he looked at biodegradable packaging lines.

When I had an idea, I would do research for maybe three weeks, and see who else was out there, if the product was feasible, and who the customers were. I would usually find a really big obstacle. Or I just found a company that does this or a big brand that does this or someone that tried to start it and it didn't work. And when I got to biodegradable plastic, I realized there was no way to compost it, so it wasn't as environmentally friendly as I had first imagined. But during this search, I came across composting technology. This seemed like a big idea and a big opportunity. The key with composting that makes it so unique is that someone is getting paid for their raw materials, which is basically trash. Companies paid to have trash hauled away, so that meant composters could get their raw material for free or even be paid to take it away.

Shane started doing research into the composting industry and was intrigued by waste conversion technology. He looked at gasification,[18] plasma arc,[19] aerobic composting,[20] and finally anaerobic digestion.[21] Anaerobic digestion caught his eye. Anaerobic digestion was a relatively proven and cheap technology, and it seemed the most viable option. Next Shane began to look at the waste stream market. He wanted to know who the largest waste producers were, what kind of waste they produced, and what the competition looked like in those industries. He looked at households and small restaurants and found that in most cases they would not generate enough waste to justify an onsite digester, and the cost of transporting the waste to a central location would be prohibitive. After further research, Shane found that the food waste produced by processing plants and supermarkets turned out to be the most promising. This was because they both were producing large amounts of food waste, and the volume was concentrated in a single location (see Exhibit 11.4).

Babson is great because there are tons of ideas floating around. The professors give us the tools to analyze whether an idea is an opportunity. You start with a problem, and if there's a problem, there's potentially an opportunity. So you have a bunch of students running around with two-page summaries on their ideas, sharing their thoughts, and seeking feedback during breaks from class. The school also has a "Rocket Pitch" event where you get three minutes to convince the audience that your idea has real potential. It takes a lot of work to learn how to pitch your concept in three minutes, but that process really helps you understand the issues around the idea.

Shane's two-page opportunity was about the company he wanted to start, which he called Biospan. He would build a large anaerobic digester that would be at a centralized plant, and he would collect food waste from restaurants, grocery stores, and even homes to feed the digester and produce compost and biogas. The basic idea made sense—taking waste and producing a usable by-product. Shane decided that this idea was worth investing time and effort to really understand it. Shane applied to Babson's Entrepreneur Intensity Track (EIT)[22] program with the idea of launching this business.

Through the EIT program, Shane met with a venture capitalist who asked him tough questions like "How are you going to get six million dollars to build a big plant, and how are you going to keep Waste Management from doing it bigger and better than you?" Six million dollars was a lot of money, and Shane didn't like the idea of competing with a company like Waste Management who did $13 billion in revenue each year. By asking the right questions, Shane also realized that a large centralized plant was inefficient. Transporting the waste to the plant and then sending the energy back to users added costs, used energy (gasoline for dump trucks), and wasn't as "Green" as a decentralized unit located where the waste was produced.

Shane then began to look at the industry and who might gain the greatest benefit from a mobile anaerobic system. Food processors, like large pig and chicken farms, already were starting

[18] **Gasification** is a process that converts organic material or biomass into gasses or liquid fuels by a combination of high temperatures and reduced oxygen supply. (Schilli, J. Using Gasification to Process Municipal Solid Waste. Environmental and Resource Management Group of HDR: *HDR Innovations*, Vol. 12.)

[19] **Plasma arc gasification** is a process in which solid waste is shredded and fed into a furnace where extreme electrical charges bring the temperature above 3,000 degrees. After an hour or so, waste material breaks down into its molecular building blocks, leaving three marketable by-products: a combustible synthesis gas, or syngas, that can be converted into steam or electricity; metal ingots that can be resold and melted down again; and a glassy solid that can be processed into material for floor tiles or gravel. (Durst, S. March 5, 2007. PROBLEM NO. 3: WASTE DISPOSAL. *Fortune*, Vol. 155, Issue 4, p. B-4.)

[20] **Aerobic composting** is the process of decomposing organic waste using microorganisms and an aerobic or oxygenated environment. (Pace, M., Miller, B., and Farrell-Poe, K. October 1, 1995. *The Composting Process*. Utah State University Extension. AG-WM 01.)

[21] **Anaerobic digestion** is a biochemical process in which particular kinds of bacteria digest biomass in an oxygen-free environment. Several different types of bacteria work together to break down complex organic wastes in stages, resulting in the production of "biogas." (Retrieved April 1, 2008, from www.oregon.gov/ENERGY/RENEW/Biomass/biogas.shtml#Anaerobic_Digestion.)

[22] EIT is a curriculum focused on deep business planning and launch of a business during the final year of a student's education.

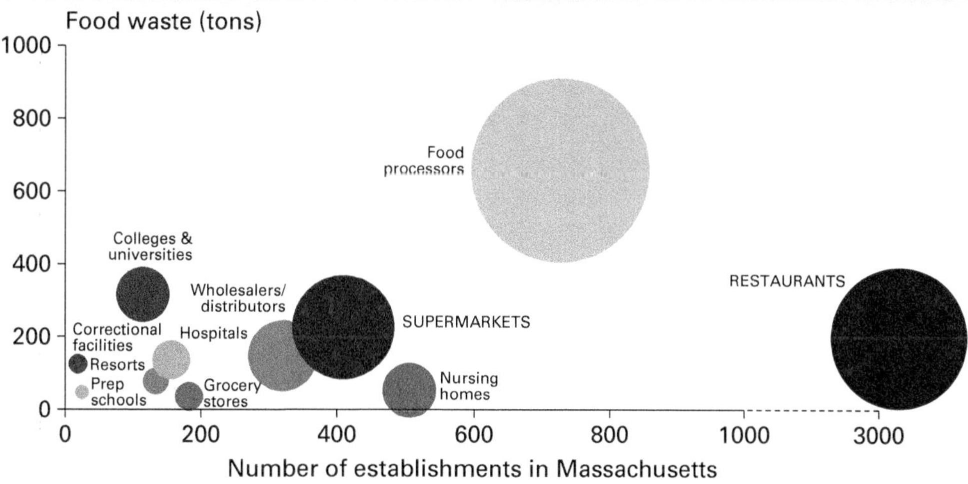

EXHIBIT 11.4 Identifying Target Waste Generation Segments.
Source: Feed Business Plan.

to use anaerobic digestion systems. After more research, Shane found that grocery stores looked like the best option. They already were sorting their waste and sending it to composters, and the volume was low enough to discourage large players from entering. This seemed like a great marketplace for his decentralized systems.

> *You didn't have to ask them to change their habits. They were already sorting their waste, and the system could be implemented on location without disrupting their day-to-day operation.*

Shane wanted to get into the industry as efficiently as possible, so he started to look for existing anaerobic systems that he could adapt to his target. He couldn't find any systems that could handle high solid content; they were mostly set up for human or animal waste. Furthermore, those companies building these systems were targeting larger scale, centralized plants, not smaller, decentralized systems that Shane envisioned. Many people, mainly the business professionals in anaerobic digestion, were saying that decentralized systems would be too small to be effective. In Europe, they were already using anaerobic digestion for food waste but only on a large scale. From the previous business models and the waste industry's frame of mind, the onsite model was not seen as profitable, but with the increases in energy prices and raised awareness in green tech, it started to make more sense. Shane believed if the technology could be produced, the idea would be easy to market in a food retail industry where the profit margins were razor thin and competition fierce.

The Product

The **feed** system, known as the R2, would utilize anaerobic digestion (AD), a clean, safe, and proven technology, to turn biodegradable waste into fuel (biogas) for a distributed electricity generation unit. AD is the breakdown of organic material by microorganisms in the absence of oxygen. Although this process occurs naturally in landfills, AD usually refers to an artificially accelerated operation that processes organic waste to produce biogas and a stable solid residue. People have been turning waste into biogas for hundreds of years, and many developing countries rely on small-scale AD systems for cooking. AD has grown rapidly in Europe, mostly in large centralized plants using advanced technologies. The R2 is a combination of the cheap, compact systems of India and China and the large-scale, expensive, and technologically sophisticated systems of Europe: a fully automated system that enables the customers to process waste and generate energy onsite without changing current waste disposal behavior.

> *The decentralized nature of our system meant that you could place the R2 (see Exhibit 11.5) at the back of the store right in the same space that the organic waste dumpster currently occupied. It was critical to our potential customers that this system didn't require more space or alter the footprint of the current store (see Exhibit 11.6).*

The automation is made possible by the integrated control technology that operates the patented pH-balancing unit to continually optimize system performance. Other novel and patented ideas that differentiate the system include an integrated biogas

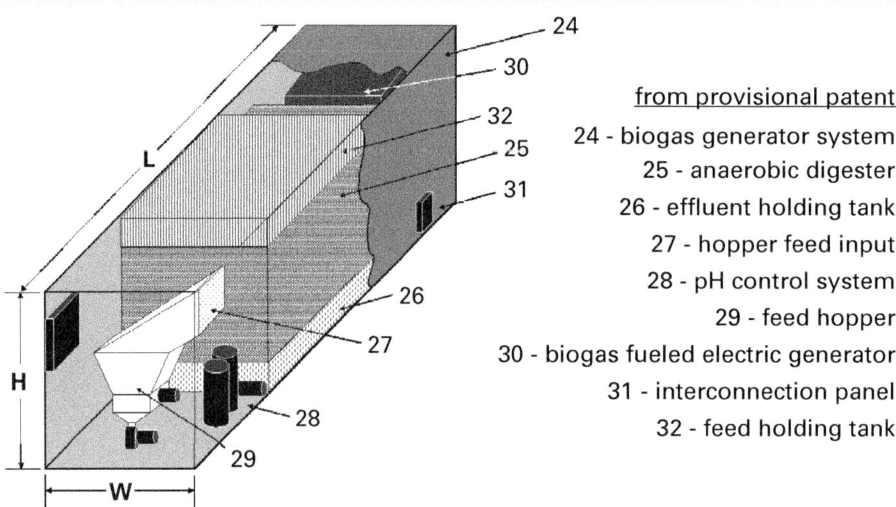

EXHIBIT 11.5 **The R2 System: Compact Onsite Waste Conversion for Supermarkets.**
Source: Feed Business Plan.

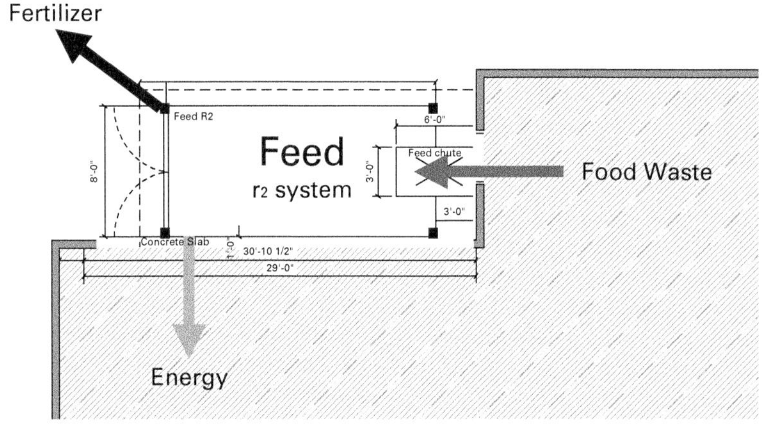

EXHIBIT 11.6 **On-Site Waste Conversion.**

generator unit, a gravity-fed system that increases efficiency while reducing cost and complexity, a multi-tank system for system reliability and flexibility, and pH balancing of the waste stream to handle diverse waste. Other than biogas, the R2 produces nutrient-rich compost that could potentially be sold to farmers. The projected price that the grocery store would pay for its R2 was around $300,000.

Lots of Interest

Craig Benson, a professor at Babson, told Shane that the best way to attract investors was to go and talk to the biggest customer you could find. "*If you can find a customer for your product, investors will be more than willing to get on board,*" Craig noted. Shane started to make as many connections as possible. He called several grocery store chains in the Northeast, including Stop and Shop, Shaw's, Walmart, and Whole Foods, but it was always hard get in front of anyone very high up in the ranks. He was always sent to someone who, even if interested, had no power to do anything about it. How could he get in front of the right person?

The success of **feed** in business plan competitions was also bringing a great deal of interest to his anaerobic digester idea. Many of the venture capitalists and investors that were present at the competitions were serious about its investment possibilities.

During the Rice Business Plan Competition in the spring when **feed** won the sustainability award, Dow Chemical Venture Group showed an especially strong interest and said they could introduce Shane to Walmart. The Dow group flew Shane to their headquarters and put him on the phone with top executives at Walmart. Shane said the conversation went something like this:

> *Does it have a 24-month payback time? I said no and they basically hung up.*

The problem was that Dow and most of the venture capitalists were looking for quick returns and proven ready technology. That meant that Shane had to figure out how to get customer payback down to two years. Moreover, once the investors realized that the final product was still in the distant future, they were reluctant to invest the time and resources needed. This meant that Shane needed to build a prototype before the venture capitalists would be interested. Shane started looking elsewhere for the needed capital.

Through the grapevine Shane heard about a Massachusetts Technology Collaborative (MTC) grant for onsite energy providers. To be eligible you needed to meet a set power output and find a buyer for the electricity that would sign on to the project. The MTC grant would then pay a certain amount of money for each kilowatt you could generate from the green energy method. Shane had a connection through a friend of the family at Ring Brothers grocery store, a small local grocery store on Cape Cod. Ring Brothers agreed to sign on as the company sponsor and **feed** won the grant for $195,000.

The grant required that **feed** first run a feasibility study before it could actually start to build the prototype, and the grant provided $20,000 for the research study. So Shane took a look at how much actual food waste Ring Brothers produced and found that they weren't producing enough waste to make the system feasible for the required energy output of 50 kw that was needed for the grant. Without the proper energy production output, they were forced to tell MTC that they were not going to be eligible for the $195,000 grant.

Team Building

Based on his experience with Ring Brothers and the knowledge that he needed to build a prototype, Shane realized that he didn't have the skill set to do this venture on his own. He needed some technical expertise on the founding team. Shane knew that he would need an engineer to run the actual research and production of the first prototype. He needed someone who could take over a large part of the company and have the ability to get things done without supervision. A friend of Shane's who worked at Raytheon told him that he worked with a young engineer who fit the profile that Shane was looking for.

Ryan Begin specialized in product development at Raytheon, where he led a multidisciplinary team of engineers in the integration of advanced missile defense hardware. Although Ryan enjoyed the big paycheck, he was looking for something different. Before Raytheon, Ryan had worked on multiple renewable energy—products through Clarkson University and other private organizations.

> *I wanted to get out of the large corporation and saw the feed concept as really interesting. It was in the green space, where I had done some work before. But most importantly, I could be on the ground floor of something potentially huge.*

When they met, Shane knew that he had found the business partner he was looking for and that Ryan would be a strong addition to the team.

> *Ryan has the unique ability to get his hands dirty in putting the prototype together, but at the same time he is also very smart and brings a lot of expertise to the table. He has a great work ethic, and he's the kind of guy that works so hard and is so driven that he makes you feel guilty if you're not working just as hard.*

After their initial meeting, Ryan began to run some of the numbers Shane had presented him regarding the biogas and electricity production of the suggested system. Although he found that many of numbers were on the high end of possibility, they still were within the range of having some real potential.

> *I could see that some of Shane's projections were off by a lot, but the potential was there. Also the fact that he already had interested customers and investors reaffirmed my feelings that this could be a great opportunity for me.*

Ryan was leaving a high-paying job at Raytheon with stability and benefits for a job with a new company and little or no salary.

> *I had a choice to make, I could continue to take the safe route with Raytheon, or I could put it all on the line to test my skills and have the chance to do something big and exciting. I didn't feel like I was doing any real engineering at Raytheon. Being able to lead product development within the renewable energy field was very appealing to me. I could also see that Shane had real business savvy and really believed strongly in his idea and had what it would take to sell it.*

To entice and reward Ryan, Shane agreed to take him on as a co-founder and to give him some founder's shares. After some back and forth on the amount of stock Ryan would receive in the company, they settled on 20% of the founder's shares and the goal of paying a salary once they had raised a significant amount of investment.

Next Steps

With the start of a team and a strong customer interest, Shane and Ryan knew they had to build a functioning prototype. They had run some preliminary numbers and put together some pro forma financials (see Exhibits 11.7–11.9 for pro forma financials). They showed that **feed** needed investment now. Where could they get the $250,000 dollars needed to build the prototype (see Exhibit 11.8)? Although most venture capitalists wouldn't invest at this stage, there were a few who might—but at what valuation and how long would it take to close the deal? Shane also could raise the money through family and friends, but this would take time as well. Shane and Ryan were anxious to get started, but they knew if they couldn't build a prototype, **feed** would never get off the ground.

Exhibit 11.7 Feed Income Statement Projections

Income Statement Years 1 to 5 ($)										
	Year 1		Year 2		Year 3		Year 4		Year 5	
NET REVENUES	320,000	100%	1,880,000	100%	6,555,000	100%	13,985,000	100%	24,345,750	100%
COST OF REVENUE	332,800	104%	1,440,629	77%	4,939,057	75%	8,794,486	63%	15,538,904	64%
GROSS PROFIT	(12,800)	-4%	439,371	23%	1,615,943	25%	5,190,514	37%	8,806,846	36%
OPERATING EXPENSES										
Sales & Marketing	**29,600**	**9%**	**96,400**	**5%**	**315,150**	**5%**	**521,550**	**4%**	**838,373**	**3%**
Salaries & Benefits	0	0%	0	0%	58,500	1%	102,000	1%	108,000	0%
Initial Branding Efforts	20,000	6%	40,000	2%	60,000	1%	0	0%	0	0%
Other	9,600	3%	56,400	3%	196,650	3%	419,550	3%	730,373	3%
Research & Development	**14,600**	**5%**	**190,900**	**10%**	**349,300**	**5%**	**727,550**	**5%**	**1,062,373**	**4%**
Salaries & Benefits	9,600	3%	90,900	5%	249,300	4%	527,550	4%	862,373	4%
Product Development	5,000	2%	100,000	5%	100,000	2%	200,000	1%	200,000	1%
General and Administration	**17,067**	**5%**	**171,100**	**9%**	**485,790**	**7%**	**742,417**	**5%**	**1,048,495**	**4%**
Salaries & Benefits	0	0%	103,500	6%	300,690	5%	405,600	3%	504,000	2%
Depreciation	667	0%	4,000	0%	9,000	0%	11,667	0%	11,667	0%
Rent & Utilities	0	0%	6,000	0%	15,000	0%	15,450	0%	15,914	0%
Legal Fees	10,000	3%	20,000	1%	30,000	0%	30,000	0%	30,000	0%
Other	6,400	2%	37,600	2%	131,100	2%	279,700	2%	486,915	2%
Total Operating Expenses	61,267	19%	458,400	24%	1,150,240	18%	1,991,517	14%	2,949,241	12%
EARNINGS FROM OPERATIONS	(74,067)	-23%	(19,029)	-1%	465,703	7%	3,198,997	23%	5,857,605	24%
TAXES	0	0%	0	0%	(149,043)	-2%	(1,279,599)	-9%	(2,343,042)	-10%
NET EARNINGS	(74,067)	-23%	(19,029)	-1%	316,660	5%	1,919,398	14%	3,514,563	14%

Exhibit 11.8 Feed Balance Sheet Projections

	Begin	Year 1	Year 2	Year 3	Year 4	Year 5
ASSETS						
CURRENT ASSETS						
Cash	250,000	174,926	140,904	866,314	3,127,462	7,174,275
Accounts Receivable		1,200	10,159	40,000	234,000	772,000
Inventories		0	0	60,000	130,000	331,200
Other Current Assets		204	1,224	60,000	130,000	276,000
Total Current Assets	250,000	176,330	152,287	1,026,314	3,621,462	8,553,475
PROPERTY & EQUIPMENT	0	1,500	16,000	29,250	32,500	31,250
TOTAL ASSETS	250,000	177,830	168,287	1,055,564	3,653,962	8,584,725
LIABILITIES & SHAREHOLDERS' EQUITY CURRENT LIABILITIES						
Short-Term Debt	0	0	0	0	0	0
Accounts Payable & Accrued Expenses		1,693	10,159	522,000	1,131,000	2,401,200
Other Current Liabilities		204	1,224	60,000	130,000	276,000
Current Portion of Long-Term Debt	0	0	0	0	0	0
Total Current Liabilities	0	1,897	11,383	582,000	1,261,000	2,677,200
LONG-TERM DEBT (less current portion)	0	0	0	0	0	0
STOCKHOLDERS' EQUITY	250,000	250,000	250,000	250,000	250,000	250,000
Common Stock						
Preferred Stock	0	0	0	0	0	0
Retained Earnings		(74,067)	(93,096)	223,564	2,142,962	5,657,525
Total Equity	250,000	175,933	156,904	473,564	2,392,962	5,907,525
TOTAL LIABILITIES & EQUITY	250,000	177,830	168,287	1,055,564	3,653,962	8,584,725

Exhibit 11.9 Feed Cash-Flow Projections

	Year 1	Year 2	Year 3	Year 4	Year 5
OPERATING ACTIVITIES					
Net Earnings	(74,067)	(19,029)	316,660	1,919,398	3,514,563
Depreciation	500	5,500	11,750	16,750	21,250
Working Capital Changes					
(Increase)/Decrease Accounts Receivable	(1,200)	(8,959)	(29,841)	(194,000)	(538,000)
(Increase)/Decrease Inventories	0	0	(60,000)	(70,000)	(201,200)
(Increase)/Decrease Other Current Assets	(204)	(1,020)	(58,776)	(70,000)	(146,000)
Increase/(Decrease) Accts Pay & Accrd Expenses	**1,693**	**8,466**	**511,841**	**609,000**	**1,270,200**
Increase/(Decrease) Other Current Liab	204	1,020	58,776	70,000	146,000
Net Cash Provided/(Used) by	(73,074)	(14,022)	750,410	2,281,148	4,066,813
INVESTING ACTIVITIES					
Property & Equipment	(2,000)	(20,000)	(25,000)	(20,000)	(20,000)
Other					
Net Cash Used in Investing Activities	(2,000)	(20,000)	(25,000)	5(20,000)	(20,000)
FINANCING ACTIVITIES					
Increase/(Decrease) Short-Term Debt		0	0	0	0
Increase/(Decrease) Curr. Portion LTD		0	0	0	0
Increase/(Decrease) Long-Term Debt		0	0	0	0
Increase/(Decrease) Common Stock		0	0	0	0
Increase/(Decrease) Preferred Stock		0	0	0	0
Dividends Declared		0	0	0	0
Net Cash Provided/(Used) by Financing		0	0	0	0
INCREASE/(DECREASE) IN CASH		(75,074)	(34,022)	725,410	2,261,148
CASH AT BEGINNING OF YEAR		250,000	174,926	140,904	866,314
CASH AT END OF YEAR	250,000	174,926	140,904	866,314	3,127,462

Exhibit 11.10 Start-up Capital Needed to Build Prototype

Components of Digester	$150,000
Engineering Salaries	75,000
Other/Misc	25,000
Total	**$250,000**

Discussion Questions

1. Is **feed** an opportunity?
2. Where can Shane raise the necessary money to build the prototype?
3. What are the implications on valuation for the different sources?

Legal and Tax Issues, Including Intellectual Property

12

Photo Credit: M. Unal Ozmen/Shutterstock

Coca Cola has kept its formula a trade secret for over 100 years.

This chapter was written by Richard Mandel, Kirk Teska, and Joseph S. Iamdioio.

Why, When, and How to Choose an Attorney

Many enthusiastic entrepreneurs are so excited about where they're going that they forget to consider where they've been. They're surprised to learn that there may be serious limitations imposed on their freedom of action arising out of their former employment. Some of these limitations may be the result of agreements signed by the entrepreneur while employed in his or her former position. Others may be imposed as a matter of law, without any agreement or even knowledge on the part of the employee. These considerations are among many that suggest that entrepreneurs obtain an early consultation with an appropriate attorney.

Unfortunately, many people perceive engaging an attorney as an unnecessary expense when beginning a new venture. However, the earlier you can consult a professional, the more likely your business will avoid costly mistakes. For example, without an attorney to advise you with regard to the drafting of a partnership or stockholders' agreement (described later in this chapter), the remaining partners may have no way of retrieving the share of the business owned by the estate of a founder who has left the business for a "better opportunity." Or the entrepreneur may be confronted by a large income tax bill for his receipt of "sweat equity."

The laws in the United States do not officially recognize legal specialties. In practice, however, the U.S. legal profession has become highly specialized. Thus, most patent attorneys do very little else, and most good litigation attorneys concentrate on litigating. The representation of start-ups and small businesses has become a specialty as well.

An attorney experienced in the problems of start-ups will be aware of the myriad issues that should be covered in a stockholder or partnership agreement and the other unique problems facing entrepreneurs. He or she will be able to advise among the various choices of legal entities available to entrepreneurial enterprises as well as to advise with regard to any residual obligations owed by an entrepreneur to previous employers. Most general corporate lawyers, representing larger, more established enterprises, are simply not as familiar with issues such as these. In addition, attorneys who practice in the start-up world will be familiar with these companies' unique cash-flow problems and may be willing to work out installment payments or other arrangements to ease the strain on tight start-up cash flow. On college campuses, student entrepreneurs can often find lawyers who provide pro-bono advice to help students understand the legal obligations and choices that may soon come when their fledgling idea develops into a viable business operation. You may also talk to a business law professor.

Leaving Your Present Position

Corporate Opportunity

The **corporate opportunity** doctrine is an outgrowth of the traditional obligation of loyalty owed by an agent to a principal. In its most common form, it prohibits an officer or director of a corporation, a partner in a partnership, or a person in a similar position from identifying a business opportunity that would be valuable to his company and using that information for his own benefit or the benefit of a competitor.

Just a few years ago, Federico Pignatelli, former CEO of Biolase, a company specialized in laser technology for the dental industry, alleged that "Biolase's former and current directors appeared to have misappropriated corporate opportunities." The example provided by Mr. Pignatelli was that a former director of the company met in secret with a start-up competitor regarding developing robotic health care technologies. He stated that this secret meeting led to some directors personally investing in the company.[1] Generally, to discharge his legal obligation to the corporation of which he is a director, a person would be required to disclose the opportunity to his board and allow the board to decide (without his participation) whether the corporation will make the purchase. Only after the corporation has been fully informed and decided *not* to take advantage of the opportunity may the director use that information for himself. Even then, as the new owner of a competitor, he would be required to resign his director position with the previous business.

The scope of this **duty of loyalty** is normally adjusted by the law to reflect the individual's position within the business. Although the president and members of the board may be required to turn over knowledge of all opportunities that may be in any way related to the business of the company, lower-level employees probably have such an obligation only with regard to opportunities that are directly relevant to their positions.

Recruitment of Fellow Employees

Another aspect of the duty of loyalty owed by an employee to an employer is the legal requirement that the employee not knowingly take action designed to harm the employer's business. This is, perhaps, pure common sense. We would not expect the law to countenance a paid salesperson's regularly recommending that customers patronize a competitor, nor would we expect the law to endorse an engineer's giving his best ideas to another company. Similarly, courts have held that it is a breach of the duty of loyalty to solicit and induce fellow employees to leave their jobs.

Once again, the likelihood that a court would enforce this obligation against an employee depends to some extent on the nature of the employee's activities and her position in the company. Generally, two budding entrepreneurs need not fear reprisals for their having convinced each other to leave. Nor would there be much likelihood of liability if they convinced another employee to leave with them, especially if these conversations took place after working hours. However, if either of them worked in the human resources department, where their job descriptions would include recruiting and retaining employees, this same activity might well expose them to liability. Further, if their plan included the wholesale resignation of a relatively large number of employees, such that the company's ability to continue to efficiently function might be compromised, a court might be more likely to intervene with an injunction or other relief. For example, recently, the boutique investment bank Perella Weinberg sued four former colleagues for allegedly trying to hire the restructuring team of the firm to create a new bank. The boutique claimed that four former partners and employees left the firm after an unsettled dispute, and since then, Perella Wienberg lost 8 of their 12 restructuring team members.[2]

Noncompetition

More general than any obligation not to recruit fellow employees is the obligation not to compete with one's employer. Like most of the obligations we've already discussed, this duty is derived from the fiduciary relationship between employer and employee—specifically, the duty of loyalty. How can we justify accepting a paycheck from our employer while we are simultaneously establishing, working for, or financing a competing business?

The law imposes this duty not to compete on all employees, officers, directors, and partners while their association with the employer remains in effect. Unlike the obligation to protect proprietary information discussed later, however, the non-compete duty does not extend to the period after the termination of the relationship. To extend the obligation, the employer must obtain the employee's contractual promise.

We can analyze noncompetition agreements along many different dimensions, like the scope of the obligation. In an extreme case, an employee may have agreed not to engage in any activity that competes with any aspect of the business his former employer engaged in, or planned to engage in, at the time of the termination of the employee's association with the company. At the other end of the spectrum, the employee may have agreed only to refrain from soliciting any of his former employer's customers or (somewhat more restrictively) from dealing with any of the same, no matter who initiated the contact. We can also measure such agreements by the length of time they extend beyond the termination of employment and by their geographic scope.

Such measurements are important because, in the employment context, many states take the position that non-compete agreements contravene basic public policies, such as encouraging competition and allowing each individual to make the best use of his talents. A few such states (such as California) actually refuse to enforce all noncompetition agreements. Most, however, purport to enforce only those deemed reasonable, recognizing the employer's interest in protecting its business and goodwill. Only those restrictions that prevent likely harm to the employer's legitimate interests will be enforced.

Thus, a company could not enforce an agreement not to compete throughout New England against a salesman whose territory extended only to portions of Maine, New Hampshire, and Massachusetts.[3] Furthermore, although a manufacturer may be able to enforce such an agreement against an officer, salesperson, or engineer who has either direct contact with customers or knowledge of the company's processes and products, it might not be able to enforce the same agreement against a bookkeeper, whose departure would have little effect on the company's goodwill. Even the officer, salesperson, or engineer might be able to resist an agreement that purports to remain in effect beyond the time that the employer might reasonably need to protect its goodwill and business from the effects of new competition.

Another factor that may affect the enforceability of a noncompetition agreement is whether the employer agrees to continue part or all of the former employee's compensation during the noncompetition period. Similarly, a noncompetition agreement that might be unenforceable against an employee might nonetheless be enforceable against the seller of a business or a major stockholder having his stock redeemed. Finally, some courts that find the scope or length of a noncompetition agreement objectionable nonetheless enforce it to the maximum extent they rule acceptable. Others take an all-or-nothing approach.

Intellectual Property

Yet another potential complication arising out of an entrepreneur's previous employment is the possible use of information or technology belonging to the former employer. Such information need not be subject to formal patent or copyright protection to be protected from such use. And usually, by the time an entrepreneur has developed a viable business, she will have created a body of proprietary information of her own. At that point, she will be forced to turn her attention to protecting that information from use by competitors, employees, and end users who have failed to pay for the privilege. Thus, an in-depth discussion of intellectual property rights would be advisable at this juncture.

Entrepreneurship and **intellectual property** (IP) go hand in hand. Intellectual property refers to creations of the mind, such as inventions; literary and artistic works; and symbols, names, images, and designs used in commerce. Business intellectual property includes patents, trade secrets, trademarks, and copyrights.

Patents protect inventions. **Trade secrets** cover proprietary information, whether it's in the form of a recipe, a customer list, or a unique way of conducting business. **Trademarks** are key in differentiating a business's products and services from those of others as well as in franchising arrangements. **Copyrights** protect authors' original creations, including literary, musical, artistic, software, and other intellectual works.

Investors need to be assured not only that a business has considered IP but also that it has implemented a plan to protect the company's crown jewels. And because IP protection costs money, it is necessary to budget for and manage it.

There are few guarantees in the area of IP. Not every patent application is granted; a name you've chosen for your company might not be available or be registrable as a trademark for a variety of reasons. Sometimes entrepreneurs must take risks. To do that wisely, entrepreneurs must understand the IP environment, which is slow to change in its legal underpinnings but continually being pushed to keep up with technological advances.

Even when it's successful, however, protecting IP is not the endgame. A patent, for example, doesn't generate revenue—it's just a document. A patent taken out for a great new idea is nothing unless people are willing to pay for that idea implemented in a product or service. Timing can play a crucial role in IP, just as it does in exploiting an entrepreneurial opportunity.

Finally, IP is everywhere. Just because a business isn't about technology, don't be misled into thinking it won't ever face IP issues. Patents today cover non-engineering subject matter such as holders for floral bouquets; trademark law is invoked in Internet search engines, pop-up ads, and Web sites in general; and even users of another company's products, for example, can be sued for patent infringement.

The Basics: What Is Protectable and How Should It Be Protected?

When someone conceives a new idea or designs a new product or method, two of the first questions to arise are these: Can I protect this? Can I keep competitors from copying this?

There are very practical reasons for protecting a new idea. Investors are loath to put money into a venture that cannot establish a unique product niche. Stockholders will challenge a corporation's investment of its resources in a program that can be easily copied once it is introduced to the market. All the time, effort, and money you invest in perfecting a product, as well as advertising and promoting it, may be wasted if imitators can enter the market on your heels with a product just like yours. Moreover, the imitators can cut prices because they have not incurred the start-up expenses you had to endure to bring the idea from conception to a mass-producible, reliable, and appealing product or service.

The next question is, "Does my new product infringe the IP rights of anyone else?" Only by understanding the basics of IP can that be answered.

Once it is determined that a new idea, product, or method is eligible for one or more forms of IP protection—*patent, trade secret, trademark,* or *copyright*—secure the rights as quickly as the budget allows. A single product can qualify for different forms of protection, each obtained in a different manner and providing a different set of rights. For example, consider computer software. It will be marketed under a brand name and will be accompanied by a set of instructions. What is protectable, and how should it be protected? Where might others have IP that must be considered? The following sections provide information to help answer these questions.

Patents

Although there are actually three different kinds of patents, the kind usually used to protect an invention is a **utility patent**. Think utility patent whenever you think "better, cheaper, faster." But don't confuse invention in the patent sense with "eureka"-type ideas. Most patents are simple combinations of well-known components. Consider the following example.

Aerogel is listed in the Guinness Book of World Records as the world's lightest substance. A block of aerogel as big as an adult male weighs less than a pound but can support a small car. Recently, numerous companies have been patenting new uses for aerogel—as insulation, in fuel cells, and as building structures, just to give a few examples. Engineers at those companies didn't invent aerogel—a Stanford University researcher discovered it in the early 1930s. Still, the Patent Office will readily grant patents for new uses of aerogel.

Technically speaking, utility patents cover these classes of inventions:

- Chemical inventions include new compounds, new methods of making old or new compounds, new methods of using old or new compounds, and new combinations of old compounds.

Assays, biological materials and methods, drugs, foodstuffs, drug therapy, plastics, petroleum derivatives, synthetic materials, adhesives, pesticides, fertilizers, and feeds are all protectable.

- General/mechanical inventions include everything from gears and engines to tweezers and propellers, from zippers to Jacques Cousteau's scuba regulator. For example, complex textile-weaving machines, space capsule locks and seals, and diaper pins are all protectable.
- Electrical inventions include everything from lasers to light switches, from the smallest circuit details to overall system architectural concepts.

Computer software is also patentable in various forms:

- Application programs, such as the software that runs in a computer used to control a chemical-processing plant or a rubber-molding machine, are patentable.
- Software for running a cash management account at a brokerage house or bank is patentable.
- Internal or operations programs that direct the handling of data in the computer's own operations are patentable.

Obtaining a Utility Patent

There is no rule that patents cover only remarkable inventions. Instead, the basic requirement for a utility patent is that the idea be different in some way from what came before. Most important, patent protection can be broad: The owner of the patent has the right to exclude others from making, using, selling, offering for sale, or importing the patented invention during the term of the patent. This "monopoly" lasts for 20 years from the date of filing. On average, though, given that a patent application takes about three years to process through the Patent Office, the patent term is usually about 17 years from the date the patent is granted.

The patenting effort begins when the inventor or inventors conceive of an invention. Typically, a registered patent attorney acting on the inventor's behalf prepares a patent application and files it in the U.S. Patent and Trademark Office. From the date the application is filed, there is a patent pending. There are no real legal rights associated with "patent pending." Full protection applies only if and when the Patent Office agrees that the invention is patentable and issues the patent. But with patent pending, a would-be competitor doesn't always know exactly what will be patented or when, and thus, he must proceed with caution in making the decision to offer the same or a similar product.

The patent application must contain a complete and understandable explanation of the invention. It doesn't have to be a nuts-and-bolts instruction manual. It is enough to convey the inventive concept so that a person "skilled in the art" can make and use the invention without undue experimentation. Further, the explanation must contain a full description of the best mode known by the inventor for carrying out the invention. For example, the inventor cannot use the second-best version or embodiment of the invention as an illustration for the patent application disclosure and keep secret the best embodiment. That could make the resulting patent invalid.

The *timing* of the filing is critical. In the United States, the patent application must be filed within one year of the first public disclosure, public use, sale, or even offer for sale of the product, or the filing will be barred and the opportunity to obtain a patent lost forever. This is known as the one-year period of grace. And if patent protection is beneficial in foreign countries, a patent application must be filed in the United States *before* any public activity occurs.

Market testing, exhibitions, or even use by the inventor himself can be a public use sufficient to activate the one-year period. One exception is a public use for experimental purposes. The test for whether a public use is an excepted experimental use is rigorous. The inventor must show that it was the operation and function of the invention that was being tested, not the appeal or marketability of the product employing the invention. Further, he should establish some evidence of the testing. For example, if samples were sent to potential customers for evaluation, it would be good to show that the customers returned filled-out evaluation forms and that the inventor considered and even made changes based on those evaluations.

The idea is that an inventor should be given only one year in which to file her patent application after she has begun to commercially exploit or to attempt to commercially exploit her invention. And it is not just an actual sale that triggers the one-year period: An offer for sale is sometimes enough, even if the sale is never consummated.

Criteria for Obtaining a Utility Patent

A patent "application" is not a form to be filled out. Instead, each patent application is unique, although all patent applications contain the same three basic sections:

- Drawings showing an embodiment of the invention
- A written description of the invention referring to the drawings akin to an engineering specification
- One or more claims—hybrid legal and technical language that "captures" the invention in words

The definition of the patented invention—the protected property—is not what you disclose in the drawings and the specification portion of the application; these are only descriptions of one or more specific embodiments or versions of the invention. Instead, the coverage of the patent is defined by the third part of the application, the legal claims.

To qualify the invention for a patent, the claims must describe something both novel and unobvious. *Novelty* is a relatively easy standard to define: If a single earlier patent, publication, or product shows the entire claimed invention, the invention is not novel, and no patent will be issued. *Obviousness* is somewhat more difficult to grasp, and, worse, the test for obviousness is fairly subjective: Are the differences between the invention and all prior knowledge (including patents, publications, and products) such that the invention would have been obvious to a person having ordinary skill in the art? If so, the invention is not patentable even if it is novel.

Obviousness is a somewhat subjective determination, but many ideas have ultimately been deemed patentable even though they were originally rejected as obvious by an examiner of the U.S. Patent and Trademark Office. In one notable case, Anita Dembiczak came up with the idea of a plastic leaf bag configured to look like a giant Halloween-style pumpkin when stuffed with leaves. The U.S. Patent and Trademark Office essentially concluded that because leaf bags were well known and pumpkins drawn on paper lunch sacks were also well known, the idea of a pumpkin leaf bag was obvious and therefore not patentable. Not so, said the Court of Appeals for the Federal Circuit: The Patent Office failed to prove there was any motivation to combine the idea of a Halloween pumpkin with a leaf bag. As a result, the patent for the leaf bag pumpkin was issued.

Consider another example of what "novelty" and "unobvious" mean in the area of patentability. Suppose a person is struggling to screw a wood screw into hard wood, and he realizes the problem is that he cannot supply enough twisting force with the blade of the screwdriver in the slot in the head of the screw. So he gets the bright idea of a new screwdriver with two shorter, crossed blades, which will give increased surface-area contact with two crossed slots in the head of the screw. The result: He has invented the Phillips head screwdriver, for use with a Phillips head screw. Certainly, the invention is "novel": No one else had made that design before. It is also "unobvious" and thus patentable. The addition of the second blade and has resulted in a wholly new screwdriver concept. The concept is patentable.

Now suppose another party, seeing the patent issued on this double-blade Phillips head, comes up with an improvement of her own. Her invention is to use three crossed blades (cutting the head of the screw into six equal areas). This design may not be patentable. Certainly it is novel, but is

June 23, 1964 J. S. KILBY 3,138,743

MINIATURIZED ELECTRONIC CIRCUITS

Filed Feb. 6, 1959 4 Sheets-Sheet 1

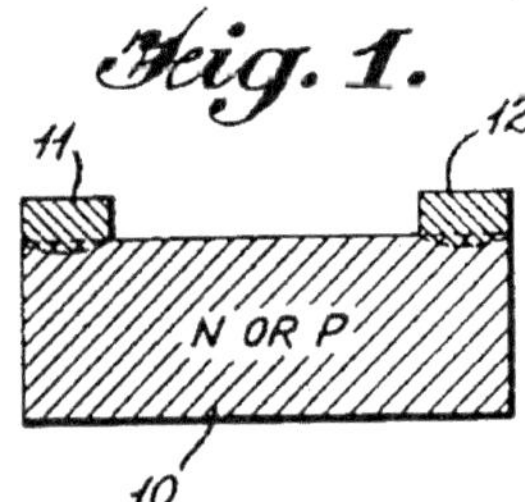

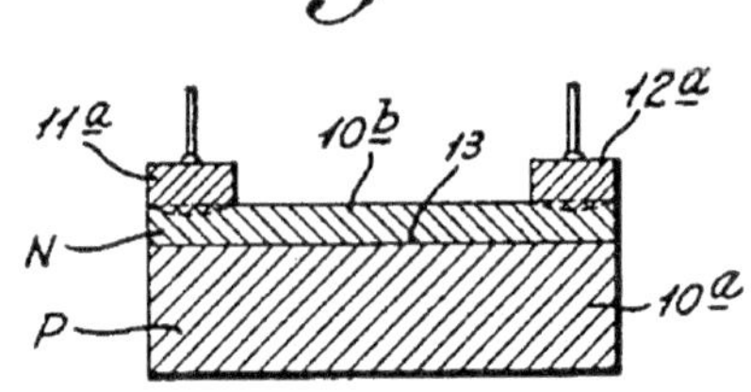

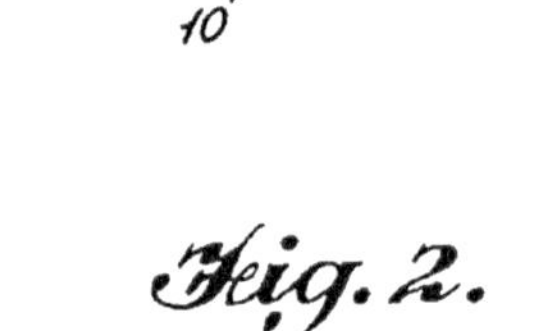

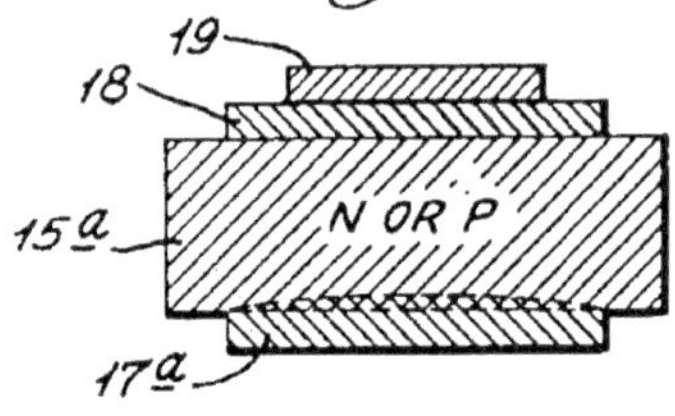

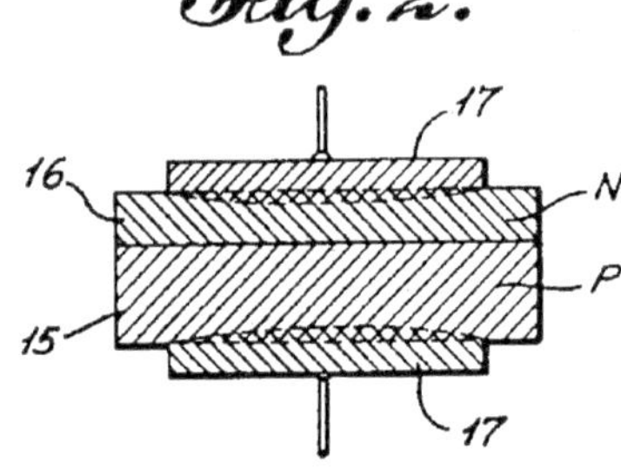

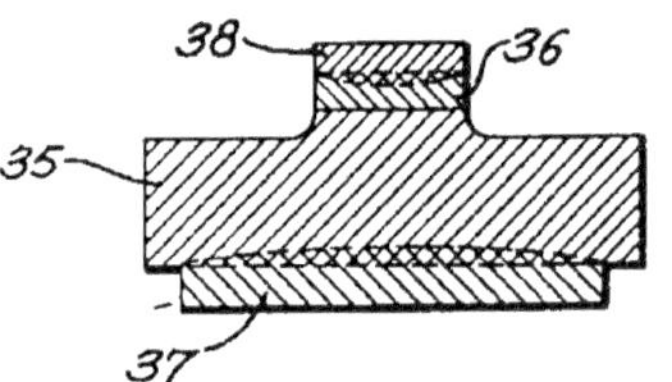

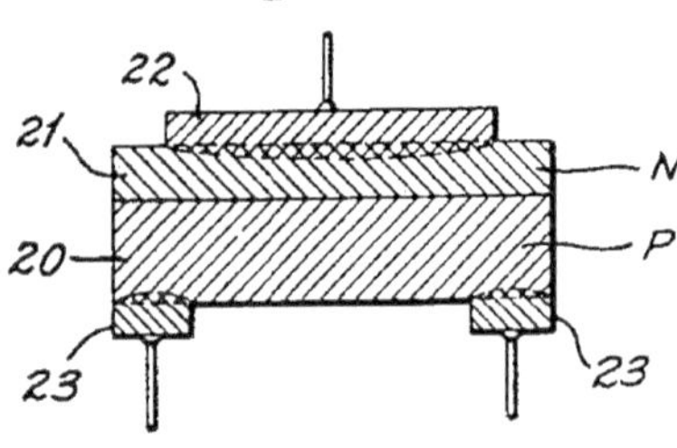

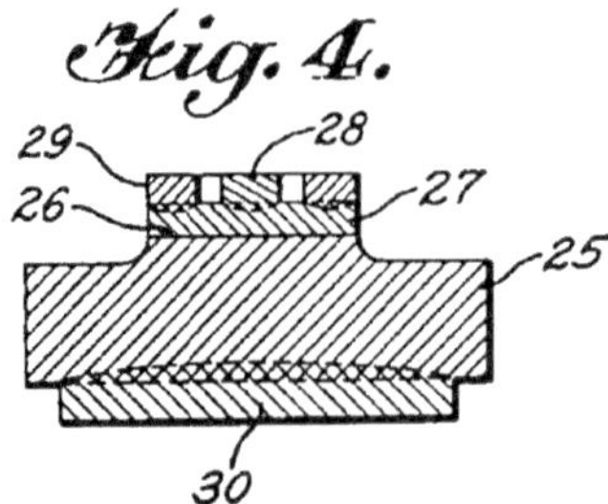

Fig. 5a

N OR P

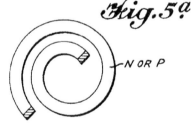

INVENTOR
Jack S. Kilby

BY
Stevens, Davis, Miller & Mosher
ATTORNEYS

Courtesy US Patent Office

Integrated circuit patent, 1958 (#3138743).

it unobvious? Not likely. Once the first inventor has originated the idea of increasing the number of blades, it may be obvious to simply add more blades.

Drafting the Patent Claims

Once you have decided that a patentable invention exists, you must protect it with properly drafted patent claims. It is the claims that the U.S. Patent and Trademark Office examiner analyzes and accepts or rejects in considering the issuance of the patent; it is the claims that determine whether someone has infringed a patent, and it is the claims that define the patented property.

Claims, then, are clearly the most important part of a patent. It is no good to have claims that cover the invention and yet do not protect your product or process from being copied by competitors. Does this sound contradictory? Study the following example and you will understand.

Suppose an entrepreneur meets with a patent attorney and shows the attorney a new invention for carrying beverages on the slopes while skiing. The invention eliminates the risk of smashing glass, denting metal, or squashing a wine skin, and it also eliminates the need to carry any extra equipment: It's a hollow ski pole. The ski pole has a shaft, a chamber, and a handle. The handle has a threaded hole opening into the hollow shaft. Partway down the inside of the hollow shaft is a plastic liner that creates a chamber for holding liquids; this plastic liner is sealed to the shaft. The chamber is closed by a threaded plug. The entrepreneur wants to patent this invention, and so he assists the patent attorney in writing a description of the ski pole. They write the following claim:

A hollow ski pole for carrying liquids, comprising:

- a hollow shaft.
- a plastic liner inside the shaft to define a chamber for containing liquid.
- a handle on the shaft.
- a threaded hole in the handle that opens into the chamber.
- a threaded plug for sealing the threaded hole.

The patent application is filed. The U.S. Patent and Trademark Office examines the application and three years later issues the patent with that claim. The inventor is happy: The claim describes exactly what the entrepreneur markets and sells. But not happy for long—because a competitor comes out with a similar hollow ski pole that doesn't use a liner. The competitor simply welds a piece of metal across the inside of the shaft to make a sealed chamber. The competitor has avoided infringing the patent because there is no liner, which was one of the requirements of the patented claim. Still another competitor replaces the threaded plug with an upscale mahogany cork. Again, the patent is not infringed because there is no threaded plug, as required by the claim. Patent claims are akin to requirements, and a competitor who can sell a competing product without meeting all the claim requirements doesn't infringe the patent.

You can avoid this problem by exploring the various ways in which you can build your product before you file the patent application. You may need input from sales, marketing, engineering, and production people as well as from the inventor. After a thorough study, a better claim might emerge as follows:

A hollow ski pole for carrying liquids, comprising:

- a hollow shaft.
- a chamber in the hollow shaft for containing a liquid.
- a handle on the shaft having a hole opening into the chamber.
- a closure for the hole in the handle.

Now the liner and the threaded plug are not required. This claim, then, would likely be good enough to keep competitors at bay. There is a limit to how broadly you can word the claim, however. Eventually, if it becomes broader and broader and does not specify the ski pole or hollow shaft, it may apply to a bottle or a pot with a cover, and the patent will not be obtainable—it is not new. Careful claim drafting is thus critical.

If you don't remember anything else about patents, remember this: It's the claims that matter.

Provisional Patent Applications

Provisional patent applications are also available. People like provisionals because they don't have to include patent claims—indeed, a paper, specification, or report can be filed as a provisional. Be careful, though. In one case, a product embodying an invention was sold in the spring of 2018, a provisional application for the invention was filed in the spring of 2019, and a full patent application was filed in the fall of 2019. But, the provisional failed to adequately describe the invention actually claimed in the full patent application. The result? The patent was held invalid because the provisional failed to provide the necessary disclosure, and thus the one-year deadline had been missed.

Provisionals have found favor because they are typically less expensive than full patent applications and allow companies to advertise "patent pending." In fiscal year 2018, almost 170,000 provisional patent applications were filed.[4] But as the preceding case proves, provisionals are only as good as the details they contain. If you don't actually draft the legal claims for the invention, you should at least envision them to ensure that the provisional application adequately supports the claims you file later in the full utility application.

Design Patents

Another type of patent is the design patent. Hockey uniforms, ladies' dresses, computer housings, automobile bodies, buildings, shoes, and game boards are all protectable with design patents. But this type of patent covers only the *appearance* of the product, not the idea, underlying concept, or functionality of the product. What you see is what you get. Design patents are generally less expensive to obtain than utility patents but typically also offer far less protection.

Managing Patent Costs

Patents are expensive: Plan on spending between $6,000 and $23,000 to prepare and file a patent application and between $5,000 and $7,500 to prosecute the patent application.[5] Prosecution is what occurs in the two to three years following filing of the application as you attempt to convince the Patent Office that the invention is worthy of a patent in the face of inevitable rejections. Foreign patents can cost thousands per country in filing fees alone. Obtaining a patent for all European countries costs around $88,000, a patent in Canada would be around $2,500, a patent in Japan around $6,000; translation fees contribute 33% of the cost.[6] But you have to put these costs in perspective. Consider the price of a mold for a plastic part, for example, or the cost of a marketing study undertaken by a consultant. Because of the potential value of a patent, the cost of filing is often well worth it. If, for example, Gillette's patent for the five-bladed Fusion razor can really be used to stop all competitors from introducing razors with similarly manufactured five blades, the cost of the Gillette patent and even the cost of patent litigation (typically $1 million or more) is well worth the protection afforded, especially given the enormous cost of Gillette's advertising campaigns surrounding the Fusion razor.

On the other hand, some patents may not have enough potential value to provide a return on the investment. Consider a patent for aerogel used as an insulating liner in deep-sea oil-well piping. If other insulating materials work as well or almost as well, the patent might not be worth the cost—unless it is worth something to advertise "the only deep-sea oil-well piping with aerogel!"

The problem is that, at the time the patenting decision must be made, the value of the patent might be hard to measure. Big companies regularly file for numerous patents and have a yearly IP budget in the millions of dollars. Entrepreneurial companies cannot typically afford those costs and thus must be particularly adept at planning and managing patents and other IP, all the while remembering the deadlines and the fact that the value of a given patent is measured by its claims. Finally, don't forget to make sure your new product or service doesn't infringe someone else's patent.

Trade Secrets

One benefit of trade secrets is they can cover everything patents cover—and much more. A trade secret is defined as knowledge, which may include business knowledge or technical knowledge that is kept secret for the purpose of gaining an advantage in business over one's competitors. Customer lists, sources of supplies of scarce materials, or sources of supplies with faster delivery or lower prices may be trade secrets. Certainly, secret processes, formulas, recipes, techniques, manufacturing know-how, advertising schemes, marketing programs, and business plans are all protectable.

Another benefit of trade secrets is there is no standard of invention to meet, as there is with a patent. If the idea is new in this context and if it is secret with respect to this particular industry or product, then it can be protected as a trade secret. Also unlike the case for patents, trademarks, and copyrights, there is no formal government procedure for obtaining trade secret protection. Protection is established by the nature of the secret and the effort to keep it secret.

Finally, a trade secret can be protected forever against disclosure by all those who have received it in confidence and from all who would obtain it by theft for as long as the knowledge or information is kept secret.

The key disadvantage of trade secrets is that, unlike the case with patents, there is no protection against discovery by fair means, such as accidental disclosure, independent inventions, and reverse engineering. Many important inventions, such as the laser, the integrated circuit, and the airplane, were developed more or less simultaneously by different persons. Trade secret protection would not permit the first inventor to prevent the second and subsequent inventors from exploiting the invention as a patent would.

But don't be misled into thinking trade secrets are a fallback position to patents or that they offer "free protection." Consider the feature of the Windows program that allows you to open two files at the same time, display them on the screen, and drag content from one into the other. Nice feature, but it cannot be a trade secret. Why not? Because you and everyone else can see the feature in operation every time you use it. Microsoft even advertises it. It's not a secret. Any competitor of Windows can write code that affords the same functionality. Microsoft's exact code that carries out that functionality is secret, to be sure, but even that is not "free" protection when you consider the overhead costs Microsoft incurs to ensure the code is always kept under wraps and that its numerous employees and consultants are subject to secrecy agreements.

Many companies use both approaches, filing a patent application and during its pendency keeping the invention secret. When the patent is ready to be issued, the company reevaluates its position. If the competition is close, they let the patent issue. If not, they abandon the patent application and rely on trade secret protection. But patent applications are now published 18 months after their earliest filing date, voiding trade secret protection unless the filer takes active steps to prevent publication (such as an agreement not to file an application for the invention in any foreign country).

Despite the problems with trade secrets, some have been appraised at a value of many millions of dollars, and some are virtually priceless. For example, Coca-Cola claims that its formula is one of the best-kept trade secrets in the world. Known as "Merchandise 7X," it has been tightly guarded since it was invented over 100 years ago. It is known by only two persons within the Coca-Cola Company and is kept in a security vault at the Trust Company Bank in Atlanta,

Georgia, which can be opened only by a resolution from the company's board of directors. The company refuses to allow the identities of those who know the formula to be disclosed or to allow the two to fly on the same airplane. Although some of the mystique surrounding the Coca-Cola formula may be marketing hype, it is beyond dispute that the company possesses trade secrets that are carefully safeguarded and extremely valuable.

Secrecy is essential to establishing trade secret rights; without it, there is no trade secret property. There are four primary steps for ensuring secrecy:

1. Negotiate confidential disclosure agreements with all employees, agents, consultants, suppliers, and anyone else who will be exposed to the secret information. The agreement should bind them not to use or disclose the information without permission.

2. Take security precautions to keep third parties from entering the premises where the trade secrets are used. Sturdy locks, perimeter fences, guards, badges, visitor sign-in books, escorts, and designated off-limits areas are just some of the ways that a trade secret owner can exercise control over the area containing the secrets.

3. Stamp specific documents containing the trade secrets with a confidentiality legend, and keep them in a secure place with limited access, such as a safe, locked drawer, or cabinet.

4. Make sure all employees, consultants, and others who are concerned with, have access to, or have knowledge about the trade secrets understand that they are trade secrets, and make sure they recognize the value to the company of this information and the requirement for secrecy.

Photo Credit: Gregor/Pixabay

In 2019, a Chinese-born scientist was arrested for allegedly trying to steal Coca-Cola's trade secrets for the technology used to coat the inside of Coke's cans and other drink containers.[7]

Trade secret owners rarely do all these things, but they must do enough so that a person who misappropriates the secrets cannot reasonably excuse his conduct by saying that he didn't know or that no precautions were ever taken to indicate that something was a trade secret. This is important because, unlike patents, trade secret protection provides no "deed" to the property.

Trade secret misappropriations generally fall into one of two classes: someone who has a confidential relationship with the owner violates the duty of confidentiality, or someone under no duty of confidentiality uses improper means to discover the secret.

Trade secret theft issues frequently arise with respect to the conduct of ex-employees. Certainly, a good employee will learn a lot about the business during her employment. And some of that learning she will take with her as experience when she leaves. We cannot prevent that. The question is, "Did she simply arrive smart and leave smarter, or did she take certain information that was exclusively the company's?"

For example, a few years back, CBS Broadcasting, Inc. brought suit against the American Broadcasting Companies, Inc. and related defendants alleging, among other things, misappropriation of CBS's trade secrets. Specifically, CBS alleged that ABC's new television show, *Life in a Glass House*, was developed using confidential, proprietary information related to the behind-the-scenes development, filming, and production of CBS's hit reality series *Big Brother*. It is further alleged that ABC obtained access to those trade secrets from 19 former CBS employees who had previously worked on *Big Brother* but had been hired by ABC to develop *Glass House*.

ABC, on the contrary, denies that any trade secrets have been employed in the production of *Glass House*. It points out that *Big Brother* has been on the air for 13 years and is one of approximately 400 reality shows to be broadcast during that period. It is highly unlikely, asserts ABC, that there is anything still secret about the production and editing of a reality show that could have been transferred to ABC by the former CBS employees.

In summary, trade secrets can be valuable, but they are not a form of "free protection," nor is protection available for secrets that can be discovered. Still, many investors rank trade secrets as at least as important as patents when they make an investment decision in a start-up company.

Trademarks

Trademarks are the stuff of advertising. Technically speaking, trademark protection is obtainable for any word, symbol, or combination thereof that is used on goods to indicate their source. Any word—even common words such as "look," "life," and "apple"—can become a trademark, so long as the word is not used descriptively. "Apple" for fruit salad might not be protectable, but Apple for computers certainly is.

Common forms such as geometric shapes (circles, triangles, and squares), natural shapes (trees, animals, and humans), combinations of shapes, and colors may also be protected. Even the single color pink has been protected as a trademark for building insulation. Three-dimensional shapes such as bottle and container shapes and building features (e.g., McDonald's golden arches) can serve as trademarks.

Although people generally speak only of trademarks, that term also encompasses other types of marks. A trademark is for products. A **service mark** is a word or symbol or combination used in connection with the offering and provision of services. Blue Cross/Blue Shield, Prudential Insurance, and McDonald's are service marks for health insurance services, general insurance services, and restaurant services, respectively. McDonald's is a service mark (fast-food restaurant services) and also a trademark (the McDonald's brand Big Mac hamburger).

If you use any such name or feature to identify and distinguish your products, then think trademark protection. Ownership of a trademark allows you to exclude others from using a similar mark on similar goods that would be likely to confuse consumers as to the source of the goods. This right applies for the duration of ownership of the mark—that is, as long as the owner uses the mark.

Trademarks can be more valuable to some companies than patents and trade secrets combined. Consider the sudden appearance and abrupt increase in the worth of trademarks such as Cuisinart, Häagen-Dazs, and Ben & Jerry's. Consider also the increased value that a trademark name such as Apple, Amazon, Starbucks, or Netflix brings to even a brand-new product or service offering. But don't be misled—trademarks and service marks protect the *names* of products and services, not the products and services themselves.

You can establish a trademark, unlike a patent, without any formal governmental procedure. You acquire ownership of a trademark simply by being the first to use the mark on the goods sold in commerce. It remains your property as long as you keep using it. And keep using it you must—because nonuse for a period of three years or more may constitute abandonment.

The mark should not be too descriptive of the goods on which you use it, and it is best to select a mark that is arbitrary and fanciful with respect to the goods. The reason is that every marketer, including a competitor, has the right to use a descriptive term to refer to its goods. Therefore, no one can secure exclusive rights to descriptive marks.

If a name is too descriptive, you cannot register it, and competitors may freely use it as is or in a slightly modified form. The more descriptive the mark, the less advertising required to inform consumers what the product is for. But so descriptive a mark enjoys a much lower level of protection.

On the other hand, a highly protectable arbitrary mark (Exxon, FedEx) requires significant expenditures in advertising dollars to inform consumers what the product or service associated with the mark actually is. Pick trademarks that are suggestive enough to adequately inform consumers but that are not too descriptive. Examples of marks held to be too descriptive include "Beer Nuts," "Chap-Stick," "Vision Center" (for an optical clinic), "Professional Portfolio System" (stock valuations), "5 Minute" (glue that sets in five minutes), "Body Soap" (body shampoo), "Consumer Electronics Monthly," "Light Beer," and "Shredded Wheat." The trademark Windows itself has more than once been the subject of legal action in which evidence existed that "windows" was descriptive before Microsoft adopted it.

A trademark owner should also take care to prevent the mark from becoming generic, as happened to Aspirin, Cellophane, Linoleum, and other product names. Thus, it is not proper to refer to, for example, a xerox—the correct form of description is a Xerox brand photocopier.

It is wise to research a proposed new mark to be sure the mark is clear before you use it; that is, verify that no one else is already using or has registered the same or a similar mark on the same or similar products. It's confusing to customers and expensive to change a mark and undertake the costs of all new printing, advertising, and promotional materials when you later discover that your mark has previously been used by another company. Moreover, in a due diligence study, whether at the time someone invests in your entrepreneurial company, at the time you make a public offering, or during a sale or merger, you can be sure a trademark search will be conducted. If you plan to enter foreign markets, make sure your mark does not mean something unintended in a foreign language.

Registering a Mark

Although trademarks don't have to be registered, there are significant benefits that make it worthwhile. You can register in individual states, or you can obtain a federal registration. A state registration applies only in the particular state that granted the registration and requires only use of the mark in that state. A federal registration applies to all 50 states, but to qualify, you must use the mark in interstate or foreign commerce. A distinct advantage of federal registration is that, even if you initially use a mark only locally—say, in New England—you can establish federal protection in all 50 states. Without a federal registration, you may later be blocked from using your mark in other states if a later user of the same mark, without knowledge of your use of the mark, federally registers it.

Also, you can file an application to register a mark that is not yet in use. After the U.S. Patent and Trademark Office examines the application and determines that the mark is registrable, you must show actual use within six months. The six-month period can be extended if good cause is shown. Nevertheless, before registration, even before actual use, the mere filing of the application establishes greater rights over others who actually used the mark earlier but did not file an application for registration.

A typical search and registration costs between $1,500 and $3,500 per mark. Given these fairly low costs, entrepreneurial companies regularly seek federal registration for all trademarks and service marks. A search increases the odds your registration will be successful because the Trademark Office primarily evaluates two things: Is the mark too descriptive, and is it too similar to another already registered mark? If the answer to both these questions is "no," the registration is typically issued about a year after you file the trademark application.

Ownership of a Mark

Be careful with your trademark properties. You cannot simply sell a trademark by itself or transfer it like a desk, car, patent, or copyright. You must sell it together with the business or goodwill associated with the mark, or the mark will be considered abandoned.

Claiming ownership of a mark can be an important business decision. When Cuisinart started selling its food processors, it promoted them vigorously under the trademark Cuisinart. A good part of the business's success was due to the fact that the manufacture of the machines was contracted out to a quality-conscious French company, Robot Coupe, which had been making the machines for many years before they became popular among U.S. consumers under the mark Cuisinart. When price competition reared its head, Cuisinart found cheaper sources. Robot Coupe owned no patents and had no other protection. Cuisinart began selling brand X under the name Cuisinart, and a wild fight ensued through the courts and across the pages of major newspapers in the United States—but to no avail. The whole market had been created under the name Cuisinart, and Cuisinart had the right to apply its name to any machine made anywhere by anyone it chose. Robot Coupe, whose machine had helped create the demand for food processors, was left holding its chopper.

Copyright

Copyrights cover all manner of writings, and the term *writings* is very broadly interpreted. It includes books, advertisements, brochures, spec sheets, catalogs, manuals, parts lists, promotional materials, packaging and decorative graphics, jewelry, fabric designs, photographs, pictures, film and video presentations, audio recordings, architectural designs, and software.

Exact copying is not always required to engage in infringement. For example, you can infringe a book without copying every word; the theme itself may be protected. One example exists in the software area, where using the teachings of a book to write a program has resulted in copyright infringement of the book by the computer program. In another case, a program was infringed by another program even though the second program was written in an entirely different language and for an entirely different computer. Copyright, then, can sometimes be a good source of protection, but be careful: It doesn't generally protect engineering, inventions, marketing or advertising ideas, or business plans. The good news is that a copyright registration is easy to obtain, protection lasts a long time, and it is inexpensive (typically less than $500). But unless your business is related to some form of the arts (music, movies, books, photography) or software, copyright usually only offers very limited protection because ideas and functionality are not generally protected by copyright.

Copyright registration is not compulsory, but it bestows a few valuable benefits. If the copyright owner has registered the copyright, special damages can be recovered. This can be a real advantage in copyright cases where actual damages can be difficult and expensive to prove or actual damages are limited.

Registration simply requires filling out the proper form and mailing it to the Copyright Office with the proper fee and copies of the work to be registered. Accommodations are made for filing

	Patents	Trade Secrets	Trademarks	Copyright
Subject Matter	Inventions and innovation, i.e., new products, features, and functionality	Only what can be kept secret	Names of companies, their products and services	Works of authorship, i.e., the arts and software
Cost	Expensive: $10–28K per patent per country	Depends on the volume of those secrets and the number of employees and consultants; definitely not "free"	Moderate: $1–3K per mark	Inexpensive: less than $500
Government Review	Yes—extensive and mandatory	No	Yes—moderate and optional but a good idea	Yes—but it is a rubber stamp
Term of Protection	On average, 17 years from issuance	Potentially forever—as long as the secret is kept secret	Potentially forever, as long as the mark is used	Long time—100 years
How Long to Achieve Protection	A fairly long time: 3–5 years	Immediately	Immediate—when the mark is used; registration takes about a year	Immediate, and registration takes only about a month
Pros	Can provide very broad protection even when an infringer didn't know about your patent	No government review; protects things not protectable by patents	Cost is moderate, and the odds of achieving a registration can be determined beforehand	Inexpensive and immediate
Cons	Value is commensurate with the claims; high level of government scrutiny; strict time requirements	Cannot be used if the "secret" really isn't; others have the right to discover the secret on their own	Only protects names—not the products or the services themselves	Outside of software and the arts, copyright usually doesn't offer extensive protection

FIGURE 12.1 IP Considerations.

valuable or difficult deposit copies; for example, deposits for large computer programs may consist of only the first and last 25 pages. Further, if the program contains trade secrets, there is a provision for obscuring those areas from the deposit because the Copyright Office's records are public. The Copyright Office doesn't really check to make sure the material is copyrightable; provided the form is filled out correctly, the Copyright Office will stamp it and you have a registration.

Figure 12.1 summarizes a few key aspects of the different avenues of IP protection.

International Protection for Intellectual Property

Obtaining protection for patents, trademarks, and copyrights in the United States alone is no longer sufficient in the modern arena of international competition and global markets. International protection often needs to be extensive and can be quite expensive, but there are ways to reduce and postpone the expense in some cases. You will want to consider protection in countries where you intend to market the new product or where competitors may be poised to manufacture your product.

A patent in one country does not protect the product in any other country: You must protect a novel product or method by a separate patent in each country. In addition, different countries have different conditions that you must meet to obtain any patent protection. The first and most important restriction is the time limit within which you must file an application to obtain a patent in a country or else forever lose your right to do so.

Patent Filing Deadlines

Not all countries are the same with respect to filing deadlines. There is no period of grace in any other country but the United States, and each country has a slightly different view of what constitutes making an invention public. In Japan, for example, public use before the filing of an application bars a patent only if the public use occurred in Japan; in France, any public knowledge of the invention anywhere bars the patent.

Thus, whereas the United States allows a business one full year to test-market its new product (see the earlier discussion), most other countries require that the patent application be filed before any public disclosure—that is, before the owner can begin to determine whether the new product will be even a modest success. Meeting this requirement is not inexpensive, especially when the U.S. dollar is down against the currencies of other major countries.

How to Extend Patent Filing Deadlines

There are ways around having to file immediately in all foreign countries. If you file in the United States and then file in another country within one year of that date, the U.S. filing date applies as the filing date for that country. In this way, by filing one application for the invention in the United States, you can preserve your initial U.S. filing date for up to one year and then immediately make the invention public through advertising, published articles, and sales. If within one year the product appears to be a success, you can then file in selected foreign countries, even though the prior public use of the invention would ordinarily bar your filing in those countries.

You can even delay up to 20 or even 30 months before incurring the costs of filing in individual countries. By filing a special Patent Cooperation Treaty (PCT) patent application in a specially designated PCT office within one year of your U.S. filing and by designating certain countries, you can preserve your right to file in those countries without further expense for 20 or 30 months after the U.S. filing date. That will provide an additional 8 or 18 months for test marketing the product. This does introduce the extra cost of the PCT application filing, but if you are considering filing in, say, six or more countries, it may be well worth the cost for three reasons:

- It delays the outflow of cash that you may not presently have or may require for other urgent needs.
- It provides for a uniform examination of the patent application.
- If the product proves insufficiently successful, you can decide not to file in any of the countries designated under the PCT and save the cost of all six national application filings.

Another cost-saving feature of international patent practice is the European Patent Convention (EPC), which is compatible with a PCT filing and which enables you to file a single European patent application and designate any one or more of the European countries in which you wish the patent to issue.

A number of international treaties affect trademark rights and copyrights as well. A "European" trademark registration is now available, for example, known as a Community Trade Mark (CTM). A single registration will cover the entire European Union (EU)—with the benefit of a single filing, you obtain plenary protection. However, there are certain drawbacks. For example, a single user in any country of the EU could block registration everywhere, and cost considerations make a CTM filing uneconomical unless you seek trademarks in at least three countries. Registration is also now possible simultaneously in the United States and other foreign countries via a treaty known as the Madrid Protocol.

Choice of Legal Form

Another important issue all entrepreneurs will confront is what legal form they should choose to operate their new venture. Many choices are available.

The most basic business form is the **sole proprietorship**, owned and operated by one owner who is in total control. No new legal entity is created; the individual entrepreneur just goes into business, either alone or with employees, but without any co-owners.

If there is more than one owner of the business, the default mode is the **general partnership**. This is the legal form that results when two or more persons go into business for profit, as co-owners, sharing profits and losses.

Another choice available to entrepreneurs is the **corporation**. This form is created by state government, as a routine matter, upon the entrepreneurs' filing an application and paying a fee. It is a separate legal entity, with legal existence apart from its owners, the stockholders.

A variation of the corporate choice is the **subchapter S corporation**. If a corporation passes a number of tests, it may elect to be treated as a subchapter S corporation, a designation that affects only its tax status. In all other respects, a subchapter S corporation is indistinguishable from all other corporations.

An increasingly popular form of business entity is the **limited liability company (LLC)**. This entity is owned by "members" who either manage the business themselves or appoint "managers" (either outsiders or a subset of the members) to run it for them. All members and managers have the benefit of limited liability (as they would in a corporation) and, in most cases, are taxed similarly to a subchapter S corporation without having to conform to the S corporation restrictions described later in this section.

Another possible legal form is a hybrid of the corporate and partnership forms, known as the **limited partnership**. Such a business would have one or more general partners, who would conduct the business and take on personal risk, and one or more limited partners, who would act as passive investors (similar to stockholders with no other interest in the business). Due to the availability of the limited liability company, this form of entity has over time faded into use in only a niches such as venture capital firms; it is no longer attractive to most businesses.

Also available is the **limited liability partnership (LLP)**, which is the entity of choice for many law firms, accounting firms, and the like, but is not widely used by other businesses.

Finally, a **not-for-profit entity** will typically take the form of a corporation or trust and elect nonprofit status as a tax matter. Although many start-ups do not make a profit, nonprofit status is available only to certain types of activities, such as churches, educational institutions, social welfare organizations, and industry associations. If an organization so qualifies, its income is exempt from taxation (as long as it doesn't stray from its exempt purpose), and if certain additional tests are met, contributions to it may be tax deductible. All profits must be devoted to the company's exempt purpose; none may be distributed as dividends to private parties.

Although we can compare these forms of business on an almost endless list of factors, the most relevant include control issues, exposure to personal liability, tax factors, and administrative costs. We discuss these in detail in the following sections, and Figure 12.2 provides an overview of the issues and how they play out in the most relevant business forms.

Control

Because there is only one principal in the sole proprietorship, he wields total control over all issues. In the general partnership, control is divided among the principals in accordance with their partnership agreement (which need not be written but should be, to encourage specificity). The parties may decide that all decisions must be made by unanimous vote, or they may adopt a majority standard. More likely, they may require unanimity for a stated group of significant decisions and allow a majority vote for others.

	Control	Liability	Taxation	Administrative Obligations
Sole proprietorship	Owner has complete control	Unlimited personal liability	Not a separate taxable entity	Only those applicable to all businesses
Partnership	Partners share control	Joint and several unlimited personal liability	Not a separate taxable entity	Only those applicable to all businesses
Corporation	Control distributed among shareholders, directors, and officers	Limited personal liability	Separate taxable entity unless subchapter S election	Some additional
Limited liability company	Members share control or appoint managers	Limited personal liability	Not a separate entity unless affirmatively chosen	Some additional

FIGURE 12.2 Comparison of Various Business Forms.

Regardless of how power is allocated in the partnership agreement, in the eyes of third parties, each of the partners will have a free hand to contract with outsiders, subject only to the internal consequences of the partner's breaching his agreement with the others. This is also true for the consequences of torts committed by any partner acting in the course of partnership business.

A corporation, regardless of whether it has elected subchapter S status, is controlled by three levels of authority. Broadly speaking, the stockholders vote, in proportion to the number of shares they own, on the election of the board of directors, the sale or dissolution of the business, and amendments to the corporation's charter. In virtually all cases, these decisions are made either by the majority or by two-thirds of the votes cast. Thus, any group of stockholders owning a majority of the voting stock, can elect the entire board.

The board of directors in turn makes all the long-term and significant policy decisions for the business as well as electing the officers of the corporation. Votes are virtually always decided by majority. The officers, consisting of a president, treasurer, and secretary at a minimum, run the day-to-day business of the corporation and are the only level of authority that can bind the corporation by contract or in tort. It is not uncommon for the corporation's attorney to act as secretary because the attorney presumably has the expertise to keep the corporate records of the company in an accurate manner.

The limited liability company can operate much like a general partnership. All members can share in control to the extent set forth in their agreement, known in most states as an *operating agreement*. However, members may choose to appoint one or more "managers" to control most of the day-to-day operations of the business.

Personal Liability

Should the business incur current liabilities beyond its ability to pay, must the individual owners risk personal bankruptcy to make up the difference? This unhappy result need not occur only as a result of poor management or bad business conditions. It could just as easily be brought about by an uninsured tort claim from a customer or a victim of a delivery person's careless driving.

In both the partnership and the sole proprietorship, the business is not recognized as a legal entity separate from its owners. Thus, the debts of the business are ultimately the debts of the owners if the business cannot pay. This unlimited liability is enough to recommend against these forms for virtually any business, with the exception perhaps of the one-person consulting firm, all of whose liability will be the direct result of the wrongdoing of its owner in any case.

If this unlimited liability is uncomfortable for the founders, imagine what it would mean to an investor. The investor no doubt has significant assets to lose and will likely have only limited control over the business decisions that may generate liability. This risk is made even worse by the fact that all partnership liabilities are considered joint and several obligations of all partners. Thus, the investor will be responsible for full payment of all partnership liabilities if the founders have no significant assets of their own.

The answer to this problem lies in the corporation and the limited liability company, both of which afford limited liability to all owners. If the business ultimately becomes insolvent, its creditors will look only to business assets for payment; any shortfall will be absorbed by the unfortunate creditors.

This solution is not quite as all-encompassing as it sounds. To begin with, creditors know these rules as well as entrepreneurs do. Thus, large or sophisticated creditors, such as banks and other financial institutions, will insist on personal guarantees from the owners of the business before extending credit.

In addition, the law allows creditors to "pierce the corporate veil" and go after the owners of a failed corporation or LLC under certain conditions. The first situation in which this can occur involves a business that was initially underfunded or "thinly capitalized." A business should start out with a combination of capital and liability insurance adequate to cover the claims to which it might normally expect to be exposed. As long as the capital was there at the outset and has not been depleted by dividends or other distributions to owners, causing insolvency, the protection of the separate entity survives even after the capital has been depleted by unsuccessful operation.

The second situation that may result in the piercing of the corporate (or LLC) veil is the failure of the owners to treat the corporation or LLC as an entity separate from themselves by

- Failing to use *Inc., Corp., LLC*, or a similar legal indicator when dealing with third parties, or
- Commingling business and personal assets in a personal bank account or allowing unreimbursed personal use of corporate assets, or
- Failing to keep business and legal records and hold regular directors', stockholders', or members' meetings.

Taxation

Income taxes, both personal and corporate, that will be paid as a result of starting up and operating a business are an important consideration in the choice of the legal entity for a new venture. The ideal entity from the perspective of income taxes should do the following:

- Minimize or eliminate any personal income tax that might result from receipt of founder stock.
- Maximize the tax shelter for the investors when the business has an annual loss.
- Minimize taxes paid by the business, founders, and investors when the business has an annual profit.
- Minimize capital gains taxes payable by the founders and investors if they sell all or some of their stock.

No entity accomplishes all the preceding income tax considerations and at the same time shields the owners from liabilities incurred by the business. Although various forms of partnership might be more favorable tax shelters for the investors, operating businesses are almost always set up as a corporation or limited liability company for reasons that we have examined and will examine in the remainder of this and the next section.

Entrepreneurs are often warned about the *double taxation* that arises when a corporation makes a profit, pays income tax on it, and then distributes part or all of its profit after tax as a dividend to its stockholders, who in turn pay income tax on that dividend; this means that the same money is taxed twice (although potentially at a reduced dividend rate the second time).

In reality, however, double taxation is more a myth than a legitimate threat to the small business. In fact, in most cases, it presents an opportunity for significant economic savings. To begin with, most small corporations lower or even eliminate their profit by increasing deductible salaries and bonuses for their owners up to the limit deemed "unreasonable" by the Internal Revenue Service. The owners then pay only their own individual income tax on the money.

On the other hand, if it is necessary to retain some of these earnings, the start-up corporation will normally pay income tax at a lower rate than the stockholders would have because tax will be imposed at the lowest marginal corporate rate rather than the stockholders' highest rate. When the corporation is later sold, the stockholders will be taxed at favorable capital gain rates, and the corporation will have had the use of the money in the meantime to create greater value. Thus, it is the rare small corporation that will actually pay double tax.

Furthermore, if the corporation meets certain eligibility requirements, it can elect, under subchapter S of the Internal Revenue Code, to be taxed essentially as if it were a partnership. Whatever profit or loss it may generate will appear on the tax returns of the stockholders in proportion to the shares of stock they own, and the corporation will file only an informational return. To take advantage of this option, the corporation must have 100 or fewer stockholders, all of whom must be individuals (with some exceptions) and either resident aliens or citizens of the United States. The corporation can have only one class of stock (with the exception of classes based solely on different voting rights) and is ineligible to participate in most multiple-entity corporate structures. Note there is no size limit on subchapter S eligibility.

The subchapter S election can be very useful in a number of circumstances. For example, if the business is expected to be profitable and investors insist on a share of those profits, one cannot avoid double taxation by increasing salaries and bonuses. Because an investor performs no services for the business, any compensation paid to him would automatically be deemed "unreasonable." But under subchapter S, because there is no corporate tax, a dividend to the stockholders would be taxed only at the stockholder level.

If the business were to become extremely successful, the founders could reap the rewards without fear that their salaries might be attacked as "unreasonable" because, again, there are no corporate compensation deductions to disallow. An early subchapter S election can also avoid double taxation should the corporation eventually sell all its assets and distribute the proceeds to the stockholders in liquidation.

Furthermore, if the business is expecting losses in the short term, the investors might be able to use their share of the losses (determined by percentage of stock) to shelter other income subject to the passive loss rules of the Internal Revenue Code.

After having considered all this, the founding entrepreneurs might wish to form a corporation, elect subchapter S treatment, and arrange their affairs such that, when an angel investor contributes his investment, he can make as much use of short-term losses as possible. However, because profits and losses in an S corporation must be allocated in accordance with stock ownership and only one class of stock is allowed, any disproportionate allocation of losses to the investor would have to be accompanied by a disproportionate allocation to him of later profits. More creative allocations of profit, loss, and control could be accomplished in a general (or limited partnership), but one or more of the owners would have to accept exposure to unlimited liability in those entities.

Limited liability companies were designed for just this circumstance. If structured carefully, they afford the limited liability and "pass-through" tax treatment of the S corporation, while avoiding the S corporation's restrictive eligibility requirements. Freed from these restrictions, limited liability companies can use creative allocations of profit, loss, and control that would constitute prohibited multiple classes of stock in the S corporation context.

The LLC is not the solution for all situations, however. The investor may have little ability to use losses due to a lack of material participation in the business as required by the Internal Revenue Code's passive loss rules. Worse yet, the investor would certainly not be enthusiastic at the notion of "phantom income" when the company's financial performance turns positive and the company begins to retain earnings.

Initial Investment of the Founders

As a general rule, founders normally arrange the issuance of their equity in the venture for very little tangible investment. After all, they intend to look to investors for working capital, and their investment will be the services they intend to perform for the business.

Of practical concern, however, is the fact that any property (including stock or LLC membership interests) transferred to an employee in exchange for the employee's services is considered taxable income under the Internal Revenue Code. Thus, whenever equity is issued to founders in exchange for services (so-called "sweat equity"), they may face an unexpected tax liability as a result.

In the LLC context, the Internal Revenue Service will, in most cases, value the ownership interest granted to the partner or member as equivalent to the amount credited to the capital account. Thus, as long as a noncontributing owner's capital account begins at zero and grows only to the extent of future profits, there will be no current taxation at the time of issuance.

However, in the corporate context, at approximately the same time that the founders are receiving their stock for minimal investment, the investors will be putting in the real money. Because the investors will be paying substantially more for their stock than the founders are paying for theirs, the Internal Revenue Service will likely take the position that they are getting a bargain in exchange for the services they are providing to their company. Thus the founders may be facing an unexpected income tax on the difference between the price per share of the investors' stock and the price of theirs.

One way to solve this problem is to postpone the investor's investment until the founders can argue for an increase in the value of the corporation's stock. Aside from the essentially fictional nature of this approach, most founders probably cannot wait that long. Instead, the parties must design a vehicle for the investors sufficiently different from the founders' interests to justify the higher price. This is taken care of in the LLC context by the difference in capital accounts. In the corporate context some form of preferred stock will serve the purpose (although the issuance of preferred stock would render a corporation ineligible for subchapter S status, as it would then have more than one class of stock).

How does all this inform the choice of entity? Essentially, the pass-through form exposes the investor to potential "phantom income" if the company does well, while failing to provide practical use of losses on his personal return if the company loses money. On the other hand, preferred stock in a C corporation provides the liquidation, dividend, participation, and conversion privileges the investor desires without the risk of phantom income. And from the founders' point of view, issuance of preferred stock to their investor has the benefit of solving their potential income tax problems. The parties will therefore likely agree on the C corporation as the best choice of entity unless the investor is looking for current distributions of profit instead of the company's retaining profits to fuel further growth.

Administrative Obligations

Start-up businesses should obtain an Internal Revenue Service federal identification number. On the state level, the business should obtain a sales and use tax registration number, both to facilitate reporting and collection of such taxes and to qualify for exemption from such taxes when it purchases items for resale. A nonprofit entity has 18 months to file for and secure nonprofit status from the Internal Revenue Service. Furthermore, all business entities will incur a certain amount of additional accounting expense, specifically for the calculation and reporting of taxable profit and loss.

Corporations and limited liability companies, however, bring some additional administrative burden and expense. They must file an annual report with the state government in addition to their tax return. This document usually reports only the business's current address, officers, directors, managers, and similar information, but it is accompanied by an annual maintenance fee. The fee, in addition to any income tax that the state may levy, must be paid to avoid eventual involuntary dissolution by the state.

In addition, corporations are sometimes formed under the laws of one state, while operating in another. In particular, the state of Delaware has a corporate law particularly sympathetic to management that has also been thoroughly interpreted by its long history of complex corporate litigation. Although these are questionable advantages in the context of a small business (where management and stockholders are generally the same people), Delaware does offer a method of calculating its fees that does not penalize a corporation for having a large number of authorized shares. This allows a corporation whose compensation strategy includes stock grants or stock options to use much larger numbers of shares in these grants, creating a psychological appearance of generosity that may not mathematically exist. Even corporations that have not adopted such a strategy often form in Delaware merely to share in an appearance of sophistication.

In all such cases, the corporation must pay not only initial and maintenance fees to the state of Delaware (or whichever state is chosen for formation), along with the costs of maintaining an address for service of process there, but also initial and annual maintenance fees to qualify to do business in each state in which it actually operates. Many large, national concerns pay these fees in virtually all 50 states.

Choosing a Name

The choice of a name for a business may seem at first to be a matter of personal taste, without many legal ramifications. However, because the name of a business may ultimately be the repository of its goodwill, the owner should choose a name that will not be confused with the name of another business.

Although partnerships and sole proprietorships need not do so, corporations and limited liability companies obtain their existence by filing charters with the state. As part of this process, each state will check to see whether the name of the new entity is "confusingly similar" to the name of any other entity currently registered with that state. Some states will also deny the use of a name they deem misleading, even if it is not similar to the name of another entity.

Stockholders' and Operating Agreements

The owners' respective investments will normally be memorialized in an operating agreement in the case of an LLC and in a combination of a stock purchase agreement, charter amendments, and stockholders' agreement in the case of a corporation. In a partnership, very similar provisions allocating equity interests and rights to distributions of profit and cash flow would appear in a Partnership Agreement. In all these cases, however, the parties would be well advised to go beyond these subjects and reach written agreement on a number of other potentially thorny issues at the outset of their relationship.

Negotiating Employment Terms

The founders should reach agreement with the investor about their commitment to provide services and the level of compensation for doing so. It would be very unusual for the founders to forgo compensation solely to share the profits of the business with their investor. For one thing, what would they be living on in the interim? For another, the profits of the business are properly conceived of as the amount left over after payment of the expenses of the business—including reasonable compensation to its employees. Thus, the founders should negotiate employment terms into the operating or stockholders' agreement, setting forth their responsibilities, titles, compensation, and related issues.

This is especially important in the case in which any individual founder may hold only a minority interest in the corporation (depending on the voting rights given to the preferred stock). She may wish to foreclose the possibility that the other owners may ally and employ a majority of the shares to remove the founder as a director, officer, or employee of the company. Given the lack of any market for the shares of this corporation, such a move would essentially destroy any value the shares had for the holder in the short run.

Although a concise description of each party's obligations and rewards is still advisable to avoid dispute, this negative scenario would be illegal in a partnership (in the absence of serious misconduct by the party being removed) because the majority partners would be violating the fiduciary duty of loyalty imposed on each partner toward the others under partnership law. Although no such duty formally exists among stockholders in a corporation, many states (not including Delaware) have imported the fiduciary duties of partners to the relationship among the founders of a closely held corporation. Similar doctrines have been developed for LLCs. Thus, in many states, were a founder to be removed without cause from her employment and corporate positions, she would have effective legal recourse even in the absence of a stockholders' agreement.

Disposition of Equity Interests

As for other items that might be covered in the agreement among the founders and investors, many address the disposition of equity held by the owners under certain circumstances.

Transfer to Third Parties

To begin with, although sale of stock in a close corporation or LLC is made rather difficult by federal and state securities regulation and the lack of any market for the shares, transfers are still possible under the correct circumstances. To avoid that possibility, stockholder and operating agreements frequently require that any owner wishing to transfer equity to a third party must first offer it to the company and/or the other owners, who may purchase the equity, often at the lower of a formula price or the amount being offered by the third party.

Disposition of Equity upon the Owner's Death

Stockholder and operating agreements should also address the disposition of each owner's equity upon death. Again, it is unlikely that each owner would be comfortable allowing the deceased owner's stock to fall into the hands of the deceased's spouse, children, or other heirs, although this may be more acceptable in the case of a pure investor. Moreover, should the business succeed over time, each owner's equity may well be worth a significant amount upon death. If so, the Internal Revenue Service will wish to impose an estate tax based on the equity's value, regardless of the fact that it is an illiquid asset. Under such circumstances, the owner's estate may wish to have the assurance that some or all of such equity will be converted to cash so the tax may be paid. If the agreement forbids free transfer of the equity during lifetime and requires that the equity be redeemed at death for a reasonable price, the agreement may well be accepted by the IRS as a persuasive indication of the equity's value, thus also avoiding an expensive and time-consuming valuation controversy.

Any redemption provision at the death of the owner, especially one that is mandatory at the instance of the estate, immediately raises the question of the availability of funds. Just when the business may be reeling from the effects of the loss of one of its most valuable employees, it may be expected to scrape together enough cash to buy out the deceased's ownership. To avoid this

	Effect on Tax Basis	Effect on Alternative Minimum Tax	Need for Adequate Corporate Surplus
Redemption agreement	No stepped-up basis	Risks accumulated current earnings preference for larger C corporations	Needs adequate surplus
Cross-purchase agreement	Stepped-up basis	No risk	Surplus is irrelevant

FIGURE 12.3 Comparison of Stock Redemption Agreement and Stock Cross-purchase Agreement.

disastrous result, many of these arrangements are funded by life insurance policies on the lives of the owners. This would be in addition to any key person insurance held by the business for the purpose of recovering from the effects of the loss. In structuring such an arrangement, however, the parties should be aware of two quite different models.

The first, and more traditional, model is referred to as a *redemption agreement*. Under it, the business owns the policies and is obligated to purchase the equity upon death. The second model is referred to as a *cross-purchase agreement* and provides for each owner to own insurance on the others and to buy a proportional amount of the deceased's equity. Figure 12.3 illustrates the primary differences between the two forms of agreement. Although a cross-purchase is more complicated, especially if there are more than a few stockholders, it has significant benefits compared with a redemption agreement.

Disposition of Equity on Termination of Employment

Stockholder and operating agreements normally also address disposition of equity on events other than death. Repurchase of equity on termination of employment can be very important for all parties. The former employee whose equity no longer represents an opportunity for employment would like the opportunity to cash in her investment. The company and other owners may resent the presence of an inactive owner who can capitalize on their later efforts. Thus, both operating and stockholder agreements will normally provide for repurchase of the interest of a stockholder or member who is no longer actively employed by the company. This, of course, applies only to stockholders or members whose efforts on behalf of the company were the basis of their participation in the first place. Such provisions would not apply to a pure investor, for example.

This portion of the agreement presents a number of additional problems peculiar to the employee–owner. For example, the company cannot obtain insurance to cover an obligation to purchase equity on termination of employment. Thus, it may encounter an obligation to purchase the equity of the former employee at a time when its cash position will not support such a purchase. Furthermore, courts uniformly prohibit repurchases that would render the company insolvent. Common solutions to these problems commit the company to an installment purchase of the affected equity over a period of years (with appropriate interest and security) or commit the remaining owners to make the purchase personally if the company is unable to do so for any reason.

Furthermore, these agreements frequently impose penalties on the premature termination of a stockholder or member's employment. For example, normally the investor is relying on the efforts of the founders in making his investment. Should the founders be entitled to a buyout at full fair market value if he or she simply decides to walk away from the venture? Often these agreements contain so-called vesting provisions that require a specified period of service before repurchase will be made at full value.

Such provisions, in addition to providing incentive to remain with the company, have complicated tax implications as well. As discussed earlier, if an employee receives equity for less than fair market value, the discount would be considered taxable compensation. The Internal Revenue Code provides that compensation income with regard to unvested equity is not taxed until the stock is vested. But at that time, the amount of income is measured by the difference between the price paid for the equity and its value *at the time of vesting*. The only way to avoid this result in the corporate context is to file an election to pay the tax on the compensation income measured at the time of the purchase of the equity, even though the equity is not then vested and may have little or no current value. And that election must be filed within 30 days of the receipt of the stock, not at the end of the year. This tax problem does not normally arise in an LLC so long as there is no initial contribution to the founders' capital accounts.

Distributions of Company Profits

Stockholder and operating agreements may also include numerous other provisions peculiar to the facts and circumstances of the particular business. Thus, pass-through entities often provide for mandatory distributions of profit to the members or stockholders at least in the amount of the tax obligation each will incur as a result of the profits of the business. Other agreements might include provisions to resolve voting deadlocks between owners because otherwise a 50–50 split of voting stock might paralyze the company. Various types of arbitration provisions might avoid this problem.

Redemption Provisions

Further, some stockholder or operating agreements provide investors with the right to demand repurchase of their equity at some predetermined formula price at a designated future time, so they will not be forever locked into a minority investment in a closely held company. Conversely, some such agreements provide the company with the right to repurchase such equity at a predetermined price (usually including a premium) should the capital no longer be needed. Other agreements protect investors against being left behind if the founders sell their equity to third parties. The presence or absence of all these provisions depends, of course, on the relative negotiating strengths of the parties.

Legal and Tax Issues in Hiring Employees

Employees as Agents of the Company

Employees are agents of the company and, as such, are governed by many of the agency rules that already affect the relationships of partners to a partnership and officers to a corporation. Thus, employees have the duty of loyalty to the company and obligations to not compete while employed, to respect confidentiality, and to account for their activities.

Possibly more interesting is the potential of employees to affect the business's relationships with third parties, such as customers and suppliers. Here, the rules of agency require that a distinction be drawn between obligations based on contractual liability and those resulting from non-contractual relationships such as tort actions.

Employees are authorized to bind their employers to contracts with third parties if such actions have either been expressly or impliedly authorized. Thus, if a company hires a sales manager and informs her that she has the authority to close any sale up to $50,000, she may wield that authority without further consultation with her principals. She also has the implied authority to do whatever is necessary to close such deals (such as sign a purchase order in the company's name, arrange delivery, and perhaps even alter some of the company's standard warranty terms).

However, the employee has authority that often extends beyond that expressly or impliedly given her. To illustrate this, suppose this sales manager decides to close a sale for $100,000. This goes beyond her express authority and is not within her implied authority because it was expressly prohibited. Yet, from the point of view of the customer, the company's sales manager appears to have the authority to close all sales transactions.

Unless the customer has been informed of the limitation imposed on the employee, he has no reason to think that anything is wrong. The law vindicates the customer in this situation by providing that the employee has apparent authority to conclude contracts within the scope of authority she appears to have due to actions of her employer. Because she was put into that position by her employer and the employer has not informed the customer of the limits imposed on the employee, the employer is bound by the employee's actions.

Outside the contract arena, the employee's power to bind the employer is based on similar considerations. The employer, under the doctrine of *respondeat superior* (or vicarious liability), is responsible for any actions of the employee occurring within the scope of her employment. Thus, if the sales manager causes a traffic accident on her way to a sales call, the employer is responsible for damages. This imposition of liability is not, in any way, based on the employer's fault. It is liability without fault imposed as a result of the economic judgment that employers are better able to spread losses among customers and insurance companies. Consistent with this approach, employers are normally not liable for the tort or criminal actions of employees *outside* the scope of their employment, such as actions occurring after hours or while the employee is pursuing his own interests. Furthermore, employers are normally not liable for the torts or criminal actions of agents who are not employees (so-called independent contractors) because they are more likely to be able to spread these costs among their own customers and insurers.

However, employers should not take this as an invitation to avoid all liability (and employee benefits, payroll taxes, withholding, etc.) by the wholesale hiring of independent contractors. To begin with, the labeling of a potential employee as an independent contractor is not necessarily binding by law. Courts will look at the level of control exerted by the employer and other related factors to make this determination. For example, in a very high profile case, Microsoft was forced to enter into a $97 million dollar settlement agreement with the IRS as a result of having misclassified thousands of "independent contractors."[8]

In addition, many activities of employers are considered non-delegable (such as disposal of hazardous waste). Employers cannot escape the consequences of such activities by hiding behind independent contractors.

Similarly, someone's status as an employee (or, for that matter, as an independent contractor) does not relieve him of responsibility for tortious or criminal acts. Notwithstanding any liability of the employer, the agent is always still jointly responsible for his own wrongful acts.

Employment Discrimination

In addition to these common-law considerations, there are, of course, a number of statutory rules of law that govern the employer–employee relationship. Perhaps the best known of these are the laws prohibiting employment discrimination. Title VII of the Civil Rights Act of 1964, the Age Discrimination in Employment Act, and laws protecting disabled and pregnant employees collectively prohibit employment discrimination on the basis of sex, race, national origin, religion, age, and disability. They do not, as yet, prohibit discrimination on the basis of sexual orientation, although a number of state and local laws do.

Prohibited discrimination can occur not only in hiring but also in promotion, firing, and conditions of employment. In fact, sexual discrimination has been found in cases of sexual harassment that created a "hostile environment" for the employee.

These statutes are exceptions to the age-old common law concept of employment at will that allowed employers to hire and fire at their whim, for any reason or no reason at all. This rule is still in force in situations not covered by discrimination laws and, of course, not involving employment contracts. Notwithstanding that rule, however, courts in many states have carved out exceptions to employment at will for reasons of public policy, such as cases involving employees fired for refusing to perform illegal acts or employees fired in bad faith to avoid paying commissions or other earned compensation to the employee. Furthermore, courts in some states have been willing to discover employment contracts hidden in employee manuals or personnel communications that employers may not have thought legally binding.

Employment Agreements

The attraction of employment agreements comes, in the main, from their protection against firing without cause. Thus, a major item of negotiation will likely be the length of the contract. Courts have universally held that an employee cannot be forced to work for an employer against her will. Thus, an employment contract is essentially a one-way street. The employee is promised employment for a period of time, with accompanying salary, bonus, and incentive provisions, but she can leave the company at any time without consequence (unless legally enforceable consequences are specifically provided). As a result, employers would be well advised to avoid employment agreements with their employees whenever possible and, if forced to grant one, at least to obtain some accompanying benefit for the company.

Such benefit usually comes in the form of the noncompetition and proprietary information covenants discussed at the beginning of this chapter. For example, a software engineer may promise, in exchange for a two-year employment agreement, not to work in the computer sales industry for a year after the termination of his employment. Yet, as mentioned, proprietary information obligations exist quite apart from any employee agreement, and courts may refuse to enforce noncompetition provisions against the employee.

Raising Money

Although it is analyzed in greater detail earlier in this book, raising money from potential investors involves another set of complex legal issues that deserve mention here.

Most businesspeople are aware of the fact that both federal and state law regulates the offer and sale of securities, but many believe that these statutes apply only to the offerings of large corporations. Small companies, they believe, are exempt from these acts. Unfortunately, this is a dangerous misconception. In fact, these laws (specifically, the federal Securities Act of 1933, the federal Securities Exchange Act of 1934, and states' "Blue Sky" statutes) apply to all issuers and their principals.

Further, some businesspeople who are aware of the reach of these acts nevertheless believe that they only apply to issuers of equity securities, mainly stock. This, too, is a misconception. All these statutes apply to issuers of "securities" not just stock. Securities include, in addition to stock, most debt (other than very short-term loans or loans for very specific purposes such as real estate mortgages), options, warrants, LLC membership interests, and any other form of investment in which the investor buys into a common enterprise and relies on the efforts of others for the investment's success.

In general, then, the securities laws prohibit the offering of securities to the public without prior (and very expensive) registration with the Securities and Exchange Commission (SEC). The SEC also punishes fraudulent activities in connection with such offerings, including not only affirmatively false statements but also mere nondisclosure of material facts about the investment. Due to the complex and expensive nature of registration, these laws provide exceptions to the registration requirement in specific circumstances, but even these offerings are generally subject to the antifraud provisions of the laws. Thus, the challenge to entrepreneurs is to identify provisions in the securities laws that will offer them an exemption from registration, understanding that they must still provide sufficient disclosure to potential investors (in the form of either an "offering circular" or, in appropriate circumstances, an unlimited opportunity to perform due diligence) to avoid "antifraud" liability.

The most popular exemption from registration under the federal act is the *private placement exemption*, which excuses from registration transactions "not involving a public offering." The SEC has relied in part on this exemption to issue regulations designed to facilitate the raising of capital by small businesses in small offerings. Thus, as of this writing, Regulation D under the act exempts from registration any offering of under $1,000,000 to over $5,000,000 of securities, depending on the Rule the company qualifies under and chooses to rely on. Above $5,000,000, the regulation requires increasing levels of disclosure (still short of full registration, however) and limits the number of non-accredited investors to 35 plus an unlimited number of *accredited* investors. For these purposes, accredited investors are certain institutions, as well as individuals with net worth or annual income at levels that argue a need for less protection. In addition, there is a "crowdfunding" exemption that allows certain companies to make use of the Internet to accept relatively small investments from large numbers of unrelated investors. These investors are limited to investing $2,000 or 5% of their annual income if they make $100,000 or less, or 10% or a maximum of $100,000 if they make more than $100,000 a year.[9] Also, it is important to keep in mind that if a private company has more than 2,000 investors (excluding crowdfunding investors), the law requires that it discloses financial information publicly,[10] an issue that forces many companies to go public even if they did not want to.

Of course, exemption from registration under the federal act does not necessarily grant exemption under state acts. In fact, offerings made to investors in a number of states require attention to the Blue Sky statutes of each such state. Fortunately, however, federal law has preempted state regulation in offerings beyond a certain size, and even in the absence of preemption, virtually all state statutes contain similar exemptions for private placements, typically exempting offerings to 25 or fewer persons.

Thus, most entrepreneurs will likely be able to seek out the investment they will ultimately need without the necessity of registering with either the federal or state governments. However, it cannot be overemphasized that they remain subject to the antifraud provisions of these acts. Thus, they will be well advised to seek professional assistance in identifying the applicable statutory exemptions, drawing up a comprehensive offering circular for their offering, if appropriate, and disclosing all that an investor would need to know about their company to make an intelligent investment decision.

CONCLUSION

Considering all the legal and tax pitfalls described in this chapter, you may be tempted to ask whether any entrepreneur would choose to go down the road of the start-up if fully aware of the complications lying in wait. But not to be aware of these matters is to choose consciously to play the game without knowing the rules. These issues are there regardless of whether the entrepreneur prepares for them. Surely you are much more likely to succeed in a venture for having taken the time to become aware of the legal and tax issues facing the entrepreneur.

YOUR OPPORTUNITY JOURNAL

Reflection Point	Your Thoughts...
1. What fiduciary duty do you have with your current employer? Does your proposed new venture rely on proprietary information belonging to your previous employer? Are you materially interfering with your previous employer's business by recruiting away key employees?	
2. When should you engage an attorney? What criteria will you use in your decision?	
3. What legal form should you choose for your new company (sole proprietorship, corporation, etc.)? What criteria will you use in your decision?	
4. What will you name your company? Have you registered your name with the state government? Are there other companies using the same or similar name (check the U.S. Patent and Trademark Office database)?	

Reflection Point	Your Thoughts...
5. What provisions should you have in your shareholders' agreement? What kind of salary will you draw? When will you draw it? What provisions do you have for disposition of equity (e.g., death, termination, etc.)?	
6. What type of equity sharing (if any) will you implement with your key employees?	
7. What type of insurance is needed to protect your company? When will you secure this insurance?	
8. What is the crucial intellectual property of your company? How will you protect it?	

WEB EXERCISE

Many Web sites offer legal form templates (e.g., shareholder agreements). Studying these templates helps you talk with your lawyer and can reduce your legal fees (time spent with lawyers), especially if you draft the documents and then have the lawyer approve them (rather than having your attorney draft the documents from scratch). Search out Web sites that offer legal templates.

NOTES

1. "BIOLASE SHAREHOLDER ALERT—Andrews & Springer LLC is Investigating Biolase, Inc. for Possible Violations of Securities Laws and Breaches of Fiduciary Duty." *NASDAQ OMX's News Release Distribution Channel.* Jul 07 2014. *ProQuest.* Web. 18 Oct. 2015.
2. http://www.ft.com/intl/fastft/410961/perella-weinberg-sues-bankers-over-recruitment-dispute.
3. *All Stainless Inc. v Colby* 364 Ma 773 (1974).
4. Performance and accountability report 2018. https://www.uspto.gov/sites/default/files/documents/USPTOFY18PAR.pdf
5. Quinn, Gene. *The Cost of Obtaining a Patent in the US.* April 4, 2015. http://www.ipwatchdog.com/2015/04/04/the-cost-of-obtaining-a-patent-in-the-us/id = 56485/.
6. http://www.smithhopen.com/patents_foreign.aspx.
7. Kate O'Keeffe & Aruna Viswanatha. Former Coke Scientist Acused of Stealing Trade Secrets for Chinese, February 14, 2019, Wall Street Journal.
8. *Vizcaino v. Microsoft Corp.*, 120 F.3d 1006 (9th Cir. 1997), cert. denied, 522 U.S. 1098 (1998).
9. JOBS Act, Title III, Crowdfunding. SEC. 301. http://www.gpo.gov/fdsys/pkg/BILLS-112hr3606enr/pdf/BILLS112hr3606enr.pdf.
10. Feld, Brad. *The 99 Investor Problem.* January 22, 2014. http://www.feld.com/archives/2014/01/99-investor-problem.html.

Case Wefunder: Leading the Growth of a New Industry[1]

In early 2018, Nick Tommarello could be proud of what he and his partners had accomplished. Their company, Wefunder, Inc., was the acknowledged leader in the equity crowdfunding industry, an industry that he and his partners were largely responsible for creating. Wefunder served as an online portal for crowdfunding investments and had raised more money for more companies than any of their competitors. Yet Nick's pride and satisfaction with these accomplishments were tempered by the knowledge that neither his company, nor the industry as a whole, had achieved the volume and size he had originally projected. Wefunder's careful vetting of the companies allowed to raise money on its site had created a reputation for quality, but the labor-intensiveness of this model was limiting the company's ability to scale up for growth. And the restrictive conditions imposed by federal law and the Securities and Exchange Commission's regulations on equity crowdfunding seemed to prohibit models of doing business deemed essential for the growth of the industry as a whole. If these challenges could not be met, Wefunder might well end up as one of many fish competing in an unfortunately small pond.

Short History of Crowdfunding

Since the humble foundings of Indiegogo in 2007 and Kickstarter in 2009, online crowdfunding had exploded to nearly a $10 billion dollar industry. Initially a way for hobbyists, artists, and inventors to realize creative projects, the industry spawned disruptive entrepreneurial ventures such as the *Oculus Rift* in 2012, a virtual reality headset ultimately sold to Facebook for $3 billion, and *The Pebble* in 2013, the first mass market smart watch.

The disruptive power of crowdfunding had arrived, but only for nonequity commitments from backers where a simple product or thank you was promised in return for financial support. The opportunity to actually invest in these companies was reserved by law generally to sophisticated, wealthy investors ("accredited investors"[2]) by a legal system founded on the principle of protecting the general public from excessive risk.

Against this backdrop, Nick Tommarello, co-founder of *Wefunder*, an equity crowdfunding platform for nonaccredited investors, set out to disrupt the world of entrepreneurial finance. He remarked, "I don't feel a sense of meaning when I buy a share of IBM—it's purely a financial transaction. But start-ups? If I could support entrepreneurs trying to change the world and still have a chance of earning a return...well, that's value beyond money. I could give back. And that's the key to making crowd investing work." According to Nick, "Wefunder is predicated upon the idea that anyone, regardless of wealth level, should be able to invest in a company." He and his co-founders Greg Belote and Mike Norman wanted to fill the frequent funding gap for start-ups between angels and that first major round of capital.

In doing so, the three entrepreneurs would be engaging in "regulatory entrepreneurship," a form of entrepreneurship gaining recognition in the field. As defined by Pollman and Barry, "some companies pursue a line of business that has a legal issue at its core—a significant uncertainty regarding how the law will apply to a main part of the business operation, a need for new regulations in order for products to be feasible or profitable, or a legal restriction that prevents the long-term operation of the business. For these entrepreneurs, political activity is generally a major component of their business models. Essentially, these companies are in the business of trying to change or shape the law."[3]

For Tommarello, Belote, and Norman, it meant working to shape the original **"JOBS ACT,"** officially known in the U.S. Congress as the 2012 *Jumpstart Our Startup Businesses Act.* The Wefunder founders actually helped craft the Crowdfunding section of the JOBS Act that President Obama later signed into law. As such, they were invited by the White House to witness the signing of the JOBS Act into law, thus setting the stage for a new age of entrepreneurial finance.

In signing the new legislation in the Rose Garden, Obama stated, "Start-ups and small businesses will now have access to a big, new pool of potential investors. For the first time, ordinary Americans will be able to go online and invest in entrepreneurs that they believe in" (April 5, 2012).

The JOBS ACT, with rules later released by the Securities and Exchange Commission (SEC), allowed anyone to invest up to 5% of their annual income or net worth, whichever is higher—up to $2,000 total per year—in start-ups, only through an online equity crowdfunding portal such as Wefunder. Those individuals with an annual income or net worth above $100,000 could invest up to 10% of annual income in a 12-month period not to exceed $100,000 in total. Securities purchased in this manner would be effectively nontransferable for a period of one year after purchase. Companies would be limited to raising no more than $1,000,000 per year in this manner. With the stroke of a pen, the new regulations created millions of new investors with the ability to make equity investments in entrepreneurial ventures but only through crowdfunding platforms.

[1] This case written by Erik Noyes and Richard Mandel.

[2] Accredited investors are a special legal class of investors either having a net worth above $1 million (excluding their personal home value) or with annual individual earnings above $200,000 or $300,000 for a couple. Accredited investors legally attest to their financial strength and have special rights to speculate with certain types of risky investment given their ability to sustain investment losses and presumed financial sophistication.

[3] Pollman and Barry, "Regulatory Entrepreneurship," 90 S. Cal. L. Rev. 383, 392 (2017).

To temper investor expectations, however, the SEC listed a number of potential hazards with equity crowdfunding (https://www.sec.gov/oiea/investor-alerts-bulletins/ib_crowdfunding-.html) including *the limited disclosure that start-ups need to share, the possibility of fraud*, and the *potential that a start-up will fail*. Equity crowdfunding for nonaccredited investors introduced new possibilities, as well as new potential risks, for investors passionate to support entrepreneurs.

The Global Crowdfunding Industry

Equity crowdfunding for nonaccredited investors was but one of four primary types of crowdfunding driving the growth of the global industry.

Rewards-based crowdfunding: In rewards-based crowdfunding (e.g., Kickstarter, Indiegogo) campaign "backers" receive no equity stake in a venture but rather a "thank you," generally a product, from the campaign creators ("creators" is Kickstarter's name for an individual or team that launches a campaign on the Kickstarter platform). By aggregating funds on these types of platforms, hobbyists, artists, and inventors alike could know they had both funding and an audience in place for costly projects—in essence preselling new products, music CDs, or even events—before beginning production. The costs to raise funds on such platforms are generally 9% of total funds raised with 5% going to the platform itself (e.g., Kickstarter) and 4% going to a payments processor such as Stripe or Amazon Payments.

Donation crowdfunding: In a donation crowdfunding campaign (such as GoFundMe), backers support a worthy cause or organization with a fundraising need. Donation campaigns have been run to cover the costs of such items as expensive medical procedures for the uninsured to emergency college costs. Costs to raise funds are generally less than with rewards-based crowdfunding and in some cases free.

Lending crowdfunding: Lending crowdfunding engages crowds to make loans to individuals, offering financial returns (i.e., interest) to backers, leveraging the borrower's social reputation and network. Examples of lending crowdfunding sites include LendingClub, Upstart, and Funding Circle. The idea is to personalize lending as differentiated from a loan made by bank or professional lender, and costs to the borrower vary. However, since all but short-term loans qualify as securities under the law, prior to the JOBS Act, the opportunities to make such loans were also essentially limited to accredited investors.

Equity crowdfunding: In equity crowdfunding, the focus of Wefunder's business model, backers acquire an equity stake in the venture raising funds. Portals charge a percentage of funds raised, on average 4–5%, plus a fee to the investors. The issuer or venture is responsible to disclose a valuation for the company, thus enabling the backer to value his or her investment in the venture. Equity crowdfunding had existed before 2012 JOBS Act but only for accredited investors. Prior to the launch of Wefunder, there were portals serving angel investor networks, or what Wefunder called "rich person crowdfunding," which Wefunder also offered until nonaccredited investor crowdfunding became legal. [4]

The Global Scope of Crowdfunding

Globally, an estimated 1,250 active crowdfunding platforms (CFPs) compete in the categories of *rewards-based crowdfunding* (Kickstarter, Indiegogo), *donation crowdfunding* (GoFundMe, Patrion), *lending crowdfunding* (Lending Club, Kiva), and *equity crowdfunding* (Wefunder, StartEngine, SeedInvest, Republic). According to the World Bank, the global crowdfunding industry is expected to raise $93 billion annually by 2025, or approximately 1.8 times the size of the global venture capital industry today, suggesting an opportunity to shake up existing models of entrepreneurial finance. Starting in 2011, Kickstarter raised more money for artists than the United States' *National Endowment for the Arts*, or over $323 million. To date, the global crowdfunding industry has transformed notions of how artists, inventors, and entrepreneurs can bring new technologies and innovations to life.

Backer Motivations

Crowdfunding relies on *backers*—short-hand for financial backers—who support a particular project, product, person, or passion. While those creating failing campaigns may assume funds simply fall from the sky—a common misconception—those leading successful campaigns activate, or roll up, a network of fans and followers, including *friends, family,* and *customers*.

With rewards-based crowdfunding campaigns, like those on Kickstarter, backers support the entrepreneurial vision or product development wishes shared by a project's *Creator*. More generally, backers support projects that reflect their unique interests and values. Three varied such campaigns are as follows:

Stompy: A successful $65,000 campaign to build a giant, truck-sized, 6-legged, rideable mechanized "insect" backed by amateur roboticists, science fiction enthusiasts, and engineers. https://www.kickstarter.com/projects/projecthexapod/stompy-the-giant-rideable-walking-robot-0/description.

The Pebble Watch: A successful $10 million dollar campaign to build the world's first mass market smart watch, beating companies such as Samsung and Apple to establish this new technology category. The campaign was backed by fans of

[4] Equity crowdfunding like that offered by WeFunder had in fact established an earlier footprint in Europe, with such platforms as CrowdCube, SeedMatch, and Seedrs. Seedrs.com alone had raised 100 million British pounds on its platform since February, 2016.

emerging wearable computing technologies and other technophiles. https://www.kickstarter.com/projects/getpebble/pebble-e-paper-watch-for-iphone-and-android/description.

FlowHive: A successful $13 million dollar campaign to create an innovative new beehive design/honey-harvesting process targeting amateur beekeepers who understand the pain and mess of traditional methods of honey-making. https://www.indiegogo.com/projects/flow-hive-honey-on-tap-directly-from-your-beehive-environment-5#/.

Each of the examples above illustrate that successful campaigns target specific target backers and subcultures (e.g., roboticists, wearable computing enthusiasts, amateur beekeepers). Backers back campaigns because:

- Often they have family and friendship relationships with the crowdfunding campaign leaders.
- They want to see the creation of a new innovation in their particular passion or interest area.
- They value the connection with the project creator and particularly the opportunity to participate—at least vicariously, but sometimes directly—in the journey to realize the innovation, including project updates.
- They want to receive the final product, deliverable or experience promised by the project creator at a discounted or promotional price.

As Yancey Strickler, co-founder of Kickstarter, once famously said, "Kickstarter is not a store!" The decision to back a project does not guarantee the delivery of a final product two days later as with an order on Amazon. Each project has real risks—which project creators are required to disclose on their project page—and over 75% of rewards have been shown to be delivered late to backers.[5] Backers can show extreme patience and support in the face of delays if the project creator is transparent about unforeseen challenges. Backers can also be merciless and turn on creators taking to comment boards, or even trolling campaigns for years after failure, if creators are seen as inept or deceptive.[6] Crowds giveth and crowds taketh away—which speaks to the deep personal nature of backing and trust between the backers and creators.

Backers most commonly are family and friends, thus the expression "no network, no funding." Just after Wefunder launched, Nick commented, "Investors who use the site are largely friends or followers of the business itself." However, certain campaigns break-out and capture the popular imagination, in some cases raising millions of dollars. At the time of the writing of this case, Kickstarter has seen over 300 $1+ million dollar campaigns (https://www.kickstarter.com/help/stats).

To date, it is unclear whether the rise of the equity crowdfunding sector threatens rewards-based crowdfunding by adding the possibility of "earning a return" on backers' monies. Alternatively, rewards-based crowdfunding motivators (e.g., exuberance for the projects and the desire for vicarious participation—and even physical rewards) may be equally important in equity crowdfunding, suggesting a likely hybridization of motives and methods.

Wefunder's Planning for Growth

Nick and his co-founders knew all too well the potential risks of bringing equity crowdfunding to the masses. Investors would have to be educated about very real risks and their expectations would need to be managed very carefully. Equity crowdfunding could not be promoted as a get-rich-quick scheme for investors, but instead as a new way *to make small investments in businesses you know and love*—ones launched by your friends or right in your own neighborhood.

As seen on the company's home page, Wefunder's managed this message carefully:

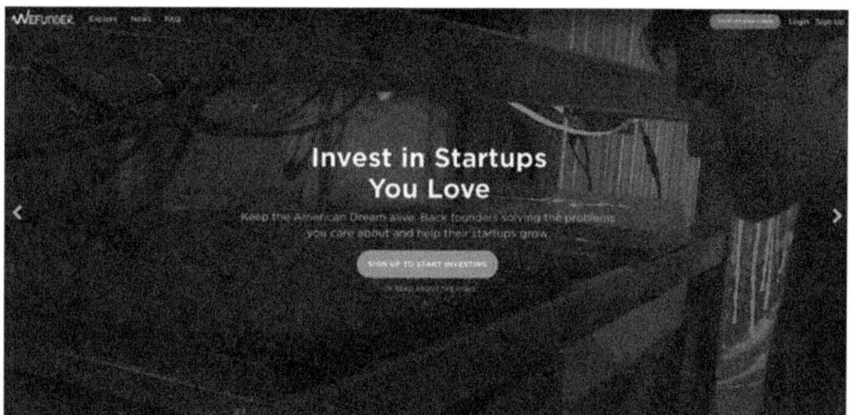

[5] E. Mollick (2014). The dynamics of crowdfunding: an exploratory study, Journal of Business Venturing, vol. 29, iss. 1.

[6] https://www.nytimes.com/2015/05/03/magazine/zpm-espresso-and-the-rage-of-the-jilted-crowdfunder.html?_r=0

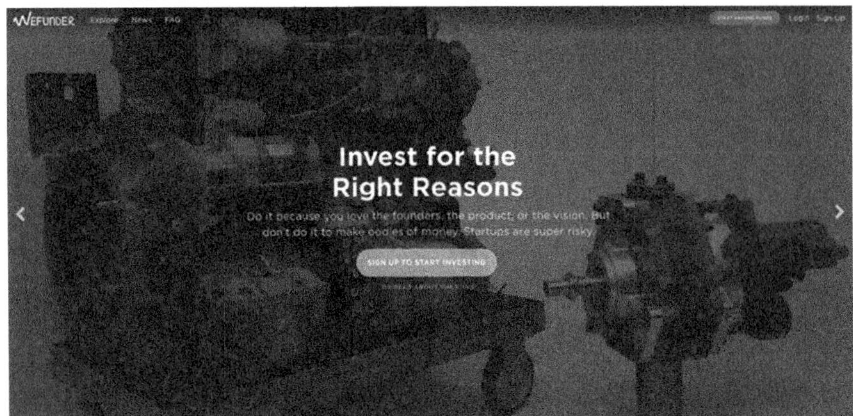

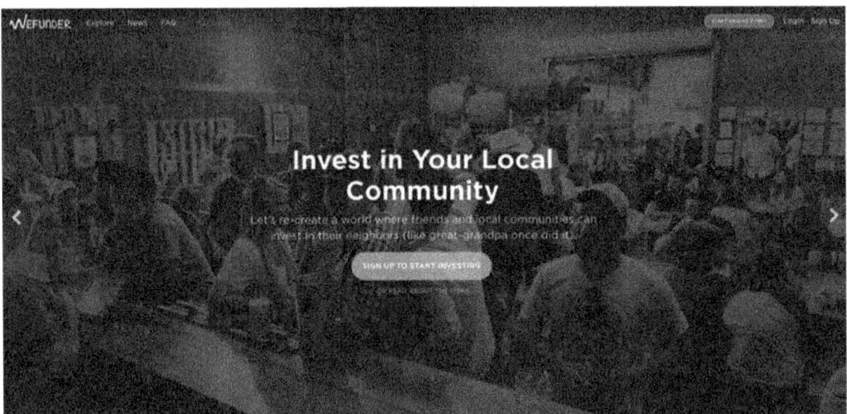

Participation with the potential for profits—but not wealth—was the value proposition. Your fellow engineering Ph.D. student developed a new technology—support her to commercialize it. Your favorite small-batch whiskey distillery wants to expand regionally—support the founder's dream and let others know how amazing the whiskey is.

However, there were broader ambitions too, as stated on the Wefunder website:

> *"Let's revitalize capitalism and keep the American dream alive. GDP is slowing. Wealth inequality is rising. Entrepreneurship is dying across America; falling from 10.6% to 3.6.% among those under 30 since 1989. We aim to reverse these trends by funding more deserving businesses. Our goal is to build a new type of stock market (a NASDAQ for riskier ventures) that lets markets allocate capital to a wide range of businesses more efficiently than banks or VCs."*

Wefunder Does a Whistlestop Tour Across America

With a priority to drive entrepreneurial community—not just financial returns—Nick and his team sought to build deal flow and identify high-quality initial campaigns for the platform. The conviction was that strong campaigns and demonstrably-capable entrepreneurs would distinguish Wefunder from other equity crowdfunding platforms with little personal interest and research into their first issuers.

Wefunder co-founder Greg Belote commented, "Our vision was always to help fund a cross-section of the economy in 'real America'—not just Silicon Valley—so our entire company hopped on a train and met hundreds of business owners across America, 12 cities in two weeks, coast to coast." The message was fairly straightforward: "Out-of-touch bankers on Wall Street don't take any risks for Main Street! Let's recreate a world where friends and local communities can invest in their neighbors."

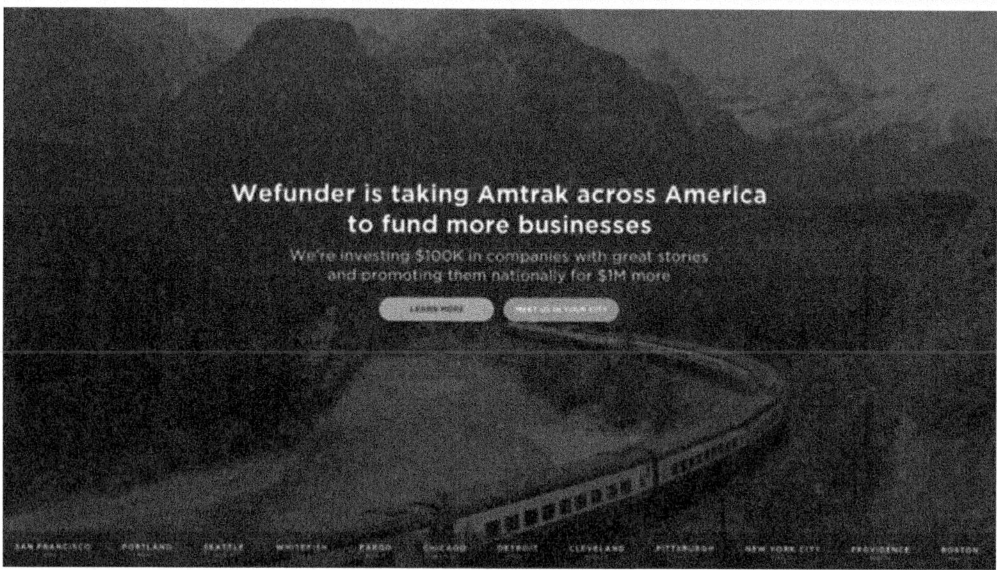

Wefunder website

Fellow Wefunder co-founder Mike Norman summed it up, "The majority of entrepreneurs are not web-tech focused businesses in the Bay Area, so it was important for us to get out there, meet folks on the ground, hear people's issues and challenges and what they're building in places like Fargo and Chicago and Pittsburgh and Providence.... We found some great companies to feature for our big launch."

When the launch date finally came, Wefunder launched with 20 companies, which ultimately raised nearly $3 million, including a donut shop, whiskey maker, a biotech company, and a Chicago entrepreneur looking to launch an African American culinary district. Nick told Crowdfund Insider, "People are going to be surprised by the quality of companies that decide to use Regulation Crowdfunding on May 16 [2016]," the first day that the new type of equity crowdfunding became legal.

Fast forward to the date of the writing of this case, and Wefunder has raised over $31 million for 90 different companies through equity crowdfunding, and was the most successful portal in the industry, "leading the pack both in the number of deals and total dollars raised"[7] (see Appendix A: Sample Wefunder Offerings). It is almost overwhelmed by the number of companies seeking to be listed on the portal and the challenges of scaling the high-touch vetting and listing process, which has led to its success. Yet, the number of companies using equity crowdfunding and the amount of money raised through equity crowdfunding portals are significantly less than initial projections.

Nick and his partners recognized that the new industry was becoming crowded with other platforms entering, so it sought to differentiate Wefunder by encouraging and enabling investors to build relationships with entrepreneurs, and as Nick stated, "help start-ups beyond the funding moment." Equity investors could provide vital product feedback and network contacts, comment on a venture's overall strategy, and even evangelize. As Nick's co-founder Mike Norman explained, "Wefunder really wants to build long term relationships between founders and investors."

Wefunder also sought to differentiate itself from other platforms by enabling investors to become part of *investment clubs* and follow lead investors. One of the founders' key values driving the creation of Wefunder (beyond giving everyone the opportunity to invest in start-ups) was that the idea that informed experts make better investment decisions than investors alone. "We believe in the wisdom of the crowd guided by industry experts," said Mike Norman. He continues, "If we allow crowd investors, experts, and fans to collaborate effectively we can allocate capital to deserving new businesses more efficiently than traditional investing." But, there were also legal obstacles to such an approach (captured in the discussion of Special Purpose Vehicles below), so some further regulatory entrepreneurship would be needed.

Challenges Remaining with the JOBS Act and Equity Crowdfunding Industry

Although the JOBS Act and the subsequent SEC regulations went a long way toward facilitating this new method of crowdfunding ventures, in the view of Nick and others in the industry, the law still contained key shortcomings, which would have the effect of drastically limiting the potential for growth. The most

[7] https://venturebeat.com/2017/05/16/equity-crowdfunding-is-1-year-old-today-wefunder-is-top-platform/ (accessed December 7, 2017).

serious of these shortcomings is derived from a failure to address the problems inherent in ventures with a large number of small equity holders. These problems fall into two main categories.

The first set of problems result from the provisions of Section 15 of the Securities Act of 1934 ("the 34 Act"). Although the Securities Act of 1933 enacted a comprehensive system of disclosures for companies issuing securities, it did not require any follow-up disclosures for the benefit of any secondary market, which might arise in such securities. Thus, without additional follow-on disclosures, investors buying and selling securities on a stock exchange would be essentially flying blind. The 34 Act remedied this by requiring publicly traded companies to register with the SEC and create and file a series of regular disclosure documents, including quarterly reports, two types of annual reports, and proxy statements, as well as reports and press releases for any of a series of significant events. It also established serious penalties for failure to disclose and misrepresentations.

This, of course, begs the question of the definition of a publicly traded company. Section 12(g) of the 34 Act includes any company that has done a registered public offering but also, in its present form, any company with 2,000 or more shareholders (or 500 or more unaccredited shareholders) and more than $10 million in assets. Obviously, a company successfully completing an equity crowdfunding offering quickly risks exceeding the 500 unaccredited investor limit, exposing itself to the highly complex and expensive reporting requirements of the 34 Act as well as its potential liabilities.

The SEC's crowdfunding rules attempted to address this problem by exempting issuers from registering under the 34 Act, even if they exceed the allowable number of shareholders, so long as they have less than $25 million in assets. Once a company exceeds the $25 million dollar limit, they will have a two-year grace period before having to register with the SEC. Thus, a successful crowdfunded company could be on track for 34 Act registration and its attendant liabilities and disclosure obligations. As such, Nick and most of the crowdfunding industry would prefer a clean exemption under which crowdfunded shares simply do not count against the Section 12(g) limits. Such an exemption is included in the omnibus Financial Choice Act (designed mostly to address alleged shortcomings in the Dodd-Frank Act) passed by the U.S. House of Representatives in June of 2017 and sent to a very uncertain fate in the Senate, as well as in standalone bills previously passed in the House and in a bill proposed to the Senate. But, this problem remains unresolved as of this writing.

Second, the existence of potentially hundreds or thousands of individual small stockholders presents a legal and recordkeeping nightmare for most issuers. Under various state corporate laws, stockholders may have rights to inspect records, attend stockholders' meetings, receive distributions, etc. Without incurring the expense of a professional transfer agent and establishing a stockholder services infrastructure, most crowdfunded companies would be unable to keep up with their obligations in this regard. Just keeping up with securities transfers and address changes could be overwhelming. And this, in turn, would likely scare off potential later round investors who much prefer "clean" cap tables.

Nick and much of the crowdfunding industry advocate the use of Special Purpose Funds (or Special Purpose Vehicles, "SPVs") to solve this problem. An SPV would be an entity formed for the purpose of investing in one crowdfunded company and would be managed by its officers or, in some cases, the relevant funding portal. Investors would invest in the SPV, not the crowdfunded company, so the crowdfunded company would have only one additional stockholder of record (the SPV). The manager of the SPV would handle the crowdfunding compliance and recordkeeping requirements of the SPV. Unfortunately, such an SPV would likely qualify as an investment company under the Investment Company Act of 1940, which regulates companies whose assets are largely securities of other companies. The cost and complexity of compliance with the Investment Company Act are substantial. And worse, the SEC regulations prohibit investment companies from using crowdfunding to raise money, thus making the SPV solution to this problem illegal.

Legislation exempting crowdfunded SPVs from the Investment Company Act is viewed as essential by the industry, but as of this writing, no such legislation has been passed. It is not included in the (likely doomed) Financial Choice Act but was included in standalone bills passed by the House and a bill proposed to the Senate.

In the meantime, many crowdfunding portals advocate the offering of alternatives to formal equity, such as debt. One increasingly popular form of crowdfunded security is the Simple Agreement for Future Equity (often misleadingly referred to as "SAFE"). This is an instrument that converts into actual equity at the time of, and on the same terms of, a future round of investment such as venture capital deal or upon a liquidity event such as a sale of the company or IPO. It addresses the administrative and state law issues created by having large numbers of small stockholders, but doesn't address the remainder of the challenges described above, such as the registration requirements of Section 12(g).

Finally, notwithstanding the careful management of investor expectations contained in most equity crowdfunding websites, it is fair to assume that some portion of crowdfunding backers (those motivated mainly by hope of return on investment) will become frustrated and angry upon discovering that they are effectively locked in to an uncertain, long-term investment in the absence of any meaningful secondary market for their shares. Such frustration might be directed against the issuing company and its founders, or even the portals themselves. This problem, it seems, can be addressed only by creation of a secondary market once the one-year holding period for crowdfunded securities has expired, but the question is will Wefunder or any of its competitors see this as one of the ways to increase the size of their business? In summary, a complex and uncertain legal landscape complicated the overall growth and development of the equity crowdfunding industry.

The Road Ahead

In a round-up of the first year of equity crowdfunding, one analyst wrote, "Wefunder got out of the gate strong, but can it stand up to the portals that have deep-pocket VCs behind them?"

Nick and his co-founders grappled with strategic questions such as how to lead and grow the industry overall, how to enlarge the current entrepreneurial opportunity by lobbying Congress and the SEC, how to scale their currently labor-intensive business model, and how to maintain a commanding lead in the industry, which was seeing new entrants. The prospect of welcoming millions of people to fund innovative, entrepreneurial ventures and help reboot the U.S. economy in the process was enticing but there were several high hurdles ahead.

Discussion Questions

1. What is regulatory entrepreneurship?
2. Given that equity crowdfunding industry growth is much lower than anticipated, what should Wefunder's immediate and longer term strategy be? Relatedly, in your view, what competitive actions will separate winners from losers in this new industry?
3. How, if at all, will the emergence of crowdfunding impact angels and venture capitalists?
4. In what cases should an entrepreneur consider—and not consider—equity crowdfunding? How should equity crowdfunding be evaluated and compared to other sources of capital?
5. How are backer motivations similar—and different—when comparing rewards-based crowdfunding versus equity crowdfunding?

Appendix A | *Sample Wefunder Offerings*

Industry: Craft Beer

HOPS AND GRAIN

Gold Medal winning craft brewery in Austin, Texas

Hops & Grain is a local Texas brewery. We brew and package all of our beers on-site and sell them throughout Austin and the surrounding areas. After 5 years of expansion in our current facility, we have finally reached max capacity and are now looking to double our capacity with a new brewery. The investment will be in a new LLC to develop the new tap room and brewery in San Marcos, TX.

OUR AMBITION

Since Day 1 our goal has been to craft high quality beers that tell a compelling story

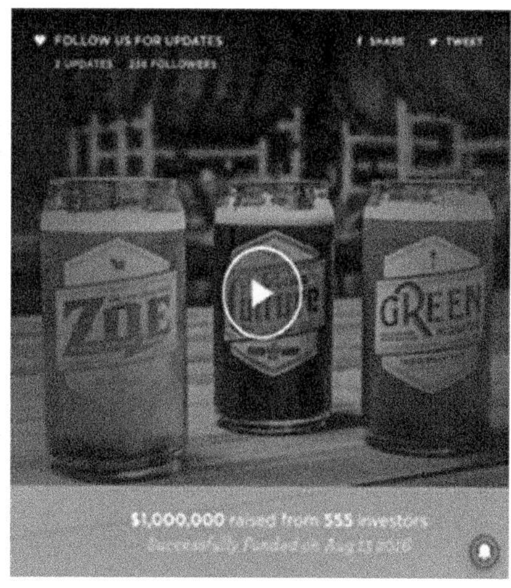

Amount Raised: $1,000,000
Date Closed: August 13, 2016
Number of Investors: 555

Terms: Annual payments of a percentage of gross revenue until twice the invested amount has been repaid.
Industry: Home Server (replacing "the cloud")

DAPLIE

Connect Without "The Cloud"

"The cloud" is just someone else's computer. When you use centralized cloud services like iCloud, Gmail, Google Drive, Dropbox, Box, Facebook, or hundreds of others, you gain the convenience of storing data on someone else's computer, but you make some huge tradeoffs in return. Daplie provides a platform for people to have the convenience of the cloud without giving up privacy and ownership of their data. At Daplie, we believe the Internet was made for people, not people for the Internet.

OUR AMBITION

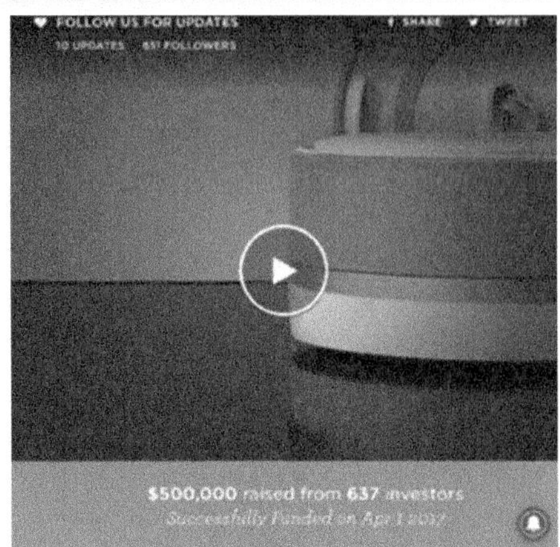

Amount Raised: $500,000
Date Closed: April 1, 2017

Number of Investors: 637
Terms: Class A Common Stock

Entrepreneurial Growth

13

Photo Credit: © Scott Eisen/Bloomberg / Getty Images

Yankee Candle Company

Whereas entrepreneurship begins with an opportunity, sustainable success comes from creating an organization that can execute on that opportunity. However, as organizations start to gain more sales and customers, managing growth becomes a critical challenge that, if not handled appropriately, can lead to venture failure.

This chapter was written by Donna J. Kelley and Edward P. Marram.

The objectives of any entrepreneur wishing to create a sustainable enterprise should include building an efficiently operating organization while developing an organization-wide entrepreneurial capability.

Why do entrepreneurs fail to manage growth? Often they have limited time and resources to spend on organization building. They're constantly fighting fires in the business's day-to-day operations or they're chasing too many opportunities, leaving little time for planning. Entrepreneurs without organizational or business skills may retreat into something they do know and are more comfortable doing, like product development. They may hire salespeople or engineers to handle sales and technical support before bringing in someone with organizational and business skills. But eventually growth overwhelms the operation. To survive and continue to grow, entrepreneurs need to pay attention to the requirements of a firm in its growth phase. They cannot neglect the planning and preparation required for long-term success.

Many believe that entrepreneurial and managerial skills are mutually exclusive and operate at different phases of the firm's life. Entrepreneurial skills *are* critical during the venture's launch, whereas managerial skills become increasingly important thereafter.

Yet the organization will need to retain its entrepreneurial spirit as it grows. It can't function over the long term by simply managing what it has previously created. Customer needs inevitably change. Competitors eventually offer superior products or services. Economic conditions, politics, technology, and a variety of other external shifts will create a constantly changing opportunity set that leads to new possibilities while rendering old opportunities obsolete.

It's no wonder that half the businesses started today will not be around in eight years. And far fewer firms will continue to grow and stay profitable—as few as one in seven.[1] What distinguishes those firms that not only survive but also thrive? Entrepreneurs and leaders who build an efficient operating organization, while maintaining the organization's entrepreneurial ability.

Making the Transition from Start-up to Growth

During start-up, the business opportunity is taking shape, but as yet there are no significant sales. The founders are acquiring resources and organizing initial operations—and they do everything. At the other end, in the mature stage and beyond, the business must deal with the problems of a well-established organization. Systems and structures can become entrenched, and the culture can impede efforts to grow further, leading to decline. In this chapter, we look at how entrepreneurs operate once they've started and, we assume, their companies have reached a point of initial success with their opportunity. The primary task beyond this start-up stage is to create a professional organization capable of managing its current growth, while setting the stage for continued entrepreneurship to ensure the organization can sustain growth as it matures and avoid decline.

The chapter is organized around four driving forces in the growth stages: leadership, the opportunity domain, resources and capabilities, and execution. Before we get to this discussion, let's review a key decision every entrepreneur must consider beyond start-up: whether to sell, maintain, or grow the venture.

Looking Forward: The Choice to Grow, or Not,... or Sell

Figure 13.1 presents post-start-up options for an entrepreneurial business. Each option presents at least two alternatives for the founder.

If a new venture is successful in generating sales, entrepreneurs can reap capital gains by finding a suitable buyer. If the entrepreneur decides to sell the business, she may stay with the acquiring company, or she may leave and either seek other employment or start another company.

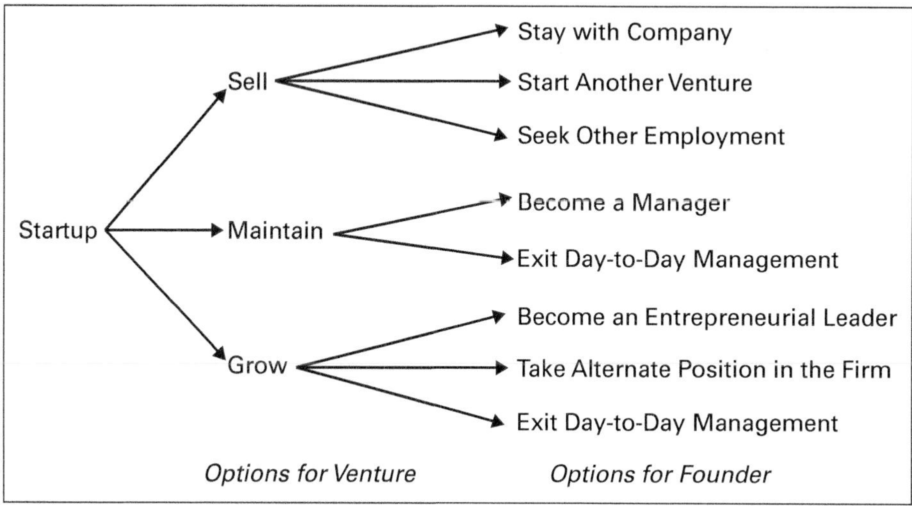

FIGURE 13.1 Post-start-up Options.

The first situation is perhaps the most common; the entrepreneur sells to reap a capital gain but stays on with the organization for several years to help in the transition. When Michael Lazerow, founder of Buddy Media, sold his company to Salesforce in 2012, Lazerow remained with the company and eventually became Salesforce's Chief Strategy Officer.[2] The buyer wants the entrepreneur to stay in order to reduce risk.

A typical acquisition might give the entrepreneur one-third of the price in cash, one-third in the acquiring company's stock (vested over the term of an employment contract), and one-third in an earn-out that is tied to the performance of the acquired company. If the acquired company meets certain milestones, the entrepreneur earns the full amount of the earn-out. If it falters, the entrepreneur's earn-out is at risk. Thus, the entrepreneur has an incentive to work hard after the acquisition takes place.

If a company is publicly traded, on the other hand, it is easier for the entrepreneur to sell and leave. Subrah Iyar, who co-founded WebEx in 1996, sold the company to Cisco Systems for $3.2 billion in 2007 and left. He focused, for a number of years thereafter, on spending time with family.[3] When selling a business, the founders often have contractual agreements to consider, like restrictions on their activities if they exit; for example, non-compete clauses may place limitations on their next venture. If you sell your business, the acquirer will prohibit you from starting a new, directly competing business.

When maintaining a business, the entrepreneur is faced with two basic choices. He can continue to lead the organization or exit day-to-day operations. Wealthfront, an online investment advisor with $10 billion in assets under management as of 2018,[4] co-founders Andy Rachleff and Daniel Carroll started the company in 2008. Whereas Rachleff was a seasoned venture capitalist and faculty member at Stanford, Carroll's motivation behind the idea was rooted in the financial crisis of the time. The two of them leveraged Carroll's passion for the idea and Rachleff's connections to young, wealthy individuals in Silicon Valley to jump-start Wealthfront by quickly adding clients and investors in the business. Carroll took on the role of CEO for a short time until Rachleff stepped in to accelerate the company's growth. Carroll's focus shifted to business development, and Rachleff soon came to understand that the complexities involved in leading an organization as CEO were far different than those of a venture capitalist. Through a connection at his previous company, Rachleff began to recruit Adam Nash as his replacement. Nash, who had never had CEO experience, was, however, a veteran in Silicon Valley, having worked at Apple, eBay, and LinkedIn. The move to CEO was a natural one for Nash, who had been serving as

Wealthfront's COO when Rachleff approached him for the top job.[5,6] Maybe, the decision wasn't wise. With increasing competition, Wealthfront was losing market position and brought Rachleff back in as CEO.[7]

Although our focus is on growing a business, it's true that many entrepreneurs choose to operate lifestyle businesses that pay enough salary for them to have a comfortable lifestyle, with less risk and complexity. These firms usually aren't large or successful enough to be sold, and the entrepreneurs don't have the desire to grow the business. One of the authors of this chapter, for example, was working with an ergonomics consulting company that hired her to grow the business. They explored a number of options, but growth would mean hiring more employees and moving out of the founder's basement. The founder decided he preferred the flexibility, lower risk, and greater control associated with staying small. After two engineers who had worked with him part-time finished college and moved on to other jobs, he maintained the business as a one-person operation, outsourcing any additional expertise, and keeping his commute to "a walk downstairs." What this example illustrates is that the decision to grow (or not) is multifaceted. It should take into account not only the ability to grow (the company could capture more customers if it were larger) but also the desires of the entrepreneur.

We'll now assume the company is currently growing, and the owner chooses to sustain a growing organization rather than selling or maintaining a lifestyle business. We'll focus on the founder as CEO, although most of the concepts also apply in the case where the founder is replaced. We next present our model of driving forces in the entrepreneurial firm's growth stages.

A Model of Driving Forces of Growth

Chapter 2 offers a model describing three driving forces that must be in balance during the start-up process: the entrepreneur, the opportunity, and resources. In the growth stage, these three driving forces shift to *leadership, the opportunity domain*, and *organizational resources and capabilities*, as Figure 13.2 illustrates. Whereas the business planning is at the core of Chapter 2's model, the growth model has *execution* as its core and fourth driving force. These forces must all come into balance and remain so during the growth phase.

Both the start-up and the growth models are affected by uncertainty and environmental conditions. Whether at start-up or in its growth phase, an organization is unable to predict many events,

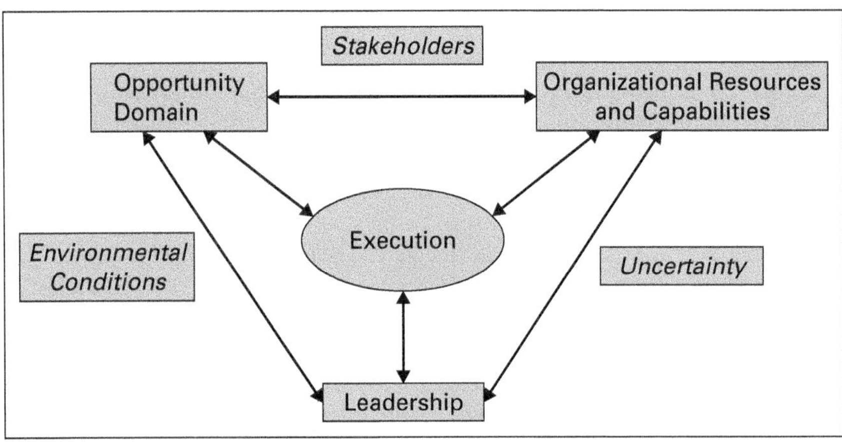

FIGURE 13.2 Driving Forces of Growth.

such as a competitor introducing a superior product soon after launch or customers adopting a product much more slowly than anticipated. Environmental conditions, such as economic cycles, the regulatory environment, and technological change, can also affect a venture's viability and success. In all phases of its life, the organization will need to balance the driving forces amid conditions it cannot control.

Stakeholders have the largest impact on a firm's growth potential. **Stakeholders** are those having a stake in the venture's success, like investors, customers, suppliers, and employees. As a new venture grows, it accumulates a range of insiders and outsiders who become increasingly dependent on the firm and exert heavy influence on its decisions. The organization will need to balance the current needs of these stakeholders with its need to think about how to sustain itself over the long term.

In 2014, the Volkswagen Group sold more than 10.2 million vehicles worldwide. By the end of 2015, however, the company was mired in a scandal, as 11 million vehicles manufactured for model years 2009–2015 were found to have cheated on emissions tests. The scandal serves as a clear-eyed example of stakeholder interests running at odds with a company's growth model. In its 2014 Annual Report, the company defined its strategy as, "positioning the Volkswagen Group as a global economic and environmental leader among automobile manufacturers."[8] Its supposedly low-emissions, fuel-efficient diesel engines were a key component to executing on that strategy. And, for a while, it paid off. The company achieved 75% market share of all diesel-powered passenger vehicles in the United States. VW sales plunged over 5% in the first month of the scandal. By 2017, sales rebounded with a 12% increase in sales from 2016 to 2017.[9] Why did VW cross the ethical line? Too many stakeholders were vested in maintaining the status quo. Volkswagen's marketing efforts for its vehicles equipped with the so-called TDI technology were based on the notion that the cars were more fuel efficient than indicated by EPA testing (the results of which were displayed alongside the car's sticker price). It is rare for a car company to outperform the EPA fuel efficiency tests, and as such, Volkswagen Group used this extensively in its marketing campaigns.[10] In the three years prior to the scandal breaking, the company spent nearly $1.2 billion in advertising on its Volkswagen brand in the United States.[11] A key point in that campaign was to appeal to car buyers who sought a low-emissions option (a car less harmful to the environment). The scandal proved costly to Volkswagen in terms of lost sales and in payouts to consumers who had purchased one of their diesel vehicles. But the diesel car market in the United States was still in its early stages and represented only about 1% of total automobile sales.[12] Less than a year after the scandal broke, Volkswagen's U.S. sales had fallen. Volkswagen's strategy with regard to diesel vehicles was bold and forward-looking but its execution fell flat and proved costly. VW agreed to compensate owners of its diesel cars, and the cost of fines and vehicle retrofits soared to $30 billion as of 2017.[13] Volkswagen failed to balance the needs of its various stakeholders—the EPA and VW customers.

The Growth Process

Figure 13.3 shows the challenges associated with the four driving forces outlined in Figure 13.2, and the key imperatives the firm needs to address to achieve overall balance among the forces.[14] The table differentiates between a venture's early and later growth stages. This distinction is important because the problems facing a company at an early stage of growth are different from those it faces later, and therefore the decisions and solutions will change. By knowing where the organization stands in the life cycle, an entrepreneur can tell which problems are normal and which require special attention. For example, whereas an entrepreneur needs to focus her firm's strategy during early growth, she will need to look toward expansion in later growth stages.

	Early Growth		Later Growth	
	Challenges	**Key Imperatives**	**Challenges**	**Key Imperatives**
Execution	Emphasis on sales over profits. Reactive orientation (fighting fires). Rapid growth overwhelms operations. Inadequate systems and planning leads to inefficiency, poor control, and quality problems. Informal communication and processes create confusion and lack of accountability.	Develop basic systems to manage cash, control receivables, inventory, and payables. Develop simple budgets and metrics to track performance and expenditures.	Profit orientation can constrain later growth. Organization outgrows initial systems and planning structure. Difficulties with coordination and control as decentralization increases.	Upgrade and formalize systems for control and planning for the longer term/future—before they are needed. Proactive planning replaces reactive approach. Maintain balance between control and creativity; ensure processes don't constrain innovation.
Opportunity Domain	Tendency to over-commit, pursue many diverse opportunities. Lack of clear strategy for how the venture competes.	Develop a focused strategy that leverages the company's unique value. Maintain the consistency of this strategy with all company activities (such as product development, marketing, operations).	Original opportunity domain may provide fewer opportunities for growth. Competitive pressures and changes in the market may threaten current businesses.	Establish competitive uniqueness and move beyond "one-product" orientation. Expansion into the periphery with products and markets. Also, develop strategy for future that provides new momentum and long-run effectiveness. Anticipate/respond to changes in industry/ market environment.
Organizational Resources and Capabilities	Financial and human resources constrained as rapidly expanding sales require more people and financing. Generalized skills increasingly incapable of handling increased complexity.	Get profitability and cash flow in check. Tap early financing sources. Hire people with specialized expertise. Protect intellectual property.	Insufficient resources for growth.	Maintain bootstrap mentality. Manage cash for internal growth resources. Secure growth financing.
Leadership	Company outgrows entrepreneur's abilities. Entrepreneur unable to delegate. Internally promoted managers often lack adequate skills.	Start the process of delegating responsibility to others. Promote/ hire functional managers/ supervisory-level managers. Invest in management training.	Management lacks the managerial sophistication required for the increasing size and complexity of a growing organization. Inadequate communication throughout organization. Tensions between professional management and entrepreneur, between new and old managers and employees.	Recruit key professional management talent. Build fully functioning Board of Directors. Ensure leadership team shares in strategic planning and preserves entrepreneurial capability. Create decentralized reporting structure.

FIGURE 13.3 Challenges and Key Imperatives for Managing Growth.

Execution

The growth model has execution at its core. Execution depends on the other components in the model—leadership, the opportunity domain, and organizational resources and capabilities—but it has the most direct link to profits. The start-up is commonly loosely managed, with few controls, very little performance assessment, and a lack of responsibility for outcomes. It often puts an emphasis on sales over profits, with chasing a new customer taking priority over considering the costs of serving that customer, for example. Growth will soon overwhelm operations, however, leaving the company capable only of reacting to inventory outages, overdue collections, diminishing cash flows, and delivery restrictions by suppliers. In addition, uncontrolled growth can lead to poor coordination between activities such as sales and inventory planning.

Without an adequate system of controls, the company can't optimize its decision making and prevent the waste of resources. One example of a start-up that failed quickly because it did not understand cost monitoring, and therefore the inherent weaknesses of its own cost structure, was Doorman[15]; a package delivery service that made e-commerce logistics easy by letting its users choose delivery time. Doorman was started by serial founder and software engineer Kapil Israni and Pixar's former Technical Director, Zander Adell in 2013. Doorman sought to revolutionize the "last mile delivery" between package transit hubs and personal residences for a one-time fee of $3.99 per package or a monthly subscription service at $19 per month. It worked by assigning subscribers the address of a nearby Doorman warehouse, where their package would stay until they notified Doorman they were home and ready for delivery.

> *Doorman had a promising start, delivering 25,000 packages in San Francisco in its first two years and winning an investment of $250,000 for 10% equity from Robert Herjavec in 2015. Doorman used the initial investment to expand to the New York and Chicago markets, and within months had raised an additional $1.5 million.[16] However, 75% of users who signed up for the app never used it to order a package.[17] For those who did become loyal users, their love for Doorman posed a clear problem for the monthly subscription pricing model: they were using the app too much. The company estimated that Doorman customers shopped online twice as much as they had previously within 6 months of signing up[18], making the subscription prices of $19 and $29 per month a net loss. By the time that Doorman realized the shift in consumer behavior, customers were used to paying a low price for the convenient service. Doorman tried to address this discrepancy between its product cost and its price by raising the premium subscription rate to $89 per month and adding a per package fee but the price hike caused its number of active customers to dwindle and in September 2017, Doorman closed its warehouse doors forever.[19]*

With only so many hours in a day and so many days in a week, it is hard to step back, develop and implement new processes, hire and train people, and ensure everything functions adequately. Yet these control tasks are essential to creating an organization that can continue to thrive and grow. Therefore, your most critical first task in transitioning beyond start-up is to create an efficient operation. This will eventually overlap with your efforts to sustain an entrepreneurial organization, but the firm will first need to catch up to its burgeoning growth—then it can set the stage for creating new sources of growth in the future. The key objectives for a control system should be to institute controls, track performance, and manage cash.

Instituting Controls

Your first **control system** in early growth should be relatively simple. The organization should quickly and easily be able to get it up and running and train people to use it. With a simple system, there's less that can go wrong, and as employees and managers get accustomed to control practices, you can upgrade the system later to handle a larger and more complex organization. You can also implement the system stepwise—for example, by starting with components having the greatest gap between actual and desired performance or with those that are easiest to put in place and therefore will have immediate impact.

An effective control system includes the following (all of which were covered in detail in Chapter 11):

- Accounts receivable and collections policies
- An inventory management system

- Account payable policies
- Assessment of performance and expenditures
- Metrics to track trends in cash, receivables, inventory, payables, expenditures, and performance

Managing costs requires both making decisions about expenditures and instituting controls that monitor spending. A growing firm's selling and administrative costs often expand rapidly with its escalation in sales. This expenditure is often appropriate because you need marketing to generate sales and administrative overhead to support the burgeoning organization. Yet you do need to monitor these areas to determine effectiveness and detect overspending. For example, certain advertising approaches may be more effective than others, or they may work in one region but not another.

As the company begins to sell more and more products in multiple markets, you will want to analyze its performance in different product or market segments, along with how effectively it is spending its resources. You need to understand what each product costs and whether you are truly making a profit. All the costs going into each product are those costs, both variable and fixed, that would disappear if the product were discontinued. What remains after these costs are deducted from the selling price contributes toward company overhead and profit.

You can also develop performance metrics to aid in decisions about investments and expenditures. Performance measures in an early-stage company are designed less for evaluating actual outcomes against a plan (as they would be in a more stable, established organization) than for helping in entrepreneurial decision making. As the company's operations expand, managers can develop metrics to help them answer the following questions:

- Which products or markets generate the highest revenues and margins?
- Which customers or customer groups are reliable accounts (make timely payments, are at low risk of default)?
- How effective are our expenditures in areas such as marketing and sales, and does this differ across markets?

Tracking Performance

Tracking performance is integral to one of the core functions of an entrepreneur, decision making. A performance tracking system is what separates decision making under uncertain conditions from merely guessing. Decisions must be sound as well as timely. A performance tracking system is about much more than simply key performance metrics, or KPIs. It is about investing the right dose of organizational effort into a simple, flexible, but deliberate plan to create and sustain a common operating picture that allows everyone in the company to see the critical variables of your business, your market, and your competition. Although tracking systems will vary as greatly as companies do, there are basic criteria that the best systems all possess.

- They identify decisions that require a true "this or that" choice, including those under most likely, best-case, and worse-case scenarios.
- For each decision, they determine the latest point in time at which the decision remains relevant to an outcome (the latest time any performance information would be of value).
- For each decision, they determine what specific questions must be answered to support a decision. They include what must be answered about the market, your own firm, and your competition.
- For each question, they determine the specific metrics (both qualitative and quantitative) needed to formulate an answer.

- They determine where, when, and how to measure each metric, and the name(s) of those responsible for measuring it.
- They remain simple so that tracking performance does not itself degrade performance.
- They assign someone responsibility for running the tracking system (using the entrepreneur as the *last choice*).

Successful entrepreneurs are careful not to invest excessive effort in tracking the activities of their competition too early on. They focus on finding, and delivering value to, their customers and keeping their own business in order. Reliable information about your competition's future actions often takes more time and resources to collect than many start-ups can spend. Focus on tracking how you are creating value for, and relationships with, your customers and how you are running your business; track just what is needed to effectively deal with your competition when they get in your way. A simple, but deliberate performance tracking system supports a focus on timely action and excellent execution because when you can efficiently determine where you stand, you will have more time and energy left to apply toward getting to where you want to be.

How do you determine what's good or bad when examining key metrics? For some financial ratios, published sources can provide industry averages for comparison. Entrepreneurial firms, however, often adopt policies that differ from those of more stable, established firms, such as spending on marketing while building brand awareness. Thus, it may be more useful to look at trends in metrics over time; for example, an increase in your collection period for receivables could indicate a relaxing in collection efforts, or a decrease in inventory turns could indicate you are at increasing risk of stock-outs. If you see significant changes and they are not the result of policy shifts in your firm, look for causes and consider making adjustments in policy.

One key point is to make performance measures as simple and inexpensive to track as possible, while providing information that helps you make better decisions. One very successful consulting firm had simple but useful measures. The entrepreneur tracked performance through his "B-Report." The B-Report was a simple Excel spreadsheet, with each consultant occupying a row, and columns representing every week of the year. If consultants expected to bill in a given week, they put a "B" in the column. If they did not, they left it blank. If the entrepreneur did not see a lot of Bs, he knew he had a problem.

Performance measures for a growing organization should be as simple and inexpensive to track as possible, while providing information leading to better decision making.

The company can also develop simple budgeting practices to estimate cash and inventory needs, schedule production, determine staffing requirements, and set sales and profitability goals. It should upgrade and formalize these controls, metrics, and budgets as it moves toward later growth. But more important, these tools should evolve to provide the best information possible in aiding the company's decision making. The value they provide should more than justify the time and effort spent to develop and maintain them.

There may be times when it's appropriate to slow the pursuit of new growth to give the company room to improve its ability to manage growth. Some indicators that your company is growing at an uncontrollable rate are the following:

- *Your workforce is stretched too thin*, and you and/or the founding team are allocating too much time hiring/training new employees at the expense of providing the necessary leadership to existing employees.
- *The percentage of your cash flows from operations is declining against your cash flows from financing*, particularly debt. At this point, your cash conversion cycle, a measure of sustainability, is too long and/or getting longer. You may need to borrow money to sustain operating activities. Growth under these conditions can exacerbate this problem and leave your business unable to respond to unforeseen costs.

- *Profit margins are shrinking as sales are climbing.* Tight margins equate to a need to run an efficient operation, or have large amounts of cash on hand that are rarely found in a rapidly growing start-up. Under these conditions the line between making a profit or incurring losses is very thin, and the overall risk posed by further growth may outweigh the benefits.
- *You are doing other peoples' jobs.* As the tempo of business increases, you are finding it harder to delegate effectively and doing more things yourself instead, which can lead to a breakdown in the organization's structure.
- *Customer complaints, in proportion to increases in sales, are increasing.* This means your company is not learning from your customers. Start-ups must "learn in order to earn." All companies receive complaints; the best companies embrace this feedback to refine their business to avoid scaling an inefficient business, or a business that does not yet understand its customer.
- *Your accountant is nervous.* Although accountants in a start-up should never be at ease, as the leader you must demonstrate the judgment required to recognize when the accountant's "worry-meter" is pegged, slow down, and listen to their counsel.[20]

Joel Kolen, former president of Empress International Ltd., a seafood distributor, emphasizes that

> *By taking a break from growth and putting in controls such as those at a large company, an entrepreneur can ease the growth transition and ensure that the qualities that helped build the company don't get lost in the rush to fill new orders.*[21]

Managing the Cash Cycle

It takes money to make money. Most entrepreneurs know this, and although most pay attention to "how much?" successful entrepreneurs focus on "how fast?" The **cash cycle** shows the amount of time that passes between cash outlays and cash inflows during the company's sales process. It also shows the relationship between three key measures: days in payables, days in inventory, and days sales are outstanding. Let's use Albercan Drilling Supply to illustrate the cash cycle—and how better controls can conserve resources. Albercan's sole business was the sale of drill pipes and collars to drilling contractors in the local area. In 2019, as the company was growing, it seemed to have a constant need for cash. At the same time, its bankers were hesitant to extend more credit. A review of the key measures in Figure 13.4 shows that all have increased substantially in two years, more than doubling the cash conversion period.

As Figure 13.5 illustrates, the cash conversion period extends from the time of cash outlay (to suppliers) to cash inflow (from customers). Looking at this diagram, you can imagine how an increase in sales would actually decrease cash inflows in the short term. The company would need to borrow money to cover the costs associated with this increase in sales until cash comes in 98 days later. In the meantime, as it makes additional sales, the company would need to cover these costs. When cash finally comes in, the company would likely need that cash for more inventory!

Albercan Drilling Supply	2019	2020	2021	Increase 2019–2021
Days sales outstanding	39	45	53	37%
Days in inventory	44	86	98	122%
Days in payables	36	38	53	48%
Cash conversion period	47	92	98	108%

FIGURE 13.4 Albercan Cash Conversion Analysis.

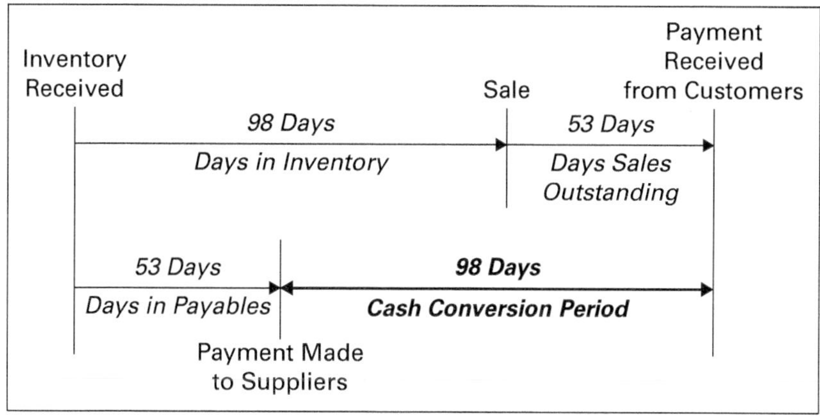

FIGURE 13.5 Cash Conversion Period for Albercan: 2019.

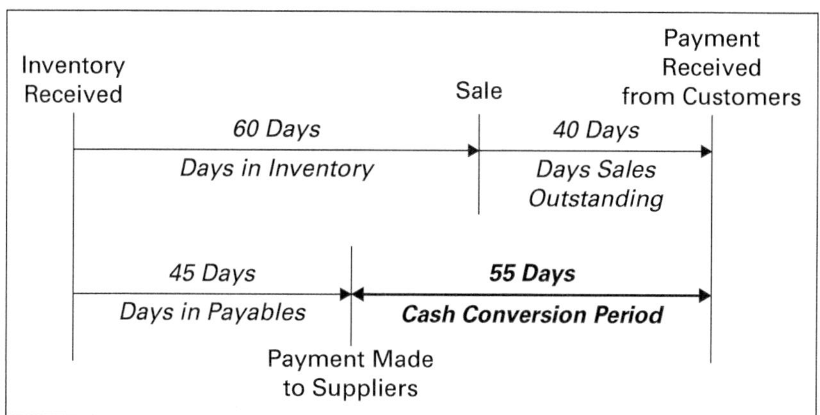

FIGURE 13.6 Adjusted Cash Conversion Period for Albercan: 2019.

Another problem revealed in this analysis is the length of time Albercan takes to pay suppliers. If typical payment terms are 30 days (whereas Albercan is paying in 58 days), the company may be testing its relationship with suppliers. This could lead them to refuse to ship additional product until Albercan pays past invoices, or in the worst case, they might refuse to do business with the company.

The easy solution would be to borrow from a bank or other debt source, preferably using a revolving line of credit that allows the company to draw funds as needed and pay them back when it receives cash. These are short-term loans designed to cover shortfalls such as this. Borrowing can get expensive, though, so why not think about reducing the average cash conversion period? This is much more difficult, but it instills a sense of resource parsimony that boosts a company's efficiency. What if Albercan can reduce its days in inventory to 60 and its days' sales outstanding to 40? We'll also assume Albercan needs to reduce days in payables to 45. This all leaves a cash conversion period of 55 days, as Figure 13.6 shows. Not only will that reduce the period of time the company would need to borrow, but also it would reduce the average amount needed because cash comes in more quickly and is therefore available for more inventory.

The cash management practices employed by Amazon provide insight into the impact that careful attention to your cash conversion cycle can have on your company. The company is known for having negative cash conversion cycles. In 2018, Amazon's cash conversion cycle was –34 days, down from –41 in 2017. This change is largely because its accounts payables period was 100 days, meaning that vendors are typically paid more than 3 months after their goods or services are rendered. In 2015, when Amazon ramped up its cloud storage services, Amazon Web Services, it used its cash management strategy to fund the necessary capital expenditures. This was largely accomplished by maintaining its collection period and increasing its accounts payable period to 314 while accelerating revenue growth.[22] From October 1, 2014 to October 1, 2015, the company's cash management efforts contributed to an overall 96% increase in share price, as compared with increases in the Dow Jones, Nasdaq, and S&P 500 indices of 1.5%, 2.8%, and 8.7%, respectively.[23]

Leveraging the Value Chain

Amateurs talk tactics, professionals talk logistics.

— Military maxim

We commonly represent a value chain as a series of steps showing the activities and entities that we need to coordinate for the company to execute its product or service. A start-up may outsource more than it wants to at first because it does not have the resources or capabilities to do everything in-house. Often it designs a product with as many off-the-shelf parts as possible to minimize design and tooling charges. On the other hand, the firm may need to take on some value chain activities because there is no reliable or ready source for them; this is particularly true for new products or services for which there is little infrastructure. Alternatively, value chain players may not cooperate, leaving the company to, for example, sell its product direct rather than creating channel conflict for distributors who deal with more stable, older companies.

As the company grows, you should decide which value chain positions are capable of creating the most value and for which you can establish unique advantage.

For example, SeatGeek.com, a mobile service for searching for the best price for tickets to performances and sporting games, started as a service that predicted the best time to buy tickets. Russel D'Souza and Jack Groetzinger co-founded SeatGeek.com because their favorite Boston teams—the Red Sox, Celtics, and Patriots—were winning game after game but getting their hands on tickets to see them was nearly impossible.[24] The founders needed information on thousands of venues, from a photo of the location to what prices were charged and at what time. So Groetzinger turned to UpWork (formerly known as ODesk), an online platform that connects businesses with freelance professionals. On ODesk, Groetzinger found freelancers from all over the world—ranging from the Philippines to Arkansas—who gathered ticket pricing data and found photographs of event spaces. Groetzinger relied upon reviews from other companies to select the most reliable freelancers.[25] Outsourcing these key functions allowed SeatGeek to scale, along with its first million in venture capital funding. As of 2018, SeatGeek has projected revenues of $125 million and has raised $160 million in venture capital. Their model has also evolved; SeatGeek.com began building out its B2B/enterprise business by partnering with the Israeli company TopTix, and before bringing the operation in-house by acquiring the company in 2017 for $60 million.[26]

Photo Credit: © David Yellen/The Forbes Collection/Contour/Getty Images

Jack Groetzinger and Russel D'Souza Founders of SeatGeek.com

Outsourcing can enable a growing company to focus on those activities it can perform particularly well and those underlying its source of competitive advantage. It makes sense to outsource those activities other companies can do more reliably and less expensively. But recognize that, although moving activities outside reduces the steps the firm performs in-house, it will also reduce the control you have over those activities—and often consume substantial time just for managing the relationship. The firm will therefore need to weigh some considerations, such as how it will maintain quality and how responsive the value chain partner needs to be in reducing or increasing production in response to fluctuations in sales.

Maintaining the Entrepreneurial Organization

With all this talk about efficiency and controls, it's hard to imagine how anything entrepreneurial can happen. That is sadly the case with many companies. A history of success creates preferences for recreating the past rather than building toward the future. Efficiency in current operations often does not accommodate new initiatives, like those requiring different sales channels or different value chain partners. Customers want the company to improve the products they know best rather than forcing them to change their behavior and endure the switching costs of adapting to a new product.

How, then, can a well-run organization maintain the ability to create new businesses? It's primarily a combination of the remaining driving forces of the growth model: how leadership views and manages its opportunity domain and the organization's people and resources.

Opportunity Domain

Whereas a start-up is focused on shaping an opportunity and bringing it to life, as the organization grows, its leadership needs to define a strategic arena that guides decisions on how it competes in its industry and creates value for its targeted markets. An organization defines this arena through a balance of the unique capabilities it builds and its ability to differentiate itself in its competitive environment. This balance then guides decisions about how the company markets and sells its products and about which opportunities it pursues in expanding its business.

The impact of Under Armour's strategic focus can be seen in many aspects of its business. Under Armour positioned itself as the company that produced higher-quality athletic apparel product, while promoting a healthy (if a little intense) image. Founder Kevin Plank began selling his products from the basement of his grandmother's home. Having played football in college, he began to supply athletes at his alma mater with his apparel. From there, the bona fide quality and comfort of his products caught the attention of the National Football League (NFL) and collegiate football programs. Under Armour landed its first major sale when Georgia Tech placed an order in 1996.[27] The firm's marketing was driven by word-of-mouth awareness as more and more college and professional athletes began to appreciate the comfort and performance of the product. The company did not have to resort to the endorsement mega-deals to compete in its early days, Instead, Under Armour gained a reputation as the gear "all about the team."[28] The company's strategy early on was focused on football, the sport its founder knew best. By 2015 their strategy had evolved to the point where the company offered products across many sports and for all seasons. As the brand's reach grew, Under Armour found itself in the place where it even began courting athlete endorsements, an expensive but effective strategy employed by rival Nike for decades.[29] After sales wavered in the United States due to increased competition from Nike, Adidas, and Lululemon, Under Armour began to focus its strategy on sneakers (such as the Curry 6 sneaker released with NBA All-Star Stephen Curry) and women's wear. As of 2018,

Under Armour's revenues had climbed to $1.39 billion, largely driven by a 28% increase in revenue outside of the United States.[30]

A focused strategy in early growth helps to guide the firm through the maze of opportunities that materialize once it experiences initial success. All too often, a start-up chases diverse opportunities without defining what it can do distinctly well. During early growth, define your firm's core focus, and develop capabilities around this, spending your limited resources and time close to this core, just as Under Armour focused on building awareness of its unique product performance.

In later growth, your company has established its competitive uniqueness and can now leverage this, while training a strategic eye on the future. It may continue to extend its advantage in its current position by, for example, upgrading its products. Over time, however, opportunities will eventually diminish in a particular product space, and you will need to combine incremental extensions with expansion into the periphery. A company may create a next-generation product that includes improvements and new features for existing customers, while exploring new products and new markets. A restaurant chain can start offering Sunday brunch to its customers, for example, or it can launch a catering business.

Pay attention, however, to new developments in the industry and market environment. These may determine where you should best focus your strategic efforts at specific points in time. For instance, you may emphasize a current product to gain maximum returns before competition comes in. Or you may seek new ground if the market is becoming crowded by large competitors or if a technology foundation is becoming obsolete.

Yankee Candle Company illustrates how a company can expand over time within an existing product/market space and into the periphery. The company traces its origins to young Michael Kittredge's home operation, which soon expanded to an old paper mill. The company grew its sales of candles through gift shops and expanded into the international market through distributors. It started selling online and through catalogs. The company also opened its own retail stores, including a flagship store in South Deerfield, Massachusetts, which serves as a tourist destination, with a candle museum, a restaurant, and sales of toys, gifts, home accessories, and other products, along with candles of all shapes and sizes.

A Cautionary Note on Expanding Through Acquisitions: Living Social

Living Social was a rising star in the e-commerce space in 2011. Rumors of an IPO swirled, and valuation estimates for the company ran above $10 billion. But in the fall of 2012, Living Social's outlook had turned sour. Revenues nearly doubled from the prior year, but the company incurred a net loss for the quarter of $566 million. Nearly $500 million of that loss was a reflection of acquisitions that had been written down by the company.[31] From 2009 to 2011, Living Social bought at least eight other companies, largely aimed at either subscriber growth or revenue growth, regardless of whether or not they were an ideal strategic fit. Those acquisitions included Urban Escapes and BuyYourFriendADrink.com. Founder, and then CEO, Tim O'Shaughnessy attributed the loss as follows, "In layman's terms, we took a charge of around $496 million because we had to revalue some of the companies we acquired last year (2011)." Among those companies were other "daily deal" sites—part of a roll-up strategy; and overseas companies as Living Social sought to go international. As rival Groupon pursued its own international growth strategy, Living Social (LS) followed suit. LS acquired DealKeren (Indonesia), Ensogo (Thailand, Philippines), and GoNabit (UAE, Lebanon, Jordan, Kuwait). One of those acquisitions was Korean e-commerce site Ticket Monster, which cost Living Social $350 million.[32] LS sold Ticket Monster and its nearly $800 million in revenue to rival Groupon in 2014 for $260 million. Even with an impressive top line, Living Social was not yet profitable itself and could no longer finance the near-term losses.[33] What was a company that employed nearly 4,500 people in 2011 has shrunk to 800 in late 2015,[34] and its valuation was estimated to have dropped from $10 billion in 2011 to only 1.5 billion in 2013.

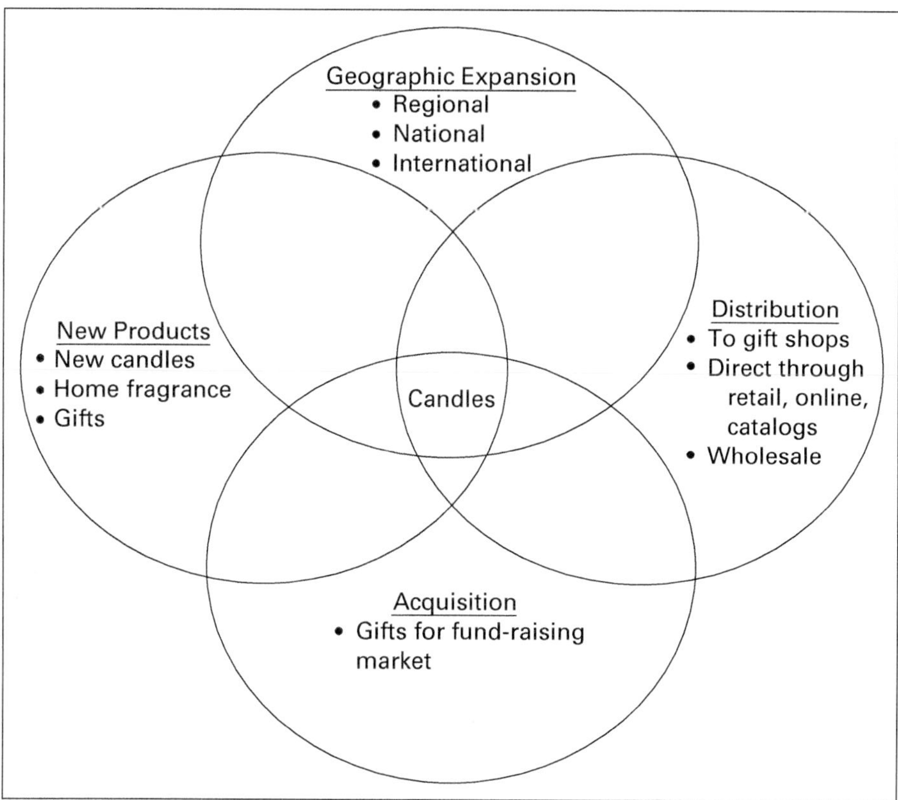

FIGURE 13.7 Yankee Candle's Opportunity Domain.

While this expansion continued, the company entered the home fragrance market with products such as electric home fragrancers, room sprays, potpourri, and bath care products. The primary target audience was still women ranging in age from 20 to 60. However, the company started to test new markets through its acquisition of GBI Marketing, a distributor of selected gift products (including Yankee Candle products) to fundraising organizations.

As Figure 13.7 shows, Yankee Candle has taken a multipronged approach to expanding its business: geographic expansion, new products, new distribution methods, and acquisition. There is a common logic surrounding all these methods, extending from core elements relating to its original product: candles. You've probably encountered small, single-operation candle shops. The Yankee Candle example[35] shows how a seemingly slow-growth business can become a high-potential venture with sales revenue surpassing $804 million prior to being acquired by Jarden Corp, in 2013.[36]

As a company grows, it may experience stagnating growth in its core business but see little opportunity for expansion into the periphery. It may need to make drastic shifts in its business. As Living Social's experience illustrates (see the box on Expanding Through Acquisitions), however, the company should make these forays outside the periphery carefully.

Acquisitions can provide inroads into new businesses for a company, but this undertaking requires an underlying logic. While Living Social attempted to move from daily deals to social media, Yankee Candle was already in the gift market when it made its acquisition. The central precept is the connection between organizational resources and capabilities and the opportunity domain, as illustrated in Figure 13.2. The growing organization should not consider external opportunities that simply appear attractive unless it has some particular ability to pursue them better than do competitors.

Obviously, a company cannot be driven only by opportunities that leverage current capabilities. Expansion opportunities will stretch these capabilities, and the company may choose to build new ones over time. Think about how this likely happened for Yankee Candle. The company can experiment or partner to reduce risk. It can adopt an options strategy, spreading exploratory resources across multiple business options with the logic that a few, as yet unknown, will warrant more substantial commitments. The company can also stage its investments, as venture capitalists do, investing a minimal amount in a new business opportunity and tying further investment to the achievement of milestones or the reduction of uncertainty. These practices minimize impact on the organization until more is known.

The one certainty entrepreneurs can count on, however, is change. You will need to anticipate, respond to, and even sometimes drive change. Professor Richard Osborne examined 26 privately held firms, all of which experienced initial success. Six of these firms were able to sustain growth beyond the entrepreneurial phase, while the rest saw their growth stalled. Factors such as inadequate resources, poor managerial capabilities of the entrepreneur, and bureaucracy were minor factors in the growth stall, according to this research. The main factor was the inability to perceive and respond to changing opportunities and conditions in their environment.[37]

The growing company therefore needs to be responsive to impending environmental shifts, maintaining its ability to transform its strategy and establish a new source of uniqueness in a changed environment. For example, college friends Peter Yang, Michael Wu, Kevin Hsu, and Kasper Hsu opened Pokéworks, a fast casual restaurant that served Hawaiian poke in 2015. Peter Yang and Michael Wu, who are brothers, knew a bit about the restaurant industry from growing up in their parents' Chinese food restaurant.[38] They got the idea to start Pokéworks after taking several trips to Hawaii and making their own poke at home. Then, in 2016 they created the poke burrito, which went viral after a Business Insider video about it was released, receiving nearly 50 million views. The Hawaiian-inspired Pokéworks dishes are colorful, fresh, and authentic, making it the perfect food for the health-conscious millennial eaters who want to Instagram their dinner plate.

"At Pokéworks, freshness and flavor reign above all else," said co-founder Peter Yang. He also notes that Pokéworks is a socially conscious brand, focused on sustainability. "Our high-quality menu includes a combination of sustainably-farmed fresh and wild caught seasonal features. Pokéworks only uses brands that are Marine Stewardship Council (MSC) certified 'Fish to Eat' or recognized by the Aquaculture Stewardship Council as certified environmentally and socially responsible seafood."[39] To add to its legitimacy and inform its flavor, Pokeworks collaborates with Hawaiian-born *Top Chef* contestant Sheldon Simeon on their menu. Social media played a role in this win too: the partnership began after they reached out to the chef on Facebook. Since poke bowls and poke burritos only require a rice cooker and a refrigerator for its fresh ingredients, each location needs only a small kitchen area, which lowers costs and enables more revenue per square foot. The company began to franchise in 2016, and has launched 120 locations as of 2018.[40]

As your company grows, its strategic planning efforts will benefit from the input of others inside and outside the company with critical knowledge that can influence the company's direction. Customers, particularly lead users, can provide information about market needs. Specialist employees who are close to markets and technologies can identify future opportunities. The firm can institute a function that gathers and monitors outside information and examines external trends and opportunities.

Organizational Resources and Capabilities

A bootstrap mentality does not end once the company is launched and successful; it is a lasting orientation toward maximizing value from resource parsimony.

Efforts to finance growth internally go hand in hand with controls. By improving its cash flow, your growing company can better avert a cash crisis and avoid being at the mercy of reluctant or expensive lenders or investors. You may even be able to self-finance some of its future growth, reducing reliance on more expensive sources of funding. The key lesson is this: A bootstrap mentality does not apply just to starting a company; it is a lasting orientation that maximizes returns through resource parsimony.

Obtaining Financial Resources for the Growing Company

Shortening operating cash cycles and increasing margins are vital for conserving cash. They essentially represent costless financing. The rapidly growing organization, however, will likely need to tap additional sources to finance its growth. Not only will you need financing to support accelerating sales, but also new policies, such as granting customer payment terms or taking on bulk orders, as well as investments in new products or services, will create a drain on cash.

Despite its success and future prospects, however, a company early in its growth cycle may have only certain options available. For example, a bank would not typically extend credit to a firm with little operating history and fluctuating sales. But as we discussed in Chapter 11, a supplier who is motivated to make a sale and gain a loyal, growing customer might. After a company has been established for a year, a bank might be willing to loan monies against a portion of its receivables, based on the founders' good credit, or with signed guarantees, perhaps requiring loan covenants to maintain certain numbers or ratios.

It's therefore useful to think in terms of stages when financing growth. Sources closed to the firm earlier in its life may open up later. Undertake periodic surveys of the firm's current financing options, and consider any changes that may open up new and cheaper financing sources. In this way, you may recognize new opportunities for refinancing at lower rates.

As we covered in Chapters 10 and 11, sources of financing for early growth include

- Investment from key management
- Founder loans
- Family and friends
- Angel investors
- Venture capital
- Loans on assets, such as receivables, inventory, and equipment
- Equipment leases
- Credit cards

As the company moves into later growth and undertakes expansion efforts, such as selling internationally or launching new products or services, it will need financing from sources more appropriate for higher-risk and longer-term investment. Banks typically will not loan substantial funds, unsecured, for riskier expansion efforts that won't generate returns for quite some time. The firm will likely need to rely on equity sources.

But there are other ways to finance future growth. Look to strategic partners who may provide more favorable financing terms. You may also decide to expand by franchising. Take the risks of these financing modes into consideration: For example, potential customers who compete with your strategic partner may view a relationship with you as too risky because your partner has some control over your firm or has greater access to information that could unfavorably affect the customer. Determine your resource needs by your firm's range of value chain activities. Reducing activities to those considered core to the business and achieving better coordination throughout the chain can reduce your resource requirements and risk, as we detailed in the execution section.

Intangible Resources and Capabilities

Resources at start-up include people, but the focus is on acquiring capital because the key human resource is the founder or founding team. As the company grows, it accumulates capital, to be sure, and fixed assets. But it also builds intangible assets—resources such as the proprietary knowledge underlying its products and services and the skills of the organization's people. You should have addressed intellectual property considerations early on, before early growth—even before starting the business. But this should also be an ongoing process requiring continual legal advice and subsequent actions to protect technologies, processes, and creative work through trade secrets, copyrights, trademarks, and patents (see Chapter 12).

Starting in early growth, you'll need to develop or hire people with specialized skills. Generalist skills are important at start-up: Everyone should be able to pitch in and help with shipping, inventory control, marketing, and so forth. As volume increases and the business becomes more complex, it becomes harder to maintain efficiency and effectiveness with generalist skills. Now you will need to hire specialists in areas such as marketing, inventory management, accounting and finance, and logistics.

An organization also develops capabilities that define what it is good at. These are processes that coordinate and integrate the organization's tangible and intangible resources to create unique sources of value. Just like inventory and equipment, they lead to revenues for a company. Think about businesses or organizations that are familiar to you and about what they do best. McDonald's has efficient processes to deliver fast, low-priced meals. Starbucks delivers quick, convenient, customizable coffee drinks. These transactions translate to capabilities. Now think about whether these organizations would be good at doing something totally different in their industry. Could McDonald's open a high-end restaurant? Could Starbucks become the new happy hour spot? In 2010, Starbucks debuted its "Evenings" menu in Seattle, where it offered wine, craft beer, and tapas such as bacon-wrapped dates after 5 pm. The company recognized that its customers also appreciated wine and beer and that it could create a similar experience to its coffee experiences. Although it originally planned to roll out to 1,000 stores across the United States, the Evenings program only reached 400 and the experiment came to an end in 2017. The Evenings concept was too different from the Starbucks brand, and poor advertising meant many customers not even aware of the program's existence. The fundamentally different attitude of someone looking for a caffeine fix to power through their day and an alcoholic drink to wind down meant that Starbucks "Evenings" were not meant to be.[41]

Instead, Starbucks has decided to break into the alcohol business in a different way, by launching Starbucks "Reserve Roastery," a new type of store entirely with a coffee bar, a full liquor bar, and a Princi Bakery in 2018. The Starbucks Reserve brand is meant to project an exclusive, elegant experience, and instead of a nationwide rollout, it has opened locations in New York, Seattle, Milan, and Shanghai, with locations in Tokyo and Chicago on the way.[42] Will Starbucks have more success by creating a fundamentally different, upscale experience under the Starbucks brand?

But there are opportunities for companies to expand into the periphery with their capabilities. For example, McDonald's began to offer salads in an attempt to attract more health-conscious, but also convenience-minded and price-conscious, eaters. In 2008, McDonald's rolled out McCafé, which offers specialty coffees such as cappuccino, lattes, and mochas and directly competes with Starbucks.[43] As of 2015, McCafé was the top third specialty coffee shop by sales, netting $1.4 billion in sales[44] across 5,000 locations. In 2018, McCafé's product line has expanded into espresso drinks and "McCafé' on the go" bottled Frappes. In its 2018 Annual Report, McDonald's identified McCafé' as a core driver of their strategy to convert casual to committed customers as part of its Velocity Growth plan to "serve more customers, more often."[45]

In another effort to increase sales from existing customers who are becoming more health conscious, McDonald's rolled out a completely new "Favorites under 400" menu to make it simpler for customers to select items based on their calorie content. With more scrutiny on food ingredients for its staple items, McDonalds started serving fresh beef, cooked-to-order quarter pounders in 2018 and has committed to removing corn syrup from its hamburgers and buns and using only cage-free eggs by 2025.[46]

Your capabilities need to be consistent with your firm's strategic focus. As the opportunity domain section of this chapter reveals, organizations define their strategy both through detecting where the opportunities are for unique advantages in the external competitive environment and through building and leveraging a set of unique capabilities. McDonald's needs to have processes that optimize efficiency and cut costs out of its operations. Microsoft needs to be constantly imagining and developing the next breakthrough operating systems and software applications, then integrating them into seamless ecosystems that help lock customers in.[47] Think again about the capabilities Under Armour and Yankee Candle needed as they started and expanded their businesses.

Sustained growth in a changing environment requires constant attention to identifying what the company does best and matching that with the potential for unique value in the competitive environment. Your company may be good at user-friendly innovations. If it does this better than rivals and users are willing to pay a premium for that, then leverage it—ensuring the right people and systems are in place to maximize the value you can gain from this capability. Meanwhile, you need to monitor the uniqueness and value of your company's capabilities over time. If competitors duplicate this ability or customers shift toward more technically complex solutions, reassess what your company does best. Renew key capabilities periodically. A research study of telecommunications and computer start-ups found that high levels of innovativeness at founding did not translate to higher growth seven, eight, or nine years out. And simply forming alliances didn't help. But those building internal technology capabilities beyond founding were more likely to achieve a higher level of sustained growth.[48]

Leadership

Figure 13.8 summarizes some key differences between entrepreneurs, managers, and entrepreneurial leaders. The entrepreneurial leader plays a distinct role, critical for sustaining a growing organization.

Entrepreneur	Manager	Entrepreneurial Leader
Locates new ideas	Maintains current operations	Leverages core business while exploring new opportunities
Starts a business	Implements the business	Starts businesses within an ongoing organization
Opportunity driven	Resource driven	Capability and opportunity driven; leverages capabilities and builds new ones to expand opportunity domain
Establishes and implements a vision	Plans, organizes, staffs, controls	Establishes a vision and empowers others to carry it out
Builds an organization around the opportunity	Enhances efficiency of organization	Maintains entrepreneurial ability as organization grows; ensures culture, structure, systems are conducive to entrepreneurship; removes barriers
Leads and inspires others	Supervises and monitors others	Develops and guides entrepreneurial individuals; bridges between individuals and groups with diverse expertise and orientation
Orchestrates change in both the organizational and competitive environment	Maintains consistency and predictability	Orchestrates change in the competitive environment

FIGURE 13.8
The Entrepreneur versus Manager versus Entrepreneurial Leader.

Starting the Delegation Process

The entrepreneur typically starts out doing everything. She answers phones, ships product, designs advertisements—in essence, performing just about all the activities needed to ensure the organization gets product sold and out the door. But sometime in early growth, the organization will outgrow her ability to keep up. She will have neither the time nor the expertise to deal with the range of challenges a burgeoning business presents. The following are symptoms revealing that the organization has outgrown the entrepreneur's capacity.

- The volume of decisions multiplies. The entrepreneur is working harder but accomplishing less.
- Decisions become more difficult to make: more complex and specialized. The entrepreneur increasingly wonders whether she has made the right decision.
- Everyone is still pitching in and doing everything, but more and more, something critical slips by or mistakes occur.
- If the entrepreneur is not directly involved in the task, no progress can happen.

Starting in early growth, the entrepreneur must delegate responsibilities to others in the organization. The process of delegation is mapped out in Figure 13.9.

As Figure 13.9 shows, the entrepreneur starts out assigning specific tasks to others. As delegation proceeds, she passes responsibility for achieving objectives to specialists, and then managers, without needing to understand or know about the underlying mechanics. Then the setting of objectives moves to others: experienced managers and teams close to the activity. This process enables the entrepreneur to spend less time on the day-to-day details of everything and focus on what she does best, while those most qualified make decisions. At the same time, the entrepreneur needs to oversee execution by providing guidance to managers and using metrics to evaluate progress, but she may need to step in when necessary, particularly when initiatives meet with resistance.

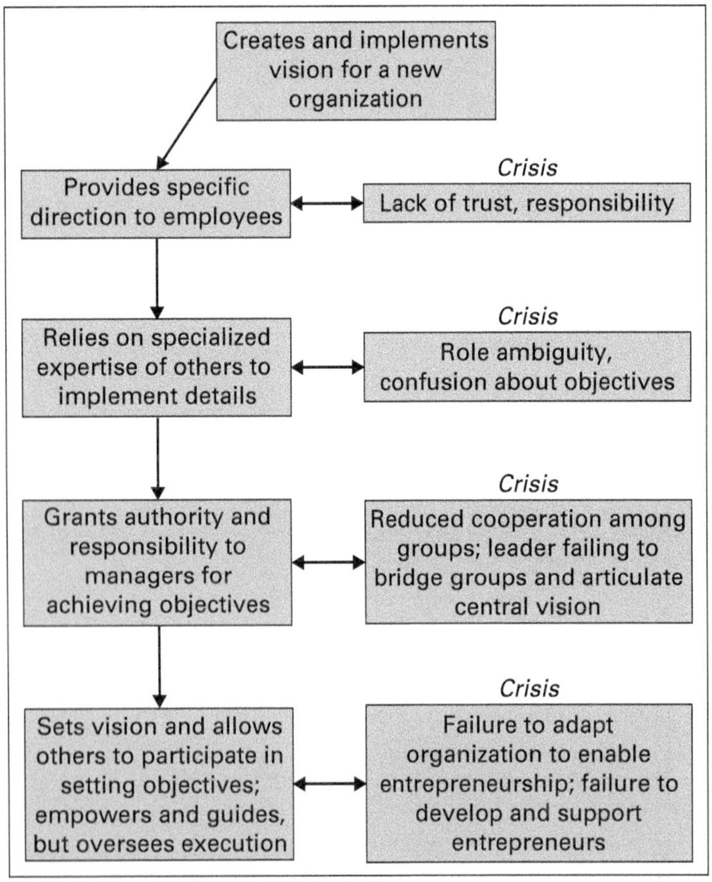

Delegation, although necessary for surviving the entrepreneurial growth phase, is typically difficult for the entrepreneur to accomplish. She may continue to attempt to do everything herself, but she's increasingly unable to do so. Faced with these challenges, the entrepreneur may revert back to what she does best, ignoring tasks she has neither the comfort level nor the capability to deal with. A technical entrepreneur may retreat to developing new products, while ignoring the company's inability to pay bills on time. What's bad is not the entrepreneur doing what she does best—it's having no one pay attention to the company's most critical problems.

Employees may not have a problem with the lack of delegation because they may prefer that the entrepreneur make decisions that they can then carry out. Then they don't need to take responsibility for outcomes. On the other hand,

FIGURE 13.9 Transition from Entrepreneur to Entrepreneurial Leader.

in allowing employees to take responsibility for decisions, the entrepreneur also needs to let them make mistakes and learn from them, circumstances neither the employees nor the entrepreneur may feel comfortable with. The entrepreneur cannot continue to be the "go-to" guy, however, when the volume of decisions mushrooms and she becomes increasingly less qualified to provide direction in many areas.

As the entrepreneur delegates, she will need to put in place managers who can be responsible for executing in specialized areas. Then, in her leadership role, she must develop the ability to inspire people with a range of expertise to organize, communicate, collaborate— and be creative in both running an efficient operation and pursuing entrepreneurial ideas.

First-Level Management

In early growth, the first set of supervisors can come from within. In some sense, they deserve to be promoted because they have been with the company since its early days and have contributed to its success. They were willing to chip in whenever and wherever needed, they have worked closely with you, the entrepreneur, and they therefore understand your vision and the purpose of the organization. They may also have the respect of their peers.

Assess whether these people have the potential to become managers, however, and whether they can develop their abilities through training and experience. There are a few things you should do: (1) set expectations up front, including setting personal performance goals; (2) provide coaching, mentoring, and training; and (3) periodically assess behavior and performance. But developing managers takes time. If the venture is late forming its management structure and is therefore playing catch-up, if internal and external conditions are rapidly changing, or if the learning gap between current employees and needed management is too wide, then allowing managers to learn on the job is too risky. You will need to hire from the outside.

Hiring from the outside has its own hazards because the workers, particularly those who have been there from the beginning, may not respect these outsiders. First, act as a broker between the employees and management during this transition. This includes advising the new manager and recognizing the cooperation and contributions of employees. The latter can mean acknowledging accomplishments through personal contact or making these visible around the organization. In addition, you (and your managers) can ensure employees have a satisfactory career path by promoting them and moving them into jobs in which they increasingly feel engaged and challenged.

Where possible, employ a mix of externally hired managers and internally promoted managers. Again, broker between these internal and external managers during the transition by setting expectations, advising and coaching, and monitoring behavior. By achieving cooperation among internal and external managers, you're more likely to accomplish broad cooperation across the organization. Also reinforce the authority of your new managers, whether they originate from the inside or the outside. For example, route to them employees who have always gone directly to you.

From Delegation to Decentralization

What starts as a process of delegation in early growth evolves into a decentralized reporting structure as the organization approaches later growth. As functions become more specialized and the product and service offering broadens, responsibility and decision making are best left to those with the expertise and day-to-day involvement in specific areas.

A decentralized structure can also aid communication flow throughout the organization, which increasingly becomes challenged as the organization grows. Although closeness to the entrepreneur in early stages helps everyone understand her vision and the organization's objectives, the complexity and changes a growing organization experiences can create confusion about direction and purpose. Communication and understanding need to happen among the members of the management team, who then ensure consistent information flow throughout their areas.

Professional Management and Boards

In later growth, the organization needs to ensure it has a leadership team in place: professional managers who share in the organization's strategic planning process and have the capability to balance the need for efficient operations with the benefits of maintaining its entrepreneurial edge. Once the organization has created control systems, a management structure, and a strategic focus, it needs to look toward its future. This job becomes increasingly complex and requires those with experience and track records. Employees who have been promoted into managerial positions are not likely to be qualified for the organization's top levels. Consequently, professional managers typically come from the outside.

With the introduction of a leadership team, the organization itself becomes more professional. This is a major change, even more so than the shift from start-up to early growth. Some employees will leave, but others will make this transition. The practices you put in place to integrate managers and employees and insiders and outsiders during early growth will be critical to your introduction of a professional management team.

By carefully selecting members of the board of directors, you can provide alternative perspectives and depth and breadth of experience. The board should include experts from outside the firm who can become key participants in the strategic planning process. What's important for the firm is a proactive, rather than a reactive, approach to seeking ways to extend and build value. The composition of the company's board of directors will typically undergo changes as the firm emerges from its start-up phase. Initially, the board may be informal—occupied by those unlikely to have high-level experience but able to provide support to the entrepreneur in her early endeavors. In early growth, boards typically evolve to include those able to provide operational guidance—for example, retired bankers, investors, and lawyers.

As the company professionalizes, the board should be more useful for strategic purposes, with members having a broader and visionary view of the market and industry—for example, other CEOs, industry experts, and senior executives in related businesses. Although many investors require representation on the board of directors, avoid stakeholders who can control the firm for their benefit through board positions, such as suppliers, customers, and the company's lenders.

Supplement the skill and experience of the company's leadership and board of directors with the skill and experience of advisory boards and consultants. For example, you may assemble a group of technology experts from universities, government labs, and corporations to examine industry technological trends, or you may bring in a marketing consulting firm to determine tactics for expanding into overseas markets.

Coordinating the Driving Forces

The driving forces model shows a link among the three elements: organizational resources and capabilities, opportunity domain, and leadership. And at the core of this is execution: ensuring the most efficient and effective coordination of these activities in a way that enhances the organization's profitability. Capabilities and the opportunity domain interact: Capabilities define where the company can best play, and opportunities extend capabilities. Leadership maps out a particular opportunity domain with its strategic focus and modifies this focus over time, as the industry and market environment changes and the company seeks future growth. Leadership also ensures its capabilities and opportunity domain are in balance. But as the organization grows, a key concern for its leaders is how to manage its people and maintain its entrepreneurial capabilities, as the next section illustrates.

Leading People; Developing Entrepreneurs

The most common "people mistakes" an entrepreneurial firm makes are preparing people inadequately and maintaining the wrong people as the organization grows. Early in the business's life, organization members do their jobs and pitch in wherever needed. It is more important for the lean team to maintain the flexibility and broad skills needed to accomplish a lot with a little. Early in the game, it is not yet apparent these employees lack the skills needed to scale up the organization. It is difficult to think about training to develop future skills when growth is consuming everyone's time.

As the need for specialists and managers arises, the tasks you expect of some employees may exceed their abilities, and you may need to place them in other roles—or even fire them if necessary. Other employees may be able to rise up to the challenges presented and assume these new functions and responsibilities. The process of adapting to these new roles takes time, however. The company will often need to do some hiring from the outside. You will have to deal with reduced motivation from setbacks or crises at the same time that employees struggle with adapting to new employees and higher-level managers coming from the outside, both of whom lack the shared experiences gained through the organization's history.

The second tier of employees, beyond the founding group, is often said to be more like 9-to-5ers who tend to view working there as a job. But in most companies, there are entrepreneurs in the mix. Although we often think that ideas come from anywhere or that anyone can be creative if given a chance, the reality is that some people don't have the stomach for ambiguity and risk. And in many companies, the entrepreneur remains the sole entrepreneurial engine.

Our research on corporate entrepreneurship suggests the organization's leaders need to:

- Identify those exhibiting passion for entrepreneurship.
- Develop their ability to work under conditions of high ambiguity.
- Ensure they have the inclination and credibility to convince others in the organization to contribute and commit to their projects.
- Facilitate, support, and guide their efforts, while also providing them with sufficient freedom and empowerment.
- Recognize their contribution to the company's innovation and growth ambitions.
- View failure as a risk associated with entrepreneurship and an opportunity for learning, therefore ensuring that well-intentioned failures are not punished.

We suspect these practices are also critical in smaller organizations. One study reports that human resource practices like training and development distinguish high-growth firms from more slowly growing ones.[49]

CONCLUSION

Starting a business is a risky endeavor, but staying in business can be just as challenging. As the entrepreneurial firm grows beyond founding, it needs to ensure its organization is capable of managing growth. We have outlined a driving forces model that integrates leadership, opportunity domain, and resources and capabilities—and has execution at the core. The entrepreneur should understand and anticipate the challenges associated with building and managing a growing organization at different stages, prepare the organization to execute effectively at each point, and set the stage for a healthy future.

These efforts, however, must not distance the company from its entrepreneurial roots. Growing companies struggle not just with such concerns as having fewer resources than big companies but also with coordinating an increasingly bigger and more complex business. The team members must work to prevent the organization from becoming a bureaucracy that inhibits entrepreneurship. They must continually foster entrepreneurial actions even when this is their biggest challenge. They have to consciously work on preserving and maintaining their entrepreneurial spirit, and if they lose it, they have to rejuvenate the company and rekindle entrepreneurship before it's too late.

YOUR OPPORTUNITY JOURNAL

Reflection Point	Your Thoughts...
1. What are your personal growth objectives for your venture? Is a "lifestyle" business going to meet your personal goals? Or a high-potential venture?	
2. What will your role within the company be at various stages of growth? Do you want to remain the CEO? Are you more interested in another aspect—say, CTO?	
3. What skills will you need to develop as the company grows to satisfactorily fulfill the roles you aspire to? Which of these skills can you learn on the job? Which skills might need further education or other outside development?	
4. What kind of controls can you establish early in your venture's life? How will these help you manage cash and other key components of your business?	
5. Which aspects of your business should you keep in-house and which should you outsource? How do you protect your competitive advantage?	
6. What is your strategic focus for early growth? How do you leverage what you do really well? What are some possible peripheral growth opportunities for later in your venture's life?	
7. What are your organization's key resources and capabilities? What should they be in the future? How do you build toward those resources and capabilities?	
8. What is your leadership plan? When and which responsibilities will you delegate? How will you promote people in your organization? When might you need to go outside to hire?	

WEB EXERCISE

Identify three companies that have experienced successful, rapid growth in your industry. Study their websites and search for articles about the companies. Can you discern their strategic focuses early in their growth cycles? What are the core areas that they are leveraging? How do their growth strategies change later in their lives? What are some peripheral markets/customers they are going for? Have they grown by acquisition? How has that worked out?

NOTES

1. Zook, C., and Allen, J. *The Facts about Growth*. New York: Bain Company. 1999.
2. https://www.dmnews.com/channel-marketing/multi-omnichannel/article/13036365/meet-the-marketer-michael-lazerow-chief-strategy-officer-of-salesforce-marketing-cloud.
3. http://www.inc.com/christina-desmarais/webex-cofounder-subrah-iyar-moxtra.html.
4. https://www.barrons.com/articles/as-robo-advisors-cross-200-billion-in-assets-schwab-leads-in-performance-1517509393
5. https://pando.com/2014/01/21/it-doesnt-always-end-in-tears-inside-wealthfronts-second-orderly-ceo-switch/.
6. http://www.riabiz.com/a/5022384834740224/andy-rachleff-is-out-as-ceo-of-wealthfront-as-former-linkedin-star-takes-his-place.
7. http://fortune.com/2016/10/31/wealthfront-andy-rachleff/.
8. http://www.volkswagenag.com/content/vwcorp/info_center/en/publications/2015/03/Y_2014_e.bin.html/binary storageitem/file/GB+2014_e.pdf.
9. https://www.nytimes.com/2017/11/01/business/volkswagen-sales-diesel.html
10. http://www.consumerreports.org/volkswagen/did-volkswagen-use-cheat-mode-as-a-selling-point.
11. *Advertising Age*. Volkswagen Group's advertising spending on Volkswagen (brand) in the United States from 2012 to 2014 (in million U.S. dollars). http://www.statista.com/statistics/467681/volkswagen-ad-spend-usa/.
12. http://www.bbc.com/news/business-34324772.
13. https://www.reuters.com/article/legal-uk-volkswagen-emissions/vws-dieselgate-bill-hits-30-bln-after-another-charge-idUSKCN1C4271.

14. Additional resources on growth stages can be found in the following references:

- Adizes, Ichak. *Managing Corporate Lifecycles*. Paramus, NJ: Prentice Hall, 1999.
- Churchill, Neil C. The Six Key Phases of Company Growth. In S. Birley and D. Muzyka (Eds.), *Mastering Enterprise*. London, England: Pitman Publishing, 1997.
- Flamholtz, Eric G., and Randle, Yvonne. *Growing Pains: Transitioning from an Entrepreneurship to a Professionally Managed Firm*. San Francisco, CA: Jossey-Bass, 2000.
- Greiner, Larry E. Evolution and Revolution as Organizations Grow. *Harvard Business Review*, 76(3): 55–63, 1998.
- Harper, Stephen C. *The McGrawHill Guide to Managing Growth in Your Emerging Business*. New York: McGraw-Hill, 1995.

15. https://techcrunch.com/2017/09/25/package-delivery-startup-doorman-is-shutting-down/.
16. https://techcrunch.com/2015/06/02/doorman-raises-1-5-million-to-eliminate-missed-package-deliveries/https://kirktaylor.com/doorman-delivers-package-shark-tank-deal/.
17. https://500.co/engagement-habit-with-doorman-app/.
18. https://techcrunch.com/2017/09/25/package-delivery-startup-doorman-is-shutting-down/.
19. https://techcrunch.com/2017/09/25/package-delivery-startup-doorman-is-shutting-down/.
20. www.startups.co.uk/is-your-business-growing-too-fast.html.
21. Kolen, Joel, and Jaffe, Susan Biddle. Knowing When to Take a Breather: Controlling Company Growth. *Nation's Business*, 83(11): 6, November 1995.
22. https://www.stock-analysis-on.net/NASDAQ/Company/Amazoncom-Inc/Ratios/Short-term-Operating-Activity#Cash-Conversion-Cycle.
23. http://finance.yahoo.com/echarts?s= AMZN+Interactive#{"range":"2y", "allowChartStacking":true}.
24. https://frntofficesport.com/seatgeek-consumer-brand/.
25. https://www.entrepreneur.com/article/204652.
26. https://frntofficesport.com/seatgeek-consumer-brand/
27. http://www.inc.com/magazine/200312 01/howididit.html.
28. http://fortune.com/2011/10/26/underarmour-gets-serious/.
29. http://nypost.com/2015/07/24/underarmour-is-using-nikes-strategies-better-than-nike/.
30. https://www.cnbc.com/2019/02/12/under-armour-reports-q4-2018-earnings.html.
31. https://www.washingtonpost.com/business/capitalbusiness/livingsocial-posts-566-million-loss-as-acquisitions-drop-in-value/2012/10/25/6c1e229c-1eeb-11e2-9746-908f727990d8_story.html.
32. http://techcrunch.com/2011/10/07/livingsocial-143-million-acquisitions/
33. http://techcrunch.com/2014/01/02/groupons-260m-acquisition-of-ticket-monster-from-livingsocial-has-closed/.
34. http://www.nytimes.com/2015/11/22/technology/livingsocial-once-a-unicorn-is-losing-its-magic.html?_r=0.
35. www.secinfo.com/d12Pk6.phtj.htm#_8.
36. http://www.reuters.com/article/2013/ 09/03/us-jarden-yankeecandle-idUSBR E98205C20130903.
37. Osborne, Richard L. Second Phase Entrepreneurship: Breaking Through the Growth Wall. *Business Horizons*, 37(1): 80 – 86, 1994.
38. https://www.inc.com/magazine/201808/helaine-olen/poke-sweetfin-pokeworks.com.html.
39. https://www.franchisechatter.com/2018/05/25/qa-with-peter-yang-co-founder-of-pokeworks/.
40. Ibid.
41. https://www.myrecipes.com/extracrispy/why-booze-at-starbucks-never-caught-on.
42. https://www.businessinsider.com/starbucks-reserve-roastery-compared-regular-starbucks-2018-12.
43. www.nytimes.com/2012/05/06/magazine/how-mcdonalds-came-back-bigger-than-ever.html?pagewanted = all&_r = 0, and also its Web site www.mcdonalds.com/us/en/food/food_quality/nutrition_choices.html, and www.huffingtonpost.com/2012/07/23/mcdonalds-favorites-under-400-calories_n_1695885.html.
44. https://www.nasdaq.com/article/heres-why-mcdonalds-is-increasing-focus-on-mccafe-cm718236.
45. McDonalds. (2018). 2017 Annual Report. Retrieved from: https://corporate.mcdonalds.com/corpmcd/investors-relations/financial-information/annual-reports.html.
46. https://www.qsrmagazine.com/finance/why-2018-could-be-mcdonalds-best-year-ever.
47. www.microsoft.com.
48. Kelley, Donna, and Nakosteen, Robert. Technology Resources, Alliances and Sustained Growth in New, Technology-Based Firms. *IEEE Transactions on Engineering Management*, 52(3): 292–300, 2005.
49. Barringer, B., Jones, F., and Neubaum, D. A. Quantitative Content Analysis of the Characteristics of Rapid-Growth Firms and Their Founders. *Journal of Business Venturing*, 20: 663–687, 2005.

Case Esporte Interativo[1]

While Esporte Interativo (EI) had grown dramatically over the last 18 years, co-founders Edgar Diniz and Leo Lenz Cesar felt overwhelmed as they thought about how to maintain that growth in an increasingly competitive industry. Edgar and Leo, along with Carlos Moreira, a former partner, started EI in 1999 when the market of live sports and media in all its forms was starting to develop in Brazil. First as consultants, later as a broadcasting business, and then as a sports channel, EI endured a rough path to get to where they were, but competition against the giants, including Globo, the fourth largest media company in the world, was becoming fierce. Could they survive? What kind of resources would they need to continue growing and fend off the competition?

The Beginning of EI

Leo and Carlos met during their MBA at Babson College. Edgar was a common friend from back home in Brazil. While all were pursing successful corporate careers, they were just counting the days until they were ready to start their own business. They had always talked about starting something in the realm of sports, and finally they each put up $35,000 and incorporated TopSports (the original name for EI) in the summer of 1999.

Luckily, they left their former employers on good terms and JP Morgan hired them to raise capital and improve the brand for one of their clients, Sporte Clube Vitoria, in Salvador, Brazil. Later, they landed a series of consulting projects with Globo, such as managing a new professional soccer tournament, developing an Internet portal, and managing the sale of the marketing properties of Brazil's most important soccer competition (Campeonato Brasileiro).

In 2003, acknowledging that their business was heavily dependent on Globo, they decided to look for an independent opportunity. They raised nearly $1.7 million from 16 friends and former colleagues and approached Rede TV! with a long-term plan to start and manage their sports channel. This partnership lasted for six months. After some disagreement, they sued RedeTV!, ended up winning the lawsuit, and left for Bandeirantes broadcasting, but this time under better terms. During their two-year contract with Bandeirantes, TopSports established ties with major mobile providers and became the only television network to offer SMS interaction with their audience, generating up to 20 million SMS responses. From 2003 to 2006, TopSports grew 522% not only due to their capacity to sell sponsorship in an innovative way but also because of their capacity to build the digital business. The Bandeirantes experience was extremely successful and a great learning opportunity. But, at the end of the day, TopSports was benefiting from a market inefficiency and Bandeirantes realized that it could replicate what TopSports was doing and therefore did not need them any longer. By the middle of 2006, TopSports, knowing that the Bandeirantes contract would come to an end soon, decided to go and build their own independent sports station.

In January of 2007, TopSports launched Esporte Interativo 24/7 with an estimated broadcast reach of 27 million households[2] with the growth objective of reaching 40 of the 53 million total households in Brazil. They started generating revenue through fan-direct programs like SMS, hotel reservations, and contests. In the first quarter of 2007, they had over six million SMS participations and about 30 million page-views on their website.[3]

Their value proposition was a success, and by the summer of 2008, EI was breaking even and had attracted six major advertisers: telcos TIM, Embratel, Gillette, Pirelli tires, DirecTV, and a manufacturer of satellite dishes. Still, they knew they had to significantly increase their media sales and distribution to achieve their profit objectives, so they came up with an aggressive growth plan that allowed them to play to their strengths. Distribution came in three main platforms: (a) free-to-air; (b) satellite dish; and (c) pay TV. The plan included the following: (a) create distribution through partnerships and/or acquisitions in order to obtain broadcasting licenses, (b) compete or collaborate with larger media companies, and (c) differentiate by adding new and better products and services to their portfolio (Exhibit 13.1 shows IE's Timeline).

EI Grows to a Major Player

By 2010, EI revenue was starting to diversify, with 70% coming from advertising, 25% from mobile telephone services, and 5% from its virtual store shop.[4] In 2011, EI regained the broadcast rights for the UEFA (Union of European Football [soccer] Association) Champions League that had long

[1] This case was authored by Andrew Zacharakis, Ed Marram and Andres Hinojoso with support from the John H. Muller, Jr. Chair in Entrepreneurship.

[2] The C Band satellite gave EI about 18 million households, and they acquired an additional nine million households for a few hours a day by contracting with affiliate broadcasters, one in Sao Paulo and one in Rio De Janeiro.

[3] By the end of their first year (2007), TV Esporte Interativo had logged SMS calls from 1.3 million separate participants, and had a registered 465,000 members collecting and spending SMS points.

[4] https://www-emis-com.ezproxy.babson.edu/php/sources/index/pub?pcid=SABINEWS&sv=EMIS. Retrieved December 14, 2016.

Exhibit 13.1 **Growth Strategy Timeline (provided by EI)**

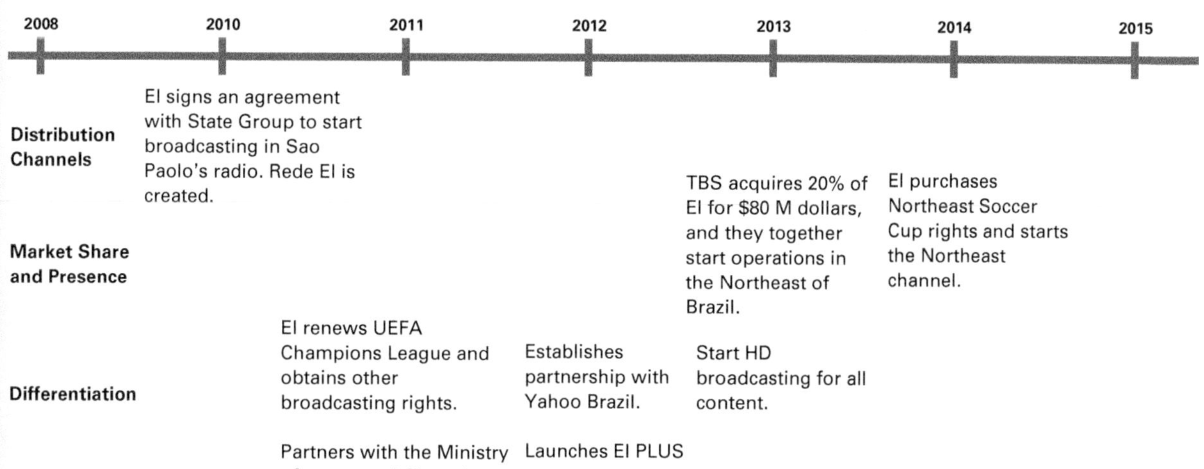
Growth Strategy Timeline
By 2008, EI has attracted the attention of powerful media interests. In order to take advantage of the momentum, the partners design a growth strategy with 3 fronts: Distribution channels, Market Share and Presence, and Differentiation.
2008
2010
2011
2012
2013
2014
2015
Distribution Channels
EI signs an agreement with State Group to start broadcasting in Sao Paolo's radio. Rede EI is created.
Market Share and Presence
TBS acquires 20% of EI for $80 M dollars, and they together start operations in the Northeast of Brazil.
EI purchases Northeast Soccer Cup rights and starts the Northeast channel.
Differentiation
EI renews UEFA Champions League and obtains other broadcasting rights.
Establishes partnership with Yahoo Brazil.
Start HD broadcasting for all content.
Partners with the Ministry of sports and Olympics.
Launches EI PLUS

belonged to ESPN.[5] Also, it added more tournaments like the U-17 World Cup soccer championship, the U-20 Football [soccer] Women's World Cup, and the National Football League (NFL) to its portfolio.[6] In the same year, EI partnered with the Brazilian Ministry of Sports and the Olympics and Paralympics Committees to publish and promote Olympic and Paralympic Sports in 2016. These additions and partnerships allowed EI to differentiate from the competition and to broaden its target market, generating new spectators and customers. In 2012, EI partnered with Yahoo Brazil to create a portal that combined the best sport videos with top news. This allowed EI to generate more value for its customers through their website and, consequently, more traffic. In August of the same year, EI launched Esporte Interativo Plus, a subscription-based online service where spectators could watch complete programming 24 hours a day live or on-demand. By the end of 2013, they started broadcasting all content in high definition (HD).[7]

Overview of the Market Place

As of 2014, Globo, SBT, Record TV, Rede TV!, and Bandeirantes are the top five players in TV Broadcasting in Brazil. Together, they account for 71.1% of the free-to-air market share by volume and they all have sports channels.

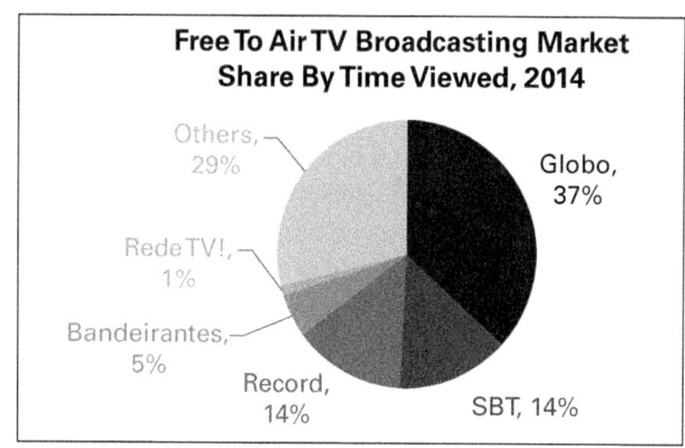
Free To Air TV Broadcasting Market Share By Time Viewed, 2014
Others, 29%
Globo, 37%
Rede TV!, 1%
Bandeirantes, 5%
Record, 14%
SBT, 14%

Chart created by authors from data from http://www.bastidoresdatv.com.br/audiencia/coluna-evolucao-nacional-das-emissoras-de-tv; http://tvfoco.pop.com.br/audiencia/confira-a-media-mes-parcial-das-emissoras-e-a-audiencia-por-faixa-horaria/. Retrieved January 23, 2017

Sport Broadcasting has been part of Brazilian television since its origins in 1950, when TV Tupi broadcast the 1950 World Cup, the first sporting event ever broadcast in Brazil. By 1964, pushed by the government, television became a mass medium and a new player, Rede Globo, started growing as the favorite TV partner of the State. During the 1970s and 1980s, Globo dominated the audience with a 60–80% market share

[5] http://maquinadoesporte.uol.com.br/artigo/espn-perde-liga-dos-campeoes-na-al_7859.html. Retrieved December 14, 2016.
[6] Ibid.
[7] Ibid.

all around Brazil, only competing against Tupi TV and Rede Bandeirantes, which was the first to introduce color TV to the country.[8] In the 1980s, Tupi TV went bankrupt and its signal was split into two companies, which are today SBT and Rede TV!. In the 1990s, with the launch of UHF television channels, Rede Record began to air its signal. Tupi's bankruptcy left the market wide open for Globo's hegemony, until 2000, when preferences of the audience and technology shifted and the whole industry suffered a significant loss in viewership. The top five players lost 4.3% of share from 2000 to 2008 mainly driven by the rapid growth in Internet access.[9]

From 2000 to 2008, the industry underwent many changes with respect to audience preferences and technology, and the players that were able to adapt quicker were the ones to gain a competitive edge. For example, Record gained the lead over Globo during some time slots on Sunday mornings and in regions such as Rio de Janeiro because it focused programming that catered to those audiences. Globo countered its losses in free-to-air TV by making significant investments in pay TV, which was starting to rapidly increase in share.

While the market share of some top players decreased from 2007 to 2014, EI increased its number of spectators substantially. Free-to-air broadcasting by volume grew at 3.1% from 2007 to 2014 while EI grew over 85% during the same period. Regarding market share of free-to-air TV Broadcasting by volume, Globo and Rede lost market share to SBT and others while EI gained between 1 and 3% of share. On the other hand, in market share of live pay TV by volume, big player Sky-Direct TV was losing share to Oi, Global Village, and Telefonica. EI was growing fast and had gained access to 30% of available pay TV distribution channels since entering in 2009.

Total TV Broadcasting by number of household connections.[10]

Household TV Viewership		2007	2008	2009	2010	2011	2012	2013	2014
Absolute size		58.05	61.06	63.46	64.23	72.13	78.17	81.33	84.84
	Growth %		*5.2%*	*3.9%*	*1.2%*	*12.3%*	*8.4%*	*4.0%*	*4.3%*
Free to air		52.7	54.74	55.99	54.46	59.39	61.98	63.31	65.27
	Growth %		*3.9%*	*2.3%*	*–2.7%*	*9.1%*	*4.4%*	*2.1%*	*3.1%*
Live Pay TV		5.35	6.32	7.47	9.77	12.74	16.19	18.02	19.57
	Growth %		*18.1%*	*18.2%*	*30.8%*	*30.4%*	*27.1%*	*11.3%*	*8.6%*

Resources

After almost eight years of broadcasting independently, EI barely had 3% of market share in free-to-air TV. Still, their financials were steady and they were profitable, but in order to continue growing, they needed cash. Pay TV had grown, gaining around 15 percentage points of market share against free-to-air TV[11] from 2007 to 2014. EI held a strong position with EI Plus featured in Apple TV[12] and other streams, but they were still competing against the same big players who had deep pockets.

EI pioneered mobile services, engaging their spectators through SMS services and this operation continued by joining the Claro TV alliance.[13] The alliance allowed them to feature their content on mobile devices through an on-demand service. Mobile broadband reached 114 million cell phone users in 2014 growing from only 4 million in 2008.[14] However, Leo noted that "while SMS was a cash cow, it was fading away. The game going forward is in social media. We've been aggressive in social media and we have huge audience engagement, even bigger than ESPN worldwide."[15]

EI has over 100 thousand paid subscribers—or as EI call them, fans—to their social media content and over one million indirect customers annually. While EI remains innovative and differentiated, its competitors are catching up. EI holds the lead in social media followers, as they have almost twice as many followers on Facebook as Globo does.

EI was an early mover in acquiring sporting rights. In 2004, EI brought the European Champions (soccer) League and the National Basketball Association (NBA) to Brazil. Leo reminisced:

> *We acquired sporting rights that the big players ignored. The Champions League was ideal. Many Brazilian superstars are recruited and play for teams like Real*

[8] https://tvefamosos.uol.com.br/colunas/flavio-ricco/2017/02/03/faturamento-da-record-da-quase-a-soma-de-sbt-band-e-rede-tv.htm. Retrieved December 14, 2016.

[9] http://www.bastidoresdatv.com.br/audiencia/coluna-evolucao-nacional-das-emissoras-de-tv. Retrieved December 14, 2016.

[10] IBOPE Media/ Media Workstation / Media Dados Brasil 2014, Company Information, Mintel.

[11] Ibid.

[12] https://www.engadget.com/2014/07/31/apple-tv-launches-sports-channel-in-brazil/. Retrieved February 2, 2017.

[13] http://www.wirelessfederation.com/news/12667-claro-launches-an-on-demand-mobile-tv-service-minha-tv-brazil. Retrieved February 2, 2017.

[14] Grupo Globo. Media Landscape in Brazil, 2014. http://cfp.mit.edu/events/2014-October-CFP-Slides/CFP_OTA_Incumbent_Oct_2014.pdf. Retrieved February 2, 2017.

[15] Interview with Leonardo Cesar. May 16, 2017.

Madrid. We gave Brazilians a chance to watch their heroes. However, when it came time to renewing these contracts, we now had competition. We had demonstrated there was an audience for these properties and now our deep pocket foes were bidding against us.[16]

Prices for the exclusive rights of tournaments and other sporting events continued to increase and EI's bargaining power was small compared to the deep pockets and dual revenue streams that the big players controlled. Specifically, the larger players not only earned advertising revenue but also revenue from cable and satellite providers to carry their channels. The rights for the Premier League, an English professional league for men's association soccer clubs, increased significantly and had been bought exclusively by ESPN for US$50 million a year through 2019, a huge increase from the US$15 million that ESPN and Fox used to pay.[17] But EI had not been totally shut out of securing important broadcasting rights. EI recently secured the rights for the Champions League for US$45 million per season through 2018, a 180% increase on the previous deal.[18]

Compete or Collaborate with Larger Media Companies

With the cost of securing broadcasting properties escalating and the barriers to entry for EI to secure Pay TV broadcast spectrum meaning that its competitors earned money both from advertising and from Cable providers paying to carry their stations, EI faced a dilemma; should they join forces with a bigger player or try to continue independently? This dilemma was partially solved in 2013, when Turner Broadcasting System (TBS) acquired approximately 30% of EI for BRL$80 M[19] (~US$35 M). Edgar noted at the time:

Having Turner as a strategic partner will significantly amplify our investment capacity and give us access to state-of-the-art content production. It will also provide the opportunity to develop new business models in the dynamic environment of multi-platform content distribution. The size of our dream has just increased considerably with this deal.[20]

In the same year, EI started operations in the northeast region of Brazil.[21] Later in 2014, EI bought rights to broadcast the Northeast Cup and other important tournaments of the Northeast region, and started Esporte Interativo Nordeste channel, reaching a whole new group of spectators.[22]

While EI's growth and reach have been impressive, Edgar and Leo wondered how they could continue to compete with ever escalating rights prices and limited access to PayTV. To not only survive but thrive, EI needed to grow on three main pillars.

1. Grow distribution
2. Maintain and increase content
3. Evolve on other platforms like mobile and Internet

Where would the capital to grow the business come from?

TBS Offer

While EI was considered an innovative leader within the sports broadcasting industry and had proven to have a loyal base of spectators, competition was straining their resources to mimic and develop new features to increase their audiences. EI's success had relied partly on taking advantage of the industry's immaturity, the size of the market, and their leadership in innovation. Now that top players were catching up, EI needed a lot of capital to compete. Recognizing their need for capital, EI sought potential suitors. Hiring Goldman Sachs, EI approached Liberty, Discovery Channel, and Viacom, but the TBS offer seemed to be the best fit. TBS already owned 27% of the company and EI had a strong relationship with them.[23] The acquisition would provide EI the resources to compete, but Edgar and Leo were reluctant to sell their "baby." As Leo said, "EI has been our life's work. If we are acquired by TBS, what happens to our entrepreneurial culture? Would we run EI as a separate division? Would they force us out?"[24]

Leo and Edgar wondered if they could find the capital elsewhere? Could they raise money on the public markets? Edgar and Leo had a lot to consider before deciding whether to accept the TBS offer.

---

[16] Ibid.
[17] http://www.sportspromedia.com/news/espn_gets_exclusive_premier_league_rights_in_brazil. Retrieved February 2, 2017.
[18] TV Sports Markets. The battle for sports rights in America. March 2015. http://www.sportbusiness.com/system/files/tvsm_sportel_briefing_march2015_full.pdf. Retrieved February 2, 2017.
[19] http://www.valor.com.br/international/news/3885390/turner-broadcasting-gets-full-control-esporte-interativo. Retrieved December 14, 2016.
[20] http://www.exchange4media.com/tv/turner-acquires-equity-stake-in-esporte-interativo_51401.html. Retrieved April 13, 2017.
[21] http://www.afaqs.com/news/company_briefs/?id=56368_Turner+Acquires+Equity+Stake+in+Esporte+Interativo. Retrieved April 13, 2017.
[22] https://esportes.yahoo.com/noticias/spt--esporte-interativo-anuncia-transmiss%C3%B5es-da-primeira-rodada-da-copa-do-nordeste-002330348.html?showMessage=1. Retrieved April 13, 2017.
[23] http://natelinha.uol.com.br/noticias/2015/01/23/turner-compra-totalidade-do-canal-esporte-interativo-veja-detalhes-84722.php. Retrieved April 13, 2017.
[24] Interview with Leo Cesar, May 16, 2017.

Exhibit 13.2 Esporte Interativo Income Sheet for 11 years[25]

					Top Sports						
Income Sheet	**2.65**	**2.34**	**2.14**	**1.78**	**2.33**	**1.74**	**1.66**	**1.86**			
in BRL (000)	**2004**	**2005**	**2006**	**2007**	**2008**	**2009**	**2010**	**2011**	**2012**	**2013**	**2014**
Total Revenue	5,729	11,466	13,655	17,626	31,923	33,906	35,633	39,042	47,985	59,577	74,038
Total Expenses	7,624	10,553	12,229	19,511	31,623	34,408	36,722	42,274	54,894	78,991	91,943
EBITA	−1,895	913	1,426	−1,885	301	−502	−1,089	−3,232	−6,909	−19,414	−17,905
Net Profit	−2,624	1,004	4,130	−4,162	−741	−854	−2,249	−4,586	−5,670	−14,610	−14,817

[25] Final 3 (2012–2014) years from *S&P Capital IQ*. https://www.capitaliq.com/CIQDotNet/Financial/CashFlow.aspx?CompanyId=137298337. Retrieved January 10, 2018. Years 2004–2010 are created by case author to illustrate trajectory of growth.

Exhibit 13.2 (continued) Esporte Interativo Cash Flow and Balance Sheet for Three Years[26]

	Cash Flow Statements		
	2012	2013	2014
Net Income	–5.670	–14.610	–14.817
Depreciation & Amort.	0.832	1.181	2.751
Other Operating Activities	–0.592	–5.686	–3.757
Change in Acc. Receivable	–2.015	–2.359	0.531
Change in Acc. Payable	4.011	19.070	–10.160
Change in Inc. Taxes	0.029	–0.516	0.898
Change in Other Net Operating Assets	0.432	–15.093	2.401
Cash from Ops.	**–2.973**	**–18.013**	**–22.153**
Capital Expenditure	–0.809	–11.223	–1.686
Cash Acquisitions			
Divestitures			
Sale (Purchase) of Intangible assets	–0.265	–0.391	–1.552
Invest. in Marketable & Equity Securt.	–12.708	–30.743	19.642
Net (Inc.) Dec. in Loans Originated/Sold			
Other Investing Activities	–1.792		
Cash from Investing	**–15.574**	**–42.357**	**16.404**
Short Term Debt Issued			
Long-Term Debt Issued	9.800	22.595	10.768
Total Debt Issued	9.800	22.595	10.768
Short Term Debt Repaid			
Long-Term Debt Repaid	–4.079	–31.577	–6.051
Total Debt Repaid	–4.079	–31.577	–6.051
Issuance of Common Stock	12.134	85.167	0.203
Repurchase of Common Stock		–15.000	
Total Dividends Paid	–	–	–
Special Dividend Paid			
Other Financing Activities			
Cash from Financing	**17.855**	**61.185**	**4.920**
Net Change in Cash	**–0.692**	**0.815**	**–0.829**

Balance Sheets			
	2012	2013	2014
ASSETS			
Cash And Equivalents	9.482	20.248	6.401
Account Recievables	10.591	14.409	13.340
Other Current Assets	17.395	33.085	14.563
Total Current Assets	37.468	67.742	34.304
Net Property, Plant & Equipment	2.946	13.242	12.626
Long-term Investments	3.552	4.082	5.560
Other Intangibles	0.667	1.068	2.170
Deferred Tax Assets, LT	0.000	11.051	17.507
Other Long-Term Assets	7.643	29.436	37.543
Total Assets	52.276	126.621	109.710
LIABILITIES			
Accounts Payable	3.057	5.152	5.392
Accrued Exp.	1.014	1.310	1.080
Curr. Port. of LT Debt	6.407	2.517	5.327
Curr. Income Taxes Payable	–	0.647	0.652
Unearned Revenue, Current	–	10.142	10.467
Other Current Liabilities	8.641	17.818	12.128
Total Current Liabilities	19.119	37.586	35.046
Long-Term Debt	6.183	7.465	10.745
Other Non-Current Liabilities	1.896	7.130	4.106
Total Liabilities	27.198	52.181	49.897
Common Stock	38.465	111.538	111.752
Retained Earnings	–17.135	–31.745	–46.575
Treasury Stock	–	–21.195	–21.195
Comprehensive Inc. and Other	3.748	15.842	15.831
Total Common Equity	25.078	74.440	59.813
Total Liabilities And Equity	52.276	126.621	109.710

[26] From *S&P Capital IQ*. https://www.capitaliq.com/CIQDotNet/Financial/CashFlow.aspx?CompanyId=137298337. Retrieved January 10, 2018.

Discussion Questions

1. Describe the challenges the team faces as they design and implement their aggressive growth strategy to increase share value.
2. Describe the causes and effects of each of the three fronts of the growth strategy.
3. Does EI have what it takes to continue competing against the giants in terms of resources?
4. Is there something they can do differently?
5. Should the partners sell the company?
6. If they accept the TBS offer, what other considerations (besides price) should the founders negotiate for? How should they broach these topics in the negotiations?

14 Social Entrepreneurship

Photo Credit: © Renphoto/Getty Images

Cheap Energy Drove the Expansion of Suburbia. With Exploding World Populations, Social Entrepreneurship Seeks New Ways of Living and Protecting Resources.

This chapter was written by Brad George and Candida Brush.

Introduction

Just imagine a world where malaria is eradicated, saving 655,000 lives each year[1] and where entrepreneurs in developing countries have access to 5 billion potential individual investors and lenders through access to the Internet. Imagine car-free cities that dramatically reduce respiratory disease, where food is grown locally in vertical farms, and buildings are made of "green concrete" made by capturing the CO_2 emitted from coal or natural gas power plants. By the year 2025, some of these things will be possible due to dramatic changes in technology, demographics, and sociopolitics. Now, further imagine a world where women in the developing world have equal access to education, resulting in a dramatic slowing of population growth and increasing economic well-being. A world where human potential is no longer ignored or marginalized based on one's race or economic background, but maximized for the benefit of all. Imagine people around the world with the ability to afford to meet their basic needs without the need for government handouts or subsidies.

Many of these social, environmental, and technological changes will be possible because of social entrepreneurs. Social entrepreneurs will be essential to creating this new future by solving complex problems, both social problems that have economic consequences and economic problems that have social impact. The intersection of social and economic problems and outcomes is more prevalent today than ever. There is a new world order, characterized by global interconnections and interdependence of business, society, communities, regions, and countries. In particular, technological innovation, decreasing natural resources, shifting demographics, social changes, and political unrest contribute to the complexity of problems as well as the opportunities for solutions (see box below). These changes in the global environment require solutions that meet the needs of many stakeholders and take into account both social and economic outcomes. This is the world of social entrepreneurship.

Turning Tragedy into Opportunity

In recent years the planet has seen an increase in violent weather patterns. The human toll of these events has increased with increasing population. In addition, other factors such as deforestation in Haiti have increased the impact of these events on society. At the same time, global and social media have raised our awareness of these problems and inspired social entrepreneurs to take action.

Realizing that access to clean drinking water is an enormous problem following these events, Tricia Compas-Markman and her professor at Cal Poly, Dr. Tryg Lundquist, invented a personal water treatment bag that can be carried as a backpack and provides individuals with the ability to collect and treat their own water, making it safe to drink. The bags are easy to transport, and one pallet of DayOne Waterbags can produce 26 times more drinking water than one pallet of water bottles. Tricia went on to found Day-One Response to make their invention commercially available.[2]

The Rise in Social Entrepreneurship

With these global changes, it is not surprising that there is a rise in the number of people creating ventures that have both social and economic goals. For example, the recently released report on social entrepreneurship from the Global Entrepreneurship Monitor (GEM) shows that nearly 7% of the population is either currently in the process of trying to start a social venture or is presently running one.[3] And these trends are not limited to new ventures or the United States as this data comes from 58 unique economies across the globe.

This increased emphasis and awareness of sustainability and social purpose creates opportunities for social entrepreneurs to find new ways to achieve these goals. Why is there a rise in social entrepreneurship? In part, it is because the assumptions on which new ventures were created have changed. Until the 1990s, energy was relatively inexpensive, labor was widely available and in some countries, very cheap. Access to credit to start businesses was relatively easy, either through credit cards or small loans, and information to start a business only required a computer, cell phone, and Internet hookup. Further, the drivers of opportunities were usually due to technology or market forces. But, more recently, the drivers of entrepreneurial opportunities have shifted, creating new assumptions and conditions for venture creation. In particular, as global social and environmental issues increasingly affect a larger portion of the world, many drivers of entrepreneurial opportunities have shifted from simply market dynamics to more complex environmental and social catalysts. Wicked problems, those that require multiple stakeholders and complex solutions, are more often driving new ventures.[4] For instance, healthcare in a barrio in a Latin American country might be driven by a configuration of the healthcare system, immigration policies, drug importation, and contaminated water. The solution requires social and economic goals and outcomes. In other words, the traditional business model of identifying the opportunity, analyzing the industry, business planning, raising money from investors, and scaling the business may not be enough. Furthermore, stakeholders are increasingly active and better equipped to communicate and coordinate with each other, making it necessary to consider a wider variety of goals for any organization. As noted by Lee Scott, CEO of Walmart:

> *"We thought we could sit in Bentonville, take care of customers, take care of associates—and the world would leave us alone. It doesn't work that way anymore."*[5]

With the increasing importance and emphasis on social entrepreneurship, it is important for any aspiring entrepreneur to have a basic understanding of some of the key elements involved. In this chapter, we begin by considering the definition of social entrepreneurship and then provide a typology of different types of ventures to illustrate different options for positioning your venture in the social context. We then show how a venture can move across the typology with different variations of social and economic purpose and impact. Finally, we will discuss ways in which you can measure the success of your venture beyond simply economic success.

Popular Definitions of Social Entrepreneurship

Process-Oriented Definitions	**Author(s)**
Social entrepreneurship is an innovative, social value creating activity that can occur within or across the nonprofit, business, or government sectors.	Austin, Stevenson, and Skillern, 2006[6]
The activities and processes undertaken to discover, define, and exploit opportunities in order to enhance social wealth by creating new ventures or managing existing organizations in an innovative manner. Social wealth is defined broadly to include economic, societal, health, and environmental aspects of human welfare.	Zahra, Rawhouser, Bhawe, Neubaum, & Hayton, 2008[7]
Social entrepreneurship is about applying practical, innovative, and sustainable approaches to benefit society in general, with an emphasis on those who are marginalized and poor.	The Schwab Foundation for Social Entrepreneurship[8]
Entrepreneur-centric Definitions	
Social entrepreneurs are the change agents for society, seizing overlooked opportunities by improving systems, inventing new approaches, and creating sustainable solutions to transform society for the better. Social entrepreneurs are constantly searching for superior ways to solve the problems that plague society.	The Skoll Foundation[9]
Social entrepreneurs play the role of change agents in the social sector, by (i) adopting a mission to create and sustain social value (not just private value); (ii) recognizing and relentlessly pursuing new opportunities to serve that mission; (iii) engaging in a process of continuous innovation, adaptation, and learning; (iv) acting boldly without being limited by resources currently in hand; and (v) exhibiting a heightened sense of accountability to the constituencies served and for the outcomes created.	Dees, 1998[10]
Social entrepreneurs are individuals with innovative solutions to society's most pressing social problems.	Ashoka[11]

Social Entrepreneurship Defined

What exactly is social entrepreneurship? The fact is that almost everyone has his or her own personal definition of social entrepreneurship, what it means, what's included, or where it applies. Further, there are multiple terms used, some of which convey the same thing—for instance, green entrepreneurship, social venture, social enterprise, nonprofit start-ups, environmental entrepreneurship, social innovation, sustainability, corporate social responsibility, ethics, social justice, and the list can go on and on.

Definitions of social entrepreneurship vary both in content and approach. Some of the most common definitions are shown in the box on definitions of social entrepreneurship. There are *process-based* definitions that focus on actions such as value creation, opportunity recognition, opportunity exploitation, and resource mobilization. Then there are *entrepreneur-centric* definitions that focus on describing those that engage in social entrepreneurship. For example, Ashoka, a premier organization that invests in social entrepreneurs, defines a social entrepreneur as an individual with innovative solutions to society's most pressing social problems. Similarly, the Skoll Foundation, which also invests in social entrepreneurs for systemic change, identifies social entrepreneurs as society's change agents—pioneers of innovation that benefit humanity. Further confusing this definitional debate is the contextual placement of environmental entrepreneurship, also known as green, sustainable, or ecopreneurship. There are a variety of definitions in this area—environmental entrepreneurship is the early adoption of environmentally responsible practices and products[12] or environmental entrepreneurship is process of discovering, evaluating, and exploiting economic opportunities that are present in environmentally relevant market failures.[13]

A Social Entrepreneurship Typology

To clarify the landscape of social entrepreneurship, we simplify the definitional debate by proposing that the process of entrepreneurship is the same across all entrepreneurial ventures. In other words, the activities of "creating or identifying an opportunity, acquiring the resources and building the team to create something of economic and social value"[14] apply across entrepreneurship of all kinds and contexts, including corporate ventures, family enterprises, technology licensing, franchising, and of course, social ventures. Although the process of entrepreneurship can be thought of as the same across all entrepreneurial ventures, most definitions focus on the fact that social entrepreneurship and social ventures are unique in their purpose and outcomes. Babson Professors Neck, Brush, and Allen map the landscape of entrepreneurship, which reflects the variety of traditional and social ventures.[15] This typology is based on two dimensions, *venture mission* and *impact*.

Every entrepreneurial venture has a mission or purpose. This purpose or reason for being is to solve a problem and almost always has both economic and social/environmental dimensions. The mission is the guide for strategy, policies, and the approach that the firm uses to reach customers, manage employees, and interact in the marketplace.[16] For example, here are three mission statements reflecting varying degrees of social and economic purpose. The first two have primarily an economic or social purpose, whereas the third illustrates a combination of social and economic factors.

> *Our mission to revolutionize car rental distribution globally by reducing distribution costs in the industry while maintaining high margins and increased revenue for our customers and suppliers worldwide. In turn, our aim is become the largest distributor of car rental globally.*[17]
>
> —CarTrawler

> *We work with people and partners to develop innovative and long-lasting solutions to the water, sanitation, and hygiene problems in the developing world. We strive to continually improve, to experiment with promising new ideas, and to leverage resources to multiply our impact.*[18]
>
> —Water for People

Ben & Jerry's is founded on and dedicated to a sustainable corporate concept of linked prosperity. Our mission consists of three interrelated parts:

***Social Mission**: To operate the Company in a way that actively recognizes the central role that business plays in society by initiating innovative ways to improve the quality of life locally, nationally and internationally.*

***Product Mission**: To make, distribute, and sell the finest quality all natural ice cream and euphoric concoctions with a continued commitment to incorporating wholesome, natural ingredients and promoting business practices that respect the Earth and the Environment.*

***Economic Mission**: To operate the Company on a sustainable financial basis of profitable growth, increasing value for our stakeholders and expanding opportunities for development and career growth for our employees.*

Underlying the mission of Ben & Jerry's is the determination to seek new and creative ways of addressing all three parts, while holding a deep respect for individuals inside and outside the company and for the communities of which they are a part.[19]

—Ben & Jerry's

The outcomes of business are both social and economic, but these may vary in the degree to which social and economic performance is measured.[20] For example, the international coffee company Starbucks spends significant time and effort to ensure that the producers of its coffee beans, the farmers in Central America, follow ethical guidelines. They approve and train third-party organizations to ensure the ethical sourcing of their coffee according to C.A.F.E. Practices.[21] Likewise, TisTik, a small jewelry retailer in Cambridge, Massachusetts, works to support artisans from the founder's home country of Mexico and ensure that they are fairly paid for their work. It also sells products made by prisoners in an effort to help them earn money so that they are better able to support themselves upon their release.

There are four specific types of entrepreneurial ventures, plus a hybrid form (Figure 14.1). *Traditional Ventures* (quadrant 1) focus primarily on economic mission and economic impact—financial performance is the primary metric. These ventures have no explicit social mission beyond running a good and profitable business through the exploitation of market-based opportunities. *Social Consequence Ventures* (quadrant 2) are similar to the traditional venture except that many of their practices have social outcomes, yet these social outcomes are not the reason for the firm's existence but it is an outcome of doing business. The popular term, corporate social responsibility, most closely aligns with the Social Consequence Venture. *Social Purpose Ventures* (quadrant 3) are founded on the premise that a social problem will be solved, yet the venture is for-profit and the impact on the market is typically perceived as economic. The fourth type of venture is the *Enterprising Nonprofit* (quadrant 4). *Enterprising Nonprofits* have earned income activities that very much apply the general principles of entrepreneurship.[22] In addition, these organizations focus on growth and economic sustainability and may be funded by venture philanthropists. Finally, there are *hybrid forms* that have a combination of behaviors and characteristics that are found in more than one type. The next section provides examples of each type of venture and their strategies.

Impact \ Venture Mission	Economic	Social
Economic	1. Traditional *Gemvara*	3. Social Purpose *BigBelly Solar* *ThinkLite*
Social	2. Social Consequence *Vera Bradley*	4. Enterprising Nonprofits *Kiva* *One Hen*

Hybrid (center): *Stonyfield Farms*, *Preserve Products*

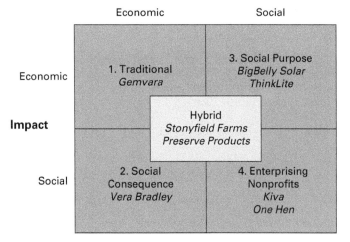

FIGURE 14.1 Typology of Ventures.[23]

1. Traditional Venture

Traditional ventures are those that we are most commonly familiar with. These are firms whose primary mission and outcomes are economic. Although it can be argued that all firms have some social outcomes through the creation of jobs and other benefits, traditional ventures view these as by-products rather than primary outcomes. Their main focus is on maximizing revenues and profits by recognizing and capturing opportunities in the market. An example of this would be Gemvara. The company, founded by two undergraduate students, sells customized jewelry online. The company follows more of a traditional business model, whereby customers design jewelry online and the company creates the design and sends it direct to the customers. As they describe it,

> *Gemvara isn't a traditional jeweler. We have the crazy idea that you deserve jewelry that's uniquely you. That's made only for you We make your design the way you would (if you were a master metal-smith with a lot of time on your hands.)*[24]

The company has a traditional economic goal orientation and measures success based on economic factors such as revenue growth, profitability, and returns on investment.

2. Social Consequence

Social consequence ventures are those that have an economic mission, but also have a firm commitment to social impact, sometimes at the expense of economic returns. Take, for example, Vera Bradley. Guided by founders, Patricia Miller and Barbara Bradley Baekgaard, Vera Bradley has earned a reputation as a leader in the gift industry. While on vacation in March 1982, Patricia and Barbara were awaiting a flight in Atlanta when they noticed a definite lack of feminine-looking luggage. The longtime friends wasted no time in correcting this situation. Within weeks, these dynamic women had created a company, named after Barbara's mother, capable of marketing and manufacturing their cleverly designed products. But, instead of just creating a company, they are also committed to breast cancer research. Each year, Vera Bradley sponsors a golf and tennis tournament, which attracts participants from all across the United States to Fort Wayne, Indiana.

"This is a group effort. To break a million dollars for breast cancer research is truly an accomplishment! Every individual, company or foundation, whether they made a $5 or $20,000 donation should be proud to be part of this success," says Catherine Hill, Vera Bradley Foundation for Breast Cancer Foundation Development Director. Since 1998, the foundation has raised more than $15 million and presently endows a chair in oncology, and a 16-member research team at the Indiana University Cancer Center. As a publicly traded company, Vera Bradley has a strong economic mission, but the impact of their business and their philanthropic activities has strong social outcomes. Retail stores sell products supporting breast cancer, several of their designs are in pink and if purchased, profits go to breast cancer research.

3. Social Purpose Venture

Similar to traditional ventures, social purpose ventures are firms that seek to make profits, but that were started with a specific social mission. The opportunity they are addressing has a specific social or environmental aspect to it. Essentially, they are looking for a profitable means of addressing a social issue. Jim Poss started Big Belly Solar in 2003. He went to Babson College to start a company, specifically an environmental company. While doing an independent study on the trash industry, Jim recognized that trash pickup and hauling represented an enormous waste of fuel and labor and that the burning of that fuel had significant environmental consequences. From there he developed the concept for BigBelly, which is a solar-powered trash compactor for use in rural and urban settings. He founded BigBelly in 2003 with a mission to reduce fossil fuel consumption through innovative cost-saving approaches to inefficient, everyday problems. Today, BigBelly Solar is changing the concept of waste collection by implementing on-site solar compaction systems. The flagship product, the BigBelly, can be found around the world, reducing pollution by cutting down the frequency of trash collection trips.

BigBelly has an explicit social/environmental mission, "We are committed to improving the environment and economies of the world by utilizing an efficient approach," but the venture is a for-profit business, seeking to grow and be financially sustainable. The company believes that it cannot solve social problems without economic success.

"Our BigBelly product was so successful, we changed our name to BigBelly Solar and refocused the company around a central business proposition: Saving fuel is environmentally and fiscally sound." Another example is ThinkLite, a lighting company founded by Enrico Palmiero and Dinesh Wadhwani, two Babson College dorm mates. They got the idea for their company from an ad for an energy-efficient lightbulb. They thought they could sell businesses on going green by putting the bottom-line savings up front, rather than the environmental benefit. ThinkLite manufactures custom energy-saving light systems. Recognizing that high costs often prevent firms from choosing more environmentally friendly products, ThinkLite uses a unique business model that eliminates the up-front costs by having the customer only pay for the energy it saves. Clients typically pay ThinkLite about 40% of the estimated two- to three-year savings. By eliminating the initial purchase and installation costs, ThinkLite reduces the financial risk to its customers. As ThinkLite describes it,

> *Thinklite is a global lighting efficiency company dedicated to helping businesses and governments go green without having to incur the upfront costs and difficulties associated with the change.*[25]

ThinkLite licenses its technologies from private laboratories in Germany, uses components from Korea, designs them in Boston, and assembles them in China. After ThinkLite installs the lighting system, the client's lighting bill drops on average by 50–80%, Wadhwani says. The company has about 100 clients, including AT&T, Kodak, and Babson College, as well as smaller businesses ranging from restaurants to offices. ThinkLite uses different efficient lighting technologies depending on the application, and tailors its design to adapt to the current lighting fixtures and infrastructure already in place, thereby making an effective and efficient retrofit possible for any type of facility.[26] As with BigBelly Solar, ThinkLite has a clear environmental mission, but uses a unique business model to drive economic returns.

4. Enterprising Nonprofit

As mentioned previously, enterprising nonprofits are firms offering products or services that generate revenue and income like other entrepreneurial ventures, but in this case that income is put to use to address a social problem rather than returned to investors or the owners. Sometimes social entrepreneurship is equated with nonprofits, but we contend that ventures that rely strictly on donations for their funding operate under entirely different principals than other entrepreneurial ventures and therefore they are not included in our typology. Enterprising nonprofits are driven by a social mission and focus on social outcomes as measures of their performance, but like other ventures they need to find ways to generate revenue and grow their business as a means of increasing their social impact.

One Hen is a nonprofit organization whose mission is to "provide education resources that engage children." The business was built around a book about a young West African boy who received a small loan to buy a hen, and then became an entrepreneur. He gradually moved from poverty to economic sustainability. It is the story of how the world can be changed, one person, one family, and one community at a time. The founders, including the author, created a board game based on the book to help students learn about business and finance in a fun, creative way. From there the business has expanded into additional enrichment curriculum that includes One Hen microfinance for kids and the Good Garden: Food Security for Kids. One Hen focuses on microfinance, which is the practice of providing financial services—such as working capital loans, insurance, and savings—to those at the poverty level. Such basic financial tools help necessity entrepreneurs to build and run their businesses, stabilize consumption, shield them from risk, and find a way out of poverty. The venture generates revenue through the sales of the book and donations, but provides lessons plans, the board game, and other teaching materials free to educators because the primary focus of their venture is to reach as many children as possible. One Hen is an enterprising nonprofit, an entrepreneurial solution to a serious social problem that is focused on social impact.

Another example would be Kiva. Kiva is an organization that provides microlending around the world. Their mission, "to connect people through lending for the sake of alleviating poverty,"[27] allows individuals to make microloans to working poor to enable them to have a business and work themselves out of poverty. Kiva is the world's first person-to-person microlending Web site, empowering individuals to lend directly to unique entrepreneurs around the globe. The organization works this way—individuals browse entrepreneurs' profiles on the site, choose someone to lend to, and then make a loan, helping a person they have identified to make great strides toward economic independence and improve life for themselves, their family, and their community. The loan period is usually 6–12 months, and the lender can receive email journal updates and track repayments. Then, when the loan is repaid, the lender can lend to someone else in need. Kiva partners with existing expert microfinance institutions. Kiva is a nonprofit with a social mission and clear social impact, but the organization is also enterprising in the way that it innovated how microlending was traditionally organized.

Hybrid Ventures

Hybrid ventures are those that pursue social and economic goals equally—for instance, City Fresh Foods, a retail grocery store in Boston, prides itself on being a minority-owned business that employs minorities from the ethnic community. If you ask the founder, he will say that the social and economic missions are equally important. Therefore, the distinction between social/economic goals and social/economic outcomes is not often clear cut because missions and outcomes are more blended.

Ten Principles of the United Nations Global Compact

Human Rights

- Principle 1: Businesses should support and respect the protection of internationally proclaimed human rights; and
- Principle 2: make sure that they are not complicit in human rights abuses.

Labor

- Principle 3: Businesses should uphold the freedom of association and the effective recognition of the right to collective bargaining;
- Principle 4: the elimination of all forms of forced and compulsory labor;
- Principle 5: the effective abolition of child labor; and
- Principle 6: the elimination of discrimination in respect of employment and occupation.

Environment

- Principle 7: Businesses should support a precautionary approach to environmental challenges;
- Principle 8: undertake initiatives to promote greater environmental responsibility; and
- Principle 9: encourage the development and diffusion of environmentally friendly technologies.

Anticorruption

- Principle 10: Businesses should work against corruption in all its forms, including extortion and bribery.

It is also important to note that customers are increasingly demanding that companies consider human rights, social justice, and environmental issues in their operations. We have seen cases where problems at suppliers for companies like Walmart, Apple, or Nike have led to customer action and damage to their brands. As customers become more aware of companies' global operations through the Internet and social media, companies are increasingly being held accountable to a wider variety of stakeholders. This is a global phenomenon as illustrated by the fact that over 8,000 firms in 161 countries have joined the UN Global Compact since its founding in 2000. Joining the UN Global Compact represents a commitment by firms to align their operations and strategies to ten principles in the areas of human rights, labor, the environment and corruption.

Being a hybrid venture does not require signing onto the UN Global Compact, but it does involve balancing both the mission and the impacts between social and economic objectives. One example of this type of firm would be Stonyfield Farms, a yogurt company in New Hampshire. The venture was started by Samuel Kaymen and Gary Hirshberg in 1983 as a farming school that taught sustainable agricultural practices with the goal of helping family farms and protecting the environment, clearly a social mission. They made and sold yogurt to fund the school. As the yogurt business grew, they focused on building an economically successful and sustainable business that would not only provide profits, but would also have social impact by supporting family farms that used organic practices. This not only gave small family farmers a market for their products, but also encouraged them to use practices that were less harmful to the environment. Stonyfield Farms extended this into its own operations and has clearly stated its economic and social goals in its mission statement:

Our mission: We're committed to healthy food, healthy people, a healthy planet, and healthy business.

- Healthy food. We will craft and offer the most delicious and nourishing organic yogurts and dairy products.
- Healthy people. We will enhance the health and well-being of our consumers and colleagues.
- Healthy planet. We will help protect and restore the planet and promote the viability of family farms.
- Healthy business. We will prove that healthy profits and a healthy planet are not in conflict and that, in fact, dedication to health and sustainability enhances shareholder value. We believe that business must lead the way to a more sustainable future.

The company also pursues social impact through the creation of their Profits for the Planet (PFP) fund, which to date has given over $15 million in support of organizations that care for the earth.[28]

Another example of a hybrid venture would be Preserve Products. Preserve Products was founded by Eric Hudson, who was concerned about the fact that recyclables were not being turned into new products. This meant that additional resources were being used to make products rather than using recycled materials. He was particularly concerned about plastic because roughly 9% of the world's petroleum usage goes into making plastic products. Preserve Products' mission is "to deliver consumer products that offer great looking design, high performance, and are better for the environment than alternative products."[29] The company uses recycled plastic to make consumer products such as toothbrushes, razors, cutting boards, tableware, and other products that it sells. As Eric puts it:

I saw an opportunity in that 45% percent of people recycled and I thought they would have an interest in products made from their efforts.

Although the company's mission is clearly focused on an environmental concern, it is still a for-profit firm that looks for the most profitable and attractive product markets as it develops new lines. At the same time, Preserve also considers environmental and social impacts. It supports the recycling industry through volunteer and community efforts and, in February 2012 it further signaled its commitment to economic and social impacts by joining over 600 other firms in becoming a Certified B Corporation™ (see box on benefit corporations).

The Rise of Benefit Corporations

Although there is increasing interest on both the customer and venture side regarding social missions and social impact, firms in the United States have been limited in the extent to which they can pursue social outcomes due to existing legal frameworks. The Michigan Supreme Court ruled in 1919 that

> *A business corporation is organized and carried on primarily for the profit of the stockholders. The powers of the directors are to be employed for that end. The discretion of directors is to be exercised in the choice of means to attain that end, and does not extend to a change in the end itself, to the reduction of profits, or to the non-distribution of profits among stockholders in order to devote them to other purposes.*

Although this ruling is over 100 years old, it has been reaffirmed in other court rulings as well. As a result, the pursuit of social impact can put its directors at risk of legal action for violation of their fiduciary responsibility if the actions cannot be shown to benefit shareholders. Without legal authority, directors may be hesitant to make decisions to pursue both economic and social impacts, even if this is part of the company's stated mission.

In response to this situation, an enterprising nonprofit named B Lab was launched in 2007. B Lab created a third-party certification system that allowed companies to become Certified Benefit Corporations (or B Corporations). Becoming a Certified B Corporation requires meeting a minimum score on a B Impact Assessment, which looks at the firm's environmental and social impacts. Next, it may be necessary to amend the firm's governing documents to allow directors to consider the impact of its decisions on its employees, customers, suppliers, community, and the environment in addition to its shareholders. However, it is important to note that this may provide some legal protection to directors in states with constituency statutes; those in non-constituency states (including Delaware, where the vast majority of U.S. companies are incorporated) are not permitted to consider the interests of stakeholders other than shareholders. Even still, as of 2019 over 2,700 firms in 150 industries in 60 countries have become Certified B Corporations.

The movement is gathering steam, and to date legislation creating a new legal entity, called a Benefit Corporation, has been passed in seven states and introduced in several others. This legislation generally addresses three major provisions: (1) a corporate purpose to create a material positive impact on society and the environment; (2) expanded fiduciary duties of directors that requires consideration of non-financial interests; and (3) an obligation to report on its overall social and environmental performance as assessed against a comprehensive, credible, independent, and transparent third-party standard.[30]

Choosing Your Venture Type

It should be clear that each of the different types of ventures requires different resources and strategies. Therefore, it might be helpful to look at how the same firm could choose to operate in the different sectors. Let's take the case of Aravind Eye Hospital in India. India has the highest rate of blindness in the world. The approximately 15 million blind people in India represent almost one-third of the total number of blind people worldwide, yet up to 80% of these cases are preventable or treatable, with cataracts being a major cause of unnecessary blindness.[31] Upon reaching the government's mandatory retirement age, Dr. Govindappa Venkataswamy, or Dr. V. as he is often called, decided to start the Aravind Eye Hospital as a means of addressing this issue.

If we consider the ways in which Dr. V. could have positioned this business, it is easy to see how Dr. V., a highly renowned eye surgeon, recognized that the demand for cataract surgery far exceeded the supply. As such, he could have created a firm whose mission was to maximize profits by providing high-quality eye surgery to patients in India. In this situation, his primary mission would be economic, or profit maximization (quadrant1). For example, he might discover that the wealthier people in India are willing to pay the equivalent of $1,000 for the surgery, whereas those in the middle class can only afford $600. His costs per surgery would be $600, a large part of this being the cost of the lenses at $300. The middle class may be a larger market, but would generate less profit per surgery. Alternatively, the upper class is willing and able to pay more, but may represent a smaller number of customers. Each may have different needs or expectations that could further affect operating expenses, so in a purely traditional venture, he might determine which market is most profitably served and then acquire the resources to meet the needs of those customers. Because profitability is the main measure of success, he could look at ways to increase his profit margins through operational efficiencies, cost reductions or by offering higher margin services. Although the business may have a social impact by improving eyesight for some individuals, the primary outcome from the businesses perspective would be economic and would be measured in net profits to the business, with minimal focus on social benefit.

If Dr. V. wanted to have a social mission, his mission statement might be revised to a primary purpose of "eliminating unnecessary blindness for the largest number of people in India" (quadrant 2). However, he would still be looking at economic impact. The difference would be that instead of simply maximizing profits, he is looking at how he can maximize profits given his social mission. In this case, rather than looking at the most profitable segment, he might consider which segment is the largest he could serve profitably. The largest markets are likely to be people with lower incomes, which makes accomplishing his mission more challenging. In this case he would focus on reducing costs, not to increase his profit margins, but to be able to serve a larger segment of the population at the same margins. By lowering his costs, for example, from $600 to $350, he would be able to charge less than $600, making him able to serve a larger portion of the population while maintaining the same margins. He may even decide that he can increase overall profitability further by decreasing his margins and reaching yet a larger group. He might decide that the best way to do this is to cut the cost of the lenses, so he could start a local lens factory that produces lenses for $50. But because he knows that the wealthy are still willing to pay $1,000, he might institute a tiered pricing scale based on ability to pay. This would allow him to maximize profits for the customer segment that can afford to pay and at the same time serve people in lower income brackets by providing the service at a lower cost. In this case, because Dr. V.'s social mission drives the cost/pricing equation for the business, he establishes a price to achieve acceptable profits while helping the largest number of people.

Alternatively, Dr. V. could decide that he is concerned about other causes of blindness in India, not just eyesight lost due to cataracts that his business is focused on. So while the firm maintains its economic mission, it looks to have greater social impact as well by taking a portion of the profits and donating these to charities that focus on nutritional issues for rural children, another source of blindness in India (quadrant 3). Operationally, the business would still be focused on maximizing profits, but the primary impact he is trying to have may be measured by considering the social outcome—the total number of individuals helped, so the business could be considered a social consequence venture in our typology.

If Dr. V. decided that he wanted to be an enterprising nonprofit (quadrant 4), then he would have a social mission and focus on social, rather than economic, impact. In some cases, such as in the United States, this may involve an entirely different legal structure for a venture if it is to be a nonprofit. As an enterprising nonprofit, Dr. V. would have a social mission, like the one stated earlier, but the outcome would be measured in maximum social impact, or people treated, rather than profits or economic returns. Dr. V. might first start by charging only $350 (the cost with the less expensive lenses) to be able to reach the largest number of people. As revenue sources to support his business, he might seek to attract donations or government grants that could pay for some of the operating expenses. In this way, he could lower price even further and reach a larger number of people.

But, what if the people most in need of eye care cannot afford to pay at all? This is a common situation for enterprising nonprofits. Often those that are not being served by society are those on the fringes, in extreme poverty. In this case, the potential to achieve revenues from the market you want most to serve is zero because the product or service needs to be provided for free. This means that the organization must raise money from government sources or philanthropists to pay for costs. Fundraising becomes a major focus of day-to-day activities because it is the source of operating funds. Reliance on volunteers keeps costs down, but this can make management of the venture more challenging. You will often see these types of companies create large boards of directors because a key function of the board becomes raising money for the venture. Although the board still has responsibility for organizational oversight, members are more often chosen for their personal or corporate connections, personal wealth, and/or enthusiasm for the mission of the organization rather than for their management or industry expertise.

This was the situation facing Dr. V. in India. His mission was to eradicate unnecessary blindness across the entire country. Although he had a primary social mission, Dr. V. took an unusual and creative approach, which is an example of a hybrid venture in our typology. He recognized that the poorest in the country could not afford even basic eye care. However, at the same time, he recognized that there was a large population with the ability to pay. As a result, he used a market-based approach similar to a traditional venture to serve the population that was able to pay. He created an assembly-line type process that enabled his doctors to perform 10 times the number of surgeries that doctors in the West performed in order to increase the revenues and profit from the business. However, because he had a social mission, he used these profits to pay for free surgeries for the poor. In other words, by charging $1,000 with a cost of $600, his profits were $400. That meant that for every three paying customers he could use the profits to perform two surgeries for free. So you can see that although his primary mission is social, he also has an economic mission to the extent that it enables him to achieve his social mission. Profit maximization is still important because it allows him to achieve greater social impact. The difference for an enterprising nonprofit is that the increase in revenues is not translated into an increase in profits but rather in operating capital. Another way to think of this is that he is essentially turning his customers into philanthropists by providing a service that they value and are willing to pay for, rather than simply asking them for donations.

So you can see that it is possible to position a venture in different quadrants of Figure 14.1, but that this requires a considerable amount of thought as it will ultimately impact all aspects of the Timmons framework (referred to in Chapter 2)—the nature of the opportunity, the resources required, and team needed to accomplish your mission. However, although you may start in one quadrant, circumstances, strategies, or values can change over time, and you may decide that you are interested in different outcomes or want to change the goals of the organization, and a venture can move between quadrants or, as in the case of Dr. V., occupy a space in more than one quadrant. However, it is important to recognize that movement between quadrants is not simple. Each type of venture has unique characteristics that affect the strategies and resources that the firm needs to succeed.

Measuring Impact

One of the critical things for social entrepreneurs to consider is how they will measure their impact or outcomes. For some ventures it is straightforward. Preserve Products can tell you how much new petroleum was saved by using recycled plastic, BigBelly Solar can determine how many pounds of CO_2 emissions were saved by decreasing the pickup frequency of trash, Aravind Eye Hospital can determine the number of cataract surgeries they performed. Each of these represents measures of the social impact related to their mission. Other social issues are more difficult to quantify. You can provide clean water to children in rural Pakistan, but measuring the impact of this is more difficult.

Social problems are often quite complex, and there are usually a number of social ventures and other organizations trying to address issues such as infant mortality or AIDS through education, health services, treatment, or other means. In these cases it is difficult to say which approaches are responsible for subsequent outcomes. Although it would be nice to think that everyone would be happy if the problem is being diminished, many organizations and companies are fighting for the same resources and often believe very strongly in their particular approach. Further, sometimes reducing the consequences may not solve the problem. For instance, medical problems with dysentery or nutrition in a barrio can be treated with medicine, but it may be that clean water and nutrition education are the causes, therefore the solutions are multipronged. It is important for social ventures to determine performance measures that are related to their objectives and that can be directly tied to their particular activities. You remember that Stonyfield Farms' mission revolved around healthy food, healthy people, healthy planet, and a healthy business. Obviously, it would be difficult to measure the health of people who buy its product and tie that back to its yogurt. Similarly, how would one determine the impact of its business on the health of the planet? However, Stonyfield Farms does realize that any waste from its production has a negative impact on the environment and represents a cost to the business. As such, they measure waste water, plastic, packaging, and other by-products of their production that do not contribute to the health of the food, people, planet, or business. By decreasing this waste, Stonyfield Farms can show that it is making progress toward social goals and it can be directly attributed to its business.

Although it is difficult, more and more companies are realizing that measuring environmental and social impact is increasingly important for their business. As Jeffrey Immelt, former CEO of General Electric, put it,

> *"It's up to us to use our platform to be a good citizen. Because not only is it a nice thing to do, it's a business imperative. If this wasn't good for business, we probably wouldn't do it."*[32]

The need to consider impacts beyond those of traditional measures of growth and profitability has led to interest in what is known as the Triple Bottom Line (TBL). The TBL is a way of measuring success that was originally proposed by John Elkington in his book, *Cannibals with Forks*.[33] Elkington argued that businesses need to look at not only the traditional financial bottom line, but also their impact on the environment and society. The key for succeeding is in finding ways to make "doing good" and "doing well" synonymous, thus avoiding the implied conflict between society and shareholders. For entrepreneurs, this will become increasingly important. As we have discussed in this chapter, companies are no longer able to divorce themselves from the communities with which their products and operations interact. And these communities are becoming increasingly informed and able to mobilize. We are also finally acknowledging that we live on a planet of finite resources and that using up or damaging those resources affects our business as well as our lives. Companies on the coasts are seeing higher insurance premiums as a result of the increasing volatility of weather events, which most scientists believe is related to global climate change and CO_2 emissions. Climate change may also result in a carbon tax or carbon cap and trade system, either of which will impact a new venture's costs, which means that even for ventures with a purely economic mission, the need to understand how they interact with society and the environment is important. And as the saying goes, you measure what you care about and you care about what you measure.

So how do you go about deciding what to measure? First, you need to think about the way in which your business touches society and the environment. What communities do your operations affect? In what way? What materials are used in your products? Where do they come from, and where do they go? Does your business produce waste products or byproducts? Where do these go and how do they affect the environment? It is important to remember that these not only represent costs or potential areas for improvement, but also potential liabilities if not measured and addressed (just ask Walmart, Nike, or Apple). Figure 14.2 gives some general examples of social and environmental impacts that ventures might consider measuring, but because every venture interacts with the environment and society in a different way and has different objectives based on its mission, it is impossible for us to provide an exhaustive list. Ultimately, it is up to the entrepreneur to determine what measure of performance and impact she needs to keep track of to best achieve her mission in the long run.

Economic	Environmental	Social
Sales	Air quality	Labor practices
Profits, ROI	Water quality	Community impacts
Taxes paid	Energy usage	Human rights
Jobs created	Waste produced	Product responsibility

FIGURE 14.2 Sample Impacts.[34]

CONCLUSION

It should be clear from this chapter that social entrepreneurs have the opportunity to enact enormous change in a variety of ways. In addition to having either a social or economic mission, entrepreneurs need to think about their impacts and how they will measure them. We presented a typology that included what we called "traditional ventures," but one might argue that this type of venture, once the most dominant in entrepreneurship, may become a thing of the past. As we illustrated, firms are increasingly being forced to consider, measure, and report their performance with regard to social impacts as well as economic returns, and leading companies are increasingly taking on a hybrid forms, illustrating the ability to move between forms. However, the entrepreneur should take the time early on to consider the type of venture he wants to have, as changing forms can be difficult and costly. It is important to recognize the cost and resource trade-offs that determine how your venture is positioned in the market.

Entrepreneurship is about doing different things or doing things differently. As Albert Einstein said,

> *We can't solve problems by using the same kind of thinking we used when we created them.*

The world is looking for answers to a wide range of social and environmental issues that have resulted from our current thinking. We believe it is up to social entrepreneurs to find the new way of thinking that will be needed to solve these problems and create a better tomorrow.

YOUR OPPORTUNITY JOURNAL

Reflection Point	Your Thoughts...
1. What social problems are of particular interest to you?	
2. What are some of the root causes of these problems, and in what ways might these be addressed?	
3. What type of venture would you want to create? Do you want to have primarily a social mission or an economic mission? Why?	
4. If you are considering a new venture, how does it interact with the social problems you are concerned with? What are the ways in which your venture could have impact on these problems?	
5. In what other ways does your venture impact society and the environment?	
6. Think about how you might measure your venture's social impact. What can you directly attribute to your business? How would you measure it and what does this measure mean?	
7. What resources would you need to have or acquire to have the type of venture you envision in terms of both mission and impact?	
8. Does it give you information you can act on to improve your impact?	

WEB EXERCISE

Think about companies you admire or aspire to be similar to. Go to two or three websites and look at their missions. Is their mission primarily economic, social, or both? Next, see if you can find how each one reports its performance. If it is a public company, this can often be found by going to the "Investor" link on the Web page and looking at the annual report. For nonprofits or other companies this can often be found under the "About" link. What is each one reporting? Are these consistent with the mission? If not, why not? What do you think each company should report? Use this information to make a list of possible ways in which you can measure performance for your own venture and describe how this information will tell you whether you are achieving your mission.

NOTES

1. www.who.int/malaria/world_malaria_report_2011/WMR2011_factsheet.pdf.
2. www.dayoneresponse.com.
3. Bosma, N., et al. 2016. *Global Entrepreneurship Monitor Special Topic Report: Social Entrepreneurship*. Global Entrepreneurship Research Association.
4. Buchanan, R. 1992. *Wicked problems in design thinking*, MIT Press, 8:2, 1–25.
5. The Debate over Doing Good, *Business Week*, Aug. 15, 2005, p. 76.
6. Austin, J., Stevenson, H., & WeiSkillern, J. 2006. Social and Commercial Entrepreneurship: Same, Different, or Both? *Entrepreneurship Theory & Practice*, January: 1–22.
7. Zahra, S. A., Rawhouser, H. N., Bhawe, N., Neubaum, D. O. and Hayton, J. C. 2008. Globalization of Social Entrepreneurship Opportunities. *Strategic Entrepreneurship Journal* 2(2): 117–131.
8. www.schwabfound.org/sf/SocialEntrepreneurs/Whatisasocialentrepreneur/index.htm.
9. www.skollfoundation.org/about/skollawards/skoll-award-for-social-entrepreneurship-glossary.
10. Dees, G. 1998. *The Meaning of Social Entrepreneurship*, p. 4. (www.caseatduke.org/documents/dees_SE.pdf).
11. https://www.ashoka.org/social_entrepreneur.
12. Schaper, M. 2002. *The Essence of Ecopreneurship*. Saltaire, UK: Greenleaf Publishing, pp. 26–38.
13. Dean, T. J., & McMullen, J. S., 2007. Toward a Theory of Sustainable Entrepreneurship: Reducing Environmental Degradation through Entrepreneurial Action. *Journal of Business Venturing*, 22: 50–76.
14. Neck, H., Brush, C. & Allen, E. 2009. The Landscape of Social Entrepreneurship. *Business Horizons*, 52:13.
15. Ibid., pp. 13–19.
16. Andrews, K. 1971. *The Concept of Strategy*. Homewood, IL: Irwin.
17. www.cartrawler.com/about/cartrawlergoals.php.
18. www.waterforpeople.org/about/mission-and-vision.
19. www.benjerry.com/activism/mission-statement.
20. Mair, J., & Marti, I. 2006. Social Entrepreneurship Research: A Source of Explanation, Prediction, and Delight. *Journal of World Business*, 41: 36–44.
21. C.A.F.E. Practices ensure that Starbucks is sourcing sustainably grown and processed coffee by evaluating the economic, social, and environmental aspects of coffee production. These aspects are measured against a defined set of criteria detailed in the C.A.F.E. Practices Evaluation Guidelines. According to an impact study performed by Conservation International, C.A.F.E. Practices have significantly benefited more than one million workers employed by participating farms. www.scsglobalservices.com/starbuckscafe-practices.
22. Dees, G. 1998. The Meaning of Social Entrepreneurship, p. 4. (www.caseat duke.org/documents/dees_SE.pdf). Massarsky, Cynthia W. and Beinhecker, Samantha L. *Enterprising Nonprofits: Revenue Generation in the Nonprofit Sector*, Yale School of Management, The Goldman Sachs Foundation Partnership on Nonprofit Ventures, 2002.
23. Neck, H., Brush, C., & Allen, E. 2009. The Landscape of Social Entrepreneurship. *Business Horizons*, 52:13.
24. www.gemvara.com/About-Us/pages/v/about.
25. www.thinklite.com/index.htm.
26. www.babson.edu/news-events/babsonnews/Pages/10-28-11Babson-Startup-ThinkLite-Ranked-2-Among-Bloomberg-Businessweek%E2%80%99s-America%E2%80%99s-Best-Young-Entrepreneurs-2011.aspx.
27. www.kiva.org/about.
28. www.stonyfield.com.
29. www.preserveproducts.com/aboutus/index.html.
30. Clark, W. H., Jr. 2012. "*The Need and Rationale for the Benefit Corporation: Why It Is the Legal Form that Best Addresses the Needs of Social Entrepreneurs, Investors, and, Ultimately, the Public*." White paper available at http://benefitcorp.net/for-attorneys/benefit-corp-white-paper.
31. www.blindfoundation.org/facts.html.
32. Quoted in "Money and Morals at GE," by Marc Gunther, *Fortune*, Nov. 15, 2004, p. 176.
33. Elkington, J. *Cannibals with Forks*. Capstone Publishing Ltd., 1997.
34. Savitz, A. W. & Weber, K. *The Triple Bottom Line*. San Francisco: Jossey-Bass, 2006.

Case | InnerCity Weightlifting[1]

I started realizing there are things that I need to do that are more important than gangbanging and wasting my life in the streets. Even though I felt stuck in it. Even though there were 10 dudes that wanted to kill me and there was no way for me to get out of the streets. I started realizing there is more important things that need to be done. I have a daughter. My father wasn't in my life and maybe if my father was in my life it would be different. If I die, then who is the man that is going to be in her life? I started looking at my family through the generations. Nobody in my family owns a house. They have been living in the poor section of the city. They don't even have an income. Nobody in my family even had a car. I was the first one to own a car. I want to break that cycle for my family. I want to own a house so that my daughter, when I leave, can take over the house and get things going. I want to get my daughter away from living in those parts of the city. I don't want her around that.[2]

~ Joe Sierra, ICW trainer and former InnerCity Weightlifting student[3]

Section 1: Is the Time Right to Expand to a Second City?

Jon Feinman, founder and executive director of InnerCity Weightlifting (ICW), was working out in one of ICW's Boston-area gyms as he did every day. ICW is a nonprofit focused on reducing recidivism by giving young men who are active in the streets the tools to turn their lives around. Jon was proud that ICW was having a profound impact on the lives of its students like Joe. Jon wanted to grow ICW so it could impact more young people involved in gangs and the streets. He was contemplating a potential major growth initiative: should ICW expand beyond Boston? He had planned to expand to other cities since founding ICW, and he and the board had chosen Philadelphia as a possible next location.

There are approximately 1,150,000 gang members in the United States distributed among 24,250 gangs, some local and some national.[4] ICW's unique program helps transform the most hardened gang members in Boston into a better life outside of gangs. Jon wondered whether ICW's high-touch model could scale. Could other cities replicate the Boston model? He wondered if ICW worked because the team really understood Boston. He worried that other cities and gangs might be very different and that the model might not fit elsewhere. As CEO of a nonprofit, Jon knew there was a lot riding on the decision. While growing ICW into a national model was his dream, expansion posed several risks, especially for the financial well-being of his company. There were lives on the line if ICW did not work in Philadelphia; worse, a misstep could potentially set the Boston operation back by damaging ICW's financial well-being and reputation. The Philadelphia move might be successful, but it could put a crushing burden on the lean management team if other cities increased pressure on ICW to expand there.

ICW works to reduce street violence and recidivism of the highest-risk youth in the city. One percent of Boston's youth is responsible for over 50% of the city's gun violence.[5] This one percent is about 400 people who live mostly in the neighborhoods of Roxbury, Dorchester, and Mission Hill. This list of 400 people, called the PACT list, includes those most likely to kill or be killed, identified by the Boston Police in its Partnership Advancing Communities Together program for reducing street violence in Boston.[6] Most of these individuals are affiliated with a gang and have done significant jail time. The Boston Police call them "high-impact players."[7] ICW identifies and recruits this group of young people to be their students.

ICW helps its students turn their lives around by building trust, instilling hope, and providing opportunity. Not many organizations are willing to work with this population, but Jon believes transforming even a few gang members will have huge benefits not only for the students, but also for the greater Boston community. He believes the model will bring systemic change by reducing violence and changing society's perceptions of the demographic that makes up his student population.

Jon always had the goal of expanding from Boston to other high-profile cities to achieve national systemic change. He feels that after almost eight years of operation, now is the time. He knows there is great demand for ICW to expand to other cities.

[1] This case was prepared by Sophia Zacharakis, Research Assistant at Babson College; Andrew Zacharakis, Professor of Entrepreneurship at Babson College; and Mary Gale, Senior Lecturer of Entrepreneurship at Babson College, with support from the John H. Muller, Jr. Chair in Entrepreneurship. *Copyright © 2018 Babson College.*

[2] Case interview with Joe Sierra, July 27, 2017.

[3] Participants progressing through InnerCity Weightlifting's program are called students.

[4] "Gang Member Statistics," *Statistic Brain*, Statistic Brain Research Institute, May 24, 2017.

[5] Case interview with Jon Feinman, June 22, 2017.

[6] "The Boston PACT Program," Mayor Thomas Menino, Justice Department, May 30, 2014, https://www.justice.gov/sites/default/files/usao-ma/legacy/2014/05/30/BostonPACT.pdf, accessed August 1, 2017.

[7] "Our Mission," InnerCity Weightlifting, https://www.innercityweightlifting.org/about1-c91a, accessed August 8, 2017.

When ESPN ran a short documentary in 2013, the ICW server crashed twice as people from all over the country and around the world posted messages and sent e-mails requesting information about how to start a chapter in their city. But big unanswered questions remain: is ICW ready for expansion? Will Jon's model be sustainable in another city? Will Philadelphia, the city chosen for expansion, have the same positive reaction as Boston? Can ICW work without Jon there at every step?

Jon knows the risk is great. While expansion could certainly transform more lives in more places, if it is not executed properly, it could also cause ICW to lose its intimate mode of operation, arguably the biggest factor for current success. Furthermore, failure in Philadelphia risks hurting ICW beyond repair, thus closing the doors not only to Philadelphia's high-impact players but also to ICW students in Boston as well. Without ICW, many might not have any option but to turn back to the streets for survival. And on the streets, the six-month outlook for these young men is jail or death.

The Beginnings of a Social Entrepreneur

Jon grew up in Amherst, Massachusetts, a small, wealthy, suburban town that provided him with plenty of opportunities. "I grew up in a family and community with connections and opportunity. I went to college because everyone I knew went to college. That was really my only focus growing up. After working with ICW students, I recognize how much I took for granted."[8]

College was Jon's primary focus. He figured he would graduate, start a career and a family of his own, and live the American dream like his parents and all the people he grew up with. With the luxury of being able to choose from various extracurricular activities, Jon took up many hobbies, including soccer. He excelled at soccer, and after graduating from high school, he was recruited to play for Bryant University. At 5′8″ and 160 pounds, Jon had always been an undersized athlete. To compete at the collegiate level, he started taking weightlifting very seriously. His dedication to weightlifting throughout his undergraduate years led him to certification and his first job as a personal trainer.

Jon started studying to be a personal trainer after college. He enjoyed the science behind the sport and later, the relationships he built with his clients. During the first year after graduation, Jon's main commitment was his work with the AmeriCorps program, Athletes in Service in America.[9] He was stationed at a kindergarten through eighth grade school in East Boston, and his role was to involve kids in after-school sports programs.

Jon was drawn to a group of young people associated with one of the nation's most violent gangs, MS-13. Other counselors told him not to bother with this group—they were too dangerous and definitely didn't care enough to change—but Jon was determined to make contact and build a connection. At first they paid him little notice; they were suspicious of Jon as he self-described himself as the "small white kid from Amherst Mass." The kids, mostly of color from the inner city of Boston, didn't relate to Jon. One day while the boys were playing soccer, Jon saw his opportunity. After showing them some tricks, Jon earned their attention. He started to break through the trust barrier by playing soccer and lifting weights with them. During this time, he got to know them for who they were as people beyond their MS-13 label and learned from them something that forever changed his perspective.

> *I recognized what I believed to be confusion between lack of care and lack of hope. People call them thugs, gang members, criminals, and whatever other word they want to throw out to basically write them off, because they think they don't care and that you can't really do much for someone who doesn't care. What I saw was very different. No one wants to end up dead or in jail, and yet they are willing to lose their life to a bullet or jail to be there for each other, to care for each other. I saw this really genuine form of care, and I saw what was lacking was not care, but hope. That realization was empowering because hope is something that I felt I could do something about, and more importantly, we as a society could do something about.*[10]

Spending time with the young people eventually helped Jon discover what drove them to the streets. They lacked hope and opportunity and a network to access opportunity. These young people only have the support of their fellow gang members, which leads to gang activity and street violence. If the lack of hope and opportunity led to violence, what is it that drains hope and opportunity?

> *I started to recognize the system. [Our students are] born into families and communities that are segregated and isolated. Unlike myself, they have to worry about rent, they have to worry about food, they have to worry about clothes. There's no way that school can be their only focus. So they turn to the streets to solve the real challenges that they face today, because they don't get to see tomorrow*

[8] Case interview with Jon Feinman, June 22, 2017.

[9] AmeriCorps recruits Americans, often students who've just graduated from college, to work in underprivileged communities. Its mission is to help others and meet critical needs in the community.

[10] Case interview with Jon Feinman, June 22, 2017.

unless they take care of those short-term obstacles that are in their way. Rather than leveraging an education to find a meaningful career, they find themselves in jail. They come out more segregated and more isolated. All along the way everyone calls them a bad decision-maker, when in reality, they don't have a single good option to choose from. This whole system gets perpetuated every time someone like myself during that year [in AmeriCorps] was told stay away from them: "Don't cross this street; it's dangerous over there." That very avoidance creates segregated and isolated pockets of communities which leads to a lack of resources, lack of opportunity, inequality, poverty, and the need for the streets in the first place, which manifests itself in violence.[11]

Jon had always been considered a good decision-maker by society, but he realized this was because he only ever had good options to choose from. On the other hand, society looks down on his students' decisions and punishes them through the criminal justice system. While these decisions might lead to actions that break the law, the decisions themselves are not illogical. Their decision-making process isn't what is flawed, it is their options, limited by a society that has written them off. Getting to know these young men helped Jon start to recognize the system of segregation and isolation that left this population with only bad options. Thus, leading to street violence with death or jail as the most likely outcomes.

Many of Jon's realizations took place during his time in AmeriCorps, but it took him a while to develop those ideas and start thinking of a solution. When Jon's year in AmeriCorps ended, his work as a personal trainer expanded from a side gig to his full-time job. After another year or two of working for himself as a trainer, at age 24, he had a full schedule of clients and a comfortable salary. Jon was uneasy with the fact that he had reached this top level of success in the field at such a young age. He knew he could continue like this and lead a comfortable life, but he wasn't satisfied. Jon decided to pursue the idea that he had been contemplating since AmeriCorps.

The Founding Story of ICW

There isn't one moment that Jon can point to as *the* moment when the idea for ICW came to him. Rather, the idea started forming as a combination of his life experiences and his feeling of being stuck in a career at age 24. While Jon was talking to one of his personal training clients about his concerns, he realized he could use his trainer skillset to make a social impact. Although he had lost contact with them, Jon had not forgotten about the young people he met during AmeriCorps. He had enjoyed working with them and was still passionate about making an impact on their lives. Using sports and lifting had worked to connect with them then, so why couldn't it work again?

Once the idea that would become ICW started forming in his head, Jon decided to take a big risk. He put himself in debt to go to Babson College to get his MBA. To this day, Jon says it was one of the best decisions of his life. Going to school for an MBA is what allowed his idea to grow. Jon started piloting his business plan while at Babson. He was able to use an acquaintance's gym space for two hours, three days a week, to start working with their target students. While in his pilot period, Jon received a piece of criticism that led to the basic approach for running ICW today. Jon was told that he had no idea what he was doing, and he agreed. "Since I had no clue what I was doing, I really only had one option. To LISTEN. I think too often, especially in the nonprofit sector, we try to solve problems from our own privileged perspective, that somehow if we can get kids onto the path we followed, their lives will be better—it worked for me, so it should work for everyone else. This is flawed logic."[12]

Jon started listening to his students and realized his original business plan wasn't going to work for ICW's target population. Originally, Jon thought he would reduce violence in the target population by using weightlifting to get kids into the Olympics or win college athletic scholarships. After listening to the students he was working with, Jon soon realized his original idea was deeply flawed. "Knowing this was the population we were working with and reducing violence was our end goal, there's probably a million different ways to get there. To succeed, we needed to let the students define their own path and shape the organization off that. Like I said, I don't know what they have to go through on a day-to-day basis."[13]

It turns out, just getting these young men in the gym, off the streets, lifting together and building a community not based on violence, was much more realistic, effective, and far-reaching in impact than trying to get them college scholarships or Olympic glory. This change in philosophy led Jon to make adjustments, including letting go of some of his original coaches because they were too focused on the lifting and not on the connection and community aspect that ICW needed to center around. Jon now viewed the gym and weightlifting as a "hook" to attract his target population. He built a community and support system to accomplish the larger mission of helping his students redirect

[11] Ibid.

[12] Ibid.

[13] Ibid.

their lives. After this change in model, ICW really started to grow into what it is today.

How ICW Works

InnerCity Weightlifting's entire philosophy is centered around a promise. "What this organization is about, is that we don't promise to solve [our students'] short-term problems, because they are too severe and honestly, we can't hope to fix them. What we do promise and commit to is being by their side so they don't have to solve these problems alone. That became pretty powerful."[14] As Joe Sierra, a student turned trainer through ICW's program notes:

> *When I talk to these kids, some of them have been shot already. I ask them what they want to be when they grow up, and they don't even have an answer. They shrug their shoulders. Some of them say they want to move bricks, you know kilos of cocaine or heroin. They think they're going to be Pablo Escobar. "You are not going to be Pablo Escobar." I try to help them. I tell them what I've been through, what I've seen.*[15]

Working individually with each person allows ICW to help students discover another way to live their lives. The incarceration recidivism rate for ICW's target population before starting the program is 80%. Among those students who continue through the program long enough to develop hope and real alternatives, the rate drops to 8.2%.[16] One of the reasons ICW is effective in reducing these rates is that they do not give up on their students. They do not require students to make it through all its stages consecutively or to "graduate" from the program. Many students are arrested, shot, or stabbed at different points while in the program; but Jon and his staff stand by their promise to help their students no matter what—visiting them in prison or in the hospital, going to court appearances, and writing to them while they are behind bars. ICW also provides formal weightlifting training so that students may achieve certification for a career as a weight trainer. The program also helps students who did not finish high school to earn a GED. This promise applies to students in all stages of the program. Once ICW reaches out to someone, the staff is there for that student no matter what. Cali, an ICW student who has started his own personal training program and attends Bunker Hill Community College, agrees with this philosophy. "At the end of the day, all anyone around here can do is do what they can do for these kids. Do what you can do and don't ever give up on these kids."[17]

ICW has developed four main sequential stages that students work through: Trust, Hope, Social Capital, and finally Economic Mobility. Originally, ICW sought students through court referrals, street workers, and juvenile detention centers. Now, ICW has grown enough in Boston that it only needs to rely on word-of-mouth, their current students bringing friends to the program. ICW works hard to ensure they are only admitting students who are truly in their target demographic, which is that 1% who are most susceptible to street violence. Most of ICW students have shot, been shot, done significant time in jail, and come from a family that makes less than $10,000 a year. If someone is referred to ICW who is not in this demographic, ICW refers them to another program.

ICW determines if a potential student is part of their target demographic during an extensive screening process. To maintain the safety and security of everyone inside the gym, it is imperative that ICW not mix rival gangs. During the screening process, ICW must establish the student's identity within gang dynamics to ensure that it is safe to bring them into the gym.

> *We recognize the fact that we just don't know. We've developed a process that takes everything off-site, and we don't give away our locations publicly. We incorporate our students in that process. If we don't know the person, our next step is to ask the people we are working with: do you know this person? Do you know this group? Our own people actually have a big say in whether or not that person ends up at the gym, and it allows us to make sure we are keeping everything safe even before we know the new candidate.*[18]

Angel LaCourt, who has been with the program for six years and is now a certified trainer and student intake coordinator, laughed when asked about his own screening process.

> *My friend brought me to the gym, and I met Jon for the first time. But, there was a whole process before I met Jon that took place without me even knowing. My boy [friend] asked Jon if I could come before he even asked me to come. Someone did intake with me, and there was a whole process and it was just crazy the way it worked. I was like "S*** when was I going to be notified that this was going on?" Jon didn't tell me until a couple months later when I asked "How come I didn't go through that [intake process]?" and he was like "You did, you*

[14] Ibid.
[15] Case interview with Joe Sierra, July 27, 2017.
[16] Case interview with Jon Feinman, June 22, 2017.
[17] Case interview with Jarreau "Cali" Pelote, July 25, 2017.
[18] Case interview with Jon Feinman, June 22, 2017.

just didn't know it happened," and I was like "That's cool"... I understood why too, because it was for everyone's safety.[19]

In his current role as student intake coordinator, Angel helps with the screening process by reaching out to potential students, talking to them, and learning about their background and goals.

The initial stage, Trust, takes place mostly outside of the gym as part of the screening process. Within the first stage, ICW measures a student's success through his willingness to communicate. The first big step is to get their phone number, which already requires preliminary trust from the student. Then ICW looks at the communication ratio they have with each student. Does the student call or text back when ICW reaches out? At a minimum, ICW likes to have at least eight points of contact within a month with each student. This can be by phone or text, appearance at the gym, or a car ride to and from the gym. During this stage, ICW staff is building trust with students by listening to them and breaking down small barriers that are preventing them from coming into the gym.

Once you start listening, you hear that someone is actually interested, but they can't get here safely. So I say, "Well, I'll pick you up tomorrow if you want." As you listen, you start hearing how someone wants to come to the gym and work out, but they don't have a pair of shorts. Well, we can buy you a pair of shorts. Someone might come here and, more often than not, they haven't eaten that day – let's go out for lunch. A lot of our guys, they get out of jail, and they don't have an ID and yet they'll still have probation fees and they need a job, but they can't get a job without an ID and they don't have any money. We take them and buy the ID for them. By listening, you start to solve problems and earn someone's trust in these seemingly simple ways, which are actually pretty profound. If you can't pay your probation fees and you can't get a job, you are left with one choice: go back to the streets and solve your problems the way know how.[20]

Stage two, Hope, is all about engagement in the gym. Success in the second stage is eight engagements beyond just small conversation. Once students start coming to the gym regularly and are comfortable at ICW, they start to have hope that long-term goals are possible. Then they move on to the third stage. As Cali notes, "You have to go through a process that allows you to grow through the levels. The majority of that process is pretty much dedication and just showing up and really being disciplined about learning about fitness, doing some of the exercises yourself, learning about program design, and stuff like that. I took it seriously coming through the door."[21]

Stage three, Social Capital, is where ICW's in-house personal trainer training comes into play. The end goal for this stage is making meaningful connections and building genuine relationships with clients to bridge social capital across socioeconomic classes. This is when student networks really start to grow; they are training clients who come from six or seven figure backgrounds, Boston area professionals who work in finance or large corporations. Building these relationships eventually connects students to opportunities either directly from or within the clients' extensive networks. Furthermore, all ICW students have access to everyone and everything in ICW. This provides all students with a network, no matter their stage or whether they have built a personal training clientele. For example, Jon found out that Mack, one of ICW's students, was interested in consulting. Jon knew someone else's client who worked for a consulting firm, and they set up an opportunity for Mack to shadow someone at this company. Opportunities like these eventually lead students to potential jobs. While these connections with clientele from the opposite socioeconomic background impact students greatly, clients are affected as well. ICW sends out surveys to its clients, and many say their perspective on this population has changed. Clients consider many of the trainers to be friends and vice versa. When asked about his relationships with his clients, Cali lit up. "Oh my clients?! Me and my clients are homies! Yeah, we're good, we're friends!"[22]

Many clients meet with their student trainers outside of the gym, inviting them to dinner or some other activity. The gap between these two populations begins to be bridged and an altered, positive perception starts to spread. "To be successful, we always need high-net-worth clients to come. We run corporate training programs to try to bridge the gap between people of wealth and people of poverty. If they don't come together, you can't grow—we need them to grow, they need us to grow—we can't do it separately."[23]

The last stage, Economic Mobility, is what ICW defines as earning over $30,000 a year. In this stage, success is measured by how much money students are making. ICW knows how much students still in the program are earning and can estimate what students with jobs outside the organization are making. In addition to income and long-term employment, ICW also looks at recidivism rates and life stability as measures of success.

[19] Case interview with Angel LaCourt, July 6, 2017.

[20] Case interview with Jon Feinman, June 22, 2017.

[21] Case interview with Jarreau "Cali" Pelote, July 25, 2017.

[22] Ibid.

[23] Case interview with Reggie Talbert, June 22, 2017.

During this stage, ICW hopes students will start to make enough money to think more about their future, instead of having to spend all their time, energy, and money on the problems of today. Joe Sierra, who has been with ICW for nearly six years, is now on salary at ICW as a trainer and is saving to buy a house.

That's my focus on life right now, is me trying to get to where I want to get to, I mean I have three jobs, I'm on salary here at InnerCity Weightlifting because I have been with them for so long. I train anywhere from 40 to 60 clients on top of what I make. I work at another gym. And then I also work at a Dorchester brewery where I also get paid well. I'm going good. I meet people in college that don't even make the money that I make. I travel a lot. Every month or two. I have 20 stamps in my passport.[24]

ICW also looks at the critical points when students reach a bump in the road. Do they have a new network that can support them through it, or do they have to return to their old gang networks? The recidivism rate of students who reach stage four is less than 8.2%.[25] For students who leave ICW before completing all the stages for another job opportunity, data shows they are more likely to go back to jail.

All students do not study to become personal trainers, as this is not the career for everyone; but regardless, all ICW students are working to become ICW certified. The ICW certification requires basic skills to run a client through a training session. Working toward this certification adds structure to a student's program as they work through stages two and three. It also allows for a sense of accomplishment when completed and inspires students to pursue a career in personal training and study for an official personal training certification. Some, like Cali, know right away that personal training is for them. "After four to six months, I was running my own show. Even though I represent ICW, I pretty much go out there and get my own clients. I have been doing that for probably about a year now."[26]

Other students take to it more slowly. Angel admitted that at the beginning, personal training was terrible for him because it was hard to get clients. It took two years for him to reach a point where his schedule was full. While Angel enjoys personal training, he wants to do something else for ICW in the future. "I definitely see myself with ICW, but doing something just a little bit different one day. [Eventually,] I want to open up an InnerCity Weightlifting Gym myself, just to give back and show dudes that there is hope. Because Jon gave a lot of us hope when we thought there wasn't any."[27]

Table C14.1 Key Performance Indicators 2017

	Goal	Notes
Fundraising	3.5–5 million	
Student Enrollment	90 students total (at 58)	Stages 2–4 + Stage 1 Priority Targets
Individual Training	760 sessions/month	Doubles current trend
Corporate Training	80 sessions/month	
Education	30 students ICW certified	2x current certifications
Placement	20 new job placements for students	

Source: ICW Business Plan (used with permission).

While ICW uses stages to track success of its students, they have a set of key performance indicators (KPIs) that allow them to track success of the organization as a whole. Table C14.1 identifies ICW's KPIs.

Todd Millay, the president of ICW's board, notes:

One challenge is how do we measure success? How do we know if this is working or not? How does a donor know that this has been a good investment relative to the other things they could've done? I think that is a really hard question. We've developed a variety of metrics that we use to measure success. I think we've done a better job measuring success on the student side, the original narrow purpose of ICW. It is very challenging to measure the broader sense of that. What impact have we had on all the clients that have come into our gym? When they see a scary-looking African American guy walking down the street, do they cross the street? Do they make an assumption about somebody? All these little things that help to ingrain the isolation and segregation of this population, are we ameliorating those or not? If we are, that is tremendously important.[28]

The ICW team is still figuring out how to best measure changes in client attitudes, but hopes that it will eventually show the national impact and systemic change that ICW promotes.

ICW's first gym location is in Dorchester. When the client training aspect of the program began to grow, ICW and the board began to believe that expansion to a second location

[24] Case interview with Joe Sierra, July 27, 2017.
[25] Case interview with Jon Feinman, June 22, 2017.
[26] Case interview with Jarreau "Cali" Pelote, July 25, 2017.
[27] Case interview with Angel LaCourt, July 6, 2017.
[28] Case interview with Todd Millay, July 21, 2017.

would help students interact with high-net-worth clients. Todd Millay understood the need for growth from the unique perspective of both client and now ICW's board chair.

I think Dorchester is awesome. I love the gym, I love going there, but it can be intimidating. I've had several people that I was surprised were just unwilling to go to that gym. People that I didn't think of as particularly timid, people who I thought would really like the experience, but just the idea of going down to Dorchester, going through a metal detector, it was intimidating. Half of ICW's mission is focused on not only the students, but the broader community that they're isolated from, and making connections with them. That was what was missing with Dorchester. Only a small subset of that [wealthier] community would be willing to go down to Dorchester. That limits the economic opportunity of the students.[29]

In the spring of 2015, ICW opened its second Boston-area location. The Kendall Square facility was designed to operate mostly as a client-training gym. ICW chose this location because it allowed ICW to focus on its goal of bridging the gap between the student population and the clientele. Kendall Square is in an area with no gang presence, which helps maintain the safety of the students and the clients they train. On the business side, Kendall Square is a favorable location, because there are not many competing gyms in the area to serve the growing presence of tech companies. While clients can still train at the Dorchester gym, its main function is offering a place for students to work out and work through the stages.

Jon's unique model and ICW's success since its launch have earned recognition for both Jon and the organization in greater Boston. Jon has won the *Heroes Among Us* award from the Boston Celtics, the *Babson College Rising Star* award, the *Outstanding Community Partner Award* from YearUp, the Lewis Institute *Changemaker Award*, along with awards from Good Sports, Cabot Creamery, Anytime Fitness, and two from Bostinno. Jon was also Social Ventures Partner Grantee in 2012, one of the Ten Outstanding Young Leaders named by the Greater Boston Chamber of Commerce in 2014, and the Ernst & Young New England Social Entrepreneur of the Year in 2015. And ICW as an organization won the *Rosoff Award* in the Nonprofit Diversity Initiative Category in 2015.[30] The local recognition has helped Jon grow ICW and garner more support.

Resources

ICW is a 501(c)3 nonprofit corporation. Its funding comes from three different sources. Around 70% of ICW revenue comes from corporate donors and philanthropic foundations such as the Lynch Foundation, Devonshire Foundation, Baupost Group, State Street Foundation, John Hancock Foundation, and Highland Street Foundation. Many of these foundations fund ICW with yearly or multi-year grants. ICW also applies for city and state grants. The second revenue category is individual donors, which brings in 15% of ICW revenue. Most of these donors are relationship-based repeat donors. Many clients who train at the gym also make contributions. ICW has a program called Elexson's Club, which has donors who give over $1,000 each year. The third source, accounting for 15% of ICW revenue, is earned income from individual and corporate training sessions which ICW runs and students provide. Individuals can purchase a one-time session, a pack of sessions, or a monthly unlimited number of training sessions. Each session costs a client $25. While this is a source of revenue, most of the $25 goes directly into the pockets of ICW student trainers.

Almost all payments now are done through credit card. At the lowest rate, clients will pay $25 a session and students keep $20 of that. We put our trainers on W-2s, unlike traditional gyms that will 1099 their trainers. That way, our students don't have to worry about the employer-side taxes. Their taxes come out of their checks and we just take care of all of that for them. They don't have to worry about [taxes] at the end of the year. Between the employer-side taxes, mind-body software, and credit card fee, we net $1.70 from the transactions.[31]

While ICW hopes to grow its earned income revenues, it does not want to do so in a way that would reduce student income. Jon stresses the importance of fundraising strategies that align with ICW's mission. "Because our clients are paying a reduced rate and because they get to change lives while changing their own, they become our donors. It creates a sustainable donor cultivation strategy. We can actually make more money off of client donations than we could trying to take an extra 20% that would come out of our students' pockets and just wouldn't feel right in any way."[32]

And clients feel good about choosing ICW. As Todd Millay highlights:

For me, I think ICW is addressing one of the fundamental problems in America. The segregation and isolation of a

[29] Ibid.

[30] "Our Team, Jon Feinman," InnerCity Weightlifting, https://www.innercityweightlifting.org/about1-c7ol, accessed August 8, 2017.

[31] Case interview with Jon Feinman, June 22, 2017.

[32] Ibid.

part of our population and the increasing disparities of wealth. I think Jon's sense that this can be a vehicle to break down that isolation on both sides is quite insightful, and personally I have benefitted from it tremendously. Because I would never know Reggie or any of these guys if it weren't for ICW. So I feel like I have forged some very meaningful relationships in my life from having that first-hand experience and just having a conversation about what their lives have been like. I think it's important for any of us on the other side of the divide to be doing something about it. This was a way that I saw that would be sustainable for me to make a meaningful contribution. Any nonprofit activity when you already have a demanding job and an active family life has to be something you're really passionate about.[33]

Despite all ICW's fundraising efforts, the budget is still tight. More resources are needed to improve ICW's operation in Boston. First and foremost, ICW needs more staff. They need more drivers to bring students to and from the gym, a larger administrative staff, and a donor outreach team. Furthermore, to better serve the target population in Boston, ICW needs an additional location. Right now, they cannot bring people from rival gangs to their gyms. This prevents ICW from reaching the PACT population at the depth their program aspires to. In the future, ICW hopes to open another site in either Roxbury or Mission Hill to serve rival gang members.

The Philly Opportunity

Jon's motivation for growing his company is unique. The more ICW grows, the more high-risk young people it can reach across the nation, and the more it can lower street violence nationwide. Jon has a larger goal than lowering street violence or even changing the lives of ICW's target population. Jon wants to grow ICW to shift the national perception of this target population and change the narrative surrounding issues of violence, incarceration, isolation, and segregation that these people face. Jon's theory is that if ICW can create this effect in key, high-profile cities, then that will be enough to start real national systemic change so that ICW doesn't have to be in every city. ICW believes it can help start a national conversation about how segregation and isolation in impoverished communities create a need for gangs, and how segregation and isolation continually fuel and are fueled by mass incarceration. Further, ICW believes this dialog will create more opportunity and inclusion on a grander scale.

ICW has identified four additional high-profile cities with significant street violence: Philadelphia, Baltimore, Chicago, and LA. Philadelphia is the logical location for the first expansion because it is geographically close to the home base in Boston. After sharing the idea of starting ICW in Philadelphia, the target population of gang members, government officials, and additional stakeholders have expressed strong positive reactions. As Josh Feinman, Jon's brother and ICW Director of Development and Communications points out, "We heard from a lot of people that they wanted us to be there tomorrow. When we were telling them that it might be a year out or so, they were like, well we could use this program tomorrow."[34]

The ICW team has chosen now as the time to expand to a new city because it recognizes the opportunity to build a national brand and spread their message. "Right now, as a society, we're still trying to solve this problem by further segregating and isolating people, first by circumstance, but then by prison and incarceration. By expanding ICW, we are hoping to build more awareness about what can be done by bringing these disparate groups together, instead of pushing them out."[35]

After eight years of experience in Boston and successful expansion to a second Boston location, the ICW team feels ready to take on this next step toward developing a national voice. Jon knows the risk is great. Failure in Philadelphia risks hurting ICW beyond repair, but not trying equates to a bigger failure in Jon's eyes. "I'll feel like we failed if we've been around for decades and we're still just in Boston and haven't made that national impact, because we won't have made the systemic change nationwide that we set out for. I think there is a bigger risk on the side of not growing. That being said, we are very aware of the risk involved with growing, especially as it relates to financial sustainability."[36]

The most important thing to the ICW team is to make sure the integrity of the mission and operation is maintained with expansion. A good leader is essential to achieving this goal. Josh Feinman, the current Director of Marketing and Communications and Jon's brother, volunteered to lead the expansion in Philadelphia. At the time Jon was piecing the idea of ICW together in his head, Josh was working with him as a personal trainer at the same studio. When Jon launched ICW in 2010, Josh was one of the first volunteers. He does a lot of work building and maintaining relationships with both corporate and individual donors. He has learned many lessons about leadership from watching Jon build ICW for the past eight years. For example, Josh is more emotional and likely to speak

[33] Case interview with Todd Millay, July 21, 2017.

[34] Case interview with Josh Feinman, July 6, 2017.

[35] Ibid.

[36] Case interview with Jon Feinman, June 22, 2017.

up if something happens that bothers him. He has learned to moderate his emotions based on Jon's example. He understands that becoming visibly upset with an unfriendly potential stakeholder can negatively impact ICW and its students in the future.

The ICW team and board are all confident that Josh is a good fit to lead the expansion. He has been with the organization from the beginning and is very passionate about its mission. "When it comes to expanding, we need to have the right leaders in place who understand our model from the ground up. I think for us to feel comfortable, we have to have leaders within the organization involved in the expansion."[37]

Road Map to Philly

The current rough plan for Philadelphia expansion is for Josh and ICW head coach, Regan Feinman, to move there for two years. During this time, Josh will be hiring and training staff and identifying local leaders who can continue the operation after he leaves. It is important that Josh build a staff dedicated to the intimate nature of ICW's program. He needs to find people who, no matter their title, will be willing to give rides, go to court dates, and always listen to their students and attend to their needs. Josh has already organically been building a volunteer staff as interest in the city spreads. The goal is for the Philadelphia operation to be self-sustaining at the end of his two years. If all goes well, Josh will then return to Boston with a playbook for further expansion.

ICW has held focus groups with the young people they have been able to contact. At these focus groups, current ICW students have been able to chat with Philadelphia's high-risk youth. From listening to people in their target population, the ICW team has learned that there are different dynamics in Philadelphia from those in Boston.

> *It's a very different city, and we're learning that as we go, again by the philosophy of listening as much as possible. I think it's different on almost every level, even though there are some similarities. In Boston, you seem to have these groups of young people who have very clear beefs with other groups and territories. In Philadelphia, so far, it seems like the lines are a little more blurred. This is something we need to learn more and more about to be effective there.*[38]

Although Philadelphia is two times bigger than Boston, Jon and Josh have learned that it still has a small city feel; you are likely to run into more people you know, and the city's population is more connected than in other large urban centers. Everything that ICW is learning from the focus groups will be further investigated on a larger and deeper scale as planning and development continue. It is essential for ICW in Philadelphia to know enough about the city's dynamic to ensure the safety and security of its students and staff.

In terms of funding stakeholders, ICW started making connections in Philadelphia after Jon spoke at the Aspen Institute in DC. Here he met a man who ran a foundation in Philadelphia and took interest in ICW. The ICW team took a trip to Philadelphia to meet with him, and networking spread from there. ICW currently has $70K in seed capital but will not launch in Philadelphia until they have raised $500K. On top of securing more funds, ICW is in the process of putting together a local advisory board to help with expansion.

ICW has the goal of making the Philadelphia model self-sustainable within two years; and to achieve this, they must build both individual and corporate clientele much faster than they did in Boston. Building clientele in Philadelphia is crucial to sustainability because there are not as many resources for nonprofit funding as in Boston. ICW is hoping to rely more on earned income from personal and corporate training for revenue. In Boston, earned income is about 15% of revenue. In the future, ICW hopes to grow this to 30% in Boston and hopefully more in Philadelphia. Jon explained his concern. "I think the big concern, from my perspective, is whether it is going to be sustainable. How do we know from year one if this is working really well, or if it is time to say, hey we learned a lot but we need to scale back and get back to Boston because this thing is going to put us under. I think any time you grow, you've got this risk of hurting the organization unintentionally."[39]

While financial sustainability, safety, and security are major risks of expansion, another is that the ICW team might dilute the effectiveness of their work back in Boston. This could happen if the team is spread too thin or distracted by the Philadelphia operation. Josh thinks the most important way to mitigate dilution is to maintain open lines of communication between the Boston and Philadelphia operations. The ICW team has adjusted operations at the two Boston sites, based on what they have learned from each location. This mutual learning must take place in regular communications. According to Josh, it is essential for the Philadelphia operation to inform the Boston operation and vice versa.

While confident, Jon has a fear of dilution but also a concern that a Philadelphia failure will let down its students.

> *The biggest fear I had with starting ICW was that even though I thought it was going to work, somehow I wasn't going to be able to sustain it as a leader because*

[37] Case interview with Josh Feinman, July 6, 2017.
[38] Ibid.
[39] Case interview with Jon Feinman, June 22, 2017.

I didn't know what I was doing. I think it is similar with Philadelphia. If we don't know what we are doing, are we going to become just another door that opens for the people we work with, to ultimately shut it in their faces because we couldn't figure it out on our end. That was my biggest fear here.[40]

ICW is changing the lives of this population and starting to have an impact on members from the opposite side of society. This program has shown amazing results, causing recidivism rates to drop from 80% to 8.3%. Failure would end access to creating opportunity for a better future, but not trying would leave high-impact players around the globe without the chance to partake in a program that is actually working.

Decision Point

The exact date for expansion is still up in the air. First, ICW must reach its set milestone of $500K in funding before starting in Philadelphia. If this goal is achieved in the next year, the earliest that ICW would move to Philadelphia is next summer (2018). Other factors could delay the move. ICW is also currently looking at possibly expanding to a third location in Boston. The South Boston Waterfront Neighborhood Association Seaport (SBWNA Seaport) has offered ICW a site. This site is in an affluent area and would function like the Kendall Square site to train clients. The problem with this project is that ICW cannot afford the rent for the building. ICW is currently discussing options with the landlord. If this project progresses, Philadelphia might be put off for a little longer.

As Jon looked at the Philadelphia expansion opportunity, he was torn. Expansion was central to his vision, but it could risk the success that ICW had achieved in Boston. As he continued lifting, Jon wondered if expansion was a good idea.

Discussion Questions

1. Should ICW expand to Philadelphia?
2. Besides financial, what obstacles would such an expansion face?
3. Can ICW replicate its Boston success in Philadelphia? What are the key factors that need replication?
4. While Josh has worked for ICW since the beginning, is he the right person to lead expansion?

[40] Ibid.

Glossary

Accredited Investor: Under the Securities Act of 1933, a company that offers or sells its securities must register the securities with the SEC or find an exemption from the registration requirements. The Act provides companies with a number of exemptions. For some of the exemptions, such as rules 505 and 506 of Regulation D, a company may sell its securities to what are known as "accredited investors." The federal securities laws define the term **accredited investor** in Rule 501 of Regulation D as:

1. a bank, insurance company, registered investment company, business development company, or small business investment company; an employee benefit plan, within the meaning of the Employee Retirement Income Security Act, if a bank, insurance company, or registered investment adviser makes the investment decisions, or if the plan has total assets in excess of $5 million;
2. a charitable organization, corporation, or partnership with assets exceeding $5 million;
3. a director, executive officer, or general partner of the company selling the securities;
4. a business in which all the equity owners are accredited investors;
5. a natural person who has individual net worth, or joint net worth with the person's spouse, that exceeds $1 million at the time of the purchase;
6. a natural person with income exceeding $200,000 in each of the two most recent years or joint income with a spouse exceeding $300,000 for those years and a reasonable expectation of the same income level in the current year; or
7. a trust with assets in excess of $5 million, not formed to acquire the securities offered, whose purchases a sophisticated person makes.

Acquisition: Acquiring control of a corporation, called a target, by stock purchase or exchange, either hostile or friendly; also called **takeover**.

Agency theory: A branch of economics dealing with the behavior of principals (e.g., owners) and their agents (e.g., managers).

All-hands meeting: A meeting of managers, lawyers, accountants, and investment bankers that sets the timetable and tasks to be accomplished prior to an initial public offering.

Angel: An individual who invests in private companies. The term business angel is sometimes reserved for sophisticated angel investors who invest sizeable sums in private companies. *(See informal investor.)*

Antidilution (of ownership): The right of an investor to maintain the same percentage of ownership of a company's common stock in the event that the company issues more stock. *(See dilution.)*

Asked: The price level at which sellers offer securities to buyers.

ASP (Application Service Provider): An ASP deploys, hosts, and manages access to a packaged software application for multiple parties from a centrally managed facility. The applications are delivered over networks on a subscription basis.

Asset acquisition: Means of affecting a buyout by purchase of certain desired assets rather than shares of the target company.

Asset-based valuation: This method considers the fair market value of fixed assets and equipment and inventory. It is most appropriate for asset intensive businesses such as retail and manufacturing companies.

Audited financial statements: A company's financial statements prepared and certified by a certified public accounting firm that is totally independent of the company.

Babson College: Babson College, located in Wellesley, Massachusetts, is recognized internationally for its entrepreneurial leadership in a changing global environment. Babson grants BS, MBA, and custom MS and MBA degrees and has a school of executive education. The Arthur M. Blank Center for Entrepreneurship was dedicated in 1998 and provides a dynamic home for Babson's world-famous entrepreneurship program.

Backlog: The sales that have been made but not fulfilled due to lack of inventory to finalize the sale.

Bake-off: When a private company compares offers from different investment banks to take it public.

Balance sheet: Summary statement of a company's financial position at a given point in time. It summarizes the accounting value of the assets, liabilities, preferred stock, common stock, and retained earnings. Assets = Liabilities + Preferred stock + Common stock + Retained earnings. *(See pro forma statements.)*

Basis point: One-hundredth of a percent (0.01%), typically used in expressing yield differentials (1.50% – 1.15% = 0.35%, or 35 basis points). *(See yield.)*

Bear: A person who expects prices to fall.

Bear market: A period of generally falling prices and pessimistic attitudes.

Best efforts offering: The underwriter makes its best efforts to sell as much as it can of the shares at the offering price. Hence, unlike a firm commitment offering, the company offering its shares is not guaranteed a definite amount of money by the underwriter.

Beauty contest: When investment banks make their best offers to take a company public.

Bid: The price level at which buyers offer to acquire securities from sellers.

Big Board: *See New York Stock Exchange.*

Blue sky: Refers to laws that safeguard investors from being misled by unscrupulous promoters of companies with little or no substance.

Book value (of an asset): The accounting value of an asset as shown on a balance sheet is the cost of the asset minus its accumulated depreciation. It is not necessarily identical to its market value.

Book value (of a company): The common stock equity shown on the balance sheet. It is equal to total assets minus liabilities and preferred stock (synonymous with net worth and owners' equity).

Bootstrap: To build a business out of nothing, with minimal outside capital.

Bottom-up forecasting: Forecasting your income sheet revenue and expenses based on a typical day and then multiplying those forecasts by the number of days in the period (i.e., month, quarter, or year).

Brain-writing: Similar to brainstorming, but the process is done with written versus oral communication. Ideas are presented, and participants add their thoughts in writing. The key is to build on the idea rather than argue why the idea can't work.

Break-even point: The sales volume at which a company's net sales revenue just equals its costs. A commonly used approximate formula for the break-even point is Sales revenue = Total fixed costs/ Gross margin.

Bridge financing: Short-term finance that is expected to be repaid relatively quickly. It usually bridges a short-term financing need. For example, it provides cash needed before an expected stock flotation.

Burn rate: The negative, real-time cash flow from a company's operations, usually computed monthly.

Business angel: *See angel.*

Business model: The way in which a business makes a profit. As an example, here is IBM's definition of its business model: "IBM sells services, hardware and software. These offerings are bolstered by IBM's research and development capabilities. If a customer requires financing, IBM can provide that too." Southwest Airlines' business model is to provide inexpensive fares by keeping costs low through being more efficient than its major competitors.

Business Model Wheel: A framework to help entrepreneurs envision all the parts of the business and how they come together to create, deliver, and capture value.

Business plan: Document prepared by entrepreneurs, possibly in conjunction with their professional advisors, detailing the past, present, and intended future of the company. It contains a thorough analysis of the managerial, physical, labor, product, and financial resources of the company, plus the background of the company, its previous trading record, and its market position. The business plan contains detailed profit, balance sheet, and cash flow projections for two years ahead, and less detailed information for the following three years. The business plan crystallizes and focuses the management team's ideas. It explains their strategies, sets objectives, and is used to monitor their subsequent performance.

Buyback: A corporation's repurchase of stock that it has previously issued; for example, a company buys its stock back from a venture capital firm that has previously been issued stock in return for money invested in the company.

Call: A contract allowing the issuer of a security to buy back that security from the purchaser at an agreed-upon price during a specific period of time.

Capital gain: The amount by which the selling price of an asset (e.g., common stock) exceeds the seller's initial purchase price.

Capitalization rate: The discount rate, K, used to determine the present value of a stream of future earnings. PV = (Normalized earnings after taxes) / (K/100), where PV is the present value of the firm and K is the firm's cost of capital.

Carbon tax: A tax on emissions caused by the burning of coal, gas, and oil, aimed at reducing the production of gases that contribute to the warming of the Earth's atmosphere by reflecting radiation from the Earth's surface (e.g., carbon dioxide and ozone).

Carried interest: A venture capital firm's share of the profit earned by a fund. In the United States, the carried interest (carry) is typically 20% of the profit after investors' principal has been repaid.

Cash flow: The difference between the company's cash receipts and its cash payments in a given period.

Cash-flow statement: A summary of a company's cash flow over a period of time. *(See pro forma statements.)*

Channel coverage: The product distribution strategy in regard to how many channels to use. It can be intensive (multiple channels), selective (a subset of channels), or exclusive (one channel).

Chattel (or property) mortgage: A loan secured by specific assets.

Classic venture capital: Money invested privately in seed-, startup-, expansion-, and late-stage companies by venture capital firms. The term "classic" is used to distinguish from money invested privately in acquisitions, buyouts, mergers, and reorganizations.

Co-Creation: Product concepts are co-created alongside the customer.

Collateral: An asset pledged as security for a loan.

Common stock: Shares of ownership, or equity, in a corporation.

Common-sized income statement: Converting the income statement into percentages with total revenue equaling 100% and all other lines a percentage of total revenue.

Comparable: Using existing industry or company financials to forecast your own venture's financials.

Compensating balance: A bank requires a customer to maintain a certain level of demand deposits that do not bear interest. The interest forgone by the customer on the compensating balance recompenses the bank for services provided, credit lines, and loans.

Conversion ratio: The number of shares of common stock that may be received in exchange for each share of a convertible security.

Convertible debt: A loan that can be exchanged for equity.

Convertible security: Preferred stock that is convertible into common stock according to a specified ratio at the security holder's option.

Cooperative (co-op): An autonomous association of persons united voluntarily to meet their common economic, social, and cultural needs and aspirations through a jointly owned and democratically controlled enterprise.

Corporation: A business form that is an entity legally separate from its owners. Its important features include limited liability, easy transfer of ownership, and unlimited life.

Cost of capital: The required rate of return of various types of financing. The overall cost of capital is a weighted average of the individual required rates of returns (costs).

Cost of debt capital: The interest rate charged by a company's lenders.

Cost of equity capital: The rate of return on investment required by the company's common shareholders (colloquially called the hurdle rate).

Cost of goods sold: The direct cost of the product sold. For a retail business, the cost of all goods sold in a given period equals the inventory at the beginning of the period plus the cost of goods purchased during that period minus the inventory at the end of the period.

Cost of preferred stock: The rate of return on investment required by the company's preferred shareholders.

Covenant: A restriction on a borrower imposed by a lender. For example, it could be a requirement placed on a company to achieve and maintain specified targets such as levels of cash flow, balance sheet ratios, or specified capital expenditure levels to retain financing facilities.

Crowdfunding: Using social media to raise small amounts of capital from a large number of individuals to finance a business venture.

Cumulative dividend provision: A requirement that unpaid dividends on preferred stock accumulate and have to be paid before a dividend is paid on common stock.

Current ratio: Current assets/Current liabilities. This ratio indicates a company's ability to cover its current liabilities with its current assets.

Customer acquisition cost (CAC): Marketing expense/Number of new customers.

Customer lifetime value (CLTV): Average revenue/Customer X How long customer is retained.

Customer relationship management (CRM): Systems designed to compile and manage data about customers.

Customer value proposition (CVP): The difference between total customer benefits and total customer costs, which are both monetary and nonmonetary.

Deal flow: The rate at which new investment propositions come to funding institutions.

Debenture: A document containing an acknowledgment of indebtedness on the part of a company, usually secured by a charge on the company's assets.

Debt service: Payments of principal and interest required on a debt over a given period.

Deep pockets: Refers to an investor who has substantial financial resources.

Default: The nonperformance of a stated obligation. The nonpayment by the issuer of interest or principal on a bond or the nonperformance of a covenant.

Deferred payment: A debt that has been incurred and will be repaid at some future date.

Depreciation: The systematic allocation of the cost of an asset over a period of time for financial reporting and tax purposes.

Differentiation: A common strategy whereby a company differentiates its product offering from its competitors.

Dilution (of ownership): When a new stock issue results in a decrease in the preissue owners' percentage of the common stock.

Discounted cash flow (DCF): Method of evaluating investments by adjusting the cash flows for the time value of money. In the decision to invest in a project, all future cash flows expected from that investment are discounted back to their present value at the time the investment is made. The discount rate is whatever rate of return the investor requires. In theory, if the present value of the future cash flows is greater than the money being invested, the investment should be made. *(See discount rate, internal rate of return, net present value, and present value.)*

Discount rate (capitalization rate): Rate of return used to convert future values to present values. *(See capitalization rate, internal rate of return, and rate of return.)*

DJIA: Dow Jones Industrial Average. The Dow Jones Industrial Average is a price-weighted average of 30 significant stocks traded on the New York Stock Exchange and the NASDAQ. The DJIA was invented by Charles Dow back in 1896. Often referred to as "the Dow," the DJIA is the oldest and single most watched index in the world. The DJIA includes companies like Apple, Disney, Exxon, and Microsoft.

Doriot, General Georges: Founder of the modern venture capital industry, Harvard Business School professor, and one of the creators of INSEAD.

Double bottom line: Captures both the financial profit the organization earns and also the social benefit it provides society; associated with social entrepreneurship.

Double jeopardy: The case where an entrepreneur's main source of income and most of her/his net worth depend on her/his business.

Due diligence: The process of investigation by investors into a potential investee's management team, resources, and trading performance. This includes rigorous testing of the business plan assumptions and the verification of material facts (such as existing accounts).

Dun & Bradstreet (D&B): The biggest credit-reporting agency in the United States.

Early-stage financing: This category includes seed-stage, startup-stage, and first-stage financing.

Earnings: This is synonymous with income and profit.

Earnings before interest and taxes (EBIT): *See operating income.*

Earnings before interest, taxes, depreciation, and amortization (EBITDA): Often referred to as cash flow. It removes non-cash charges, such as depreciation and amortization, to get a clearer view of the cash-flow-generating ability of a company.

Earning-capitalization valuation: This values a company by capitalizing its earnings. Company value = Net income/Capitalization rate.

Earnings per share (EPS): A company's net income divided by the number of common shares issued and outstanding.

Earn-out: A common contract provision when a company is sold or acquired. The founders will earn a portion of the sales price over time based on continuing performance of the new venture.

Elasticity of demand: The percentage change in the quantity of a good demanded divided by the percentage change in the price of that good. When the elasticity is greater than 1, the demand is said to be elastic, and when it is less than 1, it is inelastic. In the short term, the demand for nonessential goods (e.g., airline travel) is usually elastic, and the demand for essentials (e.g., electricity) is usually inelastic.

Employee stock ownership plan (ESOP): A trust established to acquire shares in a company for subsequent allocation to employees over a period of time. Several possibilities are available for structuring the operation of an ESOP. Essentially, either the company makes payments to the trust, which the trust uses to purchase shares; or the trust, having previously borrowed to acquire shares, may use the payments from the company to repay loans. The latter form is referred to as a leveraged ESOP and may be used as a means of providing part of the funding required to affect a buyout. A particular advantage of an ESOP is the possibility of tax relief for the contributions made by the company to the trust and on the cost of borrowing in those cases where the trust purchases shares in advance.

Employment agreement: An agreement whereby senior managers contract to remain with the company for a specified period. For the investing institutions, such an agreement provides some measure of security that the company's performance will not be adversely affected by the unexpected departure of key managers.

Equity: *See owners' equity.*

Equity kicker (or warrant): An option or instrument linked to the provision of other types of funding, particularly mezzanine finance, which enables the provider to obtain an equity stake and hence a share in capital gains. In this way, providers of subordinated debt can be compensated for the higher risk they incur.

Exit: The means by which investors in a company realize all or part of their investment. *(See harvest.)*

Expansion financing: Working capital for the initial expansion of a company that is producing and shipping products and has growing accounts receivable and inventories.

Factoring: A means of enhancing the cash flow of a business. A factoring company pays to the firm a certain proportion of the value of the firm's trade debts and then receives the cash as the trade debtors settle their accounts. Invoice discounting is a similar procedure.

FASB (Financial Accounting Standards Board): A private-sector board (industry) that establishes financial accounting and reporting standards.

Filing: Documents, including the prospectus, filed with the SEC for approval before an IPO.

Financing flows: Cash flows generated by debt and equity financing.

Finder: A person or firm that attempts to raise funding for a private company.

Firm commitment offering: The underwriter guarantees to raise a certain amount of money for the company and other selling stockholders at the IPO.

First-round financing: The first investment made by external investors.

First-stage financing: Financing to initiate full manufacturing and sales.

Five Cs of credit: The five crucial elements for obtaining credit are character (borrower's integrity), capacity (sufficient cash flow to service the debt), capital (borrower's net worth), collateral (assets to secure the debt), and conditions (of the borrowing company, its industry, and the general economy).

Fixed and floating charges: Claims on assets pledged as security for debt. Fixed charges cover specific fixed assets, and floating charges relate to all or part of a company's assets.

Floating lien: A general lien against a group of assets, such as accounts receivable or inventory, without the assets being specifically identified.

Flotation: A method of raising equity financing by selling shares on a stock market and often allowing management and institutions to realize some of their investment at the same time. *(See initial public offering.)*

Follow-on financing: A second or subsequent round of funding for a company.

Founder shares: Shares that the founders issue to themselves in exchange for their "sweat equity," meaning that the founders buy their shares for a nominal amount of cash. Founder shares are typically issued prior to the first round of financing.

Four Fs: Founders, family, friends, and foolhardy persons who invest in a person's private business, generally a startup. *(See informal investor and angel.)*

Franchising: An organizational form in which a firm (the franchisor) with a market-tested business package centered on a product or service enters into a continuing contractual relationship with franchisees operating under the franchisor's trade name to produce or market goods or services according to a format specified by the franchisor.

Free cash flow: Cash flow in excess of that required to fund all projects that have a positive net present value when discounted at the relevant cost of capital. Conflicts of interest between shareholders and managers may arise when the organization generates free cash flow. Shareholders may desire higher dividends, but managers may wish to invest in projects providing a return below the cost of capital. *(See cost of capital and net present value.)*

Future value: The value at a future date of a present amount of money. $FV_t = PV \times (1 + K/100)^t$ where FV is the future value, PV is the present value, K is the percentage annual rate of return, and t is the number of years. For example, an investment of $100,000 must have a future value of $384,160 after four years to produce a rate of return of 40%, which is the kind of return that an investor in an early-stage company expects to earn. *(See net present value, present value, and rate of return.)*

Gatekeeper: Colloquial term for a person or firm that advises clients on investments in venture capital funds; formally called an investment advisor.

GDP (gross domestic product): The total market value of goods and services produced by workers and capital within a country's borders during a specific period, which is generally a calendar year.

Gearing: British term of leverage. *(See leverage.)*

GEM (Global Entrepreneurship Monitor): An annual study of entrepreneurial activity within different countries.

General partner: A partner with unlimited legal responsibility for the debts and liabilities of a partnership.

Going concern: This assumes that the company will continue as an operating business as opposed to going out of business and liquidating its assets.

Golden handcuffs: A combination of rewards and penalties given to key managers to dissuade them from leaving the company. Examples are high salaries, paid on a deferred basis while employment is maintained, and stock options.

Goodwill: The difference between the purchase price of a company and the net value of its assets purchased.

Gross margin: Gross profit as a percentage of net sales revenue.

Gross profit (gross income, gross earnings): Net sales revenue minus the direct cost of the products sold.

Guarantee: An undertaking to prove that a debt or obligation of another will be paid or performed. It may relate either to a specific debt or to a series of transactions such as a guarantee of a bank overdraft. For example, entrepreneurs are often required to provide personal guarantees for loans borrowed by their companies.

Guerilla marketing: Unique, low-cost marketing methods to capture attention in a crowded marketplace.

Harvest: The realization of the value of an investment. *(See exit.)*

Headcount: The number of employees within a company at a particular point in time.

High-fidelity prototype: Prototypes designed to look like a final completed product concept.

High-potential venture: A company started with the intent of growing quickly to annual sales of at least $30 – 50 million in five years. It has the potential to have a firm-commitment IPO.

Hurdle rate: The minimum rate of return that is acceptable to investors. *(See return on investment.)*

Hybrid organization: Nonprofit with an earned income component dedicated to achieving social value at a level significantly higher (say, two-thirds or more) than economic value.

Income statement: A summary of a company's revenues, expenses, and profits over a specified period of time. *(See pro forma statements.)*

Informal investor: An individual who puts money into a private company—usually a startup or a small business. Informal investments range from micro loans from family members to sizable equity purchases by sophisticated business angels.

Initial public offering (IPO): Process by which a company raises money and gets listed on a stock market. *(See flotation.)*

Intellectual property (IP): Knowledge that a company possesses and considers proprietary. IP can be protected through patents, trademarks, and so on.

Interest cover: The extent to which periodic interest commitments on borrowings are exceeded by periodic profits. It is the ratio of profits before the deduction of interest and taxes to interest payments. The ratio may also be expressed as the cash flow from operations divided by the amount of interest payable.

Internal rate of return (IRR): The discount rate that equates the present value of the future net cash flows from an investment with the project's cash outflows. It is a means of expressing the percentage rate of return projected on a proposed investment. For an investment in a company, the calculation takes account of cash invested, cash receipts from dividend payments and redemptions, percentage of equity held, expected date of payments, realization of the investment and capitalization at that point, and possible further financing requirements. The calculation will frequently be quoted in a range depending on sensitivity analysis. *(See discount rate, present value, future value, and rate of return.)*

Inventory: Finished goods, work in process of manufacture, and raw materials owned by a company.

Investment bank: A financial institution engaged in the issue of new securities, including management and underwriting of issues as well as securities trading and distribution.

Investment flows: Cash flows associated with purchase and sales of both fixed assets and business interests.

IPO: *See initial public offering.*

IRR: *See internal rate of return.*

Junior debt: Loan ranking after senior debt or secured debt for payment in the event of a default.

Junk bonds: A variety of high-yield, unsecured bonds tradable on a secondary market and not considered to be of investment quality by credit-rating agencies. High yield normally indicates higher risk.

Key performance indicator (KPIs): Key measures to assess how your business is performing. Examples include number of new customers, sales/customer, delivery time, and so forth.

Key person insurance: Additional security provided to financial backers of a company through the purchase of insurance on the lives of key managers who are seen as crucial to the future of the company. Should one or more of those key executives die prematurely, the financial backers would receive the insurance payment.

Key success factors (KSFs): The attributes that customers use to distinguish between competing products or services. KSFs go beyond just product attributes and may include brand and other intangibles.

Lead investor: In syndicated deals, normally the investor who originates, structures, and subsequently plays the major monitoring role.

Lead underwriter: The head of a syndicate of financial firms that are sponsoring an initial public offering of securities or a secondary offering of securities.

Lead venture capital firm: The head of a syndicate of venture capital firms that is investing privately in a company.

Lemons and plums: Bad deals and good deals, respectively.

Leverage: The amount of debt in a company's financing structure, which may be expressed as a percentage of the total financing or as a ratio of debt to equity. The various quasi-equity (preference-type shares) and quasi-debt (mezzanine debt) instruments used to fund later-stage companies means that great care is required in calculating and interpreting leverage or gearing ratios.

Leveraged buyout (LBO): Acquisition of a company by an investor group, an investor, or an investment/LBO partnership, with a significant amount of debt (usually at least 70% of the total capitalization) and with plans to repay the debt with funds generated from the acquired company's operations or from asset sales. LBOs are frequently financed in part with junk bonds.

Lien: A legal claim on certain assets that are used to secure a loan.

Limited liability company: A company owned by "members," who either manage the business themselves or appoint "managers" to run it for them. All members and managers have the benefit of limited liability and, in most cases, are taxed in the same way as a subchapter S corporation without having to conform to the S corporation restrictions.

Limited partnership: A business organization with one or more **general partners**, who manage the business and assume legal debts and obligations, and one or more **limited partners**, who are liable only to the extent of their investments. Limited partners also enjoy rights to the partnership's cash flow, but are not liable for company obligations.

Line of credit (with a bank): An arrangement between a bank and a customer specifying the maximum amount of unsecured debt the customer can owe the bank at a given point in time.

Line of credit (with a vendor): A limit set by the seller on the amount that a purchaser can buy on credit.

Liquidation value (of an asset): The amount of money that can be realized from the sale of an asset sold separately from its operating organization.

Liquidation value (of a company): The market value of the assets minus the liabilities that must be paid of a company that is liquidating.

Liquidity: The ability of an asset to be converted to cash as quickly as possible and without any price discount.

Listing: Acceptance of a security for trading on an organized stock exchange. Hence, a stock traded on the New York Stock Exchange is said to be listed on the NYSE.

Living dead: Venture capital jargon for a company that has no prospect of being harvested with a public offering or an acquisition; hence, the venture capital firm cannot realize its investment in the company.

Liquidation value: The total amount that could be realized from selling the business's individual assets, after satisfying all of the business's liabilities.

Loan note: A form of vendor finance or deferred payment. The purchaser (borrower) may agree to make payments to the holder of the loan note at specified future dates. The holder may be able to obtain cash at an earlier date by selling at a discount to a financing institution that will collect on maturity.

Lock-up period: An interval during which an investment may not be sold. In the case of an IPO, employees may not sell their shares for a period of time determined by the underwriter and usually lasting 180 days.

Looks-like prototype: A prototype, as suggested by its name, that appears similar or identical to a final product but does not function as the final product is expected to.

Low-fidelity prototypes: A prototype that expresses the rough product concept, either in two-dimensional or three-dimensional form, often in material as basic as paper.

Management buy in (MBI): The transfer of ownership of an entity to a new set of owners in which new managers coming into the entity are a significant element.

Management buyout (MBO): The transfer of ownership of an entity to a new set of owners in which the existing management and employees are a significant element.

Market capitalization: The total value at market prices of the securities in issue for a company, a stock market, or a sector of a stock market, calculated by multiplying the number of shares issued by the market price per share.

Market-comparable valuation: The value of a private company based of the valuation of similar public companies.

Marketing: An organizational function and a set of processes for creating, communicating, and delivering value to customers and for managing customer relationships in ways that benefit the organization and its stakeholders.[1]

Merger: The combining of two or more entities into one, through a purchase acquisition or a pooling of interests.

Metric: *See key performance indicators.*

Mezzanine financing: Strictly, any form of financing instrument between ordinary shares and senior debt. The forms range from senior mezzanine debt, which may simply carry an interest rate above that for senior secured debt, to junior mezzanine debt, which may carry rights to subscribe for equity but no regular interest payment.

Microcredit: Tiny loans to entrepreneurs too poor to qualify for traditional bank loans. In developing countries especially, microcredit enables very poor people to engage in self-employment projects that generate income.

Microfinancing: Same as microcredit.

Minimum viable product (MVP): Version of a new product concept that allows a team to collect the maximum amount of validated learning about customers with the least effort.

1 American Marketing Association, 2004; http://www.marketingpower.com/content21257.php.

Modified book value: Valuation of a business in which all assets and liabilities (including off-balance sheet, intangible, and contingent) are adjusted to their fair market values.

Money left on the table: The difference between the price at the end of the first day's trading and the initial offering price, multiplied by the number of shares in the offering.

Multiple: The amount of money realized from the sale of an investment divided by the amount of money originally invested.

National Association of Securities Dealers Automated Quotation (NASDAQ): An electronic system for trading stocks. It is owned and operated by The Nasdaq Stock Market, Inc.

Necessity entrepreneurship: A business started out of necessity by an entrepreneur who cannot find a better source of income through employment.

NGO: Nongovernmental organization.

Net assets: Assets less liabilities.

Net income (net earnings, net profit): A company's final income after all expenses and taxes have been deducted from all revenues. It is also known as the bottom line.

Net income margin: Net income as a percentage of net sales revenue. In a typical year an average U.S. company has a net income margin of about 5%.

Net liquid value: Liquid financial assets minus callable liabilities.

Net present value: The present value of an investment's future net cash flows minus the initial investment. In theory, if the net present value is greater than 0, an investment should be made. For example, an investor is asked to invest $100,000 in a company that is expanding. He expects a rate of return of 30%. The company offers to pay him back $300,000 after four years. The present value of $300,000 at a rate of return of 30% is $105,038. Thus, the net present value of the investment is $5,038, so the investment should be made. *(See free cash flow, future value, present value, and rate of return.)*

Net profit: *See net income.*

Net surplus: Total revenue minus total cost and expenses in a nonprofit organization; equivalent to net income in a for-profit enterprise.

Net worth: *See book value.*

New York Stock Exchange (NYSE): The largest stock exchange in the world, located in New York. Also known as the Big Board.

Nonprofit organization: Organizations that are considered public charities are owned by the public and, as such, cannot accrue privately owned profits. These organizations have applied and been granted nonprofit status and thus do not have to pay taxes.
NPO: Nonprofit organization; also not-for-profit organization.
OECD: The Organization for Economic Cooperation and Development comprises Australia, Austria, Belgium, Canada, Czech Republic, Denmark, Finland, France, Germany, Greece, Hungary, Iceland, Ireland, Italy, Republic of Korea, Japan, Luxembourg, Mexico, the Netherlands, New Zealand, Norway, Poland, Portugal, Spain, Sweden, Switzerland, Turkey, the United Kingdom, and the United States.
Offering circular: *See prospectus.*
Operating cash flows: Cash flows directly generated by a company's operations. The cash flow from operating activity equals net income plus depreciation minus increase in accounts receivable minus increase in inventories plus increase in accounts payable plus increase in accruals. *(See financing flows and investment flows.)*
Operating income: Earnings (profit) before deduction of interest payments and income taxes, abbreviated to EBIT. It measures a company's earning power from its ongoing operations. It is of particular concern to a company's lenders, such as banks, because operating income demonstrates the ability of a company to earn sufficient income to pay the interest on its debt. *(See times interest earned.)*
Opportunity: An idea that has commercial viability and that provides the entrepreneur and company the potential to earn attractive margins and a return on their investment.
Opportunity entrepreneurship: The pursuit of a new venture because it is deemed as better than remaining in one's current job or other jobs that might be available.
Options: *See stock option plan.*
Out of cash (OOC): A common problem with entrepreneurial companies. The OOC time period is cash on hand divided by the burn rate.
Over the counter (OTC): The purchase and sale of financial instruments not conducted on a stock exchange such as the New York Stock Exchange. The largest OTC market is the NASDAQ.
Owners' equity: Common stock plus retained earnings. *(See book value of a company.)*
Pain point: A potential customer's problem that a business can relieve with its product or service.
Paid-in capital: Par value per share times the number of shares issued. Additional paid-in capital is the price paid in excess of par value times the number of shares issued.
Paper prototyping: Paper prototyping, as the name suggests, is the representation of a concept using simple materials such a paper or cardboard, markers, and tape.
Partnership: Legal form of a business in which two or more persons are co-owners, sharing profits and losses.
Par value: Nominal price placed on a share of common stock.
Patent: Granted by the government, patents protect unique devices (or combinations of components integrated into a device) and processes.
Penetration pricing: Pricing your product at a relatively lower price to gain high market share, but with lower margins.
Persona: A fictionalized description of your core customer built upon demographics and psychographics that might predict how they would interact with your product.
Piggy-back registration rights: The right to register unregistered stock in the event of a company having a public stock offering.
Pivot: Changing your business model, product, or some other major aspect of your business to better compete in the marketplace.
Pledging: The use of a company's accounts receivable as security (collateral) for a short-term loan.
Pop (first day): Percentage increase in the price of a stock at the end of the first day's trading over the initial offering price.
Positioning: A company's offering on certain product attributes—the ones customers care about most—relative to competitive offerings.
Portfolio: Collection of investments. For example, the portfolio of a venture capital fund comprises all its investments.
Post-money valuation: The value of a company immediately after a round of additional money is invested.
Preemptive rights: The rights of shareholders to maintain their percentage ownership of a company by purchasing a proportionate number of shares of any new issue of common stock. *(See antidilution, dilution, and pro rata interest.)*
Preferred stock (Preference shares): A class of shares that incorporate the right to a fixed dividend and usually a prior claim on assets, in preference to ordinary shares, in the event of a liquidation. Cumulative preference shares provide an entitlement to a cumulative dividend if, in any year, the preference dividend is unpaid due to insufficient profits being earned. Preference shares are usually redeemable at specific dates.
Pre-money valuation: The value of a company's equity before additional money is invested.
Preliminary prospectus: The initial document published by an underwriter of a new issue of stock to be given to prospective investors. It is understood that the document will be modified significantly before the final prospectus is published; also called a red herring.
Prepayment: A payment on a loan made prior to the original due date.
Present value (PV): The current value of a given future cash flow stream, FV_t after t years, discounted at a rate of return of K% is $PV = (FV_t/1 + K/100)^t$. For example, if an investor expects a rate of return of 60% on an investment in a seed-stage company, and she believes that her investment will be worth $750,000 after five years, then the present value of her investment is $71,526. *(See discount rate, future value, net present value, and rate of return.)*
Present value of future cash flows (valuation): Present value is today's value of a future payment, or stream of payments, discounted at some appropriate compound interest, or discount rate; also called time value of money. The present value of company is the present value of the future free cash flows plus the residual (terminal) value of the firm:

$$PV = \sum_{t=1}^{N} (FCF_t)/(1+K)^t + (RV_N)/(1+K)^N$$

where K is the cost of capital; FCF_t is the free cash flow in year t; N is the number of years; and RV_N is the residual value in year N.

Free Cash Flow
=Operating Income
–Interest
–Taxes on Operating Income

+Depreciation & Other Noncash Charges
–Increase in Net Working Capital
–Capital Expenditures (Replacement & Growth)
–Principal Repayments

Prevalence rate: The percentage of a population participating in a particular activity.
Price discrimination: A strategy where different customer segments are charged different prices.
Price-earnings ratio (P/E ratio): The ratio of the market value of a firm's equity to its after-tax profits (may be calculated from price per share and earnings per share).
Price points: Product pricing in standardized or fixed points.
Price promotion: Discounts from the base price for a short period to attain specific goals such as introducing a product to new customers.
Price skimming: The strategy of pricing your product high to generate high margins, but recognizing that you'll gain limited market share because prices are relatively high.
Primary data: Market research collected specifically for a particular purpose through focus groups, surveys, or experiments.
Primary target audience (PTA): A group of potential customers identified by demographic and psychographic data that will be the focus of the company's early marketing and sales efforts.
Prime rate: Short-term interest rate charged by a bank to its largest, most creditworthy customers.
Private placement: The direct sales of securities to a small number of investors. *(See Regulation D.)*
Product life cycle: A stage model of a product's life, including introduction, growth, maturity, and decline; a similar concept to the S-curve life cycle for an industry.
Profit: Synonymous with income and earnings.
Pro forma statements: Projected financial statements: income and cash-flow statements and balance sheets. For a startup company, it is usual to make pro forma statements monthly for the first two years and annually for the next three years.
Pro rata interest: The right granted the investor to maintain the same percentage ownership in the event of future financings. *(See antidilution and dilution.)*
Prospectus: A document giving a description of a securities issue, including a complete statement of the terms of the issue and a description of the issuer, as well as its historical financial statements. Also referred to as an offering circular. *(See red herring.)*
Prototyping: The process of quickly putting together working models (i.e., prototypes) to represent ideas, test various aspects of a design, and gather early customer feedback.
Psychographics: Information that categorizes customers based on their personality, psychological traits, lifestyles, values, and social group membership. It helps to understand what motivates customers to act in the ways they do and is important because members of a specific demographic category can have dramatically different psychographic profiles. Marketing strictly based on demographic information will be ineffective because it ignores these differences.
Purchasing power parity (PPP): A method of measuring the relative purchasing power of different countries' currencies over the same types of goods and services. Because goods and services may cost more in one country than in another, PPP allows us to make more accurate comparisons of standards of living across countries. PPP estimates use price comparisons of comparable items, but because not all items can be matched exactly across countries and time, the estimates are not always "robust."
Put: A contract allowing the holder to sell a given number of securities back to the issuer of the contract at a fixed price for a given period of time.
Quiet period: The period starting when an issuer hires an underwriter and ending 25 days after the security begins trading, during which the issuer cannot comment publicly on the offering, due to SEC rules.
R^2 (R-Square): The fraction of variation in the dependent variable that is explained by variation in the independent variable. A high value indicates a strong relationship between the two variables.
Rate of return: The annual return on an investment. If a sum of money, PV, is invested and after t years that investment is worth FV_t the return on investment K = $[(FV/PV)^{1/t} - 1] \times 100\%$. For example, if $100 is invested originally, and one year later $108 is paid back to the investor, the annual rate of return is 8%.
Realization: *See exit and harvest.*
Redeemable shares: Shares that may be redeemable at the option of the company, or the shareholder, or both.
Red herring: Preliminary prospectus circulated by underwriters to gauge investor interest in a planned offering. A legend in red ink on its cover indicates that the registration has not yet become effective and is still being reviewed by the SEC.
Registration statement: A carefully worded and organized document, including a prospectus, filed with the SEC before an IPO.
Regulation D: An SEC regulation that governs private placement exemption.
Reserve(s): Nonprofit organization's equivalent of owners' equity in a for-profit company.
Residual value: Market capitalization of a company at a specific time.
Revenue drivers: Elements within a business model that can be influenced to increase revenue, such as price, quantity purchased, awareness of product, availability, and so forth.
Retained earnings: The part of net income retained in the company and not distributed to stockholders.
Return on investment (ROI): The annual income that an investment earns.
Roll-up: A strategy to consolidate a fragmented industry.
Running returns: Periodic returns, such as interest and dividends, from an investment (in contrast to a one-time capital gain).
Road show: A series of meetings with potential investors and brokers, conducted by a company and its underwriter, prior to a securities offering, especially an IPO.
SBA: Small Business Administration.
SBDC: Small Business Development Centers (supported by the SBA).
SBI: Small Business Institutes, run by universities and colleges with SBA support.
SBIC: Small Business Investments Companies.
SBIR: Small Business Innovation Research Program.
S-curve: A model of new market product adoption. It illustrates market emergence, rapid growth, stability, and decline.
Schumpeter, Joseph A.: Moravian-born economist whose book *The Theory of Economic Development*, written in Vienna in 1912, introduced the modern theory of entrepreneurship, in which the

entrepreneur plays the central role in economic development by destroying the static equilibrium of the existing economy. Excellent modern examples are the roles played by Steve Jobs, Bill Gates, and Dan Bricklin in creating the microcomputer industry in the late 1970s. By the beginning of the 1990s, microcomputers (personal computers) were the principal force shaping the computer industry, and the old companies manufacturing mainframe and minicomputers, which dominated the computer industry until the mid-1980s, were in distress, ranging from outright bankruptcy to record-breaking losses.

SCORE: Service Core of Retired Executives, sponsored by the SBA to provide consulting to small businesses.

Secondary data: Market research that is gathered from already published sources, like an industry association study or census report.

Second-round financing: The introduction of further funding by the original investors or new investors to enable the company to grow or deal with unexpected problems. Each round of financing tends to cover the next period of growth.

Second-stage financing: Financing to fuel the growth of an early-stage company.

Secondary offering: The sale of stock by an issuer or underwriter after a company's securities have already begun trading publicly.

Secondary target market (STA): *See primary target audience*. A group of potential customers identified by demographic and psychographic data that will be a secondary or alternative focus of the company's early marketing and sales efforts.

Securities and Exchange Commission (SEC): Regulatory body for investor protection in the United States, created by the Securities Exchange Act of 1934. The supervision of dealers is delegated to the self-regulatory bodies of the stock exchanges and NASD under the provisions of the Maloney Act of 1938.

Seed financing: A relatively small amount of money provided to prove a concept; it may involve product development and market research but rarely involves the initial marketing of a product.

Seed-stage company: A company that doesn't have much more than a concept.

Sensitivity analysis: Examination of how the projected performance of the business varies with changes in the key assumptions on which the forecasts are based.

Serviceable available market (SAM): The segment(s) of the total available market that a company targets.

Serviceable obtainable market (SOM): The likely number of customers that a company will capture from the SAM.

Short-term security: Generally, an obligation maturing in less than one year.

Slotting fees: The fees that a product manufacturer pays a retail outlet to place products in its warehouse and then ultimately in the retail store.

Small business: The SBA defines most small businesses as ones with 500 or fewer employees.

Social capital: Networks, norms, and trust that facilitates coordination and cooperation between people for mutual benefit.

Social entrepreneur: Someone who develops social innovation through entrepreneurial solutions. A social entrepreneur recognizes a social problem or need, comes up with a solution, and creates an organization to pursue it. Business entrepreneurs typically measure performance by profit and financial return, whereas social entrepreneurs also take into account a positive return to society.

Social media: Websites and other online means of communication that are used by large groups of people to share information and to develop social and professional contacts.

Sole proprietorship: A business form with one owner who is responsible for all the firm's liabilities.

Startup company: A company that is already in business and is developing a prototype but has not sold it in significant commercial quantities.

Startup financing: Funding provided to companies for use in product development and initial marketing. Companies may be in the process of being organized or may have been in business a short time (one year or less), but have not sold their product commercially. Generally, such firms have assembled the key management, prepared a business plan, made market studies, and completed other preliminary tasks.

Stock option plan: A plan designed to motivate employees, especially key ones, by placing a portion of the common stock of the company under option at a fixed price to defined employees. The option may then be exercised by the employees at a future date. Stock options are often introduced as part of the remuneration package of senior executives.

Stock-out: Demand for a product exceeds the inventory that a company has on hand. Stock-outs may lead to lost sales as customers seek other options.

Strategic acquisition: When a company buys another company to get access to a product or service that complements its existing business.

Subchapter S corporation: A small business corporation in which the owners personally pay the corporation's income taxes.

Subordinated debt: Loans that may be unsecured or, more commonly, secured by secondary charges that rank after senior debt for repayment in the event of default. Also referred to as junior debt or mezzanine debt.

Sustainability: *Environmental Science*. The quality of not being harmful to the environment or depleting natural resources and thereby supporting long-term ecological balance.

Sweat equity: Equity acquired by the management team at favorable terms reflecting the value to the business of the managers' past and future efforts.

Syndicate: A group of investors that act together when investing in a company.

TEA Indices (Total Entrepreneurial Activity Indices): The percent of the adult population that is participating in a specific type of entrepreneurship. For example, the TEA (Overall) Index is the percent of the adult population that is in the process of starting a new business or has a business less than 42 months old.

Tertiary target audience (TTA): *See primary target audience*. A group of potential customers identified by demographic and psychographic data that will **not** be the focus of the company's early marketing and sales efforts.

Term loan: Debt originally scheduled to be repaid in more than one year, but usually in 10 years or less.

Term sheet: Summary of the principal conditions for a proposed investment in a company by a venture capital firm.

Third-stage financing: Funding to fuel the growth of an early-stage company.

Times interest earned: Earnings before interest and taxes, divided by interest (**EBIT/I**). The higher this ratio, the more secure the loan on which interest is paid. It is a basic measure of the creditworthiness of a company.

Top-down forecasting: Determining projected revenues by estimating what a certain percentage of market share translates into in terms of revenues. This method is highly suspect, and bottom-up and comparable projections tend to be better.

Total available market (TAM): Total demand for a product or service. *See serviceable available market* and *serviceable obtainable market.*

Trade promotion: Price promotions offered to retailers to induce them to carry your product.

Trade sale: This is the sale of a business to another company, often, but not always, in a similar line of business.

Trade secret: Knowledge that is kept secret for the purpose of gaining an advantage in business over one's competitors.

Trademarks: Protection obtainable for any word, symbol, or combination thereof that is used on goods to indicate their source.

Triggering event: An incident that prompts a person to take steps to start a new venture.

Triple bottom line: Captures the financial profit the organization earns and also the social and environmental benefit it provides society; associated with social entrepreneurship.

Underpricing: The difference between the closing price on the first day of trading and the initial offering price of a stock.

Underwater stock options: When the price of a stock is lower than the exercise price of a stock option. *(See stock option.)*

Underwrite: An arrangement under which investment banks each agree to buy a certain amount of securities of a new issue on a given date and at a given price, thereby assuring the issuer of the full proceeds of the financing.

Underwriter: An institution engaged in the business of underwriting securities issues.

Underwriting fee: The share of the gross spread of a new issue accruing to members of the underwriting group after the expenses of the issue have been paid.

Unsecured loans: Debt that is not backed by a pledge of specific assets.

Valuation (of a company): The market value of a company. *(See market capitalization.)*

Value-added (by investors): Many venture capital firms claim that they add more than money to investee companies. They call it value-added, which includes strategic advice on such matters as hiring key employees, marketing, production, control, and financing.

Venture philanthropy: Applying the concepts of venture capital to achieving philanthropic goals.

Venture capitalist: A financial institution specializing in the provision of equity and other forms of long-term capital to enterprises, usually to firms with a limited track record but with the expectation of substantial growth. The venture capitalist may provide both funding and varying degrees of managerial and technical expertise. Venture capital has traditionally been associated with startups; however, venture capitalists have increasingly participated in later-stage projects.

Vesting period: The time period before shares are owned unconditionally by an employee who is sold stock with the stipulation that he must continue to work for the company selling him the shares. If his employment terminates before the end of that period, the company has the right to buy back the shares at the same price at which it originally sold them to him.

Visible venture capital (formal venture capital): The organized venture capital industry consisting of formal firms, in contrast to invisible venture capital or informal venture capital.

Vulture capital: A derogatory term for venture capital.

Waiver: Consent granted by an investor or lender to permit an investor or borrower to be in default on a covenant.

Walking wounded: Venture capital jargon for a company that is not successful enough to be harvested with an IPO or acquisition, but might be worth another round of investment to try to get it into harvestable condition.

Warrant: An option to purchase common stock at a specified price. *(See equity kicker.)*

Warranty: A statement of fact or opinion concerning the condition of a company. The inclusion of warranties in an investment agreement gives the investor a claim against the company if it subsequently becomes apparent that the company's condition was not as stated at the time of the investment.

Works-like prototype: A prototype that operates like the final intended product design—demonstrating product functionality or usability—but often does not appear at all like the end product.

Yield: Annualized rate of return on a security.

INDEX

D

Q

R

Y

Z